HAMMARSKJOLD

HAMMARSKJOLD

by BRIAN URQUHART

 Alfred A. Knopf, New York, 1972

This is a Borzoi Book published by Alfred A. Knopf, Inc.

Copyright © 1972 by Brian Urquhart.
All rights reserved under International and Pan-American
Copyright Conventions. Published in the United States by
Alfred A. Knopf, Inc., New York, and simultaneously
in Canada by Random House of Canada Limited, Toronto.
Distributed by Random House, Inc., New York.

Library of Congress Cataloging in Publication Data:
Urquhart, Brian. Hammarskjold.
  1. Hammarskjöld, Dag, 1905–1961.
D839.7.H3U7 341.23'2 [B] 72–2255
ISBN 0–394–47960–2

Manufactured in the United States of America

First Edition

To Sidney

Contents

Illustrations

Following page 266

The four Hammarskjold brothers.
   (Reportagebild, *Stockholm*)

Trygve Lie welcomes Hammarskjold, April 9, 1953.
   (United Nations)

Hammarskjold and Lester Pearson of Canada in the General Assembly
   Hall.   *(George Rowen)*

Peking, January 10, 1955—with Chou En-lai.
   (United Nations)

Israel, January 1956—Hammarskjold visits kindergarten at Givath-
   Jearim.   *(United Nations)*

Cartoon by David Low during Hammarskjold's trip to the Middle East,
   April 1956.   *(By permission of the David Low Trustees and the*
   London Evening Standard)

April 1956—Hammarskjold is greeted on arrival in Amman by Prime
   Minister Samir Rifai.   *(Hammarskjold papers)*

Hammarskjold with President Nasser and Foreign Minister Fawzi.
   (Hammarskjold papers)

Reviewing Danish and Norwegian advance guard of UNEF at Abu
   Suweir, Egypt, November 17, 1956.   *(United Nations)*

Taking a question at a press conference.
   (The New York Times)

Relaxing in southern Sweden.
   (Hammarskjold papers)

In Beirut with the UN Observation Group in Lebanon.
   (United Nations)

Maps

Foreword

In 1966, I was asked by an international group of publishers to write an account of Dag Hammarskjold's Secretary-Generalship. I hesitated for some time to embark on such a difficult project, but when the trustees of Hammarskjold's papers encouraged me to do so and gave me sole access to his private papers, I decided that I should go ahead. Since I am a member of the United Nations Secretariat, I notified the Secretary-General and the United Nations Director of Personnel, both of whom agreed that I might undertake this outside activity in my spare time and that I might be granted a sabbatical leave later on to complete the project—a hope which, because of various developments at the UN, was never fulfilled.

In order to avoid any misunderstanding as to the status of this book or of my own position in writing it, I quote the following exchange of letters with Secretary-General U Thant, in which he gave me permission to publish, as required by the UN Staff Rules:

12 January 1971

Dear U Thant,

As you know, since the beginning of 1967 I have been working on a book about Dag Hammarskjold as Secretary-General, based to a very large extent on Mr. Hammarskjold's private papers, to which his Trustees have given me sole access for the purpose of writing this book.

In January 1967, in accordance with the Staff Rules, I requested, and received from, the Director of Personnel permission to engage in this "outside activity." It was understood that I had undertaken to write this book in a purely private capacity and not under the auspices of anyone or of any organization, including the United Nations.

As the manuscript is now reaching the stage where in the near future it can be given to the publishers, I now have the obligation under the Staff Rules to ask for permission to publish.

Administrative Instruction ST/AI/190 of 9 January 1970 states a.o. that "individual cases will be referred to the Secretary-General," and I have taken the liberty of approaching you directly on this matter in view of the exceptional circumstances surrounding this manuscript. When giving me sole access to the late Secretary-General's private papers, Mr. Hammarskjold's Trustees left to my discretion the form in which they were to be used. I have, in fact, written the book throughout from the point of view of an international civil servant. My basic approach has been that the story of the eight years of Mr. Hammarskjold's Secretary-Generalship should be written with forthrightness, and that any other method would be an insult not only to the late Secretary-General but also to the Organisation which he devotedly served. Although, in order to stay within the bounds of a single volume, I have had to condense and select from the very large amount of material at my disposal, I have made a conscientious effort to give an accurate, fair and objective account of all the events concerned. I have tried to let the facts and the documents speak for themselves as far as possible and have refrained from expressing personal opinions except when they have seemed absolutely necessary to an understanding of the events concerned.

I take full responsibility for the manuscript, the content of which, although relating to the United Nations, obviously expresses no official position by or on behalf of the Organisation. In the very nature of the sole access to Mr. Hammarskjold's private papers given to me by his Trustees, I could not share this responsibility even if I had wanted to do so. I will, of course, make clear in the introduction to the book the circumstances in which I have written it, my own personal responsibility for the text and the fact that it is in no sense an official United Nations venture. . . .

Yours sincerely,
Brian Urquhart

The Secretary-General replied:

14 January 1971

Dear Mr. Urquhart,

I refer to your letter of 12 January 1971 concerning the book that you are writing on Dag Hammarskjold as Secretary-General and also to a memorandum of 10 January 1967 from the Director of Personnel on the same subject. I agree that the circumstances in which this work has been undertaken are exceptional, especially in regard to the sole access to Hammarskjold's private papers which has been granted to you for the purpose of writing the book.

I note that this book has been written as a private and personal undertaking and that you will make it clear in the introduction that it is in no sense an official United Nations venture.

With this understanding, and in the light of the exceptional circumstances in which you have undertaken this work, I am glad to give my permission for you to go ahead with the publication of the book.

Yours sincerely,
U Thant

This book is written mainly from Hammarskjold's point of view as Secretary-General, and inevitably he dominates the narrative. I have not had, nor have I sought, access to the private papers of the other public figures involved, and they are described for the most part in general outline only. The book is intended mainly to give an account of Hammarskjold's Secretary-Generalship and of his own concept of his role. More detailed and more scholarly studies will obviously be required in order to explore, when other source materials become available, the depth and the full detail of the various episodes concerned.

There is little value in lengthy introductory explanations, but on one point a preliminary comment may be justified. The art of multilateral diplomacy, in which Hammarskjold excelled, consists to a large degree in long and intricate negotiations, contacts, and conversations. A detailed historical account of this process can be heavy going because it inevitably lacks much of the drama, personal tension, and pressure that prevailed at the time. Multilateral diplomacy is usually a laborious and nerve-racking process that requires great stamina as well as intuition, intellect, understanding, and negotiating ability. In an attempt to show this process at work, I have described it at some length, despite the risk that this may lead at times to a somewhat heavy and dense narrative.

A reader unaccustomed to the workings of the United Nations may well find the constant references to the Charter and to United Nations resolutions and procedures excessive, even pedantic. The fact is that these are the main guidelines of the Secretary-General's activity, and their importance as the basis for his actions cannot be played down. Because Hammarskjold was the chief administrative officer of the United Nations, and because his administrative and political functions were closely interconnected, I have also given a good deal of space to the administrative aspects of his job, even when this has the effect of interrupting the political narrative.

A brief note on my own association with Hammarskjold may be relevant. I joined the United Nations Secretariat at its inception in 1945 and worked for almost the entire period of Hammarskjold's Secretary-Generalship in the Office of the Under-Secretaries-General for Special Political Affairs, which is closely connected with the Office of the Secretary-General. Although I was continuously associated with him, I was not one of Hammarskjold's small inner circle of close associates. I did, however, greatly respect and admire him, and this attitude and the affection which many of us felt for him are, of course, reflected in this account of his time at the United Nations.

For convenience, Hammarskjold's name is spelled throughout the book without the diaeresis over the *o*, as was done in UN documentation during his lifetime. The abbreviation UN and other acronyms are printed throughout without periods for purposes of simplification.

It is impossible to thank by name the hundreds of people who have helped me in writing this book. I wish, however, to express my warm appreciation to Mr. Bo Hammarskjold and the other trustees of Hammarskjold's papers for giving me access to them, and to Dr. Uno Willers, librarian of the Swedish Royal Library, and his staff for their helpfulness in making my work on the papers as easy and as efficient as possible.

I am greatly indebted to Joseph Johnson and the Carnegie Endowment for International Peace for giving me a grant for two years which allowed me to start on the project in my spare time with the maximum effect, and for allowing my assistant to use the Endowment's facilities and library.

I am profoundly grateful to the board and to the director of the Swedish Riksbankens Jubileumsfond for their generosity in financing the project for the remaining three years and for their never-failing encouragement and confidence.

Wilhelm Wachtmeister, Gunnar Jarring, and Sven Ahman. Mrs. William

Hammarskjold's Swedish friends have been a major source of support and information. My thanks go in particular to Per and Eva Lind, Karl Ragnar Gierow, Sture Petrén, Leif Belfrage, Bo Beskow, Ranallo has also helped me greatly. Of those who have read and commented on the manuscript at various stages, I am especially beholden to Robert Rhodes James, to Walter Howard, to my wife, and to my son Robert. I have received valuable help on the Laos chapter from Colonel Hugh Toye and Dr. Edouard Zellweger, and from Izzam Azzam on the question of Bureimi. I am also grateful to all those whom I have interviewed in connection with the events described in this book.

My colleagues in the United Nations Secretariat have been especially helpful and generous with their spare time. Among them I should like to mention in particular the late Ralph Bunche, F. T. Liu, William W. Cox, William Epstein, Jacques Engers, George Sherry, Jan van Wijk, James Jonah, Beatrice Chen, May Davidson, William Marmelstein, Irene Corotneff and the staff of the United Nations Library, Jorgen Grinde, Janet Portser, Nathaniel O. Abelson, Robert Roth, and M. Bahy El-Din Hefny. Ashbel Green and Carol Janeway, who edited the manuscript for publication, have been of immeasurable assistance in giving the book whatever shape and pace it may have.

Finally, I must mention Hammarskjold's former secretary, Miss Hannah Platz, who has collaborated with me on this book from the beginning. Without her encouragement, her extraordinary and apparently effortless efficiency, and her detailed knowledge, I would not have been able even to begin, let alone finish, this book under the circumstances in which I have had to write it.

BRIAN URQUHART
January 1972

On doit des égards aux vivants,

on ne doit aux morts que la vérité.

—VOLTAIRE: Lettres écrites en 1719 . . . sur
Oedipe, Première lettre, Note.

PART ONE

PROLOGUE

THE CONCEPT OF a representative central authority working in the interest of all the people, even of one nation, has taken many centuries to evolve and longer still to become an effective reality. The rivalries of the feudal nobility periodically dislocated and laid waste the life of medieval Europe for hundreds of years before the common interest of the majority of the population in order, justice, and peace was able to assert itself through effective central authority. In our time we are witnessing a somewhat similar development on the international level. The twentieth-century world has dwelt in the shadow of great-power rivalries and conflicts which have twice erupted into world wars of an unprecedented horror and destructiveness. While these disasters have greatly stimulated the natural desire of the majority of nations for peace, the achievement of a representative world order, working in the interest of all states and peoples, is still almost as distant a possibility as orderly central government must have seemed to the hard-pressed townspeople and peasantry of medieval Europe.

The impetus given by two world wars to the search for an effective international order has been intensified by two effects of the technological revolution: the increasing interdependence of nations and the active possibility of an instant and comprehensive disaster caused by weapons of mass destruction. A third effect, the threat to the environment, has lately joined the first two as a powerful incentive to international cooperation.

Although the dangers of our situation are alarmingly clear, our world of competing sovereign states still clings to ancient prerogatives and narrow national aims, and the internationalism which is becoming a commonplace in other areas of human activity is still embryonic in the political sphere. International institutions set up in the aftermath of disaster for idealistic or enlightened purposes have so far tended to serve more as scapegoats for the failure of sovereign governments to adjust to the realities of the time—or, at best, as a last refuge from the consequences of conflicting national policies—than for the development of a reliable and equitable system of international relationships. Nonetheless, a few faltering steps forward have been made, and the search for international peace, justice, and order continues.

The United Nations is the latest and most complex of man's attempts to build an organization that would harmonize the conflicting policies and actions of nations. The first great experiment in international order, the League of Nations, after a promising start, was reduced to impotence by lack of collective resistance to the aggressions of the 1930's that culminated in World War II. Discussions on replacing the League with something more effective began in the early years of World War II. In the London Declaration of June 12, 1941, the nations fighting against Germany and Italy announced their intention of working together with other free peoples to establish "a world in which, relieved of the menace of aggression, all may enjoy economic and social security." The name "United Nations," which the later history of the Organization has often belied, first appeared in the United Nations Declaration of January 1942 and referred more to uniting in war against a common foe than to cooperating in peace after victory had been achieved.

The United Nations was very much an offspring of World War II, and two assumptions on which its new system of collective security was to be founded soon proved to be unsound. The first of these was that the alliance of great powers which had won the war would survive to supervise the peace. The role of the Security Council in deterring aggression and in dealing with threats to the peace, if necessary by the use of force, was largely based on this assumption. The unanimity rule or veto, by which any substantive decision of the Council must have the concurring votes of all the permanent members—the Republic of China, France, the U.S.S.R., the United Kingdom, and the United States—also guaranteed that the Security Council would not take enforcement action against one of the five great powers.

The harmony of the wartime alliance scarcely survived the closing months of World War II, and soon thereafter the China of San Francisco ceased to be the effective government of the most populous nation on earth. The position of two of the other permanent members, Great Britain and France, was also changing, and the influence of these two great colonial powers of the nineteenth century, weakened by war and by the new realities of the twentieth-century world, steadily declined, their predominant place being taken by two rival giants, the Soviet Union and the United States.

Even had the victorious allies remained united, a second basic assumption of the United Nations Charter was severely shaken, even before that document had come into effect, by the atomic blasts over Hiroshima and Nagasaki. The authors of the Charter, with the aggressions of the 1930's in mind, had provided that the Security Council should be able to mobilize, and if necessary use, conventional military forces to deter or defeat aggressors. The delegates at San Francisco in the early summer of 1945, with perhaps one or two exceptions, could not know that even while they were putting the last touches to the Charter, the conventional concept of war was being revolutionized by new weapons of mass destruction. The development of these weapons radically changed both the nature of war and the relationship of the greatest powers, eventually freezing them in a balance of terror that greatly diminished their freedom of action in contentious questions involving their rival spheres of influence. This fundamental change in the world political scene, and the ideological confrontation of the cold war in which the techniques of propaganda and political influence largely superseded conventional military aggression, made the Charter idea of collective military security against aggression increasingly irrelevant to postwar realities.

A world exhausted and sickened by six years of horror and destruction inevitably entertained unrealistic hopes of the international organization which was to "save succeeding generations from the scourge of war." That governments could agree with apparent ease on something so civilized after the nightmare of the preceding years was taken by many to signify a radical change for the better in human affairs. The gradual realization, after the smiles of San Francisco had faded, that the state of international relations was still much the same as before induced a disappointment and disillusionment with the United Nations as extravagant as the optimism that had attended its birth. For its member states, some of whose policies were largely responsible for dooming to frustration the Organization they had created, it was obviously easier to blame the institution itself than to admit the real causes of its ineffectiveness. Thus, soon after it had been set up, those who had always distrusted international organization were joined by those whose hopes and enthusiasms had been betrayed in a swelling chorus of criticism, derision, and even condemnation of the UN.

The frustration of the Security Council in its primary duty of maintaining international peace and security soon gave rise to a search for other expedients through which the main function of the United Nations, the maintenance of peace, might be fulfilled. In 1947, United States Secretary of State George C. Marshall proposed that the General Assembly be adapted to fill the gap left by the paralysis of the Council, and a resolution was passed, over strong Soviet opposition, providing for an Interim Committee (known as the "Little Assembly") that would be permanently available to consider international disputes, although it had none of the enforcement powers of the Council. This arrangement was never effective.

As the Security Council became increasingly a victim of the estrangement between East and West, governments began to look outside the United Nations for international security arrangements. The Brussels Treaty Organization, the first of the regional defense pacts, was established in March 1948, and in June of the same year came the Berlin Blockade. The United Nations Disarmament Commission reported deadlock in July, and in August the Security Council's Military Staff Committee announced a virtual cessation of activity, which has continued until the present. For a time at least, the divisions of its permanent members had made the international policing role envisaged for the Council—a novel feature of the Charter—a practical impossibility.

In 1950 the United Nations faced the severest test of its five-year history. The defeat of a Soviet proposal to have the representative of Peking instead of the representative of Nationalist China occupy the Chinese seat in the Security Council had led to a Soviet boycott of the Council and all other United Nations organs. Thus, when on June 25 the United Nations Commission on Korea cabled from Seoul that South Korea had been invaded from the north, the Security Council was able, in the absence of a Soviet veto, immediately to agree on an American resolution declaring the invasion a breach of the peace, calling for a cease-fire and withdrawal of invading troops, and asking all members of the United Nations to help in executing the resolution. Two days later the Council was informed that United States forces would assist the South Koreans in response to the Council's resolution, and the Council urged all member states to assist in the effort to repel the invasion and to restore peace in Korea. Sixteen governments ultimately provided forces to serve under the U.S. Commander, General Douglas MacArthur, who was designated as Chief of the United Nations

Unified Command. The Organization was thus involved, by a freak of fate, in a collective military action directed almost entirely by a single great power.

When the Soviet Union resumed its seat in the Council in August 1950, the lesson of the Korean experience led to another move in the Assembly to circumvent the paralyzed Security Council. This time the Assembly adopted the "Acheson plan," formally known as the Uniting for Peace Resolution. This arrangement provided for the Assembly to meet within twenty-four hours if the Security Council failed to "exercise its primary responsibility for the maintenance of peace and security." The Assembly further appropriated the Council's functions by setting up a Peace Observation Commission to observe and report on situations liable to endanger peace and a Collective Measures Committee to encourage member states to allocate some of their forces for use as United Nations contingents. This plan also was denounced as illegal by the Soviet Union, and the only part of it that actually became effective was the provision for mobilizing the Assembly, which, ironically enough, was invoked for the first time with Soviet concurrence in 1956 to circumvent the British and French vetoes in the Security Council over Suez.

The Korean war dragged on for three years, during which the United Nations, and especially the Security Council, became more divided than ever. Trygve Lie's support for the United States initiative over Korea caused the U.S.S.R. to veto his renomination as Secretary-General. When a deadlock ensued and Lie was "continued in office" by the General Assembly for another three years, the Soviet Union announced that it no longer recognized him as Secretary-General, thus severely limiting his effectiveness. This development excluded the possibility of turning to the political role of the Secretary-General— another of the novelties of the Charter—as a possible means of filling the vacuum in matters of peace and security which had resulted from the Security Council's inability to act. At the same time the international Secretariat became a happy hunting ground for the witch-hunters of McCarthyism in the United States, and its morale fell to the lowest level in its short history.

Seven years after its foundation, the political future of the United Nations looked dim indeed. The Charter concept of peace through collective security and disarmament seemed largely to have been abandoned by member states in favor of regional defense pacts which tacitly assumed that sooner or later the world might be at war again. Instead of the basic unity of the great powers on which the Security Council's authority was to have been grounded, the division and mutual hostility of those powers dominated the international scene and made a mockery of the hopes of San Francisco. Many governments, while paying lip service to the United Nations, scarcely concealed their contempt for the Organization they had created and reverted increasingly to various forms of realpolitik, in spite of the fact that in a nuclear age such policies were apt in the long run to be the least realistic of all.

By 1952 no foreseeable use of the mechanism set up at San Francisco seemed likely to dispel the prevailing mood of cynicism and defeatism over the political future of the United Nations. The advent of a new administration in the United States at the beginning of 1953, however, and with it the prospect of an armistice in Korea, removed one divisive element from the picture, and the death of Stalin in March of the same year gave some hope of a possible new direction in East-West relations. Even so, only dedicated leadership and skill of a new order, and a determined championing of the principles of the Charter, were likely to revive the confidence of governments in the potential of the United Nations as an organization for the maintenance of peace and security and to fill the vacuum caused by the paralysis of the Security Council. These qualities were provided in unexpectedly large measure by a more or less fortuitous arrival on the international scene —Dag Hammarskjold.

1

ELECTION

The qualities which the head of the service should possess are not easy to define. He should be young. Political or diplomatic experience, but not necessarily great fame or eminence, is an advantage. Above all, ability for administration in the broadest sense is important, implying a knowledge of when to be dynamic, to take the initiative and to force an issue; when, at the other extreme, to be content as a purely administrative official; and when, on a middle course, to be a moderator impartially smoothing over difficulties, a catalytic agent in negotiation. . . . In a new organization, it may well be that the only qualities which must under all conditions be demanded of the director are those of common sense, courage, integrity and tact.*

ON THE AFTERNOON OF November 10, 1952, the delegates to the General Assembly of the United Nations who were waiting to hear the Foreign

* From "The International Secretariat of the Future—Lessons from Experience by a Group of Former Officials of the League of Nations" (Royal Institute of International Affairs, London, March 1944). The group consisted of:
THE EARL OF PERTH, formerly Sir Eric Drummond, first Secretary-General of the League of Nations; chairman.

Minister of Belgium, Paul van Zeeland, were surprised* to hear instead a speech of resignation[1] from the Secretary-General, Trygve Lie. Lie had delayed his announcement until the Foreign Ministers of the five great powers who were the permanent members of the Security Council were gathered in the Assembly, hoping thus to facilitate a quick agreement on his successor. He had felt obliged, Lie told the Assembly, to carry on during the Korean war, but now that hopes of an armistice were in the air, a Secretary-General who was the unanimous choice of the big powers and the membership would be more helpful than he could any longer be, especially since the permanent Headquarters Building and his proposals for administrative reorganization of the Secretariat had both been completed. "I am stepping aside now," Lie said, "because I hope this may help the UN to save the peace and to serve better the cause of freedom and progress for all mankind."[2]

Lie's resignation was the culmination of more than two years of bitterness and confusion during which the Secretary-General had been at the center of the storm. In the miserable political climate of the cold war the first Secretary-General had struggled successfully to set up the administrative apparatus and the Secretariat of the UN and had directed, again with ultimate success, the search for a permanent Headquarters for the Organization. But when, despite quarrels among governments, squabbles among architects, and massive financial and practical problems, the UN Headquarters Building on the East River in New York at last began to rise, Trygve Lie's troubles had only started. His active support of the Security Council's backing of the U.S. decision to resist by force the invasion of South Korea by North Korea had brought him into head-on conflict with the Soviet Union, which after October 1950 ignored his existence and refused all communication with him.

A concurrent tribulation for the Secretary-General had begun even before the Korean war when, in 1949, the conviction, on a relatively minor charge of espionage, of a Soviet UN Secretariat member had

---

THANASSIS AGHNIDES, Greek Ambassador to the Court of St. James, and formerly Under-Secretary-General of the League of Nations.

ERIK COLBAN, Norwegian Ambassador to the Court of St. James, and formerly director of the Minorities Section of the League Secretariat.

A. PELT, director of the Royal Netherlands Government Information Bureau, and formerly director of the Information Section of the League Secretariat.

F. P. WALTERS, formerly Deputy Secretary-General of the League of Nations.

J. V. WILSON, Assistant Director of Research at Chatham House, formerly Chief of the Central Section of the League Secretariat.

* Lie in his book *In the Cause of Peace* (New York, 1954), p. 406, refers to his resignation as "the best kept secret in the United Nations history."

touched off a campaign in parts of the American press and among right-wing organizations against the Secretariat, which was alleged to be riddled with Communists and fellow travelers.

Caught in the midst of nonrecognition by the U.S.S.R., harassment and criticism in the United States, and the mounting indignation and loss of confidence of his own Secretariat, Lie had finally resigned, but his hopes that a successor would be quickly agreed upon proved unfounded. The Secretary-General of the United Nations is appointed by the General Assembly on the recommendation of the Security Council, and it was not until March 11, 1953, that the Security Council, in secret session, began the search in earnest. Originally the Council had before it three names: Carlos P. Romulo of the Philippines, the U.S.-backed candidate; Dr. Stanislaw Skreszewski of Poland, the Soviet candidate; and Lester B. Pearson of Canada, who was proposed by Denmark and supported by France and Great Britain. The United States, although unenthusiastic about Pearson because of the position he had taken on Korea, hoped to keep him as a second possibility should Romulo be blocked, although it seemed no more likely than in 1946 that Pearson would be accepted by the U.S.S.R., unless in the last resort as the sole possible alternative to Lie. On March 13, Ahmed Bokhari of Pakistan, the President of the Security Council for that month, announced that Romulo had received five votes, with two opposing votes and four abstentions. The Polish candidate got one vote, with three against and seven abstentions, while Pearson, with nine votes, was put out of the contest by the Soviet veto. The first round of the search thus ended in deadlock.

Consultations among the permanent members of the Council and further meetings failed to produce results, although a number of new names, including Mrs. V. L. Pandit of India (Prime Minister Jawaharlal Nehru's sister), Sir Benegal Rau of India, Prince Wan Waithayakon of Thailand, Nasrollah Entezam of Iran, Padilla Nervo of Mexico, Dr. Eduardo Zulcta Angel of Colombia, Ahmed Bokhari of Pakistan, Charles Malik of Lebanon, and Erik Boheman, the Swedish Ambassador in Washington, were canvassed. At this point Trygve Lie let it be known that if there was no solution, he would be willing to stay on. He at once received the support of the United States. The British and French representatives showed little enthusiasm for this idea, and Henri Hoppenot, the French representative, suggested a new approach by which four names acceptable to the United States should be suggested to Valerian Zorin, the Soviet representative, who should be asked which of them, if any, the Soviet Union could agree to. The British representative, Gladwyn Jebb, then suggested, and Hoppenot agreed, that Dag Hammarskjold, the Minister of State in the Swedish Foreign Office, should be one of the four. The others were Nasrollah Entezam, Padilla Nervo, and Dirk U. Stikker of The Netherlands. At the Council meeting on March 24, Hoppenot suggested that it was too soon to report disagreement to the General Assembly, as a new effort to reach agreement was being made by the permanent members of the Council and "certain suggestions had been received with interest."[3] At the Council meeting on March 27, Jebb asked for a further delay, saying that there had been some progress, and Zorin went so far as to say that the permanent members appeared to be "within reach of a possible agreement."[4]

Finally at a meeting at 4:30 p.m. on March 31, Jebb informed the Council that after two more informal meetings the permanent members had agreed to recommend Dag Hammarskjold, "the Director-General of the Swedish Foreign Ministry."[5]* Hoppenot made a formal proposal to this effect, and Andrei Vyshinsky, the permanent Soviet delegate, who had just returned to New York, stated that he was "happy to support the nomination of Mr. Hammarskjold to replace the person currently fulfilling the functions of Secretary-General."[6] All the members welcomed this development except the Chinese representative, who, when the President of the Council suggested a vote by acclamation, said that he would have to abstain if a vote was taken, presumably because of Sweden's recognition of the Peking government. Jebb then pointed out that no one yet knew if Hammarskjold would accept and that he was even reported to have been dismayed on hearing that his name was being discussed. It was therefore agreed that, since it was nearly midnight in Stockholm, a telegram should be sent to Hammarskjold informing him of the Security Council's agreement. "In view of the immense importance of this post, more especially at the present time," the telegram read, "members of the Security Council express the earnest hope that you will agree to accept."[7] It was also agreed that the President should inform Lie at once of the decision.

Hammarskjold was as much surprised as anyone by this turn of events. Long afterward he said, "I was simply picked out of the hat."[8] The news leaked in New York before he received Bokhari's telegram,**

---

* This title was wrong. Hammarskjold was a Minister.
** In fact the Associated Press correspondent at the UN, Frank Carpenter, was informed of the Council's decision immediately by a member of the Chinese delegation, who came out to make a telephone call as soon as the Council agreed on Hammarskjold. Carpenter thus had a lead of an hour and a half over the other newsmen, who were awaiting the official communiqué.

and Hammarskjold received the first intimation of his designation at about 10 p.m. when he was dining at his apartment with Leif Belfrage and Rolf Sohlman of the Foreign Office, by way of a telephone call from the AP correspondent in Stockholm whom he informed that his watch must be fast and that it was not yet April Fool's Day. When other calls swiftly followed the first one, however, Hammarskjold realized that his nomination was no joke, and a definitive news-agency message arrived at 12:45 a.m., followed belatedly at 3 a.m. by a message from the Swedish mission in New York. Bokhari's cable put an end to any uncertainty, and the next day began, in Hammarskjold's words, "in a glaring limelight,"[9] as he was photographed and filmed leaving his apartment.

After consulting the Prime Minister and Foreign Minister and receiving his release from the Swedish Cabinet, Hammarskjold went to see his father in Sophiahemmet Hospital before replying to Bokhari that he accepted the nomination: "With a strong feeling of personal insufficiency, I hesitate to accept candidature, but I do not feel that I could refuse the task imposed upon me."[10] Gunnar Jarring later described Hammarskjold's state of mind as follows: "It was a reaction which could best be described as an agony of doubt: 'Do I really have to accept? Isn't there somebody else who would be available?' But by then he already knew that his acceptance was unavoidable. As soon as his cable of acceptance had left Stockholm, his agony disappeared as if by a stroke of magic. There was no hesitation, no irresolution. He had decided to accept and had pledged himself to the United Nations."[11]

After replying to Bokhari's cable, Hammarskjold went to the studio of the painter Bo Beskow for a previously arranged sitting for his portrait, but spent the time talking over a glass of sherry, after which he went off cheerfully to a press conference at the Foreign Office to announce his acceptance publicly. He emphasized the unexpectedness of the nomination. He had returned from New York, he said, "two weeks ago and neither there nor in Washington had there been any inkling that I was being considered for Secretary-General."[12] In the afternoon he called Karl Ragnar Gierow, director of the Royal Dramatic Theater, to ask his help in getting a ticket for the new production of *Romeo and Juliet*, since he feared that otherwise he might miss it. The theater being sold out, Gierow gave Hammarskjold and Belfrage, with whom he was dining, seats in his own box.

Despite his initial surprise, Hammarskjold welcomed the incomparable opportunity that had been given him to use all of his ability on a much broader stage than before. In his notebook that later became *Markings** he wrote, "To be free, to be able to rise and leave everything—without looking back. To say *yes*—."[13] Hammarskjold viewed his new job with modesty and some awe. On April 4 (Easter Saturday) he asked his friend Walton Butterworth, the U.S. Ambassador in Stockholm, and Belfrage to lunch and showed them the draft of his acceptance speech to the General Assembly. Butterworth protested that it was far too humble and that the nations of the world had not appointed him Secretary-General in order to hear that he had come to New York to learn the job. Hammarskjold later revised the draft. He also told his friends that he proposed to live very simply in New York and to turn back to the UN a large part of his living allowance. They advised against this partly because it would be unfair to his successor and partly because it would be better to see what was needed before making any rash decisions. He soon found that UN pay and allowances were anything but lavish for the endless entertaining he had to do and for the life he had to lead.

Hammarskjold was not the only person to be surprised at his appointment. Although a limited circle of economists and European experts knew and respected him as an exceptionally able public servant, he was not widely known outside Sweden. Jebb had met him with Chancellor of the Exchequer Sir Stafford Cripps in the late 1940's, knew of his work with the Marshall Plan and the Council of Europe, and had met him again during the recent session of the General Assembly when Hammarskjold had been head of the Swedish delegation. Hoppenot and Henry Cabot Lodge, permanent U.S. representative to the UN, had never met him, although Ernest Gross of the U.S. mission knew him and recommended him highly. When Lodge called the State Department to say that someone called Hammarskjold had been suggested and had been accepted by Vyshinsky, Secretary of State John Foster Dulles was with H. Freeman Matthews, Acting Deputy Under-Secretary, and Paul H. Nitze, head of the Policy Planning Committee in the State Department. Matthews, remembering Hammarskjold from his time as head of the European desk in the State Department, said, "If you can get him, grab him,"[14] while Nitze recalled his negotiations over the Swedish-U.S. trade agreement and Hammarskjold's extraordinary mastery of the complex issues involved. Hammarskjold was virtually unknown in the UN Secretariat, and such information as was available was largely inaccurate and fanciful.

---

* *Markings*, translated from the Swedish *Vägmärken* (Stockholm, 1963) by Leif Sjöberg and W. H. Auden (New York and London, 1964). Where the English translations of quotations from *Markings* differ from the Sjöberg/Auden version, they will be annotated as "translated from the original Swedish."

Trygve Lie was strongly opposed to Hammarskjold's appointment and told Pearson that he would be no more than a clerk.

Carl Schürmann, for many years the Netherlands representative at the UN, later described the background of Hammarskjold's nomination: "In spite of the reputation of ability and integrity which he had acquired among those who had met him in negotiations or at conferences, it cannot be said that he was, at that moment, the obvious candidate for this high international function. His election was much more due to the wish of the Big Powers to see—after Trygve Lie who had taken a strong position in several questions—at the head of the Secretariat someone who would concentrate mainly on the administrative problems and who would abstain from public statements on the political conduct of the Organization. Such a careful and colourless official they thought to have found in Dag Hammarskjold."[15] For the most part the newspapers played up Hammarskjold's aloofness, intellectual qualities, and nonpolitical career, one French journalist even going as far as to call him the *"huître la plus charmante du monde"*[16] —the most charming oyster in the world.

On April 2, Lie cabled Hammarskjold that he was "glad that you have accepted" and urged him to arrive not later than April 7 because "there are lots of cases awaiting your decision."[17] On April 7 the General Assembly confirmed the Security Council's recommendation[18] of his appointment by 57 votes in favor, 1 against, and 1 abstention.[19] "By your election today of a Secretary-General recognized as such by all five permanent members of the Security Council," Lie said in his farewell address, "you have reopened the door of the office of the Secretary-General."[20]

When Hammarskjold, without topcoat or hat and looking very young and serious, came down the ramp from his plane at Idlewild Airport on April 9, Lie gloomily welcomed him to "the most impossible job on this earth."[21] Hammarskjold took a less somber tone in giving his first account of his own view of his new office. "In my new official capacity," he said, "the private man should disappear and the international public servant take his place. The public servant is there in order to assist, so to say from the inside, those who take the decisions which frame history. He should—as I see it—listen, analyze, and learn to understand fully the forces at work and the interests at stake, so that he will be able to give the right advice when the situation calls for it. Don't think that he—in following this line of personal policy— takes but a passive part in the development. It is a most active one. But he is active as an instrument, a catalyst, perhaps an inspirer—he serves." He concluded with a reference to mountaineering that was to haunt him for the rest of his life. "The qualities it requires are just those which I feel we all need today: perseverance and patience, a firm grip on realities, careful but imaginative planning, a clear awareness of the dangers but also of the fact that fate is what we make it and that the safest climber is he who never questions his ability to overcome all difficulties."[22]*

On April 10, Hammarskjold was officially installed by the General Assembly.[23] Lester Pearson as President of the Assembly, flanked by Lie and Andrew Cordier, the Secretary-General's Executive Assistant, was on the podium. Pearson administered the Secretary-General's oath, which Hammarskjold took with him as a bookmark on his last journey more than eight years later. It read: "I, Dag Hammarskjold, solemnly swear to exercise in all loyalty, discretion and conscience the functions entrusted to me as Secretary-General of the United Nations, to discharge these functions and regulate my conduct with the interests of the United Nations only in view, and not to seek or accept instructions in regard to the performance of my duties from any government or other authority external to the Organization."[24] Hammarskjold shook hands with the Vice-Presidents of the General Assembly, and then in his characteristically flat and quiet tones addressed the Assembly. He recalled his civil-service background in a country in which the civil service had a long tradition and was firmly founded in law. He spoke of the vital importance of loyalty, devotion, and integrity for those engaged in the international service. "Ours," he said, "is a work of reconciliation and realistic construction. This work must be based on respect for the laws by which human civilization has been built. It likewise requires a strict observance of the rules and principles laid down in the Charter of this Organization. . . . Common to us all, and above all other convictions, stands the truth once expressed by a Swedish poet when he said that the greatest prayer of man does not ask for victory but for peace."[25]

Hammarskjold's warm reception by the Assembly expressed the general relief that a difficult problem was out of the way. In the absence of reliable information about Hammarskjold himself, most delegates sang the praises of Sweden, a country, as Hoppenot put it, "in which the delicate balance between political and social democracy has been achieved. His reputation," Hoppenot went on, "had preceded him and we knew him to be a great civil servant, a leading diplomat, and a gentleman."[26]

---

* After a year's experience Hammarskjold modified this statement in reply to some impatient questioning on lack of action on the diplomatic front. "One who is really serious in his determination to reach the top," he said, "does not gamble by impatiently accepting bad footholds and poor grips."

2

DAG HAMMARSKJOLD

In the flourishing literature on the art of life there is much talk about that rare quality: maturity of mind. . . . It is reflected in an absence of fear, in recognition of the fact that fate is what we make it. . . . The dignity of man, as a justification of our faith in freedom, can be part of our living creed only if we revert to a view of life where maturity of mind counts for more than outward success and where happiness is no longer to be measured in quantitative terms. . . . There is no formula to teach us how to arrive at maturity and there is no grammar for the language of inner life. . . . The rest is silence because the rest is something that has to be resolved between a man and himself. . . . You may be surprised by an approach to international service and to the problems raised by present-day developments in international life, which, like mine today, is concerned mainly with problems of personal ethics. The so-called realists may regard what I have tried to say as just so many fine words, only tenuously related to everyday life and political action. I would challenge this criticism. The thoughts I have shared with you about international service are conclusions from a most practical experience. Politics and diplomacy are no play of will and skill where results are independent of the character of those engaging in the game. Results

*are determined not by superficial ability, but by the consistency
of the actors in their efforts and by the validity of their ideals.
Contrary to what seems to be popular belief, there is no intellectual activity which more ruthlessly tests the solidity of a
man than politics. Apparently easy successes with the public
are possible for a juggler, but lasting results are achieved only
by the patient builder.**

THESE WORDS, SPOKEN AT Johns Hopkins University in 1955, express the
main theme of Hammarskjold's adult life, the search for that "maturity
of mind" which he regarded as the essential source of individual
strength and as the indispensable basis for the successful discharge of
public responsibility.

For the Secretary-General of the UN especially, the search for
maturity of mind has a practical and compelling sense. The Secretary-
General, for all his eminence, in reality enjoys few of the normal attri-
butes of power or authority. The strength of his office resides first of
all in his own strength of character, ability, and moral courage. Without these qualities the Secretary-Generalship can be little more than
an empty shell of high-sounding aims and principles and of good but
largely unfulfilled intentions. Hammarskjold's concern with personal
ethics, maturity of mind, and spiritual strength was thus far more
than the personal idiosyncracy of a good and high-minded man. It was
also the concern of the athlete to be in the best possible condition for
the race—a race that in his case, as he himself noted when he was
reelected in 1957, turned into a marathon.

Hammarskjold often used the word "integrity," and it was the key-
note of his own character—integrity in the sense not only of purity
and honor but also of seeing life as a consistent whole, subject in all
its parts to the same rules of conduct and standards of performance.
His friend the English sculptress Barbara Hepworth came near to
describing this quality when she said: "Dag Hammarskjold had a pure
and exact perception of aesthetic principles, as exact as it was over
ethical and moral principles. I believe they were, to him, one and the
same thing."[1]

Hammarskjold's posthumously published notebook, *Markings*, is
largely the logbook of his search for maturity of mind. It is an unusual
record for a highly successful public man, and some readers have
found its earnestness and frankness embarrassing and even unattrac-

---

*SG/424, June 14, 1955.

tive. It is certainly an intensely serious book which makes no effort at all to play up the more human or charming aspects of its subject. In calling it the "only true 'profile,' "[2] Hammarskjold presumably felt that he was describing that part of himself, the inner life, which no one else could possibly know and which was the source of all his conviction and strength.

Dag Hjalmar Agne Carl Hammarskjöld, the youngest of four brothers, was born on July 29, 1905, in Jönköping, Sweden, while his father was away in Karlstad as a delegate to the negotiations on the dissolution of the Swedish union with Norway. His father, Hjalmar Hammarskjold, came from an old and somewhat impoverished family of officers and country gentlemen with a long tradition of patriotic service and literary leanings. In the elder Hammarskjold's youth a series of financial difficulties had culminated in the loss of the family estate. Hjalmar Hammarskjold was a formidable, highly disciplined, and severe man who dominated his children's youth. His son, after quoting a critic who had said that his father's reactions to contemporary problems were "a cold and bitter gust from times gone by," described him as "one of those who are firm in their roots and firm in their faith, those whose changing fates may well deepen the convictions and directions of their early years, but not change them. . . . What gave an inner unity to his life was that in the period of revolutionary development through which he lived, he remained faithful to his past, faithful also to *the* past."[3]

Of his mother, to whom he was especially close, Dag wrote: "Agnes Almquist was different from him [Hjalmar] in many respects. Her characteristics, which appear to me to reflect her family origin, had once emerged with particular clarity and with the somewhat frightening overtones of genius in the poet Carl Jonas Love Almquist, a stepbrother of her father: a radically democratic view of fellow-humans, 'evangelic' if you like, a childlike openness toward life, an anti-rationalism with warm undercurrents of feeling."[4]

Hjalmar Hammarskjold went into politics in the early 1900's and suffered the first of a series of reverses when, as Minister of Justice, he failed completely to put through a scheme of electoral reform. In the autumn of 1905 he became Minister to Denmark and two years later he was appointed Governor of the District of Uppland at Uppsala, although he was still called upon from time to time for various international tasks. In 1914, in a time of European crisis and Swedish constitutional conflict, he unexpectedly became Prime Minister. As a conservative nonparty man with stern, old-fashioned views about public service and responsibility, he was, not surprisingly, unpopular. Whatever his real motives, his policies and actions over Swedish constitutional issues were interpreted as antidemocratic and reactionary, and he soon became a national political scapegoat.

Hjalmar Hammarskjold's attitude to the 1914 war was also unlikely, at least in retrospect, to make him popular. Believing that the war would be short and indecisive, he declared a policy of unreserved neutrality which he himself called "Swedish and nothing but Swedish"[5] and which inevitably led, after the war had been won by the Allies, to accusations of partiality to Germany. Dag Hammarskjold argued that although his father's immediate objective was to keep Sweden out of the war in its own best interests, he had also wished Sweden to be in an unimpeachable position in international law to participate, when peace came, in a new effort to develop an international order as a framework for European life, an international "Civitas Legum." By abstention from opportunism in time of war he hoped to lend the country weight, which it would otherwise have lacked, in a future international order to be based on law. In a joint note to the warring powers in the autumn of 1914, which was almost certainly drafted by Hjalmar Hammarskjold, the Scandinavian governments proposed to remain the guardian of international principles. According to Dag Hammarskjold, this declaration reflected "the conviction of a man who wanted justice—wanted it in realization of how thin is the wall between culture and barbarism, presaging the bitter experience of later decades."[6] According to his son, Hjalmar was fully aware "how incomplete and fluid were the rules in which the idea of justice was reflected in international intercourse" and would not go so far as to compromise Swedish vital interests to preserve these rules for posterity, but he also realized that "for a small country, international law, in the final analysis, is the only remaining argument, and that its defense is therefore worth sacrifices even in the egotistical interest of the country itself."[7]

In 1917, in a crisis precipitated by his refusal to countenance trade negotiations with Britain, Hjalmar Hammarskjold's Cabinet resigned, and he himself left active politics forever to become once again Governor at Uppsala.* Austere, unpopular, and subject for the rest of his life to recriminations and to what he believed to be a complete misinterpretation of his wartime policies, he devoted his energies to the life of a provincial governor, to the activities of the Swedish Academy, and to his work as chairman of the League of Nations committee for the codification of international law and as a delegate to the Disarma-

---

* Around July 29, 1961, Dag Hammarskjold's fifty-sixth and last birthday, he said: "My father was fifty-six when he had to leave politics for good; I'm wondering what will happen to me."[8]

ment Conference. He ceased to be Governor in 1930, and for his remaining twenty-three years he was, in his son's words, "a man placed entirely aside."⁹ In his last speech in the Swedish Parliament, when, in advocating strong defenses, he had once again become a target for invective, he said, "Who takes the initiative, who exerts influence, is so utterly unimportant compared to the one great question: to make our country secure for the future."¹⁰ "To the nineteen-year-old listener in the gallery," his son commented, "these words epitomized a life of faith in justice and of self-effacing service under a responsibility which unites us all."¹¹ Hammarskjold's father was certainly a primary influence on Dag Hammarskjold's own character, and in describing his father he often seems to be describing himself, as when he wrote: "A mature man is his own judge. In the end, his . only firm support is being faithful to his own convictions. The advice of others may be welcome and valuable, but it does not free him from responsibility. Therefore, he may become very lonely. Therefore, too, he must run, with open eyes, the risk of being accused of obdurate self-sufficiency."¹²

The atmosphere of the Hammarskjold home in the formal splendor of the sixteenth-century castle of Uppsala cannot have been an easy one for a sensitive child, and the sense of living in the aftermath of a political disaster was kept alive by public antipathy for the father

> *A box on the ear taught the boy*
> *That father's name*
> *was odious to them,*¹³

Hammarskjold wrote in 1959, in a poem that evokes his childhood in Uppsala. A sense of loneliness, isolation, of not belonging, as well as of being someone set aside for purposes not comprehensible to the ordinary man, was certainly an important part of Hammarskjold's inheritance. Great things were not only expected but required of the children of Hjalmar Hammarskjold. The eldest brother, Bo, had a highly successful career in Swedish public life, and another brother, Åke, became registrar of the Permanent Court of International Justice at The Hague in 1922 at the age of twenty-nine and a judge of the Court at forty-three, a year before his death in 1937.

Uppsala had its compensations both for the father and his sons. "The strange, brief idyll which burgeoned all over Europe between two crises and two wars," Dag Hammarskjold wrote, "had a reflection all its own in Uppsala. The church policy of [Archbishop Nathan] Söderblom in this period made the city an international center, and Hjalmar Hammarskjold joyfully shared the burden of the ceremonial tasks which accompanied this development. Both had a strong sense of academic pomp and circumstance."[14]

Dag Hammarskjold's academic career was almost uniformly distinguished. He received degrees in law and economics from the University of Uppsala and went on to receive his Ph.D. in economics at Stockholm. At the improbable age of thirty he became Under-Secretary of the Swedish Ministry of Finance and served concurrently as chairman of the Governors of the Bank of Sweden. At the Ministry he worked under the Fabian socialist economist Ernst Wigforss, whom he once said he considered his second father, and developed his own style. His friend Sture Petrén wrote:

> In this exacting key post at the center of Sweden's state administration, which Hammarskjold was to occupy for no less than ten years, including the entire war period, he had the opportunity of developing all the legendary self-discipline he imposed on himself and which was to enable him to master the enormous burden of work he later assumed in the United Nations.
>
> Thus, for long periods, Hammarskjold was able to manage with very little sleep, he was able to absorb at breakneck speed the content of documents and books and possessed the gift of retaining the overall view of the principal lines in a large complex of problems while seizing on isolated details of it. He was, however, also able to screen off what occupied him at a given moment, so that at that time this emerged for him as of paramount importance. Taken together, these traits endowed Hammarskjold with a crushing efficiency, a concomitant of which, however, was a certain disinclination to delegate work to others. The mode of life Hammarskjold had developed also required, apart from unfailing health, the absence of family life. On the other hand, he became the natural center in the circle of his closest collaborators, whose society he sought also for his scant leisure time and to whom he became, by the radiation of his personality and the multiplicity of his interests, a superior and friend of rare inspiration and stimulus. Also in his relations to staff in general, he was an esteemed and even loved boss by virtue of his natural kindness and personal interest.[15]

Hammarskjold regarded himself as a nonpolitical civil servant even after he became a Minister in the Swedish Cabinet in 1951, and he never joined a political party. In 1947 he became Under-Secretary in the Foreign Office in charge of all economic questions, and in 1949, when he was forty-four, he was appointed Secretary-General of the Foreign Office. His activities as Swedish representative in the formative period of the Organization for European Economic Cooperation and the Council of Europe gave him a foretaste of international life.

Hammarskjold's early experience of individual responsibility in public service was a good preparation for his job as Secretary-General of the UN. "I hate talking in personal terms," he told a press conference in November 1953, "but it finally boils down to the man. . . . Where there is an uncontested right of the Secretary-General, I find it easier to stand up against whatever pressures there might be from whatever corners they might come, because then I can come down to the personal factor and say frankly this is something I would not do. That is sometimes a stronger line of defense. Where you fight it out like a lawyer is, in my experience, in the political sphere a weaker position."[16]

For all his success as a Swedish civil servant, the early part of *Markings* reveals a nagging discontent that is part of an admitted immaturity. The theme of emptiness constantly recurs in these early pages, and with it the search for a meaning, a reality, a way "to transform the mirror into a doorway."[17]

"It is not," André Malraux wrote in *Antimémoires*, "the role which makes the historical personality, but the vocation."[18] Until he became Secretary-General, Hammarskjold had not found his vocation, extraordinarily successful though he was. His new sense of vocation in that exalted position provided the keystone of the arch formed by his other qualities—intellect, courage, stamina, and political judgment. To him the challenge of the Secretary-Generalship was the greatest of blessings as well as the greatest of burdens. He gladly surrendered his life to it, and in the year of his death he wrote: "From that moment stems the certainty that existence is meaningful and that therefore my life, in submission, has a goal. From that moment I have known what it means 'not to look back,' to 'take no thought for the morrow.' "[19] He made no mystery of this sense of vocation. "For someone," he wrote in 1957, "whose job so obviously mirrors man's extraordinary possibilities and responsibilities, there is no excuse if he loses his sense of 'having been called.' So long as he keeps that, everything he can do has a meaning, nothing a price. Therefore: if he complains, he is accusing—himself."[20]

The Secretary-Generalship was a welcome bondage. "I am more of a prisoner than ever," he wrote to Rajeshwar Dayal of India in December 1954, "but it is an imprisonment for which I have only to be grateful."[21] After the Suez crisis, at the height of a bitter public campaign against him in some Western countries, he was asked if he enjoyed his job. He replied, "Well, it seems incredible but I do."[22]

The springs of Hammarskjold's sense of vocation ran deep. They were traditional, intellectual, and religious. His identification with Christian thought was not messianic, but rather in the old tradition of the imitation of Christ in sacrifice and in service to others. He was a member of that small and lonely band who throughout history have engaged at the same time in trying to deal with the hard world of political and social reality and in searching endlessly for a spiritual meaning which transcends that world. He seldom spoke, or felt the necessity of speaking, of his religious faith, although in 1954, in an interview with Edward R. Murrow, he gave a most explicit statement of the place of religion in his life, which foreshadows the substance of *Markings*:

> Frankly and squarely to build up a personal belief in the light of experience and honest thinking has led me in a circle: I now recognize and endorse, unreservedly, those very beliefs which were handed down to me at an age when it was as yet impossible for me to appraise their significance or to make them blood of my blood. . . . I inherited a belief that no life was more satisfactory than one of selfless service to your country—or humanity. This service required a sacrifice of all personal interests, but likewise the courage to stand up unflinchingly for your convictions concerning what was right and good for the community, whatever were the views in fashion. . . . Faith is a state of the mind and the soul. In this sense we can understand the words of the Spanish mystic, St. John of the Cross: "Faith is the union of God with the soul." The language of religion is a set of formulas which register a basic spiritual experience. It must not be regarded as describing, in terms to be defined by philosophy, the reality which is accessible to our senses and which we can analyze with the tools of logic. I was late in understanding what this meant. . . . But the explanation of how man should live a life of active social service in full harmony with himself as a member of the community of the spirit, I found in the writings of those great medieval mystics for whom "self-surrender" had been the way to self-realization, and who in "singleness of mind" and "inwardness" had found strength to say yes to every demand, which the needs of their neighbors made them face, and to say yes also to every fate life had in store for them when they followed the call of duty, as they understood it. "Love"—that much misused and misinterpreted word— for them meant simply an overflowing of the strength with which they felt themselves filled when living in true self-oblivion. And this love found natural expressions in an unhesitant fulfilment of duty and in an unreserved acceptance of life, whatever it brought them personally of toil, suffering—or happiness.[23]

Hammarskjold's religious faith was very personal, and non-ritual. He wished neither to impose it on others nor to have others interpret it to himself. In New York he used to attend various churches, but when the minister of one of them recognized him sitting in a back pew and wrote to him expressing the hope that he would "worship" regularly in the church, Hammarskjold's reaction was extremely negative. Religion for him was a dialogue of his own with God, and faith was the foundation for duty, dedication, and service, qualities that he considered most essential in himself and most admirable in others.

Hammarskjold was fascinated by the timelessness and variety of religious experience. His description of the religious evolution of the great Swedish naturalist Linnaeus might almost be a description of his own experience: "Wonderment at nature's proof of the Lord's omnipotence had made young Linnaeus write this comment on his first experience of the midnight sun: 'O Lord, Thy verdicts are incomprehensible.' Later, when his eye, guided by somber experiences, was directed towards the world of men, this wonderment was turned into fatalistic mysticism."[24]

In highly intelligent men, religious and mystical yearnings are often the companions of solitariness and loneliness. Of his state of mind on coming out of prison in 1918, Bertrand Russell wrote:

> Underlying all occupations and all pleasures I have felt since early youth the pain of solitude. . . . What Spinoza calls "the intellectual love of God" has seemed to me the best thing to live by, but I have not had even the somewhat abstract God that Spinoza allowed himself to whom to attach my intellectual love. . . . My most profound feelings have remained always solitary and have found in human things no companionship. The sea, the stars, the night wind in waste places, mean more to me than even the human beings I love best, and I am conscious that human affection is to me at bottom an attempt to escape from the vain search for God.[25]

Hammarskjold's experience was a more positive one, and during the last years of his life he seems to have reached a sense of fulfillment and of peace within himself through self-surrender and acceptance of his fate. In 1959 he wrote:

> Simplicity is to experience reality not *in relation to ourselves*, but in its sacred independence. Simplicity is to see, judge, and act from the point of rest in ourselves. Then, how much disappears! And how everything else falls into place!
>   In the point of rest at the center of our being, we encounter a world where all things are at rest in the same way. Then a tree becomes a mystery, a cloud a revelation, each man a cosmos of whose riches we can only catch glimpses. For the simple, life is simple, but it opens a book in which we never get beyond the first syllable.[26]

Hammarskjold's lack of close personal obligations and ties was a great advantage in carrying out the crushing duties of the Secretary-Generalship, and his remark that the Charter should include an article stating that "the Secretary-General of the UN should have an iron constitution and should not be married"[27] was more than a joke. The absence of the benign tyranny of family life left him free to work and think at all hours, and to leave for anywhere at any time and at a moment's notice. Such a situation, leading as it inevitably does to a kind of motivated egotism, did not always make life easy for his more domesticated colleagues, and there was also the risk that it might in the end produce a dangerous isolation. But for a dedicated man following the most exacting of vocations it had incomparable advantages. It certainly did not mean that Hammarskjold was ascetic or rejected human companionship. He loved the company of his close friends and delighted in small social occasions and good conversation. The food and drink produced under his supervision by his Swedish cook, Nellie Sandin, at his apartment on East Seventy-third Street were superlative, and he was the most considerate and thoughtful of hosts. On his many journeys, one of his greatest pleasures was to end the day in a favorite restaurant. He was, however, a born bachelor, and it is impossible to imagine him in the amiable but time-consuming clutter of family life or in the genial distractions of a social circle.

That Hammarskjold was aware of his loneliness, and sometimes feared and dreaded it, is clear from *Markings*, as when in 1958 he contemplates his retirement: "Another few years, and then? Life has value only by virtue of its content—for *others*. Without value for others, my life is worse than death. Therefore—in this great loneliness—serve all. Therefore: how incredibly great what has been given me, what nothingness I am 'sacrificing.' "[28]

To Bo Beskow, after the latter's remarriage in 1955, he wrote:

You ask where is the human warmth? Everywhere and nowhere. In my situation in life I suppose this is part of the price of the stakes, that you are able to give yourself wholly and without reservation only if you don't steal, even in the smallest degree, from someone else: really to "die" in the evangelical sense, that is so frighteningly realistic as a description of the situation of man—can at certain times force you to this paradoxical egoism. . . . Instead I have the light and easy warmth of contact with friends such as Greta and yourself, or, for example, the Belfrages—or Bill: a kind of comradeship under the same stars where you ask for nothing and receive so much. When I see other possibilities (like yours), I can feel a short pain of having missed something, but the final reaction is: what must be, is right.[29]

In Hammarskjold's life, sex played little if any part. Many people find the concept of a man totally dedicated to his work, to intellectual and aesthetic interests and to spiritual experience, difficult to accept. Hammarskjold himself put the problem neatly in a haiku:

Because it did not find a mate
they called
the unicorn perverted.[30]*

Stupid or malicious people sometimes made the vulgar assumption that, being unmarried, he must be homosexual, although no one who knew him well or worked closely with him thought so. When he was confronted, in the first month of his Secretary-Generalship, with the rumors to this effect then being put about by his predecessor, Hammarskjold remarked that if there had been any element of truth in the story, he would not, and could not in the prevalent state of public opinion on the question of homosexuality, have accepted the office. The homosexual rumor was resurrected from time to time by various detractors when he was under political attack. It was printed in France, for example, during the Suez crisis, and when he was shown the story he remarked, "What kind of mind must a man have to write this sort of thing?"[31] and went on with his work.

It is true that Hammarskjold was a highly fastidious man who had to make a great effort to overcome a natural shyness and diffidence. In the early part of *Markings* a number of references indicate that he found the idea of sharing his life with someone else unimaginable, and later on he certainly believed that marriage and the Secretary-Generalship were totally incompatible pursuits. The idea of physical contact made him uneasy, and he shrank instinctively from it, just as he fiercely protected his privacy from attempted invasions by well-meaning friends and colleagues.

On the personal as well as on the professional side, the turning point in Hammarskjold's life was unquestionably his appointment, at the age of forty-seven, as Secretary-General. In meeting the challenge of the position, he began to find a more positive relationship with other people as well as the inner peace he had sought for so long.

From *Markings* it is all too easy to gain the impression of a man almost overwhelmingly high-minded, serious, and self-absorbed, but nothing could be further from the truth about Hammarskjold than the image of a priggish and humorless latter-day saint regarding the world with evangelical and joyless fanaticism. To friends and colleagues his lightness of touch, quicksilver mind, humor, boundless curiosity, and powers of perception made him a fascinating companion. The main difficulty was to keep up with the speed and develop-

---

* Hammarskjold was very fond of the unicorn image. Bill Ranallo, his personal aide, once gave him for his birthday a small silver unicorn mounted on a piece of black wood, which he kept on his desk. Mrs. Ranallo has it still.

ment of his thought, and, since he tended to do people the compliment of assuming that their mental processes were as rapid as his own, failure to keep pace could cause him to make harsh judgments. His job always came first, and any attempt to infringe on this priority would incur his extreme resentment. He disliked what he called "cocktail-party talk" and meaningless distractions of any kind, but relaxing at the end of the day in the office or over a good meal, he was as entertaining as he was informal. When he was not preoccupied, nothing gave him more pleasure than arranging a party or finding a particularly appropriate gift for a friend or the right flowers to complement the beauty of a female guest.

Hammarskjold's style of life, although always well organized, was by preference informal. Although he disliked ceremonial and pomposity, his position did not always allow him to escape them, and he took the minutest pains to ensure, by personally supervising every detail, the success of formal occasions. He was apologetic about any of his public functions that might seem pretentious to his friends. He was wary of publicity and worried about the distorting effect of public success. "We have to gain a self-assurance," he wrote in *Markings*, "in which we give all criticism its due weight, and are humble before praise."[32] In pondering the dangers of complacency, he wrote of the risks of "thoughtlessly mirroring yourself in an obituary."[33]

For all his seriousness and idealism, Hammarskjold was anything but heavy or sanctimonious. In fact, his quickness and agility of mind might have made a less serious person seem almost mercurial. His slight figure and youthful face usually gave an impression of constant motion. He walked everywhere when possible, and always with a brisk, springy gait, intent on the next objective. During the long debates of the UN's deliberative organs, however, he would sit almost motionless for hours on end, moving only occasionally to write a note to a neighbor* or to answer a question from a passerby. Beneath the fair hair and high brow, the deep-set blue eyes were expressive and striking, fixed sometimes on the middle distance in contemplation, sometimes frowning and preoccupied, sometimes twinkling over a joke or a ludicrous situation, and occasionally steel-blue with anger. His shyness often gave Hammarskjold a stiff and forbidding look during public occasions. Slight, youthful, and informal as he was, he had great presence and stood out in any company.

---

* There must be thousands of Hammarskjold's notes among the papers of people who sat near him in meetings. "Why does ——— make such faces?" a typical note read. The answer came back: "He always has." To which Hammarskjold replied, "Doubtless, but this is excessive."[34]

Hammarskjold's way of life was purposeful and highly disciplined. His disposition was better late at night than early in the morning, when he tended to be irritable and moody, but when necessary he was capable of working endless hours with very little sleep. In times of crisis he never seemed tired—rather he was exhilarated—and when even he became weary, one good night's rest in the country restored him. Lester Pearson wrote, "He was a man of quiet but incredible energy. I have never worked with anyone who seemed so impervious to fatigue—or human weaknesses. At one stage during the Suez crisis, I sat more than once six, eight or ten consecutive hours with him working through the night. He seemed always as fresh, calm and unhurried at breakfast as at midnight."[35] Work and stress undoubtedly stimulated him. Harold Beeley, a British diplomat, recalls visiting him on his return from a long trip, during which, Bill Ranallo told Beeley in the anteroom, they had had no sleep for the last three nights. Beeley therefore opened the conversation with Hammarskjold by saying that he must be very tired. "Tired?" Hammarskjold replied. "That would be frivolous."[36] He was never seriously ill and very seldom even mildly indisposed, and when he was he disliked any reference to his state of health. For all the endless hours of reading and writing, he never wore glasses.

Hammarskjold's apparent indefatigability was in good part due to a firm and admittedly egotistical self-discipline. He rarely did anything he thought unnecessary, never read what he did not wish to or have to read, and wasted as little time as possible in activities, social or professional, for which he had no use. His powers of concentration allowed him to direct all his energies to whatever he was doing and then to switch completely to the next task. He was meticulously neat, and objects at home and in the office had to be in their proper place. His desk rarely had more than one or two papers on it.

Hammarskjold came to love his life in New York and to regard the city as his second home. "Funny," he wrote in August 1955, "in spite of the very deep roots in Sweden, this is after all the place where I at present feel most at home."[37] The small gatherings of friends and people with common interests in his apartment, his long walks at night, his incessant visits to bookshops, and his weekends at his retreat, an hour and a half away in the woods near Brewster, New York, provided exactly the kind of recreation he needed. In spite of the satisfactions of New York, he never lost his nostalgia for Sweden, its life, tradition, and countryside—whether for the remote seacoast in the south where he had a small farmhouse and planned to live in retirement, or the northern wastes of Lapland where he loved to walk and climb.

Hammarskjold's love of Sweden was a source of great strength and confidence. Its very specific and unique cultural tradition was embodied in the Swedish Academy, to which he was elected* in 1954; in his own rather awkward words, this election strengthened his "spiritual roots."[38] He loved to write about Sweden, and his speeches to the Academy about his father[39] and on Linnaeus,[40] and an address to the Swedish Tourist Association in February 1960,[41] show a warmth of affection and an intimacy which only his native country could arouse. One of the best things he ever wrote was an evocation of the Uppsala Castle of his boyhood ("Slottsbacken"),[42] published in the yearbook of the Swedish Touring Association after his death. He referred to his great compatriot Linnaeus as "a shining prince of the land of summer —although his mind, also, was to turn toward brooding and to get chilled by the needling winds whistling through the small-town streets; a Swede whose disciples were sent to the four corners of the earth."[43]

In his last year, when he was unable to get even a few days to himself to visit Backåkra, the farmhouse in southern Sweden which he had recently bought and which was at last in order, Hammarskjold's longing for Sweden became more acute than ever. In a letter to his sister-in-law, Britte Hammarskjold, who had described to him a trip at the time of the midnight sun to Abisko, the northern point of Swedish Lapland, a month before his death he wrote: "How I understand you! Such a night up there can be of unearthly beauty, and I am most happy to know that you got to see it in that way. Now you understand why for me it is *the* part of the world which I like the most and which I have put beyond everything else I have happened to see."[44]

FROM HIS EARLIEST DAYS as Secretary-General, Hammarskjold provided an exhilarating spectacle of principle and intellect in action. His confidence, sureness of touch, and strength communicated to others the comforting feeling that in any situation he knew what to do and how to do it, where he wanted to go and how to get there. He was a leader of men while lacking most of the outward signs of a leader. His quickness in thought and action largely concealed the intellectual preparation that made possible a seemingly effortless and fully developed mastery of the most difficult subjects. His intellectual capacity and facility were extraordinary by any standard. His learning and

---

* This was the first time since the Academy had been founded in 1786 that a son had been elected to fill a seat vacated by his father.

experience in the fields of law, politics, logic, economics, and finance were comprehensive, and his penetrating, analytical mind quickly mastered a complex problem and went on to work swiftly and creatively ahead of it, weighing possible developments and alternative courses or combinations of actions that could be taken according to the way in which the situation developed. A difficult new subject was an enjoyable challenge to his intellectual curiosity, and his phenomenal memory for dates, figures, details of past situations, and legal and constitutional niceties extended to the exact location of obscure facts in old and compendious documents. He relied very little on notes or references. When he extemporaneously delivered a long speech in Mexico in 1959[45] and the Foreign Minister later asked him for the text, he proceeded to dictate the whole thing straight out, word for word, after his return to New York. The introduction to his last annual report,[46] a document of some eight thousand words that Hammarskjold himself regarded as the final and most complete statement of his position on the controversial issues of the time, was dictated without notes and without a pause, except for one final section, in one Sunday afternoon, and he made virtually no corrections at all to the original transcript. He increasingly wrote his own speeches and communications because he found it quicker than asking someone else to do it and then having to correct the text.

Such intellectual virtuosity was not always easy to work and live with, and Hammarskjold's quickness, his shorthand explanations, complete with multilingual nuances and a slight Swedish accent and intonation, sometimes baffled his listeners.* This in turn would irritate Hammarskjold, who did not suffer slowness of mind gladly. Many people misunderstood or failed completely to understand him, and mutual resentments often resulted. His summings-up of complex problems sometimes taxed the capacities even of his closest colleagues, for his comprehensive views and philosophical references were of little help once the quicksilver thread of his argument had been lost. This tended to narrow his more intimate circle, both among national representatives and in the Secretariat, and a certain cliquishness set in during later years.

Hammarskjold spoke French, English, and German almost perfectly and with complete fluency, although he seldom employed German. His exceptional knowledge of both French and English was often

---

* Hammarskjold's enunciation was by no means always clear, and it happened more than once that a new secretary, brought in during his travels to take dictation, would sit dumfounded, pencil helplessly poised, while Hammarskjold, pacing to and fro with a small cigar in his mouth, would dictate at length and at top speed, later having to go over all of it again.

embellished by interchanging idioms and expressions between the two languages when an extra nuance or an original meaning was required, or when one language expressed his meaning better than the other. He used the phrase *constatation des faits*, for example, because he could find no usable equivalent in English.

Hammarskjold's approach to his work at the United Nations was a mixture of perception, hard work, foresight, timing, political sense, nerve, and moral courage, all activated by his sense of duty and vocation. He was so adroit, so well prepared, so quick-thinking and comprehensively acting, that he might have been accused of slickness had his actions not been so clearly based on principle as well as on a strict and self-imposed rule of behavior. In *Markings* he laid down some general rules of conduct which well describe his approach to his job:

> It is more important to be aware of the grounds for your own behavior than to understand the motives of another.
> The other's "face" is more important than your own.
> If, while pleading another's cause, you are at the same time seeking something for yourself, you cannot hope to succeed.
> You can only hope to find a lasting solution to a conflict if you have learned to see the other objectively, but, at the same time, to experience his difficulties subjectively.
> The man who "likes people" disposes once and for all of the man who despises them.
> All first-hand experience is valuable, and he who has given up looking for it will one day find—that he lacks what he needs: a closed mind is a weakness, and he who approaches persons or painting or poetry without the youthful ambition to learn a new language and so gain access to someone else's perspective on life, let him beware.
> A successful lie is doubly a lie, an error which has to be corrected is a heavier burden than truth: only an uncompromising "honesty" can reach the bedrock of decency which you should always expect to find, even under deep layers of evil.
> Finesse must not mean fear of going on the offensive.
> The semblance of influence is sought at the cost of its reality.[47]

At his best Hammarskjold was extraordinarily sensitive to the difficulties and sensibilities of the people with whom he was dealing, and he had an exceptional talent for suggesting effective solutions that could be accepted without offense by the parties to a conflict. Sir Patrick Dean, the former British Ambassador to the UN, noted after his death his "supreme ability for finding a formula for reconciling the irreconcilable,"[48] and Walter Lippmann wrote of him, "Never before, and perhaps never again, has any man used the intense art of diplomacy for such unconventional and such novel experiments."[49]

A key to Hammarskjold's success as a negotiator was his ability to retain his mobility and to avoid either getting himself boxed in or committing others to rigid public positions that they would have difficulty in changing. By preserving his freedom of maneuver, he could often make local progress even in situations that appeared hopeless. "I may plan ahead," he told a press conference in May 1957, "but I always make alternative plans."[50] His keen sense of timing allowed him both to keep alternatives open and, at the right moment, to create new and unexpected options for the parties to a conflict. In an apparent deadlock he had a talent for spinning a new concept that both the conflicting parties might be able to grasp at without losing face. Such creations as the UN "presence" and much of the apparatus of "peace-keeping" were initially symbolic and insubstantial. Their first objective was to gain time for common sense and conciliation to come in at the back door when the conflicting parties could not afford to let them be seen coming in through the front door, and in this process the ideas themselves gradually gained substance and acceptance.

All of Hammarskjold's great gifts would have had far less effect without the personal impression he made on most of the people who dealt with him. His integrity, disinterestedness, and purity of intention were clear even to those—and they were many—with whom he frequently and strongly disagreed. He was not always liked, but he was almost invariably respected. In all the worldliness of his office he preserved an almost childlike purity and innocence. Charles Baechtold, Chief of Internal Services and Security in the Palais des Nations at Geneva, put it well when he said, *"Il était comme la Bize du Nord—qui balaye tout ce qui est mauvais et assure le beau temps"*[51] ("He was like the north wind—which sweeps away all that is bad and brings good weather").

Hammarskjold began early on to show a preference for leading his troops from the front. From the time of his opening struggles with McCarthyism he had insisted on his personal responsibility, and he could be relied on to be on the scene of action with, or preferably before, the advance guard of the UN in crises such as Suez, the Lebanon, Laos, the Congo, Katanga, and Bizerte. He took both political and physical risks in stride if he thought them necessary. He disliked and discouraged special measures for his own safety and never showed the slightest interest in them. He was convinced that there was no substitute for direct personal contact with problems and people; as soon as he had settled down in New York, he set out on a concerted program of visits to as many member states and regions of the world as he could fit into the normal requirements of his job. He never tired of seeing new countries, new peoples, and new cultures, and his protracted tours were a pleasure as well as a duty. For all his awkwardness in casual personal relations, he had a flair for making contacts on a human level in the course of an official tour; and his curiosity, his untiring interest in new places and ways of life, and his love of sightseeing and photography ensured that he got the maximum out of even the briefest visit.

Hammarskjold was acutely aware of his shyness and the consequent difficulty in establishing easy personal relations. He found that the "official family" of his own office provided him with exactly the degree of friendship, support, and collaboration he needed in his work without intruding on his privacy, and this small group soon became, and remained, the mainstay of his life at the UN. In the beginning it included Andrew Cordier, his executive assistant; Bill Ranallo, his personal aide, bodyguard, and chauffeur; Loretta Cowan, the Executive Office receptionist and switchboard operator; and Per Lind, whom Hammarskjold brought with him from the Swedish Foreign Office.

Cordier, an amiable, tough, and unbureaucratic history professor from Ohio, had worked in the State Department during the Second World War and had been at the San Francisco Conference. He was an expert on the General Assembly, and kept daily contact with delegations, with all the departments of the Secretariat, and with UN missions in the field. His extraordinary memory, capacity for work, and willingness to dive headfirst into difficult problems made him an invaluable right-hand man.

Bill Ranallo, who had been Lie's chauffeur and bodyguard, was to be Hammarskjold's constant companion until the very end, and it is hard to imagine a happier or more suitable appointment. Ranallo was tough, intelligent, practical, amiable, and tactful, with an unusual understanding of other people. He excelled in all the things that Hammarskjold himself could not do. He was a first-class driver, a highly trained bodyguard, and a brilliant resolver of difficult practical situations. He could, when necessary, cook, direct the household, and fix whatever needed to be fixed in New York or in the country. Ranallo soon became expert at gauging Hammarskjold's moods and knew exactly when to be formal or informal, when to make jokes or when to be solemn and respectful. He had, as Cordier said after Ranallo's death, a "unique quality of being always available and yet never personally asserting himself."[52] Ranallo had no intellectual pretensions and no interest in political matters. He could be relied on to put Hammarskjold's safety, comfort, and peace of mind before anything—even, with her own agreement, before the convenience of his own wife. In an organization that has little tradition, no great establishments, and very little ceremony and pomp, he was the perfect assistant and companion for a shy and rather unworldly intellectual completely involved in public life. Bill Ranallo did more than anyone else to make Hammarskjold's life as easy and as comfortable as possible.

Mrs. Cowan was a switchboard operator of genius. If there was a way of getting anyone anywhere in the world on the telephone she would find it, and she recognized the voices of most of the hundreds of callers to the Secretary-General's office even before they announced their names. She was also expert in dealing firmly with cranks and nuisances. In the long days and nights to come, she was an essential and invaluable part of Hammarskjold's office.

Per Lind, an old friend, was a link with Sweden and with the past as well as an indispensable assistant and confidant. Hammarskjold was devoted to Lind and his wife, Eva, and in his first months at the UN as well as in his last, they filled a vital role as old friends with whom he could talk about any subject with perfect frankness. Lind's quiet and diffident manner and Buster Keaton expression concealed a powerful intelligence, an unshakable integrity, and an imperturbable sense of humor. Of all Hammarskjold's Swedish assistants who worked with him in New York, Lind remained the closest to him.

Hammarskjold greatly enjoyed the family jokes and banter of his hard-working team, but outside this circle his relationships were not always smooth. His judgments of people could be harsh and irrevocable, often being based on a single mistake or misunderstanding, and he resisted, often rudely, any attempt to presume on his friendship. He had little use for colleagues who in his opinion did not meet the requisite standards of dedication, intelligence, or self-sacrifice. He was capable of hurting people deeply by taking them into his confidence and friendship for a while and then suddenly dropping them or freezing them out. He could also, on occasion, be extremely curt, often in front of other people. "I am coming to see you off at the airport,"[53] a senior colleague eagerly told him in a meeting. "How kind,"[54] Hammarskjold replied coldly; and when too many officials turned out to meet him at the Geneva Airport, he would greet them with "You are here too? I thought you would be busy."[55] On the other hand, he was steadfastly loyal, sometimes to his own cost, to subordinates in difficulties, and he never hesitated to take personal responsibility for their actions, even when those actions were not what he had intended.

Hammarskjold's highly organized way of life allowed him to get through very long working days and still have time for the intellectual interests that were his principal recreation. "Personally," he said in 1955, "I am very happy if I can escape professional talk after 7 or 8 o'clock."[56] His closest friends remained for the most part outside the world of the United Nations, although a few of his colleagues also became personal friends. Lester Pearson and Hans Engen of Norway belonged in this category, and Ralph Bunche, Andrew Cordier, and George Ivan Smith would often join his small dinners at Seventy-third Street. His closest friends were mostly Swedish: Leif Belfrage, then Secretary-General of the Swedish Foreign Office; Sture Petrén, a brilliant judge and latterly on the International Court; Karl Ragnar Gierow, the poet and author who was director of the Swedish Royal Dramatic Theater and later became secretary of the Swedish Academy; Per Lind; Uno Willers, the director of the Swedish Royal Library; and the painter Bo Beskow. With these men he was constantly in touch on one subject or another, although he tended to keep them in separate orbits.

Hammarskjold was passionately interested in literature, drama, painting, and music. His activities in these fields, even during crises at the UN, were a source both of curiosity and admiration. At a press conference in May 1961 a reporter asked him: "Mr. Secretary-General, we are all ... aware of the widened responsibilities throughout this whole year which have held you close to a dawn-to-midnight schedule —the continuous waves of crisis in the Congo, the necessity to defend the UN under siege, and a long extraordinary Assembly. Yet this is a year marked by the emergence of Dag Hammarskjold in other fields: as translator of Nobel Prize winner Saint-John Perse's volume *Chronique*; as co-translator of the English play in verse, *The Antiphon*, which had a world premiere in Stockholm in February; as author of 'A New Look at Mount Everest,' complete with some strikingly beautiful pictures by photographer Hammarskjold. My question is: How did you manage it all and what about sharing with us this magical formula for extension in time?" Hammarskjold replied: "Well, frankly all this was done before the Congo crisis. There was a happy period in May and June last year when things looked much better and when I could indulge in some activities of another type. But with your permission ... I think we should not indulge in those matters now but should get back to the tasks of the UN proper."[57]

Literature, which absorbed most of his spare time, also illuminated the other sides of his life. "It is curious," he wrote to Uno Willers on his return from Peking in 1955, "how experiences can suddenly fertilize each other. Subconsciously my reaction to the Peking landscape was certainly flavored by *Anabase*.* On the other hand, reading *Anabase* after having seen northern China, it is a new poem—an overwhelming one also in its extraordinary synthesis of the very soul of that part of the world."[58]

---

* A poem by Saint-John Perse.

Hammarskjold's literary activities took three main forms: active participation in the Swedish Academy, which awards the Nobel Prize for literature; his own translating work; and a constant readiness to lend a hand in solving various literary problems. He had always been concerned with the encouragement of writers all over the world. An early case of encouragement was Andreas Labba, a nomad Lapp from northernmost Sweden, who started in life working with reindeer and later became first a salmon fisherman and then a guide, and who finally wrote a best-selling book entitled *Anta,* based on stories told him in his young days by his elders. In a letter to Gunnel Hedberg, a librarian in Göteborg, Labba wrote:

> When I was about thirty, my relatives started passing away, one by one. That was when I began understanding that I might forget their tales and fables, and I realized that I would have to take to paper and pen to commit my recollections to writing. It was a strange decision. I, who had hardly had any schooling and who felt self-conscious with paper and pen, had to seek aid from the ABC-book to be able to spell the simplest words. Sometimes it seemed hopeless. . . . When I was on Kebnekaise* in 1935 I met Dag Hammarskjold. We then hiked together to Suorva and agreed to meet again the following year. We made four long trips on foot together from then on, and also one winter trip. And it was he who patiently encouraged me to learn to write and not be afraid of there being many faults in what I wrote. He egged me on to write short letters, to note down all the recollections I carried inside me and even small everyday happenings I encountered on my path. When I walked with Dag and his friends . . . I felt I was a human being like everybody else. And without the new frankness and assurance which Dag gave me, I would surely never have dared make it my aim to write down all the old tales and stories which the old ones had told me in my youth.[59]

Hammarskjold invited Labba to New York in 1958 to show him the UN.

Hammarskjold felt that one of the main purposes of the Nobel Prize in literature was to encourage new writers, and he was much concerned with the influence and pressures of the contemporary world on them. In 1957 he wrote:

> In a mass culture, where publicity, working in the interest of sales, is constantly harping on the idea that the latest must be the best, the book, in the view of many, becomes relegated to the ranks of disposable and rapidly aging consumer goods. This may lead to an industrialization of literature, which pays attention to the indications about public taste

---

* Kebnekaise is the highest peak in the Lapland mountains and a favorite goal of Swedish wanderers in the north.

in the best-seller lists in preference to that which is essential and therefore vital. In a situation which for such reasons, and perhaps also for other and deeper ones, is characterized by the quest for novelty and by conformism, a weakening of the position of older literature would be natural. The risk is enhanced if at the same time the position of the written word as such is becoming more precarious.[60]

He developed this idea just before his death in 1961 in a letter to the Swedish poet Erik Lindegrén:

> For many reasons I am trying to follow as best I can what is done in the literary field both generally and in particular in Sweden. On the whole, the effort is not very rewarding; too little humility, too little sub-ordination to the real purpose of art, too much showing off with brilliant new techniques, too little to say. It sometimes seems to me that an industrialization of literature has come about not only quantitatively— which is only too natural—but also qualitatively in the sense that the main concern seems now to be to bring to the market a new product, the merit of which for tired consumers—in the language of an American hair-tonic ad—is that "it is different." I guess that the reason is very simple. Those who have anything to say and who have integrity to say it simply in the way it has to be said, are not more numerous today than they ever were. But general literacy has created a market which can in no way be satisfied with the trickle of true literature from these few people, and therefore the field is wide open for all the busy students of "creative writing."[61]

Apart from Swedish books, Hammarskjold's own library is an anthology of the most enduringly enjoyable books in English, French, and German, and covers also philosophy, religion, and economics in the three languages. He collected first editions of his favorites, including almost all of Joseph Conrad, E. M. Forster's *A Passage to India*, Carroll's *Alice's Adventures in Wonderland*, Livingstone's *Missionary Travels*, Fitzgerald's *Tender Is the Night*, Newman's *Apologia*, and *The Pickwick Papers*, among many others.

For times past, his tastes were simple. He regarded Benjamin Constant's *Adolphe* as almost perfect, considered Stephen Crane's *The Red Badge of Courage* as good a novel as was ever written, and thought that the first part of *Huckleberry Finn* was perfection. When asked who could write a good novel about the United Nations, he replied that Stendhal would be ideal.[62]

Hammarskjold's interest in the award of the Nobel Prize for literature coincided with his literary association and friendship with the poet Saint-John Perse—the French diplomat Alexis Saint-Léger Léger. He already knew and admired Perse's poetry when he first met him in 1955 through Henri Hoppenot, the French Ambassador at the UN. "He is a very difficult and hermetic poet," he wrote to Uno Willers, then secretary of the Nobel Committee, "but I am personally convinced that he is of the same class as Yeats or Gabriela Mistral. Apart from the sheer beauty of his poetry there is a kind of wild 'grandeur' in his vision which is more of our age than any other poetry I know of today. It is really the poetry of an 'anabasis' of mankind in a time of global conscience."[63] By the beginning of 1955 Hammarskjold was already actively sponsoring Perse's candidacy for the prize, although he admitted that Perse's French was so complex as to make translation practically hopeless.

In September 1954, Hammarskjold asked Perse if he would agree to having Erik Lindegrén translate his works into Swedish, and over the next five years Lindegrén translated and wrote about a number of them. In this connection Hammarskjold asked Perse in 1959 for an explanation of his poem *Amers* and received a reply that was published in a Swedish periodical under the heading *"Lettre de Saint-John Perse à un écrivain suédois."*[64]

In the early summer of 1960, after finishing his translation of Djuna Barnes' *Antiphon*, Hammarskjold himself translated into Swedish Perse's *Chronique*, which Perse had sent him in October 1959. In making this translation he certainly had the Nobel Prize in mind, and in August he circulated it to the members of the Swedish Academy. On October 26, 1960, Perse was awarded the Nobel Prize for literature. In the midst of a chaotic Assembly session Hammarskjold translated Perse's address to the Nobel banquet into Swedish during a night meeting, and persuaded W. H. Auden to make an English translation of it. To his great regret, he was unable to go to Stockholm for the actual ceremony.

Hammarskjold had taken immense pains with his translation of *Chronique* and continued to consult and correspond with Lindegrén and with the publishers up to the moment of publication. "I regard Perse," he wrote in November 1960, "as a rather engaged poet, and the best of his underlying emotions is mostly reflected in the rhythm and an occasional choice of words."[65] For comprehension in Swedish, he told his publishers in Stockholm, "it is wise to get the reflection of as much of the music as possible, even at the cost of less exactitude in the word-for-word translation."[66]

Hammarskjold's friendship with Perse went beyond their literary interests, and their talk and letters ranged over politics and diplomacy as much as over literature. If Hammarskjold encouraged Perse, Léger also did much to encourage Hammarskjold: *"Gardez toujours vos fers au feu,"* he wrote to Hammarskjold in 1959, *"car vous êtes, à votre façon, créateur autant qu'animateur!"*[67] ("Always keep your irons in the fire, for you are, in your own way, a creator as much as an inspirer!")

Hammarskjold had strict views about the art of translation. When asked about the possibility of translating Linnaeus, he said:

> There is just no possibility to translate . . . eighteenth-century Swedish, giving the very personal flavour. It is difficult enough, you know, in modern language, to pass from one language to another one without losing the personal flavour, and when you go back in history in this way, it becomes impossible. For that reason, I would not recommend those translations I know about, because either they are scientific and do not care much about literary form, or else they are, let us say, mildly romantic and add a flavour which is perhaps natural to the translator, but is not the somewhat harsh and very pleasant flavour which the original has got.[68]

He tended to choose the most esoteric and difficult works to translate. He had first come across the works of the American writer Djuna Barnes when he bought her *Nightwood* in Paris in 1948. In June 1958 he wrote to Miss Barnes, telling her that although he had discussed her play in verse, *Antiphon*, in England with the poet Edwin Muir, he had not yet really grasped its meaning. Miss Barnes occasionally dined with him in New York, and the idea of translating *Antiphon* in collaboration with Karl Ragnar Gierow, then director of the Swedish Royal Dramatic Theater, soon developed to the point where Hammarskjold was able to tell her that "having worked with *Antiphon*, I now share your view that there is nothing obscure in it."[69] The translation was completed in the early summer of 1960, and on February 17, 1961, it was performed by the Swedish Royal Dramatic Theater. This crisis in the Congo made it impossible for Hammarskjold to leave New York, and after the performance Gierow cabled: "Wish your play an end as fine and triumphant as *Antiphon* got tonight."[70] After the critics had spoken, however, Gierow followed up this message the next day with, "Wish your play much better end than *Antiphon* got this morning."[71]

Hammarskjold's last, and uncompleted, adventure in translation was perhaps the most difficult of all. He greatly admired the philosopher and writer Martin Buber, who had visited him in New York in May 1958* and whom Hammarskjold visited in Jerusalem in January

---

* After Hammarskjold's death, in 1962, Buber gave a talk for the Swedish Radio, later published in his *Nachlese* under the title "Erinnerung an Hammarskjöld." He said: "Damals, im Hause der 'Vereinigten Nationen' einander gegenübersitzend, erkannten wir beide, Dag Hammarskjöld und ich, was es im Grunde war, das uns miteinander verband. Aber ich spürte, ihn anschauend und anhörend, noch etwas, das ich mir nicht zu erklären vermochte, etwas Schicksalhaftes, das irgendwie mit dieser Weltstunde, mit seiner Funktion in dieser Weltstunde zusammenhing" ("When we sat facing each other, in the house of the 'United Nations,' we both

1959. An initial attempt to translate the first part of Buber's *Die Legende des Baalshem* had shown him how formidable the difficulties were, but in August 1961 he told Buber that he still hoped to translate one of his studies. Buber replied by sending him his own copy of *Ich und Du* in the special edition produced for his eightieth birthday, and he suggested that Hammarskjold should translate it. On August 26, Hammarskjold replied that he would gladly try, and he started work then and there on the translation of what he called "not only a key work in modern philosophy but moreover one of the few great poems of this age."[73] This explains, incidentally, why entries in *Markings* cease after that date. On September 12, the day before he left New York on his final journey, he wrote to Buber to tell him that Bonnier's had agreed to publish the translation. He also informed Bonnier's that the first version would be ready in two months and was intended, because of the "exceedingly difficult" nature of the work, to make the meaning crystal clear, while a second version would provide "a maximum approximation to his intensely beautiful, intensely personal, but also intensely Old Testament-German prosody."[74] He was working on this translation during his final flight.

Hammarskjold was always prepared to lend a hand in literary causes. Gierow had told him that despite the denials of Eugene O'Neill's agents, an unpublished play by O'Neill existed. Hammarskjold found out from O'Neill's widow, Carlotta, that this was indeed the case, and in September 1955 he had Mrs. O'Neill and Gierow to dinner in New York. Mrs. O'Neill then told them that the success of the Stockholm production of *A Moon for the Misbegotten* in 1953, after its unfavorable reception in the United States, had given her dying husband hope that at least somewhere in the world his plays were believed in and properly produced. On his deathbed he told his wife that he wanted his last and hitherto unpublished play, *Long Day's Journey into Night*, to be produced by the Royal Dramatic Theater in Stockholm. Although most of O'Neill's plays had been a success in Stockholm, his widow had been apprehensive and, because his later plays had not done well in the United States, she had not dared to get in touch with the Swedish Theater. She was therefore delighted and relieved when Hammarskjold and Gierow approached her about the play, which was soon thereafter produced for the first time in Stockholm. The dedication from Mrs. O'Neill in Hammarskjold's copy of *Long Day's Journey into Night* reads:

---

recognized, Dag Hammarskjold and I, what it basically was that bound us together. But I felt, looking at him and listening to him, something more, which I could not explain, something fateful, that was somehow connected with this hour of the world, with his function in this hour of the world").[72]

"Dear Mr. Hammarskjold: for you who paved the way for this play to come into its own—I send the printed word. With it goes my gratitude for the giving of your time, your interest—and your kindness to me."[75] Mrs. O'Neill remained a close friend until Hammarskjold's death.

Hammarskjold was much concerned with the postwar fate of the poet Ezra Pound and worked with Archibald MacLeish and Robert Frost to get him a permit to leave his confinement in St. Elizabeth's mental hospital in Washington. In his capacity as a member of the Swedish Academy he wrote to Assistant Secretary of State Francis Wilcox to suggest various ways in which this could be achieved, and on April 19, 1958, when Pound was at last released, he wrote MacLeish, "Congratulations to you, to common sense and poetry."[76]

Hammarskjold was fascinated by contemporary painting and sculpture. "Modern art," he said in an address for the twenty-fifth anniversary of the Museum of Modern Art in New York, "teaches us to see by forcing us to use our senses, our intellect and our sensibility to follow it on its road of exploration. It makes us seers . . . and explorers—these we must be if we are to prevail."[77] In 1954, through the good offices of the architect Wallace Harrison, he borrowed a small group of pictures for his office suite in the UN from the Museum of Modern Art. Some of them were changed over the years, but initially, from what was available, he chose works by Peter Blume, Lyonel Feininger, Fritz Glarner, Gris, Matisse, Picasso, and Rouault. Later he chose another magnificent Picasso of a different period, a Delafresnaye still-life for his own office, a fine Helion, a Braque, and a Léger, and from his own collection he brought a Hepworth and two Jean-Jacques Morvans to his office.

The UN Headquarters in New York gave Hammarskjold a practical field for his interest in contemporary art, and he never tired of walking around the building and the garden and thinking of new ways of improving them. He tried to make the official gifts of governments to the UN, which are notoriously uneven in quality, look as good as possible by supplementing them with changes in décor and the addition of original works of art.

The difficulty of reconciling popular piety with the fact that the UN is a multireligious secular organization had led to the creation in the Headquarters of a Meditation Room designed to meet the needs of the devout and the unaffiliated alike. This compromise had resulted, before Hammarskjold's time, in a meaningless and tasteless room to which he took an instant dislike, and he devoted a great deal of time and energy to creating a new one. It finally emerged as a dark, dramatic, narrow room with striking perspective and lighting. In its center is a great rectangular block of iron ore illuminated by a single shaft of light. Hammarskjold had remembered an altar made of iron ore at Malmberget in Sweden and asked his friend Erland Waldenström, director of the Grängesberg-Oxelösund Mining Company, to provide a suitable block of ore, which was cut and sent to New York. He had hoped that Braque would paint a mural for the end wall of the new Meditation Room and wrote to him that "in a setting of entire simplicity we work mainly with effects of light" and that "for the home of the United Nations only the perfect is good enough."[78] Braque, however, declined to come to New York, and Bo Beskow finally did the mural. Hammarskjold was delighted with Beskow's work, and the Meditation Room remained one of his favorite places at UN Headquarters despite what some others considered its somewhat chilling and abstract perfectionism.

One of Hammarskjold's most happy relationships with artists was with the British sculptor Barbara Hepworth. In 1956 it was arranged that Miss Hepworth would lend a piece of sculpture from her current exhibition in New York to be placed in his office. She herself suggested two possible works, one of which, curiously enough, was entitled "Antiphon." Hammarskjold visited the exhibition in January 1957 and chose a pure wooden column, "Single Form," which was placed first in his private office and later in the dining room of his suite. He also bought a drawing, "Three Views of a Young Girl," which was hung in his library at Seventy-third Street.

Hammarskjold and Barbara Hepworth shared a single-mindedness and integrity that proved a permanent bond, and in September 1960, when the Congo crisis was deepening, she wrote that she had attached a note to her will to the effect that "if anything happened to me before I make a sculpture which I feel is 'right' to offer you, you can have a choice from all my remaining works."[79]

In May 1961, Miss Hepworth, who was as diffident as Hammarskjold in personal relationships, asked if he was coming to London and, if so, might be able to visit her current exhibition at Gimpel's, in which there was a sculpture she had done specially for him. He went to the exhibition on his way back from Oxford in early June and picked out the intended piece, a wooden abstract sculpture, at that time entitled "Churinga III." When it was installed to his satisfaction in his office in New York, he wrote to its creator that it was "a strong and exacting companion, but at the same time one of deep quiet and timeless perspective in inner space."[80]*

---

* After Hammarskjold's death, through the efforts of Ralph Bunche and the generosity of Jacob Blaustein, Barbara Hepworth executed, as a memorial to Hammarskjold, the great abstract sculpture "Single Form" which dominates the entrance to the Secretariat Building at UN Headquarters.

Hammarskjold's taste in music was astringent and predominantly anti-Romantic. Music was to him an important source of recreation, and he also did much to bring it into the life of the UN. In 1954 he arranged, through a gift from Thomas J. Watson, Sr., for the construction of a movable concert stage with which the General Assembly hall could be converted in twenty-four hours into a fully working concert hall, and he took a major part in arranging the annual UN Day concerts and choosing the artists and the programs. He also established the tradition of playing the last movement of Beethoven's Ninth Symphony on each UN Day. In his last year, when on October 24, 1960, the whole symphony was performed by Eugene Ormandy and the Philadelphia Symphony Orchestra, he described it as "this enormous confession of faith in the victorious human spirit and in human brotherhood, a confession valid for all times and with a depth and wealth of expression never surpassed."[*][81]

Rooted in the European tradition yet always welcoming new ways and new experience; shy and fastidious but with a boundless regard for humanity and its possibilities; a man of deep integrity, determined to use all his gifts for the purposes and ideals he believed in; an intellectual of extraordinary range, disciplined by practical common sense and deep intuition; dazzling, difficult, considerate, exigent, aloof and charming by turns, but always consistent in the main preoccupations of his life; unshakable in his convictions but responsive to all the vital elements of the world about him—Hammarskjold was at the same time impressive and elusive. Henri Hoppenot, who had first formally proposed his name for the Secretary-Generalship, wrote of him after his death:

> Je n'ajouterai rien à tout ce qui a été dit, depuis sa disparition, sur les qualités extérieures de l'homme. Son inlassable courtoisie, la réserve et la gentillesse à la fois de son abord, et, sous la souplesse de sa démarche, l'inflexible fermeté de son propos. Quelques-unes des plus exquises traditions de la vieille Europe se sont réfugiées et maintenues vivantes dans ces oasis nordiques, à l'abri, depuis plus d'un siècle et demi, des guerres et des révolutions. Héritier de cette culture et de ses raffinements, Dag Hammarskjold avait su s'évader de cet air raréfié, et son esprit comme son coeur étaient ouverts à tous ces vents qu'a nommés le poète qu'il aimait:

---

* A year later, at the memorial service for Hammarskjold at the UN, the recording of this message was repeated, and the Ninth Symphony was played again by Ormandy and the Philadelphia Symphony Orchestra, which, in tribute to Hammarskjold and his colleagues who had died with him, and with the permission of the Musicians Union, interrupted a strike that had lasted several months.

. . . de très grands vents sur toute face de vivants . . . de très grands vents en quête de toutes pistes de ce monde. . . . Et d'éventer l'usure et la sécheresse au coeur des hommes investis.*

Il n'était rien d'usé ni de sec au coeur de l'ami que nous avons perdu, de l'homme investi des plus hautes responsabilités humaines et qui ne les assuma jamais avec plus de lucidité et de courage qu'à l'heure de ce départ, pour ce dernier vol, au seuil de la nuit africaine. . . .[82]**

---

* Saint-John Perse, *Vents*.
** Translation:

I shall not add to all that has been said, since his disappearance, of the outward qualities of the man. His unfailing courtesy, both the diffidence and the kindness of his manner, and, beneath the suppleness of his approach, the inflexible firmness of his purpose. Some of the most exquisite traditions of the old Europe took refuge and stayed alive in these Nordic oases, sheltered, for more than a century and a half, from war and revolution. Heir to this culture and its refinements, Dag Hammarskjold managed to escape from this rarefied atmosphere, and his spirit, like his heart, was open to all those winds spoken of by the poet he loved:

. . . very great winds on all the faces of the living . . .
very great winds gusting over all the trails of this world. . . .
And airing out the attrition and the drought in the hearts of men in office.[83]

There was nothing trite, nothing dried up in the heart of the friend we have lost, one whose office carried the highest responsibilities known to man, and who never assumed them with more lucidity and courage than at the hour of departure for this last flight on the threshold of the African night. . . .

3

THE FIRST
STAGE

Those who advocate world government and this or that special form of world federalism, often present challenging theories and ideas, but we, like our ancestors, can only press against the receding wall which hides the future. It is by such efforts, pursued to the best of our ability, more than by the construction of ideal patterns to be imposed upon society, that we lay the basis and pave the way for the society of the future.*

DAG HAMMARSKJOLD CAME TO HIS NEW POST with clear and realistic ideas of the nature, position, and limitations of the world organization of which he was the chief officer. "The UN," he said two years later, "reflects both aspiration and a falling short of aspiration, but the constant struggle to close the gap between aspiration and performance now, as always, makes the difference between civilization and chaos."[1]

---

* Dag Hammarskjold in a speech entitled "The Development of a Constitutional Framework for International Cooperation," delivered at a special convocation and dedicatory celebration marking the completion and occupancy of the new buildings of the University of Chicago Law School, May 1, 1960. SG/910, May 1, 1960.

Since World War II, technological progress has been steadily forcing the nations of the world to live as interdependent neighbors, although they are still deeply divided in other ways. In the face of heavy odds the United Nations represents, in Hammarskjold's words, "the beginning of an organic process through which the diversity of peoples and their governments are struggling to find common ground upon which we can live together in the one world that has been thrust upon us before we are ready."[2]

The United Nations is vested with no sovereign powers. The only exception to this principle is the power of the Security Council to enforce certain actions, provided its five permanent members are agreed—a possibility, as Hammarskjold put it, "which for obvious reasons, today is highly theoretical. It is not likely," he went on, "that a world organization embracing so many disparate and, at times, antagonistic systems of government and national cultures could be held together today on any other basis. The UN, therefore, must rely for the present mainly on the processes of negotiation, persuasion and consent to accomplish its purposes and, above all, on the exercise of enlightened and moral leadership by those in positions of responsibility."[3]

Hammarskjold saw as the primary political function of the UN the day-to-day effort to control and moderate conflicts that were a threat to peace, through a system of mediation and conciliation developed on a basis of the sovereign equality of states. This primary function went hand in hand with a long-term effort to attain wider social justice and equality both for individuals and, in the political, economic, and social senses, for nations. He believed that progress in this direction must be based on a growing respect for international law and on the emergence of a truly international civil service, free from all national pressure and influences and recognized as such by governments.

He was very much aware of the prevailing disillusionment with the UN and the impatience with which its proceedings were increasingly viewed around the world. "Aboard this new *Santa Maria*," he said in September 1953, "we have to meet the impatience of those sailors who expect land on the horizon tomorrow, also the cynicism or sense of futility of those who would give up and leave us drifting impotently. On the shores we have all those who are against the whole expedition, who seem to take a special delight in blaming the storms on the ship instead of the weather ... we have still to prove our case."[4] He was fond of quoting, apropos of critics of the UN, a phrase of Paul Valéry's, *"ceux qui préfèrent se noyer à nager dans les conditions de l'eau"* ("those who prefer drowning to swimming in the conditions imposed by the water"), as expressing the simple truth that "when trying to change our world, we have to face it as it is."[5]

Hammarskjold welcomed the demise of the early illusion that the UN would be able to enforce peace and impose the settlement of political disputes, and believed that a more realistic assessment would provide a new starting point for the Organization in a troubled world. If the UN could not impose peace, there was "no existing or conceivable alliance of nations in the world today that could do so either," despite the fact that "the policy of alliance, the policy of countervailing power . . . dominate the attention of governments and peoples alike."[6] This meant that although the quest for military security, with its prior claim on the budgets of the great powers, would go on outside the UN framework, the Western and Communist worlds had to learn to live with each other as the only alternative to a third world war fought with nuclear weapons. In such a situation the UN should be able to provide a positive and practical response to the dilemmas of the world. Its Charter was an expression of moral purpose on which all could agree. The Organization provided, in spite of the cold war, a meeting place and a center for reconciliation, as well as for constructive planning for the future. It was, Hammarskjold said, "a body where ideologies are permitted to clash inside the wider framework of a fundamental unity of purpose for peace,"[7] an organization "not created in order to bring us to heaven, but in order to save us from hell."[8]

The structure of the UN as laid down in the Charter provides for a series of principal organs that cover the main aspects of international life. Of these the Security Council, with the primary responsibility for international peace and security and a theoretical capacity to enforce its decisions, is the most prominent and most frequently in session. The General Assembly, consisting of all the member states, has one regular annual session that covers all the activities of the Organization and can also be called into emergency or special sessions by the Security Council or by a majority of the members. Its decisions are recommendatory, not obligatory. The Economic and Social Council deals with a wide range of economic and social matters, and the Trusteeship Council with territories administered and supervised under the international trusteeship system. The International Court of Justice is the principal judicial organ of the international system. The international Secretariat, headed by the Secretary-General, is the last of the principal organs of the UN.

Affiliated with the UN are the autonomous Specialized Agencies: the Food and Agricultural Organization (FAO), International Bank for Reconstruction and Development (IBRD), International Civil Aviation Organization (ICAO), International Development Association (IDA),

International Finance Corporation (IFC), International Labor Organization (ILO), Inter-Governmental Maritime Consultative Organization (IMCO), International Monetary Fund (IMF), International Telecommunications Union (ITU), United Nations Educational, Scientific, and Cultural Organization (UNESCO), Universal Postal Union (UPU), World Health Organization (WHO), World Meteorological Organization (WMO), and, after 1957, the International Atomic Energy Agency (IAEA). Although there is an elaborate mechanism for coordinating and reporting to the UN on the activities of these agencies, they are independent intergovernmental bodies operating under their own constitutions with memberships different from that of the UN. Their independence of the central organization is for the most part jealously guarded. In addition to the Specialized Agencies, there are two large semiautonomous United Nations Agencies, the United Nations International Children's Emergency Fund (UNICEF) and the United Nations Relief and Works Agency for Palestine Refugees (UNRWA).

When Hammarskjold came to the UN, this comprehensive blueprint for international order was already frustrated in a number of ways. The Security Council was frozen into near immobility on many important issues by the cold war. The Assembly was dominated, on political issues especially, by the almost automatic majority enjoyed by the United States and its Western allies, although useful work had been done in many fields, such as the passage of a Universal Declaration on Human Rights, and through deliberations on colonial questions that gave a powerful impetus to the movement of decolonization.

The Economic and Social Council, although its procedures tended to be lengthy and bureaucratic, had launched in 1948 the UN program of technical assistance for economic development of underdeveloped countries that was to become the organization's largest and one of its most effective functions. The International Court of Justice, in the somewhat rarefied atmosphere of its palace in The Hague, was infrequently resorted to on important matters in a period when governments preferred to make their own judgments on questions of international law rather than submit to a judicial determination by the International Court.

The Secretariat, the embryonic international civil service, was going through a time of travail and low morale. As a relatively new concept in international life, first experimented with in the League of Nations, the notion of an independent international civil service was not particularly popular with long-established governments and their Foreign Offices. There was a tendency to look on international officials at best as clerks and second-class bureaucrats, and at worst as interlopers and meddlers in the rightful affairs of sovereign governments. The Secretary-General, Trygve Lie, had been disowned by the U.S.S.R. over the Korean war almost at the same time that the Secretariat had become the arena for an anti-Communist witch-hunt by the U.S. authorities.

Precariously poised atop this elaborate structure, the office of the Secretary-General was far from securely established. The Charter, in five short Articles (97–101), assigns the Secretary-General two main functions. He is the chief administrative officer of the Organization, a full-time job in itself. In a radical departure from the nonpolitical concept of the Secretary-Generalship to be found in the Covenant of the League of Nations, he also has vague and far-reaching political functions. Article 98, by providing that the General Assembly, Security Council, and other organs may entrust the Secretary-General with unspecified "other functions," in effect brings the Secretary-General and the Secretariat into the arena of political conflict by charging them with carrying out political decisions which are often controversial. Article 99, a complete innovation, gives the Secretary-General the right to bring to the attention of the Security Council any matter that in his opinion may threaten the maintenance of international peace and security. This imprecise but wide-ranging mandate is the constitutional basis for an important part of the political work of the Secretary-General, implying as it does a broad discretion to conduct inquiries and to engage in informal diplomatic activity on matters relating to international peace and security. The Secretary-Generalship has become, among other things, a novel experiment in active multilateral diplomacy, and the political side of the Secretary-General's work has tended more and more to overshadow his administrative functions.

For all his prestige, the Secretary-General has little or no power, and while he may be able to influence events, he can seldom if ever control them. It is with and through sovereign governments, which are not always responsive to the hopes and ideals which he represents, that he must deal. It is in their relations with each other that he must play the part of a discreet, objective, and indefatigable go-between and face-saver, well knowing that he is a convenient scapegoat when things go wrong and that he can seldom afford the luxury of publicly being right. The Secretary-General is an embodiment of the hopes of mankind for international peace and justice, but when peace and justice are traduced he can seldom, if he wishes to preserve his usefulness, point the finger of judgment. He is at the same time the appointed head of a still embryonic experiment in world order and the director of a series of desperate last-minute efforts to avoid or limit conflict. Real authority tends to be vested in him only when things have reached a stage so dangerous and so confused that his intervention seems to be the only remaining hope, and by that time it is already very late to make good use of what support and authority he may be given. If the Secretary-General, as Hammarskjold once half-jokingly remarked, is a sort of secular Pope, he is also for much of the time a Pope without a church.

The UN, being primarily an association of sovereign governments, has no sovereign powers of its own. Thus the Secretary-General, as its chief officer, has great responsibilities but an extremely limited capacity for independent action. His position, in theory Olympian, is in practice threadbare and largely improvised. Behind the world's first international civil servant there are no great resources, no tradition, no revered establishments, not even an adequate budget. By comparison with the statesmen of the present, not to mention the great proconsuls of the past, the material trappings of the Secretary-General's office are modest indeed. The eminence of his position is symbolized by no heart-thrilling ceremonial or traditional grandeur, such as is associated with the leader of even the smallest sovereign state. The Secretary-General usually travels the world in pursuit of peace and justice with one or two assistants and by ordinary commercial aircraft.

Although the Secretary-General has become increasingly a political figure, his task as the chief administrative officer of the UN is extremely important and difficult. He is the chief official of the international civil service, a concept still in a rudimentary stage of development. When Hammarskjold arrived in 1953, he was responsible for a staff of some 5,700 people of 67 nationalities scattered all over the world, and by 1961 the staff had increased to some 7,000 members from 87 countries. Constantly confronted by urgent political tasks, the Secretary-General must also administer this organization, in which the normal difficulties of a civil service are compounded by the number of the member nations and by the conflicting pressures of an exiguous budget and an ever-increasing program of activity. Since the Secretary-General is the only elected official, much of his responsibility, even in administration, cannot be delegated.

One element in the existing UN setup proved extremely important to Hammarskjold's method of work. The establishment at the UN Headquarters of permanent national representatives provides the Secretary-General with the possibility of practically uninterrupted informal contacts and negotiations on problems with expert and highly experienced diplomats from all over the world. The work of the permanent national representatives may well, Hammarskjold wrote in 1959, "come to be regarded as the most important 'common law' development which has taken place so far within the constitutional framework of the Charter."⁹ The permanent representatives provide a kind of continuous diplomatic conference which, through the close relationships and friendships of those concerned, makes possible a businesslike mutual exploration of the most delicate problems far beyond the scope of regular diplomatic contacts. Hammarskjold increasingly used the permanent national representatives at UN Headquarters as his collaborators and confidants in the complex operations of his later years—sometimes even to the point where the representatives concerned experienced a conflict of loyalty between the UN and their own governments.

Hammarskjold's relationships with permanent representatives and with their governments did not develop quickly or always smoothly. Initially, his most important contacts were with the United States and the Soviet Union, since he had inherited Lie's strained relations with both of them. The confidence and understanding of the American authorities were particularly essential to his purposes. He had not been the U.S.-backed candidate for Secretary-General, and his first duty was to question, and even to challenge, much of the U.S. internal loyalty procedure. Nor did it seem likely that Hammarskjold and Henry Cabot Lodge, Jr., the U.S. representative, would at first sight see eye to eye on difficult matters. Lodge, who had just been defeated for election to the U.S. Senate by the relatively little known John F. Kennedy, was the patrician political representative of a new U.S. administration that had yet to prove itself; Hammarskjold was a foreign civil servant and intellectual who was almost entirely unknown in the United States.

Secretary of State John Foster Dulles did not seem inclined at first to take the new Secretary-General very seriously and was evidently irritated by early indications that this quiet, young-looking Swede had strong ideas of his own about what was right and wrong. Hammarskjold's first official visit to Washington, on May 6, 1953, was a low-key and inconsequential affair; except for an hour with President Eisenhower, he was dealt with by second-rank officials. Eisenhower seemed to understand better than Dulles Hammarskjold's insistence on his right of independent judgment in loyalty questions, and after a frustrating exchange of views Hammarskjold told Dulles flatly that U.S. public opinion should be satisfied if the UN succeeded in having a politically neutral staff. Serious political problems such as Korea were not discussed, and he left Washington under no illusions about his standing in the capital of the United States. The President ended the meeting by saying that he hoped for a chance for future talks. Hammarskjold commented, in his own notes on the meeting, "and he *may* have meant what he said."¹⁰

Hammarskjold's first dealings with the U.S.S.R., also about personnel matters, went smoothly in comparison with his confrontation with the U.S. authorities. On April 21 Andrei Y. Vyshinsky had told him than Constantin Zinchenko, the top Soviet Secretariat official, would not be coming back to New York from his leave in Moscow and suggested the name of a successor as Soviet Assistant Secretary-General, referring to this function as "liaison with the Secretariat."[11] Hammarskjold heard this request with what he described as "extreme caution"[12] and asked Vyshinsky for alternative candidates. When Vyshinsky persisted in his original suggestion, Hammarskjold told him that, at thirty-five, the candidate was too junior to occupy the top Soviet post in the Secretariat and that he was not prepared thus to weaken it, nor would he buy a "cat in a bag"[13] whom he had not even had the chance to interview. Vyshinsky retorted that Hammarskjold himself had been a cat in a bag but the U.S.S.R. had accepted him nonetheless, to which Hammarskjold replied that that might have been imprudent of the Soviet Union since that particular cat insisted on having its own way. Vyshinsky accepted this exchange with a broad smile, and Hammarskjold then suggested that Ilya S. Tchernychev, whom he had known well as Soviet Ambassador in Stockholm, should become the Soviet Assistant Secretary-General. Tchernychev's appointment was announced on May 26.[14]

Hammarskjold's relations with Vyshinsky were amiable, and both men seem to have enjoyed capping each other's metaphors. At lunch in August, for example, Vyshinsky asked him how he felt about his job. Hammarskjold answered that it would take time to develop it into an institution free from group interests and yet trusted by all concerned. Vyshinsky commented that it was always easier to make a new suit than to mend an old one and expressed the hope that Hammarskjold would not regard his role as passive. Hammarskjold replied, with reference to his usefulness to governments, that "good husbands always know when and where to find a midwife."[15] When Vyshinsky said that husbands did not always call the midwife in time, he asked if Vyshinsky meant that the midwife should tell the husbands when the day was drawing close, to which Vyshinsky replied that the midwife might do a useful job by taking the initiative and teaching the husbands a few things. Although Hammarskjold never hesitated to take up contentious matters with him, he remained on good terms with Vyshinsky until the latter's death in November 1954.

After the long political winter of the Korean war and the cold war there were, from the beginning of 1953, some signs of spring on the international scene. In January the Eisenhower administration had been installed in Washington, and in March Stalin died. The agreement of the great powers on Hammarskjold's appointment was in itself an indication of the changing climate, and on April 18, a week after his arrival, the General Assembly, after hearing unusually conciliatory speeches from both the United States and the U.S.S.R., unanimously adopted a resolution[16] calling for an armistice in Korea.

In this relatively encouraging atmosphere, the pace was almost leisurely, and the demands on Hammarskjold, although many, left him time for thought and even for recreation. He was accessible, diffident, and friendly. Administrative matters occupied the bulk of his time in these early months, and he made a determined effort to bridge the gap that had developed between his predecessor and the UN staff. On April 15, he[17] wrote to all staff members saying that he hoped to visit all of them informally in their offices, and this he managed to do in the course of the next six weeks. He also tried to eat as often as possible in the staff cafeteria.

For three weeks after Hammarskjold's arrival, Lie remained ensconced in an office on the thirty-eighth floor, ostensibly to assist and advise his successor. For Hammarskjold, who was fully aware of what Lie had been saying about him, this was a considerable embarrassment, and on May 1, to provide Lie with an opportunity to say a final farewell, he arranged a general meeting of the staff that both he and Lie would address. In the nature of things this was a somewhat stilted occasion. Although Hammarskjold's delivery was clipped and stiff, he took an informal personal line, urging the staff not to lose a sense of unity and partnership in a common venture and asking its confidence and trust in his handling of current difficulties, even if its members might not always agree with him in every detail. "The principles," he said, "on which the independence of our Secretariat is founded will be staunchly defended and firmly applied,"[18] but there would be no rapid or revolutionary changes in the administration. He turned Lie's gloomy welcome of three weeks before into a valedictory compliment. "You, the creator of this vast administration," he told Lie, "have said that the job of the Secretary-General is the most impossible job in the world. If so, you have done the impossible."[19] Lie responded with an emotional account[20] of the trials and the achievements of the past seven years, and finally left New York on May 8.

Hammarskjold returned to Europe in May to visit the UN European Office in Geneva and meet the heads of the Specialized Agencies, which make up the so-called United Nations family. He went on to Stockholm to wind up his personal affairs and returned to New York via London, where he attended the coronation of Queen Elizabeth II as a guest of the British government. In Geneva he made an immediately favorable impression on the Directors-General of the Specialized Agencies by his mastery of their problems and interests. To the Geneva staff, which had been deeply concerned over the attacks on its colleagues in New York and over efforts to extend the McCarthy-inspired U.S. investigating machinery to Europe, he spoke[21] of his plans for restoring the status and morale of the Secretariat. The independence of the staff, he told them, was both a right and a duty, since the right of the Secretariat to full independence could be defended only on the basis of the full recognition by every staff member of his own unlimited obligation to remain politically independent.

Back in New York, Hammarskjold set about the process of getting to know the permanent representatives of all the member nations, the New York State and City authorities, and the press. With the UN press corps he remained on terms of mutual affection and respect, tempered later by occasional irritation and frustration on both sides. Correspondents permanently accredited to the UN often face days, weeks, and even months when the world Organization produces very little news. The Secretary-General is an obvious, permanent, and major source of news, but since absolute discretion and confidence, especially in political activities, are essential for the maintenance of any useful relationship with the governments he is dealing with, he tends more often than not to be a disappointment to newspapermen.

"I will tell you openly," Hammarskjold said at his first formal press conference, "all I can tell you without doing harm to the interests I have to serve, and I will accept with gratitude, and will learn from it, all such criticism from your side as is based on facts and put forward with that sense of responsibility which I know animates you all."[22] He realized from the beginning that the news media were an essential element in making the UN effective and that his relationship with them was crucial to his own performance. He was equally aware that publicity, however favorable, seldom if ever mixes with effective quiet diplomacy, and he made a series of experiments in an attempt to solve this dilemma. At his first press conference he asked the correspondents themselves to suggest ways of solving the problem of finding "a proper balance between my wish to help the press and serve the public, on one side, and on the other side, a strong personal desire to be able to work—and live—as much in quiet as possible."[23] With the help of Wilder Foote of the UN Public Information Department he tried different forms of press conference, ranging from small meetings with a group of correspondents in the Press Club, through "background" press briefings, to full-scale public press conferences. A year of experiment showed that of these arrangements only the full-scale, on-the-record press conference was really practicable, since in a background press conference it was almost impossible to distinguish clearly between what was on the record and therefore usable and what was not. He eventually settled for regular press conferences about every two weeks when time permitted, except during the General Assembly sessions, and he seldom gave interviews to individual journalists. This pattern continued until the summer of 1960, when the pressures and complications of the Congo operation caused a gap of nearly a year— from June 30, 1960, to May 29, 1961—in which he held no press conference at all.

Hammarskjold developed an increasing taste for press conferences and enjoyed the intellectual challenge of answering questions—which he rarely ducked—without committing an indiscretion or a breach of confidence. Over the years, he perfected a technique of escaping into a cloud of metaphor or abstraction, with a style at the same time articulate and obscure, brilliant but hard to grasp, apparently forthright but often uninformative. His performances evoked a grudging admiration among the journalists, who not infrequently found themselves, at the end of a long press conference in which important matters had ostensibly been discussed, with no spot news and little to write about. Bruce Munn of United Press International, then chairman of the United Nations Correspondents Association, put it well at a luncheon in Hammarskjold's honor in June 1957, saying "we have him not and yet we see him still," to which Hammarskjold immediately responded with another quotation from *Macbeth*, explaining that the recent months had been " 'a tale told by an idiot, full of sound and fury'... and those who, in all modesty, have tried to go against the remaining part of that quotation—the part which says 'signifying nothing'—and have tried to have it all make sense have really had a somewhat busy time."[24]

After Hammarskjold's death, the UN correspondents paid him a tribute that he would certainly have appreciated: "We ... enjoyed a special relationship with the Secretary-General, who often referred to the press as an integral part of the United Nations. We are proud of that relationship. But we also knew him as a man, a great man, and came to have a deep respect and affection for him."[25] The Correspondents Association also set up a Hammarskjold Memorial Scholarship Fund to bring young journalists from the developing countries to UN Headquarters.

HAMMARSKJOLD'S MOST PRESSING and immediate challenge concerned the status and future of the Secretariat itself, and in his first two years his administrative functions took priority over everything else. Since he approached the problems of the UN Secretariat from the mature Swedish tradition of a nonpolitical civil service, a measure of disillusionment was perhaps inevitable, but he never gave up the struggle and in his last year he found himself again fighting for the principle of independence in defending his own office. In an organization of competing sovereign states, the building up and operation of an international civil service is a long-term problem with no quick or easy solutions. "Sometimes, when I look ahead," he said in September 1953, "the problems raised by our need to develop a truly international and independent Secretariat seem to me to be beyond human capacity. But I know that this is not so. . . . We are in the fortunate position of pioneers. . . . Every people has its own standards of judgment, its own need of ethics and its own laws of behavior. We are only at the very beginning of the development of such standards inside this Organization."[26]

The first attempt to create an international secretariat by the Secretary-General of the League of Nations, Sir Eric Drummond, was a radical innovation in international affairs to which, more than fifty years later, governments are still by no means entirely reconciled. The debates of the Preparatory Commission on the UN in 1945 had revealed two basically different views on the crucial question of the appointment of members of the Secretariat. The majority view, in the interest of assuring the freedom, independence, and international character of the Secretariat under Articles 100 and 101 of the Charter,* placed exclusive responsibility for appointments on the Secretary-General. The minority view held that Secretariat appointments should be subject to the consent of the government of the member state of which the candidate was a national and which alone could vouch for his qualifications. Although the majority held that this latter approach would effectively destroy the independence of the Secretariat, it was conceded that common sense required that Secretariat officials should as far as possible be acceptable to their own governments, but that it would be "undesirable to write into the text anything which would

---

* Article 100 reads:

1. In the performance of their duties the Secretary-General and the staff shall not seek or receive instructions from any government or from any other authority external to the Organization. They shall refrain from any action which might reflect on their position as international officials responsible only to the Organization.

2. Each Member of the United Nations undertakes to respect the exclusively international character of the responsibilities of the Secretary-General and the staff and not to seek to influence them in the discharge of their responsibilities.

Article 101 concludes:

3. The paramount consideration in the employment of the staff and in the determination of the conditions of service shall be the necessity of securing the highest standards of efficiency, competence, and integrity. Due regard shall be paid to the importance of recruiting the staff on as wide a geographical basis as possible.

give national governments particular rights in this respect. or permit political pressure on the Secretary-General."[27] It was also conceded that Secretariat officials should not engage in subversive activities, but that if such cases should arise the Secretary-General alone should be the judge of the facts.

Although the U.S.S.R. had championed the minority view of the Secretariat in 1945, it was the spirit of McCarthyism in the United States that constituted the first major challenge to the accepted view of the majority. In facing this challenge, Hammarskjold based his stand on the twin foundations of independence and integrity and pursued a policy designed at the same time to protect the staff from pressures from without and to improve its quality from within. A third and allied objective was to build up the confidence of governments in the Secretariat. "The most important thing," he told the press in Stockholm, "is that the Secretariat maintains such a position that it will always have the confidence of all parties concerned. I must defend this position."[28]

Hammarskjold was convinced that the future effectiveness of the UN, as an international organization capable of meeting the demands of a world of sovereign but interdependent governments, would depend in large measure on resisting all efforts by governments to interfere with and put pressure on the international Secretariat. Lie's dealings with the U.S. authorities, with the various intergovernmental organs of the UN, and with the Secretariat itself had left an unhappy legacy. Just before his resignation, in a defensive reaction to the activities of Senator Pat McCarran's Internal Security Subcommittee* and of the U.S. federal grand jury, Lie had tried to establish a new basis for dealing with the problems of the Secretariat by appointing a committee of three jurists—American, Belgian, and British—to advise him in detail on problems arising from U.S. investigations of American members of the Secretariat.[29] These problems included resort by American Secretariat members to the constitutional privilege against self-incrimination by pleading the Fifth Amendment, the refusal of the U.S. government to grant passports to American Secretariat members, allegations of disloyalty, and the like. The jurists had concluded "that persons convicted of subversive activities against the U.S.A., those refusing to answer questions concerning their activities, and members

---

* The McCarran Subcommittee of the Senate Judiciary Committee had begun its inquiries as early as May 1952 and had held hearings in New York in October and November 1952, at which international officials of U.S. nationality were called on to testify. The Subcommittee's members issued various public statements throughout the course of these proceedings.

of organizations regarded as subversive, should not be considered eligible for employment by the U.N. Organization, and that foreign employees of the U.N. must refrain from activities regarded as subversive"[30] in any country where they might be stationed. Lie had already fired those staff members on temporary contracts who had resorted to the Fifth Amendment, and as soon as he received the opinion of the three jurists he also dismissed, on December 5, the permanent staff members who had done so.

In other circumstances the conclusions of the three jurists might have appeared to be common sense, but in the heated and confused atmosphere of the time they did little either to strengthen Lie's position vis-à-vis the U.S. authorities or to restore the confidence and morale of the Secretariat, and they also gave rise to a highly confused debate in the General Assembly. On December 2, 1952, the U.S. federal grand jury, although it gave no names and made no indictments, published the sweeping conclusion that there was "infiltration into the U.N. of an overwhelmingly large group of disloyal U.S. citizens"[31] and that this situation constituted a menace to the security of the United States. Lie's request for the evidence on which this conclusion was based was refused. The Senate Internal Security Subcommittee, completely disregarding the fact that twenty-seven of the persons on the list were no longer employed by the UN, contributed to the general confusion by publishing, in a report[32] to the Senate Judiciary Committee on January 2, 1953, a list of thirty-eight names of U.S. members of the Secretariat who were the subject of unfavorable comment, presumably for alleged Communist affiliations.

Finding himself more than ever pressed by the rising tide of McCarthyism on one side and the indignation of the Secretariat and of many of the member governments on the other, Lie decided to put the issue of personnel policy before the General Assembly when the session was resumed in March 1953, and he then presented for the first time a full report[33] on his problems. Meanwhile, in January and February the situation had become even more complicated. On January 9, President Truman, by Executive Order 10422, introduced a procedure by which the U.S. government would provide the Secretary-General with information on U.S. candidates for employment and would empower the U.S. Civil Service Commission to investigate the loyalty of Americans already employed by the UN. In the same month, the Eisenhower administration's new representative to the UN, Henry Cabot Lodge, Jr., as one of his first official acts asked the Federal Bureau of Investigation (FBI) to investigate all members of the U.S. mission to the UN as well as U.S. members of the Secretariat itself. For the latter purpose Lie permitted the FBI to operate in the UN

Building, for the convenience, as he explained it, of the large number of Secretariat officials who would have to be interrogated and finger-printed. To the Secretariat, the presence of the FBI in the "extra-territorial"* Headquarters Building symbolized yet another capitulation to the witch-hunters.

In introducing the item on personnel policy to the General Assembly on March 10, 1953,[34] Lie gave a survey of his problems as Secretary-General that in other circumstances might have aroused considerable sympathy and interest. The already exposed and delicate situation of the Secretariat had been vastly complicated by the cold war and the "great conflict of policy and ideology between the Western world and its supporters, on the one hand, and the Soviet Union and its associates, on the other."[35] In this situation the location of the UN Head-quarters on the territory of one of the protagonists in the cold war created a special problem for the Secretariat, for the United States, and for the UN as a whole. The UN staff had had to be recruited very rapidly, no fewer than 2,500 staff members having been appointed in the UN's first year of operation in 1946–7, and careful selection had been impossible. The fact that member states had widely differing concepts regarding the rights and status of any civil service, especially an international one, further complicated the Secretary-General's task. Lie noted that while he had been vilified and boycotted for three years by the U.S.S.R. as a stooge of the United States, the Secretariat had at the same time been violently attacked in the United States for exactly opposite reasons.

The debate that followed revealed little support for and much criticism of Lie's position, and at the end of it he remarked bitterly that he had been "left alone by the member states to deal with a situation which all delegations have since come to recognize as an extremely difficult one."[36] On April 1, after Hammarskjold's nomination, the Assembly finally passed a resolution[37] in which it recalled the international character of the Secretariat and asked the Secretary-General to submit a full report on personnel policy to its next session. Hammarskjold thus formally received, as his first major UN assignment and even before his arrival in New York, the Secretariat loyalty problem in its fully unresolved state.

In facing this first test, he had certain advantages. He was new, largely unknown, and completely uncommitted to his predecessor's policies and views. From his attendance at the Assembly session in the previous autumn as chairman of the Swedish delegation, he was to

---

* The term is used in a popular sense; in a strictly legal sense it should read: "UN Headquarters, made inviolable by treaty dispositions of the United States."

some extent acquainted with the problems involved, and the international climate was better than it had been for many years. He had five months in which to get to know the situation and the people involved, to establish confidence, and to work out the elements of a solution. Although the actual situation could hardly be worse, the circumstances were not unpromising.

In confronting the problems of the Secretariat, Hammarskjold decided to avoid, for the time being at least, general statements of policy or principle, and to deal with individual cases on their merits, judged in the light of twin criteria—the independence and the integrity of the Secretariat. He hoped, through the settlement of individual cases, to develop pragmatically a sound case law of rules and principles that through its internal strength would withstand future external pressures. "It is not possible," he later wrote, "to keep this house in order—in a nonpolitical sense—on the basis of more narrow legal rules than those applying in the foreign service of any mature national administration. And if it is not kept in order, how can I say 'no' to those who try to interfere for political reasons, intentionally mixing nonpolitical and political criticism?"[38] His aim was to develop a broad system of rules, very strictly applied, that would give him "the necessary strength because it enables him [the Secretary-General] to get rid of the bad nonpolitical cases on a basis of law, strictly interpreted, and at the same time to defend himself against political pressures by the very strictness of his adherence to law. The previous legal system had been perforated by decisions which strained the text to the extreme. I have no reason here either to justify or to criticize those decisions. I just note that they have made it necessary for me, in order to be able to defend our rights on the basis of law, to recreate the law so as to put beyond doubt what are the limits to what I could do and what are the rights I have to do what I should do."[39] His plan was to reassert and redefine his own authority as Secretary-General under the Charter, so that his capacity and his right both to defend the Secretariat and to maintain its discipline were properly recognized in a revised text of the UN Staff Regulations, which he would ask the General Assembly to approve.

By early May, Hammarskjold had already completed a preliminary study of the Secretariat situation and had reached some tentative conclusions. An immediate problem was President Truman's Executive Order 10422 of January 9, 1953. On receiving this order, Lie had instructed his legal staff to engage in preliminary discussions on its application and had supplied the U.S. government with lists of American citizens employed or being considered for employment by the UN. He had not, however, specifically ordered UN staff members to comply with the order, so that the investigations that it required were, theoretically at least, a matter between individual American Secretariat officials and their own government. Thus if an American official failed or refused to cooperate, he had not violated any UN instruction and was presumably not subject to any disciplinary action by the UN, but it was an open question whether his failure to comply with U.S. procedures made him unsuitable for further UN employment. The relevant UN regulations were vague, merely stipulating that staff members should "regulate their conduct with the interest of the UN only in view,"[40] and that they should "conduct themselves at all times in a manner befitting their status as international civil servants" and "avoid any action ... which may adversely reflect on their status."[41]

As a first step to remedy this ambiguity, Hammarskjold set out to reach a decision on each of the cases where an American Secretariat official had resorted to the Fifth Amendment, with a view eventually to formulating rules that would cover more adequately the conflict between national procedures and international status. To determine whether resorting to the Fifth Amendment tended to make American staff members undesirable members of the Secretariat, he ordered a detailed inquiry into one such case both to establish the reasons for resorting to the Fifth Amendment and to determine whether the UN rules called for disciplinary action.

The Executive Order of January 9 provided that the U.S. government give the Secretary-General information on American citizens employed or being considered for employment by the UN. Hammarskjold felt that this provision seriously infringed upon his own exclusive responsibility under the Charter for the selection and retention of UN staff. Facts were one thing, but he must reserve his exclusive right to interpret and to judge those facts as far as they affected UN employment. Early in May he began to try to get this position clearly understood and accepted by the U.S. authorities. This proved difficult, not so much because the State Department officials concerned disagreed with him but because they themselves were in a state of alarm and defeatism over the inroads of McCarthyism into their department. Regardless of what Lodge or his deputy, Ambassador James J. Wadsworth, or even President Eisenhower himself might wish to do, at the operational level the ogre of McCarthyism was dominant, and officials were frankly fearful of the effect of any departure from Lie's supine acceptance of U.S. procedures.

Hammarskjold and Andrew Cordier, his Executive Assistant, took a more positive line and showed from the first a strong determination to defend the rights and position of UN staff members on their own merits. On May 7, Hammarskjold suggested an amendment of the U.S.

Executive Order based on his Charter obligation to act in relation to the staff in full independence of all outside influences. Information provided to him, he said, could and must be factual only; conclusions and judgments were his exclusive right, although the conclusions of government agencies might be received if they were purely "advisory." Although these ideas were initially received with some gloom by the U.S. State Department, Cordier was able to inform Hammarskjold in Geneva on May 30 that his proposed changes to the Executive Order had been accepted. The order itself was amended on June 2, and it was also agreed that the appropriate U.S. board was to transmit to him its determinations as "advisory opinions"[42] only. When he informed the General Assembly of this development five months later, he was also able to state that none of the information so far transmitted referred to "reasonable doubt"[43] of the loyalty of any American staff member.

Another problem inherited from Lie was the presence of the FBI in the UN Building. The extent of that agency's activities was revealed on June 20 during an incident in the public gallery of the Security Council, when an American agent in plain clothes attempted to take a demonstrator away from the UN guards. Hammarskjold demanded a full investigation of this incident and protested vigorously to the U.S. mission. He had also learned of the case of a senior official who had been given a detailed questionnaire on his relations with various people and his views on Communism. The fact that the official had felt obliged to reply raised in Hammarskjold's mind a serious question of principle. Did a government have the right to question a respected official of the UN with a long and good record of service on the basis solely of suspicion and rumor? Surely the proper course was for the government concerned to tell the Secretary-General of its suspicions, leaving it to him alone to decide what action, if any, should be taken and what questions should be put to the official concerned. He therefore instructed the members of the Secretariat that until he could get the FBI off the premises their reaction to inquiries about their colleagues could in no circumstances go beyond the duty of everyone to help the law. A member of the Secretariat must make it clear that there were questions that, as an international civil servant, he had no right to answer and these included questions relating to his UN work and to the activities of the UN itself, as well as the political or religious views or past relationships of himself or of his colleagues. This meant, in fact, that only nonpolitical criminal activities were a legitimate subject for investigation by the FBI. In November 1953, making use of the opportunity provided by a remark[44] to the McCarran Subcommittee by FBI Director J. Edgar Hoover that the extraterritorial status of international organizations in the United States made it impossible for the FBI to operate on their premises, Hammarskjold asked for the immediate removal of the FBI from the UN Headquarters. "The sooner we get the exceptional arrangements agreed to by Mr. Lie and their aftermath wound up," he wrote to Wadsworth, "the better it certainly is for all parties."[45]

Another way in which the U.S. authorities were able to influence the operation of the Secretariat was by withholding the passports of American Secretariat officials, or by denying visas to non-Americans. Considerable difficulties had been caused by this practice, and Hammarskjold asked Lodge's assistance in putting an end to it. Lodge, who had been impressed by his forthright statement on the undesirability of political engagement by the UN staff, was sympathetic and helpful.

The effects of McCarthyism were not limited to American members of the Secretariat. The Headquarters Agreement between the United Nations and the United States provides, among other things, for the free access to UN Headquarters in New York of all persons who have legitimate business with the world organization. This provision, which is vital both to the proper functioning of the UN and to its prestige and dignity, was also threatened. A serious case had occurred just before Hammarskjold's arrival in New York when Mrs. Alva Myrdal, the director of UNESCO's Department of Social Sciences, a Swedish national and the wife of the renowned economist and sociologist Gunnar Myrdal, had arrived on official business only to be informed at Idlewild Airport that she would not be granted legal entry on the basis of her U.S. visa, and would be permitted to proceed into New York only on the condition of signing a parole agreement, the object of which was to keep her under obligation to respond at any time to the call of the U.S. immigration authorities and to give them notice of her movements in the United States. This situation was insulting both to Mrs. Myrdal and her husband, as well as being in violation of the spirit of the Headquarters Agreement. Lie's inquiry to the State Department on the case remained unanswered, and on May 1, Hammarskjold issued a statement[46] on the facts, taking the opportunity to announce that negotiations with the United States were in progress with the object of settling once and for all, in a mutually satisfactory way, the question of access to the UN Headquarters.

The Myrdal case brought home forcefully to Hammarskjold the indignity and foolishness of the current state of affairs. "Alva's trouble made me see red," he wrote to Gunnar Myrdal on May 12, "so utterly unreasonable and humiliating as it is."[47] With the help of Lodge and Wadsworth, he persuaded the U.S. authorities to make a statement that what had happened was no reflection on Mrs. Myrdal's integrity, but he remained in no doubt that this situation too had to be cleared up.

Hammarskjold's approach to the problem of access to UN Head-quarters was typical of his method of dealing with delicate problems. He took the position that, while no single government could be per-mitted to interfere with the access to the world organization of people legitimately assigned to take part in its work, the United States, as host country, also had a right to keep out of its territory people who might justly be suspected of plotting against its security. He con-cluded that in order to reach a common-sense agreement on a problem that was insoluble in theory, it would be necessary first to define accurately what was meant by "access to Headquarters" and then to agree on a procedure to be followed in case that definition should produce a serious security risk for the host country. Even if this could be agreed upon, there remained the problem of visitors to the UN Headquarters in New York who wished to visit other parts of the United States as well. Although the UN had no legal rights in such a case, restrictions on the movements of UN representatives could only reflect unfavorably on the status of UN delegates and officials and complicate the relations between the UN and the United States as host country. He concluded that while freedom to travel about the United States was unquestionably a matter between the United States and the government or person concerned, there might be cases where he could intervene to avoid useless controversy and conflict on the basis of his own judgment of the facts, thus avoiding the more undig-nified repercussions of spy mania and McCarthyism.

In Geneva in July, Hammarskjold was able to report to the Eco-nomic and Social Council that there was already a measure of agree-ment that might help to remove difficulties over the matter. The U.S. representatives had assured him that if any serious problem should arise concerning access to the Headquarters district or sojourn in its vicinity, the United States would consult him at once in order to ensure that the decision made was in accordance with the rights of the parties concerned. Having elucidated the basic principles and respective rights of the parties, he refused to formalize them by legal agreements, which were liable to end in disagreement and frustration. "I do not consider the negotiations finally concluded," he told the ECOSOC, "while, on the other hand, the report leads up to a point where no further action is suggested."[48] In practice, no further prob-lems arose.

Until the General Assembly could receive and act on his report[49] on personnel policy, Hammarskjold postponed major changes in the Secretariat and in the budget, although he gave notice that he was by no means happy with the current state of affairs. "As you know," he told the Advisory Committee on Administrative and Budgetary Questions in June, "I am an old treasury hand. From that point of view I did not like my position this spring when I inherited a budget which did not leave me any possibility of a serious consideration of the main approach."[50] In his own executive office he saw no reason for immediate changes, and in fact most of the original incumbents remained with him as close collaborators for the next eight years.

For the staff outside his own office, Hammarskjold accepted for the time being the existing setup and even pronounced himself impressed with the general standard and performance. He worked closely with Wilder Foote of the Department of Public Information, who advised him on relations with the press and helped him with his many public speeches, and with the Legal Counsel, Constantin Stavropoulos, on the complexities of the various loyalty cases. Soon after his arrival in New York he also asked Ernest Gross, the former deputy permanent representative of the United States to the United Nations and a distinguished international lawyer, to act as his personal adviser on problems involving relations with the U.S. government.

During the summer a U.S. federal grand jury, the International Organizations Employees Loyalty Board, and two U.S. Senate Subcommittees continued to investigate present and former American Secretariat members. On August 21 the Administrative Tribunal, the Secretariat's highest court of appeal, rendered judgments in twenty-one cases of American staff members who had appealed against their dismissal or termination by Lie for having invoked the Fifth Amendment during investigations by the U.S. authorities. The Tribunal found in favor of eleven of the applicants, awarding compensation to seven of them and ordering the reinstatement of four. Hammarskjold declined to reinstate the four on the grounds that it was "inadvisable from the points of view which it is my duty to take into consideration,"[51] whereupon they too were awarded compensation. His decision simultaneously dismayed a large part of the UN staff, who believed that their colleagues should have been reinstated, and enraged the anti-UN faction in the United States led by Senators Joseph McCarthy and William E. Jenner, who saw it as a recommendation for the payment of some $189,000 in compensation to traitors. The attitude of the senators was later reflected in U.S. opposition in the General Assembly to Hammarskjold's request for an appropriation to pay the compensation awards.

As the summer wore on, Hammarskjold was increasingly preoccupied with ensuring as good an atmosphere as possible in the forthcoming annual meeting of the General Assembly. He met with Dulles,

Lodge, and Robert Murphy of the State Department in early September to pursue his idea of using the session to encourage an East-West détente and urged that, as far as possible, the traditionally harsh and offensive language of the cold war should be avoided. Dulles said that he was certainly prepared to speak with a low voice to get the debates down to a more businesslike level and would welcome Hammarskjold's good offices in smoothing out contentious matters. When, at the end of this meeting, Lodge asked him if he had any message for McCarthy, with whom Lodge was lunching on the following day, Hammarskjold told him to tell McCarthy that he would disregard any information that McCarthy tried to "slip into the house."[52]* Lodge was pleased with this reaction and said he felt that Hammarskjold had "the situation extremely well in hand."[53] Hammarskjold followed up this statement by informing Murphy that he would disregard the taking of the Fifth Amendment by a member of the Secretariat before the McCarthy Committee if he was satisfied with the staff member's explanation. He would also disregard previous Communist Party membership if an American staff member's present record was clean, and that he would insist in the General Assembly on the payment of indemnities to the dismissed staff members, even if the United States opposed it. Being firm on security and loyalty questions, he said, was in the interest of the United States as well as the United Nations, and both would suffer from any weakness on basic principles.

These basic principles were set out in Hammarskjold's report[54] to the General Assembly on personnel policy. His objective was, as he told the Geneva staff on December 4, "the building up of a Secretariat proud of its own standards, safe from outside criticism, capable of developing its own laws and its own inner discipline, truly independent, not because of paper rules, but by the sheer strength of its quality and maturity. What in the short run may seem harsh is in the long run in the best interest of all. . . . The Secretariat," he added, "has an essential part to play in the world affairs of today. We *will* play it if we accept the price for building up our position of strength. We must reject a role of insignificance subject to constant criticism and shirking the risks of a full part in our world. We must choose a role of responsibility and independence, sacrificing part of the illusory safety you may derive from a locked door."[55]

Hammarskjold gave a further preview of some of his ideas to the New York staff on September 8,[56] in particular expressing his conviction that Secretariat members must abstain from unsuitable political

---

* This was an allusion to a visit that McCarthy's assistant, Roy Cohn, had made to UN Headquarters without Hammarskjold's prior knowledge.

activities. He correctly foresaw that his policy of strength through discipline would initially please neither the Secretariat nor its persecutors. While the witch-hunters fumed at his concern for those under attack, many in the UN Secretariat were uneasy at the sternness of the new rules and principles he was suggesting, and some member states were openly apprehensive that he was arrogating too much power to himself.

Although Hammarskjold had engaged in intensive consultations on personnel policy with the heads of the Specialized Agencies and with the Assembly's Advisory Committee on Administrative and Budgetary Questions, the ideas put forward in his report[57] were very much his own. His six months' experience of UN administration had convinced him that the UN Staff Regulations suffered from serious ambiguities and omissions, and he began his report by outlining his ideas of the desirable standards of the integrity, conduct, and suitability of UN officials and of his own responsibility for maintaining them. Partly as a result of the haste with which the Secretariat had had to be set up, the rules for termination of staff members were very restrictive. The Secretary-General could terminate a permanent official only for unsatisfactory service, if his post was abolished, if he was incapacitated, or for misconduct, and even then a dismissed official could always appeal to the Administrative Tribunal, which functioned under its own separate statute. The Tribunal, applying strictly legal standards, tended to find that the Regulations did not permit the Secretary-General to terminate staff members who had, in his opinion, failed to meet the standards required by the UN Charter. This was the first problem that his proposed changes in the Regulations were designed to meet.

Another problem that had never properly been considered was the appropriateness of political activities by a UN staff member, and here Hammarskjold took an uncompromising line. "It is my considered view," he wrote, "that the sound operation of the Organization requires that ... such a staff member choose between continuing his political activities or remaining an employee of the United Nations."[58] Under the existing Regulations, the Secretary-General's right to put such a choice before an employee was at best doubtful. He therefore proposed that a new regulation be added stating that political activities, except for voting, should be prohibited unless authorized by the Secretary-General.

The next area where clarification was needed was the Charter concept of "integrity" as applied to UN service. The existing Regulations about "misconduct" or "unsatisfactory service" did not adequately cover this concept or allow the Secretary-General enough scope to make decisions, and this inevitably led to serious disagreements between the Secretary-General and the Administrative Tribunal, i.e., between the administrative and the legal approach. Hammarskjold proposed that a finding of lack of integrity based on an evaluation by the Secretary-General of the established facts, always subject to the possibility of an appeal by the official concerned to the Administrative Tribunal, should be made a legitimate ground for termination.

These two changes, he wrote, were the "minimal programme I consider necessary to enable the Secretary-General to fulfil his duties under the Charter as regards the standards to be maintained by the Secretariat."[59] They had, however, certain consequences that would require further changes in the Regulations. As a practical matter, a staff member who showed a serious lack of balance or judgment must be dealt with, but a finding of "lack of integrity," "misconduct," or "unsatisfactory service" might in such a case be unjustifiably harsh. He therefore asked for the right in such cases to terminate appointments "in the interest of good administration of the Organization and in accordance with the standards of the Charter,"[60] with a further right to pay a suitable indemnity.

Hammarskjold proposed, as a check on his own authority, a regular review by the General Assembly of the criteria applied by him in cases of termination as well as procedures by which staff members could give a complete answer to charges made against them and could get qualified legal counsel without undue expense. He also proposed a revision of the Statute of the Administrative Tribunal that would make the granting of compensation to a terminated staff member the normal result of a successful appeal to the Tribunal. The object of these proposals, he explained, was to give the Secretary-General clear powers to match his obligations under the Charter, to be balanced by new checks on himself and by fuller protection for the staff.

During the debate on his report in the Assembly's Fifth Committee, which deals with administrative and budgetary questions, Hammarskjold took an active part in answering criticisms and suggesting ways around objections.[61] As an additional check on his new powers, he proposed a special advisory board that would examine cases in detail before he terminated a staff member for the reasons given in the new Regulation. He went to great lengths to explain his proposals but strongly opposed efforts to postpone a decision on them, and on December 9 a text[62] was adopted that suited his purpose very well.

Hammarskjold's proposed amendments to the Statute of the Administrative Tribunal proved more controversial, for the majority felt that they would deprive the Tribunal of its power to recommend the restoration of an applicant's rights and would leave it only with a limited power to award damages, thus destroying its status as an impartial judge between the organization and its staff. He finally agreed that the Tribunal should be able in exceptional cases to grant compensation greater than that indicated as a maximum in his own proposal and that the time limit for his decision on the possible reinstatement of an official, following the judgment by the Tribunal, should be reduced from sixty to thirty days. He thus got more or less what he wanted, in that the Tribunal had to fix the amount of compensation at the time of a decision in favor of an applicant, rather than waiting until the Secretary-General had refused reinstatement.

On September 30, Hammarskjold appeared for the first time before the Fifth Committee to present the UN budget for 1954, which was half a million dollars less than for the previous year. In his presentation[63] he gave special attention to the compensation he had decided to pay to the successful appellants to the Administrative Tribunal, for which he had made provision in the budget. This move, which was interpreted in some quarters as meaning that the U.S. contribution to the UN would be used to finance subversive activities, aroused considerable public indignation in the United States, and a violent controversy ensued both within and outside the Assembly. Both Houses of the U.S. Congress reacted by adopting, without objection, a resolution deciding that no funds appropriated by Congress for the U.S. contribution to the UN could be used for payment of the compensation awarded by the Tribunal. On December 9 the Assembly postponed the vote on the matter by deciding[64] to request the International Court of Justice for an advisory opinion on whether the General Assembly had the right to refuse to give effect to the Tribunal's award of compensation. To give the United States a way out, Hammarskjold proposed a Special Indemnity Fund financed from the assessments levied on staff salaries—the UN's internal system of income tax—from which awards by the Tribunal would be paid. The United States accepted this device, by which the awards would not be paid directly out of a Congressional appropriation. The Court's opinion, which was finally received in July 1954,[65] endorsed the view of the majority that the UN was legally bound to carry out the judgments of the Tribunal and to pay compensation as awarded. The Assembly then voted[66] that compensation be paid to the dismissed officials, and the awards were finally paid in January 1955.

FEW YEARS PASS at the UN without some new attempt to streamline and reduce the cost of the international bureaucracy, and Hammarskjold had inherited a request for such a report from the previous session of the General Assembly. His other major report[67] to the General Assembly, therefore, was on the organization of the Secretariat.

The UN Secretariat, recruited with a strong emphasis on equitable geographical distribution among member states and with a top level of posts that are to a considerable extent political appointments, was very different from Hammarskjold's tidy Swedish notions of public administration. "I myself come from a small administration which has a tradition of highly developed elasticity both horizontally and in a vertical sense," he told the Advisory Committee on Administrative and Budgetary Questions in June 1953. "I don't know to what extent I shall be able to translate the experiences of such an administration into UN terms, but I feel that I should make a serious effort in that direction. As for the present, the UN administration seems to me to be strongly influenced by the philosophy typical of a big administration. I feel that the streamlining, which is an obvious objective for me as Chief Executive, would not be successful unless and until a real elasticity has developed which makes it possible to carry the same burden with a reduced staff because of a somewhat changed approach."[68]

Seeing the importance of tighter administration and economy, both for the sake of efficiency and also as a way of increasing member governments' confidence and respect for the Secretariat, Hammarskjold undertook a complete review of the tasks that the Secretariat had been assigned over the years, in the hope of weeding out projects no longer of high priority. He also ordered a temporary freeze on new appointments to the staff in order to make reductions easier. By November he had reached some conclusions about structural changes in the top level of the Secretariat, and these, together with the general lines of a policy for the future, he submitted to the Assembly on November 12.[69]

The Secretariat in its original form consisted of eight departments headed by Assistant Secretaries-General working under the direction of the Secretary-General and his Executive Office. Hammarskjold's idea was to change this pattern by adding a Personnel Office, a Finance Office, and a Legal Office to his own Executive Office, and thus do away with the Department of Administrative and Financial services as such. This concentration of administrative responsibilities at the center would, in his view, simplify and strengthen day-to-day administration. He also recommended that the departments of Economic and Social Affairs should be made into one department, whose work would be coordinated with the Technical Assistance Administration by the Secretary-General himself.

The vexed question of the top-level organization of the Secretariat remained with Hammarskjold until his death eight years later. The eight Assistant Secretaries-General were intended to be politically representative of the spectrum of member states, and under each of them a Principal Director was responsible for the day-to-day work of the department. The Assistant Secretaries-General were originally supposed to provide a form of political liaison with their own governments or regions. This function, however, had more or less lapsed with the establishment of permanent national delegations at UN Headquarters, which provided the Secretary-General a much better channel of close and continuous communication with the member governments. The old arrangement, in Hammarskjold's opinion, was difficult to justify, and he also felt strongly that he could not delegate the political powers vested in him by the Charter by setting up a sort of international Cabinet. He therefore proposed that the main departments should be headed by one echelon of officials instead of two. These officials in principle would be administrative, and would undertake political responsibilities only at the direction of the Secretary-General. Their title would be changed from Assistant Secretary-General to Under-Secretary. These proposals, if approved, would also make possible a reduction in the UN budget of about one million dollars in the coming fiscal year.*

Hammarskjold's ideas received a large measure of support in the General Assembly, although his proposal to change the nature of the top-level Secretariat posts was at first opposed by the U.S.S.R. on the grounds that it would downgrade a politically significant post to an essentially administrative one and would violate the 1946 London "gentleman's agreement" on the allocation of five of the Assistant Secretary-General posts to the five permanent members of the Security Council.** With the Soviet bloc voting against it, the General Assembly adopted a resolution[70] giving Hammarskjold full authority to proceed with Secretariat reorganization along the lines he had suggested, although a number of members expressed concern that in centralizing so much authority in his own office, he might become overburdened

---

* Budget estimates approved by the General Assembly were: for 1953, $48,327,700; for 1954, $47,827,110; for 1955, $46,963,800. Actual expenditures for these years were: 1953, $49,292,552; 1954, $48,510,009; 1955, $50,089,808.
** In accordance with this understanding, a Soviet national was to be Assistant Secretary-General for Political and Security Council Affairs, and an American for Administrative and Financial Services. The U.S.S.R., although it accepted this arrangement as the best it could get, never gave up its preference for some form of representative group of officials acting as a Cabinet to the Secretary-General, an idea that reemerged in a different form in Khrushchev's 1960 "troika" proposal.

with administrative work that would not leave him enough time or energy for political responsibilities.

Even though the acceptance by the General Assembly of his proposals on personnel policy gave Hammarskjold a much firmer basis upon which to run the Secretariat and to deal with both the U.S. authorities and the UN staff on the loyalty problem, the hunt for subversives in the Secretariat was by no means over. If anything the field widened, taking in at one time Ralph Bunche,* the most distinguished American official in the Secretariat, who had recently been awarded the Nobel Peace Prize for negotiating the Middle East armistice agreements. The hunt also spread to the UN Geneva Office and to the Specialized Agencies in Europe, where resentment was bitter and vocal. In November, Hammarskjold wrote to Lodge asking that the remaining U.S. investigations of American employees be speeded up so that the process could be ended as soon as possible, and by June 1954 he was able to reply to a question about the investigations: "On the present legal basis which we have in this house, I do not in any way feel concerned about what may happen in this sphere."[72]

Secretariat staff members had initially been wary of, and in some cases even hostile to, Hammarskjold's idea of protecting them by stiffening the required standards of conduct and by strengthening his own authority to take disciplinary measures. When, however, they saw the firm line he took against all outside interference, his fair and meticulous dealing with individual cases, his forthright and seemingly effortless handling of the debate on personnel policy in the Assembly, and his insistence, against the strong opposition of the United States, upon the payment of full indemnities to those whose contracts had been ended ("terminated," in the language of the UN rules), they gained a confidence in him that soon verged on enthusiasm. One observer summed up his achievement after his first Assembly as follows:

> It is a tribute to Mr. Hammarskjold's standing with governments and to his forceful intelligence and diplomatic skill that in less than one year he has got the Assembly's full support for a coherent approach to the problem of the independence and efficiency of the Secretariat, and has

---

* Hammarskjold gave Bunche unwavering support and detailed his own legal adviser, Ernest Gross, to assist him in the Loyalty Board hearings, where he was confronted by professional informers. When Bunche was completely cleared, Hammarskjold stated that Bunche "has always had my unreserved confidence as a man of outstanding integrity. He is an honour to the Organization which he serves."[71]

publicly reaffirmed the principle that the Secretariat is an international civil service, and not merely a playground for the pressures of individual governments or a repository for their less useful or usable officials. These decisions may prove to be of the utmost importance to the satisfactory long-term development of the organization. . . . The new Secretary-General's firm and subtle influence and his discreet but forceful diplomatic activity contributed much to the relative calm and reasonableness of the session as a whole. This in itself is a very encouraging development.[73]

President Eisenhower's speech to the General Assembly on December 8, 1953,[74] also marked a turning point in the UN's relations with the United States. His proposals for a UN role in developing the peaceful uses of atomic energy opened up a new and important field of activity for the Organization as well as heralding a new period of détente between the superpowers.

Hammarskjold himself summed up the hopeful if cautious mood in a speech on December 17 in the Albert Hall in London. "It was," he said, "a session characterized by caution—a caution that prevented far-reaching steps in any direction but also diluted the effects of harsh debate on several bitterly contested issues."[75] Eisenhower had sounded a new and inspiring note that Hammarskjold characterized as "the first response to the challenge facing the United Nations at this Assembly, fully on a level with the hopes voiced in many quarters at the beginning of the session . . . a proposal for a new beginning toward the ultimate resolution of the central problem of our time—as he put it, 'to find the way by which the miraculous inventiveness of man shall not be dedicated to his death, but consecrated to his life.' "[76]

4

SETTLING
DOWN

WITH HIS FIRST ASSEMBLY OVER, Hammarskjold could start in earnest
to carry out his ideas for reorganizing the Secretariat. He was determined to review the whole operation in person before making detailed
changes. "To be efficient," he wrote at the end of 1953, "the Secretariat
must act with unity of purpose, and the Charter has put the responsibility for such unity on the Secretary-General."[1]

He set out to secure effective organization not merely by cutting
out certain activities and jobs for the sake of economy but by reviewing all the activities of the Secretariat to see how they had originated
and to judge whether they were still justified. This review was carried
out by a working party of which he himself was chairman. He set
himself a twofold objective. First, the activities of the United Nations,
no matter how widespread, should be adjusted to general political
needs. Secondly, those activities should be staffed in a practical way
by means of the most efficient combination of units.

Hammarskjold had inherited a work program which had grown
up piecemeal over the years and which consisted of a mass of unrelated and uncoordinated activities. By themselves, such unrelated
efforts were bound to be ineffective if not futile. "In order to get
something which really makes sense," he said in March 1954, "you have

to see to it that efforts in various directions—education, community development and such matters as taxation—come into a sphere where they mutually support each other, because if you get a series of efforts spread over a wide field each will be insufficient without the coordination which really puts them together under one single aim with one single direction. That is really what I feel we must achieve, and we have not done it so far."[2]

On economic and social projects alone Hammarskjold held more than seventy-five meetings to find out what was going on, to establish tentative policy lines, to decide what organizational pattern best fitted these policy lines, and whether a particular task was one that an international Secretariat could and should perform. In general, he wanted UN programs to concentrate more on direct assistance to governments in formulating economic and social policy, and less on pure research or factual compilations that could be done equally well by national academic institutions.[3]

The budget reductions that resulted from his survey of the work of the Secretariat abolished the posts of some three hundred staff members. In order to avoid making a large number of career officials redundant, Hammarskjold froze all posts that became vacant until these three hundred officials had been reassigned and at the same time made the system of interdepartmental transfer of staff far more flexible than it had been. Although he was anxious to improve the geographical distribution of the Secretariat, he refused to do so at the expense of people already working there. "After all," he told the Fifth Committee of the Assembly, "there are two possibilities in an administration of this kind. One is to have a very great number of people, highly specialized, working rather independently. That is an extremely costly operation. The other is to have a comparatively much smaller staff of people working down the line, of whom you ask a much higher degree of flexibility, a much higher degree of intensity in their specific efforts. This is the cheaper approach, but it does require very strong leadership and also strong supervision."[4]

The obvious effectiveness of Hammarskjold's reorganization put him in a position to ask for a freer hand within the budget than the Secretary-General had previously had, and in July 1954 he asked the Advisory Committee on Administrative and Budgetary Questions for certain financial margins for new initiatives "as a price for dynamic development, even to let the Secretary-General run the risk of losing some money and making a fool of himself."[5]

The top level of officials, until then called Assistant Secretaries-General, were most affected by the reorganization of the Secretariat. Under Lie these officials had for the most part run their departments without much supervision, pursuing their own enthusiasms and preferences and keeping in touch to a varying extent with their own national authorities. They had attended occasional so-called "Cabinet" meetings with Lie, where the trivia of bureaucracy usually took up far more time than serious questions of policy. Although Hammarskjold was prepared to keep some of the incumbents, he was determined to change both the attitude and the method of operation that Lie had allowed to develop. His first move was to do away with the semi-independent administrative apparatus that had grown up under the American Assistant Secretary-General, Byron Price, by concentrating administrative, personnel, financial, and legal matters in his own office. Price resigned on January 29, 1954, leaving the top U.S. Secretariat position unfilled.

In February, Hammarskjold moved Ralph Bunche, who was then director in the Trusteeship Department, into his own office, telling him that he wanted him to be "more fully available to me in connection with special high-level problems."[6] By this move, Bunche in effect became his principal assistant in active political work and peacekeeping. Bunche was one of two new Under-Secretaries Without Portfolio, the other of whom was to be a Soviet official, who were to take on special and delicate assignments under Hammarskjold's direct supervision. Ilya Tchernychev and Anatoly Dobrynin successively filled the second of these positions. In February 1954, Hammarskjold appointed Henry Labouisse, an old friend from the Marshall Plan days, as Director-General of the huge United Nations Relief and Works Agency for Palestine Refugees, based in Beirut.

In March, Hammarskjold asked Ahmed Bokhari, the permanent representative of Pakistan, who had been President of the Security Council when he was designated, to join the Secretariat as head of the Office of Public Information. Bokhari was the first of a series of senior recruits from outside with whom Hammarskjold was initially extravagantly pleased and later disappointed. The brilliant and amusing Bokhari, like some others after him, found the anonymity, discipline, long hours, and dedication that Hammarskjold required of his collaborators increasingly irksome. Hammarskjold's search for perfect colleagues from outside the Secretariat was doomed to a series of disappointments and frustrations, and he seems later to have concluded reluctantly that in the long run he was best served in important posts by career UN officials.

Some of the former Assistant Secretaries-General were doubtful of the wisdom of concentrating all political direction in the Secretary-General's own office and person. Adrian Pelt, the director of the UN European Office in Geneva, who had also worked in the League of

Nations, felt that Hammarskjold's relations with some governments would become unnecessarily strained if he only occasionally delegated political tasks to senior officials and thus abolished the original idea of the function of the Assistant Secretaries-General. Guillaume Georges-Picot, the French Assistant Secretary-General, a man of great intelligence and integrity whose Social Affairs Department was to be merged with the Economic Department, strongly and openly disagreed with Hammarskjold's reforms. He considered that the suppression of the Assistant Secretary-General system destroyed the original idea of having a kind of college of senior officials who represented the five great powers and the three main regions of the world, and who, in helping to plan policy, would ensure that all parts of the world had some direct relationship with the Secretary-General's work. Georges-Picot's views irritated Hammarskjold, who had in any case already made up his mind.

In early March, Hammarskjold felt impelled to deliver to his senior colleagues a strongly worded appeal for solidarity:

> Without in any way dramatizing the situation, I feel that the United Nations is entering, or has already entered, a most critical stage in its history. Political problems of great delicacy are piling up, and in one of the key sections of the world the very position of the United Nations is threatened. In such a situation it is more essential than ever that we maintain a close co-operation within the Secretariat in a spirit of true teamwork, with the loyalty that such work requires. . . .
>
> You should understand, in the light of what I have said, how I look, and must look, on various reactions from the outside, which can only have their origin in the house, expressing concern about the future of this or that special activity of the UN Secretariat—a concern which sometimes seems to reflect the view that a blow is aimed at an essential interest of the United Nations in a mistaken effort to achieve economy.
>
> I heard too much of such reactions last autumn, also concerning aspects of our work where it was difficult not to see a reflection of personal interest. I preferred to disregard these reactions and, as you remember, the vote in the Assembly for the reorganization plan gave 53 votes in favour and the five votes of the Soviet states against. The Assembly vote is today to be considered as unanimous, as I understand that these states have withdrawn their criticism in the light of later developments.
>
> I chose to disregard the reactions last autumn, but that does not mean that they did not shock me as symptoms of a tendency to put other interests before those of the United Nations and—in some cases—of what I must call personal disloyalty.
>
> Now, seeing similar tendencies emerging again, I cannot let them pass by in silence. . . .
>
> Anybody in the Secretariat is perfectly free to express to me personally

his concerns or his criticism, but if he prefers to express those same concerns and criticisms not to me, but to outsiders, he should understand that he renders future cooperation between himself and me impossible. And from that rule I know no exception.[7]

By mutual consent Georges-Picot left the Secretariat at the end of 1954. Although he remained on friendly, if distant, terms with Hammarskjold and returned briefly as French permanent representative, he was not converted to Hammarskjold's ideas about the international Secretariat. His place as senior French official was soon taken by a brilliant young economist, Philippe de Seynes, who had been suggested to Hammarskjold by the French Premier, Pierre Mendès-France, during the Indochina Conference in Geneva in the summer of 1954, and who soon became and remained one of Hammarskjold's closest and most trusted colleagues.

For the period of the review of the staff and the transition to the new organizational system, Hammarskjold put Alfred Katzin in charge of personnel arrangements. Katzin, a South African who had played a leading role in the reorganization of the United Nations Relief and Rehabilitation Administration, the vast agency set up at the end of World War II, and who had subsequently served, among other things, as Lie's representative in Korea, was accustomed to taking responsibility and making unpopular decisions. His tough common sense and good nature were invaluable at a time when many officials had to be transferred to new positions.

Hammarskjold proposed to replace the Assistant Secretaries-General by Under-Secretaries, and in August he announced[8] that the new organizational plan would take effect as of January 1, 1955. In announcing the change, he emphasized that when necessary he would delegate political responsibilities to the Under-Secretaries, who had Deputy Under-Secretaries of the same rank to help them run their departments. This new double-echelon system did not commend itself to everyone, not least because it multiplied the number of senior officials of Under-Secretary rank. He was determined, however, to go ahead with it, and when Thanassis Aghnides, the chairman of the Advisory Committee on Administrative and Budgetary Questions, remonstrated with him about the unworkability of having nearly thirty Under-Secretaries, some of whom were subordinate to others, Hammarskjold curtly replied, "It works in Sweden."[9]

From a practical point of view the most important change was on the political side, where Hammarskjold had created two Under-Secretaries Without Portfolio, Ralph Bunche and Ilya Tchernychev, the new senior Soviet official. This innovation signified his intention to keep the active political work of the Secretariat at a high level close to his own office, and with a balance between East and West. The new Under-Secretaries were both men whom he knew and trusted. Bunche, as a distinguished scholar and Nobel Peace Prize winner, was the member of the Secretariat best known in the outside world. Tcherny-chev, an amiable, straightforward, and very able career official, was well known to Hammarskjold from his days as Soviet Ambassador in Stockholm. Their title of "Under-Secretary Without Portfolio" con-tinued to cause mystification and some amusement, and Hammarskjold was at pains to explain it, not always with success. "Their work-load," he told a press conference, "will be one based on *ad hoc* assignments mostly of an interdepartmental character. You know that there are very, very many questions which overlap between departments. Now, they more or less fall on me. It is not a very practical arrangement. I develop very quickly and very easily into a bottleneck. It is much better if those problems are handled by those people who can play over the whole range and can cooperate with various departments. They can get on with such and such a problem independently."[10] The arrangement worked well enough to begin with, but as Hammar-skjold's political involvements increased, the responsibility for direct-ing peacekeeping operations increasingly fell on Bunche, whose experience and permanency inevitably gave him a more influential position than his Soviet counterpart, who was changed every two years or so. Hammarskjold decided at the end of 1957, at the instance of the U.S.S.R., to revert to the old system whereby the senior Soviet official in the Secretariat was in charge of the Department for Political and Security Council Affairs, and at the beginning of 1958, Anatoly Dobrynin became the head of the Political Department instead of Under-Secretary Without Portfolio. The resulting impression of polit-ical imbalance in his own office was to cause Hammarskjold much trouble in his final year.

When Hammarskjold reported[11] to the General Assembly in Sep-tember 1954 on his year of reviewing and reorganizing, he was able to show a decrease in the budget of approximately one million dollars. Although this tended to make the members receptive to his ideas, doubts about some aspects of his plans persisted. The long-term effect of so large a proportion of posts in the Secretariat carrying the highest rank was again questioned, and a heated debate took place over the salaries of senior officials. The mystification of some members was scarcely dispelled by his explanation of why the Deputy to each Under-Secretary should also be of Under-Secretary rank. "Perhaps the terms I have used in my report in describing the status of these officials as co-ordinate with rather than subordinate to that of Under-Secretaries require some amplification," he told the Fifth Committee, and he went on to say that the system proposed was "not one that is based on a system of strict formal division of authority, but one which involves an agreed sharing of total operational responsibilities."[12]

There was also a persistent feeling that in reorganizing the Secretariat, Hammarskjold had overextended his personal and direct responsibility and had taken on too heavy a burden. He strongly denied that this was the case, and pointed out that whereas previously some twenty Assistant Secretaries-General and senior directors had dealt directly with the Secretary-General, under the new arrangement this number would be at most sixteen. Besides, better-defined and more clear-cut lines of authority would also ease the pressures that had formerly arisen from the diffusion and uncertainty of responsibility and authority among the top echelon of officials. Nor did he agree that his assumption of direct control over financial, personnel, and legal matters would overtax his time and energy. On the contrary, it was right and proper that he should assume personal responsibility for these important questions. Partly in response to suggestions that too much of his time was taken up by duties at Headquarters, he announced plans to visit all the member countries over the next few years.

Many people remained unconvinced, and Aghnides went so far as to tell the Fifth Committee that Hammarskjold's ideas on the top echelon had caused the Advisory Committee "the greatest difficulty and embarrassment,"[13] because it meant that the Deputy Under-Secretaries would have equal status with their chiefs. This comment infuriated Hammarskjold, and Aghnides, in turn, resented his resentment. Hammarskjold knew that Aghnides' good will was necessary if interminable wrangles over budgetary and administrative matters were to be avoided in the years to come. He discovered that Aghnides, who had known his brother Åke well when the latter had been Registrar of the International Court in The Hague before the war, shared some of his own tastes in music and literature, and he and Aghnides remained friends long after he had lost his first enthusiasm for international administration.

Hammarskjold was particularly incensed by attempts to decrease the salaries of top-level officials because of the change in their status and title, and stated flatly that he could not be responsible for recruiting adequate senior officials on the basis of the suggested reductions. To Aghnides in private he was far more outspoken. Aghnides had unwisely whispered to him during a meeting that people felt there were only one or two really good senior officials in the Secretariat anyway and that the reduced scale of pay was therefore justified. Hammarskjold regarded this as a slur on his colleagues and replied with an angry personal letter. Such a view, he said, was utterly unjustified and

> will wreck this Organization if it is permitted to continue. . . .
>
> When we finally promote one of the most brilliant negotiators of our time [Bunche] to the position he should have held for years, we reduce the salary for him in that position.
>
> When we recruit the head of a mission [Bokhari], who certainly is the one with the greatest "erudition," a man of very broad political experience and who once organized the All India Radio, we reduce the salary, thus increasing his loss because of the transition with an added $2,000. . . .
>
> When we merge the Economic and Social Departments and finally give the man in charge full responsibility for the whole of the Economic and Social field, to which, in due time, will be added Technical Assistance—when we try in this whole sphere to get a new start for the most essential practical work of the Organization, something the League of Nations never even imagined, and get for that post a highly intelligent and extremely energetic young man [de Seynes], we give him $5,000 less than his predecessor.
>
> When I finally am in a position to give compensation to the man who has carried the heaviest burden for the Secretary-General through the lifetime of the Organization and done so with a skill unequalled in my administrative experience [Cordier], I may not be able to give him even the salary of the counsellor of the British Delegation.
>
> And as a reason for this somewhat unusual policy it is said that people who have already established world fame or who have, during nine years, proved that they are able to keep this extremely complicated Organization running against heavy odds, are not good enough. . . .
>
> The full impact of what is now happening is perhaps best illustrated by the fact that a logical demand would be that you should at the same time reduce the salary of the Secretary-General, giving as a reason that the Organization had not turned out to be so important as people held in San Francisco. As a private person I would not mind. As Secretary-General I would have to ask how you believe that such a step would be understood by the public and how you thought that such a step could help the Organization to come closer to the ideal. The difference between the reaction to such a move and to what is now happening in the cases of Bunche, Bokhari, etc. is only one of degree.[14]

Hammarskjold was at his best when standing up for the people who worked for him, and in a dozen interventions in the Fifth Committee he publicly and heatedly defended his plans. Even so, it took all his powers of exposition to maintain what he believed to be a fair level of pay for the Under-Secretaries, namely a basic salary of $18,000 gross plus a representation allowance of $3,500 and a special allowance of up to $6,000 at the discretion of the Secretary-General. It was an indication of the low esteem in which the Secretariat had hitherto been held by the member governments that even this disputed scale compared very unfavorably with the emoluments of most ambassadors accredited to the UN. Hammarskjold was determined to change this attitude, and in the end he got the result he wanted in the form of appropriations that he himself could allot for representation purposes and an undertaking that the matter would not be reopened every year.

EISENHOWER'S ADDRESS to the General Assembly on December 8, 1953, on international cooperation in the peaceful uses of atomic energy had included a proposal for an international scientific conference to be held in the late summer of 1955.[15] To help the Secretary-General organize this large and complex meeting, the Assembly appointed an Advisory Committee, of which Hammarskjold became chairman. At his insistence the members of this committee were high-level scientists, and the group, which assembled for the first time in January 1955, could hardly have been more distinguished. I. I. Rabi of the United States and Sir John Cockcroft of Great Britain were both Nobel Prize winners; D. V. Skobeltzin was a highly distinguished member of the Soviet Academy; both Homi Bhabba of India, a brilliant mathematician, physicist, artist, and musician, and W. B. Lewis of Canada were the heads of their countries' atomic-energy programs, and Bertrand Goldschmidt of France had been associated with the atomic-energy program in Canada and the United States from the very beginning. At first the scientists seemed prone to the same political stresses and suspicions which had so long dominated the relations between their governments. The UN itself was new and suspect to most of them, and they were also initially suspicious of this expedition by a primarily political organization into the virgin fields of science. By skillful chairmanship and tactful handling, Hammarskjold soon converted these initial reservations into enthusiasm for a highly complex and unprecedented task.

The planning for the scientific conference went forward with exemplary speed and soon became a competitive exercise in the declassification of scientific material by East and West. The scientific importance of the conference was matched by its political significance as a sign of improving East-West relations. It placed enormous demands on the Secretariat in terms of organization, translation, document production, and programming; but with Hammarskjold's constant support and interest, and under the inspired leadership of its organizing secretary, Professor Walter G. Whitman of the Massachusetts Institute of Technology, it turned into an administrative, scientific, and political triumph that earned the UN a new position in the scientific world.

The Scientific Advisory Committee remained in existence, and Hammarskjold looked forward eagerly to its meetings. Most of its members became his friends, and the quick and efficient dispatch of the Committee's business by highly disciplined intellectuals was a refreshing change from the dilatory and inconclusive ways of the political organs of the UN.

IN HIS EARLY YEARS as Secretary-General, Hammarskjold gave many public speeches in an attempt both to improve the public image of the UN and to make his own ideas known. He was an unimpressive speaker, and it sometimes seemed as if he made a deliberate effort to avoid using even the simplest of oratorical techniques. He tended to speak with a tubular Swedish intonation and in a flat, unemphatic voice that often did scant justice to his texts, many of which have stood the test of time far better than they stood the hazards of his delivery.

Hammarskjold was convinced of the importance of mass public opinion as a living force in international affairs and as what he called the "expression of a democratic mass civilization that is still in its infancy, giving to the man in the street and to group reactions a new significance in foreign policy."[16] He felt that neither governments nor public opinion were yet fully accustomed to this new phenomenon, made possible in part by the new mass media of communication, and the result tended to be timidity and rigidity on the one side and over-reaction on the other. One of the objectives of his many public addresses was to bring about public acceptance of the lasting consequences of the interdependence of the twentieth-century world and to persuade the public to accept the necessity for give-and-take and compromise in international politics. "The more I get on the inside of the UN problems," he wrote to the French statesman Robert Schuman in August 1953, "the stronger do I feel the need for a development of our approach to the broad public as well as the intellectual groups in the member countries. . . . I feel strongly that we have to strike the imagination of the common man, not by an exaggerated emphasis on achievements or even by just simply demonstrating the need for the kind of approach represented by the UN, but that we have to go deeper, in order to activate in support of what we are doing, the deep urge in all of us, intellectuals as well as the man in the street, to realize the simplest and most basic ideals of life. At the same time I think we have to try to work for a greater awareness of the realities of our world of today, in terms of mutual interdependence, and of the impossibility of any group or any country—even as strong and prosperous a one as the United States—to be 'an island unto itself.' "[17] It was an ambitious goal, and his own achievements in the end did far more than his speeches to make progress toward it.

HAMMARSKJOLD GAVE MUCH THOUGHT to improving the facilities and the appearance of UN Headquarters, a task of which he never tired, even in times of crisis. Although some of the worst features were not susceptible to improvement, he never lost heart. He reorganized the dining room and cafeteria, had the podium in the General Assembly Hall redesigned, and enforced a policy about gifts to the Organization designed to avoid the imminent danger of making the UN a dumping ground for unwanted objects and dubious works of art. He substituted a more lively color scheme for the previous battleship-gray décor of the building, and started to develop the garden. He looked with distaste on the fountain in the entrance circle, which at that time consisted of two static fire hoses projecting dispirited jets across the pond, and asked for a new design. His efforts to induce Georges Braque and Rufino Tamayo to do murals for the building came to nothing, as did a suggestion that Persian tiles be applied on the dome of the General Assembly Building.

During his first year, Hammarskjold came to know and love New York. By the end of 1954 he was well settled in his apartment on Seventy-third Street and in his small country house in the woods up near Brewster. He still had plenty of time to see people outside the international world, to go to plays and galleries, and to walk and visit bookshops, recreations that later pressures seriously curtailed. "It is good," he told members of the New York State Legislature at Albany, "for the United Nations to be working in the midst of so great and vibrant a city. The challenge which confronts the UN in all its work is, in essence, the challenge to bring to bear upon the diversity of this world the healing influence of neighbourliness. There is no other city anywhere which could offer to those who work in the UN opportunity equal to New York's to live in close and personal contact with this process in their daily lives."[18]

By the end of 1954, having put into effect his administrative reforms and having largely won the confidence both of governments and of the Secretariat, Hammarskjold was in a position to turn his attention to the political matters that would absorb him more and more for the rest of his life.

5

THE POLITICAL
CHALLENGE

WHEN HAMMARSKJOLD ARRIVED in New York, the most immediate
political preoccupation of the world organization was the Korean situation. In April 1953 the General Assembly, after calling for an armistice,
had decided, pending the results of the armistice talks at Panmunjom,
to recess until it could usefully meet again to consider a political
settlement. Although there was little the UN as such could do until the
armistice was concluded, Hammarskjold kept in close touch with
Lester Pearson, President of the General Assembly, a contact that soon
developed into a close collaboration and an abiding friendship.

On June 9, on his return from Europe, Hammarskjold had welcomed the signs of an armistice in Korea as "great and grand and very
encouraging . . . for the future,"[1] an enthusiastic endorsement balanced
nine days later by a statement deploring South Korean President
Syngman Rhee's unilateral release of North Korean prisoners of war
and other actions that added to the UN's difficulties in starting on the
task of rehabilitation in Korea and in taking the first steps toward
unification of the country. Such actions, he noted, "come strangely
from the government of a country . . . which has for years been the
beneficiary of so much effort and sacrifice by Members of the UN."[2]

On June 26, Hammarskjold visited Pearson in Ottawa to discuss the timing of the reconvening of the General Assembly in relation to the conclusion of the Korean armistice agreement and arrangements for the further discussion of a peace settlement. These arrangements were complicated by the question of Chinese representation in the UN and by U.S. policy on China, as well as by the intransigence of Syngman Rhee. Hammarskjold and Pearson were well aware that they could play, at best, a peripheral role in the Korean question. Nonetheless, the interest and prestige of the UN were involved because, if the armistice talks were to fail, the General Assembly would inevitably have to take up the matter again.

In some remarks[3] to the UN Correspondents' Association on July 10, Hammarskjold set out his own position on the Korean problem, obviously with an eye to its effect on future developments and on the UN's role in maintaining world peace. His recent statement about "wars without victory for any single party but for a principle and peace without vengeance,"[4] which some people had found rather defeatist, was, he pointed out, merely a restatement of the principles of the Charter and of the 1950 Security Council decisions to repel aggression in Korea. While expressing confidence in the line followed by the Unified Command in Korea as represented by spokesmen of the U.S. government, he once again referred to Rhee's disruptive policies and to the "obligations of the victims of aggression to the community of nations assisting them. It is a curious sight, indeed, when a victim of aggression voices intentions which might themselves call for repression in the name of those very principles which have given him protection when he was attacked."[5]

Hammarskjold did not believe that a General Assembly meeting before the armistice was signed would do any good, although from his correspondence with Prime Minister Nehru he knew that if the armistice meetings dragged on too long there might be strong pressure for it. He was increasingly alarmed by Rhee's irresponsibility and asked the U.S. mission for information on the conversations then being conducted with Rhee in Seoul by Assistant Secretary of State Walter Robertson, and their likely effect on the Panmunjom armistice talks. Secretary John Foster Dulles was not, apparently, in favor of keeping Hammarskjold informed but instead treated Korea, Hammarskjold told Pearson, as "a pure U.S. business,"[6] but on July 17 he finally received a full briefing on the Panmunjom negotiations over the prisoners of war from Lodge's deputy, Wadsworth.

On July 26 it was announced from Panmunjom that the Korean armistice would be signed and go into effect the next day, but there were still plenty of difficulties. On August 6 Robert Murphy and Wadsworth asked Hammarskjold's help in finding out China's views on the forthcoming political conference on Korea, and a week later, on the basis of questions put to Chou En-lai through the Swedish Ambassador in Peking, he was able to tell Lodge that the Chinese Foreign Minister seemed as anxious to know the U.S. attitude as the United States was to know his. Wadsworth asked him if he would be willing to act as letter box for Peking and North Korea and if the UN would service a political conference on Korea in Geneva. Hammarskjold agreed, with the reservation that he must first consult Vyshinsky.

In a discussion over lunch on August 13, he told Vyshinsky that he hoped that the UN would be able to get back to its normal functions and to a spirit of detached universality now that the military action in Korea was ended. Vyshinsky agreed with him on the desirability of a "round-table" approach at the conference on Korea, which would avoid labeling any country as belonging to any group and would make it possible for China and the U.S.S.R. to take part. Vyshinsky evidently favored political initiatives by the Secretary-General as a go-between, and even as a leader, in the forthcoming negotiations. When Hammarskjold raised the question of the "letter-box" function, Vyshinsky replied that the Secretary-General could at the present juncture be most valuable by serving as a mediator, a role that Hammarskjold felt would be excessive in the circumstances.

The General Assembly reconvened to discuss Korea from August 17 to 28. Hammarskjold continued to be the "letter box" in the discussions over the political conference, which continued through the rest of 1953. The Foreign Ministers of France, Great Britain, the United States, and the U.S.S.R. finally agreed on February 18, 1954, that the Korean Peace Conference should meet in Geneva on April 26, a move that Hammarskjold hoped would mean "that the stalemate at Panmunjom which has hitherto prevented calling the conference . . . is now broken."[7] The Geneva Conference produced no result on Korea, and the division of that country persists to this day.

IN THE KOREAN QUESTION Hammarskjold was dealing, largely from the sidelines, with the aftermath of an international conflict in which the role of the UN was strictly secondary to that of the powers directly concerned. The Guatemalan affair of June 1954, despite the efforts of the United States to keep the question away from the UN, involved Hammarskjold in his first—and entirely unsuccessful—major clash with a member government.

Nearly ten years later, Eisenhower described the Guatemalan episode thus: "There was one time when we had a very desperate situation, or we thought it was at least, in Central America, and we had to get rid of a Communist government which had taken over, and our early efforts were defeated by a bad accident and we had to help, send some help right away."* Late in 1953, Washington apparently decided that the regime of President Jacobo Arbenz Guzmán, which had been in power in Guatemala since March 1951, must go. Although the Central Intelligence Agency was to organize the coup, the State Department and the Joint Chiefs of Staff were aware of the plan, which was to take the form of an invasion by a U.S.-trained Guatemalan exile, Colonel Carlos Castillo Armas, backed up by P-47 fighter-bombers and C-47 transports flown by CIA personnel from bases in Nicaragua. Already on January 29, 1954, the Arbenz government had charged that there was a plot between the United States and Castillo Armas, and at the Tenth Inter-American Conference in Caracas in March Dulles had pushed through an anti-Communist resolution that Guatemala alone had opposed.

On June 18 Colonel Castillo Armas, with a force of 150 men, invaded Guatemala from Honduras. Even at the time this improbable action was widely believed to be an effort by the CIA to topple the Arbenz regime, although on the opening day of the invasion the State Department stoutly maintained that it had no evidence "that this is anything other than a revolt of Guatemalans against the government,"[8] a statement that was to be repeated by Lodge in the Security Council.

Dithering and incompetence were the order of the day on both sides, and the invasion, planned as an overnight coup, dragged on for twelve days. Washington had to provide three extra fighter planes to replace two P-47 Thunderbolts that had been shot down while attempting to bomb Guatemala City, while on his side President Arbenz proved unable to mobilize the Guatemalan Army to protect his regime. Castillo Armas and his group waited just inside the Guatemalan border until Arbenz capitulated on June 27. Power was first assumed by a military junta. "The situation," Dulles asserted in a broadcast, "is being cured by the Guatemalans themselves." Castillo Armas, who arrived in triumph in Guatemala City in the U.S. Ambassador's plane, became President on July 8. He instituted a dictatorial regime, took back 800,000 acres given to the peasants under Arbenz' land-reform scheme, returned the United Fruit Company's sequestrated land, started a witch-hunt for Communists, and was finally assassinated on July 26, 1957.

In a cloak-and-dagger situation engineered by a great power, it was

---

* Quoted in Wise and Ross, *The Invisible Government* (New York, 1964), p. 166. Eisenhower gave a longer account of the Guatemala affair in *The White House Years: Mandate for Change—1953-1956* (New York, 1963), pp. 504–11.

unlikely that either the stately procedures of the UN Security Council or the good offices of the Secretary-General would have much effect. On June 19 the government of Guatemala requested[9] an urgent meeting of the Council. Lodge, who was President of the Council for June, maintained firmly that the obvious procedure was for the matter to be referred to the Organization of American States, a course that had also been formally suggested by Cuba.[10] When Hammarskjold advised strongly against this idea, Lodge invoked Article 52 of the Charter,* which he maintained even made a reference to the regional organization compulsory. Hammarskjold countered with paragraph 4 of Article 52, which indicates that the Council is in no way barred from action by the activities of a regional organization. On June 20 the Council, after a resolution[11] referring the matter to the Organization of American States had been vetoed by the Soviet Union, adopted a resolution calling for "the immediate termination of any action likely to cause bloodshed" and requesting all members to abstain "from rendering assistance to any such action."[12] This bland formula, which concealed the resentment of the Western European members of the Council at the highly embarrassing position into which the CIA adventure had put

---

* Text of Articles 52, 34, and 35:

Article 52

1. Nothing in the present Charter precludes the existence of regional arrangements or agencies for dealing with such matters relating to the maintenance of international peace and security as are appropriate for regional action, provided that such arrangements or agencies and their activities are consistent with the Purposes and Principles of the United Nations.

2. The Members of the United Nations entering into such arrangements or constituting such agencies shall make every effort to achieve pacific settlement of local disputes through such regional arrangements or by such regional agencies before referring them to the Security Council.

3. The Security Council shall encourage the development of pacific settlement of local disputes through such regional arrangements or by such regional agencies either on the initiative of the states concerned or by reference from the Security Council.

4. This Article in no way impairs the application of Articles 34 and 35.

Article 34

The Security Council may investigate any dispute, or any situation which might lead to international friction or give rise to a dispute, in order to determine whether the continuance of the dispute or situation is likely to endanger the maintenance of international peace and security.

Article 35

1. Any Member of the United Nations may bring any dispute, or any situation of the nature referred to in Article 34, to the attention of the Security Council or of the General Assembly.

2. A state which is not a Member of the United Nations may bring to the attention of the Security Council or of the General Assembly any dispute to which it is a party if it accepts in advance, for the purposes of the dispute, the obligations of pacific settlement provided in the present Charter.

3. The proceedings of the General Assembly in respect of matters brought to its attention under this Article will be subject to the provisions of Articles 11 and 12.

them, had no effect whatsoever on what was happening in Guatemala.

Late on June 22, Hammarskjold received a letter[13] from the Guatemalan Foreign Minister, Guillermo Toriello, complaining that the Council's resolution was not being complied with and asking for a further meeting. Lodge, who called him early on the next day, maintained, after hearing the Guatemalan letter, that the whole business was a Communist plot. When Hammarskjold pointed out that even if that was the case it did not justify a deviation from the law, Lodge inquired whether he was proposing to use Article 99.* When Hammarskjold replied that the current situation would not warrant it, Lodge merely said that such a step would have been fantastic and that he would tell him as soon as he had decided on a time for the Council meeting.

Twenty-four hours later Hammarskjold was still trying to get a decision from Lodge on convening the Council, which the Soviet representative, Semyon Tsarapkin, was now also demanding.[14] Lodge eventually phoned to say that the Council would meet on the next day, June 25, at 3 p m at the request of Brazil and Colombia, and that he would be discussing the agenda with the Council's secretary, an unusual and insulting procedure that prompted Hammarskjold to say that if he disagreed with the agenda he would take it up with Lodge. He soon found that he did disagree, for Lodge's proposed agenda consisted only of the second Guatemalan letter[15] and did not include the original Guatemalan request[16] for a meeting, an omission which, Hammarskjold told the U.S. mission, was inconceivable. The French Ambassador, Henri Hoppenot, who, despite his instructions, was indignant at the U.S. position, told Hammarskjold that Lodge had arranged for the Latin-American members of the Council—Brazil and Colombia—to oppose the adoption of the agenda, even though they themselves had requested the meeting. In fact, the Latin-American request for a meeting was simply a pretext to counter the Soviet request for a meeting.

When the Council finally met on June 25, Lodge, claiming that "international Communism" was using the Guatemalan complaint to "secure for the Security Council, where it had the veto power, a monopoly of authority to deal with international disputes,"[17] opposed the adoption of the agenda on the grounds that the investigation of the Guatemalan complaint was a matter for the Organization of American States and not, in the first instance, for the Security Council. The Council supported him by rejecting the agenda by a narrow vote of

---

* Article 99 gives the Secretary-General the right to bring to the attention of the Security Council any matter which in his opinion may threaten the maintenance of international peace and security.

4 in favor and 5 against, with France and Great Britain abstaining.

Hammarskjold had anticipated this negative result and had prepared a statement on the question of the respective jurisdiction of the UN and regional organizations, to be made if the vote on the agenda was negative. Before and during the Council meeting he showed this draft statement to Hoppenot, Sir Pierson Dixon of Britain, and Wadsworth. Hoppenot was all for his making the statement, while Dixon implored him not to make it on the grounds that it would force him to change his speech and vote against the United States instead of abstaining, and also that it would almost certainly cause the United States to walk out of the Council. Wadsworth merely commented that the statement would be a mistake and that Hammarskjold would be severely criticized for taking the initiative. Although Hammarskjold felt that a matter of principle with serious moral implications had arisen, he decided in the end not to make the statement public, but he told Dixon afterwards that Lodge's statement to the Council was the most serious blow so far aimed at the Organization and that if the matter were pushed any further he would be forced "to reconsider my present position in the United Nations."[18]

There was no longer any possibility of the UN's having any practical influence on the situation in Guatemala, for the Arbenz government had fallen on June 27. Hammarskjold, however, was determined to put his views on record without creating a useless disturbance. On June 30 he wrote to Lodge that the line taken by the United States in the Guatemala case concerning the relative responsibilities of the UN and the OAS in matters of peace and security had serious consequences for the future constitutional development of the UN, and that he considered it part of his duties to "try and help the members to develop the UN activities in a way consonant with the basic principles of the Charter and providing consistency in the practices followed."[19] He sent Lodge a legal study of the texts and records of the Security Council and the San Francisco Conference relating to this matter. Although this was an internal Secretariat document, he informed Lodge that he would "consider it in line with my obligations to put it at the disposal of delegations"[20] and especially of the members of the Security Council, but he wanted Lodge to have a look at it first. "You will find," he wrote, "that it is a rather dry, factual review without evaluations or conclusions."[21]

This "dry, factual review" provoked, as Hammarskjold must have known it would, an uproar in the State Department, which was still uncomfortable over the public reaction to the Guatemala adventure. His theme was that regional action within the framework of the

Charter was a complement of universal action and that, according to Article 103 of the Charter, if a conflict arose between members' obligations under the Charter and other obligations, those under the Charter should prevail. He maintained that regional agreements themselves also recognized the paramountcy of the Charter, especially in the maintenance of peace and security, and in support of this position he quoted the report[22] which the chairman of the U.S. delegation to the San Francisco Conference had made to the President of the United States. He also mentioned the right of any member or nonmember of the UN, under Article 35 of the Charter, to bring any situation to the attention of the Security Council or the General Assembly, recalling that at San Francisco there had been an understanding that no permanent member of the Security Council would be entitled to use the veto to prevent the Council from considering a situation brought to its attention.

The initial U.S. reaction was that Hammarskjold's analysis of the relationship between the UN and regional organizations could not be accepted as valid and that the Security Council, even when a member state had submitted a dispute or situation to it under Article 35, was obliged to promote pacific settlement through the regional agency. The memorandum pointed out that a majority of ten out of eleven members of the Council had agreed that the Guatemalan appeal, the first case to come before it that fell within the scope of a regional agency, should be referred "to the appropriate agencies of the O.A.S."[23] and had been frustrated only by the Soviet veto.

The fact that a majority of the Council had, however reluctantly, followed the U.S. line made Hammarskjold's position extremely weak, and the fall of the Arbenz government had in any case made the controversy largely academic, but the strong U.S. reaction to his memorandum indicated that his effort to put on record a point of principle had hit a sensitive nerve. A further note from the United States strongly objected to the circulation or disclosure of his memorandum on the grounds that it showed evidence of bias, was a "warped presentation" and a "thinly disguised and tendentious attack upon the position taken by the U.S., the Latin American Members of the Security Council and the O.A.S. in the Guatemalan case."[24] Its disclosure, the U.S. note warned, would gravely affect the impartial standing of the Secretary-General and of his legal adviser.

In Hammarskjold's absence in Geneva, Andrew Cordier responded strongly to Wadsworth's presentation of this second memorandum, which he termed tendentious and unacceptable. He commented particularly on the way in which the memorandum had offhandedly referred to the Security Council resolution of June 20, which called for all members to abstain from any action likely to cause bloodshed, as "another resolution concerning the matter,"[25] and on the fact that the American disregard for this resolution had led to the new Guatemalan request of June 23 and the further meeting of the Council on June 25. Cordier, who had been a member of the U.S. delegation at San Francisco, also recalled that it was the United States that had initiated the idea behind paragraph 4 of Article 52, which was designed to keep the door of the Security Council open to a nation that found itself in just such a position as Guatemala had been in.

Hammarskjold's memorandum was given to the representatives of France and Great Britain, and little more was heard either of it or of the Guatemala question at the UN, although in a letter to Lodge in August he remarked that he now found that among delegations the general interpretation of the point of principle involved in the Guatemala affair was along the lines indicated in his own memorandum.

The Guatemalan affair gave Hammarskjold a lesson in the practical weakness of the Secretary-General's position when confronted by a determined great power. It also put a considerable temporary strain on his relationship with Lodge, but in August the Lodges invited him for the weekend at their home at Beverly, Massachusetts. Hammarskjold had accepted uneasily, but he enjoyed himself thoroughly in the Lodge family circle, and after this his official disagreements with Lodge were offset by personal friendship and mutual understanding.

THE AMERICAN COMMITMENT to Chiang Kai-shek and violent suspicion of the Peking regime of Mao Tse-tung had given rise to Washington's policy of nonrecognition of the People's Republic of China. The predominance of the United States in the UN General Assembly meant that, whatever their doubts as to its wisdom, a majority of the members of the UN also accepted, from 1949 until 1971,* the exclusion from the world organization of representatives of the actual government of the largest nation on earth. The brief moment in 1950 when there had seemed to be some possibility of a change in U.S. China policy came quickly to an end with the onset of the Korean war. The belated and limited intervention of Peking in that war, after General Douglas MacArthur's troops had crossed the 38th parallel and were advancing

---

*On October 25, 1971, the General Assembly decided to seat the representatives of the People's Republic of China.

toward China itself, only served to confirm in the eyes of the American public at large the aggressor image of Peking, and anti-Peking feeling was raised to new heights.

Questions on the Secretary-General's view concerning the problem of Chinese representation were for over twenty years a perennial standby for correspondents when the going was slow at UN press conferences. Hammarskjold's publicly expressed views on the subject were less forthright than his predecessor's. Such questions, he told a press conference in June 1953, had "to be judged at each single juncture on the basis of (a) principles, (b) what is practicable at the moment, and (c) a consideration of the general political balance and the psychological aspects."[26] The principles he referred to were universality of membership and the direct representation of the major powers in the UN. "If you want to negotiate with somebody," he remarked in 1954, "it is rather useful to have them at the table."[27]

Even Hammarskjold's mildly expressed disagreement with U.S. China policy had from time to time aroused hostile reactions from conservative members of Congress. He had also had occasional disagreements with the U.S. mission on the question. On July 30, 1954, Lodge had severely criticized his decision to release to the press a communication[28] from the Peking government protesting against U.S. air incursions over China and the shooting down of two Chinese aircraft. Lodge, reflecting the missionary anti-Communist mood of the U.S. administration at the time, called the Peking government "a clique flagrantly contemptuous of the UN."[29] A similar situation later arose over another communication from Peking, about which Lodge wrote to Hammarskjold on October 12 that the fact that China was the aggressor was "enough justification to disregard all their communications" and that Hammarskjold should "not permit the abuse of your high office intended by the Chinese Communist regime."[30] On the following day Hammarskjold circulated the Chinese communication[31] as a note to all the members, telling Lodge that "the correct discharge by the Secretary-General of his formal responsibility cannot in any sense be regarded as an abuse of his office."[32] In a personal letter he told Lodge that he regarded his letter of October 12 as an attempt at pressure, while his own reaction had been the "maximum adjustment of an established practice which I could defend in the light of my duty to strict impartiality."[33] In response to press inquiries, he recalled that in the previous four years, thirty-seven communications from the People's Republic of China had been circulated and that he saw no justification for departing from a well-established procedure.[34]

The end of the Korean war in July 1953 did little to alleviate anti-

Peking sentiment in the United States, and the inspirer and spokesman of the new administration's attitude on China was Secretary of State John Foster Dulles. The war left in its wake a number of highly difficult and sensitive problems. Of these, the imprisonment in China of a small number of U.S. Air Force personnel who had come down in China while serving under the United Nations Unified Command in Korea gave rise to particularly violent feelings in the United States and added a dangerous and emotive element to the already overheated rhetoric on the China problem in Washington. When in December 1954 the United States—after trying many other approaches in vain— brought this question to the Ninth Session of the General Assembly, the UN was faced with an apparently insoluble problem. It seemed unlikely, to say the least, that an organization that had excluded and rejected the government of the largest nation on earth would have much success in prevailing on that government to release hostile airmen who had landed in China and had already been convicted as spies. The Assembly, in passing on this labor of Hercules to Hammarskjold, put in motion a train of events that was to show the member states of the Organization that their Secretary-General was not merely the talented bureaucrat whom many of them believed they had selected but also an international negotiator of exceptional resource, daring, and competence, with the capacity to get positive results even out of the most apparently hopeless situations.

On June 10, 1954, at the Geneva Conference on Indochina, U.S. Ambassador U. Alexis Johnson gave Wang Ping-nan, the Secretary-General of the Chinese Communist delegation to the Conference, lists of various categories of civilian and military personnel who were believed to be in Chinese Communist custody. These lists included eleven crew members of a B-29 which had been shot down on January 12, 1953, while conducting leaflet-dropping operations over North Korea, and four U.S. Air Force jet pilots who had been shot down between September 1952 and April 1953 during the Korean war. The Chinese confirmed that these men were being held for investigation for "violation of Chinese territorial air."[35] No further information was forthcoming until November 24, 1954, when Radio Peking announced that eleven U.S. airmen, as well as two other Americans, John T. Downey and Richard G. Fecteau, both of whom were described as special agents of the CIA, had been convicted of espionage by a military tribunal and sentenced to prison terms ranging from four years to life.

The case of the prisoners had already become an emotional public issue in the United States. Lodge expressed the prevalent mood when he said on August 18, 1954: "The fifteen American fliers* held illegally by Red China as 'political prisoners' should be a matter of grave concern to all civilized people. . . . The Chinese Communists should understand that just as they cannot shoot their way into the United Nations, they cannot blackmail their way in by holding innocent prisoners as hostages in a game of political warfare. This is one more indication that Red China remains totally unfit for a seat in the United Nations, whose Charter is devoted to peace and common justice."[36]

The announcement of the sentencing of the airmen in November further heightened this mood of righteous indignation. President Eisenhower described it as "a deliberate attempt . . . to goad us into some impulsive action in the hope of dividing us from our allies, breaking down and destroying all the work which has been going on over the past years, to build up a true coalition of free governments."[37]

On November 26, 1954, the United States, through the British chargé d'affaires in Peking, Humphrey Trevelyan, made a strong protest against the sentences imposed on the airmen, rejecting the charges of espionage and saying that their detention was in patent violation of the Korean armistice agreement. On November 28, Radio Peking announced that this protest had been returned to the British chargé d'affaires because the Chinese authorities had concrete evidence of the crimes committed by the airmen, and a further protest by the U.S. consul general to the Chinese consul general in Geneva on November 30 was also rejected. In the United States, the reaction to these developments was stormy. Senator William F. Knowland, the Republican leader in the Senate, called for a naval blockade of China unless the airmen were promptly released. The suggestion was hastily disowned by Secretary Dulles, who stated that although the U.S. government would react vigorously to the imprisonment of the airmen, it would not resort to "war actions."[38] On December 3, President Eisenhower pledged his tireless efforts but opposed warlike measures to gain the release of the airmen, which, he declared, was the responsibility of the United Nations since the prisoners had been serving the United Nations Command in Korea.

Official relations between the United States and China had steadily deteriorated since the representatives of the two countries had sat together in the Geneva Conference in the summer. Earlier in the ses-

---

* This number comprised the B-29 crew and the four jet-fighter pilots. Downey and Fecteau, as civilian agents, were not included in the list of airmen whom the U.S. regarded as prisoners of war who should be repatriated under the Korean armistice agreement.

sion the General Assembly had heard an acrimonious and abortive debate between Vyshinsky and C. D. Jackson, for the United States, on a Soviet-sponsored item alleging American "acts of aggression"[39] against the Chinese People's Republic and accusing Taiwan of "piratical acts"[40] in seizing a Soviet tanker and two Polish vessels.* The Chinese shelling of the offshore islands of Quemoy and Matsu, which started on September 3, 1954, had been followed by the formalization of U.S. support for Chiang Kai-shek in a mutual defense treaty which committed the U.S. to defend Taiwan if it was attacked from the mainland. This treaty was signed on December 2 while the U.S. administration was preparing to take up in the UN the issue of the prisoners.

On December 4, Lodge sent a letter to Hammarskjold asking the UN to act "promptly and decisively"[41] in bringing about the release of the survivors of the B-29 crew and drawing attention to the serious situation created by the action of the Chinese Communist authorities for the UN, which had called for the action in Korea to repel Communist aggression and had requested the United States to provide a Unified Command for the UN forces in Korea. At the same time the United States and the fifteen countries that had provided forces in Korea began to discuss the terms of a resolution to be put before the General Assembly. The United States was insistent that this resolution contain a strong condemnation of the Peking government, a provision reluctantly accepted by the Western European countries which argued that if any result was to be achieved the emphasis should rather be on some arrangement to negotiate for the release of the prisoners.

Hammarskjold took an active part in these discussions and from the outset told Lodge and Wadsworth of his concern over the U.S. approach, which gave condemnation of Peking priority over negotiation. The other key question was to decide who might act for the Assembly in negotiations with Peking. The original idea had been to ask the President of the Assembly, Eelco van Kleffens of The Netherlands, and van Kleffens got as far as drafting a message to Chou En-lai and looking for an expert on China to be his representative. Hammarskjold had felt obliged to point out that the President of the Assembly did not function as such after the session was over and that there would therefore inevitably be procedural complications. Additional disadvantages were the Netherlands' sponsorship of the resolution condemning Peking and its membership in NATO, both of which might well disqualify van Kleffens as a negotiator with Peking.

---

* Earlier in 1954, Hammarskjold had arranged for the delivery of letters home and other conveniences for the crew of two of these ships pending their release by the Taiwan authorities.

On the morning of December 6, Lodge informed Hammarskjold that Washington's ideas had changed and that the intention was to involve him personally in conducting the negotiations, since it was believed that he was more likely to get results than anyone else. To Lodge's request for his own reactions, Hammarskjold replied that if he was requested by the General Assembly to undertake a mission of this kind under Article 98 of the Charter, he clearly could not refuse.

On the evening of December 6, at an American Foreign Policy Association dinner for van Kleffens, Hammarskjold learned that Great Britain and France had agreed to the U.S. plan that he should undertake the negotiations with Peking. He spent the dinner considering his line of action and took Andrew Cordier home with him to discuss the problem further. Hammarskjold had first thought of using an intermediary, perhaps of Swiss nationality, but he soon came to the conclusion that such an arrangement would not carry enough weight. After another two hours of thought he decided that he personally must make the effort, as he called it, "to crash the gate"[42] by asking for a personal interview with Chou En-lai in Peking. His old Swedish friend the judge Sture Petrén, who was staying with him and returned from another dinner at 1:30 a.m., was immediately plunged into a night-long analysis and discussion of Hammarskjold's conclusions.*

On December 7, the resolution[44] on the prisoners was put before the General Assembly. It declared that the detention and imprisonment of the eleven American airmen and the detention of all captured UN personnel desiring repatriation were violations of the Korean armistice agreement, condemned as contrary to the agreement the trial and conviction of the prisoners of war illegally detained after September 25, 1953, and requested the Secretary-General in the name of the UN to seek the release of the eleven airmen and all other captured UN personnel. The Western European delegations had succeeded in including, in the request to the Secretary-General, the words "by the means most appropriate in his judgment."[45]

Hammarskjold told his press conference on December 7 that he was late because he had just received the final text of the sixteen-power resolution. When asked to comment on Eisenhower's statement that "it is the responsibility of the UN in this case to take care of its own,"

---

* Hammarskjold organized another all-night legal seminar before leaving for Peking. He asked Ernest Gross and Philip Jessup, also a former U.S. representative to the UN and later a judge of the International Court in The Hague, to dinner. Far into the early hours he led them through a discussion of legal problems he might encounter in Peking—alleged espionage, the rights of prisoners of war, and many others. Gross later described it as a "kind of dress rehearsal for an expedition into the unknown."[43]

he replied: "Let me switch the ground a little bit. I would not comment on what the President said, but I would say that it is definitely the responsibility of the United Nations to take as its own responsibility any matter which gives rise to increased international tension, and this matter obviously does."[46] When asked by a correspondent if he would consider going to Peking, he replied, "You are rather dramatic."[47]

In fact Hammarskjold was already gathering moral support for an attempt to visit Peking. Later in the day he talked to Anthony Nutting, the British Minister of State who had been an eloquent supporter of the U.S. position in the General Assembly. Nutting, although somewhat taken aback at the idea of Hammarskjold himself going to Peking, was not negative. Hammarskjold lunched with Lester Pearson, who asked for time to consider the proposal so that they could talk it over again after a dinner to be given that evening by Jehan de Noue, the UN Chief of Protocol. In the evening Pearson expressed his full agreement with Hammarskjold's plan and merely suggested a few changes in the messages to Chou En-lai that Hammarskjold had already drafted. On Wednesday, December 8, Hammarskjold showed the texts of these cables to the representative of France, Henri Hoppenot, during a meeting of the General Assembly's Political Committee. Hoppenot asked in some surprise, "Does this really mean that you would go?"[48] On the same day before lunch, he informed Lodge of his own interpretation of the mandate the General Assembly was likely to give him. He did this in order to give the United States the chance to back down if it wanted to, but Lodge was enthusiastic over his ideas even when Hammarskjold pointed out that his concept of the mission "takes us far into the field of China policy."[49]

During the morning of December 10, Hammarskjold saw Pierson Dixon and Nutting. Although they were generally in favor of his plan, they suggested that it might be wise for him first to sound out Chou En-lai on his willingness to receive him and volunteered that Humphrey Trevelyan, the British chargé d'affaires in Peking, might be entrusted with that task. Hammarskjold replied that he realized that if he approached Chou directly he risked a flat refusal, but that to sound him out in advance was much more liable to produce a refusal than a more direct approach. An indirect approach, through Trevelyan for example, could not, if it failed, even be put on the public record. He therefore thanked the British for their offer and their advice, but informed them that he intended to communicate with Chou En-lai directly.

After a heated debate, the Assembly adopted the resolution[50] on the afternoon of December 10. The Soviet bloc voted against it, and India and Yugoslavia were among the seven abstentions, but Hoppenot expressed the general mood when he said of the Secretary-General's task that "the entire moral authority of the United Nations will be behind him in an action in which he remains completely free."[51] After the resolution had been adopted in the Assembly, Hammarskjold spoke briefly to say that he accepted his responsibilities under the resolution "with a deep sense of the importance of the issue."[52] He drew attention to the resolution's words "by the means most appropriate in his judgment,"[53] which he interpreted as applying to his task in general, and, further to underline his independence of action, he referred to Hoppenot's support of this interpretation.

After the Assembly's decision, Hammarskjold sent two communications[54] to Chou En-lai, one of which, a cablegram, was published four hours later. It read as follows:

New York, 10 December 1954—The General Assembly of the United Nations has requested me to seek the release of eleven United Nations Command personnel captured by Chinese forces on 12 January 1953 as well as of all other captured personnel of the United Nations Command still detained. Taking into consideration all facts and circumstances the Secretary-General must, in this case, take on himself a special responsibility. In the light of the concern I feel about the issue, I would appreciate an opportunity to take this matter up with you personally. For that reason I would ask you whether you could receive me in Peking. I would suggest a visit soon after 26 December and would, if you accept my proposal, ask you what date at about that time would be suitable to you.

DAG HAMMARSKJOLD, Secretary-General, United Nations[55]

He had originally intended to send this cable through Swedish diplomatic channels, but finally decided to send it by commercial cable so that it would arrive in Peking as soon as possible after news reports of the General Assembly's decision. In a first exercise of his "completely free" role, he did not formally transmit to Peking the full text of the Assembly's resolution.

In a second message, sent confidentially to Chou through Indian channels, Hammarskjold mentioned the "extraordinary nature of the initiative, this being the first time that the Secretary-General of the United Nations personally visits a capital for negotiations."[56] He suggested that they establish a confidential contact through the Chinese Ambassador in Stockholm, through whom practical arrangements could be made, and mentioned that he himself would be in Stockholm on December 19 and 20.

Late in the afternoon of December 10, Hammarskjold informed Jacob Malik, head of the Soviet delegation, of the messages to Chou En-lai. Malik, who had not received instructions on the matter, expressed his own approval. Hammarskjold also saw the Indian representative, Arthur Lall, and gave him the texts of his messages to Chou En-lai to send to Nehru. He also asked Lall to convey to Nehru his request for the services of Rajeshwar Dayal, the former Indian permanent representative at the United Nations, as his political assistant on the mission.*

In approaching Chou En-lai directly, Hammarskjold was risking a rebuff that would both destroy his possibility of getting the release of the prisoners and be a serious blow to his prestige as Secretary-General, but the increasing tension between the United States and China, the angry mood of the American public, and the condemnatory nature of the General Assembly resolution had combined to put him in an extremely delicate position, and he had concluded that nothing but a bold move had any chance of success. As Lodge put it six months later, in offering to go to Peking Hammarskjold "put his life's reputation as a diplomat on the chopping block"[57]

In a letter to Anthony Eden on December 15, Hammarskjold analyzed his concept of his mission. The method he had chosen was the one that he felt would give him the maximum chance to overcome the natural reluctance of Peking to accept an approach from the UN on the prisoner issue, which was of key importance not only for the prestige of the UN in the United States but also as a factor in a highly significant international conflict. It was deplorable that the situation could not be met in a less hazardous way, but he had been unable to think of any other possibility to save the face of the United Nations and at the same time to have some chance of finding a solution. Everything would depend on Peking's interest in having any contact with the United Nations in any form. If there was no such interest, the venture was doomed to failure in any case. If Peking did prove to be interested, he would try to find a way, far from the limelight and from new sensations, to get results in Peking without making any inappropriate commitments to Peking either for the United Nations or for the Secretary-General.

Chou En-lai replied on December 17 that "in the interest of peace and relaxation of international tension, I am prepared to receive you in our capital, Peking, to discuss with you pertinent questions."[58] In another long cablegram on the same day, to emphasize the distinction between Hammarskjold's mission and the General Assembly's resolution, Chou En-lai stated that "no amount of clamor on the part of the

---

* Nehru refused this request because India did not approve of the Assembly resolution and he felt that Dayal's appointment would not be good either for Hammarskjold or for India.

United States can shake China's just stand of exercising its own sovereign right in convicting the United States spies,"[59] and referred to the General Assembly resolution as "absurd."[60]

Hammarskjold decided that from the Secretariat he would take along his personal assistant, Per Lind; Ahmed Bokhari, the chief of the Department of Public Information; Bill Ranallo, his personal aide; and Aase Alm, his secretary. From Sweden he recruited as an interpreter a former missionary in China, Gustav Nyström. He was particularly anxious to make his talks with Chou En-lai legally and diplomatically solid, and with this in mind he asked the British Foreign Office to produce the best international legal adviser it could find. As a result Sir Humphrey Waldock, Chichele Professor of International Law at Oxford University, joined his team.

On December 17, Hammarskjold left New York for the annual meeting of the Swedish Academy, at which he was to make his inaugural speech on taking the seat formerly occupied by his father. This occasion served as a useful cover for his meeting, as arranged by Chou, with the Chinese Ambassador in Stockholm, General Keng Piao, to discuss the final arrangements for the trip to Peking. He met Keng Piao on December 19 at a private lunch that he had asked Uno Willers* to arrange at his own house. The two men agreed that the talks would be of four or five days' duration and that Hammarskjold would be the only representative on the United Nations side. The discussions would be on "pertinent questions"[61] and there would be no agenda, though it was understood that the question of the U.S. airmen was "pertinent."

Hammarskjold returned to New York on December 21. When asked on his arrival in Stockholm about both the U.S. atomic energy proposals and his role concerning the U.S. prisoners in China, he had replied "it is imperative for me at present to play both issues and myself down,"[62] and for the remaining nine days at UN Heaquarters until his departure this was his main problem. The decision of the U.S. government to use the United Nations in an attempt to free the prisoners was by no means popular in Congress, while the General Assembly resolution had infuriated Peking. Hammarskjold was thus in a precarious and exposed position where any sudden movement or unexpected blast from either direction could easily throw him off balance. His difficulties were compounded by a flood of speculation in the press about the line he was going to take in Peking, and at his press conference on December 22 he made an attempt to discourage this trend, repeating what he had said in Stockholm: "To succeed means to realize the possible. The

---

* Formerly in the Swedish Foreign Office, and Director of the Swedish Royal Library.

possible has to be realized. I should just hate to see any development which would reduce our chances of realizing what was possible."[63] When asked if his mission was not humiliating for the United Nations, he replied, "I am not going anywhere to beg anybody for anything."[64] On December 24, he made another attempt to discourage publicity by issuing a statement[65] emphasizing that his visit to Peking was a diplomatic contact on an important question and not a propaganda expedition or a "state" visit or a "good-will" mission. For this reason he declined all requests to take any press correspondents with him.

Hammarskjold and his party left New York on December 30 for the first leg of his trip, landing at London, where he spent the evening with Eden at Dorney Wood, his official residence as Foreign Secretary. He found Eden strongly in favor of his mission but deeply concerned over its outcome. He flew on via Paris, where he saw Premier Mendès-France, and then to Delhi, where he had a long talk with Nehru. From Delhi the party flew on to Canton, and thence to Hankow in a Chinese aircraft. After staying overnight in Hankow, where they were joined by Hammarskjold's nephew, Peder Hammarskjold, who was serving in the Swedish Embassy in Peking, the party finally arrived in Peking at 1:45 p.m. on January 5. After lunch with the Swedish Ambassador, Hugo Wistrand, Hammarskjold paid a courtesy call on Chou En-lai, who that evening gave a reception for him in the Palace of Purple Light, after which he dined privately with Chou.

It was bitterly cold in Peking. Bokhari, describing the trip later, complained: "I was the only person in the party that had been used to a reasonable climate. Everybody else in his weaker moments had been an Alpine climber."[66] In spite of the cold, Hammarskjold went bare-headed as usual, donning a hat only for the benefit of photographers. He and his personal staff stayed in the Swedish embassy, while the rest of the party lived in a Peking hotel. In between the official meetings the Chinese did everything possible to make their guests' stay enjoyable, and there were outings to the Forbidden City, the Summer Palace, and the Ming Tombs. Peking made a tremendous impression on Hammarskjold, and he loved every minute of these visits. "On these occasions," Bokhari said later, "about the worst person in the world to follow is Mr. Hamarskjold, because he walked at a terrific pace without a hat—which was uncommon in China—and faster than anybody else."[67]

The actual talks took place in the sitting room of the Premier's office, in the old palace called the Hall of Western Flowers. They started each day at three in the afternoon and usually broke off between five and six o'clock except on one occasion when they went on until after eight. Only Hammarskjold, Chou En-lai, and the interpreter spoke, with no other sound in the room. Chou's man did all the interpreting, with Nyström following and checking the interpretation.

From the very first Chou En-lai and Hammarskjold seem to have made a good impression on each other, and their mutual respect and understanding was an important factor in the subsequent talks. Both were intellectuals as well as highly professional diplomats, and the talks were conducted at a level of finesse and courtesy that complemented rather than concealed the strong intellects of the two protagonists and their determination to stick to their own positions.

Hammarskjold's limited aim in Peking was essentially to make a good case for the release of the prisoners without calling in question the legal rights of the Chinese authorities or putting them on the defensive over their treatment of the prisoners or their attitude toward the United States. The immediate object was to establish a basis of understanding and fact upon which in due time the Chinese could take the necessary decisions to release the prisoners without appearing to be bowing to U.S. pressure or overruling their own courts. The discussions were therefore deliberately left at a loose end. Characteristically, Hammarskjold had acquired in advance a comprehensive grasp of the facts and the legal implications of the case.

At the first formal meeting on January 6, he took pains to clarify his own position. Chou had agreed, in informal talks over dinner the previous night, to begin with the prisoner-of-war issue, on which Hammarskjold had a mandate from the General Assembly, and to turn later to other pertinent questions that Chou wished to discuss, on which Hammarskjold's scope would be limited to listening and making general comments. Hammarskjold explained that in fulfilling his obligation to try to reduce international tensions anywhere in the world, the Secretary-General did not work for any one nation or even for a majority of nations as expressed in a vote in the General Assembly but under his constitutional responsibility for the general purposes set out in the Charter, which were applicable to members and nonmembers of the United Nations alike. It was on this basis that he had come to Peking. The General Assembly resolution had brought to the fore a case where Hammarskjold had both the right and the duty to act as Secretary-General, but the Charter of the United Nations, not the condemnation of the General Assembly in its resolution of December 10, formed the legal basis for his present visit. This formulation of the basis for independent intervention by the Secretary-General later became known as the "Peking formula."*

---

* See also Chapter 18, p. 495.

Hammarskjold then proceeded to give his own considered view of the question of the American prisoners. The emotional reaction in the United States to the conviction of the eleven surviving members of the B-29 crew and to the plight of the four jet pilots and other prisoners was matched on the Chinese side by the fear of a threat to Chinese security and the feeling that the Chinese authorities had been unjustly accused. The essential thing was to straighten out these emotional reactions on the basis of facts and law.

He emphasized that in trying to present the truth of the case as he saw it he was not competing with the autonomous procedures of the Chinese courts or questioning their sovereign right to convict. He was, however, firmly convinced from his own inquiries that the eleven survivors of the B-29 were on a mission for the UN Command in Korea and that their aircraft, which was part of the Resupply and Communications Wing of the 13th U.S. Air Force, was in fact fully under orders of the UN Command in Korea. The leaflet-dropping operation in which they had been engaged on January 12, 1953, had been specifically ordered by the UN Command, and all the targets designated were within North Korea. The crew of the B-29 could therefore be legitimately regarded as prisoners of war. The facts were no less conclusive in the case of the four jet-fighter pilots, who were also entitled to be regarded as UN military personnel captured in lawful combat and to be treated as prisoners of war.

Hammarskjold concluded his first statement with a broader appeal:

When the Secretary-General of the United Nations has engaged himself and his office, with all the weight it carries in world opinion, for the fate of the prisoners—and although I refer primarily to the eleven plus four, I have also all the others in mind—it does not mean that I *appeal* to you or that I *ask you* for their release. It means that—inspired also by my faith in your wisdom and in your wish to promote peace—I have considered it my duty as forcefully as I can, and with deep conviction, to draw your attention to the vital importance of their fate to the cause of peace. . . . Their fate may well decide the direction in which we will all be moving in the near future—towards peace, or away from peace. . . . This case is one of those which history suddenly lifts up to key significance—as is evidenced by the sheer fact that, against all odds, it has brought me around the world in order to put before you, in great frankness and trusting that we see eye to eye on the desperate need to avoid adding to existing frictions, my deep concern both as Secretary-General and as a man.*

Chou En-lai replied that this was not a lawsuit and that whatever

---

* All quotes from the Hammarskjold/Chou talks are from Hammarskjold's own record of the talks.[68]

the outcome neither party to the discussions would be committed, because on the one side was the Secretary-General of the United Nations talking with a country that was not a member of the UN and could not be bound in relation to the Secretary-General, and on the other side was China, which had no right to ask the Secretary-General to agree to take any special steps. The General Assembly resolution had no binding force for China, and was indeed totally unacceptable, while the jurisdiction of the Chinese courts was, of course, a domestic affair.

After a brief contretemps over this statement, it was agreed that Chou En-lai would recognize that the relations between the General Assembly and the Secretary-General were outside the field where he had any right to speak, while Hammarskjold would recognize that their discussion did not imply the acceptance by China of any part of the General Assembly resolution. Hammarskjold further insisted that since in his view the airmen had prisoner-of-war status and were not spies, international law did in fact apply to them, regardless of the Chinese courts.

This exchange caused Chou to say that on legal questions they were not even using the same language and he did not believe they would be able to find a solution without approaching the matter from the angle of general political questions, while Hammarskjold continued to insist that their difference was rather as to the facts on which the judgments were based. On this uncertain note the first meeting ended.

The following day Chou told Hammarskjold that he did not see anything in his first statement that had not already been stated by the U.S. representative at the United Nations, whose object had been to cover up the facts about intrusion and espionage. To begin with, the number of persons involved was thirteen and not eleven, and they were carrying out duties for the CIA and not for the UN Korean Command. Downey and Fecteau were shot down on November 29, 1952, while trying to pick up a special agent in Antung Province.* Chou maintained that the B-29 crew were also working for the CIA and were shot down while they were trying, as he put it, to "sneak into Antung Province." The B-29 had a portable transmitter of the type used by intelligence agents. Both planes came from Japan and both were of the type used for intelligence operations against China. The B-29 crew were wearing uniforms in order to take advantage of the Korean War for the purposes of espionage in China. Since the United States and

---

* Downey and Fecteau were not included in the U.S. presentation to the General Assembly, and it seems to have been tacitly conceded by the U.S. that they were in fact working for the CIA. This is also strongly implied in Wise and Ross's *The*

the People's Republic of China were not at war, the question of prisoner-of-war status did not arise, nor did international law apply. These men were simply a part of the American effort to overthrow the new regime in China.

The policy of the Chinese government, Chou went on, had been to try to reduce the sentences of American nationals if they were convicted, so as to speed up their exit from China, and the conviction of the B-29 crew and others had taken place in the course of carrying out this policy. The Chinese government had no desire to increase tension, as was shown by the fact that Downey and Fecteau had not been sentenced to death even though they were engaged in dropping and picking up agents. Nonetheless, in its complaint before the UN the United States had not said a word about the fourteen nationals who had been allowed to leave China or of the three who had been deported, nor had the Chinese students and other nationals detained in the United States been mentioned. The United States had simply created an uproar about the airmen. There were more than five thousand innocent Chinese nationals in the United States, of whom at least 356 had asked to return to China; only ten had been allowed to leave. On the basis of these facts Chou asked Hammarskjold to make a fair comparison of the situation on both sides. There was, of course, no question of an exchange, since there was no way of exchanging innocent for sentenced persons.

Chou then turned to political questions. Although China supported the purposes and principles of the Charter, the United Nations attitude to China was unjust in many ways. The representation of China in the United Nations by Chiang Kai-shek to the exclusion of a government representing one quarter of the world's population was a grave injustice, which Chou realized probably could not be remedied for some time to come. Taiwan had not been restored to China as had been promised at the end of World War II, and it was now cut off from the mainland. The U.S. government had ignored China's appeal for a

---

Invisible Government, pp. 106–8, although at the time the United States maintained that they were "civilian personnel employed by the Department of the Army in Japan. They were believed to have been lost in a flight from Korea to Japan in November 1952." In September 1957 an unauthorized American visitor to China saw Downey and Fecteau and asked Fecteau if he had worked for the CIA, to which he had replied in the affirmative. This conclusion was also reached by Charles Edmundsen, a former USIA official, in an article in the *Nation* in October 1957. That Hammarskjold was somewhat disconcerted by the Chinese inclusion of these two in the case is shown by an inquiry he sent to Cordier in New York during the talks with Chou, asking whether Downey and Fecteau had been in uniform when they were captured. The answer was that they were wearing denims without military insignia.

peaceful settlement in Korea and had crossed the 38th parallel toward the Yalu River, forcing China to take action in self-defense, whereupon China had been declared an aggressor. By such actions the United Nations had become an instrument of the United States. China had readily agreed to the Korean armistice negotiations during which Syngman Rhee had forcibly detained 27,000 prisoners, and the United States had violated the repatriation agreement by sending 14,000 prisoners to Taiwan without giving them the option to which they were entitled under the armistice agreement. About all of this the United Nations had remained silent, but now, on the American complaint about the airmen, it had taken action.

The Assembly's condemnation of China had caused an angry reaction among the Chinese people because they felt that right and wrong had been reversed. The United States had prevented the Assembly from reaching any agreement on Korea and had opposed the end of the war in Indochina. It had then devised the Southeast Asia Treaty Organization (SEATO) to create a further division in Asia, and its actions in South Vietnam were against the agreement on Indochina reached in Geneva. The United States was also supporting Chiang Kai-shek in his harassment against the Chinese mainland and disruption of navigation along the coast. The treaty between the United States and Chiang of December 2, 1954, was the most serious international act since World War II, because its result had been the occupation of one nation by another in violation of international agreements and the UN Charter.

In order to cover up all these actions, the American government had created an uproar in the United States and in the United Nations over the spy cases, and the UN had timidly followed the U.S. lead. The Chinese government was wholly in favor of peaceful coexistence irrespective of social systems, and Chou expressed the hope that Hammarskjold would try to persuade his American friends to support peaceful coexistence by withdrawing from Taiwan and the Taiwan Strait. This action would be the greatest possible contribution to world peace, although China would never agree to a neutral or independent Taiwan, for it could not and would not settle for peace at the cost of its territory or sovereignty.

The next and longest meeting lasted from 3 p.m. to 8:10 p.m. on January 8. Hammarskjold remarked that the fears and resentments that Chou had expressed on the previous day about other countries, especially those concerning American "imperialism," were fully matched by the attitudes of other countries toward China, especially in regard to the urge for world revolution or world domination that they believed to be a part of Communist ideology. "Thus," he said, "we have run into what I would call a tragedy of errors, in a most serious form reflecting the situation in that little Peking opera which we saw yesterday night where two men were fighting each other in the dark, each of them believing that he had been threatened by the other man."

Someone had to begin by improving the general atmosphere and preparing the ground for a solution of some of the major problems. Regardless of which points of historical interpretation they agreed or disagreed on, the real question to be considered was what could be done to improve international relations. Hammarskjold agreed that the United Nations had not always acted as he, for one, thought it should have done, nor had it always been consistent, but such a view did not justify Chou En-lai's reaction over the case of the eleven airmen. The opinion of the strong majority in the United Nations in this case was not cooked up under U.S. leadership. The Assembly had not, as Chou had said, "timidly followed" the U.S. lead. The reaction of the great majority was perfectly honest and was also explained by the fact that governments felt a special responsibility for the airmen because they were serving the United Nations itself in a cause endorsed by the United Nations. Chou admittedly had a perfect right to disapprove of the UN operation in Korea, but for the UN and for Hammarskjold himself there could be no hesitation on this point.

Hammarskjold reaffirmed his conviction that the eleven airmen were on a lawful mission and that it was unjustifiable to lump them with Downey and Fecteau and say that all were working for the CIA. They came from the 581st Air Wing, which was part of the UN Military Command, and had landed in Antung Province, immediately adjacent to North Korea. If the aircraft had been attacked over North Korea, the fact that it had come down in Antung Province was neither surprising nor sinister. Nor did he share Chou's doubts about the transmitter found on the B-29, which was part of the standard survival equipment of large American aircraft and had been included on the plane which the U.S. Air Force had provided for his own journey from New York to London.

As regards the question of Chinese representation in the United Nations, Chou certainly knew from his public statements Hammarskjold's view that it was a weakness and an anomaly of the Organization that China, representing one-fourth of mankind, was not represented, and he shared Chou's realistic view that it would take some time to solve this problem. As for the Chinese nationals and students in the United States, he would do anything he could on humanitarian grounds to improve the situation. There could be no question of a deal linking the release of the prisoners with the return of the students, since they were in quite different categories, although

Hammarskjold himself considered both groups to be innocent. Such a deal would, in any case, be beneath the dignity of the two governments concerned and of the United Nations. As regards Americans detained in China, he asked Chou to do all that he could to speed things up and shorten the time of detention and the period of uncertainty for all concerned. Meanwhile, he asked that before his departure he might be given information on the health of the prisoners and on other matters of importance to their families.

Chou expressed his regret that there were few points on which he and Hammarskjold saw eye to eye. If they looked at things objectively, however, they might reach a wider understanding. Efforts on either side to try to prove something would not be productive, but provided that was not necessary, the conversations could still be a beginning and not an end. Chou did not feel that the mutual fears that Hammarskjold had described were justified. China had shown that it was capable of appreciating U.S. actions for peace, as during the Korean armistice negotiations and at the Geneva Conference, where China had recognized the United States although the United States did not recognize China. The American interpretation of all China's actions as expansionist was contrary to China's intentions, whereas China had to judge the United States by its acts, such as the treaty with Chiang and the occupation of Taiwan. Under American protection, Chiang could occupy coastal islands and detain ships in the Taiwan Strait and he might well soon attack the mainland. Chou could not feel that Hammarskjold's views on this question were impartial, for to tolerate such a situation was like tolerating Japanese aggression in northeastern China in 1931, which had been the first spark of World War II.

Chou then returned to the Chinese charge that the American airmen were spies, adding further details of the findings of the Chinese courts concerning their mission. He noted the B-29 had carried a specially trained agent called Benjamin, and that at Geneva the United States had not referred to these men as being prisoners of the Korean war. Nonetheless, the Chinese government would respond to Hammarskjold's specific requests and would certainly be prepared to give information on the health of the prisoners, as well as photos of them to comfort their families. Chou added that if the prisoners' families wanted to come to China to see them, including Downey and Fecteau, the government would give them every assistance, and the Chinese Red Cross would be made responsible for arranging the visits and receiving the families.

Hoping that a lawyer's debate could be avoided, Hammarskjold limited himself to replying at once to a few specific points of detail in Chou's presentation. He explained, for example, that the presence of an extra crew member in the B-29 was due to the fact that Colonel John K. Arnold and the rest of his crew were flying for the first time in the area and therefore took along someone who had previous experience.

Chou, while remarking that the Chinese government had the necessary evidence, as well as confessions, upon which the courts had based their judgment on the B-29 case, the four jet pilots had in fact not yet been convicted although they had admitted freely that they had intruded into Chinese airspace. This was proof enough that the simple act of intrusion was not a sufficient basis for the Chinese courts to convict American aviators of espionage.

Hammarskjold concluded the meeting by saying that even if they could not reach common conclusions on the facts, he felt that they had built up a mutual respect "which makes us trust that the other party will reach its *final* conclusion in a spirit of justice and fairness—before his own conscience."

The fourth, final, and shortest meeting took place from 4 p.m. to 5:20 p.m. on January 10. When Hammarskjold said that the personal contacts established would have justified his visit even if nothing else had come out of it, Chou replied that the situation in China, the voice of the Chinese people, and the intentions of the Chinese government were not so easily accessible to the Secretary-General, and their views should be worthy of his consideration and attention. He hoped that Hammarskjold would be able to tell the countries concerned, especially the United States, about China and the views of the Chinese government. If the United States would give up its policy of aggression and war against China, then China and the United States would be able not only to coexist but to cooperate in a friendly way.

After a valedictory exchange of compliments, Hammarskjold said "bluntly and frankly" that what he might say about China would carry much more weight if the Chinese government saw its way to accept his viewpoint on the prisoner question, and he felt that it could do so without disavowing its own legal conclusions or by-passing its own courts. The text of a joint communiqué on the talks was agreed on without discussion. It concluded: "In these talks reference was made at the same time to questions pertinent to the relaxation of world tension. We feel that these talks have been useful and we hope to be able to continue the contact established in these meetings."[69]

On Hammarskjold's last night in Peking, Chou En-lai gave a magnificent dinner for his whole party.

Hammarskjold and his companions left Peking at 7 a.m. on January 11 by air for Canton. From there they went by special train to Sungching, the border point, where they changed to another train for Kowloon and Hong Kong. After an overnight stop they flew to Tokyo, where a U.S. military transport plane picked them up for the trip to New York, which they reached on January 13.

Cordier and Wilder Foote joined the party in San Francisco and warned Hammarskjold that the brevity and lack of substance of the joint communiqué from Peking had already given rise to stories in the U.S. press that the mission had been a failure. As a result Hammarskjold issued a brief explanatory statement[70] designed, as he later told Lester Pearson, "to ward off desperate reaction when unrealistic expectations not fulfilled."[71] "My visit to Peking," he said at the airport, "was a first stage in my efforts to achieve the release of the eleven fliers and other UN Command personnel still detained. I feel that my talks with Mr. Chou En-lai were definitely useful for this purpose. We hope to be able to continue our contact. The door that has been opened can be kept open, given restraint on all sides."[72]

His first step in New York was to give Lodge a preliminary account of his talks in Peking, and on the following day the UN press corps greeted him with applause at his press conference. Hammarskjold had a heavy cold but was otherwise cheerful. He took personal responsibility for the Peking communiqué's being so short and factual and for the complete secrecy that had surrounded the talks. Premature publicity, he said, had in the past "often frozen positions in a way which has rendered the situation much more difficult."[73] He had given Chou En-lai "the full and complete case for the release of the convicted men"[74] and had listened to the Chinese point of view. The other questions discussed were entirely apart from the prisoners, and there had been no suggestion from either side of any deals, especially on the Chinese students in the United States. The press conference provided a foretaste of what he might expect from the U.S. side. Thomas J. Hamilton of the *New York Times* asked what was holding up the prisoners' release and why Hammarskjold was hopeful. Hammarskjold replied: "This seems to be some kind of Christmas game—asking funny questions. I think both questions can be replied to quite easily. You know very well, or should know, what has been the history of this case. You should, with that background, easily understand that a change in the situation is something which is self-significant and a thing that is not too easily achieved. On the other hand, if the situation is one where you can see that possibilities are there to achieve that very thing, it is, I think, a good basis for the optimism to which Mr. Hamilton refers. I have not myself said that I was optimistic. I used another expression. I have said that the door was open and could remain open with due restraint. I have said that I hoped to be able to continue contacts. That is a temperature somewhat lower than that reflected in the word 'optimism.' "[75]

Hammarskjold's desideratum of "restraint on all sides"[76] was noticeably lacking in some quarters. On the evening of January 13 the U.S. Assistant Secretary of State, Walter S. Robertson, delivered a blast in Philadelphia against "China's gangster role."[77] Lodge was summoned to the U.S. Strategic Air Command Headquarters in Omaha to report to Dulles on Hammarskjold's mission; but when inquiries were made about this unusual rendezvous, he issued a statement saying that the meeting at SAC Command had "nothing to do with a show of power diplomacy and is not primarily concerned with the captured fliers."[78] On January 17, Senator Knowland attacked the mission as "a failure by any standard or yardstick" and accused the United Nations of "a massive propaganda build-up . . . to silence those who would analyze the facts."[79] He warned of a "Far Eastern Munich."[80] President Eisenhower evidently thought this attack so serious that he invited the Senator to breakfast in the White House on January 19 and later in the day told his press conference that the United States was not concerned with the Tachen Islands (off the Chinese coast south of Hang-chow) and was committed only to the defense of Taiwan and the Pescadores. He went on to suggest that the UN should negotiate a cease-fire in the strait. On January 18, Dulles told the press that the United States was "standing aside to let the UN try to work this problem out," but added, "I don't think that can go on forever."

On January 17, Hammarskjold had given Lodge the photographs of the prisoners and other personal details and also informed him of Chou's offer to arrange for visits by the relatives of the captives. On January 19 he went to Washington to meet with Dulles, Lodge, and Robertson. The meeting was not wholly satisfactory, since there was only time for him to give a condensed account of the Peking talks and there was no opportunity to discuss the next steps to be taken, and especially the U.S. reaction to Chou's offer of family visits. Hammarskjold felt, however, that Dulles agreed with him that "matters must settle down somewhat"[81] before he took new action. On January 21 the Associated Press published part of Hammarskjold's account of his conversation with Chou, notably on the question of Taiwan. This leak caused him to send a letter to Lodge regretting that he had not been consulted before part of a very confidential discussion had been revealed.

Of the U.S. attitudes that were now the central factor in achieving the release of the airmen, Hammarskjold wrote on January 25 to Waldock, "I am afraid that their emotions have run away with their political wisdom." He went on to quote part of a prayer that had been given in the Senate: "Fanatical foes whose pledged word is worthless . . . who, for their own ends, callously traffic in normal human affections and family ties. . . ."[82] He felt, however, that it was a good sign that Chou En-lai had still made no public reference to the talks. Chou himself, as Hammarskjold told Eden a month later, had been meticulous in avoiding propaganda or embarrassing Hammarskjold and had made no attempt to bargain over the U.S. airmen. By far the greatest risk was a premature and violent reaction in the United States that would make it impossible for the Chinese to find a pretext for releasing the prisoners. He had no doubt that Chou's main worry was to avoid the impression that he had given in to American pressure. If this was so, the visits of the prisoners' families would serve as an excellent pretext for their eventual release; some observers even believed that if the families were to go to China, the prisoners might be allowed to go home with them.

This possibility was quickly demolished on January 21, when the Chinese offer of family visits to the prisoners was announced both in Peking and at the UN.[83]* The State Department's immediate reaction was to state: "The United States government cannot of course in good conscience encourage those who may wish to go into an area where the normal protections of an American passport cannot be offered." The statement went on to denounce the motives of the Chinese in putting the families in a "harrowing dilemma" and ended sententiously, "It is by releasing those they hold that the Chinese Communists can convincingly show concern for the human sufferings they have caused."[85] Hammarskjold at once stated publicly that he had "no doubt about the safety of those members of the families wishing to visit China to see their men."[86] Some of the families themselves also showed great interest in the Chinese offer and were undaunted by the State Department's announcement. Mr. and Mrs. Harold Fischer, the parents of one of the jet pilots, wrote to Hammarskjold: "We believe there can be a lot gained by going over there and it could also bring the release of Captain Fischer and the other boys."[87] Other relatives visited United Nations Headquarters to make inquiries. This development led, on January 27, to a letter from Dulles himself to all the families referring to "the increasingly belligerent attitude and actions of the Chinese Communists in recent days." This attitude made it

---

* On January 24 Lodge protested this UN announcement, which, he said, gave the offer "the apparent accreditation—and consequent respectability—of a UN dateline." This, Lodge said, had caused "surprise and chagrin in the State Department."[84] Hammarskjold replied that Peking had in fact announced the offer first and that there was nothing inappropriate about the UN press release.

"imprudent for the time being to issue passports valid for travel to Communist China to any American citizens," Dulles wrote, adding that "we do not think it prudent to afford the Chinese Communists further opportunities to provoke our nation and strain its patience further."[88] Only on the following day was Hammarskjold officially informed of this letter, which was released to the press at 9 p.m. on January 27.

Who was increasingly belligerent, who was straining whose patience, was a matter of some controversy both at the time and later,* for the cautious and peaceful pronouncements of President Eisenhower on January 19 shortly gave way to a very different atmosphere in Washington, in which preventive war against China was openly discussed. The Eisenhower administration decided to ask Congress for advance approval for the authority of the President to use U.S. forces not only to defend Taiwan and the Pescadores but also to act against concentrations of mainland forces that might appear to be part of an attempt to invade Taiwan. The President's request was approved by overwhelming majorities in the House of Representatives on January 25 and in the Senate on January 28, creating an atmosphere of crisis and tension that was increased by the sending of the U.S. Air Force 18th Fighter Bomber Wing to Taiwan and the alerting to full combat readiness of the Seventh Fleet.

Ignoring as far as he could this wider crisis, Hammarskjold wrote personally to Dulles on January 27 that there was a very important link between the offer of family visits and the possible release of the prisoners, and that the whole way in which the question had been handled by the United States had seriously jeopardized the possibility of a successful outcome. It had been essential, he explained, to announce the offer simultaneously in New York and Peking, since this was the procedure agreed upon with Chou En-lai, and he was surprised that the State Department had been so critical of this action. He was also much concerned that the State Department evidently considered the offer to be propaganda, whereas he himself was convinced that it was intended to be a bridge to a solution of the prisoner problem. He had not been consulted, or even informed in advance, about the State Department's refusal to grant permits to the families, although this was a question absolutely vital to future negotiations for which he would almost certainly be responsible. He also noted that the United States had not consulted with him at all about the Taiwan crisis, which was now about to come up in the Security Council, and he ended by expressing a hope for better cooperation with Dulles. That this was not immedi-

---

* A vivid and critical contemporary analysis of U.S. policy is given in *I. F. Stone's Weekly*, "The Hidden History of the Formosa Crisis," February 7, 1955, and "The Inner Politics of a False Alarm," February 14, 1955.

ately forthcoming was indicated by Hammarskjold's remark a month later that "the special characteristics of Mr. Dulles have made it extremely difficult for me to maintain even in the most modest way the contact which I need with Washington on the Peking issue."[89]

Dulles for his part apparently felt that Hammarskjold had been overimpressed by Chou and that he had completely failed to use the "strong moral position"[90] bestowed on him by the General Assembly, although how he could have done this without immediately putting an end to the talks in Peking was not explained. On January 28 Dulles replied coldly to Hammarskjold's letter, saying that he had to delegate responsibilities, that he could not be tied personally to the prisoner question, and that he saw no link between the release of the prisoners and the offer of family visits, in fact quite the contrary. He was, however, prepared to reconsider the matter and asked Hammarskjold to talk it over with Lodge.

Hammarskjold's feelings about his recent experiences in Peking and with Washington were reflected in a personal letter of January 31 to Uno Willers:

> The mission to Peking was not only unique in diplomatic history but also unique as a human experience. It is a miracle that everything went well, because the risks we were taking were extraordinary; but it did—in every detail. The contacts with Chou En-lai and with this whole very foreign world made an enormous impression on me, and I would wish that other policy makers had got it. What is so appalling is the basic lack of realism as to assumptions on which very much of Western policy is built. And now I am thinking not only of the situation in China, but of China's role in Asia and of the position of the present regime in Peking. It is a little bit humiliating when I have to say that Chou En-lai to me appears as the most superior brain I have so far met in the field of foreign politics. Of course, that does in no way mean that I have found a wider area of agreement than I anticipated, but it does mean that policy making without taking into account his personal qualities is likely to lead to disaster. As I said to one of the Americans: "Chou is so much more dangerous than you imagine because he is so much better a man than you have ever admitted."[91]

Hammarskjold had intended to make a new démarche to Chou En-lai at the end of January on the four jet pilots, whose early release, since they had not been convicted of espionage, was a distinct possibility. In the meantime he was anxious to prevent well-meaning governments from making uncoordinated moves, especially in the form of pressures on or threats to the Chinese. His aim was to reduce outer pressures to the minimum while increasing inner pressures to the maximum, but the sudden crisis over the Taiwan Strait made it very difficult to pursue either of these objectives.

Immediately after the U.S. Senate's approval of the Taiwan resolution, New Zealand, with U.S. support, brought to the Security Council the question of hostilities between Communist and Nationalist Chinese forces in the Taiwan Strait,[92] the declared purpose of this move being to seek a cease-fire. On January 31 the Council voted to invite Peking to send a representative to take part in the Council's proceedings and adjourned to await Peking's reply. After formally conveying this invitation to Peking on January 31,[93] Hammarskjold sent a personal message on February 2, through Swedish channels, to Chou, stressing the opportunity that this invitation offered to come to grips with essential political problems, starting with a concrete and limited issue. This view, he said, was based on his impression that "we have reached a state of deadlock, characterized by a sincere wish for peace on both sides,"[94] and he strongly urged Chou to send a representative to the Council. Before this personal message reached Peking, Chou En-lai responded, on February 3, to the first and formal message from Hammarskjold in a long and strongly worded message refusing the Council's invitation.[95] Hammarskjold thereupon tried to recall his personal message, which could no longer serve any purpose, but on February 4 Chou, who had been warned to expect it, sent him a message asking where it was, so that it was delivered anyway together with a further message saying that it had already been by-passed by events. Hammarskjold knew that the Taiwan issue was a strong political irritant to Peking, which he compared to France's feelings about Alsace. Obviously, until some arrangement could be made through the Security Council to cool down the Taiwan situation, the prisoner question would have to remain in abeyance.

When the United States took strong exception to Hammarskjold's abortive initiative, he replied that he had felt morally bound to make a personal representation to Chou En-lai. Lodge told him that there was "no 'personal' existence in an affair of this kind" and that the United States objected both to the Council's invitation and to his personal message, "which we think exceeds your authority"[96]—a contention that Hammarskjold vigorously contested. On February 5, Chou told Hammarskjold that the initiative by the Council was useless since it equated the Chinese government with Chiang Kai-shek. Chou pointed out that the Taiwan Strait was an internal affair of China and that Hammarskjold should persuade his "American friends" to negotiate directly. In spite of U.S. objections, Hammarskjold replied to Chou that there was now no hope of the Council discussions' going beyond the New Zealand item and the question of a cease-fire in the offshore islands. He noted that Chou eliminated the possibility of Security Council action but not, he assumed, an approach under UN aegis "if another appropriate form could be found."[97] Chou replied on February 10 that he could not accept the cease-fire proposal or a recognition of two Chinas, that the United States must negotiate directly, that China was indignant at the representative of Chiang occupying China's seat in the Council, and that direct negotiations might take place, if necessary with the help of the Soviet Union, Great Britain, or India.

On February 4, with U.S. assistance, the evacuation of Chinese Nationalist troops from the Tachen Islands began and was completed without incident two weeks later. The members of the Security Council, who were divided on the cease-fire question and the treatment of the offshore islands, agreed on February 14 to adjourn the question, and the crisis subsided.

Despite the Taiwan diversion and the U.S. rejection of the family visits, Hammarskjold was determined to press for the release of the prisoners "after the Formosa [Taiwan] gale has calmed down somewhat."[98] His plan was to approach Chou concerning the four jet pilots as soon as photographs and personal details on them had been received from Peking. When these were received on February 17, he immediately wrote to Chou pointing out again that the four jet pilots had not been convicted, that no charge against them seemed to exist other than that of intrusion into Chinese airspace, and that the time they had spent in jail was already far in excess of the normal pretrial detention period. The debate on the prisoner question in the United States, he pointed out, was now moderate and restrained, although this comparative tranquillity had not been achieved without some effort. A favorable action on the four pilots by the Chinese government in line with Peking's declared humanitarian policies would not now be misinterpreted as a disavowal of the sovereign rights of the People's Republic of China or of the status of its courts. He also referred to the family visits, which he hoped could still come about, although the recent situation had certainly not been favorable for them. He himself, he told Chou, appreciated the Chinese offer "not as an alternative but as a bridge"[99] to solutions of the overall problem, and he would revert to the offer when he felt it would be helpful to do so.*

Chou took more than a month to reply to this message, but on March 21 he told Hammarskjold that the case of the four jet pilots

---

* Hammarskjold believed that the offer of the family visits had been made because Chou felt he had to give him something, and that it was even possible that the visits might provide the occasion for releasing the prisoners of war as a sort of grand gesture. This view was borne out later on by Ambassador Henryk Birecki of Poland, who told him in June 1955 that if the family visits had been allowed in February the problem would have been solved because the Chinese were prepared to release the prisoners just as soon as the families arrived.

was being dealt with seriously and earnestly. "This will not be influenced by the clamors on the U.S. side," he wrote, "though I appreciate the efforts you have made."[100] The American refusal to allow the family visits was hard on the men themselves and showed that the U.S. government was not really concerned with them, but Chou promised to inform Hammarskjold immediately of the result of the investigation of the cases of the four jet pilots. Hammarskjold replied briefly, saying that he was sending letters to Chou from the families of the prisoners. Lodge, when informed of Chou's reply, expressed his warm appreciation of Hammarskjold's efforts but commented that there was "very little encouragement in what has happened so far."[101]

The atmosphere on the U.S. side was still anything but encouraging. In March, Dulles visited Taiwan for the ratification of the Mutual Defense Pact, an event accompanied by a liberal amount of tough talk to which Peking replied in kind. He then went on to Bangkok for the first Foreign Ministers' meeting of the Southeast Asia Treaty Organization and, on his return to Washington, told Eisenhower that the situation was far more serious than he had thought. "The Chinese Communists," Dulles said, "are determined to capture Formosa. Surrendering Quemoy and Matsu won't end that determination. If we defend Quemoy and Matsu we'll have to use atomic weapons. They alone will be effective against the mainland airfields."[102] On March 28 in a letter to Lodge, Hammarskjold explained again that Chou En-lai must seem to act without pressure from outside and that his patriotic pride had to be considered and his prestige preserved if he was to get the agreement of the Peking government to release the prisoners. This was why he, Hammarskjold, urgently needed the cooperation of the United States government in reducing public pressures to the minimum and increasing private pressure.

The letters from the families to Chou were one form of private pressure. Another was through various Asian leaders. Early in April, Hammarskjold had asked the permanent representatives of India and Thailand in New York to urge Prime Minister Nehru and Prince Wan to use their presence at the Bandung Conference of Asian and African States* to urge Chou to make concessions on the prisoner-of-war issue in the general interests of Asia. He felt that he himself must also make further moves and asked Anders Österling, the secretary of the Swedish Academy, if it would be possible, in violation of the Academy's tradition of meeting each Thursday evening, to arrange a meeting on Friday, April 22, since he had to be in New York for a Security Council meeting on Thursday, in order to provide a cover for a meeting with

---

* April 18–24, 1955.

the Chinese Ambassador, Keng Piao.* Österling agreed, and, to ensure absolute secrecy, Uno Willers arranged a luncheon rendezvous for April 23 at his mother's house, which was near the Chinese embassy.

At luncheon on April 23 the two men spoke for two and a half hours with only the Ambassador's interpreter present. Keng Piao, after expressing regret that the family visits had not come about, asked Hammarskjold how he would solve the problem of the four jet pilots. Hammarskjold replied that he did not accept the Chinese view of the facts but that the Chinese courts, on the basis of their assumptions, could note that the four had intruded but that the prosecution had not proved the charge of espionage, so that they could be convicted only for intrusion. The normal punishment for intrusion was extradition. The Chinese Ambassador doubted whether this approach could be reconciled with Chinese law. Hammarskjold replied that the legal systems he knew of gave only limited time to the prosecution to prove its case and then dismissed it if no conclusion had been reached. He conceded that the case of the eleven airmen who had already been convicted was more difficult and would require another solution.

He asked the Ambassador to tell Chou En-lai that he was impatient to the point of deep disappointment. He realized that Chou could not disavow the Chinese courts or give the impression of yielding to pressure or tie his actions to the Assembly resolution, of which he disapproved. But in the improved climate Chou had already missed opportunities for action on the prisoners, for example the Chinese Nationalist evacuation of the Tachen Islands or the Bandung Conference, and thus they were still only at the stage reached in Peking in January. The Ambassador replied that in January Chou En-lai had been prepared to shorten the terms of imprisonment, but new intrusions into Chinese airspace during the Tachen evacuation, and a sabotage incident in which an aircraft carrying Chinese delegates to Bandung had been blown up in the air,** had changed the assumptions on which Chou could act. Hammarskjold said he knew nothing of these incidents, to which the Ambassador replied that the Indians or the Indonesians could give him the full story.

Hammarskjold asked the Ambassador to send a short message to

---

* Hammarskjold announced this visit to his press conference on April 19[103] as follows: "For private reasons, and also in order that I may finally attend a working session of the Swedish Academy, I shall be taking a couple of days over the weekend in Stockholm." When asked whether he would "have any contact with the diplomatic corps" in Stockholm, he replied, "You are very subtle" and repeated his previous statement.
** On November 21, 1967, John Discoe Smith, an American defector in Moscow, charged in an article in the weekly *Literaturnaya Gazeta* that the CIA was involved in sabotaging the Air India plane on which Chou En-lai himself had been scheduled

Chou asking "if there was anything I now could do in order to facilitate for him the solution of the prisoner problem; I ask that question solely as a representative of a general interest which, however, being general, must *also* be China's interest."[105] He pointed out that his possibilities of maintaining contact with Peking must depend on action being taken on the prisoners. He noted later that in the two-and-a-half-hour discussion the question *whether* the prisoners should be released never arose but only *how* they should be released, and that this had seemed perfectly natural to the Ambassador.

On his return to New York, Hammarskjold answered affirmatively a question on whether his contacts on the prisoners had been "intensified" during his visit to Europe, but when asked how, he rejoined, "Will you leave a few family secrets to me?"[106] He did, however, inform Lodge, Pierson Dixon, and A. A. Sobolev, the Soviet permanent representative, in general terms of his conversation with Keng Piao.

On May 16, he asked Chou En-lai for a reply to the message he had sent through the Chinese Ambassador in Stockholm. He also asked if Chou was going to reply to the letters from the families, saying that he desperately needed some evidence to reinforce persons in the United States who had advocated restraint and patience. Chou's reply was handed to the Swedish Ambassador in Peking on the evening of May 29 and reached Hammarskjold on the next day. It referred to Hammarskjold's two previous messages and stated that on May 24 the Chinese Supreme Court had ordered the deportation of the four jet pilots and that they would probably reach Hong Kong on May 31.* As for the other prisoners, Chou deeply regretted that their families had not been permitted to visit them.

Peking announced the release of the four jet pilots on May 30,[107] and Hammarskjold in his own public comment[108] stated that he would not relax his efforts until the other eleven aviators were released. Dulles publicly expressed his deep appreciation for Hammarskjold's efforts and his hope for the release of the others in the near future, and British Foreign Minister Harold Macmillan, in congratulating him, said that he was sure "that it must have a helpful effect in reducing

---

to travel to Bandung. Chou had changed his plans at the last minute, but all fifteen passengers had been killed when the plane crashed in the South China Sea off Sarawak. Smith claimed that he had delivered a suitcase containing the explosive mechanism to a Chinese Nationalist in Hong Kong. This mechanism was later recovered from the wreckage, and the Hong Kong police had called the incident a case of "carefully planned mass murder."[104]

* In Peking, Peder Hammarskjold was annoyed with his Ambassador for waiting until the next day to send this message, and in fact this delay allowed V. K. Krishna Menon to make a public announcement first.

tension in the Far East."[109] In his press conference on June 2, Hammarskjold repeated that there would be no relaxation of his efforts, although he was more hopeful than ever before on this matter. When asked if he agreed with Krishna Menon's statement that the four pilots had been released at the request of the Indian government, he replied, "I read that in the paper and perhaps with a little surprise, but I do not see that I have any reason to comment on the statement at all."[110]* In fact, there could be little doubt on this point since Chou En-lai had specifically referred to Hammarskjold's approaches on the four jet pilots, and the decision to extradite them had been taken on May 24 before Krishna Menon saw Chou.**

Krishna Menon's freewheeling activities had for some time been a source of uneasiness for Hammarskjold. In the middle of March he had sent Menon Humphrey Waldock's notes on the prisoner problem and had asked for India's cooperation in an effort "which after the Peking talks I consider as detached from the General Assembly resolution in a way which should make it possible for the Indian Government to cooperate actively.[111] To this, as well as to his message to Nehru concerning the Bandung Conference, he had received no response whatsoever, although Menon himself had been to Peking in the meantime. On May 31, the day after the release of the four jet pilots, Hammarskjold spoke to Arthur Lall, the Indian representative in New York, about the failure to reply to his messages, saying that regardless of what Menon might have said in the past, he himself was interested in the future and wanted to know Menon's views on the case of the eleven aviators still in jail. In line with his request to other governments not to take uncoordinated initiatives on the prisoner question, he wished to know what Menon was doing, for he had an uneasy suspicion that Menon had been crossing wires in Peking on the prisoner issue.

On June 11, Menon himself appeared in New York and told Hammarskjold that Chou En-lai was "adamant" on the release of the eleven. On June 16 he again visited Hammarskjold, apparently in a very bad humor. He appeared to have no specific points to discuss but argued for a general relaxation of tension and for direct talks between

---

* Although Lodge and the Chief of Staff of the U.S. Air Force, General Nathan Twining, credited Hammarskjold with securing the release of the four pilots, Dulles sent notes of appreciation to both Hammarskjold and Nehru.

** In a press conference in Delhi on June 4, Krishna Menon modified his original claim and stated that the four jet pilots had been released "maybe in response to our request." In Michael Brecher's *India and World Politics—Krishna Menon's View of the World* (Oxford, 1968), p. 108, however, Menon states in an interview with the author: "I had the greatest difficulty in persuading Chou En-lai to release the American fliers (1955) on account of Hammarskjold."

the United States and China, in which he appeared to Hammarskjold to have assumed, at least in his own mind, the role of go-between. This conversation did little to relieve Hammarskjold's fear that Menon, for his own purposes, might seriously complicate his efforts to secure the release of the eleven aviators. He had noted that Chou's attitude toward himself had noticeably changed immediately after the Indian's visit to Peking in late May, and to make matters worse, it was clear from his own talks with Menon that Menon was convinced that all the American prisoners were spies. Later on, Hammarskjold commented that Menon's interference might have cost one or two months in the effort to get the remainder of the prisoners released. Nor was Krishna Menon by any means Hammarskjold's only unwanted associate. Hammarskjold was infuriated to learn in mid-May that the Swedish Ambassador in Moscow, Rolf Sohlman, had taken it upon himself to visit Peking, a visit that Hammarskjold in a letter to Leif Belfrage, then head of the Swedish Foreign Office, characterized as "an example of political innocence in a state of rare purity."[112]

On June 2, immediately after the release of the four jet pilots, Hammarskjold made a new démarche to Chou En-lai. He told Chou the family visits would now almost certainly be acceptable to the United States, but that he could not formally take the matter up with the U.S. government before he had some indication about the eleven aviators still detained. The world reaction to the release of the four pilots showed that the release of the eleven would not cause any misunderstanding or embarrassment, and he therefore urged that they be released before the tenth-anniversary meeting of the United Nations, which was to take place in San Francisco on June 20.

Hammarskjold let a month elapse before his next approach, which was delivered to Chou En-lai by the Swedish Ambassador in Peking on July 8. In this message he pressed for an urgent reply to his previous démarche on the eleven remaining prisoners, saying that he very much hoped he would not be obliged to report the failure of his mission. Chou En-lai quickly replied that the United States, judging from Dulles's speech at the anniversary celebrations at San Francisco and from Lodge's remarks on the Taiwan question, did not seem to have any desire to reduce tension. Indeed, the United States appeared to wish to prevent China from releasing the prisoners, and if China did release them it would only be said that they had been freed because of American pressure. Chou characterized Hammarskjold's latest message as an example of such pressure and cautioned him that pressure could not be put on China by the threat of reports to various organs of the United Nations. He concluded this stern message by stating his intention to continue the discussion with Hammarskjold on the basis of the friendly attitude that had inspired their talks in Peking. Hammarskjold received this message through the Chinese consul general in Geneva, through whom he replied that while he recognized Chou's rejection of the General Assembly resolution, the resolution had a binding force on himself that did represent a certain pressure on him. He told Chou that he would be in Geneva again in the early days of August and that the Chinese consul general in Geneva would therefore be the best channel of communication.

All these delays provided additional opportunities for other developments calculated to hinder Hammarskjold's efforts to obtain the release of the eleven fliers. Apart from the public statements of Dulles and Lodge, two of the four jet pilots who had been released—Parks and Fischer—published articles in *Life* (June 27) and *U.S. News & World Report* (June 24) respectively, which might almost have been specifically written to discourage the Chinese from releasing any more prisoners. As Hammarskjold told Lodge, this kind of reporting was dangerous for those in China who were trying to secure the release of the prisoners and also dangerous for the prisoners themselves, who as a result of such publications would undoubtedly be subjected to far stricter control. Worse still, this kind of publicity gave the Chinese further excuses for delay. At this juncture Hammarskjold felt the possibility of failure more keenly than at any other time. "Difficulties," he wrote to Lodge, "have piled up in a way entirely outside the control of the United Nations."[113]

Not all the signs were gloomy. At Hammarskjold's suggestion, Willers, writing to the Chinese chargé d'affaires in Stockholm about an exhibition of Chinese books in the Swedish Royal Library, dropped a hint that Hammarskjold would be on holiday in the south of Sweden in the last week of July and could always go to Stockholm if necessary. At a luncheon earlier in July, when the Chinese chargé had asked what present Hammarskjold would like for his fiftieth birthday, Willers replied that the release of the eleven American prisoners would be by far the best gift. Similar inquiries about his birthday, which was July 29, had also been made of the Swedish embassy in Peking.

Hammarskjold was in Geneva from July 10 to 23 for the usual round of summer activity in the Economic and Social Council and with the Specialized Agencies, as well as for the Big Four summit meeting held in the Palais des Nations. On July 23 he went to Sweden for a holiday from which he was due to return to Geneva in time for the opening of the First International Conference on the Peaceful Uses of Atomic Energy on August 8. He was staying in his small house —a *stuga*, as it is called in Sweden—by the sea near Löderup in Skåne. He had been anxious to stay out of the limelight and to celebrate his fiftieth birthday quietly. "In fact," he said later, "I went cod-fishing, and I did not catch a single cod, so even the cod kept out of the picture, which was quite appropriate and in line with my intentions."[114] On August 1 he received, through the little post office at Löderup, a message from Chou En-lai passed through Swedish diplomatic channels and, fifteen minutes later, a telephone call from Cordier telling him that a radio report had been monitored to the effect that Radio Peking would announce the release of the eleven fliers at 10 a.m. Chou En-lai's message had been given orally to the Swedish Ambassador at 1 a.m. (New York time) on August 1. At 10 a.m. on the same day the Associated Press in Tokyo gave the text of the Peking message, which stated that the eleven "criminals who sneaked into the territorial air of China" had been released because during their sentences they "observed discipline and behaved themselves fairly well," and that the court had therefore felt that they should be treated with leniency.

Cordier agreed with Hammarskjold by telephone on the wording of the UN communiqué: "We are delighted by the news of the release of the eleven fliers and share the profound joy that has come to the immediate families."[115] Hammarskjold immediately set out for Geneva, where he arrived on August 2. Awaiting him there was a cable from the Swedish Ambassador in Peking, which had arrived in Bern at 8:15 on the evening of August 1. The cable read as follows:

> I was called today by Chou En-lai at 1 o'clock who asked me to transmit the following:
> 1. Thanks for cable from Geneva.
> 2. The Chinese Government has decided to release the imprisoned U.S. fliers. This release from serving their full term takes place in order to maintain friendship with Hammarskjold and has no connection with the UN resolution. Chou En-lai expresses the hope that Hammarskjold will take note of this point.
> 3. The Chinese Government hopes to continue the contact established with Hammarskjold.
> 4. Chou En-lai congratulates Hammarskjold on his 50th birthday.[116]

Hammarskjold immediately answered Chou En-lai with a message which he later described as "restrained in substance but warm in tone."[117] He expressed his deep gratification for the Chinese action,

> an action which will strengthen the position of the People's Republic of China as well as contribute to an improvement of the political atmosphere in general. I am looking forward to continued contacts with you and feel that the basis for such contacts has been reinforced by your action. The efforts to help towards an objective interpretation and appreciation of the problems of your country, in which—as you know—you

may see an expression of my interpretation of my duties as Secretary-General, have got added possibilities to carry weight. I wish to express to you personally my great appreciation for the spirit in which you have approached our long discussions. I thank you also for the kind birthday greetings which you added to your message.

DAG HAMMARSKJOLD.[118]

The restrained tone and involved syntax of this message were necessitated by several considerations. Continued contacts were essential with Chou because Hammarskjold was now obliged to raise questions concerning military personnel of other nationalities who were still in China as a result of the Korean war, although he did not wish to move on this problem before he could see where the Chinese-American talks in Geneva that had begun on August 1 might lead. On the other hand, Chou's message was also a clear attempt to make a distinction between Mr. Hammarskjold and the Secretary-General, an attempt that Hammarskjold felt impelled to discourage strongly but in such terms as not to disturb the friendly atmosphere that Chou at this time evidently wished to preserve.

The release of the prisoners was unquestionably a triumph for Hammarskjold and was acknowledged generously and immediately by Eisenhower* and Lodge among many others, but to this acclaim too he reacted very cautiously. He was under no illusions that his own efforts and his fiftieth birthday were the sole motive forces. The United States had finally agreed on July 25 to ambassadorial meetings with China in Geneva to discuss the repatriation of nationals of both nations and "certain other practical matters now at issue between both sides."[119] When Peking announced the release of the American airmen, the Chinese Ambassador in Warsaw, Wang Ping-nan, who was also to be the representative in the Geneva talks, had expressed the hope that "this measure taken by the Chinese Government will have a favorable effect on our talks."[120] In a Telex conversation with Cordier on August 2, Hammarskjold said that he found the UN perhaps a little too much in the middle of the picture and added, "I rather prefer not to have more of an accent than there is already. That reason in itself speaks against the release of the Peking message."[121]

Chou En-lai would certainly not wish the message to be released, and in any case it would not be a good idea to publicize Chou's attempt to draw a distinction between Hammarskjold's activities and the General Assembly resolution. For these reasons it would be best,

---

* It is interesting to note, however, that in his memoirs, *Mandate for Change*, Eisenhower, in referring to the release of the eleven airmen, makes no mention whatsoever of Hammarskjold.

Hammarskjold felt, to keep himself as far as possible out of the picture, and in Geneva he confined himself to commenting that the release of the fliers "showed what could be achieved through international cooperation in the right spirit."[122] Twelve days later in New York he commented: "In a complex story of this type, all sorts of factors do influence the outcome, and all sorts of personalities necessarily come into the picture. I think it is very premature to try and evaluate the significance of any single personality or any single action. That really belongs to history, and I think it would be rather presumptuous on my part to try and interpret the arguing and the reasoning of a government when I have no special right to look behind closed doors; that is to say, I would leave this question to the future and to history."[123] He did, however, permit himself to add: "I would say that no event or anything which I have been permitted to do ranks higher on that list of causes for gratitude than my trip to Peking."[124]

His misgivings about Chou's attitude were soon justified. On August 6 he received a message about the Chinese-American talks then going on in Geneva, in which Chou wrote, "I hope you will persuade the American side to respond also by deeds."[125] Although Hammarskjold was anxious to eliminate any temptation on the Chinese side to use him as a spokesman, he did not believe that Chou was making these requests as a price for the gift of the release of the prisoners, but rather that he might want to use him as a third party in dealing with such problems as the Chinese students in the United States or the American citizens still detained in China.

Congratulations now came pouring in from all parts of the world. Among them were a warm message of thanks from General Twining of the U.S. Air Force and congratulations from Moshe Sharett, the Foreign Minister of Israel. The Nebraska legislature passed a resolution honoring Hammarskjold for his part in securing the release of the prisoners. But the letters from the families of the prisoners, to judge by Hammarskjold's replies to them, gave him more satisfaction than anything else. In September, Colonel John A. Arnold, Jr., the commander of the B-29, came to New York to express to Hammarskjold his "tremendous appreciation"[126] for Hammarskjold's personal efforts in securing his crew's release.

Hammarskjold's other main source of satisfaction was professional pride in an intricate diplomatic operation carried through against extremely difficult odds to a successful conclusion. On August 13, in reply to a letter of congratulations from Humphrey Waldock, he wrote, "all of us who had the privilege of being on this new Argonaut expedition for the golden fleece can share the feeling of gratitude and satisfaction."[127]

The friendly contact with Chou En-lai was not destined to last much longer. On September 10, as a matter of courtesy, Hammarskjold had cabled to Chou the text of the report[128] that he was obliged to make to the General Assembly on the outcome of the question of the American prisoners. The report was purely factual, even laconic, and gave little idea of the complexity of the negotiations or of the obstacles and pitfalls that had had to be surmounted. Its concluding and most emotional paragraph read: "Mr. Chou En-lai has expressed his hope that the contact established will be continued. In reply I have stated that this hope is shared by me."[129] The next day Chou cabled that he could not agree to Hammarskjold's report since China, in releasing the prisoners, had acted on its own initiative, which had nothing to do with the General Assembly resolution or with any report to the General Assembly. He went on to point out that the report was not objective since the airmen were spies and not UN personnel. They had been released, Chou wrote, only to ease tension and not because of any resolution of the General Assembly. Furthermore, although Hammarskjold had discussed with him only the eleven fliers and not "all the other captured UN personnel"[130] who were mentioned in the illegal resolution of the General Assembly, the report gave the impression that the contact with Chou En-lai was to be continued on behalf of these others. Finally, the report made no mention of the 14,000 Chinese prisoners of war who had been shipped to Taiwan. If the report was not withdrawn, China would make the necessary statements "based on truth and on all the facts."[131]

It is possible only to speculate on the reasons for this drastic change in Chou En-lai's attitude over a document that stated the bare minimum required by Hammarskjold's obligation to report to the General Assembly on a task that it had formally assigned to him. In any event, Chou's reply seemed clearly intended to break off further contact.

On September 12, Hammarskjold replied that his report was a "factual account of my activities"[132] as required by his constitutional relationship to the General Assembly, which he had already explained to Chou, and that there had been no question of giving his views or anyone else's. As a concession to his objections, he told Chou, the press had been given background information to the effect that the release of the airmen by China had been on China's own initiative based on its sovereign rights and was not connected with the General Assembly resolution, and that in releasing the prisoners China had been inspired purely by a wish to ease tensions. He expressed the hope that future contacts would be possible and not simply as a means of discussing this or that particular issue, and he urged that a public exchange be avoided, because it would damage the continuing contact, which was "valuable in its own right."[133]

This conciliatory approach evoked renewed thunder from Peking, this time in the form of an oral message delivered on September 12 through Swedish channels from the Vice-Foreign Minister, Cheng Han-fou, who repeated in more violent terms the Chinese objections to Hammarskjold's report and also objected to the statements made in his press conference on August 12. For good measure Cheng accused Hammarskjold of lack of impartiality because he had never given the Chinese viewpoint. To this message Hammarskjold could only reply at some length that he greatly regretted the loss of confidence in him that the message clearly indicated. He went ahead with his report to the General Assembly, but the Chinese, having effectively cut all contact, did not pursue the matter and the only further reverberation was an article on October 22, 1955, in *Jen Min Jin Pao* ("People's Daily") containing a relatively mild attack on Hammarskjold's report as being "not very objective."

A week later, on September 18,[134] when asked if negotiations with Chou En-lai were continuing, Hammarskjold referred to the U.S.-Chinese talks in Geneva and excused himself from comment, and he continued to take this line when the question arose periodically in the succeeding years.

On January 5, 1956, Hammarskjold sent Chou a message on the anniversary of his arrival in Peking, to which Chou duly replied thanking him and hoping for new progress in the cause of international peace and cooperation. On September 26, 1957, after his reelection as Secretary-General, he wrote a long letter[135] to Chou in order, as he put it, "to remain in touch." In this letter he pleaded for the two American prisoners who were still in captivity, Fecteau and Downey,* who were "caught in the web of circumstances and history." They had, he said, been on his mind as a person "who once got personally engaged in the fate of these two men," and he hoped very much that the Chinese government would see its way to treating them with its traditional leniency. He also hoped that during his second term as Secretary-General he would be able to maintain his personal contact with Chou En-lai. On this note his contact with Chou effectively ended.

In September 1958 Hammarskjold considered using the "Peking formula" in an attempt to solve the dangerous deadlock over the off-

---

* On November 15, 1971, three weeks after the decision of the General Assembly to seat the representatives of the People's Republic of China, the *New York Times* reported from Hong Kong that Downey's mother had visited him in prison in Peking and was hopeful that her son would soon be released. She also saw Fecteau, who was freed on December 13, 1971.

shore islands in the Taiwan Strait and discussed with Dulles the possibility of negotiating with both sides an arrangement by which the islands would become a kind of no man's land to which, pending a final settlement, neither side would assert its alleged rights of possession. He suggested that if both the United States and the U.S.S.R. were agreeable to the idea, a group of governments might exercise their good offices with Peking and Taipei, or alternatively he himself, in full knowledge of the risks involved, might tackle the question using the "Peking formula," i.e., on the basis of an acceptance of the office of the Secretary-General as an international, neutral institution established by international agreement and entitled under the Charter to go into questions of peace and security, irrespective of whether the parties concerned were members of the United Nations or not. Any chance of success, he said, would depend on his being able to support a solution of the question of Chinese representation in the United Nations. Dulles's reply to this suggestion was noncommittal, and the matter was not pursued.

Although Hammarskjold's hope of continued contacts with Peking, and especially with Chou En-lai, was disappointed, the Peking affair had other important results. The success of his mission established him once and for all as a major resource of the international community for dealing with difficult problems and as an important international figure in his own right. It also transformed his relations with the United States. Up to this time his relations both with Lodge and with Dulles had been marked by a series of strongly expressed disagreements and had tended to be marred by a mixture of condescension and irritation on the U.S. side and a sometimes shrill reaction on Hammarskjold's part. Much to the credit of all concerned, these attitudes were superseded, as the affair of the U.S. prisoners developed toward its successful outcome, by a large measure of mutual respect and understanding that easily survived future disagreements.

Hammarskjold enormously enjoyed the challenge of the Peking experience. It stimulated in him a new taste and new ideas for using his office and his position to tackle difficult problems, and in later years he tended to recall it as a measure of the tension and quality of other crises. After August 1955 his style changed noticeably, as if, at the completion of the affair of the American prisoners in China on his fiftieth birthday, he had come of age as Secretary-General.

6

THE MIDDLE EAST, APRIL–MAY 1956

THE YEAR 1955 HAD SEEN the effects of the first major improvement in the international atmosphere since World War II. Summing up the situation during that July, Hammarskjold wrote:

> During its first nine years the UN has had to operate in an atmosphere poisoned by the failure to reach agreed settlements of problems arising out of the Second World War and its aftermaths in Europe and in Asia. Now the Treaty of Austria has at last been concluded. The first meeting since 1945 of Heads of Governments of four of the Great Powers will have taken place. . . . In the Far East, the Bandung Conference of Asian and African nations reflected an attitude and approach that may bear increasing fruit in the future. . . . These developments give reason for hope that they may be followed by others in the same direction.[1]

In June 1955 the celebration of the tenth anniversary of the UN had brought together many Foreign Ministers in San Francisco. Three other events contributed further to making 1955 something of an *annus mirabilis* on the international scene. The heads of state of the Big Four met in Geneva;[2] Hammarskjold had his first great personal success as an international go-between and negotiator in the release by Peking of the U.S. airmen; and the first UN Conference on Peaceful Uses of Atomic

Energy was an unexpectedly successful demonstration of the possibilities of East–West rapprochement through the machinery of the UN. During the General Assembly session in the fall the deadlock on the admission of new UN members was broken at last, letting in sixteen new states.* At the end of the year the Organization was, as Hammarskjold put it, in an unprecedented state of flux, and there was a "beginning of a thawing of fixed patterns ... with a groping towards a new orientation on a more strict national basis, with less of overriding ideological considerations."[3]

This state of flux, although it produced new uncertainties and new problems, was a fertile environment for Hammarskjold's ideas for developing the UN's potential as an instrument of multilateral diplomacy, and the events of the second half of 1956 in the Middle East provided an unexpected opportunity for practical experiment and radically changed both the Organization's method of functioning and his own position as Secretary-General. He responded to this challenge with enthusiasm and ingenuity, using the limited resources of the Secretariat to the practical extreme and developing whatever new resources and sources of support that he could find. In this process the UN managed, in Hammarskjold's words, "to renew itself administratively, and in some respects politically."[4]

Of all the problems inherited by the United Nations from former colonial powers that gave rise to the form of UN crisis management later known as "peace-keeping," the Palestine problem was one of the earliest and the most intractable. The sudden relinquishment by Great Britain in May 1948 of its League of Nations mandate over Palestine had led in rapid succession to the proclamation of the state of Israel, its recognition by the UN, fighting between Jews and Arabs in Palestine, and the invasion of the former mandated territory by the armies of Egypt, Iraq, Saudi Arabia, Syria, and Transjordan. The confused fighting that followed was temporarily halted in June by a four-week truce called for by the UN Security Council, which in July, after further fighting, ordered an indefinite cease-fire. United Nations military observers were deployed to supervise the truce under the direction of the UN mediator, Count Folke Bernadotte of Sweden, while he himself set about the search for a long-term settlement between Israel and its Arab neighbors. When Bernadotte was assassinated in Jerusalem by Jewish terrorists on September 17, 1948, his function as mediator was taken over by Ralph Bunche. Sporadic fighting soon

---

* The new members, admitted on December 14, 1955, were: Albania, Austria, Bulgaria, Cambodia, Ceylon, Finland, Hungary, Ireland, Italy, Jordan, Laos, Libya, Nepal, Portugal, Romania, and Spain.

broke out again, and Bunche, after obtaining a new cease-fire, began at the end of 1948 a series of negotiations on the island of Rhodes which ended, in the spring of 1949, with the conclusion of armistice agreements between Israel and her four Arab neighbors. These agreements were intended only to be a first step toward a permanent peace settlement. They were supervised on the ground by mixed armistice commissions for each front and by the military observers of the United Nations Truce Supervision Organization (UNTSO), based in Jerusalem and operating under the direction of the Secretary-General and the general authority of the Security Council.

When Hammarskjold arrived at the UN in 1953, the uneasy truce in the Middle East was based largely on the armistice agreements and on a later, and unconnected, arrangement, the Tripartite Declaration of France, Great Britain, and the United States of May 1950. This Declaration was designed to maintain the status quo and to deter aggression by any of the governments concerned against their neighbors in the Middle East.

After the collapse of the Turkish Empire in the First World War, Britain and France had become the dominant powers of a relatively subservient Middle East, and their postwar arrangements had already sown the seeds of the Arab-Israeli problem as it finally emerged in its full insolubility in 1948. With the creation of Israel the United States joined France and Britain as the patron states of the Middle East, a position formalized in the Tripartite Declaration, but the new hegemony was not to stand unchallenged for long. The growth of Arab nationalism and the steady increase of Soviet influence in the Middle East, and the simultaneous decline in the influence of France and Great Britain, had begun to make the Tripartite Declaration an anachronism long before the desperate attempt of France and Great Britain to reassert by force their former influence finally dealt the Declaration its death blow.

The armistice agreements and UNTSO, although originally intended as a short-term transitional arrangement, survived despite a steady erosion throughout the early 1950's. Although they were pitifully inadequate as a means of stemming the rising tide of hatred, violence, and recrimination between Israel and its Arab neighbors, they still provided the best available legal and practical basis for the maintenance of some kind of order along the boundaries of Israel. Nevertheless, growing friction and bitterness led to constant violations of the armistice agreements by both sides. After the abortive Arab invasion of Palestine in 1948, the problem of Palestine had become a main focus of the policies of the surrounding Arab states, in which the presence of large numbers of Palestinian refugees was a constant reminder of

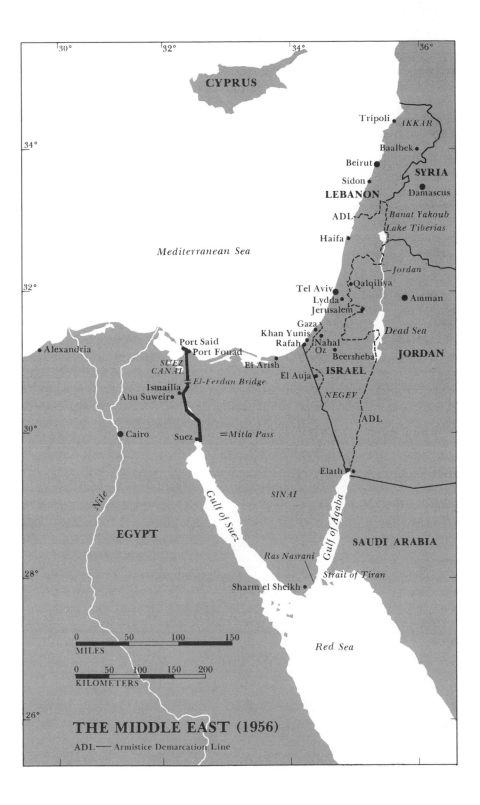

CYPRUS

Tripoli • *AKKAR*

Baalbek •

Beirut •

Sidon •

SYRIA

LEBANON

Damascus •

ADL *Banat Yakoub*
Lake Tiberias

Haifa •

Mediterranean Sea

—Jordan

Tel Aviv • • Qalqiliya

Lydda • • Amman

Jerusalem •

Gaza • *Dead Sea*

Khan Yunis •

Rafah • • Nahal
Oz

JORDAN

• Beersheba

ISRAEL

• Alexandria

Port Said •
Port Fouad •

SUEZ
CANAL

El Arish •

El Auja •

NEGEV

Ismailia •
El-Ferdan Bridge

Abu Suweir •

ADL

• Cairo

Suez • =*Mitla Pass*

Elath •

SINAI

Gulf of Suez

Gulf of Aqaba

SAUDI ARABIA

Nile

EGYPT

Ras Nasrani

Strait of Tiran

Sharm el Sheikh •

Red Sea

| 0 | 50 | 100 | 150 |
MILES

| 0 | 50 | 100 | 150 | 200 |
KILOMETERS

THE MIDDLE EAST (1956)

ADL —— Armistice Demarcation Line

the failure to crush, or at least to curb, Israel. The resulting desire for revenge increasingly dictated policies and courses of action that ensured the permanent instability of the armistice lines. Israel for its part, having narrowly survived as a fledgling state the onslaught of 1948, adopted, as it grew stronger, a harsh defensive policy of strong reprisals for incursions and incidents on its borders. Isolated in the midst of hostile states which refused to recognize even its right to exist, Israel developed a single-minded siege mentality that not infrequently entailed treating the UN truce-supervision machinery with scant courtesy. A long-term Palestine settlement, which had been discussed at the UN since 1947, was less and less spoken of in the Middle East and became an increasingly remote possibility.

In the early 1950's the Middle Eastern policies of states outside the area were changing, as was the Middle East itself. By March 1954, the U.S.S.R. had shifted sufficiently far from its earlier support of Israel to veto an attempt[5] by the Security Council to reaffirm its 1951 resolution[6] calling on Egypt for complete freedom of navigation in the Suez Canal. A month later Colonel Gamal Abdel Nasser became President of Egypt, and that autumn the Arab role in the Algerian war swung French policy in the Middle East in favor of Israel. On October 19, 1954, the British and Egyptian governments concluded the agreement on the evacuation of British troops from the Suez Canal area. Israel, after one last attempt to force the British to make freedom of navigation in the Canal a condition for their withdrawal by trying to run the Israeli ship *Bat Galim* through it, was compelled to consider seriously whether force might not be the only way left to secure this objective so crucial to its economy. Even when British troops were still in the Canal Zone and Egypt had stopped ships bound to and from Israel, British policy had been that Egypt, which claimed still to be at war with Israel, had the right under the Constantinople Convention of 1888 to stop Israeli ships. Even after the Security Council resolution of 1951 calling on Egypt to lift the ban, the British did nothing to persuade Egypt to carry out the resolution. According to Anthony Nutting,[7] later British Minister of State, Foreign Secretary Eden was still supporting Egypt's position as late as January 1954.

The relations between Israel and its Arab neighbors steadily deteriorated through 1954. During the summer a series of incidents on the armistice demarcation line between Jordan and Israel led General E. L. M. Burns, the Canadian Chief of Staff of UNTSO, to warn the Security Council that such incidents unless checked could spread "like bush-fire,"[8] and in January 1955 increasing friction between Israel and Syria caused Burns to urge a negotiated revision of all the armistice agreements.[9] On February 28,[10] two platoons of Israeli paratroopers crossed into the Gaza Strip and attacked a military camp near the railway station in Gaza, while a subsidiary Israeli ambush on the road from Rafah to Gaza caught the Egyptian reinforcements, killing thirty-six Egyptian or Palestinian soldiers and two civilians, and wounding twenty-nine soldiers and two civilians. In Burns's words, "It was a crucial event in this dismal history, and set a trend which continued until Israel invaded the Sinai in October 1956."[11]

Although Nasser later called the Gaza raid a turning point in Egypt's relations with Israel, Egypt remained relatively conciliatory through the summer of 1955 and even proposed a mutual pullback of troops one kilometer from the armistice line to avoid unnecessary incidents, a suggestion received with no enthusiasm by Israel. The subsequent discussions between representatives of the two governments under the chairmanship of Burns at Kilometer 95 on the demarcation line reached an impasse by the end of June because the Egyptians refused to have any direct contact with the Israelis until the Palestine refugees were either repatriated or compensated. An Israeli raid into Gaza on August 22[12] was followed by the first sabotage and terrorist raids into Israel by the Egyptian-trained Palestinian "fedayeen" from the Gaza Strip. A week later the Israelis raided Khan Yunis in the Gaza Strip, killing thirty-six Egyptians; and on September 21, over the strong protests of Hammarskjold and Burns, they occupied the Demilitarized Zone of El Auja, the strategic key to both the Negev and Sinai.

The Security Council and UNTSO were almost helpless in this anarchy of raid and reprisal, and Hammarskjold's frequent protests were also unavailing. The fedayeen presented a new and particularly difficult problem since no Arab government would admit responsibility for them, and moves by the Security Council to condemn such raids were subject to the Soviet veto. The UNTSO machinery was powerless to give any effective protection against this type of clandestine and ostensibly unofficial activity. Israel's massive reprisals, on the other hand, were a clear violation of the clause in the armistice agreements forbidding hostile acts against the other party, and were almost invariably condemned by the Security Council. This anomaly added to Israel's increasing embitterment with the UN.

Nasser's approach to the Soviet bloc in May 1955 for the arms the Western powers had hesitated or refused to give him, and the public announcement of the Egyptian-Czech arms agreement on September 27, 1955, were a turning point for the Western powers and for Israel. Egypt also began to tighten its control over the Strait of Tiran, which gives access to the Gulf of Aqaba and to the Israeli port of Elath, and prohibited Israeli civilian aircraft from flying over the Gulf. Although Hammarskjold did not know it at the time, on October 23 David Ben-

Gurion, then Israel Defense Minister, recalled General Moshe Dayan, the Chief of Staff of the Israeli Army, from a vacation in Paris to tell him "to be prepared to capture the Strait of Tiran."[13] On November 2, Ben-Gurion became Prime Minister.

Both Egypt and Israel were now engaged in an arms race which, since the Eastern and Western powers were their respective suppliers, inevitably brought the cold war into the Middle East situation. Western attempts to counter Soviet influence, such as the setting up of the Baghdad Pact, a mutual security agreement among Great Britain, Iran, Iraq, Pakistan, and Turkey, further polarized the conflict and also embittered inter-Arab relations. In December 1955, in another attempt to pre-empt Soviet influence, the United States and Great Britain offered to defray the foreign-exchange costs of Nasser's primary domestic project, the Aswan High Dam, a matter of $56 million and $14 million respectively for the two countries, and the World Bank announced that it was prepared to grant Egypt a $200-million loan.

Hammarskjold became increasingly preoccupied by the steady deterioration of the Middle East situation, but it was only in January 1956, in the course of his first world tour,[14] that he visited Israel, Syria, Jordan, Egypt, and Lebanon for the first time and got some direct idea of the personalities and the problems of the area. Asked on his return to New York if he was planning any personal initiative in the Middle East, he replied: "It is not a good idea for the Secretary-General to jump up on the stage and try to assume a role unless and until he is called for. For that reason, my reply to your question, if it is interpreted in that more pretentious sense is, for the present, 'no—not unless asked for.' "[15]

The call was not long in coming. British, French, and U.S. concern over the situation in the Middle East was rapidly increasing. In January 1956, British efforts to bring Jordan into the Baghdad Pact were thwarted by riots in Amman that threatened the government itself, and on March 1 King Hussein dismissed Glubb Pasha, the architect and for twenty-six years the commander of the Arab Legion. This act, for which the real reasons were almost certainly domestic, was variously interpreted in different parts of the world. Eden, who had succeeded Churchill as British Prime Minister a year before, believed that Glubb's dismissal was Nasser's doing, and his reaction, in Nutting's words, was "that the world was not big enough to hold him and Nasser."[16] Nasser told British Foreign Secretary Selwyn Lloyd, who was then on a visit to Cairo, that he thought Glubb's dismissal was a British trick. The truth seems to have been that King Hussein felt that a foreigner should no longer command his army and that Glubb was far too cautious in his attitude toward the Israelis. Burns, who had dealt extensively with Glubb, feared that his removal would seriously imperil the stability of the Jordanian régime and the relatively peaceful relationship between Jordan and Israel, for Glubb had always been at pains to try to prevent infiltration from Jordan into Israel. As the Algerian War became more intense, the French attitude to Nasser also steadily hardened.* On May 16, Nasser recognized the Peking government—which Israel had recognized more than six years before.

In early March, Hammarskjold still had doubts as to the utility of any new move by the Security Council on the Palestine question. "The role of the United Nations," he said on March 7, "should be to help those who are responsible, all of whom want peace, to work towards peace. They can do that by introducing whatever means they have at their disposal to reduce borderline tensions, to engage in intelligent discussion of the major underlying problems and to help in keeping down the temperature by as realistic an appraisal of the situation as possible."[18] A day later he told the press:

> If you mean what can the United Nations do about it from day to day, or even from hour to hour, I think there is no need for very great imagination to see it does quite a lot. It does quite a lot directly in current negotiations concerning small matters and major matters. It does quite a lot to bridge the gulfs, to act as a lightning conductor service for bringing high tensions down by explanations. It cannot and it will never make news because no single piece of it is news, and the whole thing, the continuous operation, should not be news, because it is a matter of course. But it is an operation; it is very much like the constant attendance of a good nurse, which may be just as important as the operation itself. Surgeons' operations are news, the work of nurses is not.[19]

Western frustrations and anxieties had now reached a point where the governments concerned were no longer content with nursing care and were prepared to risk a more drastic move through the UN. On March 13, Lodge and Pierson Dixon told Hammarskjold that they were planning to propose that the Security Council should establish an agent-general in the Middle East with far-reaching political authority. At first sight this struck him as an empty and unconvincing gesture that would also be extremely unfair to Burns, the hard-working Chief of Staff of UNTSO, and as a Western creation the "agent-general" would certainly be suspect both to the Arabs and to the Soviet Union. "Laying myself open to serious misunderstandings,"

---

* At this time Nasser was for the first time compared to Hitler, by Colonel Louis Mangin, an aide to the French Defense Minister, Maurice Bourgès-Maunoury. This inappropriate and emotive comparison was to be taken up by other Western statesmen in the coming months.[17]

Hammarskjold noted in recording this discussion, "I had to say that I feared that the only man with a task like the one suggested who would be swallowed by the Soviet Union and tolerated by the Arabs, was the Secretary-General as Secretary-General."[20]

Hammarskjold found out from Hervé Alphand, the French representative, that the "agent-general" was a purely American idea and also, as he had feared, that his own comment had been misunderstood by Lodge as an expression of his wish to fill the role. The idea of the Secretary-General's involvement had been planted, however, and the next day Dixon asked Hammarskjold if he really believed that he himself could do something useful in the Middle East. Hammarskjold replied that he considered that most uncertain, but that the risk would be worthwhile if only to kill what he regarded as a potentially disastrous American initiative. The situation was further confused when, on March 15, stories in the *New York Times* and the *Christian Science Monitor* gave the impression that the United States was taking a strong lead on the Middle East in the UN with Hammarskjold as its collaborator. He told Sobolev that such articles were a symptom of increasing pressures about the Middle East in the Western world and suggested that the only useful course of action would be to start sounding out the countries of the Middle East on a possible intensification of UN assistance in a general settlement, a process during which the Secretary-General might have to visit the governments concerned.

Hammarskjold soon learned that the French and U.S. governments approved of his ideas, even to the point of his proposing to the Security Council a resolution on what problems should be tackled. In an attempt to clarify the confusion caused by further press speculation, he put in writing to the three Western members of the Security Council— France, Great Britain, and the United States—his reactions to their various proposals, pointing out that if any intervention by the Secretary-General was to succeed he must make direct approaches to the governments in the Middle East. The operation must be accepted by them, must not appear to be undertaken in the interest of any one of the big powers, and should be so organized as to be entirely outside the cold-war orbit. If this could be arranged, he would be prepared to go immediately to the area to explore with the governments concerned "an intensified attack on the major problems within the framework of the United Nations."[21] He hoped that the Security Council would formally request him to undertake this mission. He had no wish to reserve any special position for himself in the Middle East, not least "because the effort itself is hazardous and not without great personal risks,"[22] but he would accept these risks if there was a reasonable hope that he could make a useful contribution.

The Security Council met from March 26 to April 4. Despite the cold-war tone of the debate, both Arabs and Israelis finally welcomed a resolution, introduced by the United States, of which the main proposal was that Hammarskjold should proceed immediately to the Middle East. The Soviet representative also agreed to it, and on April 4 the Council adopted the resolution[23] unanimously. Its operative part read:

> The Security Council . . .
> 2. Requests the Secretary-General to undertake, as a matter of urgent concern, a survey of the various aspects of enforcement of and compliance with the four general armistice agreements and the Council's resolutions under reference;
> 3. Requests the Secretary-General to arrange with the parties for the adoption of any measures which, after discussion with the parties and with the Chief of Staff, he considers would reduce existing tensions along the armistice demarcation lines, including the following points: (a) Withdrawal of their forces from the armistice demarcation lines; (b) Full freedom of movement for observers along the armistice demarcation lines, in the demilitarized zones and in the defensive areas; (c) Establishment of local arrangements for the prevention of incidents and the prompt detection of any violations of the armistice agreements;
> 4. Calls upon the parties to the general armistice agreements to cooperate with the Secretary-General in the implementation of this resolution;
> 5. Requests the Secretary-General to report to the Council in his discretion but not later than one month from this date on the implementation given to this resolution in order to assist the Council in considering what further action may be required.

The mission was primarily for fact-finding and to negotiate whatever measures might be necessary in order to ease the tension along the armistice demarcation lines, and Hammarskjold interpreted it simply "as permitting me to negotiate for the fullest possible compliance with the armistice agreements,"[24] as a stage that had to be passed in order to make progress on the main issues possible. The Security Council had not asked him to deal with those main issues—freedom of navigation in the Suez Canal and in the Strait of Tiran, the problem of the Palestine refugees, the project for diverting the waters of the River Jordan, or the state of belligerency that the Arab states insisted on maintaining with Israel. Nor would he be able to influence the international rivalries that provided the wider context of the Arab-Israeli conflict.

Hammarskjold departed for the Middle East on April 6 amid considerable speculation in the press. All observers were agreed on the extreme difficulty of his mission.* The Arab press was generally distrustful of the Western initiative in the Security Council and even speculated that he shared this distrust and might refuse to undertake the mission—a story that, to Hammarskjold's annoyance, had originated in Washington three weeks before. From London Joseph Alsop wrote that the gloom over Middle East developments was "so deep that it all but approaches despair."[25] Alsop foresaw a Communist takeover in many Arab countries as the inevitable aftermath of the dismissal of Glubb, and his dire prophecies reflected, if nothing else, the growing feverishness of Eden and his Cabinet over the Middle East in general and Nasser in particular.

The news from the Middle East added a note of emergency to Hammarskjold's mission. On April 5, Israeli shelling of Gaza had killed 59 and wounded 93 Arabs, and Egypt responded by stepping up the fedayeen raids.[26] Burns worked desperately to persuade both sides to delay further reprisals, and Hammarskjold cut down the time he had intended to spend in preliminary consultations in Rome with Burns, whom he asked to return to the area after one day.

Hammarskjold arrived in Beirut at 2:30 a.m. on April 10 and immediately flew on to Tel Aviv, where Burns met him. A four-week diplomatic marathon followed. Burns later wrote of Hammarskjold that "throughout this gruelling programme his stamina was astonishing; he never seemed weary nor did his perceptions flag. His name had become synonymous with diplomatic skill, and he deployed his great resources throughout the four weeks of his mission. At the beginning of it he found a situation in which all-out war seemed possible within hours; at the end, though he had not accomplished all that he had hoped for, he had secured engagements from all countries which, had they been kept, would have ensured stability under the general framework of the armistice agreements."[27]

Hammarskjold had set the ball rolling for his negotiations[28] on April 8 in a letter to Ben-Gurion, endorsing the Prime Minister's request that Burns get an undertaking from Egypt to observe Article II, paragraph 2, of the general armistice agreement in its entirety,**

---

* William Frye in the *Christian Science Monitor* of Thursday, March 22, stated the general reaction: "The principal issues are so serious and run so deep that it will be extraordinary if Mr. Hammarskjold is able to make major progress in the month he is to be given by the Security Council. Almost certainly his mandate will have to be extended."

** Article II, paragraph 2, of the general armistice agreement between Egypt and Israel reads:

No element of the land, sea or air military or para-military forces of either Party, including non-regular forces, shall commit any warlike or hostile act against the military or para-military forces of the other Party, or against civilians in ter-

and at the same time he requested the government of Israel to give a similar undertaking, pointing out to Ben-Gurion, in a reference to Israel's policy of reprisal, that "you are undoubtedly aware of the limits this paragraph of the said article puts on your freedom of action." He also sent a message to Nasser, expressing his concern at the recent incidents in the Gaza area and drawing his attention "to the vital need of breaking the present chain of actions and reactions." Ben-Gurion agreed unconditionally to comply with Article II, paragraph 2, of the armistice agreement on the understanding that Egypt would do likewise.

The Egyptian reply, received from Mahmoud Fawzi, the Egyptian Foreign Minister, on April 10, was more circumspect, saying merely that Hammarskjold's and Burns's imminent visit to Cairo would afford an admirable opportunity for thorough discussion of all the points raised. This reply disappointed Hammarskjold, and he told Fawzi that if the requested assurance, which was for him a precondition of his mission, was not given, "I would find myself obliged to reconsider my plan now to enter upon discussions with the Egyptian Government in implementation of the Security Council resolution."[30] He flew to Cairo on the afternoon of April 10, and that evening held preliminary talks with Fawzi. With Nasser and Fawzi on the following morning, he immediately took the offensive, pointing out that if raids and shooting across the armistice demarcation line continued, intervention from outside the region would probably be unavoidable. He asked Nasser, as a precondition to discussions on wider matters, to put a stop to the shooting and the fedayeen raids. Nasser retorted that the United Nations in the last few days had been adding to the tension by a series of démarches that were almost like the ultimatums received from the Israelis, to which Hammarskjold replied that exactly the same démarche had been presented to Ben-Gurion.

Nasser agreed to give Hammarskjold a reply on Article II, paragraph 2, that could be published at once to match the Israel assurance, which Ben-Gurion had already released to the press. Hammarskjold said that he proposed to tie up this particular arrangement by writing to Ben-Gurion, noting the Israeli assurances and informing him of Nasser's orders to stop all firing and line-crossing, in the hope that the acute tension that had caused the chain reaction of reprisal

---

ritory under the control of that Party; or shall advance beyond or pass over for any purpose whatsoever the Armistice Demarcation Line set forth in Article VI of this Agreement . . . and elsewhere shall not violate the international frontier; or enter into or pass through the air space of the other Party or through the waters within three miles of the coastline of the other Party.[29]

and counterreprisal might be broken that very day. Nasser also tentatively agreed to restrain the fedayeen, although Burns warned Hammarskjold privately that the Egyptian authorities would not be able to control the fedayeen who were already in the field because there was no communication with fedayeen parties once they had been launched. The truth of this observation became apparent when, on April 12, in response to Hammarskjold's letter transmitting Nasser's reply, Moshe Sharett, the Israeli Foreign Minister, reported new attacks by the fedayeen on the previous night, concluding that "the utter worthlessness and falseness of Colonel Nasser's assurances stand exposed"[31] and demanding public condemnation by the UN of Nasser's "revolting behavior."[32] In reply to this message, which he received on returning to his hotel late in the evening after driving out to see the Pyramids, Hammarskjold asked Ben-Gurion for restraint over what was probably the last fedayeen flare-up. "It is not for the Secretary-General to add to the tension by public statements," he wrote. "He has refrained from doing so after the events of last week.* He will refrain from doing so now. The proper body for such condemnations is, as you well know, the Security Council."[33]

Having broken the ice with Nasser, Hammarskjold began to realize that his main difficulties probably lay with Ben-Gurion. The last fedayeen raid[34] had been a particularly outrageous one in which three children and one adult had been killed and fifteen persons wounded. Ben-Gurion, in his indignation, had published his protest to Hammarskjold before it had even reached Hammarskjold himself and seemed inclined to humiliate Nasser and to discredit his assurances. In an effort to rescue what progress had already been made with both sides, Hammarskjold therefore published in full his exchange of letters concerning assurances on Article II, paragraph 2, of the armistice agreement.

Hammarskjold next turned to Burns's earlier suggestion for making UNTSO's supervision of the armistice lines more effective, in the hope that the tenuous assurances he had extracted from the two governments might hold for long enough to build up the confidence of each side in the other's good intentions. To dramatize the possibility of restoring calm on the Gaza line, he decided to fly to Gaza and then to drive along the armistice line and cross into Israel. "My reason for this proposal," he told Cordier, "is the effect it would have on international public opinion, signalizing the new state of affairs which we all hope will result from the last few days' negotiations."[35] On April 14, in spite

---

* A reference to the Israeli shelling of Gaza.

of the anxiety of his Egyptian hosts over his safety,* he carried out
his plan, driving from Gaza along the armistice demarcation line in a
convoy of white UNTSO jeeps to the UN checkpoint at Kilometer 95,
where he said good-bye to the Egyptian representatives. One hundred
meters down the road he was greeted by the Israeli delegate to the
Mixed Armistice Commission and a military escort. The crossing went
off without incident, and Hammarskjold drove to Lydda Airport and
flew on to Beirut on the evening of April 14.

The danger of renewed incidents on the Gaza line was not the only
obstacle to Hammarskjold's progress. On April 13 Ben-Gurion asked
him to find out whether Egypt considered itself still at war with
Israel and whether Egypt realized that the Armistice Agreement
required her to discontinue the closure of the Suez Canal to Israeli
shipping. This major question, according to the sponsors of the
Security Council resolution, was not within his formal mandate. Con-
sequently, Hammarskjold pointed out to Ben-Gurion, he could discuss
it with Egypt only if Egypt was willing to discuss it with him in his
capacity as Secretary-General. This limitation would obviously weaken
his hand in negotiations with Ben-Gurion, and in a long personal letter
on April 15— "sent," as he put it, "from a man with heavy responsibility to a man with even heavier responsibility, and of great experience and courage,"[36]—he told the Prime Minister that it was vitally
important to encourage the forces for peace that were now in control
in Egypt.

April 16 being Israel's national day, Hammarskjold was not due
in Jerusalem until the seventeenth and had a little time to contemplate
his next steps. He also had an afternoon free to walk around Beirut,
and he set off at his usual fast pace. The Lebanese security men,
used to riding in cars, were soon exhausted, and one of them, puffing
painfully, drew abreast of Ranallo to inquire if Hammarskjold was
married. When told that he was not, the security man remarked,
"That is the reason he can walk so fast at his age."[37]

With Ben-Gurion, and in Israel, Hammarskjold found a far more
receptive audience than he had expected. After their first meeting,
Ben-Gurion, who admired toughness and ability and had already
found that Hammarskjold's detailed knowledge of Middle Eastern
problems was as formidable as his skill in negotiation, jokingly asked,
"And where did they find *you*?" On Hammarskjold's arrival in Jerusa-

---

* The Egyptians were not the only ones to worry. Bill Ranallo, who was responsible
for Hammarskjold's personal security, felt that the demonstration was silly, since
if anything went wrong it would only demonstrate conclusively how bad things
were on the Gaza line.

lem, Ben-Gurion had confirmed that orders would be enforced as of 6 p.m. on the following day, April 18, prohibiting any firing by Israeli forces across the armistice demarcation line and the crossing of the line by military or paramilitary forces for any purpose whatsoever. Hammarskjold also received assurances from Fawzi that strict orders had been given to the Egyptian forces in Gaza, and UNTSO observers on the ground confirmed that Egyptian officers permitting violations of these orders had been threatened with court-martial. He was therefore able, on April 19, to announce simultaneously in Jerusalem and in Cairo the first milestone in his negotiations,[38] reciprocal arrangements for the implementation of the cease-fire.

This announcement was on the whole well received. The Israelis took it as meaning the cessation of fedayeen raids, and the U.S.S.R. reacted by stating that it would support all UN Middle East moves.[39] In New York, Arkady Sobolev stayed for an unusually long time at a reception given by the Israeli mission and predicted peace in the Middle East. Hammarskjold himself was especially pleased with a cable from Alphand which read simply, "Bravo Dag."[40] The Beirut newspaper *L'Orient* of April 17, with more enthusiasm than accuracy, sported a front-page banner headline, *"Le Liban et l'Egypte acceptent le plan Hammarskjold."*

On his way to Beirut on April 20, Hammarskjold commented: "This particular job is a little bit like building an arch. I feel that I have now added a second stone to the first one, and that it is just as good as the first one. However, you know that, in building an arch, the construction is not stable until all the stones have been fitted in. I may add that I know that we are on the right road, and I don't see why we should lose it."[41]

Lodge, who was the President of the Security Council, was less tentative in a message on the nineteenth. "Publication of the Secretary-General's statement will be received with gratification throughout the world,"[42] he wrote, and in a public statement on the following day he was even more enthusiastic. "This looks like the real thing," he said. "Last year, we saw Secretary-General Hammarskjold going to Peking, and, as a result, our 15 U.S. aviators were released from the prisons of Communist China. This year Mr. Hammarskjold has gone to Palestine and has achieved this wonderful result. May it last a long time. We can all be thankful, I think, that the position of the Secretary-General of the United Nations exists, and that it is filled by such a capable individual as Mr. Hammarskjold, when we think of how much we all want to avoid war."[43]

"God knows where we are," Hammarskjold told Cordier on April 21, "but with the present attitudes not only in the two leading countries, but, as it seems, among the big powers, we may find that we are at a juncture where things may be given a new direction."[44]

His next problem was to get cease-fire assurances from Jordan, Lebanon, and Syria. Such an assurance from Syria would mean that the Syrians would not be able to shoot at the Israelis if they resumed work on the Jordan water diversion project at Banat Yacoub, but in line with his views on Israeli reprisals he had told Ben-Gurion on April 19 that he would tell the Syrians that no Israeli work at Banat Yacoub would justify armed reprisals, because the cease-fire obligation in the armistice agreements could not be canceled by noncompliance with any other clause in the agreements. There was the further problem of Israeli interference with Syrian fishing rights on Lake Tiberias as well as a standing dispute between Israel and Syria over some parts of the Israel-Syria border in the Demilitarized Zone.

On the evening of April 22 there was a scuffle between Israeli and Syrian fishermen on Lake Tiberias during which shots were fired and the Israelis had had to retire leaving their nets behind. Sharett lost no time in protesting this incident to Hammarskjold, who was in Damascus, saying it was exactly the kind of thing that had compelled the Israelis to send police launches to protect their fishermen. At a preliminary meeting with Burns on April 23 the Syrians took a hard line, saying that Israel must relinquish all claims to sovereignty in the Demilitarized Zone and abandon forty-five Israeli settlements in the Zone that the Syrians claimed to be more military than agricultural. They further suggested that fishing permits on Lake Tiberias be given out by the UN and not by the Israelis. There were difficulties on other fronts as well. On April 23, Ben-Gurion demanded the cessation of the blockade of Israel, and the next day Sharett reported another fedayeen ambush in the Negev.

In Damascus Hammarskjold was able to record, in a letter to the Syrian Foreign Minister, understandings relating to the watering of cattle and drawing of water by the inhabitants on the Syrian side of the lake and a 250-meter limit for Israeli police craft. It was also agreed that UN observers should be stationed on the Syrian side to deal with incidents on the lake. Hammarskjold undertook to get a solution to the problem of Syrian fishing rights on the lake, while the Syrians reaffirmed their determination to respect the provisions of the armistice agreement with Israel, which enjoined them to refrain from warlike acts.

Hammarskjold left Damascus on the afternoon of April 24 for Amman, where he dined with King Hussein. The next day was occupied with meetings with Samir Rifai, the Prime Minister of Jordan, and a tour of the Old City of Jerusalem, which was under Jordanian control. Although Hammarskjold was still optimistic, distracting and unhelpful trends persisted. The *Jerusalem Post*, in a report from Washington, quoted Abba Eban,[45] Israeli Ambassador in Washington, as cautioning against excessive optimism about the Secretary-General's mission and saying that it merely restored the situation that had existed when the Security Council sent him to the Middle East. This expression of doubt caused Hammarskjold to appeal to Sharett to make a new series of unconditional assurances to observe the cease-fire, "which as an interlocking system of newly assumed obligations would cover the whole region"[46] and would form a starting point for a new approach from all sides. "I have made myself a personal hostage for your will," he wrote to Sharett, "not only to maintain the cease-fire but to work for peace and nothing but peace. I am sure that I have been right in doing so, but I am also sure that you fully realize that when I put the full prestige of my office in the scales in this way, I feel entitled to your full cooperation."[47] Referring to recent incidents, which he deeply regretted, he begged the government of Israel to refrain from making judgments and give his efforts a fair chance. "It is easy," he wrote, "to undo what is on the verge of being achieved: it requires nothing but that the governments discredit the result and start again the old round of discrediting each other."[48]

By April 26, when Hammarskjold left Amman for Beirut, other arrangements were beginning to show signs of coming unstuck. Ben-Gurion, in reaffirming Israel's unconditional agreement to comply with the cease-fire clause of the Israel-Syria armistice agreement, asked for confirmation of full reciprocity from Syria, while on the same day the Damascus press announced that the Syrian government had agreed to the cease-fire on condition that Israel would give up the Banat Yacoub water-diversion project. From Amman, Hammarskjold immediately cabled the Syrian Premier that this could only be a misunderstanding, since the cease-fire pledge was clearly unconditional and could not therefore include the acceptance by the Israelis of an unrelated obligation.

While he awaited the necessary assurances from Jordan, Lebanon, and Syria, Hammarskjold became acutely apprehensive. He instructed his press officer, George Ivan Smith, who was being incessantly badgered about his future arrangements, to say only that they remained fluid and flexible.* The various governments would either come through with firm and categorical assurances or, by making conditions and misleading public statements, would seek to escape

---

* At this time Hammarskjold and Smith took to addressing each other as Mr. Fluid and Mr. Flexible, a habit that lasted for some time in their correspondence.

from the oral assurances given in their talks with him. It was a nerve-racking moment.

Arriving in Cairo at noon on April 28, he was more preoccupied with the Syrian than with the Egyptian position. He told Damascus that he expected to put on record the assurances of both Syria and Israel in the next few days and asked for an immediate confirmation of the Syrian position on the cease-fire. The deadline for reporting to the Council was rapidly approaching and he still awaited definitive assurances from Lebanon and Jordan on the cease-fire. To add to his problems, the Israelis were now expressing doubts about the arrangements for strengthening the UN observer organization in Gaza to which Fawzi had agreed.

By this time Hammarskjold was both exasperated and very tired. Realizing that a demonstration of firmness was required, he asked the Syrian Premier for a meeting on Wednesday, May 2, at 2:30 p.m., "where I trust that we, at the table, will fully and definitely cover the points so far left open. I intend to leave the Middle East the same evening."[49] He told the Premier that such a meeting could be useful only if he could be given the information concerning the Syrian attitude that had to go into his final report to the Security Council, to be dated May 3. He also informed the government of Lebanon that, in the absence of a reply, he would have to report its noncompliance with the Security Council resolution. The tenuous structure of interlocking agreements on the cease-fire was further threatened by sporadic fedayeen activity against Israel. Another Israeli was killed on April 29 at the kibbutz of Nahal Oz, and one more died when his vehicle struck a mine. In a personal message to Fawzi, Hammarskjold asked the Egyptian government to punish the criminals involved, an action that alone could put these incidents in the right perspective as far as the Israelis were concerned.

On the evening of May 1, Henry Labouisse reported from Beirut that he had received the government's reply, and in Damascus the next afternoon Hammarskjold succeeded in getting the assurances he had sought from the Syrians. He was thus able to state in an interim report to the President of the Security Council that he had reciprocal assurances from all the parties to the armistice agreements that they would observe the cease-fire unconditionally. This, he reported, in effect "establishes anew the legal situation on which the armistice régime was to be founded."[50]

Earlier in his mission, Hammarskjold had told his team that an essential rule in such negotiations was never to stay in one place for a moment longer than was necessary. This technique had been effective for the time being, but the stir caused in the capitals of the

Middle East by his interim report to the Council showed that the hypnotic effect of his incessant communications and lightning visits was already wearing off. On May 4 the Lebanese Foreign Office voiced surprise at his claim of unconditional assurances of a cease-fire from Lebanon, Syria, and Jordan, saying that Lebanon had made a reservation concerning the Jordan River diversion project, while from Damascus Henri Vigier, Burns's political adviser, reported "confusion and polemics" following Hammarskjold's expressed intention to publish his exchanges of letters with the governments. At dawn on May 4, Hammarskjold arrived in Rome, where he worked on his final report.

Despite the rumblings of dissent from the Middle East, the world press, which ten days before had been prophesying his failure, was almost unanimous in interpreting Hammarskjold's interim report[51] as a triumphant conclusion of his mission. Alphand went as far as to say that "the road is now open for a solution to the many problems which do exist in the Middle East,"[52] while from Paris it was reported that the Western Big Three Foreign Ministers had decided to leave the explosive Middle East situation entirely in the hands of the UN and outside the terms of the Tripartite Declaration of 1950. The International News Service correspondent at the UN reported that "UN diplomats promptly declared Hammarskjold's mission as Security Council peace emissary 'a rousing success.' "[53]

Hammarskjold was more than ever inclined to caution. In his airport statement in New York on May 6 he said only that the trip showed that the UN "can be directly helpful to member governments in their wish to reestablish order and maintain peace; helpful, not by imposing its will, but by bringing out what is common ground for agreement to the parties in a conflict and crystallizing it in a way which gives the governments a firm point from which they can move forward."[54] Ambassador Wadsworth of the United States shared this caution: "It would be wrong—and the Secretary-General, I am sure, would be the first to agree—to consider this accomplishment a miracle. His successful negotiations do testify both to his own ability and persistence and to the cooperation of the parties in agreeing on practical steps to relieve tension. . . . We await with great interest the full report. . . . Now we simply express thanks for his safe arrival and say 'well done.' "[55]

Hammarskjold went straight from Idlewild Airport to his office to complete his final report.[56] It began with a masterly summary of the problems of the area and of the position of the various governments, and proceeded to a detailed analysis of his own efforts to secure full compliance with the armistice agreements as a first step toward improving the political relations among the various governments. It was too early to say what had really been achieved, but what had been done might open the door to fruitful developments if only the governments of the area could build up mutual confidence and demonstrate their wish for peaceful conditions. "I believe," he concluded, "that the present situation offers unique possibilities. If we have previously experienced chain reactions leading to a continuous deterioration of the situation, we may now have the possibility of starting a chain of reactions in the opposite direction. The final settlement is probably still far off, but even partial solutions to the harassing problems of the region would be a contribution to the welfare of the peoples concerned and to the peace of the world."[57]

"Neither Israelis nor Arabs," noted the *Jewish Observer and Middle East Review* of May 25, "feel that they can afford to ignore the Hammarskjold findings. That in itself is already a considerable step forward." Hammarskjold enjoyed the confidence and trust of Nasser and Ben-Gurion,

> to a degree which no president, premier, or foreign secretary has yet enjoyed simultaneously from both sides since the outbreak of the Palestine war. This is something which cannot be rated too highly. For the first time in this sorry diplomatic story here is a man trusted by the Israel and the Egyptian Governments not to play power politics and to woo one side or the other by the offer of advantageous terms. For the first time in fact since the partition resolution of 1947 the stock of the United Nations in the Middle East stands higher than that of any of the great powers in the eyes of the Arabs and of the Israelis. This has happened not as a result of any kind of appeasement or mediation, but simply as a consequence of the rigid honesty of purpose displayed by the Secretary-General and the cooperation which it has won for him from the two premiers who mattered—Nasser and Ben-Gurion.

As events were to show, this was the most lasting—in fact perhaps the only lasting—achievement of Hammarskjold's mission.

He himself was very well aware of the limitations of his success and of the dangers that lay ahead, and feared that the optimistic reaction in the United States and elsewhere in the world would arouse false hopes. His own conclusions from his dealings with the leaders in the area were pessimistic. In the Middle East there were those who genuinely wished for peace, and yet the political and emotional pressures of the area, with the accompanying and incessant incidents on the cease-fire lines, had created a state of mind among leaders on both sides that made peace infinitely difficult to obtain. He had sensed especially that the contrasting temperaments of Nasser and Ben-Gurion created the constant danger of a clash between them, and yet he was convinced that neither planned to attack the other and that

both wished to avoid war. The trouble lay in their deep mutual suspicions and in the different ways in which each believed it necessary
to protect his nation's security. Nasser, though relatively patient, was
partial to conspiratorial activities and to guerrilla tactics, while Ben-
Gurion was impatient and would respond to any Egyptian move by
forceful and open retaliation. Both honestly believed that they were
always right, and Ben-Gurion portrayed every Egyptian move publicly
as further evidence of Nasser's bad faith. While Hammarskjold sym-
pathized with the preoccupations of both leaders, their attitudes
involved great risks both for the Middle East and for the UN. "When
everybody is playing safe in the way you do," he told both Ben-Gurion
and Nasser, "the result is a state of utmost insecurity."[58]

Perhaps the most useful lesson of Hammarskjold's month in the
Middle East was that political activity and diplomatic skill were not
enough and that he had to establish with Middle Eastern leaders personal relationships and mutual understandings sufficiently strong to
survive both their own mutual antagonisms and their periodic irritations or disillusionments with the UN. Of these relationships the most
important were with Ben-Gurion and with Mahmoud Fawzi of Egypt.
After the April mission both became valued and trusted friends with
whom Hammarskjold could correspond or talk with the utmost frankness in bad times as well as in good.

This aristocratic and determined Swede, carrying out the often
irksome directives of the United Nations Security Council and as convinced as Ben-Gurion himself of the rightness of his own position,
was not, at first sight, the sort of person whom Ben-Gurion would
trust or like, but Hammarskjold and Ben-Gurion quickly perceived
each other's exceptional personal qualities and over the years of often
violent disagreement they developed a strong friendship and mutual
sympathy which was reinforced by a common taste for conversation
on broad philosophical subjects.*

In Fawzi, Hammarskjold found a friend and a colleague with whom
he could speak his mind on even the most difficult issues without fear
of being misunderstood. Fawzi's position in Egypt was more delicate
than Ben-Gurion's in Israel, and Hammarskjold appreciated his difficulties and the limitations on his possibilities for action. He saw that
beneath Fawzi's urbanity and sophistication lay wisdom and goodness,
and their friendship survived the disappointments of later years and

---

* In May 1956, Hammarskjold wrote to Per Lind: "The greatest individual experience certainly was to be able to get to know Ben-Gurion thoroughly, whom I have
learned to like very much notwithstanding the fact we are disagreed on much and
have had very violent exchanges of views."[59]

even the bitter experience of the Congo. Hammarskjold was privately criticized, especially in Great Britain, for being too close to Fawzi and for being unduly influenced by him,* but from his correspondence with Fawzi over the years, whether they agreed or disagreed on the question under discussion, there seems little basis for these criticisms. He immediately recognized in this kind, civilized, and wise man both a friend and an important influence for moderation in an area of the world where that quality was becoming increasingly rare.

Reasonable and farsighted as he was, Fawzi lacked real power and could very easily be compromised by any too obvious effort to use his influence with Nasser in peace maneuvers. Hammarskjold did not immediately take to Nasser, although their conversations had been highly satisfactory. He was much impressed by Samir Rifai, the Prime Minister of Jordan, although his influence on events was small because of the weakness of his government. Moshe Sharett he regarded as able but excessively emotional, and Dayan as intelligent but trigger-happy. He feared especially that the unsettled state of Syria could easily lead to dangerous and irresponsible adventures and thought that Syrian reactions to any resumption by the Israelis of work on the Jordan River diversion project was the most likely immediate cause for a new war.

Although he had failed to achieve wider objectives, Hammarskjold believed that it might still be possible soon to secure the lifting of the Suez and Tiran blockades, the Israeli withdrawal from El Auja, and the dispersal of troop concentrations on both sides. These were the "related, unilateral moves"[61] referred to in his final report as the essential next step, and he emphasized that they could only be taken by the governments themselves without outside pressure, and if peace could be maintained on the borders through the efforts of the UN observers for long enough to build up some degree of mutual confidence. The problem, as so often in the Middle East, was to get one of the parties to take a first step that would allow the other side to make a responsive move.

For all his exertions Hammarskjold had scored, in the end, only a limited and temporary success in a situation which, he wrote to the Swedish Foreign Minister, Östen Undén, "had elements of 'A Thousand and One Nights,' of 'The Merchant of Venice' and of 'Oedipus Rex.' "[62] For himself he had gained an education in the Arab-Israeli struggle. "For the first time in my life," he told a press conference

---

* During the Suez crisis the British Secret Service solemnly warned the government to distrust anything agreed to by Fawzi "on the grounds that he was too close a friend of Hammarskjold."[60]

on May 11, "I believe that I understand it."[63] On June 4 the Security Council unanimously commended[64] him for his efforts and asked him to continue them, but the debate both before and after the vote reflected the emotional divisions and mutual fears and suspicions that persisted between the conflicting parties.

BY EARLY JULY, Hammarskjold's mission was already being superseded by a train of events that had started long before. As Burns wrote later, "By the spring of 1956 the currents which were bearing the antagonists in the Middle East towards the whirlpool of war were too strong to be stemmed just by diplomatic interventions, or changed by simple mediation by third parties, including the United Nations and its agent the Secretary-General. If the Three Powers had remained firmly determined to enforce their declaration, peace could have been maintained—but in a few months, Nasser's nationalization of the Suez Canal would put an end to that, making enemies of two of the Three Powers that had undertaken to keep the peace."[65]

Already in June the progress toward disaster, arrested briefly by Hammarskjold's impressive but unavailing efforts, was picking up speed again. On June 19, Ben-Gurion, in a speech to the Knesset, delivered the epitaph for Hammarskjold's efforts and those of the Security Council. "The armistice agreements are not an ideal solution and cannot last forever.... We are willing to implement the entire agreement on condition that the other side does the same. Otherwise the agreement does not exist and is not binding for us.... We must be prepared for attempts by great powers to dictate a settlement. We must muster all our strength so that we can say No to the greatest powers in the world...."[66]

The arms race continued. In June two Soviet destroyers and nineteen Czech torpedo boats arrived in Alexandria, while on the other side the original twelve Mystère fighter-bombers for Israel showed, in Eisenhower's words, "a rabbit-like capacity for multiplication."[67] Burns, who saw Ben-Gurion on June 28 in an effort to follow up Hammarskjold's arrangements to reinforce the cease-fire on the Gaza line, found him in a dangerous mood. On July 18, Hammarskjold himself returned to the Middle East, but his brief tour served mainly to show how much his influence had waned since April. He had gone to Jerusalem because he felt that his links with Ben-Gurion had worn very thin since the publication of his report to the Security Council. Ben-Gurion seemed to be under the impression that Israel had been treated less than fairly in the report and apparently also believed that the resolution in the Security Council had been watered down under Arab pressure at the suggestion of the Secretary-General. In eight hours' private conversation with Ben-Gurion, Hammarskjold succeeded to some extent in dispelling the Prime Minister's distrust, and he was more than ever convinced that his personal relationship with Ben-Gurion was the only basis on which he could ever hope to influence the Israelis, "super-sensitive as they are to the supposed element of pressure attached to my official capacity as agent of the Security Council and, through the Security Council, of the much suspected big Powers."[68] He could not know of the more dynamic aspects of current Israeli policy, which Ben-Gurion, not surprisingly, did not mention.

In Amman Hammarskjold sensed a feeling of great insecurity, and from Cairo he came away empty-handed and told Fawzi as much. He arrived in Cairo at the worst possible time, for Dulles had just formally notified the Egyptian Ambassador in Washington that no U.S. financing would be forthcoming for the Aswan High Dam, and the British and World Bank offers lapsed at the same time. This abrupt decision, which was taken and announced in a way that could hardly have been more insulting to Nasser and to Egypt,* opened a new chapter in the Middle East crisis. The Aswan High Dam, which Eugene Black, the President of the World Bank, called "the largest single structure ever undertaken in the history of the world,"[70] was the keystone of Nasser's plans for a dignified and prosperous Egypt. Its power and irrigation capacity were believed to represent the difference between catching up with the twentieth-century world and probably starving within a generation. Nasser had made clear his preference for Western aid in building the dam and had been in negotiation with the World Bank and with the United States over the terms for such aid since the previous October. The United States and Great Britain, for their part, were apparently anxious to forestall Soviet backing of such an important project. The World Bank was satisfied both with the desirability and feasibility of the project and with Egypt's capacity to play its part in realizing it. On July 15 the Egyptian Ambassador, Ahmed Hussein, had returned to Washington from Cairo with the news that Nasser had accepted the Western terms for giving assistance on the dam.

When Dulles, after minimal consultations with Eisenhower, informed Hussein on July 19 that the U.S. offer was canceled, he gave

---

* The British decision had in fact leaked in the *Times* of London for July 14 in an article that stated, "The attempt to stabilise the Middle East in cooperation with Egypt is now over."[69]

as a reason that the economic situation of Egypt made it not feasible for the United States to take part. The implication was that Egypt, in buying Russian arms, had mortgaged its economy to the U.S.S.R. to the point where Egypt could not fulfill its part of the dam project. The World Bank did not hold this view, and Senator J. William Fulbright later pointed out that since the Russian arms deal was one of the main reasons for the U.S. offer on the dam, it could hardly, in logic, also be the reason for withdrawing the offer. Eden, who was informed but not consulted about Dulles's decision, has written that Dulles called off the deal "for reasons connected with the Senate's attitude to foreign aid and the critical climate towards neutralism then prevalent in Washington,"[71] while Lodge told Nutting that the reason was internal U.S. political pressures resulting from anti-Arab lobbying in Congress and the reaction to Nasser's recognition of Peking. Eisenhower and others later alleged that Nasser had refused to discuss the details of the project, and Dulles developed the rationale that Nasser deliberately provoked the United States to renege on its offer in order to have a pretext for nationalizing the Suez Canal. Of all these confusing and contradictory explanations, the most likely seems to be that Dulles's emotional and missionary anti-Communism was aroused by Nasser's recognition of Peking, by his neutralism, and by the idea of Nasser as a traitor in the cold war. Certainly the decision seems to have been very much Dulles's own. "It was," Eugene Black said later, "a classic case where long-term policy was sacrificed because of short-term problems and irritations. And war came shortly after."[72]

Whatever the reasons for the withdrawal of U.S. aid for the Aswan High Dam and the consequent withdrawal of the British and World Bank offers, the effects were dramatic. When the news came through, Nasser was in Brioni, Yugoslavia, with Tito and Nehru. He seems to have decided quickly that if the door to Western financial aid for the dam had been closed, he would open a new door by taking over the foreign-currency earnings of the Suez Canal twelve years before it was to revert automatically to Egypt, a gesture which would also repay the United States and Great Britain for their rebuff to himself.

On July 26 Nasser announced the nationalization of the Canal and declared martial law in the Canal Zone. One of the most important results of this action was its repercussions in London. Eden, who had waited so long to inherit the leadership from Churchill, by mid-1956 was being labeled as indecisive and a ditherer even in the British Conservative press. He had been infuriated by Glubb's dismissal, which he wrongly attributed to Nasser, and was ready for any enterprise that would hurt the Egyptian leader. The nationalization of the Canal was the long-sought chance to go over to the offensive against Nasser. In Paris, the French government, with its increasing difficulties in Algeria, in which it suspected Nasser of being involved, needed little such stimulus, and Israel, by the nature of its position, was a ready and willing accomplice.

In the matter of the Egyptian nationalization of the Canal, Hammarskjold had as yet no formal status. He had refused to comment on Dulles's announcement of July 19, saying that "The United Nations has not that kind of judgment independent of its component members"[73] and that he himself was insufficiently informed to express any personal view. When asked on August 2 whether he believed that the nationalization was in violation of international law and, if not, whether the hysteria created in some Western countries had increased world tension, he dodged the question by saying: "My advice has not been considered that interesting on this question. I have been informed about certain aspects by the permanent representative of Egypt. That is all. We have not discussed it."[74]

The crisis over the Canal did not cause him to give up his efforts to get compliance with the armistice agreements. Serious incidents on the Israel-Jordan armistice demarcation line near Jerusalem on July 24 and 25,[75] starting on the Jordan side and leading to heavy Israeli reprisals, led him to appeal bluntly to both governments against any repetition of such incidents and to threaten the possibility of even calling a meeting of the Security Council under Article 99 of the Charter if things got worse.

In late August, perturbed by further raids and reprisals across the Gaza Line, Hammarskjold canceled a trip to Latin America. On August 23, Ben-Gurion wrote of Nasser's intentions, "You understand so much —can you not also understand that, for us, this is a matter of life and death? Can you expect us to share the complacency of Mr. [Foreign Minister D. T.] Shepilov and Mr. Dulles?"[76] In an interview with Burns, Ben-Gurion remarked bitterly that it was apparently easier for Hammarskjold to report to the Security Council on Israeli interference with the freedom of movement of UN observers than on the failure of his talks in Cairo. Then, in what later appeared to be an indication of Israeli plans, he said that the UN observation posts in Gaza had been useless and that Israel would be unlikely to accept them after October 31. Burns's report of this talk riled Hammarskjold sufficiently for him to write to Ben-Gurion of "your consistently negative attitude,"[77] and to complain bitterly that in all the months of effort Israel had not given him one card to play. Unless Israel's attitude changed, he told Ben-Gurion, he saw no point in visiting the Middle East again in October as he had planned, a piece of news that in the circumstances was probably more welcome to Israel than he had intended.

New and serious incidents on the Jordan-Israel line in mid-September caused Hammarskjold again to protest strongly to both countries.[78] Although he still refused to regard the cease-fire agreement achieved in May as defunct, he knew that the real challenge now lay elsewhere. "We have to live," he told Burns, "with the fact that, for the time being, all our problems will develop in the shadow of the Suez crisis."[79] He increasingly suspected that the Israelis were exploiting incidents to demonstrate their strength by intimidation, but he still refused to believe that they intended to embark on any major military operation. On September 26, he again brought the Jordan-Israel situation to the attention of the Council.[80] If the governments of Israel and Jordan did not bring the situation rapidly under control, he felt that the Council should take the matter up and decide what further measures should be taken.

Hammarskjold's final report[81] on the task the Security Council had given him in April recorded the failure of his effort to make the cease-fire clauses of the armistice agreements into independent and binding reciprocal legal obligations. It also recorded the collapse of his attempt to make a new kind of international arrangement in which the parties to a conflict, instead of engaging in direct negotiations, would give the Secretary-General assurances that would then be reported to the Security Council.

The last week of September saw new outbreaks in the Jerusalem sector that exacerbated Hammarskjold's dealings with Ben-Gurion, who commented that his condemnation of Israel's retaliation had had the effect of encouraging Egypt and Jordan to commit outrages. Hammarskjold replied:

> You are convinced that the threat of retaliation has a deterrent effect. I am convinced that it is more of an incitement to individual members of the Arab forces than even what has been said by their own Governments. You are convinced that acts of retaliation will stop further incidents. I am convinced that they will lead to further incidents. . . . You believe that this way of creating respect for Israel will pave the way for sound coexistence with the Arab peoples. I believe that the policy may postpone indefinitely the time for such coexistence. . . . I think the discussion of this question can be considered closed since you, in spite of previous discouraging experiences, have taken the responsibility for large-scale tests of the correctness of your belief.[82]

After this acrimonious exchange, Hammarskjold was surprised to receive a letter from Ben-Gurion regretting the increasing gulf between them. He had no desire, Ben-Gurion wrote, to find himself in disagreement with the representatives of the United Nations and he was abundantly aware of Israel's interest in maintaining the best possible relations with world public opinion and with the organs of the UN. He urged Hammarskjold to come to Israel again soon. "I am convinced that our talks in the past have been not only pleasant, but also useful, and—for me at least—instructive. . . . Whenever you may come, you will be a dear and honoured guest of my country. And if you are able to secure reciprocity in the observance of the armistice agreements, you will have achieved a very great thing for the welfare of all the peoples of the Middle East, and for the peace of the world."[83]

Hammarskjold responded warmly and appreciatively. Inevitable though it might be, he wrote, in the different situations each had to confront, that they drift apart, "I don't think that either of us would have respected the other one for compromises or evasions accepted solely in order to smooth out our differences. For me, however, the understanding established in our direct contacts has always remained a kind of 'ultimate reality.' "[84]* The Security Council meetings on the Suez question made it impossible for him to go to the Middle East immediately, he told Ben-Gurion, but he would look at the possibilities again in the next week or two.

Hammarskjold could not know that other plans were already afoot which would forcibly postpone his visit to Jerusalem for many months to come.

---

* A reference to the philosophical talks to which Hammarskjold and Ben-Gurion were both especially partial.

7

THE SUEZ
CRISIS

FROM AUGUST 1956 ONWARD, the Suez crisis developed on two separate levels—public efforts by governments within and outside the UN to find a peaceful solution, and clandestine maneuvers and preparations to break the Canal problem by force.[1] Although Hammarskjold must have had some inkling of the latter activities, his position as Secretary-General excluded him from publicly taking account of them. It later became known that there had been discussions between France and Israel as early as 1955 on the possibility of coordinated military action against Egypt, and the nationalization of the Suez Canal intensified these contacts. In early August there were more specific discussions in Paris, and on September 1 France informed Israel that Britain had now joined her in a contingency plan for action against Egypt called "Operation Musketeer."[2] On September 20, Premier Guy Mollet told Ben-Gurion that France was prepared to undertake a joint operation with Israel against Egypt.

The UN has no intelligence service, and Hammarskjold felt strongly that any intelligence-gathering activity would be entirely inappropriate for an international Secretariat serving a membership of sovereign states. In crises the Secretary-General must rely for the most part on his own judgment and knowledge and on such information as he may get from governments, UN field offices, and other more or less public sources. Thus over the Suez crisis, as in most other political conflicts, Hammarskjold was engaged in an international game of blindman's buff in which he was at a considerable initial disadvantage.

Although Hammarskjold had no direct knowledge of the British and French plans for using force to settle with Nasser or of the efforts of the U.S. government[3] to dissuade them, the mobilization of reserves in Great Britain and reports of military activity there and in France were alarming enough. The United States finally prevailed on the British to withhold military action until a conference of Suez Canal users could be called in London in mid-August to consider a peaceful solution to the Canal problem. Hammarskjold had maintained personal contact on Middle Eastern questions with Selwyn Lloyd, the British Foreign Secretary, throughout the difficult summer, and on August 7, in response to a personal message from Lloyd, he sent him "a few thoughts in the margin to the problem."[4] Although the maritime conference might serve a purpose if the object was to win over world opinion in support of a continued international management of the Canal, he thought that it was a mistake to have made no reference to the UN in announcing the conference. "You must remember," he told Lloyd, "that to a large part of the world the Canal Company* has not appeared as being 'universal' but as an agency of the most interested powers."[5] He himself believed that the Canal should be under international control "in the broadest sense of the word,"[6] and this meant that the UN would eventually have to be brought into the picture as "the only way to avoid making this a conflict between Europe and Asia."[7] This did not mean that the UN should have direct executive authority but rather that it might register an Egyptian declaration promising full freedom of passage, controlled perhaps by a UN commissioner who would report to the organization on the implementation of the declaration. Even this much would be difficult to sell to the Asian world, but it might be just within the limits of the possible.

When the proposals of the London Maritime Conference for the continued international control of the Canal with the participation of

---

* The Compagnie Universelle du Canal Maritime de Suez, a "state within a state," as the French consul-general in Egypt called it just before the Canal opened in November 1869, held the concession for the Suez Canal, in which Egypt had, at the beginning, 44 percent of the capital shares and a perpetual right to 15 percent royalties on the company's profits. In 1875 the Khedive Ismail sold all his shares to the British government, and in 1880 the 15 percent royalty was sold to a French investment syndicate. Thus Egypt, although claiming to have borne 40 percent of the cost of building the Canal, had no equity in the immensely profitable company at all, and retained only the concession agreement by which after ninety-nine years the Canal would revert to Egypt upon payment for the company's assets.

Egypt were rejected by Nasser, Dulles came up with another formula, the Suez Canal Users Association (SCUA). At the same time, Eden decided to make an appeal to the UN in a further attempt to persuade Egypt to accept the proposals of the London Conference. Dulles refused to join in this appeal, and on September 12 the British and French governments sent a note[8] to the President of the Security Council declaring that Egypt's refusal to negotiate the Suez problem on the basis of the London proposals was an aggravation of the situation that might well become a threat to peace and security. The letter contained no request for a Council meeting, and it seems to have been intended largely as a formal warning of trouble to come.* A second London Conference was to convene on September 19 to discuss the SCUA.

The gap between the British and French on the one side and the United States on the other over the Suez Canal question steadily widened. When the House of Commons was recalled on September 12 for a special debate on Suez, Eden declared, amid a tumult of derisive questions from the opposition, that if Egypt interfered or refused to cooperate with the SCUA, the British and other governments would feel free to take whatever steps were required, either through the UN or by other means. Dulles, on the other hand, stated in a press conference on September 13 that even if Egypt used force to block the Canal, "we do not intend to shoot our way through," and added that, as he understood it, Eden had not given any pledge to shoot Britain's way through the Canal either. This bland statement, coming in the midst of the emergency debate in the House of Commons, exasperated Eden still further. For good measure Premier Nikolai A. Bulganin, in a letter dated September 11, told Eden that the existence of the UN made it impossible any longer to issue threats and brandish weapons and that the principles of the Charter made it impossible for the Soviet Union not to side with Egypt on the question of the Canal. The reactions from both Washington and Moscow could hardly have been a clearer or more painful reminder to Eden of the new imperatives of superpower politics and of the waning world position of the former great colonial powers.

Hammarskjold continued to urge that the Canal problem, if it was not solved in the near future by other means, should be brought to the Security Council before the crisis became even graver, and he pointed out to Lloyd that if this was not done, he himself might feel obliged

---

* Selwyn Lloyd, speaking of a recourse to the UN, told Nutting, "We must set the stage." When Nutting asked if he meant setting the stage for war, he replied, "for war or for negotiation."[9]

to bring the matter to the Council under Article 99.* He told Lloyd that he believed that an arrangement could be found within the framework of the principles enunciated at the first London Conference that would fully safeguard Egyptian susceptibilities, while providing strong international guarantees, "stronger indeed than you had under the previous system,"[10] but he believed that such a solution could be found and given proper status only through the machinery of the United Nations.

In contrast to Eden's thinly veiled threats and to the accusatory tone of the Anglo-French note to the President of the Security Council, Egypt had, on September 10, made a conciliatory gesture. Cairo pointed out[11] that so far no other government had taken up Egypt's own declaration of its willingness to sponsor, with the other signatories of the Constantinople Convention,** a conference to review the Convention and to consider the conclusion of an agreement reaffirming and guaranteeing freedom of navigation in the Canal. Egypt believed that solutions could be found on three points: the freedom and safety of navigation in the Canal, the development of the Canal to meet future requirements, and the establishment of just and equitable tolls and charges. With this end in view, Cairo proposed the immediate establishment of a negotiating body that would represent the different views held by states using the Canal.

Hammarskjold wrote a commentary on this declaration, the text of which he later gave to the French, British and U.S. representatives. He urged the necessity of a negotiated solution of the Suez problem, although he felt that for practical reasons the negotiating body should be smaller than the total number of all the users of the Canal. It

---

* In a private memorandum at this time, Hammarskjold noted that Article 99 expected the Secretary-General to take action if the parties to a conflict, for reasons irrelevant to the main objectives of the Charter, did not themselves bring to the Security Council a matter threatening the maintenance of international peace. In such circumstances the Secretary-General would be obliged to bring the matter to the Council himself to prevent the machinery of the Charter being put out of action because the parties had not met their explicit obligations to use it.

** After the British occupation of Egypt in 1882, France, in the hope of weakening Britain's physical control of the Canal, unsuccessfully tried to mobilize European opinion in favor of internationalizing it. As a second-best objective, France sought the neutralization of the Canal, and in October 1888 the major powers of Europe joined in the Constantinople Convention, which declared in its first article that the Canal should always be free in time of war as in peace "to every vessel of commerce or of war, without distinction of flag."[12] Article X, however, provided that this declaration should not "interfere with the measures which His Majesty the [Ottoman] Sultan and His Highness the Khedive . . . might find it necessary to take for securing by their own forces the defense of Egypt and the maintenance of public order."[13] It was this article, originally a British reservation, which Egypt invoked to prohibit Israel, with which it was technically at war, from using the Canal.

seemed natural to him that the matter should be brought before the Security Council under Article 37 of the Charter* with the single aim of asking the Council to invite a restricted number of member nations to set up a committee on the Suez question that might explore ways and means of achieving the three objectives mentioned by Egypt. If the committee could agree on something, the results might be submitted to the Security Council, which might then pass them on either to all the users of the Canal or to the General Assembly, where all the users were represented. To these suggestions Fawzi replied that the Egyptian government also wished to form a small negotiating body, to be agreed upon either through diplomatic channels or otherwise.

On September 16, Eden took a more moderate tone in reply to Bulganin's warning. The British government's aim, he said, was to seek a peaceful solution through negotiation, inquiry, mediation, and conciliation. He reminded Bulganin that in 1946 the Soviet government had proclaimed its support for international control of the Canal. This was precisely the aim of his own government and was fully consistent both with Egypt's sovereignty and with the Charter of the UN. On September 15 many of the non-Egyptian Canal pilots had walked out, apparently at the instigation and inducement of the French and British governments. This action, which was confidently expected in some British quarters to paralyze the Canal, had little if any effect, and the Egyptian Canal Authority was soon able to announce that normal traffic was going through with no difficulty whatsoever.

The second London Conference on the Canal ended on September 21 with the decision to establish a Suez Canal Users Association to protect the rights of the Canal users under the Constantinople Convention, with due regard also for the rights of Egypt. The possibility of SCUA's success was summed up by Dulles when, in his concluding remarks at the Conference, he said, "The extent of its practical utility will of course depend much, though not wholly, upon Egypt's attitude."[14]

British and French lack of confidence in the future of SCUA was underlined in a joint letter to the President of the Security Council in which the two governments asked him to convene the Council to consider the "situation created by the unilateral action of the Egyptian Government in bringing to an end the system of international operation of the Suez Canal, which was confirmed and completed by the Suez Canal Convention of 1888."[15] Dulles, with whom Lloyd had dis-

---

* Article 37, paragraph 1, provides that if the parties to any dispute liable to endanger the maintenance of international peace and security fail to settle their dispute by peaceful means, they shall refer it to the Security Council.

cussed the possibility of a further approach to the UN, was not informed in advance of the Anglo-French letter.* On the following day, September 24, Egypt filed a counteritem, asking for a meeting of the Council to consider "Actions against Egypt by some Powers, particularly France and the United Kingdom, which constitute a danger to international peace and security and are serious violations of the Charter of the United Nations."[17]

While the Council was meeting on September 26 to consider both of these items, Eden and Lloyd flew to Paris to consult with their French counterparts, Guy Mollet and Christian Pineau, who, although they did not yet disclose their joint military plans with Israel, wholeheartedly endorsed Eden's view that if the Security Council failed to agree on a just solution, Britain and France should be ready to use all the measures necessary to resolve the dispute, including force. The Council adjourned its meeting until October 5 so that the Foreign Ministers of Egypt, France, and Great Britain could attend. Elsewhere, and in the greatest secrecy, time was not being wasted. On October 1, General Dayan and Shimon Peres, the Director General of the Israel Ministry of Defense, were in Paris for talks with the French general staff and although there were no precise discussions of the Suez expedition, Dayan on his return to Israel the next day gave orders for the preparation of an operation against Egypt to commence on October 20.

In September there had been serious incidents between Israel and Jordan that had led to talk of supporting Iraqi forces entering Jordan, and this provided a useful cover for Israeli military preparations. Ben-Gurion had already agreed in principle to provide the pretext for a French expedition to seize the Canal. British participation was desirable, especially to provide initial airstrikes from Cyprus to destroy the Egyptian air force on its airfields. It seems likely that Eden heard of this plan on October 3 from Pineau, who visited London on his way to the Security Council meeting in New York, for on the same day he was reported to have told the Cabinet that "the Jews had come up with an offer"[18] which might give Britain and France an opportunity to launch Musketeer. Eden's disillusionment with Dulles had been intensified when the Secretary of State, after attending the meeting to inaugurate SCUA, had told a press conference that there were "no teeth"[19] in SCUA and had pointedly dissociated the United States from the attitude of "so-called colonialism."[20] Pineau on his arrival in

---

* Macmillan, who was in Washington, describes in his Memoirs, *Riding the Storm*, Dulles's indignation at this Anglo-French move: "From the way Dulles spoke you would have thought he was warning us against entering a bawdy house." Dulles prophesied that Britain and France would "get nothing but trouble in New York."[16]

New York told Dulles there was no peaceful way out of the crisis and that the capitulation of Nasser was the only solution. On October 6, General Sir Charles Keightley, who was to command the Suez expedition, ordered his task-force commanders to prepare a "winter plan"[21] for Operation Musketeer to be ready at ten days' notice. In the midst of these conspiratorial doings, about which the United States had its suspicions but was not informed, Eisenhower asked himself what Britain and France were really doing in the Security Council and was "apprehensive"[22] that they might merely be "setting . . . the stage for the eventual use of force in Suez."[23]

Notwithstanding all of this clandestine activity, on October 5 the Foreign Ministers of France and Britain were at their places at the horseshoe table of the Security Council and ostensibly ready to discuss the Suez problem with the Foreign Minister of Egypt. Among other Foreign Ministers also present were Dulles, Paul Henri Spaak of Belgium, Shepilov of the U.S.S.R., Koča Popović of Yugoslavia, and Krishna Menon of India.

France and Britain immediately introduced a draft resolution,[24] which, among other things, endorsed the proposals reached by the majority of the London Canal Users Conference, including the establishment of an International Board for the Canal, as a basis for negotiations with Egypt. Although Shepilov categorically opposed the Anglo-French proposal, Fawzi, perhaps partly because of pressures on Egypt to negotiate a settlement of the Canal dispute from Europe, the oil-producing Arab states, and India, showed a desire to compromise and suggested that any negotiations should be based on three principles: cooperation between Egypt and the users of the Canal to take account of the former's sovereign rights and the latter's interests, a fair system of tolls and charges, and the earmarking of a reasonable portion of the Canal's revenues for its development and improvement. The concession by Egypt of the principle of user participation appeared to establish a basis for negotiations that had not existed since the Canal had been nationalized. With the support of Dulles, who was alarmed at the growing evidence that Britain and France wanted, and were preparing for, war with Egypt, Hammarskjold therefore took the initiative of calling Lloyd, Pineau, and Fawzi into private consultations in his office to see if some agreement could be reached. "I will be acting merely as a chaperon," he told Dulles, who replied, "My understanding of a chaperon is a person whose job is to keep two people apart. Your job is to get the parties together."[25]

The first of these consultations took place on October 9. It was agreed that the talks were purely exploratory and without commitment for any of the participants. Fawzi reaffirmed that the basis for exploring existing possibilities was the full acceptance by Egypt of its obligations under the Constantinople Convention of 1888, and went on to discuss how the principles of that convention could be guaranteed by a system of cooperation between Egypt and the Canal users, organized in some form of association. There would have to be some form of arbitration machinery to settle differences expeditiously and effectively, and also a procedure for enforcing arbitration decisions on both parties. Fawzi was noncommittal on the method of payment of tolls and charges and on the question whether pilots could be provided by the Users Association as well as by the Egyptian Canal Authority. He also sidestepped a question from Lloyd about freedom of navigation for Israel, saying that he would prefer to discuss it at a later stage. He agreed, however, that the operation of the Canal should be insulated from the influence of the politics of any one nation.

The next day there was a discussion of the Constantinople Convention and of a name for the "system of cooperation"[26] proposed by Fawzi. Lloyd and Pineau asked pointedly whether Egypt accepted the Users Association recently set up in London, to which Fawzi reacted noncommittally and cautiously, pointing out that some clauses in the Association's statute would be impossible to reconcile with the system envisaged by Egypt. Lloyd urged the advantages of the Association for both parties. Fawzi was noncommittal on the method of payment of decisive importance to the success of the talks. There was an inconclusive discussion of the Association's role in the collection and payment of dues.

On October 11, Fawzi, after receiving no reply to his questions about the nature of the Users Association, volunteered to produce suggestions on arbitration machinery and on tolls and charges. Pineau suggested brusquely that the Western powers should submit to the Egyptian government a clear questionnaire requiring clear replies, and he dropped this suggestion only when Hammarskjold objected to it on the ground that the new system had to encompass both the insulation of the Canal from national politics and the question of the guarantee of free passage. Lloyd then suggested five principles for discussion, but Fawzi objected that these five principles were simply a quotation of the London principles, on which he understood that they had all agreed to turn their backs. Hammarskjold intervened to say that the fact that principles had been stated in London should not necessarily bar them from discussion, and Fawzi then admitted that Lloyd's principles might be acceptable if they were presented in a new context.

The next morning, Hammarskjold put before the three Foreign Ministers his notes on the previous discussion as to principles, arrangements, tolls, and compensation for the old Canal Company. Fawzi suggested only two very minor editing changes, and Pineau had no objection to the principles. He could not, he said, discuss other matters and wished to avoid giving the impression of greater progress than had actually been made. At the time, Hammarskjold noted that "everybody was in various ways protecting himself in relation to his own government, while, in fact, he was agreed on the paper."[27]

He had noticed in particular that Pineau's attitude had become totally negative by the last day of the talks, and that Lloyd was upset at the news that France had sent seventy-five Mystère aircraft to Israel. While Hammarskjold realized that Pineau wished to slow down the talks, he could not know the extent of Pineau's dilemma and learned the full truth only two years later when Anthony Nutting dined with him in New York in May 1958. Unlike Lloyd, who became aware of the Anglo-French-Israeli collusion plan only on his return to London on October 14, Pineau was already fully aware of his government's joint plans with Israel. For those plans to be put into action, it was essential to maintain the deadlock over the Canal at the United Nations. The obvious way to do this was to insist on the eighteen-power London proposals that Nasser had already rejected, and it must have been a blow to Pineau when Hammarskjold persuaded Fawzi on October 11 that the London principles, as put forward by Lloyd, would be acceptable if framed in a new context. With this basis for negotiation clearly in sight, Pineau was in serious difficulty, for he either had to go along with the negotiations for a peaceful settlement and spoil the military plans or else go back on all his government's public statements of the need for such a settlement.

On October 11, Reuters quoted Pineau as saying that there was no progress in the talks and no basis for negotiation. "There has only been a lot of words," he said. "Tomorrow will be the last meeting. I am leaving Saturday afternoon as planned." Fawzi, who later told the British Ambassador in Cairo that he realized all along that Pineau was negotiating in bad faith, ignored this blatant attempt to break up the talks and continued to work for an understanding. The result of his and Hammarskjold's persistence was that on the afternoon of October 12 the three Foreign Ministers agreed that Hammarskjold could use his summary of the previous day's discussion as he liked in reporting to the Security Council. It was also agreed that the Foreign Ministers and the Secretary-General would meet again in Geneva on October 29 to work out practical methods of implementing the principles. The following six principles were accepted:

1. Free and open passage through the Canal;

2. Respect of Egypt's sovereignty;
3. Insulation of the operation of the Canal from the politics of any country;
4. Egypt and the users to agree on tolls and charges;
5. Allotment of a fair proportion of the dues to development of the Canal; and
6. Arbitration to settle affairs between Egypt and the old Canal Company.

Fawzi, urged on by Hammarskjold, had made significant concessions.* Although he had rejected the London proposals for an international body to control the Canal, he had accepted the principle of organized cooperation between Egypt and the Canal users and even a measure of control by the users over the allocation of Canal revenues for maintenance and development. He had agreed to the arbitration of disputes, to negotiation of tolls and charges, and to acceptance of the Constantinople Convention and of all previous rules and regulations for the administration of the Canal. In fact, he had undertaken to negotiate an agreement which gave the maritime powers most of what they wanted and which would convert the Users Association into a working body that would cooperate with the Egyptian government rather than defying it. At last it seemed possible that the Canal might after all be run as a partnership between Egypt and the users.

That this was not to be became evident when Hammarskjold presented his report on the Foreign Ministers' talks to a private meeting of the Security Council. Ignoring Fawzi's warnings, Lloyd, on instructions from Eden, and Pineau proceeded to make a pointed comparison with the London proposals and entirely omitted to repeat what they had said in Hammarskjold's office about their willingness to recommend what had been agreed.

Developments outside the UN were no less confusing and discouraging. Substituting at the last minute for Lord Salisbury, Anthony Nutting on October 11 delivered Salisbury's militant speech to the Conservative Party Conference. "Britain and France," he said, ". . . mean business and will stand firm. If the United Nations does not do its duty, we must do ours. . . . If this hard test should come upon us . . . I do not believe this country will flinch from it."** The next evening

---

* Macmillan, on the other hand, maintains in *Riding the Storm* that the British made a major concession in accepting Egyptian management of the Canal and an international committee empowered to act if the principles were disregarded, but that Fawzi in return offered only "fair words."[28]
** Nutting's doubts about delivering this speech were followed by his eventual resignation over the Suez adventure.

Eisenhower underlined the lack of rapport among the Western allies by saying on television, "A very great crisis is behind us. . . . We sat down and we were determined to pursue a course that would not lead to war. We were certain a negotiation could settle this problem."*

On October 13, Eden further showed his dissatisfaction with the prospect of a negotiated settlement by instructing Lloyd to press to a vote in the Security Council the substance of the original Anglo-French resolution. The resolution[30] introduced by Lloyd, after stating the six principles agreed to by Fawzi, went on to insist on the eighteen-power London proposals as the only right and proper method of putting these principles into practice. It ignored Fawzi's concessions and curtly invited Egypt to formulate precise proposals "promptly." As was evidently intended by its authors, Fawzi rejected the whole operative part of the Anglo-French resolution, and his rejection was backed by the Soviet veto. This rejection, by which the original deadlock survived the perils of Fawzi's concessions, also made it possible to show Egypt and the Soviet Union publicly allied against the West, thereby relieving Eden and the French government of the unwelcome possibility of a negotiated settlement.

Apprehensive though he was about the attitude of the British and French, Hammarskjold felt obliged to try to maintain the momentum toward agreement that had developed during the talks in his office. In the Security Council, Dulles had suggested that Hammarskjold might "continue to encourage"[31] direct interchanges between Egypt, France, and Great Britain, and Hammarskjold announced[32]** that he would pursue his efforts to promote an agreement. His consultations with Fawzi resulted, on October 24, in a letter[33] to the Egyptian that pinned down the concessions made by Fawzi in New York and proposed a plan for the operation of the Canal and a method of cooperation between Egypt and the body representing the Canal users, the object being at the same time to protect the users' rights and interests and to avoid interference with the administrative functions of the Egyptian Canal Authority. He received Fawzi's reply on November 2,[34] four days after the Suez fighting had started. It confirmed that, with the exception of one small point, Fawzi shared Hammarskjold's view that the framework he had suggested was sufficiently wide to make another search for a basis for negotiation worth trying. By the time Hammarskjold received this reply, however, all hope of an agreed settlement had van-

---

* In his memoirs Eisenhower corrected this lapse into optimism, remarking only that "On Tuesday afternoon, the 9th, the French, British and Egyptians got together but nothing productive resulted."[29]
** After the Council adopted Resolution S/3675 of October 13, 1956.

ished in the confusion of the Anglo-French-Israeli military adventure.

While the Canal talks were going on in New York, developments on the Israel-Jordan line[35] served to divert attention from the real course of events. In an unusually massive reprisal raid, Israel attacked the town of Qalqiliya, northeast of Tel Aviv, on the night of October 10, and forty-eight Jordanians and eighteen Israelis were killed before Burns managed to arrange a cease-fire the next morning. Egypt, Iraq, and Syria offered help to Jordan, and Britain announced that it would go to the assistance of Jordan if Israel reacted with force to the stationing of Iraqi troops in Jordan, which Eden had suggested in an attempt to forestall a request from Jordan for Egyptian help. France, in an effort to save the projected Anglo-French-Israeli effort against Egypt, put pressure on Eden to stop the Iraqi move, and Israel demanded that it be called off altogether. Dayan later noted in his diary: "I must confess to the feeling that, save for the Almighty, only the British are capable of complicating affairs to such a degree. At the very moment when they are preparing to topple Nasser, who is a common enemy of theirs and Israel's, they insist on getting the Iraqi Army into Jordan, even if such action leads to war between Israel and Jordan in which they, the British, will take part against Israel."[36]

On October 15, Jordan asked for an urgent meeting of the Security Council.[37] Ben-Gurion, after paying due tribute to Hammarskjold's efforts, attacked the UN in the Knesset for the "double standard"[38] by which it ignored Arab violations of UN decisions but stigmatized Israel for reprisals. He also denounced the UN's failure to enforce the 1951 Security Council decision on freedom of navigation in the Canal. Hammarskjold regarded this statement as "a sweeping public indictment of the United Nations and its agents. . . . In my treatment of the Palestine problem," he told the Israel representative, Reginald Kidron, "nothing now seems to remain but the duties of the Chief Executive Officer of the Organization, concerning the role of which Mr. Ben-Gurion has so clearly indicated his views."[39]

This was a sideshow while the real drama was being prepared elsewhere. Premier Mollet had apparently decided that the best way to overcome Eden's reluctance to call off the move of Iraqi troops into Jordan was to broach the idea of a concerted Anglo-French-Israeli move to seize the Canal. On October 14, Eden was informed in detail by French emissaries of the plan to use an Israeli attack as the pretext for a French—and at best an Anglo-French—expedition to secure the Canal. Selwyn Lloyd, who had been ordered back from New York by Eden on October 16, arrived in London in a mood of cautious optimism over the possibility of a negotiated Canal settlement. He was soon persuaded that Nasser could not be trusted to honor any agreement and was whisked off by Eden to Paris the very same afternoon for talks with Pineau and Mollet. The four leaders, in a magnificently obscure communiqué on October 17, concluded that they had "decided to maintain constant contact . . . in the spirit of the closest Anglo-French friendship."[40]

Not surprisingly, Hammarskjold heard no more from Lloyd and Pineau about a new meeting with Fawzi on October 29, nor was there any response when he sent them a copy of his letter to Fawzi. There followed instead a brief, uneasy lull, during which rumors flourished. To many people it seemed that Israel was about to attack Jordan, and Eisenhower speculated[41] that the days preceding the U.S. Presidential election might be a tempting time for Ben-Gurion to embark on a major military expedition. American suspicions were heightened by a sudden absence of contact with France and Great Britain and a dramatic increase in coded radio traffic between Paris and Tel Aviv. The U.S. Ambassador in London, Winthrop Aldrich, reported that Walter Monckton, who had resigned from the British government ostensibly for reasons of health, had told him that he believed that the use of force against Egypt would be a great blunder.[42] On October 25, Egypt, Jordan and Syria announced the Pact of Amman, providing for increased military cooperation and placing all their armed forces under an Egyptian commander in the event of war. Reports of mobilization in Israel brought a plea from Eisenhower for restraint, to which Ben-Gurion replied that such moves were purely defensive.[43]

Another grave crisis had now arisen. On October 22 the first news of disturbances in Hungary began to reach New York, and the next day it became clear that a full-scale uprising was in progress and that Soviet forces would be brought in to deal with it. Widespread fighting was soon reported between the insurgents, Soviet forces, and Hungarian forces loyal to the Hungarian regime, and on Sunday, October 28, the UN Security Council voted to consider the question of Soviet action in Hungary.[44]

The following day, France complained to the Security Council that a vessel intercepted off the coast of Algeria contained arms and munitions loaded by Egyptian troops in Alexandria and was accompanied by six French nationals from Algeria "who had attended terrorist courses at Cairo."[45] Dulles, whose suspicions of British and French intentions had steadily increased, summoned the British and French chargés d'affaires in Washington, both ambassadors being absent, to tell them that if fighting started in the Middle East, the United States would ask the UN to stop it and would request and expect full support from Britain and France.

Israel launched its attack against Egypt on October 29, with the avowed intention of eliminating the fedayeen bases from which terrorist raids had been made against Israeli territory. A parachute battalion dropped in the Mitla Pass, forty miles east of Suez, was soon reinforced by Israeli troops driving through the Sinai Desert. Another column drove for Ismailia in the middle of the Canal, while a further expedition, launched against Rafah and El Arish at the southern end of the Gaza Strip, effectively sealed off the Strip from Egypt. Yet another force headed down the west coast of Sinai on the Gulf of Aqaba to take Sharm el Sheikh and Ras Nasrani, the positions from which Egypt could shell Israeli shipping entering the Gulf of Aqaba.

Hammarskjold heard the news of the Israeli action just before the Security Council was due to meet on the French complaint about Egyptian assistance to the Algerian rebels. The Council adjourned in some bewilderment at 3:25 p.m., and Hammarskjold let it be known that he would, if necessary, take the initiative in bringing the new crisis before the Council, but that he could do this only when more complete information was available. Eisenhower and Dulles had already agreed on a statement of U.S. determination to stand by the 1950 Tripartite Agreement, which pledged support to any victim of aggression in the Middle East, and Eisenhower told the British chargé d'affaires in Washington, "We plan to get to the United Nations the first thing in the morning—when the doors open, . . . before the U.S.S.R. gets there."[46] Actually the U.S. decided to ask that very evening for an immediate meeting of the Security Council on the Israeli invasion of Egypt.[47]

Hammarskjold heard of the U.S. decision over the radio at 9 p.m. but was unable to contact Lodge, who was attending the opening night of the Metropolitan Opera. He finally managed to contact James Barco, Lodge's deputy, who said he would call back as soon as he received definite instructions from Washington. Barco hurried to the Metropolitan Opera House to tell Lodge of Washington's decision to call an emergency meeting of the Security Council to try to stop the Israelis. When Lodge told Pierson Dixon, who was also at the opera, of the U.S. decision, Dixon went pale and snapped, "Don't be so damned high-minded."[48] This reaction gave Lodge the perhaps mistaken idea that Dixon knew a great deal more about the situation than he was prepared to admit. Meanwhile the President of the Security Council, Bernard Cornut-Gentille of France, told Hammarskjold he was shocked to have first received news of the U.S. initiative over the radio, since, as President of the Council, he should have been informed before it was published. Hammarskjold visited Cornut-Gentille in his apartment and found him in an aggressive mood since he felt that the U.S. had both by-passed France and slighted him as President of the Council. Cornut-Gentille thus inadvertently proved his personal innocence of the collusion. His government, he said, was against the U.S. move.* Hammarskjold sought to mollify him, saying that the United States probably had information not available to either of them and that in any case the President of the Council must act on a request from a member, irrespective of his views either on the procedure adopted or on the substance of the request. At this point Lodge and Barco arrived from the opera and confirmed the U.S. request for an immediate meeting of the Security Council.

On October 30, Mollet and Pineau flew to London, ostensibly to draw up the Anglo-French ultimatum to Egypt and Israel, although it had in fact been written some days before. The ultimatum, which was delivered at 4 p.m. on the thirtieth, gave Egypt and Israel twelve hours to cease hostilities, called upon their military forces to withdraw to a distance of ten miles on each side of the Canal, and further requested Egypt to allow Anglo-French forces to be stationed temporarily on the Canal at Port Said, Ismailia, and Suez with the aim of separating the belligerents and ensuring the safety of shipping. By previous arrangement the ultimatum was accepted at once by Israel, but its anticipated rejection by Egypt opened the way for the Anglo-French invasion, which was to start with bombing of Egyptian airfields and other military installations by British aircraft based on Cyprus.

Hammarskjold gave the Security Council[49] the gist of messages[50] received from General Burns, who in the early hours of October 30 had requested Israel to withdraw its troops from Sinai and to cease firing. The cease-fire request was also made to Egypt. Burns also reported the expulsion by Israel on the previous day of the UN observer team from El Auja on the main axis of the Israeli advance. The first news of the Anglo-French ultimatum became generally known during the Security Council meeting when Sobolev read out an Associated Press report. Dixon, much taken aback, said lamely that he was waiting for the text of an important statement by Eden to the House of Commons, and the Council adjourned until the afternoon, at which time Dixon, obviously shaken, read out Eden's statement and the Anglo-French ultimatum. Lodge then introduced a resolution[51] demanding Israeli withdrawal and stating that compliance by Israel with the resolution would remove the basis for the Anglo-French ultimatum. The Council was then treated to the unprecedented spectacle of a U.S. resolution being vetoed by Britain and France. In an only slightly less surprising sequel, the Soviet Union resubmitted the U.S. resolu-

---

* On October 31, Cornut-Gentille collapsed from heart trouble brought on by nervous exhaustion.

tion, in an amended form[52] suggested by Nationalist China and Iran which omitted the clause calling on all UN members to refrain from the use or threat of force. This too was vetoed by Britain and France.

The Anglo-French ultimatum shocked and outraged Hammarskjold. In spite of rumors, hints, and disturbing pieces of evidence, he found it hard to believe that two permanent members of the Security Council, the two Western European countries which he most admired and which he believed to represent the best traditions of European civilization, could be guilty of so shoddy a deception or of so disastrous a course of action. His feelings were reflected in the statement of principle he made at the opening of the next meeting of the Security Council on October 31. For the first time he publicly rebuked two governments, and two great powers at that, and served notice that there were situations in which he felt obliged to enter the political arena as an active participant:

> The principles of the Charter are, by far, greater than the Organization in which they are embodied, and the aims which they are to safeguard are holier than the policies of any single nation or people. As a servant of the Organization the Secretary-General has the duty to maintain his usefulness by avoiding public stands on conflicts between Member nations unless and until such an action might help to resolve the conflict. However, the discretion and impartiality thus imposed on the Secretary-General by the character of his immediate task may not degenerate into a policy of expediency. He must also be a servant of the principles of the Charter, and its aims must ultimately determine what for him is right and wrong. For that he must stand. A Secretary-General cannot serve on any other assumption than that—within the necessary limits of human frailty and honest differences of opinion—all Member nations honor their pledge to observe all Articles of the Charter. He should also be able to assume that those organs which are charged with the task of upholding the Charter will be in a position to fulfill their task.
>
> The bearing of what I have just said must be obvious to all without any elaboration from my side. Were the Members to consider that another view of the duties of the Secretary-General than the one here stated would better serve the Organization, it is their obvious right to act accordingly.[53]

The immediate result of this statement was a series of speeches by Lodge, Cornut-Gentille in his dual capacity as President of the Council and Representative of France, Sobolev, Dixon, and other members of the Council, assuring Hammarskjold of their confidence and asking him to continue in office. The statement was misinterpreted by some as signifying his intention to resign, although in order to avert any such misunderstanding he had shown it to the permanent members before the Council meeting. Dixon had at first reacted angrily, saying that Hammarskjold wasn't playing fair, to which Hammarskjold replied that he well knew what he was doing and that it was hardly the moment for the British representative to be talking about "playing fair." Lodge characterized it as a "major bomb," while Cornut-Gentille told Hammarskjold that he appreciated both the motive and aim of the statement.

With the Security Council frustrated by the French and British vetoes, the Yugoslav representative offered a resolution[54] under the Uniting for Peace resolution,* proposing that the current crisis be referred to an Emergency Special Session of the General Assembly. This proposal was adopted over the objections of Britain and France, which, since it was a procedural matter, had no power of veto. The British bombing of Egyptian airfields and other military targets started that night.

What Hugh Gaitskell, the leader of the Opposition in the British House of Commons, called "an act of disastrous folly,"[55] produced an unprecedented atmosphere of shock and disbelief at the UN. The representatives of France and Great Britain, ignorant of their governments' intentions, found themselves in an agonizing position, and while their public statements caused general indignation, their personal dilemma and obvious dismay evoked considerable sympathy. "The effort of concealing these feelings," Sir Pierson Dixon wrote later, "and putting a plausible and confident face on the case was the severest moral and physical strain I have ever experienced."[56] It was in this atmosphere that the first Emergency Special Session of the Assembly[57] opened at 5 p.m. on November 1 and continued, with a two-hour break, until 4:20 a.m. the following day. The Assembly adopted a cease-fire resolution[58] that also urged the withdrawal of the Israeli, French, and British forces and the reopening of the Suez Canal, which the Egyptians had blocked at numerous points as soon as the British bombing began. Lester Pearson, speaking for Canada, announced that he would abstain from voting on the cease-fire resolution on the ground that it was "inadequate to achieve the purposes which we have in mind at this session."[59]

---

* The Uniting for Peace resolution—377 A(V) part A of November 3, 1950, para. A.1— reads as follows: "Resolves that if the Security Council, because of lack of unanimity of the permanent members, fails to exercise its primary responsibility for the maintenance of international peace and security in any case where there appears to be a threat to the peace, breach of the peace, or act of aggression, the General Assembly shall consider the matter immediately with a view to making appropriate recommendations to Members for collective measures, including in the case of a breach of the peace or act of aggression the use of armed force when necessary to maintain or restore international peace and security." The constitutionality of this device, originally designed by the United States to circumvent the Soviet veto in the Security Council, had always been challenged by the U.S.S.R.

Before the emergency meeting of the Assembly, Pearson told Hammarskjold that he thought a United Nations force might become necessary. Hammarskjold was initially very doubtful of the practical possibility of such an idea, and Pearson himself, although his government had given him a free hand, was evidently having trouble in formulating such a proposal for public presentation, for he withdrew his name from the speakers' list several times before he presented the idea to the Assembly in the early hours of the morning of November 2.* Pearson suggested that the Secretary-General be authorized "to begin to make arrangements with Member States for a United Nations Force large enough to keep these borders at peace while a political settlement is being worked out . . . a truly international peace and police force,"[60] and he added that he would be willing to recommend Canadian participation in such a force. Dixon endorsed Pearson's suggestion saying that "if the United Nations were willing to take over the physical task of maintaining peace in the area, no one would be better pleased than we."[61] At about the same time in the House of Commons, Eden suggested somewhat condescendingly that "a United Nations force should eventually be associated with the Anglo-French police action."[62]**

During a political crisis at the UN the days and nights are filled with endless contacts, meetings, maneuvers, arrangements, drafting of cables, speeches, telephone calls, interviews with ambassadors, dealings with the press, and making formal reports to the Security Council or the General Assembly. In all this hubbub the Secretary-General must keep a clear head and a balanced picture of the situation. He must preserve an imaginative, constructive, and forward-looking approach to a constantly shifting series of problems and a kaleidoscopic panorama of changing national policies. Hammarskjold, by his capacity for concentration and thinking ahead, was a master at this game and dominated these hectic periods by his stamina, intellectual energy, imagination, and skill in political and legal drafting and in thinking out ways around apparently insurmountable obstacles. He was instantly and instinctively aware of the ramifications and possible repercussions

---

* Pearson encountered another difficulty when he called the Canadian Minister of Defense to ask what military units Canada might make available for a UN force. The units available were the Queen's Own Rifles and the Black Watch, two names which, as Pearson noted, could hardly have been more unfortunate.

** The idea of a United Nations force was not quite as novel as was generally thought at the time. In November 1955, General Burns had discussed with Anthony Nutting, the British Minister of State, the possibility of introducing UN troops between the armed forces of Israel and Egypt. Burns said at the time that he didn't think this would be possible without prior military intervention by the great powers. "This turns out," Burns wrote later, "to have been a good prediction."[63]

of any given course of action and almost automatically thought out in advance the combinations of results, both good and bad, that could be expected from a particular move, as well as the alternative moves that might be made. His quiet but commanding personality was very effective in periods of crisis, not least because there is a tendency at such times for everyone to believe that he is playing a unique and indispensable role. In such circumstances only firm and unquestioned leadership can provide the impetus required to keep all the various participants moving in relative harmony and in the same direction.

Before anything else could be done, it was essential to secure compliance with the Assembly's call for a cease-fire. The Anglo-French air offensive against Egypt was now in full swing, while the Israeli forces appeared to have achieved their first objectives and were approaching the Canal from the eastern side. Anglo-French landings were presumed to be imminent, but the troops were in fact making the five-day sea trip from Cyprus, and the first parachute drop on Port Said and Port Fouad did not take place until dawn on November 5, followed up by landings from the sea.

The idea that the cease-fire should actually be negotiated by the Secretary-General first came up late on the night of November 2 when Hammarskjold was visited at home by Djalal Abdoh, the permanent representative of Iran, who asked him on behalf of the Afro-Asian group to intervene personally to negotiate a cease-fire. Hammarskjold pointed out that the Assembly resolution had not requested the Secretary-General to take any initiative for the implementation of the cease-fire but said that he would not object to a proposal that might authorize him to negotiate the cease-fire himself.

On November 3 the first reaction of Great Britain and France to the Assembly's cease-fire resolution was received. With the Anglo-French invasion force at sea between Cyprus and Egypt, both governments could hardly do otherwise than proclaim their firm intention to persevere in their adventure. Their initial replies[64] to Hammarskjold, therefore, maintained the fiction that they were carrying out a police action to stop the Israeli-Egyptian hostilities now threatening the Canal and to pave the way for a settlement of the Arab-Israeli conflict. They were prepared to stop their own military action as soon as Israel and Egypt agreed to accept a UN force to keep the peace and ensure a satisfactory arrangement on the Suez Canal. Egypt had accepted[65] the Assembly's cease-fire resolution on condition that the attacking armies did not continue their aggression, but after hearing the Anglo-French response the Egyptian permanent representative asked for a meeting of the Assembly that same night to consider the continued failure of the British and French to honor the cease-fire.

The Israeli forces had achieved all their objectives and, in accordance with the Anglo-French ultimatum, were waiting for the Anglo-French expedition to take over in the Suez Canal area. There was no reason, therefore, why Israel should not agree to an immediate cease-fire, and Israel announced its acceptance "provided a similar answer is forthcoming from Egypt."[66]

In the meantime, the Afro-Asian group had gone ahead with the plan to involve Hammarskjold in the negotiation of the cease-fire. Their resolution in its original draft had merely "requested" the Secretary-General to undertake this duty, but Hammarskjold said he preferred the word "authorize," as this would make it clear that he would negotiate on behalf of the General Assembly. The resolution, adopted[67] early on the morning of November 4, authorized the Secretary-General and General Burns to obtain compliance of France, Great Britain, and Israel to the withdrawal of all forces behind the armistice demarcation lines.

Hammarskjold's second pressing task was to develop the concept of the UN force. Despite prolonged discussions with Pearson, he was still skeptical of the practicability of Pearson's idea, which originally envisaged a combination of UN troops and the Anglo-French forces, with the objectives of legitimizing the Anglo-French invasion, getting the British and French off the hook, and staving off a permanent split in the Western alliance and perhaps also the collapse of the Commonwealth. Hammarskjold saw the political impossibility of such a move, but in discussion with Pearson the two men began to see a way out of the difficulty. Hammarskjold's doubts about establishing an effective UN force persisted up to November 4, when he cabled to Burns: "Our main concern is of course whether it is at all possible within a reasonable time to establish such a group with the peculiar conditions which must apply in the choice of nations from which recruitment can take place. My personal lack of optimism is of course no excuse for not exploring the field."[68]

Pearson had written a draft resolution suggesting the establishment of an Assembly committee to explore the possibilities of a UN force, but Lodge suggested that to save time Hammarskjold himself should undertake the necessary explorations instead of an Assembly committee. Pearson introduced his resolution in the Assembly, which adopted it in the early morning hours of November 4. The operative part read as follows:

> The General Assembly . . . requests, as a matter of priority, the Secretary-General to submit to it within forty-eight hours a plan for the setting up, with the consent of the nations concerned, of an emergency inter-

national United Nations Force to secure and supervise the cessation of hostilities in accordance with the terms of the aforementioned resolution —(997(ES-I)).[69]

After consultations with representatives whose countries might supply troops, Hammarskjold asked the Assembly on the same day for an immediate decision on the establishment of a UN command for an emergency international UN force and on the appointment of General Burns as commander. He further proposed that Burns be authorized to organize a small staff from his own military observers in UNTSO, that these officers should be drawn from countries that were not permanent members of the Security Council, and that Burns also be authorized in consultation with Hammarskjold to recruit directly from various member states the additional number of officers he might need for his headquarters. Omar Loutfi, the Egyptian representative, telephoned Cairo and through Fawzi got Nasser's agreement in principle to the idea of a UN force. The British and French, who now wished the UN force to take over from their own forces and settle the Canal problem, were disappointed at the vagueness of the Assembly's definition of the functions of the force. Nonetheless they began to accept Hammarskjold's concept of the force as the best, and perhaps the only, way out of their military-political dilemma.

The Assembly quickly approved Hammarskjold's proposals, and invited "the Secretary-General to take such administrative measures as may be necessary for the prompt execution of the actions envisaged in the present resolution."[70] In the vote on this resolution, the nineteen abstentions included the entire Soviet bloc as well as Australia, Egypt, France, Israel, Great Britain, South Africa, New Zealand, Portugal, Turkey, and Laos.

Early on November 5, Hammarskjold acknowledged[71] Israel's reply to the cease-fire request, brushing aside the questions that Israel had asked to be put to Egypt as being irrelevant in the present situation. Late in the afternoon he received from Israel another reply[72] that contained a general cease-fire assurance. He had also received from Egypt a declaration[73] accepting the resolution of the Assembly on the setting up of the UN command. He could thus use three new factors— the Egyptian acceptance, the Israeli reply, and the plans for the United Nations Emergency Force (UNEF)—as a basis for making a new formal démarche[74] on the cease-fire to Britain and France. Hammarskjold asked the governments "whether they would recognize the decision of the General Assembly, establishing a United Nations Command, as meeting their condition for a cease-fire"[75] and requested the British and French representatives to transmit his proposal to their Foreign Ministers with the utmost speed. British and French paratroops had dropped into the Port Said area at the northern entrance to the Suez Canal at dawn on the same day, but by the evening it was still uncertain whether or not Port Said had surrendered. Port Said and Port Fouad officially surrendered on November 6, but contrary to the expectations of the military planners the Anglo-French expedition did not make swift progress southward down the Canal.

At the request of the Soviet Union, the Security Council met on the evening of November 5 to consider a Soviet proposal[76] that France, Britain, and Israel withdraw their troops within three days and that the Soviet Union, the United States, and other UN members having at their disposal powerful air and naval forces give armed and other assistance to Egypt unless Britain, France, and Israel complied with the Assembly cease-fire resolution by a fixed date. The U.S.S.R. proposed that the action should be an enforcement action under Article 42 of the Charter, and offered to make its contribution "to the cause of curbing the aggressors . . . and of restoring peace, by sending to Egypt the air and naval forces necessary for the achievement of this purpose."[77]

This new development gave added urgency to the cease-fire. In an attempt to give the debate a positive accent, Hammarskjold informed the Council[78] that as of midnight New York time on November 4 the governments of France and Britain had stated that as soon as Israel and Egypt had signified their acceptance of, and the UN had endorsed a plan for, an international force as envisaged by the Assembly, France and Britain would cease all military action. With Israel's and Egypt's acceptance of the cease-fire, "the conditions for a general cease-fire," he stated, "would thus, it seems, depend on the possibility of an agreement concerning the plan for an international force,"[79] which he hoped to present on the following day. In the event, the Security Council refused to adopt the Soviet agenda item after Lodge had said "that the draft resolution embodied an unthinkable suggestion" since this would "convert Egypt into a still larger battlefield."[80]

Nonetheless it was now more urgent than ever to persuade the British and French to relinquish their military adventure and thus to allay any possibility of further military escalation in the Middle East. Just before lunch on November 5, Hammarskjold started writing his main report[81] on the establishment of the United Nations Emergency Force (UNEF). This document both laid the foundations for an entirely new kind of international activity and set out principles and ideas that were to become the basis for future UN peace-keeping operations. By lunchtime, he had dictated three pages, which he read during the meal to Pearson and Cordier, and during the afternoon he dictated the remainder in bits and pieces between other commitments. The first full draft of the report was brought to him while he was sitting in the Security Council that evening, and after the Council meeting ended at 10:25 p.m. he went over it with Bunche, Cordier, and Stavropoulos, his legal counsel, and then with Pearson and his assistant, John Holmes. By 2 a.m. on November 6, the report had been retyped in final form. A copy of it was given to Dixon at 2:30 a.m. to be cabled to Selwyn Lloyd, and Hammarskjold himself cabled it directly to Pineau.

Before lunch on Tuesday, November 6, Dixon informed Hammarskjold that a cease-fire "by the Franco-British forces" would come into operation at midnight on November 6.[82] A statement to this effect, Dixon said, was to be read in the House of Commons in "about ten minutes," and the British government hoped that the text could be published simultaneously in New York. Hammarskjold immediately summoned a press conference[83] to which he read the British text, pointing out that although all the belligerents had now agreed to a cease-fire, he would delay his formal reply until the Assembly had pronounced itself on his second and final report on UNEF. The British decision, as he noted later, had been influenced not only by a study of this report but also by intensive pressure from Ottawa. In the early hours of November 6, Pearson, with Hammarskjold's agreement, had telephoned the text of the report to the Canadian Prime Minister, Louis St. Laurent, who had immediately contacted London to impress on Eden the importance that Canada attached to it and to warn of the risk of a split in the Commonwealth if it was not accepted by London. Returning from his press conference at 1:30 p.m., Hammarskjold summoned Eban and Loutfi to inform them of the British communication and of the fact that he had orally confirmed to the British representative the Israeli and Egyptian cease-fire commitments.

It was now vital to get the UNEF to Egypt as soon as possible so that the British, French, and Israeli forces might withdraw. At a meeting of the Assembly on November 7, Hammarskjold presented his second and final report[84] on the UN force. He only wished, he said, "to express my earnest hope that a decision in line with my proposals will be taken promptly so as to permit us to get going. There should not be left in the minds of people any uncertainty about the determination of the UN."[85] He told the Assembly that he had instructed Burns to go at once to Cairo, and Burns had also established direct radio contact with the Anglo-French headquarters in Cyprus "which will be necessary for clearance and aircraft passage and, later, for other purposes."[86]

That evening, the Assembly adopted two resolutions.[87] The first approved Hammarskjold's guiding principles for the organization and functioning of UNEF, authorized him to go ahead in setting it up, and established an Advisory Committee for the UN force under his chairmanship. It also requested all member states to afford assistance as necessary to the UN command. Although France and Great Britain voted in favor of this resolution, the whole Soviet bloc, Egypt, Israel, and South Africa abstained. Vasily V. Kuznetsov explained the Soviet abstention by saying that the resolution constituted a tacit acceptance of the presence of the Anglo-French and Israeli forces in Egypt pending the arrival of UNEF and meant in effect the removal of the Canal from Egyptian administration. He also maintained that the creation of the force by the Assembly was in violation of the UN Charter, since the Security Council alone was empowered to take such an action. The second resolution called again on Israel, Britain and France to withdraw their forces from Egypt immediately.

While sitting in the General Assembly on the morning of November 7, Hammarskjold had received from Burns the text of a statement Ben-Gurion had made in the Knesset earlier in the day in which he had said that the armistice agreement with Egypt was dead and could not be restored, that there were in consequence no valid armistice lines between Israel and Egypt, and that on no account would Israel agree to the stationing of a foreign force on her own territory or in territory occupied by her. Hammarskjold told Eban that he considered it his duty to regard the Israeli position on the armistice agreement as in contradiction with the legal stand of the United Nations. Eban asked him whether, if the Israeli troops withdrew, Egyptian troops would come up to the demarcation line. He replied that obviously Egyptian troops had the right to move freely on Egyptian territory, to which Eban responded that this would complicate Israel's acceptance of withdrawal because there might be a renewal of the fedayeen raids. Hammarskjold replied that the current situation was far too dangerous to allow for consideration of such future security problems, involving as it did the possibility of a major new intervention in the area unless UNEF was quickly established and the withdrawal process began at once, and he urged Eban to take this as the expression of his most serious considered opinion. Just before his talk with Eban, he had asked Lodge to request Eisenhower to send a personal message to Ben-Gurion, urging immediate Israeli withdrawal and acceptance of the UN force.

The approaches to Eban and to Eisenhower brought results on the following day, when Kidron informed Hammarskjold that the Israeli government had approved a text drafted by Eban which covered both the Secretary-General's request for withdrawal and the acceptance of the UN force. As soon as Ben-Gurion had understood the world political context of the situation he changed his policy, and the Israeli message stated that "the Government of Israel will willingly withdraw its forces from Egypt immediately upon the conclusion of satisfactory arrangements with the United Nations in connection with the emergency international Force."[88]

In presenting the Israeli message, Eban asked Hammarskjold to use his influence "with one Security Council Member"[89] to try to prevent activities from that side. Hammarskjold at once sent a note to Kuznetsov, informing him of the Israeli message and adding: "This brings the situation under full control unless unrest breaks out in the northern part. I have had the most disturbing information on the situation in Syria. May I ask you to do what *you* can do in order to make us avoid renewed fedayeen activities or anything that might disturb the extremely delicate but promising situation."[90] He concluded by saying that it might do good if they could talk the matter over, but Kuznetsov did not follow up the suggestion.

Although the fighting had stopped by November 7, tension remained high. The Western alliance was in disarray, British and French embassies all over the world were being attacked by infuriated mobs, and the British pound and the oil supply for Western Europe were gravely threatened. The cease-fire had not eliminated U.S. economic pressure on Britain, and U.S. Secretary of the Treasury George H. Humphrey informed Harold Macmillan, Eden's Chancellor of the Exchequer, that he would oppose a loan or any drawing from the International Monetary Fund until British and French troops had left Egypt. In Egypt itself the British and French forces found themselves in an uneasy proximity with the Egyptian forces and the civilian population in Port Said and Port Fouad, and the Israelis were in occupation of Sinai almost up to the eastern bank of the Canal. The Canal itself was blocked along its entire length by vessels sunk by Egypt and by the wreckage of the bombed El-Ferdan Bridge.

THE CREATION OF UNEF was the condition upon which the cease-fire had been brought about; its effective deployment was the condition upon which the British, French, and Israeli troops would withdraw. The first necessity, therefore, was to make UNEF into a reality as quickly as possible. The two main problems were to recruit, mobilize, organize, and transport the force to Egypt, and to negotiate with the Egyptian government the terms upon which it could accept this novel international experiment upon its sovereign territory.

While the Assembly debate was still in progress on November 4,

Hammarskjold had invited the representatives of Canada, Colombia,* India, and Norway to meet with him for a first exploratory meeting on the availability of troops, and he later also consulted Denmark, Finland, Sweden, Brazil, Mexico, New Zealand, and Iran. He also had to consider what sort of military formation was required, and he cabled Burns asking for his views on its size, organization, and equipment. He instructed Burns to be prepared to fly to Cairo to establish contact with the government of Egypt before coming to New York to consult in detail about setting up of the force, and also told Cairo that the force could arrive without delay and that he had called on Canada, Colombia, Denmark, Finland, and Sweden to provide contingents. He asked if Egypt would have any objections to the participation of troops from any of these countries, saying that as soon as a reply was received he would address a formal request to the governments asking them to make contingents available immediately. He asked Cairo to consult with Burns on the plans for the stationing of the projected force.

To deal with practical problems, Hammarskjold constituted the military representatives of the countries which had troops immediately available to the UN as a working group, over which he, Cordier, and Bunche presided at various times. Until the arrival of General I. A. E. Martola of Finland, whom he had asked for as his military adviser, he assigned Lieutenant General John B. Coulter of the U.S. Army, then the Agent-General of the UN Korean Reconstruction Agency, to serve temporarily in this capacity. Two U.S. military representatives also joined the group to coordinate the U.S. airlift which was to transport the contingents from their home countries and to take the necessary logistical support to a staging area outside Egypt.

The securing of Egyptian agreement on the composition and nature of the force and on the conditions under which it would operate in Egypt proved to be the most difficult of the problems involved in establishing UNEF. The Assembly had set up the force and established the command, but had left to the Secretary-General the task of negotiating its entry into Egypt. The stationing of a UN force on the sovereign territory of a member state had never occurred before and

---

* Francisco Urrutia, the Colombian representative, was urgently summoned from Washington, and Hammarskjold asked if Colombia would provide a contingent for the Force. Urrutia called the President of Colombia from Hammarskjold's office. When the President expressed astonishment at the request, Urrutia said, "If this was 1902 and the UN had existed and could have put in a peace force, Colombia would not have lost the Panama Canal." The President thereupon agreed to provide a contingent, and Hammarskjold telephoned Washington to request U.S. aircraft to pick it up in Bogotá.

would have aroused the sensibilities of any sovereign government. In Egypt's case a history of foreign occupation and the recent invasion of its territory by the armies of three other powers had heightened the sensitivity of the government on all questions relating to its sovereignty. After his initial doubts, Hammarskjold had become optimistic about UNEF. "I have been very much heartened," he told Burns on November 6, "by the support that has been given to this plan both in terms of the kind of support required in the Assembly as well as by those countries in a position to provide forces for the Command."[91] Since it was of the utmost urgency to get UN troops on the ground as quickly as possible, on November 8 he asked Burns what might most usefully be sent to Egypt within the next thirty-six to forty-eight hours as an advance party, how such an advance party could be maintained, and where it could land. It was a considerable surprise and setback when Burns warned him from Cairo that a delay in the Egyptian agreement to the stationing of UNEF was to be expected.

Fawzi had told Burns that although he was as anxious as anyone for speed and although the Egyptian government had agreed in principle to receive the force, it was essential for his government to know the function of the force in clearer terms before the troops actually arrived on Egyptian territory. Egypt wished to know whether, when the force reached the former armistice line, the governments concerned would agree to the areas to be occupied by it, how long the force would stay, whether it was supposed to have any functions in the Canal area apart from observing the withdrawal of the Anglo-French forces, and whether it would stay in the Canal area after the Anglo-French withdrawal. Disturbed by this new complication, Hammarskjold cabled a private message to Fawzi through Burns:

> You know the firm line we have taken in respect of the fact that the UNEF can be temporarily stationed on your territory only with your consent. I would be less than frank with you if I did not tell you how worried Burns' report made me as an indication of the possibility that a delay in your consent might jeopardise the speedy action which at present is so vitally needed. . . . Any wavering from Egypt's side now would undoubtedly isolate Egypt in world opinion which so far has been its best protection. It would further open possibilities which you know as well as I, and which if they were to materialise, would be just as much against what I know to be your hopes as against the interests of us all.[92]

Fawzi replied through Loutfi on the following morning, saying that he understood Hammarskjold's concern but wished him to understand that he also was facing some very real difficulties. Some clarifications would be necessary, and the requisite questions would be sent through Burns.

On November 9 another snag arose. Fawzi warned Burns that there might be difficulty in accepting a contingent from Canada because Canada was a part of the Commonwealth and owed allegiance to the British Queen. Although Pearson's helpful attitude was much appreciated, the Egyptian in the street would inevitably see the Canadian troops as being apparently British. Hammarskjold answered that while he understood Fawzi's difficulties psychologically, his objection to the Canadians might be catastrophic. "The Canadian role in this operation from the beginning of the crisis is such that I consider it necessary to maintain my stand that Canadians should be included,"[93] he told Fawzi, and there was no possibility of a compromise.

Nasser and Fawzi told Burns that no firm decision on the entry of the force could be taken by Egypt until clear answers were forthcoming on the question of what would happen in the Canal area after the French and British had departed, on the final location of UNEF when it reached the armistice demarcation line, and whether it would be stationed in Israel as well as in Egypt. He must, Nasser explained, be able to explain his government's agreement to the entry of UNEF to his people in terms they would understand. He was also apprehensive that the Canadian contingent might act in accordance with British policy as regards the nationalization of the Canal.

"I frankly fail to see," Hammarskjold commented to Burns, "how, as constructed, the UN Force could be instrumental in forcing on Egypt a solution of the Canal question other than one freely negotiated."[94] There also seemed to be some misunderstanding in Nasser's mind about the question of the force's being stationed in Israel. The objective of the force was to get the Israeli Army back behind the armistice demarcation lines and international frontier, and there was no intention that it should thereafter take over the functions of UNTSO. (Hammarskjold did not, of course, anticipate at this time the later decision of the Assembly to station the force on the line between Israel and Egypt.) Hammarskjold instructed Burns to point out that cooperation with the UN was to the decisive advantage of Egypt and would not infringe on Egyptian sovereignty, detract from Egypt's power freely to negotiate a Suez Canal settlement, or submit Egypt to any control from outside. The force provided a guarantee for the withdrawal of foreign forces from Egypt, and since it would come with Egypt's consent, it could not stay or operate in Egypt if that consent was withdrawn. "Any further delay in reaching agreement," he concluded, "would force me to continue negotiation through open notes, although I fear consequences of resort to such procedure."[95]

Notwithstanding these difficulties, Hammarskjold announced on November 9[96] that arrangements were nearly complete for the dispatch of the first units of the force and that within twenty-four hours advance parties from Danish and Norwegian contingents would be flown to a temporary staging area at the Capodichino Airport outside Naples, where they would shortly be joined by advance parties of other contingents. The troops were to be flown from their home countries to the staging area in U.S. transport aircraft. Thereafter, in order to respect the principle that military forces of the permanent members of the Security Council were not to take part in the actual operation, he had arranged with the Swiss government for Swissair aircraft to ferry the troops from the staging area to Egypt.

On November 10, Loutfi asked Hammarskjold to state whether Egypt's consent was indispensable to the participation of a specific nationality in UNEF. Hammarskjold replied that he found it impossible, constitutionally, to accept such a condition, which would imply that he had permitted Egypt to infringe upon his authority under the Assembly resolution and would allow Egypt to stop the movement of UNEF by refusing to accept certain of its contingents. This position of principle, however, was not the full reply, since obviously, as a practical matter, the UN must give serious consideration to the views and wishes of Egypt on the point and give them full weight in deciding on the composition of the force. Loutfi also asked whether, since Egypt had accepted a Canadian as the force commander, Canada would feel slighted if a Canadian contingent was refused. This proposition Hammarskjold declined categorically to accept, and he later informed Loutfi that the Canadian government took the matter very seriously and would even have to reconsider its permission to Burns to become UNEF's commander if Egypt were to refuse to accept the Canadian contingent. Pearson was, however, prepared to discuss the possibility of substituting supply units for the infantry battalion that had originally been detailed.

Loutfi urged Hammarskjold to go to Cairo himself as soon as possible, but Hammarskjold felt obliged first to make another attempt to get his views across to Nasser. He assured Nasser once again that the force would be purely international in character and warned him that any effort to introduce considerations extraneous to the aims of the UN in this operation "is to distort the character of the Force and to create difficulties which may lead to the failure of the whole initiative. I need not elaborate what such a failure might mean."[97] He himself, he told Nasser, would come to Egypt with the first troops, who were likely to be Colombians. He further warned Nasser that Egypt's objection to Norwegian and Danish units, on the grounds that those governments were members of NATO, would jeopardize the participation of any Scandinavian country, and concluded by expressing his deep concern at "a stand which involves such risks for international cooperation, for peace and for Egypt itself, the cause of which has been endorsed by so many who would fail to understand the line you now indicate."[98] After seeing Burns on November 12, Nasser said that he trusted "that we all work for the same purpose of speedily ending the present crisis."[99] He accepted Danish and Norwegian participation in UNEF but said nothing about the Canadian contingent.

It was Hammarskjold's intention to move the initial units of the force—Colombians, Danes, and Norwegians—to Egypt on Tuesday, November 13, and he asked what airfields in Egypt should be used. On November 12, after further contacts with Fawzi, he felt sufficiently confident of his position to call a press conference[100] to announce that agreement[101] had been reached with Egypt on UNEF and that the first troops would arrive shortly. He himself, he said, would visit Cairo "at the very first stage of the operation for discussion of details with the Egyptian Government"[102] and to inspect the staging areas of the force. He planned to leave New York on the afternoon of November 13 and to spend a maximum of two days in Cairo. Although this announcement had been agreed with Loutfi, it soon proved premature, for later that afternoon Burns reported, after a further interview with Nasser, that the Egyptian objection to Canadian troops still stood; and a news-agency report from Cairo, giving the official Egyptian announcement of agreement, stated once again the necessity for Egypt's agreement to the composition of the force and to each separate entry and shipment of troops, as well as to the location of the force, adding that the force would withdraw immediately if Egypt so ordered.

At his apartment that evening, Hammarskjold described his difficulties to Pearson and the Foreign Ministers of Norway, Sweden, Finland, and Denmark. He assured them that he was maintaining a firm line and was going immediately to Cairo for talks with Nasser and Fawzi. He advised Pearson, who was worried about the effect on Canadian public opinion of any leakage of Nasser's objections to Canadian participation in UNEF, that the advance party of the Canadian contingent should be flown to Naples regardless of the difficulties with Nasser, and he also agreed that the Canadian move should be released to the press.

On November 13, Fawzi declared that Egypt could not subscribe to Hammarskjold's interpretation of the agreement for the arrival of the force, which would be an infringement of Egyptian sovereignty, and asked that the agreement remain inoperative until all misunderstanding was dispelled. To this Hammarskjold replied that no one had ever questioned Egypt's sovereign right of consent to the presence of the force, and he urged Fawzi to agree to the force's arrival in Egypt without further delay. He explained that he had to go on record as reserving his right for a discussion with Egypt concerning the withdrawal of UNEF if Egypt were to ask the UN force to leave when its task was obviously still not fulfilled. "What would the situation be," he asked, "if I accepted your obvious constitutional right without reserving my own position as to the way you exert it to the extent that your reaction might go against your own acceptance of the General Assembly resolution on the Force of 5 November?"[103] Obviously they both had to reserve their freedom of action, he told Fawzi, "but all the same we can go ahead hoping that the controversial situation will not arise."[104] He warned Fawzi that he would have to postpone his visit to Cairo again* unless Cairo agreed to the entry of the first UNEF troops, because he did not feel he could expose the UN to a situation "where I would come in before the troops, so to say to pave the way for them."[105] He reminded Fawzi that the UN was not begging for permission but was offering assistance as friends, and member governments would undoubtedly find it humiliating if the Secretary-General arranged his visit to Cairo in such a way as to confuse this point. He concluded: "I have done my best to help you. On this specific point I feel entitled to trust that in the name of our joint interest you will help me by putting the stand I must take on my own rights in the right perspective."[106]

On the morning of his departure, November 14, Hammarskjold met with the UNEF Advisory Committee for the first time. "For my whole operation," he told the Committee, "the very basis and starting point has been the recognition by the General Assembly of the full and unlimited sovereign rights of Egypt."[107] He explained that in spite of the unsatisfactory nature of some of the Egyptian conditions, the early arrival of UNEF was so essential that he had thought it best to establish a *fait accompli* of the acceptance in principle of UNEF's arrival, even if there might be things still to be cleared up. "In order to gain the necessary time," he told the Committee, "I accepted a certain lack of clarity."[108]

Pearson, while congratulating Hammarskjold on his wisdom and patience, expressed anxiety over the current state of affairs. He was especially concerned by Egypt's claim of its sovereign right to determine the composition and functions of the force and to demand UNEF's withdrawal at any time, although he agreed that the advance

---

* Hammarskjold had already decided not to leave on November 13, since he was also awaiting a reaction to his proposal to go to Budapest.

parties of UNEF must be moved into Egypt while Hammarskjold tried to work out the problems with Cairo. The Indian representative, Arthur Lall, maintained that it would be intolerable if the force were to stay in Egypt or have its composition decided without Egypt's consent, and he urged Hammarskjold to organize it on the basis of contingents that Egypt was likely to accept. Hammarskjold felt that his only possible course was to assert, in his negotiations, the right of the Secretary-General on behalf of the UN to determine the composition of the force, while agreeing, as a practical matter, that it would make no sense to send contingents to Egypt without Egypt's agreement. If the UN action could not be based on a reasonable degree of good faith, then it had embarked on an extremely dangerous adventure, and his main object in going to Cairo was to emphasize the good faith of the UN and the international nature of the force. The words "good faith" were to acquire a special significance a little later on. The Advisory Committee meeting ended on an optimistic note with a summary by Ralph Bunche of the military situation, showing there were twenty-one offers of troops for the force and 650 officers and men already in Naples. "This is the most popular army in history," Bunche said, "an army which everyone fights to get into."[109]

Hammarskjold's last message to Fawzi had the desired effect, and on November 14 the latter gave Egypt's agreement to the entry of UNEF on the basis of Hammarskjold's previous assurances and the assumption of full respect for Egypt's sovereign rights. Hammarskjold left New York for Rome that evening. From Rome he flew in an Italian Air Force DC-3 to Capodichino Airport near Naples. The first transport of troops to Egypt, part of the Danish contingent, had taken place on November 15. On the sixteenth he took off at 7 a.m. with the advance guard of the Colombian contingent, and landed five hours later at Abu Suweir, west of the Suez Canal. After a brief inspection of the bomb-damaged facilities at Abu Suweir and Ismailia, he flew on to Cairo.

Hammarskjold's three-day stay in Cairo was filled with intensive negotiations with Fawzi and Nasser on the various problems of the presence, composition, and stationing of UNEF in Egypt. He spent the seventeenth with Fawzi and then met with Nasser from 6 o'clock in the evening until 2 a.m., returning to his hotel to work for the rest of the night. He made little progress on the participation of a Canadian infantry battalion in the force, and doubted whether any argument of his could open the door for a Canadian ground force, although Canadian air units had already been accepted. He thought it better to accept this situation for the time being until Pearson had a chance to talk to Fawzi in New York the following week. Later in the day, however, Burns suggested that UNEF's major requirement was for administrative supporting units that Canada alone seemed capable of providing, and Fawzi found this acceptable. Hammarskjold also instructed Burns to get UN observers into Port Said as soon as possible to forestall trouble between the Anglo-French forces and the civilian population.

Having taken the risk of bringing the advance elements of the force into Egypt, Hammarskjold's main task in Cairo was to develop a firmer basis for continued cooperation with Egypt, a basis that must also command the approval of the General Assembly. He would have greatly preferred a direct undertaking by Egypt to maintain its consent to UNEF's presence as long as the force's task was not completed, but he had found the Egyptians unprepared for such a commitment, and he knew that any hint of an enforcement function for UNEF would lead to its immediate termination. There was no question of Egypt's agreeing that UNEF's withdrawal could take place only if the Assembly so decided, nor would Nasser accept the idea that withdrawal should be subject to an agreement between the UN and the Egyptian government. Hammarskjold therefore suggested to Nasser a formula that was, as he later described it to the Advisory Committee, "a combination of one-sided but interlocking declarations,"[110] the so-called "good faith" agreement. The object of this formula was to recognize Egypt's undisputed right to request the withdrawal of UNEF, but to get from Egypt an agreement by which the government would limit its freedom of action by making any request for withdrawal of the force dependent upon the completion of the force's task, a question that obviously would have to be submitted for interpretation to the General Assembly.

In the final agreement,[111] the government of Egypt declared that "when exercising its sovereign rights on any matter concerning the presence and functioning of UNEF, it will be guided, in good faith, by its acceptance of General Assembly resolution 1000 (ES-I) of 5 November 1956."[112] The Secretary-General, on behalf of the UN, made a reciprocal commitment "that the activities of UNEF will be guided, in good faith, by the task established for the Force" and undertook to maintain the force until its task was completed. Both parties agreed to explore jointly "concrete aspects of the functioning of UNEF, including its stationing and the question of its lines of communication and supply."[113]

In a second memorandum, Hammarskjold and Nasser set out the basis for the arrival of UNEF in Egypt, with the following understandings:

1. The area to be occupied by UNEF after the Israeli withdrawal would be subject to agreement;
2. The Force would have no function in Port Said and the Canal area after the Anglo-French withdrawal;

3. Appropriate staging areas for the Force would be subject to agreement with Egypt;
4. Hammarskjold would negotiate with Egypt on the addition of any new nations providing troops for UNEF;
5. UNEF could not stay or operate unless Egypt continued to consent, although it was understood that Hammarskjold's "approach to the question of the UNEF had been based on his understanding of Egypt's acceptance of the General Assembly resolution of 5 November 1956" which created the Force.

A third memorandum elaborated on this agreement and specifically separated the function of reopening the Canal, as called for by the Assembly in its November 2 resolution, from the functions of UNEF.

Hammarskjold had intended to publish these last two memoranda as well as the "good faith" agreement in a report to the General Assembly, but their restrictive definition of the functions of the force was an embarrassment to Lloyd and Pineau, whose governments had justified their acceptance of the concept of the UN force to their critics at home by indicating vaguely that it would take over from the Anglo-French forces and, by implication, would continue the effort to impose an international regime for the Canal. On Hammarskjold's return to New York, Pineau and Lloyd asked him not to publish the second and third memoranda; and, seeing no reason to make life more difficult than it already was for the French and British governments, he agreed to their request, although he informed the Advisory Committee of the contents of the memoranda.

Before leaving Cairo, Hammarskjold agreed in principle to Nasser's request for UN assistance in clearing the obstructions in the Suez Canal[114] as soon as the Anglo-French forces had withdrawn from Port Said and the Canal area. He undertook to prepare immediately to give such assistance on his return to New York, and in fact he had already, on November 8, alerted the salvage firms of Smit in Rotterdam and Svitzer in Copenhagen.

Since he had received no positive response to his proposal to go to Budapest, Hammarskjold returned to New York on Monday, November 19. He reported to the UNEF Advisory Committee that the arrangements "are becoming almost metaphysical in their subtlety. I have no complaint about that because if, from the beginning of this operation, we had attempted to be specific, we would not have had an operation at all."[115] Although Pearson and other members of the Committee were not entirely happy about it, in the end the Committee concurred that he should put his agreement with Nasser on record before the General Assembly. He concluded these meetings by remarking that it was very pleasant from his point of view that "every responsibility in this whole Middle East context that falls on me automatically falls on this Committee."[116] The private thoughts of the Committee members on this assumption are not recorded.

The terms that Hammarskjold had been able to get in Cairo, although just adequate to allow the operation to go ahead, were in many respects vague and far from satisfactory, especially after the Assembly gave UNEF a new task on the line between Egypt and Israel in February 1957. Their weakness became abundantly clear a decade later in May 1967, when Nasser finally requested the withdrawal of UNEF. Certainly Hammarskjold himself was anything but satisfied with what he had been able to achieve. In February 1957, during the long discussions on the withdrawal of Israeli forces from Sinai, Eban, referring to UNEF's presence in Sharm el Sheikh, asked whether the General Assembly would be given notice before UNEF was withdrawn.[117] Hammarskjold replied that the "indicated procedure" would be for the Secretary-General to inform the Advisory Committee, which would determine whether the matter should be brought to the attention of the General Assembly. In describing this answer in his annual report to the Assembly four months later, he went further, saying that "the Assembly would have an opportunity to ensure that no precipitate changes were made which would increase the possibility of belligerent acts."[118]

On August 5, 1957, Hammarskjold wrote, as was his habit when a problem worried him, a private *aide-mémoire*[119] putting in perspective his negotiations with Nasser and Fawzi, and dealing especially with the question whether Egypt's right of consent to the presence and functioning of UNEF on Egyptian territory should or could in some way be limited in the interest of the political balance and stability of the UNEF operation. According to Hammarskjold, Nasser had recognized that even the "good faith" agreement had serious implications for Egypt's political freedom of action. The definition of UNEF's task was extremely loose and would, in the event of a disagreement, have to be interpreted by the General Assembly.* Nasser realized that in accepting it he had agreed to "a far-reaching and unpredictable restriction."[121]

---

* In May 1967, when Nasser demanded the withdrawal of UNEF, Hammarskjold's successor, U Thant, referred the question to the UNEF Advisory Committee in accordance with the procedure Hammarskjold had suggested. Although some members of the Committee were deeply disturbed at Nasser's request, the Committee did not determine that the matter should be brought to the General Assembly. Despite this fact, U Thant was widely blamed for deciding that he had no alternative, either legally or as a practical matter, to acceding to Nasser's request. In fact, the Egyptian army had already taken over UNEF's posts in Sinai and at Sharm el Sheikh and Ras Nasrani before the official request for UNEF's withdrawal was received.[120]

He had, in fact, accepted it only after Hammarskjold had threatened three times that if it was not accepted by Egypt he would have to propose the immediate withdrawal of UNEF. "If any proof would be necessary for how the text of the agreement was judged by President Nasser," he wrote, "this last-mentioned fact tells the story."[122] Hammarskjold concluded that the "good faith" agreement superseded the whole previous exchange of views "by a formal and explicit recognition by Egypt of the stand I had taken all through, in particular on 9 and 12 November,"[123] and, since only the "good faith" agreement had been approved by the Assembly, it alone had any standing. Although his anxiety over the frailty of his arrangements with Nasser was to be justified by the events of 1967, Hammarskjold had in fact succeeded in establishing a basis for cooperation between the UN and Egypt upon which UNEF operated smoothly and effectively, and solely on Egyptian territory, for nearly ten and a half years.

Hammarskjold's energy and resourcefulness attracted considerable attention at this time, and his reputation, except in France, Britain, and Israel, had never stood higher. It was the honeymoon period when the worst of the crisis was over and relief had not yet given way to criticism and recrimination. Certainly, acting on Pearson's initiative, he had created in UNEF a face-saving operation of a unique kind. In doing so he had risen to a level of influence and executive authority that the Secretary-General had never hitherto enjoyed. Eisenhower indicated the new position of the Secretary-General in world affairs when he said at a press conference on November 14: "The last thing we must do is to disturb any of the delicate negotiations now going on under the leadership of Secretary-General Dag Hammarskjold. We must do nothing that could possibly delay his operations, impede them, or hurt them in any way. I should like to take just a moment to say what he has been doing. The man's abilities have not only been proven, but a physical stamina that is almost remarkable, almost unique in the world, has also been demonstrated by a man who night after night has gone with one or two hours' sleep, working all day and, I must say, working intelligently and devotedly." In a letter to Eisenhower, Hammarskjold wrote, "I assure you that there is nothing particularly unusual about the energy that I have devoted to my task, except that I have had a deep sense of the great importance of timing, lest the catastrophe, already serious, should degenerate into something even worse."[124]

8

THE AFTERMATH
OF SUEZ

ON HIS RETURN FROM CAIRO, Hammarskjold found progress toward a solution to the Suez conflict barred by the apparently irreconcilable positions of the various parties. The Egyptians were determined that their attackers should reap no reward or advantage from their adventure and were suspicious of almost any move from outside. The British and French, smarting under the dual indignity of an almost unanimous international rebuke and of an ignominiously unsuccessful politico-military adventure, could be expected to welcome and encourage any development that would discredit the UN in general and Hammarskjold in particular. The Israelis, who, after achieving military success on their own, had been castigated by the UN and let down by their partners in the adventure, were both resentful of demands for their withdrawal and fearful of a restoration of the *status quo ante*. The United States found itself playing the unexpected role of critic and coercer of Britain, France, and Israel in collaboration with the Soviet Union, which in turn was being widely denounced for crushing the uprising in Budapest.

Hammarskjold presented the text of the "good faith" agreement with Egypt to the General Assembly on November 20,[1] and reported on his discussions in Cairo about clearing the Canal.[2] On November 24 the

Assembly approved[3] the content of his report on his dealings in Cairo, including the agreement. While the immediate problem was to secure a firm date for the Anglo-French withdrawal, which in turn depended on the building up and effective operation of UNEF, he also had to negotiate the legal instruments governing the status of UNEF in Egypt and its relations with the Egyptian authorities. A final step would be to secure the withdrawal of the Israelis behind the armistice demarcation line.

Hammarskjold urged General Burns, who had returned to Cairo from New York on November 22, to deploy UNEF troops as soon as possible in Port Said and Port Fouad and in the areas along the Canal occupied by British and French forces, and Burns quickly interposed a screen of UN troops between these forces and the Egyptians. Burns received unexpected help from the British military authorities, who agreed, since the UN troops were arriving by air without vehicles or heavy stores, to turn over vehicles, medical supplies, and rations for their use. Hammarskjold's constant pressure for speedy deployment increased Burns's anxiety over supply and logistical organization. In reply to his persistent questions as to why some UNEF troops were still in Naples, Burns patiently replied that an administrative basis had to be established if the force, which was being built up by improvisation* without any normal logistical support, was to operate without a series of disasters and indignities.

In the view of the British and French governments, the Anglo-French withdrawal depended upon a convincing buildup of UN troops in Egypt. In talks in New York, Selwyn Lloyd insisted on a four-week period for the Anglo-French withdrawal and urged that the Canal clearance operation should start independently of the withdrawal. Fawzi, when informed of the British position, was equally firm that the clearing of the Canal could begin only on the day after complete withdrawal by the British and French.

By November 27 the British position seemed to have moderated to the point where it was possible to discuss the procedure for withdrawal. Lloyd planned to announce in the House of Commons that the withdrawal would be completed within two weeks, provided he could give the House a convincing presentation of the effectiveness of UNEF as well as of the UN plans for clearing the Canal. Somewhat ironically, he also wished to get an assurance that the Egyptian acceptance of Hammarskjold's proposals of October 24, which had been given two days after the Anglo-French attack had started, still stood as a basis

---

* In the early stages one of the main sources of rations for UNEF was food bought from the ships stranded in the Canal.

for negotiating a settlement of the Canal problem. Fawzi told Hammar-skjold that he might have difficulty in gaining agreement to the two-week margin in Cairo but would do his best, and suggested that Lloyd might say that the Egyptian government confirmed that the clearance operation could start as soon as the withdrawal was completed and that technically it would be possible to start clearing the Canal in mid-December. Fawzi assumed that the French would fall in with the British decision and that the Israelis would move back from the Canal sufficiently to allow the clearance operation to start.

On November 28, Hammarskjold announced[4] that 4,500 officers and men had been accepted for UNEF from eight of the twenty-three nations that had offered to make military units available. Of these, 1,374 were already in Egypt. In just three more days it was expected that 2,700 troops would be deployed in the Canal area and the whole force of 4,100 would be in Egypt, with 300 air personnel backing it up from Naples. He stressed that in view of UNEF's special nature and its good reception, in terms of potential effectiveness it should be rated as the equivalent of a much larger conventional military force.

On the same day, Hammarskjold learned that Lloyd would not be in a position to make the promised statement on withdrawal in the House of Commons because further consultations with the French were necessary. In his statement to the House on November 29, Lloyd only repeated Britain's willingness to withdraw from Egypt as soon as he was convinced of UNEF's effectiveness, and he went on in unmis-takable terms to link the Anglo-French withdrawal with the Canal clearance and a general Canal settlement. Hammarskjold was worried both by the tone and by the possible effect in Cairo of Lloyd's state-ment, which was also likely to limit Lloyd's own freedom of action when he next spoke in the House. Still, appreciating Lloyd's difficulties, he decided against sending him a personal message. Also on November 28, he received a new message from Lloyd, which among other things raised the question of freedom of passage through the Canal for British and French ships and referred to a statement by Nasser that Egypt was in "a state of war" with France and Britain. Fawzi remarked that this "state of war" was not so much a legal statement as a description of the actual situation, which would presumably change when the invading British and French troops had left, but he agreed that Hammarskjold might give the desired assurances on the freedom of passage through the Canal for British and French ships.

Lloyd was due to speak again in the House of Commons on Decem-ber 3, and Hammarskjold learned that once again he was unlikely to give a firm date for the Anglo-French withdrawal. In order to avoid mis-understandings in Cairo, he agreed with Sir Pierson Dixon that he should explain to the press[5] that the target date for the withdrawal was the middle of December. He instructed Burns that UNEF should be ready to assume its responsibilities in the Port Said area by mid-December, but Burns discovered from the Anglo-French commander, General Keightley, that the British and French commanders felt that they could not get out before December 20. Burns himself believed that he did not yet have enough troops to secure the situation in Port Said during the last stages of the Anglo-French withdrawal. Although Hammarskjold chartered extra aircraft to fly in more troops and urged Burns to try to maintain the date of December 14, the last Anglo-French troops left Port Said only on December 22. Although there were a few minor incidents, and on one or two occasions the UN troops came under fire in Port Said during sniper attacks upon the British troops, the interposition of UNEF worked well, and the withdrawal behind a screen of UNEF troops was carried out smoothly and without loss of life.

The way was now open for the clearance of the Canal. Hammarskjold later described the preliminary stages of the clearance operation as "the most time- and nerve-consuming operation I have ever tried."[6] Egypt would accept nothing which might give the impression that the Anglo-French invasion had in any sense been justified. The British and French governments, on the other hand, far from publicly accepting any culpability for the Suez affair, persisted in the fiction that the UN would simply take over their self-appointed policeman's role. Eden expressed this point of view on his return from convalescence in Jamaica. "The formation of a United Nations force," he said, "could be the turning point in the history of the United Nations. Does anyone suppose that there would have been a United Nations force but for British and French action? Of course not."[7]* It followed, according to London's thinking, that the UN, and even Egypt, would welcome with open arms the Anglo-French salvage fleet, which the British staunchly but mistakenly claimed to be the only fleet in the world capable of clearing the Canal. The resulting delay in getting the clearance operation started made Hammarskjold an easy target for accusations that the UN was amateurish and even that he was deliberately delaying the clearance operation to penalize the British and French.

When Lloyd came to New York in mid-November, "struggling," as Eden explained in his memoirs, "to inject some sense of values,"[9] he brought with him a vice-admiral and a list of 34 British salvage ships, which were, he said, the best in the world and the only fleet fit to clear

---

* Denis Healey, an Opposition M.P., dismissed this claim as being "like Al Capone taking credit for improving the efficiency of the Chicago police."[8]

the Canal. The UN, he pointed out, was an amateur at the salvage game. Knowing the inevitable Egyptian reaction to a British salvage fleet, Hammarskjold set out to make the UN professional as soon as possible. On November 20 he proposed to the General Assembly that he should negotiate agreements with "firms in countries outside the present conflict"[10] and that he also be authorized in consultation with the Advisory Committee to make the necessary financial commitments. While actual work could not begin until "non-Egyptian" forces were withdrawn, negotiations and a survey of the Canal should proceed immediately. He told the firms of Smit and Svitzer to get their ships on the way and appointed General R. A. Wheeler* to organize the operation; John J. McCloy, the chairman of the board of the Chase Manhattan Bank, as his financial adviser on the clearance project; and Alfred G. Katzin, one of his Under-Secretaries, to assist him in the Secretariat side of the work.

It was only on November 29 that the question of using the Anglo-French salvage fleet was formally raised. Lloyd suggested that these ships, most of which were British naval vessels, could fly the UN flag and that their crews might wear civilian clothes. Although Hammarskjold had Fawzi's agreement that he would be free to use any equipment he considered necessary for the quickest possible clearance of the Canal, Fawzi was unwilling even to consider the use of British and French crews so soon after the Anglo-French assault on Egypt.

On December 4, Hammarskjold reported to the Advisory Committee that there were fifty-one obstructions in the Canal, of which two were demolished bridges and forty-nine were sunken ships or other obstructions. The first objective of the clearance operation would be to provide a twenty-five-foot-deep channel without necessarily actually removing all the obstructions. Apart from the ten British and French salvage ships doing limited salvage work in Port Said harbor, there were twenty-eight chartered salvage vessels on their way to the area as well as spare crews to man the six British ships with non-British crews if necessary.

Hammarskjold was determined to take a pragmatic line because, he told the Advisory Committee, "when matters of this type are treated on a practical level, very often the question of principle never arises,"

---

* General Wheeler was borrowed from the International Bank for Reconstruction and Development. He had been chief of the Corps of Engineers in the U.S. Army from 1945 until 1949, when he retired. He had served as Engineer of Maintenance of the Panama Canal in 1940 and 1941, and had been responsible for major salvage operations during World War II, including the clearance of the ports of Cherbourg and Singapore. He later supervised the reopening of the port of Matadi in the Congo for the UN in 1960.

but such a common-sense approach did not prove easy. In an all-or-nothing approach to the salvage operation, the British stated that the Anglo-French salvage fleet must either stay or leave as a whole, while the French tried to link their part in the salvage operation with the timetable for the withdrawal of their troops. Hammarskjold told both governments that such attitudes created an impossible dilemma for him and might well produce a new political deadlock as well. Egypt, for its part, was not prepared even to discuss the use of British or French salvage ships or crews until all the Anglo-French troops had been evacuated.

General Wheeler, who had arrived in Egypt with a team of surveyors on December 8, resolutely resisted attempts by the press to elicit from him a comparison of the possible rate of clearance by the Anglo-French fleet with the estimated rate of clearance by the UN operation. (Wheeler in fact cleared the Canal for the UN in less than four months at a cost of $8.2 million, compared with the British estimate, for an Anglo-French salvage operation, of six months and $40 million.)

Hammarskjold found out that in order to bolster their all-or-nothing line, the British had informed various European capitals that although he had accepted the Egyptian position, the UN was quite incapable of running the clearance operation. On December 14, statements to the press[11] by the First Lord of the Admiralty, Lord Hailsham, who was visiting the British naval units in Port Said, confirmed Hammarskjold's worst suspicions. Hailsham, when asked where the UN could assemble a salvage fleet comparable to the Anglo-French one, spoke forcefully for ten minutes. The idea, he said, that a comparable fleet could be assembled in less than a number of months was "nonsense," and after saying that even if Wheeler used some of the Anglo-French craft the UN operation would take four times as long as the Anglo-French one, he pronounced himself "rather speechless." Hailsham was also reported to have referred to Wheeler as "an old Middle Western grocer."

Hammarskjold was angered at this cheap and ill-informed attack on Wheeler and drafted a strong letter of protest to Lloyd, but on second thoughts apparently realizing the difficulty of Lloyd's position at home, he did not send it and merely showed it to Dixon. "I can understand," he had written, "the need to safeguard certain domestic political interests, but I do react deeply when that is to such a large extent done at the cost of the UN, its prestige and my possibilities to get something done."[12]

At 4 p.m. on December 15, Hammarskjold learned, to his astonishment, that in about forty hours the whole Anglo-French salvage fleet would be withdrawn unless agreement was reached on its use by the UN. This ultimatum included a further condition that if the crews were to remain, protection must be provided, including UN guards on the ships themselves, UN covering forces on the banks of the Canal, and UN protection of road convoys. These conditions were stated to apply also to two German heavy-lift salvage vessels whose charter had been transferred to the UN by Britain. He told the British that he hoped this order would not stop the ten Anglo-French salvage ships from finishing the limited tasks on which they had already embarked. He had told Wheeler that six of the British salvage ships should remain with UN crews to assist the UN fleet, but he could see no practical justification for the protective measures required by the British, which would in any case be an extension of UNEF's functions in the Canal Zone that Egypt was most unlikely to accept. Egypt now stated categorically that British and French crews on the salvage ships were not acceptable. An immediate decision had to be made. On December 17, Hammarskjold told Dixon that he had decided to dispense with the six ships altogether, but he asked that the Anglo-French ships be allowed to complete the tasks on which they were actually engaged. On December 18 this was agreed, and Egypt gave the necessary assurances for their security.

Even if the British and Egyptian positions had not finally proved irreconcilable, Hammarskjold felt that he could not take the risk of sending British crews down the Canal in the prevailing state of tension in Egypt. This was not, he remarked to the Advisory Committee, a question of "giving in to Colonel Nasser" but a question simply of the safety of the crews.* He explained to Dixon, who had complained that "political considerations" had been allowed to interfere with the clearance operation, that "the arrangements made by the United Nations reflect only such political considerations as were germane to the organization itself in planning a Canal clearing operation shortly after the Anglo/French military action and with Anglo/French forces still in occupation of part of Egypt's territory."[13] A statement by Lloyd in the House of Commons,[14] putting the responsibility for the difficulty squarely on the UN, taxed his patience still further. Noting that the UN side of the case had never been presented publicly, he told the Advisory Committee: "I have abstained from so presenting it because I did not think it would help the negotiation if we were to get drawn

---

* The safety of the British crews was a very real problem for Wheeler, especially with the ships *Dispenser* and *Uplifter* working in Port Said harbor. The Egyptian authorities were extremely suspicious of them and even attempted to board them, and Wheeler was much relieved when they finally left in mid-January.

into any kind of public polemics. I hope we solve it without that."

General Wheeler, unperturbed by the fulminations of Hailsham and others, completed his survey and reported that there were twenty-nine obstructions actually blocking the Canal, of which the nine that blocked passage of all ships would be priority targets for the clearance operation. Despite further difficulties with the Egyptian authorities, the clearance operation got fully under way on December 31 with a fleet of thirty-two UN vessels and, initially, eleven English and French salvage ships in Port Said. After initial delays, the operation went unexpectedly fast. In mid-February the worst obstacle, the cement-filled LST *Akka*, which had been sunk in the main channel, was lifted, and on March 25, Hammarskjold himself was able to watch, from the salvage tug *Atlas*, the lifting of the tug *Edgar Bonnet*. The first ships went through the Canal on March 29, and it was declared open to all traffic on April 8.

WHEN THE LAST Anglo-French troops departed on December 22, the withdrawal of the Israeli forces had reached only its first stage. On December 1, Hammarskjold had been told that Israeli forces would be moved back from a fifty-kilometer belt along the east side of the Canal. Burns, who had been instructed to interpose UNEF between the Israeli and Egyptian forces, urged him to try to persuade Egypt to agree to keep all of its troops west of the Canal or at least within a limited distance of the Canal on the eastern bank. Hammarskjold had no authority to restrict the movement of Egyptian troops on their own territory, but he urged Cairo to hold its troops back and pressed Burns not to allow a vacuum to develop in the Canal area. In its withdrawal the Israeli Army appeared to be taking no chances that it could be closely followed up by the Egyptians, and reconnaissance parties of the Yugoslav UNEF contingent, which had advanced twenty miles into Sinai from the Canal, found their progress impeded by minefields, craters, and torn-up roads as well as by drifting sand. Hammarskjold asked Eban to ensure that there would be no further destruction of roads, railroads, or other facilities and that no more minefields would be laid.

When on December 11 Hammarskjold learned that Israel was ready to make further withdrawals, he instructed Burns to meet General Dayan in Lydda. Dayan advised Burns that the Israeli forces would withdraw from Sinai at the rate of twenty-five kilometers a week, which would mean that their withdrawal would take from four to six weeks. While Burns, having doubts as to the capacity of UNEF to follow up the Israelis, initially acquiesced in this program, Hammarskjold told the Israelis that such a slow pace would create dangerous political complications and was unacceptable. On December 21[15] the Israelis presented a new plan under which no Israeli forces would be west of El Arish after the first week of January except for detachments on the Strait of Tiran. The date for the second phase, full withdrawal behind the armistice demarcation lines, was not specified. Hammarskjold assured the Israelis that despite all difficulties, UNEF would move forward at whatever pace the Israeli withdrawal required, and he told Burns, "I hope you will inject this spirit into your troops."[16] Burns was also to take over the Coptic monastery of St. Catherine in Sinai and to have its unique collection of manuscripts and icons inspected.

After the first withdrawals the Israeli attitude hardened. On January 5 there was still no indication of Israeli intentions after January 7, and the future of the Gaza Strip and the entrance of the Strait of Tiran had not even been mentioned, although Eban's questions concerning freedom of navigation in the Suez Canal, the prevention of any renewal of the fedayeen raids from Gaza, and the right of innocent passage through the Strait of Tiran into the Gulf of Aqaba indicated that hard bargaining would be required if a complete Israeli withdrawal was to take place. On January 14 the Israelis gave Burns a new withdrawal plan[17] stipulating that they would leave all of the Sinai except for Sharm el Sheikh on the Strait of Tiran by January 22.

The real test was now approaching, for the General Assembly was again in session and in no mood to brook further delay. Israel's three sticking points were basically the reasons for which it had gone to war. Sharm el Sheikh and Ras Nasrani, where Egyptian coastal batteries dominated the Strait of Tiran, were unquestionably on Egyptian territory, but they also dominated the only sea access to the Israeli port of Elath on the Gulf of Aqaba, a fact that might well be considered to justify the right of innocent passage for all ships through the Strait. The Gaza Strip, placed under Egyptian administration in the Egypt-Israel armistice agreement, had been used as a base for the fedayeen raids, which were the other stated cause for Israel's invasion of Sinai. Finally, there was still no Egyptian commitment on future freedom of navigation for Israel through the Suez Canal. Israel was naturally unwilling to withdraw without serious guarantees on these points. Hammarskjold's dilemma in negotiating for the Israeli withdrawal was that, however much he might sympathize with Israel's misgivings, he was obliged to proceed according to the resolutions of the General Assembly, which demanded unconditional Israeli withdrawal from the territory it had occupied by force.

On January 17, Ceylon introduced a resolution[18] requiring Hammarskjold to pursue his efforts to secure Israel's withdrawal and to report within five days. The resolution was adopted on January 19[19] with only Israel and France in opposition.* Hammarskjold's subsequent discussions with both Eban and Fawzi were totally unsatisfactory and included an acrimonious exchange with Eban over Israel's denunciation of the armistice agreements. Since he had no right to ask for conditions from Egypt for the Israeli withdrawal, he privately consulted Fawzi about the attitude to be expected of Egypt after the Israelis had withdrawn, especially in relation to the fedayeen raids, the limitation of forces on and near the armistice demarcation line, and the possibility of the UN participation in the administration of Gaza. He also asked if Egypt would desist from "all acts of belligerency" in line with the Security Council's 1951 decision on freedom of navigation in the Canal and would agree that the International Court be asked for an opinion on whether the Gulf of Aqaba was part of the high seas.

Further meetings produced little progress. Hammarskjold rejected a suggestion that Israel should continue to administer the Gaza Strip under UNEF occupation and proposed instead that the armistice agreement be formally reinstated, with UNEF guaranteeing it and being formally associated with Egypt in the administration of Gaza.

On January 23, Ben-Gurion delivered in the Knesset a strongly worded demand for UN guarantees on Gaza, Aqaba, and the Canal as a condition for Israel's withdrawal, and suggested again that, for the good of the inhabitants, Israel should stay in the Gaza Strip. In New York on the same day, an Israeli *aide-mémoire*[20] suggested that UNEF occupy Sharm el Sheikh until a permanent way could be found of ensuring freedom of navigation in the Strait and preventing belligerent acts. As for Gaza, Israel recommended that UNEF not enter the Strip and that after the Israeli troops were withdrawn Israel should continue the functions of administration and security.

Ben-Gurion's public statement of Israel's conditions for withdrawal further complicated Hammarskjold's task of finding a pragmatic solution. Faced with a deadlock, he felt that in his report to the Assembly the only hope was to go back to fundamentals. He decided first to outline the legal limits of UN action, pointing out that there were certain things the UN could not do and could not decide. He would then suggest positive steps for solving these problems, not as a condition for the Israeli withdrawal but as a natural part of the UN effort to establish peace in the region. In his view, the armistice agreements were the only legal basis on which the UN could provide for a new

---

* Harold Macmillan had succeeded Eden on January 9 and had already begun the process of "Riding the Storm,'" which included turning his back on the Suez crisis.

settlement in the area. Egypt had expressed a wish to see all raids and incursions from both sides of the armistice demarcation line brought to an end, and the fact that no Egyptian military forces had been moved into Sinai in the wake of the Israeli withdrawal implied a willingness to establish a state of affairs on the Israel-Egypt Armistice Demarcation Line quite different from that which had prevailed before the Suez crisis.

While he could not specifically suggest the use of UNEF as a pacifying element in a future arrangement until the withdrawal of the Israeli forces was complete, Hammarskjold hoped that the Assembly might provide a framework for the kind of pragmatic use of UNEF that he had in mind. The immediate problem was to make certain political moves easier for both parties—for the Egyptians by not formalizing the future arrangements, and for the Israelis by providing a formula under which they could maintain their stand in principle on Gaza and the Gulf of Aqaba and yet withdraw their forces.

In his report to the Assembly[21] on January 24, Hammarskjold sketched out the principles that he believed should guide future UN activity. Military action could not be allowed to change the *status juris*. The use of a military force by the UN other than under Chapter VII, the enforcement chapter of the Charter, required the consent of the states on whose territory the force was to operate and could not be used to force a settlement in the interest of one party only. The UN must respect international agreements such as the armistice agreement, which had given Egypt control of the Gaza Strip. Thus any broader function for UNEF in Gaza would require Egypt's consent. He urged a return to full observance of the armistice agreements, suggesting that the presence of UNEF on the line between Egypt and Israel might be the new element, the lack of which had doomed to failure his efforts of the previous spring to reestablish the armistice regime. UNEF, by preventing the cycle of raids and reprisals prevalent before the Suez crisis, could make it easier for both Israel and Egypt not to deploy large forces on the armistice demarcation lines. When the Israeli troops withdrew from Sharm el Sheikh, UNEF would follow them in, as elsewhere in Sinai, and UNEF detachments might well stay in the area if necessary.

The Assembly spent the next week discussing Hammarskjold's report. In order to avoid linking the Israeli withdrawal with subsequent arrangements, two resolutions[22] were offered, one demanding Israel's withdrawal without further delay and the second following up Hammarskjold's suggestions to interpose UNEF on the line between Israel and Egypt.

Hammarskjold was as much concerned with Egypt's attitude as

with Israel's, and on January 26 "in the quiet of a Saturday afternoon"[23] he dictated a message to Nasser that he asked Fawzi to pass on at once if he thought it advisable. He was convinced, he told Nasser, that it was unwise to link the Canal issue to the withdrawal problem and that there must be no return to the pre-crisis situation concerning the Canal, although the change should be in spite of and not because of Israel's military action. He also urged Nasser to expedite the agreement on the status of UNEF, which his legal counsel, Stavropoulos, was negotiating in Cairo. "We may have a chance," he wrote, "to re-open the door which was closed last year, arriving finally at a state of affairs where Egypt could devote its main interest to the crucial problems facing the nation within its own boundaries."[24]

While the Assembly publicly debated the draft resolutions, private negotiations went on among Lodge, Pearson, Fawzi, Eban, Hans Engen of Norway, and Krishna Menon in consultation with Hammarskjold. At the end of the debate Fawzi declared[25] that his government's position was based on immediate withdrawal by Israel, followed by UNEF taking positions exclusively on both sides of the armistice demarcation lines, while Eban stood firm[26] on Israel's proposals of January 23. The Assembly reacted unfavorably to Eban's statement, and there was talk of sanctions against Israel. The first draft resolution was therefore strengthened to cover the complete withdrawal of Israel rather than a purely military withdrawal, while the second remained studiously vague about the "measures" to be adopted for Sharm el Sheikh and Gaza and was specific only on stationing UNEF on the armistice demarcation lines and the international frontier.

The Assembly's adoption of two resolutions on February 2,[27] although providing a new function for UNEF, once again left the Secretary-General to carry out the vague and ambiguous measures suggested. Walter Lippmann described the situation well when he wrote: "The General Assembly is a place where nobody can afford to stand up in public and be reasonable. He will be regarded at home as a traitor. It has, therefore, become necessary in practice to circumvent the General Assembly by letting it speak ambiguously, and then be silent, while secretly and quietly things are talked over in private, perhaps even agreed to in private, that could never be discussed in public."[28]

Despite Hammarskjold's efforts, the deadlock over withdrawal and the preconditions for withdrawal persisted, and Israel's attitude toward accepting UNEF on its soil seemed likely to add another major problem. "If Israel would not accept the stationing of UNEF, in fulfillment of its functions, on the Israel side," Hammarskjold told the Advisory Committee, "how could I at any stage and with any hope of success

raise the question of an additional stationing on the Egyptian side?"
His discussions with Eban were hard and at times bitter. Eban maintained that his government could formulate its position on outstanding
issues only after Egypt had declared that it would abandon the state
of belligerency after Israel's withdrawal. Hammarskjold asked Eban
whether, if Egyptian troops were occupying part of Israel, Israel would
not find an Egyptian request for a nonaggression pact somewhat
unusual and tantamount to a dictation of conditions. As to UNEF's
being stationed in Gaza and in Israel, Eban said that no country had
ever accepted a non-national force on its soil without any definition of
its purpose, to which Hammarskjold replied that in that case Eban
must find it remarkable that Egypt had ever consented to UNEF's
being stationed in Egypt.

Israel's negative position on withdrawal put Hammarskjold in a
serious quandary, for he knew that it would not be long before the
Assembly demanded further action and that it was he who would be
asked to take it. The Afro-Asian countries were already drafting a
resolution demanding sanctions against Israel, and a new debate could
not be long postponed.

Other pressures on Israel were, however, coming into play. The
U.S. government was interested in an immediate and full implementation of the Assembly's withdrawal resolution, and the fact that Eisenhower, Dulles, and Lodge were known to be engaged in an effort to
persuade the Israelis made it possible to get Fawzi to agree to the
postponement of a new debate in the Assembly until February 21.

Other developments were more encouraging. At the end of January,
with the Canal clearance operation in full swing, it appeared that the
original $40-million cost estimate might be reduced to $20 million. In
the previous December, Hammarskjold had asked a number of governments for interim advances of funds to finance the operation and had
received assurances amounting to some $13 million.[29] He had arranged
with the International Bank for Reconstruction and Development to
act as the fiscal agent of the UN and to receive, hold, and disburse the
funds made available. In late January he suggested a number of
alternative methods of financing the Canal clearance operation: by
ordinary UN assessment, by an assessment of the interested parties, by
an assessment based on responsibility for the damage (which would
be extremely difficult to establish), by voluntary contributions, or by
letting the Canal traffic carry the cost by a surcharge on the normal
tolls. He himself was inclined to favor the surcharge, because the
burden on the Canal users would be slight. He also suggested that
pending a settlement of the whole Canal question, the International
Bank might also act as a collecting agent for the surcharge.

Another negotiation to which Hammarskjold attached great importance ended successfully on February 8 with the conclusion of the agreement with Egypt on the status of UNEF in Egypt. The Cairo authorities had initially been suspicious of this novel legal arrangement, and its negotiations had taken Hammarskjold's legal counsel, Constantin Stavropoulos, nearly two months. Hammarskjold, who regarded it as an important innovation in international law and as a model for the future, had followed the negotiations closely. At one point, in mid-January, he cabled Nasser concerning one of the novelties in the text which provided for the personnel of UNEF to remain under the criminal jurisdiction of their own countries while serving in UNEF and which was, he told Nasser, a great advance on any similar previous arrangement, such as that for NATO forces. He was particularly proud of the delicate balance maintained in the UNEF status agreement[30] between national sovereignty and international organization, and the agreement eventually served as a model for later peace-keeping operations.

After Hammarskjold reported[31] deadlock in the negotiations for Israeli withdrawal, the center of activity shifted to Washington. Dulles told Eban that the United States stood firm on the armistice agreements as determining the status of Gaza and also supported the international status of the Gulf of Aqaba as requiring free and innocent passage for all vessels. Ben-Gurion replied that Israel was not prepared to go back to the *status quo ante* in Gaza, and that Israel would accept UNEF troops at the entrance to the Gulf of Aqaba provided they would stay until a peace treaty was signed or permanent arrangements were made for free navigation.

Between its obligations to the UN and the widespread pro-Israel feeling in Congress and in the country, the U.S. government was in a dilemma. Eisenhower, after consultation with Dulles and Lodge, decided that a stand must be made on Israel's withdrawal, and on February 20 he cut short a quail-shooting vacation in Thomasville, Georgia, to meet with Congressional leaders in Washington. After a tense and uneasy meeting Eisenhower decided that he himself must shoulder the burden, if necessary alone. In a television broadcast the same evening, he announced his decision: "If the United Nations once admits that international disputes can be settled by using force, then we will have destroyed the very foundation of the organization and our best hope of establishing a world order. That would be a disaster for us all."[32]

The General Assembly was to resume its discussion of the Middle East on February 22. On the same day, the Afro-Asian group introduced a resolution[33] that called on all states to deny all military, economic, or financial assistance and facilities to Israel in view of its continued defiance of the Assembly's call for withdrawal. As a result of his own discussions, Hammarskjold told the Assembly,[34] he could state with confidence that it was the desire of Egypt that the take-over in Gaza, which in the first instance would be exclusively by UNEF, would be orderly and safe. Egypt would also be willing, in view of the UN's responsibility for refugees in the Gaza Strip and of the special complexities and problems of the area, to make "special and helpful arrangements" with the UN. UNEF would be deployed on the armistice demarcation line and its help would be accepted in putting an end to incursions and raids across the border from either side and in safeguarding life and property, guaranteeing good administration, and fostering economic development. The debate in the Assembly adjourned to await the outcome of the talks in Washington.

On February 24, Eban returned from Jerusalem and had a long talk with Dulles. After this talk Lodge informed Hammarskjold that the Sharm el Sheikh situation was solved on the basis of Dulles's declaration to Eban on February 11, and that Israel would withdraw from Gaza "on the face value"[35] of Hammarskjold's statement to the Assembly on February 22. Eban would be coming to see Hammarskjold the next day in order to get some clarifications on his statement, which Eisenhower hoped that Hammarskjold would be in a position to give. This arrangement soon proved not to be as simple as it sounded. While Lodge was still talking with Hammarskjold, Bunche reported that Pearson had been officially informed that Israel was insisting that there could be no Egyptian return to Gaza in any way, shape, or form. When Lodge checked this report with Dulles, Dulles stated that as far as he knew from his talks with Eban, it was quite unfounded.

On the morning of February 25, Eban asked Hammarskjold a number of questions. After the Israeli withdrawal, would UNEF's function be to prevent acts of belligerency? Would the Secretary-General give notice to the General Assembly before withdrawing UNEF from Sharm el Sheikh? Would a naval unit be added to UNEF to ensure free and innocent passage in the Gulf of Aqaba? Hammarskjold replied in the affirmative to the first question, noting, however, that UNEF would never be used to force a solution to a controversial political or legal problem. As to UNEF's withdrawal from Sharm el Sheikh, the "indicated procedure would be for the Secretary-General to inform the Advisory Committee . . . which would determine whether the matter should be brought to the attention of the Assembly."[36] The question of a naval unit was beyond the authority given to the Secretary-General by the Assembly.

Eban also asked whether a de facto UN administration in Gaza would exclude Egypt's return to the area. Hammarskjold replied that the armistice agreement gave Egypt an unquestioned legal right to control the Gaza Strip. He had therefore concentrated on making arrangements to secure peace and quiet in the area within the legal framework established by the armistice agreement, and these arrangements could not be understood as limiting the rights given to Egypt in Gaza under the agreement. He also told Eban that only after Israel's unconditional withdrawal from the Gaza Strip could the practical possibilities of a satisfactory arrangement and a de facto UN administration be fully explored.

Hammarskjold was determined to proceed as far as possible pragmatically and without raising in the Assembly problems on which both Israel and Egypt would be compelled to take intransigent and conflicting positions. For example, he hoped that UNEF might be stationed in Sharm el Sheikh as part of its general deployment in Sinai without going into the question of how long it would stay. On this "pragmatic" basis UNEF eventually stayed in Sharm el Sheikh for ten and a half years.

On February 28, Pineau showed Hammarskjold the text of an agreement reached on the previous day by Mrs. Golda Meir of Israel, Dulles, and himself concerning the assumptions on which the Israeli withdrawal from Gaza would take place. Hammarskjold noted that the agreement had originally read "initial take-over"[37] by UNEF in **Gaza** but that the word "initial" had been crossed out in ink. This text was later used by Mrs. Meir in the Assembly. When Hammarskjold expressed his doubts, Pineau agreed that it meant, at the least, that no Egyptian *troops* should return to Gaza. That evening, he gave a dinner for Mollet at which Pineau and Alphand told him that the Israeli statement was intended to exclude the return of *any* Egyptians to Gaza. When he pointed out the legal impossibility of such a line for the UN in view of the armistice agreement, Alphand replied that if that was the case there was no solution and that the UN simply had to see to it that no Egyptians returned. Hammarskjold replied that if that was so, the proposal was based on impossible assumptions.

Before the Assembly met on March 1, Hammarskjold pointed out forcefully to Lodge and Pearson that an intolerable situation would be created for the UN if withdrawal statements were to be based on an assumption that was neither legally possible nor supported by a majority of the members. He had no doubt that Egypt would insist at least upon a token administration in Gaza and he could not be sure that it would not go further than that, although he believed that for the moment there was no intention of Egyptian military forces returning to Gaza.

Whatever Hammarskjold's reservations about it, the Washington scenario was about to be enacted in New York, and he felt that since he had made his views clear in private, it would be irresponsible to protect himself publicly at the risk of wrecking the slender chance the Washington talks provided of getting around a difficult corner in an atmosphere of studied vagueness.

Mrs. Meir announced to the Assembly[38] Israel's plan for full and prompt withdrawal from the Sharm el Sheikh area and the Gaza Strip on the basis of the various assurances given by the United States and the Secretary-General concerning the Gulf of Aqaba, and in the light of the understanding on Gaza agreed upon in Washington under which UNEF would take over exclusive military and civilian control and would provide security and administration "for a transitory period ... until there is a peace settlement ... or a definitive agreement on the future of the Gaza Strip."[39] Mrs. Meir was followed immediately by Lodge,[40] who read out in full Hammarskjold's February 22 statement on the UNEF take-over in the Gaza Strip, thus restoring the two time qualifications for UNEF's take-over, "in the first instance" and "in the transitional period," which Mrs. Meir had dropped from her quotation of the statement. Lodge went on to say that the future of Gaza must be worked out within the framework of the armistice agreement between Egypt and Israel and finished by noting Egypt's "commendable forbearance ... during these last trying weeks."[41] At the end of the meeting Hammarskjold informed the Assembly[42] that he had instructed Burns to meet with Dayan on the following day to complete the plans for immediate Israeli withdrawal and the UNEF take-over.

Lodge's statement in the Assembly caused a violent reaction in Israel.* The Israeli Cabinet went into emergency session, and Burns's projected meeting with Dayan was postponed. Lodge's statement, according to the Israelis, did not correspond to what had been promised in Washington and did not give the necessary basis for withdrawal. As a result of new talks in Washington and a further message from Eisenhower to Ben-Gurion, Mrs. Meir repeated her withdrawal commitment in the Assembly on March 4,[43] while Fawzi repeated his reservation of Egypt's rights[44] in the Gaza Strip. The next day Burns reported that he had agreed with Dayan to take over in Gaza on the night of March 6–7 and in Sharm el Sheikh on March 8.

In a series of talks on March 5, Hammarskjold emphasized the

---

* Others also were surprised at the tone and the emphasis of Lodge's statement. Guillaume Georges-Picot, the French representative, who had watched Lodge on television, called Pineau to ask if he should change his own prepared statement to conform to Lodge's but was told to stick to the original text.

basic contradiction between the Israeli interpretation of the understandings, the well-known majority position, and the official legal
stand of the UN on the situation in Gaza. It was out of the question
to ask the Assembly to clarify its views on this subject since there
was no possibility that the members would agree. On the other hand,
when reporting on the completion of the Israeli withdrawal, Hammarskjold would have to say something about the situation that was to
follow that withdrawal. Since no one could think of any solution to
this theoretically impossible problem, all agreed that Hammarskjold
should try to muddle through in the hope that no move on the
Egyptian side would bring the contradiction into sharp focus. There
should be no difficulty in the initial period of take-over by UNEF in
Gaza, but that period would be very short.

"So far," Hammarskjold told the UNEF Advisory Committee, "we
have had to indulge very much in a somewhat extraordinary policy;
that is, the policy of taking step after step in an atmosphere of great
ambiguity." He would, he said, be only too happy to disregard the
legal side. "I am not in any way fond of it, although commentators
think so," but the fact of the matter was that they now had to face
hard facts with some legal basis. A number of inescapable questions
were bound to arise when UNEF entered Gaza. Was the Secretary-
General, for example, to make an agreement with Egypt on the extent
and form of UNEF's activities in the administration of Gaza? Even
more difficult, was or was not UNEF to open fire if the Egyptians tried
to return to Gaza? What was to be done about the fact that the
Assembly resolution of February 2 not only permitted but contemplated the deployment of UNEF in Israel as well as in Egypt? These
were the reasons why "much as I will try to slip around all corners
and avoid saying whether the cat is white or black, because it is so
dark all around, I am very much afraid that someone may have a
torch and discover the sad secret the very moment the cat tries to
catch a rat; that is to say to do something."

Despite these difficulties, Dulles urged Hammarskjold to go ahead
with the entry of UNEF into Gaza, saying that he had never denied
the legal status of Egypt in Gaza under the armistice agreement.
Fawzi agreed that the only common ground that existed seemed to be
for the initial stage of the take-over by UNEF with a completely
indeterminate interpretation of the word "initial," which might be
taken to mean that the initial phase would last until the Egyptians
"raised their eyebrows."[45] When Hammarskjold said that a fairly long
initial period might be needed so as to provide opportunities for an
orderly settlement of some of the problems of the Gaza Strip, Fawzi
merely nodded approval.

With this somewhat vague encouragement from Dulles and Fawzi, in the hope that the initial period might be long enough to allow feelings to cool down and in the knowledge that the official record was reasonably clear despite what might or might not have been said in private, Hammarskjold felt justified in ordering UNEF to enter Gaza. Indeed, failure to do so could only throw the whole matter back into a state of acute crisis. On March 6, therefore, he sent General Burns detailed instructions on the initial take-over in Gaza, including matters such as currency, administration, and policing, but told him to avoid making any public statements about the arrangements.

Early on March 7, Burns reported that UNEF troops were in position all over the Gaza Strip and that, despite considerable administrative problems, so far all was going well. On the afternoon of the following day UNEF took over in Sharm el Sheikh. "We skate on very thin ice," Hammarskjold told the Advisory Committee, "but I think that that is ice that may bring us close to the other shore, and that is all we have to play for."

Ralph Bunche, whom Hammarskjold had sent to the Middle East on March 6, was told to stay on in order to coordinate UN activities in the Gaza Strip and generally to hold the fort until Hammarskjold himself arrived on March 21. There were, Hammarskjold told Bunche, intensive developments involving the position of both Egypt and Israel concerning the Gaza Strip, and he attached the greatest importance "to a correct handling, even of seemingly innocent administrative matters, in terms of the possible interpretation that may be attached to them."[46] The Secretariat had to risk taking responsibility "for solutions and arrangements with undefined background and for that reason open to challenge although, of course, tacitly so developed as to be consistent with our basic stand."[47]

In spite of the Israeli withdrawal, Hammarskjold was still worried over Ben-Gurion's statement that Israel reserved its freedom of action in case Egypt returned to the Gaza Strip and the implication that there was some "understanding" on this matter. Ben-Gurion had expressed surprise at a statement attributed to Bunche that UNEF was in the Strip with the agreement of Egypt. "It is not in the power of the Egyptian dictator," Ben-Gurion said, "to agree or disagree to this, since he was ignominiously expelled from the Strip."[48] To guard against the possibility of being asked to keep Egypt out of the Strip by force, Hammarskjold informed Britain, France, and the United States of his fears, pointing out that as far as he knew, Ben-Gurion's position had not been endorsed by any other member of the UN.

Clouds soon began to gather over UNEF's deployment in Gaza. Brigadier Amin Hilmy, the Egyptian liaison officer with UNEF in

Cairo, announced that he was going to Gaza on March 10 or 11 to open the post office. Burns himself entered Gaza officially at 8:30 a.m. on March 10, and although at first the main street of the town was reasonably clear, a series of demonstrations and parades soon began outside UNEF headquarters, mostly with banners demanding the restoration of Egyptian rule in the Strip. The UNEF military police guarding Burns's headquarters were compelled to use tear gas, and at one point Danish and Norwegian troops fired over the heads of the crowd. The situation was further complicated by an Egyptian demand, received at the moment when the Canadian armored reconnaissance squadron was about to be airlifted to Egypt from Naples, that no more Canadians join UNEF. The Egyptian authorities gave as the reason for this demand Pearson's alleged advocacy in the Assembly of the internationalization of Gaza. Hammarskjold told Bunche to explain to Nasser at once that it was impossible for him to go back on arrangements of long standing now very near completion, and Fawzi undertook to support Bunche's approach.

On March 10, Hilmy requested Burns's agreement to the setting up of an Egyptian liaison headquarters in Gaza and added that the Palestine Office Section of the Egyptian Foreign Office would also like to set up an office there. Burns told Hilmy that the initial take-over would be exclusively by UNEF and that Egypt should not send personnel into the Strip pending negotiations on the final arrangements. When Cairo announced the appointment of General Hassan Abdel Latif as administrative governor of Gaza, Hammarskjold warned Fawzi that if things went on in this way there would soon be a meeting of the Assembly. Fawzi left at once for Cairo to explain the situation to his government.

While some Western newspapers "in a somewhat perverse mood seem to take pleasure in difficulties," as Hammarskjold told the Advisory Committee, the Egyptian press was hinting at a plot to fill the vacuum in Gaza without the participation of Egypt, and Nasser was under strong public pressure to take a stand on Gaza. Hammarskjold himself could see no legal basis whatsoever for objecting to an Egyptian administrative governor in Gaza, much as he might deplore the timing and form of the proposal, nor, although the Israelis were bound to object to such a development, could he maintain that it was UNEF's exclusive function to police the Strip and that the Egyptians had no right to challenge UNEF's arrangements.

Hammarskjold instructed Bunche and Burns to separate the problems they were facing in Gaza, where the state of mind of the population was highly emotional, into those relating to a final settlement on the role of UNEF, which should be discussed only on his own arrival in the Middle East, and those immediate problems which could be solved without prejudging that final settlement. He hoped thus to establish pragmatically the role of UNEF in Gaza before the final settlement was discussed. He told Bunche to do his utmost to delay measures concerning Gaza contemplated by the Egyptians until he himself had had a chance to talk to Nasser. The two most vital immediate objectives were to avoid the return of Egyptian troops to Gaza and to stop the resumption of fedayeen raids.

Pressures were now building up on all sides. On March 12 the *New York Times,* under the headline "Nasser Moving to Take Over Gaza ... Hammarskjold Deferring Action," asserted that there were disagreements between the Advisory Committee and the Secretary-General. Both Hammarskjold and the Committee members themselves found this story, with its implication that he and the Committee were emotionally taking sides, harmful to the UN effort as well as untrue, and they agreed to a public statement[49] characterizing the report as inaccurate and misleading and denying that there had been any disagreement in the Committee.

Misleading newspaper stories were also having their effect in Cairo, where strong suspicion had developed that the UN was engaged in a plot to internationalize Gaza. A civilian had died as a result of a ricocheting bullet when UNEF soldiers fired over the heads of the crowd on March 10, and this too would inevitably inflame public opinion against the UN, especially since the Egyptian press alleged that the shot had been fired by a Canadian—a piece of misinformation that Bunche hastened to correct with Nasser when he saw him on March 13. Nasser agreed to convince his Cabinet that the Canadian reconnaissance squadron should be allowed in. Egypt, he said, was in no hurry to send military forces to Gaza, but UNEF must be present on both sides of the armistice demarcation line, and there might perhaps be a half-mile buffer zone on either side of the line. He volunteered that there would be no more fedayeen raids if the Israelis also refrained from raids across the line. Nasser insisted that the administrative governor be allowed to proceed to Gaza, and neither Bunche's arguments nor later representations by U.S. Ambassador Raymond Hare were of any avail in dissuading him.

Hammarskjold did not receive Bunche's report on his talk with Nasser until 8 a.m. on the following day, two hours before the expected time of arrival of the Egyptian administrative governor in Gaza, and it was therefore impossible to make any further intervention with Egypt or to warn the Advisory Committee in advance. When he informed the Committee of the governor's arrival, none of the members questioned the right of the Egyptian administration to return there.

Although Hammarskjold was anxious to get to Cairo as soon as possible, he decided to postpone his departure until March 18 or 19 in view of Mrs. Meir's imminent arrival in New York. In informing Fawzi of his plans, he wrote: "We are passing a delicate period with much at stake. I feel sure you fully realize the significance of a policy which avoids highlighting issues which we know to be controversial from the international point of view and which we hope to overcome in a gradual development in a spirit of mutual confidence and will to create conditions necessary for peace."[50] The Israelis were naturally much concerned at the arrival in Gaza of the Egyptian administrative governor, and further confusion arose out of a statement by the Canadian government that the UN must stand in equal partnership with the Egyptians in administering Gaza, a position which contrived to infuriate both the Egyptians and the Israelis. General Latif's arrival and imaginative press accounts of its implications had also aroused strong and confused feelings in some of the countries providing troops for UNEF. "I have been called a Zionist stooge down here," Pearson commented, "and then I went up to Ottawa where I am known as Nasser's catspaw. I must be following a reasonably neutral policy.... The role of the press in these matters, I must say, is deplorable."[51]

The role of the press during delicate negotiations is indeed of incalculable importance. When information is withheld, journalists understandably enough fall back on speculation. Such speculation, although usually inaccurate, is often near enough to the truth to be accepted as such by large sections of public opinion, and even by governments. The Secretary-General in particular must maintain the absolute discretion on which his confidential relationship with governments is based. The parties to a conflict, on the other hand, may sometimes find it advantageous to leak part of the story to the press in order to build up public support for their own position, and on occasion such activities grow into a fully orchestrated press campaign. In such circumstances it is extremely difficult, if not impossible, for the Secretary-General to set the record straight without destroying his position of confidence with the governments with which he is dealing, and he must usually suffer in silence the criticisms aroused by false accounts of his own activities.

In a conversation with Pearson, Eban described the arrival of the Egyptian governor and five assistants in Gaza as a complete take-over, saying that UNEF had been pushed into the background contrary to the assumptions and expectations upon which Israel had withdrawn.

It was, he said, a triumphant return of Nasser as a victor, and Egypt was dictating the deployment and functions of UNEF. He accused Bunche of "an attitude of subservience"[52] in Cairo. Pearson urged Eban to exercise restraint and moderation on a matter where Nasser also was under severe political pressure, to avoid making a scapegoat of the UN, and to seek clarifications in Washington, where the arrangement had originally been made. Mrs. Meir used even more forceful language to Pearson, referring to the UN's "unconditional surrender"[53] to Nasser and dismissing Pearson's suggestion that a good way to strengthen UNEF would be to allow it to be deployed in Israel as well.

In a message delivered by Bunche, Hammarskjold told Fawzi that what had already happened in Gaza had caused a serious deterioration of UN prestige and had had a very bad influence on the general situation. He was anxious that his visit to Cairo should not be made on false assumptions that would lead to a risk of a humiliating situation for the UN. Fawzi answered this message evasively, and Bunche commented to Hammarskjold: "Your road here will not be inviting. But I believe much of the road is still open though most suspiciously and grudgingly so."[54]

There were some encouraging signs. Gaza was completely peaceful and UNEF was in full evidence all over the Strip. There were no demonstrations, no Egyptian troops, no incitements against Israel, and the Egyptian governor's demeanor was moderate and unprovocative. Nevertheless, Hammarskjold was apprehensive that a story in the *New York Times* that Egyptian troops were moving toward Sharm el Sheikh, although totally unfounded, might produce some new and disastrous turn in the situation. To anticipate the Israeli fear of being faced with a *fait accompli* at Sharm el Sheikh, he instructed Burns that UNEF should not leave or hand over to Egyptian troops there before reporting to him so that he could inform the Advisory Committee, which could then decide whether to alert the General Assembly.

By the time he left for Cairo on March 19, Hammarskjold was extremely tired. Three days before, he wrote to his old friend Per Lind:

It is a pity that you are not around. It would have been refreshing to have you in the 24-hour working team which has been running this show now for five months, I can well say, without any interruption whatsoever. And you know, the team spirit is fine and for that reason, in spite of the incredible pressure and the unreasonable responsibilities, we have on the whole had quite a good time and on the human level quite some fun. The solidarity is admirable and the spirit is anything but weak, but I would dress up reality if I did not tell you that I think all of us by now are quite tired, and it therefore becomes increasingly difficult every morning to activate the energy for new initiatives and new decisions rendered necessary by the sometimes maddening difficulties which arise every day. . . . Personally I still feel, as I have done from 30 October onwards, that no one in my job can run this properly, short of a miracle, without breaking his neck politically. So far it has not happened, but that is, by God, no guarantee for the future. However, so what. . . . The position of the Secretariat seems to me to be more respected among delegates than ever. . . . On the American stage our popularity has increased in direct proportion to its decline in Europe. But God save me from any further statements by Eisenhower to the effect that the U.S. Government will accept whatever arrangements I make! Such votes of confidence make them just as ridiculous as they make me and, anyway, are not true.[55]

In the five days of intensive discussions with Fawzi and Nasser that followed his arrival in Cairo on March 20, Hammarskjold insisted on the necessity of Egyptian cooperation if the UN's efforts in the Middle East were to continue. The appointment of the Egyptian administrative governor and Egypt's uncompromising position on the Suez Canal, he told Fawzi, had created a serious problem of confidence in the UN and had given rise in some circles to the belief that Egypt had deceived the Organization. Such steps could easily wreck the progress made in the last few months. UNEF must be given an effective role, and the Canal problem must be settled. Fawzi replied that the Egyptians felt that Israel had accepted nothing and had even refused to allow UNEF into Israel, while Egypt was expected to accept everything.

Because Egypt's belligerency affected the whole concept of the Armistice Agreement as the basis for a settlement in Gaza as well as for free passage through the Canal, Hammarskjold formally raised the question. Fawzi hinted that acceptable arrangements on the role of UNEF in Gaza and in the Gulf of Aqaba could be made if the question was not pressed too hard or too formally. He was, however, not at all forthcoming over the settlement of the Suez Canal, which was to be reopened for all traffic by April 10.

At dinner at Nasser's home on March 21, Hammarskjold warned of the dangers of a unilateral approach by Egypt and of the unwillingness of Arab states to accept the simple truth of Israel's existence. Nasser expressed his confidence in Hammarskjold and said that Egypt would never use the UN in a crisis and then abandon it when the crisis was over. He was worried, however, about Israel's refusal to accept UNEF and did not see how the force could function except in a neutral buffer zone running along both sides of the line. As to Egypt's belligerency, it would continue until the refugee problem and the question of boundaries had been settled, but in the meantime

Egypt wanted "peaceful conditions without a settlement."[56] Nasser assured his guest that there would be "no surprises"[57] concerning the return of Egyptian troops to Gaza or to Sharm el Sheikh.

While Hammarskjold's talks with Fawzi continued, General Burns and Brigadier Salah Gohar of the Egyptian Foreign Ministry began to work out a detailed plan for Egypt's cooperation with UNEF. Hammarskjold and Bunche met with Nasser again on the morning of March 23 at the resthouse near the Nile irrigation barrage. They sat under an old banyan tree in the garden, and the talks reverted to the Canal problem. Egypt's proposed declaration on the Canal, which had been made public without any consultation, had put Hammarskjold and the interested governments in a difficult situation, made even more embarrassing by the unexpectedly early date for the Canal's reopening. Nasser said that no one ever appreciated Egypt's problems and that "Mollet will not be satisfied unless he has the Canal and my throat too."[58] Both Nasser and Fawzi were adamant against Hammarskjold's insistence on freedom of navigation for Israeli ships, maintaining that the state of Egyptian public opinion and the resulting security problems would make it impossible. They recalled that even the British, with eighty thousand troops in the Canal Zone, had been unable to let Israeli ships through. Hammarskjold pointed out that this was a dangerous argument because the world would say that Egypt had the responsibility to protect all ships going through the Canal on the basis of equality and justice. "It must happen some time," he said, "and it is a sad, sad story from my point of view,"[59] but all he could get was Fawzi's agreement to redraft the Suez Canal declaration, to consult various governments before issuing it again, and ultimately to register it with the UN.

Although there was no progress on the Canal, the arrangements for UNEF began gradually to take clearer shape. Nasser indicated that Egypt did not intend to move troops back into Gaza and that if UNEF stayed on at the mouth of the Gulf of Aqaba Egypt would, in Fawzi's phrase, "close its eyes."[60] Nasser in return asked impatiently about Israeli troops in the Negev and El Auja and repeated his suggestion of a neutral zone on both sides of the line. Hammarskjold's suggestion, however, that there should be "some arrangement whereby the parties can talk across the frontier to each other"[61] was received in silence.

Hammarskjold spent March 25 with General Wheeler on the Canal watching the raising of the last main obstruction, the sunken tug *Edgar Bonnet,* and returned to Cairo in time to dine with Nasser. After dinner general agreement was reached on a twelve-point plan for UNEF's cooperation with Egypt. Hammarskjold readily agreed with

Fawzi that it would be unwise to state publicly and specifically what had been understood in the talks. He would, of course, have to report to the Advisory Committee and could not guarantee what its reaction would be to the various arrangements made. He had in particular been surprised that Nasser had not made Egypt's cooperation conditional on Israel's accepting the force on the Israeli side of the Line.

From his talks in Cairo, Hammarskjold was convinced that the Egyptian government sincerely wished to have UNEF deployed in such a way as to make it effective for the prevention of raids and other border disturbances. On the other hand, the situation in Gaza was liable to give rise to spontaneous waves of marauding that, even if not instigated by the Egyptian government, would be of legitimate concern to the Israelis. This risk had to be reduced to the minimum by the proper arrangements between UNEF and the Egyptians, who would have to steer public emotion in Gaza in a peaceable direction. The delicate nature of these arrangements, however, was such that it would be unwise to publicize them. "This is not one of the fields," he told the Advisory Committee, "where it is easy for any government to have on public record what it wants to do or what it does not want to do, as the practical administrative arrangements. In fact, it is one of those areas where a government can do much more in fact than it can do in form. It is one of those areas also where something can be fully understood, but would cease being a fact the moment it was in the papers."

This paradox was both the key to the effectiveness of UNEF and the reason why UNEF's actual usefulness was so difficult to explain, because Hammarskjold's purpose was to solve problems on a practical level without raising questions of principle on which it was impossible to get general agreement. Thus in Cairo he had simply asked Burns to set down what he considered to be the necessary practical arrangements for UNEF to be effective on the armistice demarcation line, and Burns's twelve points had become the agreement with Egypt. The agreement covered infiltration across the line and the acceptance of UNEF's role in preventing it, including the right to fire on infiltrators provided Israel accepted the same arrangement, the duty of Egypt to make these arrangements known to the population of the Strip, freedom of movement for UNEF on land and in the air, and various other administrative arrangements. The Advisory Committee accepted these arrangements, although they were unlikely, as Hammarskjold pointed out, to be 100 percent effective because there was no reciprocal arrangement on the Israeli side.

It was Hammarskjold's intention to pursue the unresolved problem of freedom of navigation through the Canal with Egypt while at the same time pressing the Israelis on the deployment of UNEF in Israel. He thought it probable that this approach would cause the American press to allege that Egypt had made UNEF's deployment in Israel a condition for concessions on the Canal, although this was the opposite of the truth, and he therefore asked for the support of the Advisory Committee before he approached the Israelis. He hoped, he said, that the Committee would act as "a cloud of angels over my head" as it had during his negotiations in Cairo, and the members all agreed.

By March 29 there were unmistakable signs of another press campaign against UNEF. An Associated Press dispatch from Jerusalem quoted the Israeli Director of Armistice Affairs as stating that Arab police under Egyptian command had joined UNEF patrols in the Gaza Strip. This assertion was alleged to show "how the Egyptian dictator, Colonel Nasser, is trying to turn the UN Force into a tool of his policy of belligerency against Israel.... These events prove that the return of Egyptians into the Gaza Strip is in full swing."[62] This press campaign presented Hammarskjold with a typical dilemma. The allegations of concessions to Egypt could most easily have been dealt with by publishing the arrangements made in Cairo, had not the Egyptians specifically requested him not to announce them publicly. The fact was that Egypt had made concessions which, if published, might create a serious problem for Nasser, but as long as the arrangements were not published some important segments of the world press would continue to proclaim that Hammarskjold had surrendered to Nasser. He asked Bunche, whom he had left behind in Cairo, to find out whether the Egyptians would agree that at least a part of the twelve-point agreement could be made public, while Dulles urged that the entire plan be published immediately. Fawzi told Bunche that he had no objection to a public statement by the Advisory Committee approving the Gaza arrangements, but he did not want the terms of the actual agreement revealed. Egypt finally agreed to the publication of a paraphrase of the first two points concerning the prevention of infiltration and of the point concerning UNEF facilities, stores, and installations on Egyptian territory.[63]

The press offensive, which continued in spite of this limited announcement, gave Hammarskjold serious cause for worry, for it inevitably had an effect on the governments whose support made UNEF possible. On April 12, Joseph Alsop proclaimed an "as yet unannounced deal that has been virtually signed and sealed between UN Secretary-General Dag Hammarskjold and his assistant Dr. Ralph Bunche, on the one hand, and Egypt's President Nasser on the other."[64] Alsop also denounced the nonexistent joint UNEF-Egyptian patrols as radically altering the whole character and purpose of the UN force and transforming UNEF into a shield for Egypt against Israel. It seems probable that this story arose from garbled reports of a very different development. To deal with UNEF's difficulty in communicating with Bedouin shepherds who tended to drift across the line with their flocks, Bunche and Burns had considered the possibility of a Palestine police interpreter accompanying UNEF patrols to talk to the Bedouin in Arabic, an idea for which the Egyptians had shown no enthusiasm whatsoever. Foolish though Alsop's story was, Hammarskjold was sufficiently alarmed by its possible repercussions to issue a statement[65] that the "deal" to which Alsop was presumably referring was the understanding with Egypt recently approved by the Advisory Committee and communicated to a number of other governments—an understanding that had involved no "concessions" to the government of Egypt.

On April 10, Hammarskjold learned of Egypt's intention to move troops into Sinai. Although he had no legal right to demand a halt to this movement on sovereign Egyptian territory, such a move would undoubtedly be widely misinterpreted, and he told Burns to take the matter up urgently with Fawzi. The Foreign Minister replied that the troops were being moved into Sinai because the government had learned that French naval vessels had left Toulon for an unknown destination, and Cairo believed they were to be used in support of an effort to send an Israeli ship through the Canal. Should this experiment be made, said Fawzi, Egypt would sink the ship. Fawzi reacted strongly to Burns's approach, saying that no one had any right to object to Egypt moving its troops within its own territory. He complained that Egypt, the victim of aggression, was always being told what it should or should not do, while little or nothing was being done to restrain the movements of the aggressors.

On March 29, Hammarskjold had given Loutfi his preliminary comments on the revised Egyptian declaration on the Canal, which reaffirmed Egyptian respect for the 1888 Constantinople Convention and Egyptian ability to manage navigation and other matters in the Canal. The declaration also provided that the system of Canal tolls, now to be paid to the Egyptian Canal Authority, should remain as it had been under the last agreement between Egypt and the Suez Canal Company, and it also provided for arbitration on compensation and claims.

Hammarskjold did not like several aspects of this declaration. He thought that a unilateral declaration that was merely registered with the UN would not have very much weight and suggested the possibility of a Users Association of a truly universal and representative kind with which Egypt could cooperate. Bunche and John McCloy were instructed to discuss his ideas in Cairo before the Canal opened for normal traffic. McCloy came away from a three-hour meeting with Nasser on April 1 with the impression that Nasser suspected that all proposed revisions of the Canal declaration were designed to ensure, through various pressures, the passage of Israeli ships through the Canal, which McCloy was convinced Nasser would never allow. On April 3, Hammarskjold wrote a personal letter to Fawzi strongly urging that Egypt renounce the blockade of Israeli shipping as a token of "the will of Egypt to contribute to a stabilisation of the political conditions in the world and to co-operate with the world community."[66] The dropping of the blockade would be much more likely, he believed, to result in some progress on the refugee question than the effort to maintain it as a bargaining point. Belligerency now meant no more than the simple fact that there was so far no Middle East settlement. "Why insist on this fact," Hammarskjold asked Fawzi, "and so maintain the present dangerous state of confusion and the present basis for repeated attacks on Arab policy and on Egypt in particular?"[67]

Bunche, whom he had asked to read this letter before delivering it, found it persuasive but questioned its timing. Nasser had flatly told both McCloy and a group of American newsmen that Israeli ships would never go through the Canal. Fawzi told Bunche that Egypt considered the freedom of passage in Suez or Aqaba for Israeli ships to be just one aspect of the Palestine question. There were many other aspects, he said, on which no one seemed to be pressing for an immediate settlement, such as the presence of the Israelis in Galilee, the failure to internationalize Jerusalem, the denial of the rights of one million refugees, and the military presence of the Israelis in the Demilitarized Zone in the Negev. If so soon after the triple aggression against Egypt the Egyptian government were to allow Israeli ships to pass through Egyptian waters, "the people would sink the ships and we would have to call Wheeler back,"[68] to which Bunche replied that this could happen only if the government made no attempt to prevent it.

When Bunche gave Hammarskjold's letter to Fawzi for transmission to Nasser, he also passed on to Fawzi Hammarskjold's warning that some governments were seriously considering taking the Canal issue to the Security Council and that "intransigence ... would have political repercussions out of all proportion to the underlying interests."[69] Fawzi assured Bunche that Egypt would do its best to reach a satisfactory conclusion on the Canal issue.

On March 29 the first convoy of small freighters went through the

Canal, and on April 8 Hammarskjold cabled his heartiest congratulations to Wheeler on the completion of his task.[70] On April 24 the United States requested a meeting of the Security Council[71] to discuss the question of passage of shipping through the Canal. Fawzi submitted Egypt's Canal declaration[72] to be formally registered with the Secretariat of the UN. The fact that this declaration showed no change in the Egyptian attitude toward Israeli shipping was a heavy blow to Hammarskjold and a serious impediment in future negotiations with Israel.

RELATIONS WITH ISRAEL over UNEF showed little sign of improvement. Disregarding the fact that UNEF's principal weakness in dealing with infiltrators was that it could operate only on the Egyptian side of the line, an Israeli spokesman declared in late April, in reference to stories of infiltration, that "all this showed . . . that the UNEF has apparently lost all its effectiveness on the border. It has been turned, at Abdel Nasser's will, into nothing more than a symbolic array of foreign troops."[73] When Hammarskjold refused, with the Advisory Committee's full support, to allow UNEF soldiers to accept an Israeli invitation to spend Easter in Jerusalem on the grounds that such an arrangement would be both improper and confusing in view of Israel's otherwise total rejection of UNEF, the same Israeli spokesman stated that the "United Nations feared that acceptance would displease Abdel Nasser."[74] "I wonder," Hammarskjold commented to the Advisory Committee on the Easter problem, "if we will ever be able to write the exact story of all these matters, because there is such a wealth of information, more or less misleading, that it will be somewhat difficult to dig out and present the real story."

These difficulties convinced him of the need to reestablish contact with Ben-Gurion, and on April 19 he wrote: "Ages seem to have passed since I last had the privilege of hearing from you personally. The long time of silence has been one of grave disappointments on both sides. I firmly believe that some things might have looked different had we managed to maintain a direct personal contact." In a new effort to reach "the target we have in common—in your case peace for Israel, in my case perhaps just simply peace,"[75] Hammarskjold suggested he should visit Ben-Gurion to discuss the full implementation of the armistice agreement and the deployment of UNEF on the armistice demarcation line.

Ben-Gurion replied in a frank but friendly letter that while he would be happy to see Hammarskjold, their discussions would not touch upon the two questions mentioned in Hammarskjold's letter.

The only point to be discussed was whether Egypt would be prepared to put an end to the state of war it maintained against Israel and in particular to terminate its blockade of Israeli shipping and commerce and to abandon the dispatch of fedayeen gangs into Israel.

Ben-Gurion's unwillingness to discuss the questions of UNEF and the armistice agreement put Hammarskjold in an awkward position, and he told Ben-Gurion he could not, and had no right to, accept a negative reply on these points. He agreed, however, that there would still be scope for a joint exploration of the issue of peace in the Middle East even if they were not likely to get very far on the two General Assembly requests. "I can promise," he wrote, "that you will again find in me a very careful listener, animated by a strong desire to assist in achieving for Israel the life of peace its people deserve. I trust that you, on your side, will listen to my problems with the full understanding that the differences of approach reflect differing responsibilities rather than divergence in views as to the ultimate goal."[76]

Hammarskjold's visit to Jerusalem proved unexpectedly fruitful. Even if it left the major problems unsolved, he said later, "it brought us out of that somewhat sickly atmosphere in which these matters have been discussed for six months."[77] He found it surprisingly easy, in ten hours of talks, to reestablish a feeling of mutual trust and understanding with Ben-Gurion. When he asked Ben-Gurion how tensions in the area could be lowered, the Premier asked how the incessant and warlike declarations of the Arab states against Israel could be stopped. Hammarskjold said that he had done and would continue to do his best to get Arab leaders to desist from such statements, which were, he felt, to a large degree in the nature of ritual incantations. It would, however, certainly be difficult to alter the attitudes of Arab leaders until the Palestine refugee question was solved.

By the time Hammarskjold returned to New York on May 12, there was a notable relaxation of tension. The situation in Gaza and the Gulf of Aqaba was peaceful, and the Israelis seemed far less concerned about unwelcome developments. Although the one-sided deployment of UNEF still made its position basically unstable, Hammarskjold had been impressed by Ben-Gurion's frankness and seriousness as well as by his unaffectedly friendly attitude, and he felt less inclined to push for the deployment of UNEF in Israel until it could be balanced by some progress on the question of the Canal. Israel had recognized the right of UNEF to fire on infiltrators coming from Israeli territory into the UNEF security zone on condition that UNEF would also fire on persons coming into Israel from Gaza. In practical terms, however, the absence of a "security zone" on the Israeli side of the line made Israel's permission to shoot more or less academic.

Despite the qualified success of his visit to Jerusalem, the press campaign abated only slowly. Having spent the previous six months dealing with the results of the Anglo-French-Israeli invasion of Egypt, including clearing the Canal and trying to make a solid arrangement with UNEF on the line between Israel and Egypt and in the Gulf of Aqaba, Hammarskjold was especially irritated by a *New York Times* editorial of May 20, 1957, about the Suez Canal entitled "The UN on Trial," the final paragraph of which read: "It is therefore all the more amazing that both the Western powers and the UN Secretary-General have adopted a defeatist attitude which may still give Nasser a victory by default. . . . The fate of the League of Nations should warn against such a course."

On June 8 the London *Daily Telegraph* published an article stating that the fedayeen were now training in Rafah and Gaza and that UNEF was to all intents and purposes under the control of Egypt. The article stated large numbers of Egyptian soldiers were in the Gaza Strip as well as two thousand Palestine Arab policemen. On top of these completely untrue statements, it went on to accuse UNEF soldiers of black-market activities. Even the long-suffering Burns was sufficiently irritated by this attack to comment that it was typical of Western journalism at the time and followed strictly the Israeli line.

On July 24, Hammarskjold was able to report[78] that UNEF was functioning very well and the area was completely quiet, although occasional rumors and stories in the press still aroused uncertainties about its future. The arrangements with Egypt were being observed meticulously by the Egyptians. His main fear was that Israel's refusal to accept UNEF might still cause Egypt to demand its withdrawal and put an end to the relatively peaceful atmosphere that was essential if long-term solutions were to be found. In early September he expressed his concern forcefully once more to the Israeli representative in New York and suggested that even if the actual stationing of UNEF in Israel was not possible, Israel might at least grant rights to UNEF to cross the armistice demarcation line and to function on both sides of it. Nothing came of this approach.

This problem was much in Hammarskjold's mind when, on September 21, he put before the Advisory Committee the text of his report on UNEF to the General Assembly.[79] If the Egyptians were to demand UNEF's withdrawal, he said, "what would happen, of course, would be that the matter would be brought to the General Assembly. If the Assembly happened to agree, well and good. If it did not agree, there would be a problem to be settled because of the lack of agreement as to the extent of the task." Thus was left hanging a problem that was to fall with some force on his successor ten years later. For the time being, however, both sides seemed anxious to keep UNEF where it was.

The Assembly session, during which Hammarskjold was reelected for another five-year term as Secretary-General, was, by comparison with the drama of the preceding year, surprisingly quiet. "Everybody," he wrote to Per Lind, "behaves as if he had a major headache and for that reason is rather afraid that anybody else will make too much noise. We have had enough reasons for big noises but on each occasion people have started busily to play the stories down."[80] This was especially the case with Middle Eastern problems, and Hammarskjold noted that incidents and issues that in previous years would have caused trouble were quickly swept under the rug. He was particularly relieved that the question of UNEF's deployment in Israel was mentioned only once in a single sentence by Fawzi, and it seemed possible that another difficult and potentially dangerous corner in the Middle East had been turned. The Assembly also decided on a sound basis for financing UNEF by regular assessment of the members,[81] so that the period of improvising by securing advances from governments was ended at last.

On November 29, Hammarskjold made a one-week trip to Beirut, Amman, Jerusalem, and Damascus with the object, as he put it, of "keeping the car on the road."[82] In Jerusalem he found the Israeli attitude toward UNEF significantly changed. "The important, and I must say the highly encouraging thing which I noted both with the Prime Minister and with the Commander-in-Chief, General Dayan," he later told the Advisory Committee, "was that, unhesitatingly, they considered UNEF a major factor in the maintenance of reasonably peaceful conditions—not only around Gaza, where UNEF's contribution was fully recognized, but also in the whole region."

After visiting Sweden for the customary annual meeting of the Swedish Academy, he went on to Cairo on December 22 and from there to Gaza to spend Christmas with UNEF. Traveling mostly by jeep or Otter light aircraft, he visited all the contingents in their posts on the line as well as the headquarters and the UNRWA refugee camps in Gaza, and he shared in the various Christmas festivities. It was for Hammarskjold a moving visit, "a Christmas experience I would not have missed for anything."[83] He repeated it in 1958, when he combined it with talks with Nasser in Cairo and a visit to Ben-Gurion at his kibbutz home at Sde Boker in the Negev.

UNEF so rapidly became an established feature in the Middle East that in March 1958, Hammarskjold was able to say that "the operation has simply succeeded."[84] Apart from occasional minor alarms, the force functioned smoothly for the rest of his time as Secretary-

General. A perennial and worrying factor in the situation was criticism by other Arab states of Egypt's relation to UNEF. In time of stress there was a tendency, especially by Radio Amman, to refer disparagingly to the fact that UNEF stood between Egypt and the forces of Israel. Hammarskjold did his best to discourage such broadcasts. On November 17, 1958, for example, he wrote to Prime Minister Samir Rifai about Jordanian criticism of UNEF, "which was bound to lead to a conflict between the U.A.R. and the UN, as the majority of the UN would insist on the continued presence of UNEF while your criticism might force the U.A.R. to ask for withdrawal."[85]

Certainly this possibility was never far from Nasser's mind either. On January 7, 1959, Hammarskjold expressed to Nasser his fears that various Egyptian moves, such as the introduction of jet fighters at El Arish and a request to increase the powers of the Palestine police in Gaza, might threaten the existence of UNEF by tempting Israel to take countermeasures. If he concluded, he told Nasser, that UNEF was being used as a screen for an Egyptian military buildup, the force might have to be withdrawn. To this Nasser replied that the moves in Sinai were a reaction to the tension on the Israeli-Syrian armistice demarcation line and that he certainly did not want UNEF to withdraw. The time might come when he would have to ask UNEF to leave, but he assured Hammarskjold that when that time came he would go straight for it and not try to operate indirectly by a change of working conditions that would force the UN to take the initiative. In the light of the events of 1967, these remarks have a prophetic ring.

UNEF was an important innovation in the technique of crisis management by the United Nations, and Hammarskjold was anxious to distill its experience as a basis for possible future ventures of this kind. In the summer of 1957 he set up a study group, consisting of Bunche, Dobrynin, Stavropoulos, and UN Controller Bruce Turner, to study the UNEF experience and extract from it lessons for the future. He was averse, however, to branching out into far-reaching proposals for permanent peace-keeping arrangements, for he realized how potentially controversial the whole issue was. "This is, after all," he said, "a new departure. It is certainly not contrary to the Charter, but it is in a certain sense outside the explicit terms of the Charter. For that reason, I think it would be highly preferable if we could indulge in a short period of more organic growth, without making it a political issue now."[86]

The Secretariat study group submitted its report during the summer of 1958. Hammarskjold read it politely and then dictated his own version as a report to the General Assembly[87] that set out the principles on which subsequent peace-keeping forces in the Congo and in

Cyprus were based. The object of this report was to register agreed notions on such delicate matters as the UN's relationship with the sovereign government in whose country a UN force was operating, arrangements that Hammarskjold called "a formula of mutual acquiescence in irreconcilable rights."[88] In doing this he hoped to set out a sound legal basis, so that in future crises "we are not in the open sea to the extent that we have been"[89] and governments would have a firm body of information to go upon.

Although he emphasized that his report was primarily a pragmatic exercise, the concepts involved were already viewed in some quarters as containing the seeds of a dangerous infringement of national sovereign rights. This was not the only reason for his reluctance to carry his studies to the point of practical proposals for the future. No one was better aware than Hammarskjold of the extreme delicacy and difficulty of using international forces of the UNEF type, but the success of UNEF had given rise to unrealistic hopes and enthusiasms for the use of international forces in all sorts of unsuitable situations. The pressure to send a UN force to deal with what was essentially a civil war in Lebanon during the summer of 1958 was only one example of this trend.

John Foster Dulles in particular showed an unexpected enthusiasm for using the UNEF experiment as the basis for establishing a standing UN peace-keeping force. The success of both UNEF and the UN Observer Group in Lebanon (UNOGIL)* prompted the U.S. House of Representatives and the Senate to pass resolutions calling for the establishment of such a force. Nonetheless Hammarskjold presented his study of the UNEF experience to the Assembly[90] with the greatest reserve, pointing out that its main object was to avoid on future occasions the degree of improvisation which had been inevitable with UNEF. He also hoped that the report might make clear the "legal restrictions imposed on the Organisation by national sovereignty, as recognized in the Charter,"[91] and especially the need for the consent and cooperation of the host country. "I would emphasize," he said, "that our approach to this problem is guided by the strictest respect for the rules of the Charter. It is entirely pragmatic in nature. It does not involve, even by implication, the creation of any new obligations for Member Nations. It does not affect, or seek in any way to affect the competence of the UN organs or their interrelations under the Charter. It does not try to freeze a pattern of action, nor would it give rise to arrangements conducive to a premature or inappropriate use of similar means in the future. It does not presume to lay down

---

* See Chapter 10.

legal rules binding in all circumstances. But it does, I hope, create a preparedness for such action as may later be found necessary, in so far as our previous experience of more general application can be utilized." Although the Assembly took no formal action on his report, Hammarskjold concluded that if need should develop for another operation employing military personnel on the model of the UNEF or the UNOGIL operations, he would necessarily turn to the basic principles he had set out in his report. This was in fact what he did in mounting the Congo operation, and three years after his death the same principles were used as the basis for the United Nations force in Cyprus.

Hammarskjold continued to oppose the idea of a permanent UN force, not only because he knew that it was politically premature and unacceptable to much of the membership but also for practical reasons. "We need," he said in 1959, "really to cut the suit to the body . . . more carefully in these various cases of which UNEF is an example than in any other cases which are of concern to the UN. That is to say, to have one ready-made suit hanging somewhere in New York or stored I do not know where and to hope that it will fit the situations in various parts of the world is just to dream. We cannot afford, or usefully have, a wardrobe sufficiently rich and varied to be able to pick out just the right suit as the situation arises. It is much better to have the cloth and go into action as a good tailor quickly when the need arises."[92]

A month later he took pains to discourage the idea of a UN force for Berlin. "What would be the functions of a UN force in Berlin?" he asked a press conference in May 1959.[93] "It would be something very different from what it has been in the case where a UN force has been used. Which parties would such a force separate? . . . What kind of military functions . . . would such a force have? Against whom would they protect whom?" How, he asked, could the UN, in its present form, give orders and directives to a potential fighting force? Where could such a force be recruited from in Europe? "If you give some thought to these various considerations, I think that you can easily see that . . . a UN force which had military functions like the forces of the Four Powers, either together with them or instead of them—would be rather a curious thing . . . and basically quite unsound."[94]

A UN peace-keeping force is a delicate organism requiring special circumstances for its functioning and survival. Its evolution into something more durable and versatile will inevitably be a long process, a process that Hammarskjold was determined should not be ended prematurely by overenthusiasm, overexploitation, or misunderstanding of the nature of the problems involved.

9

HUNGARY

THE CLIMAX OF THE CRISIS in Hungary coincided almost exactly with the Suez crisis, and the two situations were dealt with at the UN in a series of round-the-clock meetings.* The outcome, however, was in

---

* The timetable of public meetings for the week of October 28–November 5 gives some idea of the stress under which the UN was working at this time:
SUNDAY, October 28, 4 p.m.–9:50 p.m. 746th Security Council meeting on Hungary.
MONDAY, October 29, 3 p.m.–3:25 p.m., 747th Security Council meeting on a French complaint of Egyptian assistance to Algerian rebels.
TUESDAY, October 30, 11 a.m.–1:10 p.m., 748th Security Council meeting on Suez.
TUESDAY, October 30, 4 p.m.–7:55 p.m., 749th Security Council meeting on Suez.
TUESDAY, October 30, 9 p.m.–11:05 p.m., 750th Security Council meeting on Suez.
WEDNESDAY, October 31, 3 p.m.–7:20 p.m., 751st Security Council meeting on Suez.
THURSDAY, November 1, 5 p.m.–7:40 p.m., 561st General Assembly meeting on Suez.
THURSDAY, November 1–2, 9:50 p.m.–4:20 a.m., 562nd General Assembly meeting on Suez.
FRIDAY, November 2, 5 p.m.–8:50 p.m., 752nd Security Council meeting on Hungary.
SATURDAY, November 3, 3 p.m.–6:50 p.m., 753rd Security Council meeting on Hungary.
SATURDAY, November 3–4, 8 p.m.–3 a.m., 563rd General Assembly meeting on Suez.
SUNDAY, November 4, 3 a.m.–5:25 a.m., 754th Security Council meeting on Hungary.
SUNDAY, November 4, 4 p.m.–8:10 p.m., 564th General Assembly meeting on Hungary.
SUNDAY, November 4–5, 9:45 p.m.–12:25 a.m., 565th General Assembly meeting on Suez.
MONDAY, November 5, 8 p.m.–10:25 p.m., 755th Security Council meeting on Suez.

almost every way different. The Hungarian crisis was a situation in which Hammarskjold had no hope of acting effectively and in which his impotence, reflecting the impotence of the Security Council and of the General Assembly of the UN, appeared in striking contrast to the effectiveness of the Organization and its Secretary-General in dealing with the simultaneous crisis over Suez. The Hungarian crisis aroused in many countries violent emotions and a sense of frustration that in turn gave rise to a general search for a scapegoat—a role which Hammarskjold as Secretary-General was unusually well fitted to fill. For those, especially in France, England and Israel, who resented the UN's activity in the Suez crisis, it was also comforting to be able to point to the UN's inability to act in the Hungarian crisis as further evidence of a "double standard" in UN affairs.

The insurrection against the régime in Hungary had begun with mass demonstrations on October 22, 1956. Martial law, censorship, a curfew, and the disorders themselves obscured the exact course of events from the outside world, although it was known that at dawn on October 24 the Hungarian government had invoked the Warsaw Treaty and had appealed to Soviet forces to help restore order. In the following week the insurgents established control of a number of provincial cities, while heavy fighting against government and Soviet forces went on in Budapest itself.

On October 28, at the urgent request[1] of the United States, Great Britain, and France, the Security Council met in emergency session to consider the situation in Hungary and heard from Arkady Sobolev a violent denunciation of the three powers for interference in the internal affairs of Hungary, whose government, he maintained, had legitimately asked for military assistance from the U.S.S.R. On the very next day the Anglo-French-Israeli expedition against Egypt came before the Council and temporarily overshadowed the Hungarian crisis.

On October 30, Imre Nagy announced the formation of a national government and stated that the Soviet forces had agreed to withdraw, and on October 31 *Pravda* published a "Declaration by the Soviet Government on the Principles of Development and Further Strengthening of Friendship and Cooperation between the Soviet Union and Other Socialist States." This declaration stated that the U.S.S.R. and its Eastern European neighbors could "build their mutual relations only on the principles of complete equality ... and of noninterference in one another's internal affairs" and that troops could be stationed in other countries only with the consent of the host state. The Soviet troops would withdraw from Hungary "as soon as the Hungarian government considered that withdrawal necessary."

This and other developments created a short-lived feeling that the crisis was over. Even so experienced a cold warrior as Allen Dulles, the head of the American Central Intelligence Agency, told Eisenhower on November 1: "The occurrences in Hungary are a miracle. They have disproved that a popular revolt can't occur in the face of modern weapons."[2] On the same day, however, in a cable to Hammarskjold, Imre Nagy protested against the entry of further Soviet troops into Hungary, announced Hungary's withdrawal from the Warsaw Pact, appealed for a great-power guarantee of Hungary's permanent neutrality, and asked that the Hungarian question be put on the agenda of the General Assembly.[3] Although the first three days of November were relatively quiet in Hungary, Soviet forces were reported to be pouring in and encircling Budapest, and on November 2, Nagy sent another message to the UN[4] drawing attention to Soviet moves and repeating his government's wish for neutrality under a UN guarantee.

At 3 a.m. on Sunday, November 4, forty-five minutes after the General Assembly had voted that Hammarskjold should submit within forty-eight hours a plan for a new and unique international instrument—the UNEF—in the Middle East, the Security Council met to consider a resolution[5] tabled by Lodge demanding that the U.S.S.R. desist from military action and withdraw from Hungary. This resolution was vetoed by the Soviet Union at about the same time as the Red Army began its final operation in Budapest, and, like the Suez crisis before it, the matter was transferred to the General Assembly.[6] Before the Security Council rose, Hammarskjold recalled the statement of conscience he had made to the Council over the Suez crisis. "Last Wednesday," he said, "I had the honour to make before this Council the declaration concerning the views I hold on the duties of the Secretary-General and my understanding of the stands that he has to take. It is certainly not necessary, but all the same I would like to put on record that the observations I made on that occasion obviously apply also to the present situation."[7]

Over the Suez crisis the General Assembly had been dealing with one small and two big powers sensitive both to public opinion and to pressure from outside. In Hungary it was faced with action in its own sphere of influence by a superpower on which no other country could exert effective pressure except possibly by a military threat that might well prove to be the start of a war between the superpowers. "The launching of the Soviet offensive against Hungary," Eisenhower wrote, "almost automatically had posed to us the question of employing force to oppose this barbaric invasion.... Unless the major nations of Europe would, without delay, ally themselves spontaneously with us (an unimaginable prospect), we could do nothing. Sending U.S. troops alone into Hungary through hostile or neutral territory would have involved us in general war. And too, if the UN, overriding a certain Soviet veto, decided that all the military and other resources of member nations should be used to drive the Soviets from Hungary, we would inevitably have a major conflict."[8] This dilemma was transferred from the Security Council to the General Assembly amid mounting public indignation and horror at the stories which were beginning to come out of Budapest.

At 8 a.m. on November 4, Radio Budapest, after playing the Hungarian National Anthem, suddenly went off the air, its last words being "Help Hungary!—Help us!—Help us!" Later in the day Free Hungarian radio stations in other parts of the country kept broadcasting appeals to the outside world that asked again and again, "What is the United Nations doing?" In Budapest itself a desperate battle was raging. Radio Moscow announced that a "Hungarian revolutionary workers' and peasants' government" had been formed by János Kádár, who had "appealed to the Soviet command for help in putting down the mutineers protected by the Nagy government." The Kádár government, which was then under Soviet protection at Szolnok, southeast of Budapest, lost no time in cabling to Hammarskjold its objection to any discussion by the UN of the Hungarian question, which "is within the exclusive jurisdiction of the Hungarian People's Republic."[9]

At 8:10 p.m. on November 4, the General Assembly adopted, by fifty votes with the eight Communist countries opposing and fifteen members abstaining, a resolution sponsored by the United States calling on the U.S.S.R. in the strongest terms to cease its intervention. The resolution asked the Secretary-General to "investigate the situation caused by foreign intervention in Hungary, to observe the situation directly through representatives named by him, and to report thereon to the General Assembly at the earliest moment, and as soon as possible to suggest methods to bring an end to the foreign intervention in Hungary in accordance with the principles of the Charter of the United Nations."[10] Although the resolution went on to call on Hungary and the U.S.S.R. to admit the Secretary-General's observers to Hungary and to urge all states to cooperate with him, the fact was that the responsibility had been transferred once again, this time to a single individual with no sovereign powers and no military or other resources, who was already fully engaged in carrying out the General Assembly's instructions of that same morning in another major crisis. The Assembly also asked Hammarskjold to look into the humanitarian needs of the Hungarian people and to coordinate the sending of the necessary supplies.

Hammarskjold's approaches both to Hungary and to the U.S.S.R.

had so far been met with a restatement of the position taken by the Soviet representative in the Security Council and in the General Assembly. It was not in his character to harbor or to foster illusions in a serious situation or to make any attempt to give false comfort to those governments which, like himself, were horrified at the agony of Hungary. At the close of a meeting on the Middle East on November 7, he informed the Assembly:

> Despite the responsibilities which the Middle Eastern question has placed upon me and my staff, we are giving serious consideration to our responsibilities under the resolution on the question of Hungary [1004 (ES-II)]. . . . That resolution has been formally called to the attention of the two Governments most directly concerned. I shall shortly be in a position to report on further steps that will be taken in implementation of the resolution. In the meantime, the Office of the UN High Commissioner for Refugees is working with other welfare agencies to meet the need for food, medicine and similar supplies.[11]

It was a bleak statement that did nothing to check the already rising tide of international criticism over his alleged inactivity in the Hungarian question.

The General Assembly discussed the Hungarian question all through November 8 and 9 and for an hour on the afternoon of the tenth, by which time resistance in Hungary itself had virtually ceased. Hammarskjold published the *aide-mémoire* he had sent the Hungarian government on November 8,[12] asking whether it would admit his observers as soon as possible and allow them to travel freely and report. He intended, he told the government, to select these observers "on the assumption that the Government of Hungary will meet the request of the General Assembly."[13] He had already taken some steps to investigate the situation caused by foreign intervention, but "it is obviously not possible to reach a final result before the end of the investigation just referred to, and without the cooperation of the Hungarian Government."[14]

By this time the representative of the Kádár government had arrived in New York and protested strongly against the General Assembly's considering the Hungarian question at all. The two days of sessions produced much oratory and four new resolutions[15] but little that could help the people of Hungary except for pledges of relief aid of various kinds. In the circumstances, it was not surprising that governments should wish to disguise their own impotence behind the pretense of waiting for Hammarskjold to produce significant results. The Secretary-General was invoked by some as a pretext for delay and by others as the cause of it. The representative of the U.S.S.R. was of the former persuasion. "Before the ink of the previous General

Assembly resolution [1004 (ES-II)] . . . has had a chance to dry," Vasily Kuznetsov said, "before the Secretary-General of the UN has been able to say a single word about the measures taken in connection with that General Assembly resolution, further draft resolutions are submitted."[16] The representative of Italy typified the latter tendency. "We have not heard anything from the Secretary-General," he said, "because the Secretary-General probably has not received any information. Nevertheless, events in Hungary are becoming more and more grave, and while the Secretary-General studies, investigates, and reports, the Hungarian people is being massacred."[17] Krishna Menon also stressed the Secretary-General's responsibility and, in a later meeting, said that "when a reference of that kind has been made to the Secretary-General on a reasoned basis, then we have an obligation to receive the report and consider the whole of this issue in a calm manner."[18] In his closing remarks congratulating the Assembly on its progress with the Middle East problem, the Acting President of the Assembly stated: "As regards the Hungarian question, lack of time, resulting from the complexity of the grave problems created by the outbreak of hostilities in the Near East, has prevented the Secretary-General from submitting a report to the present session."[19] Such a remark could only give further support to the fiction that lack of time and a preference for the Middle East crisis, rather than the nature of the Hungarian problem itself, were responsible for Hammarskjold's failure to get results.

On November 10, he addressed the Hungarian government again, expressing disappointment that he had as yet received no reply "although the situation is one of the greatest urgency."[20] He sent a copy of this message to the Soviet mission asking its support for his demand for the entry of observers into Hungary.[21] The Hungarian government replied the next day that "for technical reasons the official text of the resolution in question is not yet available to it"[22] and on November 12 repeated at length the original Soviet position that since the Hungarian situation was an internal matter exclusively between the Hungarian and Soviet governments, the sending of observers by the Secretary-General was not warranted. The government would, it added, gratefully accept "all food, clothing, and medicine for Hungarian families who face a difficult winter."[23] The Hungarian position was supported strongly in the Soviet reply on November 13.[24] Hammarskjold again invited the Hungarian government to reconsider its decision on the observers and urged it "to cooperate with the great majority in the clarification of a situation which has given rise to such concern in the General Assembly."[25]

Despite these discouraging exchanges, Hammarskjold tried to set up a mechanism for carrying out the tasks given him by the Assembly. On November 9 he had asked Judge Emil Sandström of Sweden, Alberto Lleras of Colombia, Galo Plaza Lasso, a former President of Ecuador, and Judge Oscar Gundersen of Norway to serve as observers for Hungary. His idea was to set up two separate groups, an investigation team in New York and an observer organization in Hungary itself. He told a press conference on November 12[26] that if the observers had begun functioning in time, he would definitely consider the possibility, at some point on his way to or from Cairo, of consulting with them, either in Hungary or outside. On November 16 he announced[27] the establishment of the first group, consisting of Gundersen, Lleras, and Arthur Lall of India, to prepare a report on the situation caused by the foreign intervention in Hungary.

When Hammarskjold left New York for Cairo on November 14 to negotiate with Nasser the entry of UNEF into Egypt, it was with a deep sense of frustration over the knowledge that the pressures and conditions which were making swift and effective action in the Middle East possible were totally lacking in the Hungarian affair and that, in their absence, his directive from the Assembly was more or less meaningless. It was already obvious that the only time at which he might have achieved something in Hungary was in the critical four days from November 1 to 4 when the Nagy government was in power in Budapest. At that time, however, no suggestion had been made that he should go to Budapest because, as he later said, "There was certainly not a single member of the Security Council who at that stage either felt that the situation was clear enough to make such a proposal or felt that it was a good idea to send the Secretary-General away. There was never any choice for the Secretary-General from that point of view."[28] When the General Assembly had at last given him a mandate, his offer to go to Budapest personally to discuss humanitarian matters had been rejected out of hand, as was his request to send observers.

Hammarskjold's sense of frustration over Hungary was not lessened by developments while he was in Cairo. On November 15, in response to his suggestion to the Hungarian Foreign Minister that he come to Budapest, the Kádár government replied that its representatives would be glad to meet him in Rome to "negotiate about the aid offered by the United Nations as well as to exchange views about the position taken by the Hungarian government regarding the resolution of the UN."[29] He refused this invitation, saying that "I made my offer to discuss in Budapest in view of the value of a broader personal contact with those who would be directly concerned with the matter on your side," and added he would see the Hungarian Foreign Minister on his return to New York, "which, for other reasons as well as this one, should take place as early as possible."[30]

Hammarskjold's awareness that he was being groomed as a scapegoat in the Hungarian case was intensified by a cable from Andrew Cordier reporting that the U.S. mission in New York was urgently requesting him to make a major effort on behalf of Hungarians who were "at this moment"[31] being deported to Siberia in boxcars by the Soviet authorities. "Your mission in the Near East is vital," the U.S. request read, "but the Soviets must not be allowed to use it as a smokescreen behind which they can hide their brutality."[32] Even less reassuring was the anxiety of the U.S. mission to release this message to the press immediately, a course that Cordier had strongly opposed because of its probable effect on Hammarskjold's efforts both in the Middle East and on Hungary. Hammarskjold himself was indignant. He cabled Cordier from Cairo on November 16:

> Question should be, whom does it help, whom and what does it harm? I fail to see how it could help Hungarians but it will harm the Office of the Secretary-General, me personally and what I am trying to achieve. While I am engaged in most serious and complicated operation exposing Secretary-General to unique political risks, the public is given to understand that Soviets use this as smokescreen (how?) and that I may need sharp prompting to take interest in Hungarian case. It harms me also in what I try to do in Hungarian context. I have thrown the office into big struggles of today more than perhaps can ever be justified and taken on myself personally burdens which certainly reach limits of anybody's capacity. It must be understood that in both respects there is a point beyond which I should not be pressed, either in normal forms or by public exposure. I find it also most serious that instead of a Government in prescribed forms addressing one of main organs with Government responsibility for data presented, and Assembly or Council responsibility for decision on action, in this case a Delegation seems to act on its own in a public but informal letter to Secretary-General which he cannot use as source or justification in any context, thus exposing him to full responsibility, formally and in substance, where his office should not carry it.[33]

When, at Hammarskjold's request, Cordier showed this reply to Lodge, the matter was dropped and the question of deportations from Hungary was put before the General Assembly.

Hammarskjold returned to New York from Cairo on November 19. There could now be no doubt that despite the majority vote of the Assembly, the Hungarian government would not cooperate with him in any way except on the question of humanitarian relief, on which he reported to the Assembly on November 19.[34] On November 21 he reaffirmed to the General Assembly his offer to go to Budapest.[35] He noted that in suggesting Rome as a rendezvous the Hungarian government had indicated a wish to discuss political as well as humanitarian matters. "If it had not been for matters of extreme urgency, known to this Assembly," he said,

> I would myself already, in the last two days, have taken up that thread and continued the discussion which, as appears from what I have said, I cannot regard as concluded. It follows from the previous exchange of views that it is natural to take up the thread in personal talks here where we left it. It also follows that there is no refusal from the side of Hungary which makes it impossible for me to say that I wish to maintain my offer to go personally to Budapest and, in that context, to discuss not only humanitarian activities but, likewise, the wider aspects which the Government of Hungary itself brought into the picture.[36]

This pallid gleam of hope soon faded. On November 27, he received a letter from Imre Horvath, the Foreign Minister and chief Hungarian delegate, asking him to use his influence to avoid a new discussion in the General Assembly of the Hungarian issue, "because the Hungarian delegation is under the impression that its Government is seriously considering the question of your visit to Budapest. One can understand that in the present situation the visit of the Secretary-General of the United Nations must be properly prepared. Therefore at a stage when our Government has both its hands full, it cannot be expected to decide promptly regarding your journey. The Hungarian Government would, therefore, request Your Excellency's patience and that of the General Assembly."[37] On November 28 he asked the Hungarian Foreign Minister for his reaction to the Assembly's resolution of November 21, which dealt with deportations from Hungary, especially in relation to the question of UN observers going to Hungary, on which he had to report to the Assembly. He also raised again the question of his own visit to Budapest, saying that he could be there from December 16 to 18 and would send Philippe de Seynes, to whom he had delegated responsibility for humanitarian and relief matters, a week in advance. He also asked Kuznetsov if he had any information that might be included in his report to the General Assembly.

The response was anything but encouraging, and on November 30 Hammarskjold told the observer group that its admission by Hungary was extremely unlikely. On the same day he made a comprehensive report to the General Assembly,[38] including the reply he had received from Kuznetsov on the previous day reiterating the negative stand of the U.S.S.R. and denying allegations that any deportation of Hungarians was going on. He noted that he had no reply from Hungary on the admission of UN observers and that his own offer to go to

Budapest was still unanswered. The observer group, he said, had already been examining material available to the Secretariat but had found it an insufficient basis for a report without direct observation in Hungary.

On December 4, Hammarskjold reported to the Assembly[39] a conversation with the Hungarian representative on the time and arrangements for his visit to Budapest, in which the dates of December 16–18 seemed to have been agreed. He was sufficiently encouraged by this development to ask the Austrian government on December 5 for permission for the UN observers to go through Austria to Hungary. Meanwhile another round of resolution-making in the Assembly reemphasized the role of the Secretary-General in finding a solution by reason and negotiation to a problem which had already been resolved by force. On December 12 the Hungarian mission to the UN told Hammarskjold, after announcing it first on the radio, that the date of December 16 was "not appropriate for the Hungarian Government,"[40] and on December 15 the members of the investigation group suggested that their activities be suspended because they could not possibly do anything useful or get any new information unless they could go to Hungary and have the full cooperation of the authorities. On the same day, he wrote to Horvath again appealing to him on humanitarian grounds for General Pál Maleter and others then on trial, and repeated his wish to come to Hungary personally. On December 25 he was informed by Horvath that his letter had raised questions which were exclusively the internal affairs of Hungary.

Clearly the original idea of sending observers to Hungary was now out of date as well as being unacceptable to the Kádár government. If the General Assembly was to continue to consider the Hungarian problem, a new approach must therefore be found. On January 5, 1957, Hammarskjold informed the Assembly[41] of the suspension, at its own request, of the activities of the investigating group on the basis that they had access to no information which was not already common knowledge. As he pointed out:

> So far, there has been no possibility for representatives of the UN to make direct observations in Hungary, nor has the cooperation necessary for the investigations been forthcoming from the Governments directly concerned. Under these circumstances, the only source of new and direct information possibly available might be hearings with refugees from Hungary, conducted, in the first place, in neighbouring countries. . . . In order to yield results of value, such hearings must be extensive and organised in a juridically satisfactory form. . . . This might be the proper time for a reconsideration of the form to be given to the investigatory activities. In view of the active and continued concern of

the General Assembly for the development, the Assembly may now wish to establish a special *ad hoc* committee which would take over the activities of the group of investigators established by the Secretary-General and follow them up under somewhat broader terms of reference.[42]

Such a committee, Hammarskjold felt, should serve as an organ of the General Assembly and might do more than "what could be achieved through an investigation of the kind with which the Secretary-General has been charged."[43] It would report directly to the General Assembly.

On January 10 this suggestion became the subject of a draft resolution[44] proposed by twenty-four governments, including the United States, Great Britain, and France. It called for a special committee composed of representatives of Australia, Ceylon, Denmark, Tunisia, and Uruguay, with wide powers to observe, to hold hearings, and to collect evidence. The resolution, which was adopted on the same day[45] by a vote of fifty-nine to eight with ten abstentions, immediately evoked a protest from the Hungarian government as an "unprecedented, gross interference,"[46] and as the committee began its work the protests continued. This type of investigation could not be flatly rejected as Hammarskjold's efforts to introduce observers in November had been. The new group was a committee of government representatives set up by a large majority in the Assembly and reporting directly to the Assembly itself. Moreover, in Austria and elsewhere there were now large numbers of refugees from Hungary available and anxious to bear witness to the events in Hungary. The members of the committee, K. C. O. Shann of Australia, R. S. S. Gunewardene of Ceylon, Alsing Andersen of Denmark, Mongi Slim of Tunisia, and Enrique Rodríguez Fabregat of Uruguay, were able, distinguished and energetic and went about their business with speed and the greatest seriousness. The committee held its first meeting in New York on January 17, 1957, and made its first interim report[47] on February 20. Its final report,[48] a detailed account of the Hungarian uprising and its suppression, was published on June 18, 1957.

The Hungarian crisis was a bleak reminder of the impotence of the United Nations in the face of determined opposition by a powerful sovereign state. Lester Pearson described the true nature of the UN dilemma in a speech in Toronto on December 7, 1956. "What can we do," he said, "to help these people fighting for the right to be free, a right which we take so much for granted in this country? It is not an easy question to answer. It is easy to pass off answers, but it is not easy to make sure the answer will do more good than harm if it were carried into action." To pretend that force could have been used was a "cruel deceit ... The people who would suffer first and suffer most by that kind of action on the part of the free world would be the Hungarians themselves." And, referring to the contrast between Hungary and the Middle East, he pointed out that UNEF was in Egypt with the unanimous agreement of the members of the UN, including Egypt. "There is no possibility of getting that kind of agreement in the UN Assembly in the case of Hungary, and at the Assembly we can only act, not by compulsion, but by agreement."[49]

For Hammarskjold, the sense of frustration was especially acute because at the height of the crisis the General Assembly, in desperation, had given him special and unfulfillable responsibilities, the only real result of which was publicly to focus the responsibility for failure on the Secretary-General and to establish him as a scapegoat for the inability of the member governments themselves to take any effective action. The comparison between UN action over Suez and over Hungary was persistently made, both at the time and later, as an indictment both of the Secretary-General and of the UN. In his introduction to his Annual Report for 1956–57,[50] he addressed himself to the problem firmly and deliberately. In both cases, he wrote, there had been a difference of opinion between a large majority and a small minority on the facts of the case and the remedial action to be taken, but in the vital matter of compliance with the Assembly's resolutions the two situations differed completely. There was, eventually, full compliance by France, Israel, and Great Britain with the Assembly's demand for withdrawal from Egypt.

> In the case of Hungary there was no compliance with the Assembly's political recommendations. . . . In these circumstances, the question arose as to the means which the General Assembly might use to secure compliance. The Assembly may recommend, it may investigate, it may pronounce judgement, but it does not have the power to compel compliance with its decisions. . . . At one stage, when there was delay in compliance with the General Assembly's resolutions calling for withdrawal of foreign troops from Egypt, the possibility of recommending sanctions arose but no formal proposal to that effect was presented in the Assembly. Likewise, in the case of Hungary, when compliance was refused, no delegation formally proposed a recommendation by the General Assembly to the Member States that they apply sanctions or use force to secure the withdrawal of foreign troops. The judgement of the majority of Member States as to the course to pursue in this latter case was, instead, reflected in the General Assembly's resolution of condemnation and decision to order an investigation. Both of these measures were appropriate to the General Assembly's own constitutional authority.

This dispassionate and realistic analysis was unlikely to dispel the emotions and recriminations aroused by the Hungarian tragedy, which continued to haunt Hammarskjold, especially in the press and at press conferences. Knowing all too well the tragic reality of the Hungarian disaster, he declined to defend himself against accusations which were as unfair as they were irrational. "I did what I could," he said, "and it did not yield the results I was hoping for. That can also happen in public diplomacy. It certainly often happens in private diplomacy."[51] Why, he was asked in Copenhagen in May 1959, did he not visit Budapest on November 1–2, 1956, during Imre Nagy's brief tenure of power? He replied, "At that time no one in the Security Council knew what the situation in Budapest was. But we did know what it was in Suez."[52] This answer provoked further questions in New York as to whether Hammarskjold was implying that in some sense the Suez crisis had a higher priority than the Hungarian crisis. "I do not like," he replied,

> to write history without having the documents before me, but if I remember correctly, the situation was roughly this one, to take the real crucial stage. It was only in the night between the 3rd and 4th of November that the General Assembly reached the first decision on UNEF. That first decision, as you know, was a very meagre one. It was really only asking the Secretary-General to make a proposal within forty-eight hours. It was in the morning of the 4th, that is to say in the late night of that Saturday, the 3rd, three o'clock in the morning, that the Security Council met in the final and decisive meeting on Hungary which later on led, as you know, to the question being transferred to the General Assembly. If you disregard all other aspects and look at this time sequence, I think it is perfectly clear to you that Suez had a time priority in thinking and in the policy making of the main body in the UN. That was not their choice. It was history itself which, so to say, arranged it that way. On the 4th I had in my hand a request for a report on UNEF within forty-eight hours. I do not think that the General Assembly or any member of the General Assembly would have asked me to do that and at the same time to check what was going on in Budapest. They could not have done it. I was facing a priority because they had taken a decision which they considered necessary. But mind you, from all this, it does follow that there was never, either from my side or, as I understand it, from the Security Council or the General Assembly, any ranking of the two problems, because if you look at history, the two problems never presented themselves in such a way as to provide for a choice.[53]

On the basis of the Special Committee's report, the General Assembly adopted, on September 14, 1957, a resolution[54] which found that the U.S.S.R. had, among other things, deprived Hungary of its liberty and independence, imposed the Kádár government, and carried out mass deportations; and it condemned these acts. This time the Assembly requested its President, Prince Wan of Thailand, to take steps to get compliance with the General Assembly resolutions on Hungary and report back to it. Prince Wan finally reported with regret on December 9[55] that he had been rebuffed in all his efforts by the U.S.S.R. and Hungary. "Hungary is more or less forgotten," Hammarskjold wrote to Per Lind in November. "For moral reasons I react against this tendency. Politically it may be wise to go a bit soft for the moment when so much clse is at stake. Anyway, nothing very much could be done. . . ."[56]

A BIZARRE and ultimately tragic episode[57] in the aftermath of the Hungarian crisis provided an example both of Hammarskjold's method of dealing with personnel problems and of the kind of mythmaking to which the Secretary-General of the UN is especially vulnerable in certain circumstances. The designation of a Danish Secretariat member, Povl Bang-Jensen, as deputy secretary of the Special Committee on Hungary had seemed to some of his colleagues an ill-advised appointment to a sensitive post. Bang-Jensen was a frustrated and nervous man, suffering from considerable delusions about his own importance and ability, and from the first he seemed to be jealous of his colleagues on the staff of the Committee on Hungary, as well as being critical of the Committee members. One of the main activities of the Special Committee, since it had been refused entry into Hungary, was to interview refugees, of whom 81 out of 111 wished to testify anonymously for fear of reprisals against family and friends who were still in Hungary. The taking of highly confidential testimony was not a new problem for the UN and had been arranged without mishap in previous situations.

Bang-Jensen's task as deputy secretary included the administrative arrangements for the appearance of witnesses, and he, as well as other members of the Committee's staff, had preliminary interviews with some of them. He apparently resented the fact that the names of confidential witnesses were inevitably known to some of his colleagues, and later on he was to charge that this was "sabotage" of the Committee's work. The Committee returned to New York in late April 1957 to prepare its report, a process in which Bang-Jensen played a relatively minor part, but in late May he began to assert that parts of the report contained serious errors of commission and omission, which he also characterized as "deliberate sabotage." The chairman of the Committee, Alsing Andersen of Denmark, and the rapporteur, K. C. O. Shann of Australia, patiently went over Bang-Jensen's suggestions point by point, but in the end they rejected almost all of them. After this experience, according to Andersen, "the possibility of working with him came to an end. We had found that his judgment was completely faulty." Bang-Jensen's behavior soon became stranger, and there was a scene in the Delegates' Lounge at the UN—a public place if ever there was one—when Bang-Jensen "engaged in the wildest of allegations and threats" against Shann, and grasped him "firmly by both arms, spilling his papers on the floor of the Lounge." In protesting about this episode, Shann mildly observed, "I do not believe that Mr. Bang-Jensen is quite himself."

After the Committee's report was published on June 18, 1957, Bang-Jensen continued his attacks in the form of memoranda to Hammarskjold or to Cordier, alleging that essential facts had been suppressed and that the Committee had been "sabotaged," and threatening to inform the press and others of the changes he had unsuccessfully tried to have made. Hammarskjold was determined, even though a member of the Secretariat in a sensitive post and in a highly unstable frame of mind was threatening to precipitate a public scandal, to give Bang-Jensen "every possible chance as a fellow man and as a staff member." As a first step, he ordered an inquiry into Bang-Jensen's conduct and into the allegations made by him, and his patience lasted through a whole year and through four separate and exhaustive inquiries. Ambassador Shann later wrote that "the Secretary-General has treated Bang-Jensen with kindness and generosity in circumstances which would have sorely tried the patience of many other men." In this process Hammarskjold laid himself and his senior colleagues open to attack from an increasingly bizarre group of public accusers, including a number of professional anti-Communists in the United States.

The Special Committee's report could not, by the wildest stretch of the imagination, be regarded as anything but a crushing indictment of the repression of the Hungarian uprising. Bang-Jensen, however, on his return from leave in August 1957, immediately renewed his attack on the report and its authors, telling Hammarskjold that his removal from his post as deputy secretary "is likely to have the effect of a green light to further efforts to sabotage the Committee."[58] Hammarskjold asked Ralph Bunche to make another effort to find out what evidence, if any, existed for Bang-Jensen's allegations, but again Bang-Jensen could produce no substantial evidence of any kind.

The case took a curious turn in October when a Hungarian refugee who was faced with deportation from the United States wished to prove, in his own defense, that he had testified anonymously before the Special Committee. It now transpired for the first time that Bang-Jensen had retained in his personal possession some highly confidential papers, including a register of witnesses who had appeared before the Committee anonymously. Hammarskjold at once requested, and then formally instructed, Bang-Jensen to deliver all such papers for safe-keeping to the Secretary-General, in accordance with the Secretariat's unvarying practice. This Bang-Jensen refused to do, and Hammar-skjold, faced with a grave disciplinary offense, suspended Bang-Jensen with full pay and without prejudice. He immediately set up another investigation committee, headed by Ernest A. Gross, an eminent inter-national lawyer and former U.S. deputy permanent representative to the UN, to look into all aspects of the case. It soon became obvious that Bang-Jensen had taken his case to the press. In a press conference on December 16 a correspondent asked a question so detailed as to provoke Hammarskjold to comment, "It is somewhat unusual to hear a member of the staff speaking with the voice of a correspondent in a press conference."[59] When the correspondent indignantly protested, he blandly replied that although the questions really belonged in the investigation committee rather than in a press conference, he would gladly answer them at once.

The Gross Committee supported Hammarskjold's view that the only safe place for confidential documents was in the Secretary-General's custody, adding that Bang-Jensen's documents had probably already been so compromised that they had best be destroyed. They noted especially Bang-Jensen's "ignorance of rational security pro-cedures. He told the Committee that when travelling he usually carried the papers on his person. When he went out in the evening, and felt they might not be safe on his person, he would 'conceal them in the hotel room in some odd manner.' ... He has refused to say where the papers are maintained at the present time." Hammarskjold accepted the recommendation that Bang-Jensen's papers be destroyed, and on January 24, 1958, in a strange ceremony on the roof of the UN Head-quarters, they were burned in the presence of Bang-Jensen and UN officials. The Committee had also concluded that Bang-Jensen's con-tinued employment would be incompatible with the best interests of the UN, noting his "marked inclination to see duplicity everywhere, especially on the part of those who disagreed with his opinions." The Committee suggested that under the UN Staff Rules he should undergo a medical examination, although when Bang-Jensen refused this last suggestion it was dropped.

During this time Bang-Jensen continued to talk to journalists and even managed to provide some ammunition for the Hungarian Foreign Ministry, which, in a reference to the burning of the Bang-Jensen papers, stated on January 25 that "it is a certain satisfaction to us that the UN Secretary-General has himself expressed doubts about the sources on which the report is based."[60]

On February 19, 1958, formal charges of grave misconduct were filed against Bang-Jensen and were considered by the UN's Joint Disciplinary Committee, the function of which is to consider such charges and the defense made against them and to present its conclusions to the Secretary-General. On the unanimous recommendation of this Committee, Hammarskjold on July 3 finally dismissed Bang-Jensen, who was to be given three months' pay and an indemnity of $29,000.

Bang-Jensen's appeal against this ruling to the UN Administrative Tribunal, a body elected by the General Assembly as the highest court of appeal for United Nations civil servants, was unanimously dismissed on December 5. Despite the unanimous findings against him of all the various bodies concerned, Bang-Jensen had by this time, in Ambassador Shann's words, "attracted to himself a great deal of quite undeserved sympathy." He had characterized the Secretary-General's letter of dismissal as "sheer libel," called the indemnity granted him under the normal UN rules "a bribe," and spoke of "a world-wide slander campaign" against him. In fact Hammarskjold had refused to use his powers of summary dismissal because he felt that Bang-Jensen was unbalanced and had to be given a chance to rehabilitate himself, and had instead terminated him for administrative reasons and awarded him an indemnity. At this point Robert Morris, a former chief counsel for the Senate Internal Security Committee and a veteran of the Joseph McCarthy days, recommended that there should be a public inquiry into the Bang-Jensen case. Hammarskjold had everything to gain by a full publication of all the facts, but was anxious to make it possible for Bang-Jensen, whom he knew to be a sick man, to get out of his impossible situation with dignity. A more ruthless course would certainly have spared him and the UN a great deal of trouble and adverse publicity.

After the Administrative Tribunal had ruled against him, Bang-Jensen had no further recourse except to rally outside sympathy as a self-appointed martyr in the cause of anti-Communism. With the help of Robert Morris and others he had considerable success among the extreme Right in the United States, to the point where threatening calls and the discovery that Hammarskjold's car had been tampered with caused the UN security office, much to his distaste, to provide him with special guards around the clock.

The final chapter was pathetic and tragic. After nearly a year, during which he was under psychiatric care for some time, Bang-Jensen vanished from his home on November 23, 1959. Three days later he was found shot dead in Alley Pond Park, Queens, New York. Although the verdict was suicide, rumors of assassination by Communist agents were quickly and assiduously put about. In a letter to his friend Stig

Sahlin on December 1, Hammarskjold, after commenting on the tragedy of Bang-Jensen's final breakdown, continued: "On another level, however, it is just as sad to see the curious blend of sentimentality, wishful thinking and McCarthy-ish hysteria which his suicide has stirred up. Of all the knights in shining armour who now so energetically plead the cause of fairness, not one has checked his knowledge of the facts and not one has given an even remotely correct picture of why Bang-Jensen was terminated. . . . It is a useful reminder of how myths are created."[61]

The mythmaking continued. In January 1960, Senator Thomas Dodd attacked Hammarskjold in the Senate for his treatment of Bang-Jensen; the Associated Press commissioned a story on the case that had to be scrapped when the AP correspondent at the UN pointed out twenty-eight separate errors of fact in it; and in 1961 a scurrilous book entitled *Betrayal at the UN—the Story of Paul Bang-Jensen*[62] freely cast aspersions on Hammarskjold and his senior officials. In a final attempt to draw attention to the facts, Hammarskjold authorized the publication, on December 22, 1959, of "A Chronological Record of Facts Concerning Mr. Povl Bang-Jensen's Period of Duty in the Secretariat Assigned to Serve the Special Committee on the Problem of Hungary and Subsequent Developments Ending in His Dismissal," and on January 1, 1960, of "A List of Facts about the United Nations and the Case of Mr. Bang-Jensen." "It has not," the latter paper stated, "been the wish of the UN to reopen the record concerning a man who has died. However, there is also a duty to the Organization itself, to those who serve it, and to all who believe in its aims."

PART TWO

PROLOGUE

Working at the edge of the development of human society is to work on the brink of the unknown. Much of what is done will one day prove to have been of little avail. That is no excuse for the failure to act in accordance with our best understanding, in recognition of its limits but with faith in the ultimate result of the creative evolution in which it is our privilege to cooperate.*

ON SEPTEMBER 26, 1957, the General Assembly unanimously reelected Hammarskjold to a second five-year term of office, to begin on April 10, 1958. This was no surprise and, as he wrote to Per Lind, "not a single delegation during the weeks preceding the election came to me with any wishes or suggestions, indicating implied assumptions for their acceptance of re-election."[1] Although the unanimous renewal of his mandate strengthened the authority of the Secretariat, Hammarskjold was under no illusions about underlying motives. "What created unanimity," he told Lind, "was the fact that, whatever the national

---

* Dag Hammarskjold: Address on "The Development of a Constitutional Framework for International Cooperation," at a special convocation and dedicatory celebration marking the completion and occupancy of the New Law Buildings of the University of Chicago Law School, Chicago. S/G 910, May 1, 1960.

grudges, everybody felt that they could not afford to run into a conflict over this issue and that they knew that anything short of unanimity probably would lead me not to accept re-election. Politically important was of course the fact that, in the case of the three so-called aggressors of last year, all of them sincerely wished re-election. France and the U.K. were emphatic, and Israel really went out of its way, mainly I guess due to Ben-Gurion's personal influence, although the delegation reported that their vote had been submitted to the Cabinet and supported unanimously."[2]

Hammarskjold's own feelings on being reelected were mixed. "From my personal viewpoint," he wrote, "it may be considered mad to continue but, first of all, my choice was in no way more free than in 1953, and in the second place you well know that I would never hesitate to put the UN interest first. So, finally I had no problem."[3] He both welcomed the new responsibility and, to some extent, dreaded it. "At all events, it is a situation in which personal considerations have to be put aside," he told Henri Vigier, "and therefore I have to forget both the solid nostalgia and some feelings of worry when I see a sprinter-run turned into a marathon operation."[4]

"Nobody, I think, can accept the position of Secretary-General of the United Nations, knowing what it means," Hammarskjold told the Assembly in his acceptance speech,[5] "except from a sense of duty. Nobody, however, can serve in that capacity without a sense of gratitude for a task, as deeply rewarding as it is exacting, as perennially inspiring as, sometimes, it may seem discouraging." He did not share his more personal feelings with anyone at the time. The crisis months of 1956–7, in which he played a vital role, had also been a time of stringent self-criticism, and it is clear from *Markings* that in the weeks before his re-election he gave much thought to his personal state of mind and to his future role.

> *You are merely the lens in the beam.*
> *You can only receive, give, and possess the light as the lens does.*
> *If you seek yourself, "your rights," you prevent the oil and air*
>   *from meeting in the flame, you rob the lens of its*
>   *transparency. . . .*
> *You will know life and be acknowledged by it according to your*
>   *degree of transparency, your capacity, that is, to vanish as an*
>   *end, and remain purely as a means.*[6]

Attached to Hammarskjold's own copy of his acceptance speech was a slip of paper on which, while on the podium after making the speech, he had written in pencil:

Hallowed be Thy name

Thy Kingdom come
Thy will be done
    26 September 57
       5:40

From the time given, the prayer was evidently written about ten minutes before the end of the meeting during a series of congratulatory speeches, a type of tribute he particularly disliked, and it may have been his antidote to this wave of compliments. His reply to his secretary when he came back to his office after the meeting was in the same vein. "You'll be all right," she said, seeing him look rather pensive. "I hope so," he answered, "with God's help and a sense of humor."[7]

Hammarskjold's acceptance speech stressed the problem of the UN "as a venture in progress towards an international community living in peace under the laws of justice."[8] He recalled the views on the role of the UN he had expressed in his introduction to the Report to the General Assembly[9] for the current year and his statements to the Security Council during the Suez and Hungary crises on his interpretation of the responsibilities of the Secretary-General. In preparation for his second term, he went on to expand this interpretation. The Secretary-General should not be asked to act if no guidance for his action was to be found either in the Charter or in the decisions of the main organs of the United Nations, although within these limits it was his duty to use his office and the UN machinery to its utmost capacity. "On the other hand," he added, "I believe that it is in keeping with the philosophy of the Charter that the Secretary-General should be expected to act also without such guidance, should this appear to him necessary in order to help in filling any vacuum that may appear in the systems which the Charter and traditional diplomacy provide for the safeguarding of peace and security."[10] Not a single government representative commented on this highly significant statement of intention at the time, but in *Markings* Hammarskjold noted on the day of his reelection that the course was now set "into the storm."[11]

Hammarskjold had always had precise views on what he should do, and especially on what he should not do. The Secretary-General can be effective only as long as governments have full confidence in his objectivity and independence of judgment. If he feels compelled by overriding circumstances to take a political stand in public, as Hammarskjold did in the Suez, Hungary, and Congo crises, it is always with the possibility that his future value as an accepted intermediary may be endangered, if not lost.

Hammarskjold had moved slowly in developing the political possibilities of his office. His first two years had been spent in quietly and unobtrusively learning the job, dealing with the immediate problems of the Secretariat, reestablishing its position, morale, and direction, and building up the confidence and understanding of governments. During that period, although he did nothing to avoid political involvement when it was necessary, he did not seek it either. "Basically," he said, discussing his powers of initiative in 1954, "the Secretary-General's responsibility, as I see it, is to use whatever right he may be given, and may be acknowledged to have, with the utmost flexibility and a very quick reaction, because time means so very much in these matters. . . . The Secretary-General's initiative . . . is, in principle, a supplementary one. When governments reach a deadlock, he may be the person to help them—and help them with their complete acceptance—out of the deadlock. . . . If governments are seized of a matter, if there is no deadlock, if discussions are going on and if contacts have been established . . . the Secretary-General—no matter how concerned he may be—should keep back. . . . He has no reason to jump on the stage and take over the part of any responsible government."[12]

Hammarskjold's ideas of the Secretary-General's independent political responsibilities were mainly based on Article 99 of the Charter, which authorizes the Secretary-General to bring to the attention of the Security Council any matter which in his opinion may threaten the maintenance of international peace and security. "Article 99 is all right," he told a London audience in 1954, "but it does not go far enough. Article 99 entitles the Secretary-General to take the initiative in the Security Council when he feels there is a threat to peace and security; but the real significance is not that he is entitled to take that kind of initiative, the real significance is that this Article does imply that the Governments of the UN expect the Secretary-General to take the independent responsibility, irrespective of their attitude, to represent the detached element in the international life of the peoples. . . . Sometimes he will have to voice the wishes of the peoples against this or that government."[13] This relatively conservative concept of his powers of political initiative was infused with an increasing activism by his experiences in the affair of the American prisoners in China and by his role in the Middle East crisis of 1956 and 1957. In April 1957 he described the role of the Secretary-General and the Secretariat by quoting a contemporary description of the fourth-century B.C. Chinese philosopher Sung Tzu and his followers:

> Constantly rebuffed but never discouraged, they went round from State to State helping people to settle their differences, arguing against wanton attack and pleading for the suppression of arms, that the age in which they lived might be saved from its state of continual war. To this end they interviewed princes and lectured the common people, nowhere meeting with any great success, but obstinately persisting in their task,

till kings and commoners alike grew weary of listening to them. Yet undeterred they continued to force themselves on people's attention.[14]

In his earlier years as Secretary-General Hammarskjold often spoke of the value of "quiet diplomacy" as a complement to the conference diplomacy of the United Nations. He defined "quiet diplomacy" as a "diplomacy where you can nuance what you say with all the richness which is possible in a private talk, where you can retreat without any risk of losing face and where you can test out ideas, it being understood as only a testing out of ideas and not a putting forward of proposals."[15]

By 1959, after six years' practical experience, he had developed his ideas much further—further perhaps than future events were to justify. "The philosophy of the Charter," he said, "as reflected in Article 99, gives the Secretary-General wide political and diplomatic possibilities of action of a less formal and less public nature. It is within the field of those possibilities that we have seen a very fruitful development in recent years. . . . I do hold that it is his duty to respond, without consideration of the risks, to the extent that member governments, in the spirit of the Charter, call for his assistance in such respects. I have tried to do so, and out of it is growing a new and encouraging relationship between the Secretariat and member governments. . . . Let me . . . assure you that whatever the shortcomings, I shall do what I can to develop the office, within the terms of the Charter, to as high a usefulness for member governments as circumstances permit."[16]

There are some compensations for the Secretary-General's lack of real power. "Because he has no pressure group behind him," Hammarskjold said in April 1957, "no territory and no parliament in the ordinary sense of the word, he can talk with much greater freedom, much greater frankness and much greater simplicity in approaching Governments than any Government representative can do." Given a clearcut policy line by the General Assembly or the Security Council, "the lack of means of 'pressure' . . . is in a certain sense a weakness which, however, is compensated for, and in some respects perhaps more than compensated for, by the freedom of action, the freedom of expression, which the Secretary-General can grant himself and which, I am happy to note, Governments do grant him."[17] This again proved in the end to be an overoptimistic estimate.

After his reelection in 1957, Hammarskjold steadily developed the idea of an active role for the United Nations through practical demonstrations of what the Organization could do. "The policy line, as I see it," he said in 1959, "is that the UN simply must respond to those demands which may be put to it. If we feel that those demands go beyond the present capacity, from my point of view that in itself is not a reason why I, for my part, would say no, because I do not know the exact capacity of this machine. It did take the very steep hill of Suez; it may take other and even steeper hills. . . . My policy attitude remains . . . that the UN should respond and have confidence in its strength."[18]

Hammarskjold was increasingly convinced that in the political field the UN should concentrate on preventive action rather than corrective action, which was far less effective and in the long run far more expensive, and he developed this idea a step further in the introduction to his Annual Report for 1960. "These efforts [to prevent conflict]," he wrote, "must aim at keeping newly arising conflicts outside the sphere of bloc differences. Further, in the case of conflicts on the margin of, or inside, the sphere of bloc differences, the UN should seek to bring such conflicts out of this sphere through solutions aiming, in the first instance, at their strict localisation. . . . Preventive action in such cases must in the first place aim at filling the vacuum so that it will not provoke action from any of the major parties, the initiative for which might be taken for preventive purposes but might in turn lead to counter-action from the other side. . . . The UN enters the picture on the basis of its non-commitment to any power bloc, so as to provide to the extent possible a guarantee in relation to all parties against initiatives from others. The special need and the special possibilities for what I here call preventive UN diplomacy have been demonstrated in several recent cases, such as Suez, Gaza, Lebanon and Jordan, Laos and the Congo."[19]

As more countries became independent and the UN membership steadily grew, Hammarskjold saw the Organization more and more as the champion and the rallying point of the smaller nations in a world still largely dominated by the great powers. King Hussein of Jordan once called the UN "the Summit Meeting of the small nations,"[20] and Hammarskjold felt that the Organization was a place where, by combining together, the smaller countries could make their voice heard even in the dialogue of the superpowers. "The UN," he wrote in 1960, "has increasingly become the main platform—and the main protector of the interests—of those many nations who feel themselves strong as members of the international family but who are weak in isolation. . . . They look to the Organization as a spokesman and as an agent for principles which give them strength in an international concert in which other voices can mobilize all the weight of armed force, wealth, an historical role and that influence which is the other side of a special responsibility for peace and security."[21] He went on to comment that the emergence of a group of newly independent states had created a new force in international politics that to some extent compensated for the failure of the traditional great powers to assume their responsibilities as a directing influence in the world community. A few months later, in answering Khrushchev's demand that he resign, it was this constituency of medium and small powers that Hammarskjold claimed as his own. "I would rather say," he said three months before his death, "that I see the future of this Organization very much as one of an organ which primarily serves the interests of smaller countries which otherwise would not have a platform in world affairs—these smaller countries, however, within the Organization intimately cooperating with the big powers."[22]

In carrying out both corrective and preventive peace-keeping operations, Hammarskjold turned increasingly to the middle powers and to their representatives. Lester Pearson of Canada, Hans Engen of Norway, Frederick Boland of Ireland, Carl Schürmann of The Netherlands, and Mongi Slim of Tunisia were the type of level-headed, widely respected, able, high-minded, and practical men who could provide the support and understanding which alone made it possible to set up and maintain the complex, novel, and difficult mechanisms of UN peacekeeping operations. His feelings about such collaborators were well expressed in an exchange of letters with Pearson on his ceasing to be Foreign Minister of Canada in June 1957. Pearson had written, "It has been a wonderful experience to work with you and your colleagues, particularly all those in your own office."[23] Hammarskjold, deeply touched, replied: "Your understanding of the numerous problems with which we had to deal from time to time was so perfect that the distinction between our separate status, you as Foreign Minister and head of the delegation and we as members of the Secretariat, seemed always non-existent. . . . Canada was a key in the solution of many issues confronting the United Nations."[24]

In the end, however, the support, or at least the tacit consent, of the great powers was crucial, and Hammarskjold's steadily increasing activism and initiative set him on a hazardous course between his own sense of responsibility and the interests and sensibilities of the most powerful sovereign states. He interpreted his responsibilities more and more as a duty to use his position and influence to overcome deadlocks affecting world peace by private diplomacy. In Lebanon and Laos he took calculated risks as to how much initiative by the Secretary-General the great powers would be prepared to tolerate. The risks were considerable, not least because one of the avowed objectives of his activism was to keep international problems as far as possible outside the cold war. "I consider it a very natural function for the Secretary-General," he said in 1959, "to keep problems as much as possible outside the cold war orbit and on the other hand, of course, to lift problems out of the cold war orbit to all the extent he can. That is for many reasons. One of them is that it is one way in which we can get over the difficulties created for the UN and UN operations by the cold war. It is one way, so to say, if not to thaw the cold war, at least to limit its impact on international life."[25] How far he might go in interpreting his rights under the Charter without arousing the opposition of the giants was a gamble that included both procedural ingenuities, as when he brought the Laos situation to the Security Council by means of a report without invoking Article 99, and various practical innovations such as "UN presences" and the dispatch of personal representatives to potentially dangerous areas "with the task of assisting the Governments in their efforts."[26] Such activities, including the provision of "good offices" in disputes between governments, were sometimes undertaken without any specific authorization by the Security Council, although its members were kept informed.

For a time Hammarskjold overestimated the extent to which some governments would tolerate his activism. "It is not," he said in 1959, "by suppressing his views, but by forming his views on an independent basis and by consistently maintaining them that a Secretary-General can gain and maintain the confidence on which he is dependent. Following such a line of independence, he may antagonize one group today and another group tomorrow, or a third group the day after tomorrow, but that is nothing to worry about as member governments come to realize they have much to gain and little to lose through such independence of the Secretary-General in international conflicts. Thus, the creation and maintenance of the right relationship to member states, without exception, is not destructive of the integrity of the Secretary-General. On the contrary, it depends on his integrity."[27] To more than one government Hammarskjold's independence, if not his integrity, was in the end to become entirely unacceptable.

Hammarskjold made no attempt to hide his ideas on developing the powers of his office. When he set them out in the introduction to his Annual Report for 1959,[28] he fully expected them to be challenged. To his surprise, only Krishna Menon of India even referred to them in the Assembly,[29] saying quite rightly that they were statements of political philosophy and theory having an important bearing on the UN's future, to which proper attention had not been given by the General Assembly. He had given a public dress rehearsal of his ideas in a speech in Copenhagen in May 1959,[30] which he later referred to as "a little 'handbook' concerning UN practices, UN history and UN law" designed to show "what possibilities exist in the UN."[31] In this speech he developed the idea of the UN having an existence and possibilities of action independent of the will and policies of member governments. These possibilities arose from the emergence of an "independent position" for the Organization, rooted in the existence at the UN "of an opinion independent of partisan interests and dominated by the objectives indicated in the UN Charter."[32] This was provocative stuff, and only six days later he had to deny that he had meant these ideas as a proposal. "I have shown what possibilities exist in the UN," he told a press conference. "That is not the same as to say that those possibilities should be used."[33]

A perceptive observer of the UN described Hammarskjold's position well when he wrote in January 1960: "At present Mr. Hammarskjold is on an extended safari through Africa, characteristically meeting trouble halfway by going out to look at the problems of its many emergent states, which will soon be flooding into their seats in the Assembly. His whole political pilgrimage in recent years has been as bold, as dedicated and as lonely as David Livingstone's plunge deep into an earlier Africa. But is anybody going to send a Stanley to make sure he is all right, or will the world go on comfortably 'leaving it to Dag'? There is much that could be done to support his ventures and relieve their loneliness; and little sign—apart from a few shrewd but negative remarks by Mr. Krishna Menon—that anybody is bothering to think about it."[34]

Hammarskjold proceeded to put his ideas into practice whenever he felt the situation demanded it. In doing this he based himself on the proposition that some kind of international order and international conscience were taking shape at the UN of which he, as Secretary-General, was best placed to be the spokesman and even the executive, because, by the nature of his office and his election as Secretary-General, he was lifted above the conflicts that divided the Organization. It was when the crosscurrents of the Congo crisis finally dragged him down into the conflicts of member governments that his concept of a new international order began to run into violent opposition.

Hammarskjold developed his Copenhagen theme a year later in Chicago, saying that his position as the only elected international official representing all the member governments had involved him in increasingly widespread diplomatic and political activities. While in the early stages of this development such activities had had to be on a "fairly personal basis" and in an experimental form, "in the long run they are likely to require imaginative and constructive constitutional innovations."[35] It was a course full of complex implications and risks, where "steadfastness of purpose and flexibility of approach . . . alone can guarantee that the possibilities which we are exploring will have been tested to the full."[36]

The storm, when it came in the fall of 1960, was violent, and much of Hammarskjold's last year was spent in defending his ideas and his actions. It was not only the Soviet Union which reacted strongly. De Gaulle, although more temperate in language than Khrushchev, accused the UN of "an ambition to intervene in all kinds of matters. This is especially true of its officers. It is anxious to assert itself—even by force of arms—as it did in the Congo."[37] Other governments also certainly had serious misgivings.

Under this new and heavy attack, Hammarskjold was determined to defend at all costs two positions—the independence of the Secretary-General and of the Secretariat, and the concept of the UN as a politically active organization that could, if necessary, take practical measures in conflict situations. In defending these two basic concepts his style changed radically, and he hit back against his critics and detractors with a spirit, frankness and single-mindedness that bore little resemblance to the cautious and cryptic utterances of earlier years. He lost no opportunity to put before the member governments the choice of alternatives for the future of the UN: on the one hand "a vast conference machinery, . . . a framework for public multilateral negotiations . . . robbed of its possibilities of action in the preservation of peace,"[38] a reversion to the pattern of the League of Nations, or, on the other, the active peace organization that had slowly been emerging during the previous five years.

Hammarskjold was convinced that the independent and impartial conduct of the Secretary-Generalship was at the heart of this choice. "I believe very strongly," he said in June 1961, "that the basic principle of internationalism, as established especially in Article 100, is decisive, because if it were not applied, if it were not respected, what would we have? We would have executives or Secretariats which in fact were a lower-level government and party representation. That being so, of course, you would have not an impartial execution of a decision or an agreement, but you would have, in a sense, a continued negotiation or a continued effort to reach decisions."[39]

In his last public speech, at Oxford in May 1961,[40] he warned against sacrificing the idea of an objective international civil service led by an independent Secretary-General. Such a development, he said, "might well prove to be the Münich of international cooperation as conceived after the First World War and further developed under the impression of the tragedy of the Second World War. To abandon or to compromise with principles on which such cooperation is built may be no less dangerous than to compromise with principles regarding the rights of a nation. In both cases the price to be paid may be peace."

10

LEBANON, 1958:
PREVENTIVE DIPLOMACY

THE CRISIS THAT DEVELOPED in the early summer of 1958, although very different in nature and origin from the Suez crisis, posed another serious threat to peace in the Middle East with ominous overtones of big-power involvement. The confused relationships of the Arab states, plus the obsession of the Western powers with President Nasser, which had been a major factor in the Suez debacle, transformed the outbreak of civil war in Lebanon into a major international confrontation, the possible repercussions of which were, in Eisenhower's word, chilling.[1] The situation was beclouded by misinformation, rumor, and preconceived ideas to an extent that urgently demanded an objective and disinterested go-between and some realistic and unbiased fact-finding. Such a role, although unlikely to be popular with the protagonists, was vital if the Lebanese crisis was not to develop into something far more serious.

Even before the Suez crisis, Western policy in the Middle East had been focused on an effort to underpin the older and more conservative regimes against the forces of reform and revolution, sponsored, it was widely believed, by the Soviet Union and personified by President Nasser, although Eisenhower was frank enough to say that Nasser's "exact political leanings were still something of a mystery."[2]

After the Suez crisis, Western fears of a Soviet-sponsored take-over by Nasser in the Middle East steadily increased. In late January 1958, Nasser announced that Egypt and Syria planned to unite, forming a new nation, the United Arab Republic,* and the merger was formally concluded on February 1. This development caused considerable anxiety in other Arab nations and in the West, as well as in Israel. The Kingdoms of Jordan and Iraq reacted by deciding to form a federation, the Arab Union, which was officially announced on February 14. This in turn infuriated Nasser, who went to Damascus to denounce the Arab Union in a series of public meetings in which some of his sympathizers from Lebanon took part. In late March, King Saud of Saudi Arabia, one of the more pro-Western Arab leaders, handed over to a brother, Prince Faysal, then reputedly a Nasser supporter, full powers over Saudi Arabia's foreign, internal, and financial policies. These events all influenced the Western interpretation of the internal crisis in Lebanon, which, combined with a later misapprehension about the nature of Brigadier Abdul Karem Kassem's July coup d'état in Iraq, gave rise to an anachronistic exercise in gunboat diplomacy that for a time posed a major threat to international peace.

By 1958 the delicate and almost equal balance between Christians and Moslems in Lebanon had been tipped toward a slight Moslem majority by the influx of Palestine refugees and by the higher birthrate of the Moslem population. President Camille Chamoun's pronounced pro-Western policy had aroused increasing opposition in his own country, and this opposition was further encouraged by the denunciations of Radio Cairo. Of these developments Eisenhower wrote, "It seemed likely that Lebanon occupied a place on Colonel Nasser's time-table as a nation to be brought under his influence."[3]

When, in late April, it became known that President Chamoun was supporting an amendment to the Lebanese constitution that would give him a second term, opposition to his government immediately intensified. During the second week of May serious antigovernment disturbances, involving considerable loss of life, started in the city of Tripoli and spread to Beirut, Sidon, and the northern and northeastern areas of Lebanon near the Syrian border. The situation was obscure, but by May 20 it appeared that the Lebanese Army had reestablished control in most of Beirut and Tripoli and that government forces were gradually moving into the northern border areas. The situation was

---

* For purposes of clarity, the two parts of the U.A.R., Syria and Egypt, are referred to as such in this chapter when reference is made specifically to one or other part. The union was dissolved in the autumn of 1961, and Syria and Egypt took up their separate membership in the UN again on October 13, 1961.

watched from Washington and London with growing concern through a haze of unevaluated reports and preconceived ideas. As Eisenhower put it, "Behind everything was our deep-seated conviction that the communists were principally responsible for the trouble, and that President Chamoun was motivated only by a strong feeling of patriotism."[4]

In mid-May Chamoun inquired what the U.S. reaction would be if he were to request American assistance. While a call from the lawful Lebanese government for assistance could be regarded as a legitimate reason for U.S. intervention, Eisenhower recognized that "the consequences could easily become drastic."[5] An evasive answer was given to Chamoun's request, but certain preliminary military moves were made. Amphibious elements of the U.S. Sixth Fleet were moved to the eastern Mediterranean, and army airborne battle groups in Europe were put in a state of alert for a possible move to Beirut.

Inevitably, the Soviet Union reacted to these moves. On May 17 a Tass statement declared that U.S. or Western intervention in the Lebanese crisis could have "serious consequences not only for the future of the Lebanese State and its independence but also for peace in the Middle East." The statement went on to allege that preparations were being made to land U.S. marines on the Lebanese coast "under the false pretext that the massive outbursts of the Lebanese people against foreign intervention . . . have allegedly been inspired by the United Arab Republic."

In London a British spokesman described the Tass statement as "a collection of untruths and unsupported innuendoes" and referred to the Lebanese Foreign Minister's statement of May 13, in which Dr. Charles Malik had publicly accused the U.A.R. of "massive interference" in Lebanon's internal affairs. In the House of Commons on May 19, Selwyn Lloyd invoked the Tripartite Declaration, admitting at the same time that the situation "does not, however, at the present seem to be the sort which the Tripartite Declaration was designed to meet." When asked to make it clear that the Western governments had no intention of intervening militarily in Lebanon, he replied: "I cannot make such a statement. What I will say is that no action will be taken contrary to the Charter or the established rules of international law." On the same day, the British Admiralty announced the switching of a NATO naval exercise from the western to the eastern Mediterranean so that British and American warships could be available if necessary to help in evacuating British and American nationals from Lebanon.

On May 22, President Chamoun requested an urgent meeting of the Security Council to consider Lebanon's complaint "in respect of a situation arising from the intervention of the United Arab Republic in the internal affairs of Lebanon, the continuance of which is likely to endanger the maintenance of international peace and security."[6] The intervention, he stated, included "infiltration of armed bands from Syria into Lebanon"[7] and acts of terrorism by U.A.R. nationals, as well as the arming of the rebels. On May 27 the Security Council inscribed the Lebanese complaint on its agenda but, at the request of the representative of Iraq, agreed to postpone its debate to permit the Arab League to attempt to find a settlement to the dispute.

When the Council finally began to discuss the Lebanese complaint on June 6, the Lebanese Foreign Minister accused the U.A.R. of "massive, illegal and unprovoked intervention"[8] in his country's internal affairs, to which the Egyptian representative, Omar Loutfi, replied[9] that the charge was slander and that the Lebanese troubles were an internal matter related to President Chamoun's wish to renew his candidacy for the presidency in contravention of the constitution. It was only Lebanon's insistence on bringing this matter before the Council in order to make propaganda against the U.A.R., Loutfi said, that had prevented the Arab League from solving it as a dispute between sister nations. The United States, Great Britain, and France backed the Lebanese contention of U.A.R. interference, while Sobolev, for the Soviet Union, said that the threat to Lebanon came not from the U.A.R. but from "certain Western Powers which are openly preparing for armed intervention in Lebanon."[10] Dr. Mohammed Jamali, the Foreign Minister of the strongly pro-Western government of Nuri es-Said in Iraq, supported the Lebanese complaint, saying that the matter concerned the whole of the Middle East, the threat of Nasserism to other Arab countries, and the influence which the Soviet Union exercised through the United Arab Republic. Gunnar Jarring, for Sweden, announced that he would submit a resolution that would provide for the Security Council to keep a close watch on the situation. The East-West battle lines were thus drawn up with Sweden firmly in the middle.

When, on June 10, Jarring showed Hammarskjold the draft of a resolution that the United States and Great Britain had suggested he should put forward, he was surprised to find that Hammarskjold had not been consulted by either country. Hammarskjold was totally dissatisfied with the draft text, which simply decided to send an observation group to Lebanon to ensure there was no illegal infiltration of personnel or arms across the Lebanese borders but gave no authority to the Secretary-General to provide the necessary observers and administrative support. The Council session was therefore suspended while Jarring negotiated a new text that would authorize the Secretary-General to take all the necessary decisions and actions.

The Swedish draft resolution[11] was put before the Council on the evening of June 10, and the Council discussed it until 12:30 that night. During the evening Hammarskjold asked the Norwegian, Ecuadorean, and Indian representatives to find out whether General W. Hansteen, ex-President Galo Plaza of Ecuador, and Rajeshwar Dayal, former permanent representative of India to the UN, would be available to serve as members of the three-man Observation Group that would control and evaluate the reports of the UN military observers in Lebanon. Hammarskjold informed the Lebanese representative, Karim Azkoul, Lodge, and his Soviet Under-Secretary, Anatoly F. Dobrynin, of his ideas, knowing that in this way the whole Council would be informed before the night was over. The Council adopted[12] the Swedish proposal on the morning of June 11 by ten votes, with the Soviet Union abstaining on the grounds that, although it considered the Lebanese charges unfounded, it did not think it appropriate to oppose the Swedish resolution since neither Lebanon nor the U.A.R. had done so.

After the adoption of the resolution, Hammarskjold told the Council that the necessary preparatory steps had already been taken. The Observation Group proper, he said, would be made up "of highly qualified and experienced men"[13] to be collected from various corners of the globe, and these would be serviced by a group of military observers, some of whom, from UNTSO, could be in Lebanon on the very next day. He sent David Blickenstaff, the director of the United Nations Paris Office, to Beirut at once as secretary of the observation group, telling him that the Lebanon operation was "a classical case of preventive diplomacy,"[14] the main object of which was to keep the cold war out of the Middle East.

Hammarskjold had emphasized from the beginning that the Observation Group in Lebanon was not a police force like UNEF. Nonetheless, on June 13, Karim Azkoul called on him at 2 a.m. with a request to send one to two thousand men to Lebanon at once "for the protection of the observers."[15] Hammarskjold immediately ruled out such an action because it would completely change the nature of the operation required by the Security Council, quite apart from the problem of cost, which would be of the order of $10 million. Azkoul's subsequent attempts to persuade the United States to back his request for a UN force also came to nothing.

Egypt's support for the Security Council decision to send observers temporarily allayed Western fears of Nasser's intentions. Eisenhower wrote, "The failure of President Nasser to object to a UN observation team in Lebanon was puzzling."[16] On June 15, Hammarskjold asked Mahmoud Fawzi to do all that was possible to tone down Radio Cairo's broadcasts on the Lebanese situation and suggested that he might visit Cairo.

The first five military observers arrived in Beirut on June 12 and began active reconnaissance on the morning of the thirteenth in Beirut and the surrounding countryside. On June 14, Hammarskjold announced the appointment of the three members of the Observation Group: Galo Plaza, Rajeshwar Dayal, and Major-General Odd Bull of Norway.[17] Andrew Cordier, who had been in Jerusalem, reported from Beirut that since rebel groups occupied all but some eighteen kilometers of the whole Lebanese frontier, the observers initially had no access to the border area. He suggested that aerial reconnaissance might be the only effective form of observation. On June 14, Hammarskjold told Blickenstaff that he was arranging for sixty observers to be provided by seven governments and was also looking into the possibilities of getting helicopters and small reconnaissance aircraft. It was essential to avoid any development by which the UN Observation Group in Lebanon (UNOGIL) might tip the scale in either direction in the civil war. On the other hand, some kind of contact with the opposition was obviously essential if observation was to be carried out in the areas where the government alleged the infiltration was going on. On June 16 the situation was further obscured by heavy fighting of uncertain origin in Beirut itself. Because of the confusion and the extreme political delicacy of UNOGIL's task, Hammarskjold decided to go to Beirut to preside over the first meeting of the Observation Group himself.

On the morning of his departure for Beirut, Charles Malik, claiming that there were five thousand Syrian infiltrators in Lebanon, complained that after six days nothing had been done to protect Lebanon from illegal infiltration. Hammarskjold explained that everything possible had been done but that at the time of the Security Council decision no one had known that the Lebanese government was not in control of the frontier areas, and this fact had made it difficult so far for the observers to operate on the borders. He also suggested to Malik that captured Syrian infiltrators should be made available for interrogation by the Observation Group.

Hammarskjold arrived in Beirut, after a brief stopover in London, at 5 a.m. on June 19. Shooting was still going on in the city, and he was taken to his hotel with an escort of four armored cars. He held a preliminary meeting with the three members of the Observation Group at 8 a.m. before paying a courtesy visit to President Chamoun, whom he found barricaded in his residence and surrounded by tanks and barbed wire. He informed the President that he would be going to Cairo on Sunday, June 22, to talk to Nasser.

During his stay in Beirut, Hammarskjold set a furious pace. On the day of his arrival he worked straight through until 2:30 the follow-

The Hammarskjold brothers:
(left to right) *Bo, Dag, Ake, Sten.*

Trygve Lie welcomes Hammarskjold to the "most impossible job on this earth," April 9, 1953.

Hammarskjold and Lester Pearson of Canada in the General Assembly Hall.

Peking, January 10, 1955—with Chou En-lai. Bill Ranallo is behind them.

Israel, January 1956—
Hammarskjold visits kinderg[...]
at Givath-Jearim, a village for
immigrants from Yemen.

"THE U.N.? HOW MANY TANKS HAS *IT* GOT?"

...on by David Low during
...marskjold's trip to the
...le East, April 1956.

1956—Hammarskjold is
...ed on arrival in Amman
...ime Minister Samir Rifai
...rge Ivan Smith in aircraft,
...Ranallo on right).

*Hammarskjold with President
Nasser and Foreign Minister Faw*

...iewing Danish and ...wegian advance guard of ...EF at Abu Suweir, Egypt, ...ember 17, 1956.

...ing a question at a press ...ference.

Relaxing in southern Sweden.

In Beirut with the UN Observation Group in Lebanon: (left to right) *Galo Plaza, Hammarskjold, Rajeshwar Dayal, Major-General Odd Bull.*

Hammarskjold's photograph of Annapurna—one of a series of the Himalayas taken from an Indian Air Force aircraft. Some of these were later published in the National Geographic *and the* Times *of London.*

With Martin Buber in Jerusalem,
January 1959.

Welcoming Chairman Khrushchev
and Mrs. Khrushchev, September
18, 1959. Others in front row:
(left to right) *Arkady A. Sobolev,*
V. V. Kuznetsov, Mikhail A. Men-
shikov, and Anatoly F. Dobrynin.

Dag,

Thanks — to you, to your photographic skill and to that solemn little beast — for my favorite portrait of all time and a cherished souvenir of our unforgettable African safari.
Ralph

Hammarskjold's photograph of Ralph Bunche in Addis Ababa, and Bunche's inscription.

With Prime Minister David Ben-Gurion in the General Assembly Hall, March 1960.

At Idlewild on return from the Congo, August 6, 1960: (left to right) *Henry Labouisse, Mongi Slim, Andrew Cordier, Hammarskjold.*

*With Prime Minister Patrice
Lumumba in New York,
July 24, 1960.*

Hammarskjold addressing the Security Council, February 15, 1961—the day after Lumumba's death became known. Left to right, visible at table: *Armand Bérard (France), Turgut Menemencioglu (Turkey), Valerian Zorin (U.S.S.R.), Omar Loutfi (U.A.R.), the Secretary-General, Sir Patrick Dean (U.K.). Heinrich Wieschhoff and Andrew Cordier are behind Hammarskjold.*

"Who does he think he is—a man of destiny?"

Cartoon in Sunday Telegraph
of London, July 30, 1961

Hammarskjold inspects guar[d]
honor on arrival in Leopoldv[ille]
September 13, 1961. Front ro[w,]
General Joseph Mobutu, Prin[ce]
Minister Cyrille Adoula, and
Hammarskjold. Sture Linné[r,]
the United Nations Force
Commander, General Sean
McKeown, are in the second [row.]

Hammarskjold's last journe[y]
to Uppsala.

ing morning. At one point in the evening Dayal complained that he was getting hungry, but it was too late to get any food from the hotel. Dayal finally produced a box of mangoes and a bottle of whisky for dinner—an eccentric meal that Hammarskjold later recalled with great pleasure. When in the small hours Hammarskjold at last adjourned the discussions, he asked Dayal if he had any books, since in the hurry of departure he had neglected to bring enough to read. Dayal produced a work on Hindu mysticism, *A Vision of the Soul*, and when they met at eight o'clock the next morning Hammarskjold returned it, saying he had found it most refreshing and illuminating.

On June 21, Hammarskjold told Bunche to inform the members of the Security Council that the observers were pushing out successfully to key points close to the borders and that there was as yet only very meager evidence of foreign elements in the military picture. The situation was extremely confused, and the observers might not be able to make any firm findings for some time because of the difficulty of establishing authenticated facts. In the meantime he hoped that the widespread presence of UN observers would have a restraining influence and that the time gained would be used for diplomatic and political efforts to stop pressures from outside and to straighten out the internal situation. "Of all Middle Eastern conflicts into which I have run," he told Bunche, "this is the one in which it would shock me most if it were to develop into a wide international clash."[18]

Hammarskjold's own presence in the area was also an important factor in cooling the situation down. Eisenhower, when asked at a press conference on June 18, "Under what conditions would we be prepared to take military action in connection with the Lebanese crisis?" answered: "Secretary-General Hammarskjold is taking this whole matter under his earnest and personal view. I should say that it would be dependent somewhat upon the judgments of the armistice team and the Secretary-General as to what we might have to do."[19] This relatively cool appraisal irritated President Chamoun and his immediate supporters, and Eisenhower found it necessary to remind him that it was Lebanon which had invoked the support of the UN and that the United States could not possibly intervene with military force unless the UN admitted failure in preserving the peace. If, however, Eisenhower assured Chamoun, a real crisis arose, "we would not require the concurrence or the recommendations of the Secretary-General before providing military assistance, but pending the occurrence of such a crisis the efforts of the UN should not be impeded."[20]

Bunche reported that Lodge's reaction to Hammarskjold's initial summing up of the situation on the spot was positive and cordial, but the permanent representative of Great Britain, Sir Pierson Dixon, was far less favorably disposed and was pressing for an early report on the facts of the situation, even if it contained only meager authenticated evidence. Hammarskjold found a disturbing feeling among diplomats in Beirut that the British were eager to become involved in the Lebanese situation and also to have the U.S. involved, although Lloyd, in their brief talk in London, had given the opposite impression and had recognized that any Western intervention would almost certainly mean the sabotaging of the oil pipelines, the stopping of transport of oil through the Suez Canal, and other anti-Western manifestations in the Arab world. Lloyd's concluding remark had been, "The UN simply must succeed."[21]

After a talk on June 20 with the Prime Minister, Samy es-Sohl, in which both men agreed that a fight between the Christian and Moslem population must be avoided at all costs, Hammarskjold flew on to Amman, where he reassured Samir Rifai, the Jordanian Prime Minister, that he would make no compromises over Lebanon in Cairo. In the afternoon he went to Jerusalem and talked with Ben-Gurion all through the evening. Ben-Gurion, to Hammarskjold's surprise, did not seem unduly worried over the situation in Lebanon, which he regarded as an Arab squabble, although his ideas about putting in a UN force seemed to Hammarskjold unrealistic.

On June 22, Hammarskjold flew to Cairo and, after a preliminary talk with Foreign Minister Fawzi, met with Nasser, Fawzi, and Ali Sabry, the Minister for Presidential Affairs, at 8:30 p.m. This talk, which lasted for four and a half hours, was a turning point in the Lebanese crisis and gave him the confidence to go ahead in the face of all subsequent doubts and difficulties. His main point was the necessity of getting results under the Security Council resolution if far more dangerous developments in Lebanon, including foreign intervention, were to be avoided. He told Nasser frankly that he was convinced there had been some military cooperation from outside with the Lebanese opposition in the form of infiltration and delivery of arms. If evidence of this were to be found by the UN Observation Group, the General Assembly, in case the Council were paralyzed by the veto, might well find the U.A.R. an aggressor or potential aggressor. Such a finding would produce all sorts of complications, including the question of whether UNEF could be maintained on Egypt's soil. An intervention by the United States and Great Britain in Lebanon could also not be ruled out, and all the U.A.R.'s links with the West would be broken. The U.A.R., he told Nasser, had overplayed its hand badly in Lebanon and had to change its course quickly. Military infiltration must stop and the radio propaganda of the "Voice of the Arabs," which was an open incitement to rebellion in Lebanon, should come to an end.

Nasser asserted that when he visited Damascus "half a million Lebanese,"[22] including opposition leaders, had approached him and insisted that he go ahead with some kind of union between the U.A.R. and Lebanon. He had been at pains to discourage these ideas as quite unworkable because of the inevitability of strong opposition in Lebanon. He fully agreed with Hammarskjold that Lebanon should be a meeting ground between East and West with an established and generally recognized kind of neutrality. He had done his best to discourage the Lebanese opposition from starting a civil war, but when Lebanon had taken the case to the UN Security Council he could no longer maintain this line and had lifted all restrictions. The result had been a flow of small arms on muleback into Lebanon from Syria. Nasser soon gave Hammarskjold his promise that all infiltration of a military nature and all traffic in arms would be stopped. Hammarskjold replied that he did not want Nasser's promise, since he himself could promise nothing. What was important was that Nasser fully understood what he had wished to say, so that he would draw the right conclusions and act accordingly. When he encountered unflattering talk about him, Hammarskjold told Nasser, he invariably gave one reply: "However that may be, he has never gone back on anything he said to me personally."[23] Nasser answered, "I wish to maintain that record."[24]

On the following day, Fawzi confirmed Nasser's undertakings and told Hammarskjold that orders had been given to discontinue all military assistance to the rebels across the Lebanese border from Syria. Fawzi was worried about press speculation or leakage on Nasser's decision, which would be very badly received in Cairo, in Syria, and by the Lebanese opposition leaders. This meant that Hammarskjold would have to persuade Chamoun to moderate his own actions without being able to tell him of Nasser's decision, which would have been by far his strongest argument. Hammarskjold was well satisfied with his talks with Nasser but realized that Nasser's decision could very easily be upset by speculation or publicity. He cabled Bunche that he was "hoping strongly that anxious friends will stay out of the sickroom."[25] Bunche passed on this advice to Lodge, who agreed with its wisdom but reported that Washington's attitude was still largely unchanged, although Hammarskjold's efforts had had some effect in discouraging the supporters of direct U.S. intervention.

Hammarskjold flew back to Beirut on June 24 for lunch with the Premier. When asked about his visit to Cairo, he replied that he was "reasonably confident on the possibilities of the UN operation,"[26] which seemed to satisfy his host. At the end of the meal an enormous glazed cake was brought in, on which was inscribed, around the Lebanese national coat of arms, the words *"ONU, sauvez le Liban"*

("UN, save Lebanon"). Hammarskjold commented loudly for the benefit of the press, *"Excellence, je ne peux accepter cette inscription, parce que c'est pour le Liban de sauver le Liban"*[27]* ("Excellency, I cannot accept this inscription, because it is for Lebanon to save Lebanon"). He and the Premier were then extensively photographed with the cake.

Later in the afternoon Hammarskjold told Chamoun that while he could not divulge the substance of his talks with Nasser, he felt much more confident than before that the UN effort, of which the Observation Group was only one element, might well stop infiltration and arms smuggling, so that the Lebanese could decide for themselves on the country's internal affairs. His confidence now had to be tested against events, and it would be best to put off any further steps until diplomacy and the UN observation operation were given a chance to show results.

Before his departure for New York on June 25, he again saw Chamoun, who raised once more the possibility of stationing a UN force along the Lebanese-Syrian border. Hammarskjold explained the difficulties that would arise if such a force had to fire on Lebanese citizens, as well as of finding contingents for a force to deal with a delicate internal situation. To seal the border would require a force of at least two divisions—in fact one three times as large as the Lebanese Army itself—and in any case at the moment the need for such a force had not been established. On taking leave, he told Chamoun that the Premier's parting word had been *"Espérons"* ("Let us hope"), to which Hammarskjold had replied, *"Non, attendons"*[28] ("No, let us wait"), but after his second talk with Chamoun he was prepared to accept the Premier's terminology. This somewhat cryptic leave-taking formula was soon to give rise to controversy and misinterpretation.

From their own observation of the situation, Galo Plaza and Dayal had concluded that General Fouad Chehab, the army commander, and Kamal Jumblatt, the chief opposition leader, wished to avoid the use of force, and that if Chamoun could be persuaded to relinquish his ambitions for reelection, Chehab would be generally acceptable as an interim President. Dayal had managed to visit Jumblatt, who had confirmed this conclusion. The opposition leaders also seemed inclined to give free passage to UN observers in opposition-controlled areas. The key to the situation, therefore, was Chamoun's attitude.

Before leaving Beirut on June 25, Hammarskjold sent a message to Fawzi saying that he believed he had managed to work effectively in Beirut in the direction of "peace and fairness on which, I know, we are agreed. I have done so on the basis of our talks without, however,

---

* I.e., ". . . *parce que c'est au Liban* . . ." Hammarskjold's French was practical but not idiomatic.

in any way giving away what came out of those talks. My way of trying this has been to engage myself personally, saying that the optimistic judgement I now hold about the possibility of getting out of the present troubles, in a sound way, is a judgement passed 'with the strongest sense of responsibility and with full integrity.' . . . I have made myself a hostage to the implementation from your side of the policy which you indicated, but about which nothing has been said here. This has been possible for me in the light of our talks seen against the background of what I referred to, to the President, as his record of never having backed down on anything he has told me. I am sure that now as before my trust will prove justified."[29] He hoped, he told Fawzi, that the way might now be clear for the Lebanese to decide their own future without further international complications.

Hammarskjold's confidence was put in question while he was still on his way back to New York, when Samy es-Sohl called for Galo Plaza to complain about the disturbances in Beirut on June 25 and the continuation of radio propaganda from Cairo. He asked again for a large international police force to seal the border and seemed to fear that General Chehab might overthrow the government, which had given him command of all Lebanese forces only four days previously. The Premier hinted that he was thinking of seeking outside assistance if UN intervention was not forthcoming.

On his return to New York on June 26, Hammarskjold told reporters that he considered that the Observation Group, which now had ninety-four observers in the field, had got off to a very satisfactory start.[30] This statement prompted the representative of Lebanon in New York to declare that infiltration and arms smuggling were continuing and even increasing, and that the Lebanese forces were in action against infiltrators in the north while intensive fighting was going on in Beirut, Tripoli, and elsewhere. "It appears, therefore," he said, "that there is no ground for the optimism that has been lately expressed in some quarters."[31] Hammarskjold limited himself to commenting through a spokesman[32] that this statement had been brought immediately to the attention of the Observation Group in Lebanon and that the Lebanese authorities would undoubtedly wish to provide the Group with all the evidence they might have. Plaza was astonished at the Lebanese statement, for there had been no significant change in the situation since Hammarskjold's departure and the battles described were vastly exaggerated. The observers had so far been unable to find any evidence for the alleged illegal infiltration of men and arms, and for the previous two days the broadcasts from Cairo had been unexpectedly restrained.

The Lebanese campaign to discredit the Observation Group and to cast doubt on Hammarskjold's own conclusions received support on

June 27 from Foreign Minister Jamali of Iraq, who repeated the allegations of Nasserism and infiltration and also argued that a UN force should deal with the rebels. This line was pursued on June 28 by Azkoul, who maintained that the relaxation in international tension over the Lebanese situation was due solely to Hammarskjold's statements and "optimism." Hammarskjold pointed out that it was Chamoun, and not he himself, who had told the press that he was optimistic. He warned Azkoul that if a proposal for a UN force in Lebanon were to be put to the Security Council or the General Assembly and if the Secretary-General were to be asked to execute such a decision, he would be compelled to state that in the present circumstances he could not accept such a mandate.

Hammarskjold's main objective was to isolate the Lebanese internal struggle from outside influences. He was convinced that as soon as all the parties in Lebanon realized that no outside power was going to come to their help with armed force, they would settle their own affairs among themselves. He emphasized to the United States the importance of not forcing Nasser to resume military assistance to the Lebanese opposition by making highly publicized deliveries of arms to the Chamoun government, and he explained his views in long letters to Dulles and Lloyd. He pointed out that Nasser seemed to have acted, as he had asked him to do, to stop arms smuggling and infiltration, and it was to be hoped that no irresponsible statements from Beirut would reverse this trend. Although Chamoun had told the outside world that he was not a candidate for a new term as President, he had not told the Lebanese people, and until he did this reconciliation in Lebanon was impossible.

A long-term solution for Lebanon, Hammarskjold told Dulles, could be "a guaranteed neutrality of a somewhat Swiss type, based on the fact that Lebanon is a meeting ground between Christians and Arabs—in the same way as Switzerland is a meeting ground between French and German elements."[33] Lebanon could then be a stabilizing element in the Middle Eastern situation. "It is my belief," he wrote, "that only by an action of Chamoun, of the kind indicated, can a lessening of the Western influence in the Middle East be avoided. Were the Lebanese Government to push the conflict to the point where they publicly ask for outside assistance, in principle going beyond what we are at present providing through the United Nations, I fear very much that whatever reaction the West were to give, it would end in a defeat for the Chamoun regime *and* a weakening of the position of other Western-oriented governments in the region. It is also only through an early action along the lines indicated that I think that it can be avoided that the future developments of the internal political situation in Lebanon will get the appearance, in Arab eyes, of a victory, however modest, for Nasser."[34]

Ben-Gurion, presumably working for a U.S. intervention in Lebanon, now unexpectedly joined the critics of Hammarskjold's efforts, which he described as "the abandonment of Lebanon to the intrigues of the ruler of the U.A.R. . . . I do not know," he wrote Hammarskjold on June 30, "what promises the President of the U.A.R. gave you . . . but I do know that arms, ammunition and armed men cross the border daily from Syria into Lebanon. . . . Is not a Middle Eastern Munich in the making?"[35] Fawzi, on the other hand, wrote on July 2 that he believed, as Hammarskjold did, that "without international complications, the Lebanese have to make their own decisions and adopt their own line of action for the settlement of their internal problems."[36] He promised the U.A.R.'s full support for his efforts and said that the "Voice of the Arabs" would certainly be toning down its broadcasts.

In times of crisis one overworked word or phrase sometimes comes to express a stereotyped criticism. In Hammarskjold's handling of the Lebanon case the word was "optimism," of which he was constantly accused, especially by British, American, and Lebanese sources. "Those who challenged the expression 'optimism,'" he said on July 3, "were the ones who had characterized my stand as optimistic. I never did."[37]

In early July, President Chamoun announced publicly that he would leave office when his term expired on September 23, and it began to seem possible that the Lebanese crisis would pass, as Eisenhower later put it, "without Western military assistance."[38] In its first reports on July 3 and 5,[39] the Observation Group freely admitted that it was having difficulty in gaining access to much of the frontier area held by the rebels and could provide no substantiated or conclusive evidence of infiltration from Syria into Lebanon. The Lebanese government, on the other hand, based its dramatic allegations on vast dossiers of rumors of infiltration, smuggling, and terrorism, many of which, although unsubstantiated and unprovable, were made available to the press.

The first report of the Observation Group and Hammarskjold's comment that there was no evidence as yet of "mass infiltration" immediately gave rise to new and strong Lebanese criticisms. The Lebanese Minister of Information claimed that three thousand armed Egyptians, Syrians, and Palestinians were fighting with the Lebanese rebels and that the U.A.R. had supplied the rebels with thirty-six thousand guns, including light and heavy artillery and mortars. The Premier attacked Hammarskjold's assertion that there was no mass infiltration of arms or men into Lebanon and again demanded that the UN set up a police force to seal off the border with Syria. In New

York, Charles Malik said that his government took strong exception to the UN report and insisted that the U.A.R. was continuing "massive, illegal and unprovoked intervention in the affairs of Lebanon."[40] The Lebanese government's official reply to the Observation Group's report, published on July 8,[41] criticized its "inconclusive, misleading or unwarranted"[42] conclusions.

Reflecting on the development of the Lebanese problem, Hammarskjold recalled that Malik had told him that there had been little infiltration from Syria until Lebanon had taken its case to the Arab League and to the Security Council, and this appraisal had been confirmed by Nasser in Cairo. The Security Council proceedings and threats of Western intervention had turned the Lebanese question into a matter of prestige for Nasser. It was essential, therefore, to calm the situation down to a point where it no longer involved Nasser's prestige in the Arab world, so that he would be able to continue to honor the undertakings he had given Hammarskjold in Cairo.

The Lebanese government and much of the Western press showed no sign of cooperating in any effort to reduce tension and publicity. On July 6 the London *Daily Mail* published an allegedly exclusive interview with President Chamoun in which he made highly derogatory remarks about the UN observers, adding that Hammarskjold had allowed Nasser to understand that he could take the whole Middle East without any objection on the part of the UN. The UN observers, Chamoun was reported to have said, were acting like tourists. Hammarskjold protested strongly to the Lebanese mission in New York about this story, asking whether the report was true, whether the Lebanese government really thought that there was still massive infiltration going on across the border, and if so, why no Syrians or alleged Syrians had been made available to the UN observers for questioning. The mission's response was to repudiate the *Daily Mail* interview.

There were also widespread press reports that the U.S. and British governments were dissatisfied with the first reports of the Observation Group. Hammarskjold was irritated at this press campaign, which was, he knew, to a considerable extent officially inspired. "I did not expect anything better," he wrote to Lloyd, "in view of the far more grotesque theories which developed during the Suez crisis, when I was considered to be fooled by, if not the stooge of, Nasser, but I think that the outcome of the various arrangements with Egypt during and after the Suez crisis, for which I was responsible, should have led the papers to the conclusion that they might all the time have been wrong. However, what does it matter? The straight line often looks crooked to those who have departed from it."[43]

At lunch in Washington on July 7, Dulles showed him a lengthy list of alleged infiltrations, which seemed to Hammarskjold to be put together irrespective of sources or verification. Dulles told him that the United States was under heavy pressure from Iraq, Turkey, Iran, and Israel to intervene in Lebanon. De Gaulle had let it be known that if the United States and Great Britain were to intervene, France, because of its traditional position as a great power in the Middle East, must also take part, although Dulles had done his best to discourage him. Dulles still appeared to be anxious to find a solution that would make intervention unnecessary. Hammarskjold told him that he believed Nasser was sincere in not wishing Lebanon to join the U.A.R. but he too was under heavy pressure both from the Syrians and the Lebanese opposition. It was essential, therefore, to create a situation in Lebanon that would give Nasser the strongest possible reason for disinteresting himself in Lebanon, in the same way that UNEF had given him an excuse to disinterest himself in Israel. With this end in view, he suggested that UNOGIL might eventually be transformed into a semipermanent, though smaller, body with wider terms of reference relating to the independence and integrity of Lebanon. Dulles seemed much interested in this idea and asked for time to think it over. He congratulated Hammarskjold on the success of his talks in Cairo and told him that U.S. intelligence had confirmed that, after his talks with Hammarskjold, Nasser had given strict orders that no further assistance would be given to the Lebanese opposition.

Hammarskjold was still unsure of the extent to which infiltration from Syria had effectively ceased. Some of UNOGIL's first reconnaissance flights did nothing to dispel his doubts, for they purported to show that on the first two nights of reconnaissance, July 7 and 8, convoys of thirty to fifty motor vehicles had been detected on roads crossing Lebanon's northern border from Syria. As a result of these reports, he began to have doubts whether Cairo's influence in Damascus was sufficient to give full effect to Nasser's agreements with him. He expressed his concern to Loutfi, who sent a strong message to Cairo conveying Hammarskjold's request that Cairo dissociate itself at once from any such activities. Cairo immediately replied that the U.A.R. was keeping its undertakings to him and that his information was incorrect, but further air reconnaissance reports of convoy activity caused Hammarskjold to make yet another strong démarche to Cairo on July 11. He also suggested that UN observers be stationed on the Syrian side of the border as a means both of stopping whatever infiltration there was and of clearing Cairo of any responsibility for it.

Hammarskjold urged Galo Plaza to evaluate the aerial reconnaissance reports without delay. The Observation Group would be held responsible, he said, if some buildup from Syria resulted in an attack on Tripoli before the Group had submitted any information at all to the Security Council on the night reconnaissance reports. He also urged Plaza to send one of the Observation Group members to contact Rashid Karame, the opposition leader in the north, in order to warn him that any obstacles put in the way of UN ground observation would tend to confirm the evidence from aerial reconnaissance of military support from outside, which, when reported to the Security Council, would have very serious repercussions. He repeated this warning in even stronger terms to Cairo, urging the government publicly and unambiguously to dissociate itself from the policy of infiltration.

Direct observations by UN observers of suspicious movements had to be evaluated by the three-man Observation Group before a report was made to the Security Council. General Odd Bull, an experienced pilot, was aware of the unreliability of initial reconnaissance flights over unknown territory by inexperienced pilots, and he made intensive efforts to correlate the night aerial reconnaissance reports with observations on the ground in the same area. By July 11, arrangements had been made for the UN observers to operate in the opposition-controlled northeastern area of Lebanon. Bull made a personal survey of the northern region and reported, on the afternoon of July 13, that there was no sign at all of the sort of military build-up that would be necessary for an attack on Tripoli. Bull also learned that there was a large summer traffic of grain, fruit, and vegetables from the Akkar plains on both sides of the border, and that this traffic went largely by night in order to preserve the freshness of the garden produce. Karame emphatically denied to Bull that there was any movement of arms by road convoy across the border. Another opposition leader, Sabri Hamade, said that ordinary civilian supplies for much of the northern area around Baalbek came from Syria anyway, but because of daylight attacks by Lebanese government aircraft much of this traffic now had to go by night. Both Plaza and Dayal were inclined to agree with Bull in accepting these assurances at their face value, and they also accepted Bull's conclusion that there was no concentration of men or arms in the north that would make possible an attack on Tripoli. When the UN air observers were cross-examined on their reports, it turned out that they were by no means sure of the exact location of the vehicle movement or exactly what it was they had seen, and further efforts to check their observations on the ground failed to identify many of the features they had reported. In the light of all these factors, the Observation Group finally concluded that the air reconnaissance reports of infiltration were worthless.

This episode, although more startling events soon eclipsed it, left a legacy of mistrust. The British embassy in Beirut had somehow learned of the pilots' unevaluated reports and had passed the story on to London, where it became the basis for a thinly veiled attack on the integrity and objectivity of UNOGIL by Macmillan and Lloyd, as well as for officially inspired, and far less veiled, stories in the press. The most notable of these was an editorial in the *Times* of London for July 18, entitled "A Question of Facts," which quoted Lloyd's and Macmillan's allegations about rebel convoys crossing the border from Syria into the area round Tripoli and bluntly accused the Observation Group of suppressing evidence. Hammarskjold was sufficiently irritated by this editorial to issue a statement[44] pointing out that the Observation Group did not report findings until the evidence on which they were based had been evaluated.

EARLY ON THE MORNING of July 14, the world heard the first news of the overthrow of the Hashemite monarchy and the pro-Western government of Nuri es-Said in Iraq. The army and the mob had engulfed the Royal Palace and murdered Crown Prince Emir Abdul Illah and, it was learned later, Prime Minister Nuri es-Said and King Faisal as well. Foreign Minister Jamali, who only a few days before had been representing Iraq in the Security Council, was also at first reported to have been killed. Although the origin and motivation of the Iraqi coup were obscure, there was an initial tendency in the West to believe that it was part of a Communist plan to take over the Middle East, the specter that had haunted Western intelligence agencies for so long. "We feared the worst," Eisenhower wrote. "This somber turn of events could, without vigorous response on our part, result in a complete elimination of Western influence in the Middle East. Overnight our objective changed from quieting a troubled situation to facing up to a crisis of formidable proportions. Lebanon again came into our conscious concern because of the internal conflicts in that country and the pressure exerted by Syria."[45] The almost complete absence of reliable information on which to base such conclusions seems only to have increased the inclination of the U.S. government to take some form of urgent action, and the only place where such action could be taken was in Lebanon, which had no common frontier with Iraq. The sacking of the British embassy in Baghdad during the coup put the British foursquare behind the United States, and by the time it became clear that Brigadier Abdul Karim Kassem's revolution in Iraq had no connection whatsoever with the alleged Nasser-Moscow plot in Lebanon, the Western interventions had already occurred.

Realizing at once the virtual inevitability of American intervention,

Hammarskjold informed Plaza that the coup in Iraq made a Lebanese request for Western military assistance an imminent possibility. It was no surprise when Dulles called him at 1:30 p.m. on July 14 to warn him, as he had promised to do, that the request for U.S. intervention had been received from President Chamoun, and that the Iraqi coup had completely changed the U.S. policy he had explained to Hammarskjold over lunch a week earlier. Dulles hoped, however, that the Lebanese question would stay within the UN framework. Chamoun had in fact publicly invoked the rather vague U.S. commitment to him without even consulting Washington, thus putting the United States in a highly awkward position in which, as Dulles put it, "the U.S. were damned if we did and damned if we didn't."[46]

Events now moved rapidly. In Washington, Eisenhower spent the day in anxious consultation with Dulles and his brother Allen, the director of the CIA, reviewing the news and the rumors that were coming in from the Middle East and considering the possible repercussions of various courses of action. Eisenhower was haunted by the notion that an American intervention would be equated with the Anglo-French attack on Egypt in 1956. In his consultations with a bipartisan group of Congressmen he found wide support for intervention in Lebanon, although Senator J. William Fulbright, chairman of the Foreign Relations Committee, was extremely skeptical of the idea that the crisis was Communist-inspired and argued that Hammarskjold's lack of success in identifying support from across the Syrian border for the Lebanese rebels should preclude any American intervention.

Eisenhower believed that the risk of general war with the Soviet Union as a result of an American intervention in Lebanon* was less than the risk of doing nothing, although he admitted to himself that "the possible consequences in each case, if things went wrong, were chilling."[48] He finally directed that an American landing should take place on the following day, July 15, at 3 p.m. Lebanon time. In the meantime the United States would call an emergency meeting of the Security Council to take place on the morning of the fifteenth. No public statement would be made until the landing was actually taking place. Eisenhower then telephoned Prime Minister Macmillan, whom he found "completely in accord with my decision, almost eager,"[49] and who informed Eisenhower that he himself had received a request for

---

* Khrushchev told Nasser, who arrived in Moscow at dawn on July 17, that "the Americans had gone off their heads and 'frankly, we are not ready for a confrontation. We are not ready for World War III.' Khrushchev told Nasser that, if attacked, he would have to lean with the storm; there was no other way because Dulles could blow the whole world to pieces." (Mohammed Heikal, *Nasser: The Cairo Documents.*)[47]

support from King Hussein of Jordan. Macmillan, remembering Suez, was insistent on an American assurance that the British and Americans were in this together all the way.

Lodge came to see Hammarskjold at 9:30 a.m. on July 15 to inform him of the U.S. decision to land troops in Lebanon, acting under Article 51 of the Charter* at the request of the Lebanese government. Hammarskjold told Lodge that in his opinion this legal form was extremely thin since the United States was quite obviously moving in because of the coup in Iraq and not because of any new developments in Lebanon. The fact that U.S. forces would soon be fighting on the government side would require a new decision from the Security Council on the position of UNOGIL, for if the U.S. Marines were to go to the Lebanese border and seal it, UNOGIL would become quite useless. There could be little doubt, he told Lodge, that as soon as the first U.S. ship appeared on the horizon all Nasser's restrictions on infiltration from Syria would inevitably be lifted. Lodge himself seemed to be almost as disturbed as Hammarskjold at the new situation.

To the Observation Group in Lebanon the American landing represented a setback to almost everything they had tried to do or had succeeded in doing. Dayal heard the news on his way back from a meeting in Tripoli with the opposition leader, Karame, whom he had assured of his personal conviction that there would be no foreign intervention. The landing took place at the very moment when a political settlement seemed at last to be in sight, for General Chehab—who, by keeping the army out of the internal struggle, had prevented a total disaster in Lebanon—seemed likely to become the President-elect. If the American intervention was not directly related to the Lebanese situation but was in response to the events in Iraq, it was even more difficult to understand, since Lebanon could not possibly be used as a beachhead for intervention in either Jordan or Iraq, being contiguous to neither.

When the Security Council met at 10 a.m. on July 15, Hammarskjold gave an account of his actions under the mandate given him by the Council's resolution of June 11.[50] He also mentioned his own diplomatic efforts in support of the observation operation, which, he pointed out,

---

* Article 51 reads:
   Nothing in the present Charter shall impair the inherent right of individual or collective self-defense if an armed attack occurs against a Member of the United Nations, until the Security Council has taken measures necessary to maintain international peace and security. Measures taken by Members in the exercise of this right of self-defense shall be immediately reported to the Security Council and shall not in any way affect the authority and responsibility of the Security Council under the present Charter to take at any time such action as it deems necessary in order to maintain or restore international peace and security.

now had full freedom of movement in the northern areas as well as in the rest of Lebanon.

Lodge informed the Council that the United States had responded positively to a request for assistance by the government of Lebanon. The U.S. forces that were landing in Lebanon were not there to engage in hostilities of any kind but only to help the Lebanese government in its efforts to stabilize the situation and to protect American lives. Some indication of the inaccuracy of the information available to the United States on the Iraqi coup appeared in the second paragraph of Lodge's speech,[51] which was devoted to a description of the supposed murder of Foreign Minister Jamali.*

Both Lodge and Eisenhower emphasized that the American action had been taken not to supplant the UN but only to fill the gap until such time as the UN could take measures to preserve Lebanon's independence, thus permitting the early withdrawal of U.S. forces. While the Council was meeting in New York, Blickenstaff, from the window of his hotel-room office in Beirut, saw vessels of the Sixth Fleet and reported by cable to Hammarskjold: "One destroyer and three troop transports on horizon outside our hotel obviously proceeding toward airport where they will arrive in about half an hour. We have withdrawn all personnel from airport."[52] A little later he reported that the airport had been seized by five hundred U.S. Marines and that some fifteen hundred more were just being landed.

The American action produced strong repercussions. In Beirut, army units led by General Chehab went out apparently prepared to resist the U.S. forces, and some kind of *modus vivendi* was achieved only at the last minute in conversations between Chehab and the American Ambassador, Robert McClintock, who met between the advance guards of the two armies. Blickenstaff reported that both Dayal and Plaza were considering notifying the Secretary-General that their mission as members of the Observation Group must be considered to be at an end with the first American landings. Hammarskjold urged Blickenstaff to persuade the members of the Group not to take any decision before reading the statements that had been made in the Council, no matter what their immediate personal reactions to the situation might be. Later, sensing the tension among the three members of the Group, he sent them his personal comments on the proceedings in the Council.

---

* Jamali was in fact tried from September 20 to 25, 1958, and sentenced to death on November 10. Hammarskjold immediately appealed to the Iraqi government, and the sentence was never carried out. In March 1960, Kassem commuted Jamali's sentence to ten years' imprisonment, and in July 1961 he was granted amnesty on the third anniversary of the Iraqi revolution.

When Lodge had informed the Security Council that the U.S. forces in Lebanon "are being instructed to cooperate"[53] with UNOGIL and to "establish liaison"[54] with it immediately upon arrival, Hammarskjold gave instructions that "there was no basis for establishing any contact or working relationship, formal or informal, between UNOGIL and any non-Lebanese forces in Lebanon, beyond what is necessary for the actual functioning of our operation, such as access to the airport."[55] Blickenstaff was authorized to put out a press statement saying that the UN was in Lebanon solely to observe infiltration by any foreign troops and that any active cooperation with the U.S. forces was impossible.

The Soviet Union submitted a draft resolution under which the Security Council would call upon the United States "to cease armed intervention in the domestic affairs of the Arab States and to remove its troops from the territory of Lebanon immediately."[56] The representative of Lebanon stated that Lebanon's situation had been worsened by the events in Iraq and demanded that the Council urgently take more effective measures to prevent the continued infiltration of arms, men, and materiel.

Commenting on the day's meetings in the Council, Hammarskjold cabled Blickenstaff, "temperature much lower than expected with obvious lack of positive feelings about latest steps."[57] The United States was obviously anxious that UNOGIL survive but also that it be enlarged in order to provide a justification for a U.S. withdrawal. Although no specific proposal had been made, Washington seemed to have in mind some kind of international force to create stability in and around Beirut. If the Council decided to send such a force, he told Blickenstaff, "it cannot be excluded that their terms of reference or use will prove to be such that they will just be a new quixotic element added to the already unique picture."[58] Privately, Hammarskjold made it clear to the United States that if American troops were to be actually deployed in Lebanon, he would have no option but to recommend the immediate withdrawal of UNOGIL. The probable consequences of withdrawal were such, however, that he was determined if possible to avoid it.

On July 16 the United States introduced a resolution under which the Security Council would, among other things, request the Secretary-General "immediately to consult the Government of Lebanon and other Member States as appropriate with a view to making such additional arrangements, including the contribution and use of contingents, as may be necessary to protect the territorial integrity and independence of Lebanon and to ensure that there is no illegal infiltration of personnel or supply of arms or other materiel across the Lebanese borders."[59]

This resolution, the United States explained, would make it possible for the U.S. forces to withdraw promptly.

On the same day, Hammarskjold drew the attention of the Council to the interim report of UNOGIL[60] setting out "the complete success with which they have met in their arrangements for inspection all along the Lebanese border. . . . The fact that this result—of which I gave a first, short indication in my statement yesterday—is reached at this stage, that is to say the day of the renewed debate in the Security Council and the landing of the U.S. units, is a coincidence, the results achieved by the UN yesterday being the logical and successful outcome of its previous efforts."[61] He hoped, he told the Council, that no later developments would cause a setback and that the Observation Group would retain its key position. "A retreat on my side on UNOGIL," he cabled Blickenstaff, "would mean leaving the situation entirely in the hands of the U.S., which I will *not* do. I believe that, in cooperation, we may have a chance, building on UNOGIL, to widen the [UN] beachhead to a solid position from which the necessary political steps can be taken for a straightening out of the situation, leaving the UN as the only non-national element in Lebanon."[62]

In taking this position, Hammarskjold found himself violently opposed from an unexpected quarter. On July 16, Östen Undén, the Foreign Minister of Sweden, instructed his representative at the UN, Gunnar Jarring, to present to the Council a resolution stating that "the action now taken by the United States Government has substantially altered the conditions under which the Security Council decided, on 11 June 1958, to send observers to Lebanon," and requesting the Secretary-General "to suspend the activities of the observers in Lebanon until further notice."[63] Hammarskjold was appalled at this initiative from his strong-willed former chief, and Jarring was equally embarrassed, not least because he knew that the only possible support that the Swedish resolution would get in the Security Council would be that of the Soviet Union.

As the Foreign Minister of a neutral country that had made the original proposal for the Observation Group, Undén took the position that the circumstances in which the Swedish government had proposed UNOGIL had ceased to exist as a consequence of the American landing. When Jarring told him on the telephone that the resolution would only get the Soviet vote and the Swedish vote, Undén replied cheerfully that one vote plus the Swedish vote was quite enough to make the point of principle. In a total departure from his normal practice, Hammarskjold called up Undén to remonstrate with him, but his sole reward was an agreement by Undén to give him and Jarring twenty-four hours to see what they could do about the situation.

Hammarskjold was firmly convinced that to remove the UN observers on legalistic grounds at this critical juncture would be irresponsible and would destroy the last possibility of a peaceful solution. His fears of a sudden widening of the crisis were increased when at 10 p.m. on July 16 Lodge informed him that the U.A.R. had urged the Lebanese opposition to resist forward moves by the U.S. troops and not to support any effort at a compromise or cease-fire. The United States also had information that paramilitary operations among the refugees on the West Bank of the Jordan were to be organized immediately. He knew already that such a reaction by Cairo was inevitable, but the news about the West Bank was especially disturbing. After careful consideration, at midnight he gave Loutfi a message to Fawzi conveying his own alarm at the possible breakdown of UNOGIL, the strengthening of which seemed to provide the only hope of persuading the United States to withdraw. He also stressed the dangers of any stirring up of the Palestine refugees in Jordan or Gaza at this critical point and begged Fawzi to do what he could to avoid adding to the already explosive situation "new elements which might only too easily prove to be the fuse finally lighting the explosive charge which we have so far miraculously managed to isolate from fire."[64]

Undén's agreement to postpone his proposal for twenty-four hours put Hammarskjold under heavy pressure to secure immediate support for expanding the UNOGIL operation. He asked the Observation Group for an immediate further report on its work and organization that would explain its significance in the present situation. He himself provided an outline of the kind of report he would like to receive, including a suggestion to increase the number of observers and possibly to add a quota of noncommissioned personnel to be used for ground reconnaissance work. The Group duly submitted a report along these lines on July 17,[65] recommending an increase in the number of observers in Lebanon from the existing 113 to 200.

President Chamoun was not the only Arab head of state to be alarmed by the Iraqi coup, and on July 16 King Hussein of Jordan, whose cousin, King Faisal of Iraq, had been murdered in the coup, asked for British military support. The British responded to Hussein's appeal by sending 300 paratroops, who landed in Amman on the morning of July 17 and were reinforced on July 18 by 1,700 more. It was only with the support of Washington that Britain obtained Ben-Gurion's permission for the British troop-carrying aircraft to be flown over Israel, and there was strong pressure on him both in Israel and from the Soviet Union to withdraw this authorization at once. Two days later the United States politely sidestepped a suggestion made by Selwyn Lloyd in Washington that the Jordan expedition be a joint

U.S.-British affair. On July 17 the Jordanian government asked for an urgent meeting of the Security Council[66] on U.A.R. interference in its internal affairs, and on July 20 it severed diplomatic relations with the U.A.R. in protest against the latter's recognition of the new republican regime in Iraq.

On July 18 the Security Council rejected the Soviet resolution demanding the withdrawal of U.S. troops from Lebanon and the British troops from Jordan. The U.S. resolution was then vetoed by the Soviet Union, and the Council also rejected the Swedish resolution, as Jarring had foreseen, with only Sweden and the U.S.S.R. voting for it. The United States then proposed a special session of the General Assembly to make appropriate recommendations concerning the Lebanese complaint, while the U.S.S.R. made a similar proposal in order to consider the intervention of the United States and Britain in Lebanon and Jordan respectively. The Council then adjourned to await a compromise proposal that was being formulated by the representative of Japan.

The British attitude on the Lebanese crisis had worried Hammarskjold from the beginning. Lloyd flew to Washington on July 19, and Hammarskjold could not avoid the suspicion that one of his objectives was to dissuade the United States from withdrawing from Lebanon. A luncheon he gave for Lloyd and his entourage on July 20 did little to reassure him. Hammarskjold explained his view that the easiest way to get the U.S. troops out of Lebanon was to expand UNOGIL. As to the British troops in Jordan, he himself would rather like them to stay, since the British presence meant that the Secretary-General could for the moment forget about the Jordan-Israel problem. The British, he felt, had every reason in the world to get out of Jordan as soon as possible before they ran into that problem in an acute form, quite apart from incurring mounting resentment in Jordan itself. Lloyd answered that the British were indeed anxious to get out of Jordan and that it would be disastrous if the United States got out of Lebanon on the pretext of an expanded UNOGIL without some device being found for getting the British out of Jordan at the same time. Hammarskjold suggested that if it was possible to build up the UN observer capacity on the Israel-Jordan armistice line and along the Syrian border and to get a four-power guarantee for Lebanon and some sort of UN presence in Jordan, disaster might be averted at least for a time.

The U.S. landings caused the UN observers in Lebanon to be treated for a time with extreme distrust and obstructionism, especially in opposition-held areas. The flight of American jet-reconnaissance aircraft all over Lebanon made the population uneasy and also provided an incidental hazard to the observation flights of the much slower UNOGIL aircraft. Washington soon reappraised its initial and hasty diagnosis of the Iraqi coup, and Robert Murphy, Eisenhower's special envoy, flew to Iraq to give Washington's assurances to Kassem and then proceeded to Cairo to confer with Nasser. The panic and misapprehension were dying down, and once again the time was coming to save faces and to resume the long, slow haul toward a peaceful solution.

On July 19, Khrushchev proposed a meeting of heads of government on the Middle East, to be held in Geneva on July 22 with the Secretary-General participating.[67] France, India, the U.S.S.R., the United States, and Great Britain were to take part, and the recommendations made at the meeting would be given to the Security Council for review. Hammarskjold told Sobolev that for the immediate future he would go ahead with expanding UNOGIL, whether or not the resolution to be proposed by Japan was adopted by the Security Council, since everyone agreed that a way must be found to get the American troops out of Lebanon. Sobolev was uneasy about Hammarskjold's authority to expand UNOGIL without a Security Council decision, but Hammarskjold told him that if he did not overplay his hand he might say he had such authority under the Charter. He also told Sobolev that he would not be a party to putting a UN force into Lebanon and, if necessary, would say so publicly before such a notion was voted on.

The United States did not accept the Soviet proposal for a meeting of heads of government, on the grounds that the resources of the UN for maintaining peace in the Middle East were far from exhausted and that the five powers could not sit down to decide the fate of the Middle East without the participation of Israel. As an alternative, Eisenhower suggested that a summit meeting might be held within the framework of the Security Council.

On July 21 the Japanese representative, Koto Matsudeira, introduced in the Security Council a resolution requesting the Secretary-General "to make arrangements forthwith for such measures, in addition to those envisaged by the resolution of 11 June 1958, as he may consider necessary in the light of the present circumstances, with a view to enabling the United Nations to fulfill the general purposes established in that resolution, and which will, in accordance with the Charter of the UN, serve to ensure the territorial integrity and political independence of Lebanon, so as to make possible the withdrawal of United States forces from Lebanon."[68] It was not his intention, Matsudeira told the Council, "to create a police force of any kind,"[69] but only to provide for a strengthened UN Observation Group in Lebanon. All the members of the Council except the Soviet Union reacted positively to the Japanese initiative, with Lodge going so far as to say that the resolution "could lead to conditions which would make possible the withdrawal of U.S. forces from Lebanon."[70]

Sobolev, however, opposed it on the ground that it amounted to a tacit moral sanction for the continued presence of the U.S. and British forces in Lebanon and Jordan, and that since it did not specify what other measures the Secretary-General was required to take "the Security Council would, so to speak, be buying a pig in a poke."[71]

Although Sobolev vetoed the Japanese resolution, his proposed amendments to it had included one that authorized the enlargement of the Observation Group in Lebanon, and this encouraged Hammarskjold, despite the failure of the Council to reach a decision, to inform the Council of his own intention[72] to take the practical steps that were needed without delay. In doing this, he recalled both his statement at the time of the Suez crisis that the Secretary-General's task should not be allowed to "degenerate into a policy of expediency"[73] and his statement to the General Assembly on his reelection that he believed it to be in keeping with the philosophy of the Charter that the Secretary-General also should be expected to act without guidance from the Assembly or the Security Council, should this appear to him necessary, toward helping to fill any vacuum that might appear in the systems which the Charter and traditional diplomacy provide for the safeguarding of peace and security. In the present case he felt that it was his duty to help prevent a further deterioration of the situation in the Middle East and "to assist in finding a road away from the dangerous point at which we now find ourselves."[74] "Were you to disapprove," he told the Council, "of the way in which these intentions are translated by me into practical steps, I would, of course, accept the consequences of your judgment."[75] In the absence of any dissent, he assumed that the Council tacitly endorsed his intentions.

As soon as the Council adjourned, Hammarskjold asked the Observation Group to provide at once a detailed plan for the strengthening of UNOGIL, and on July 24 the Group replied that a total of 636 military personnel plus ten aircraft and four helicopters would be required for the new establishment. Hammarskjold immediately set to work to recruit this very large additional team.

Hammarskjold had pushed his powers of independent initiative to a new limit in his last statement to the Council, leaving behind him a vacuum of constitutional authorization. With the precedent of the UNEF Advisory Committee in mind, he set about filling this vacuum in an informal way by asking the same countries—Argentina, Brazil, Canada, Ceylon, India, Norway, and Pakistan—to serve as a consultative group on Lebanon. Announcing the appointment of the group on July 24, "in view of the growth in size and significance of the UN operation in Lebanon,"[76] he emphasized that its members were appointed in an "exclusive personal capacity,"[77] and at the group's first meeting on July 25, he described it as a "strictly extra-constitutional group, not unconstitutional at all."[78] He then proceeded to try out his ideas for the future on the group. The basic idea was that a clearly visible UN physical presence within Lebanon, as well as on its borders, would have a calming effect, especially in the somewhat delicate period that might follow an election. He hoped to develop UNOGIL on these lines until it provided the pretext for the U.S. withdrawal.

There were soon a number of signs that the U.S. withdrawal might not be too long delayed. On July 25 the *New York Times* reported a statement by Chamoun that if the Lebanese presidential elections produced an acceptable compromise candidate, the U.S. troops might withdraw within a month. In a Senate subcommittee hearing on the same day, U.S. Ambassador Wadsworth said that the U.S. troops in Lebanon "may be withdrawn 'quite soon.' "[79] In Beirut General Chehab indicated that he would be willing to accept the presidency if it was offered to him, and that the U.S. troops should withdraw within four-teen days after the elections. On July 31, Chehab was elected President.

The relationship both of Hammarskjold and of the Observation Group with the Lebanese government had been strained throughout the crisis. It had been impossible to avoid the impression that both Charles Malik in New York and Chamoun in Beirut, sometimes with the assistance of the United States and Britain, had persistently tried to undermine the credibility of the Observation Group because its findings did not help Chamoun politically and also reduced his chances of getting active military support from the United States. Times were changing, however, and on July 28 Malik agreed both to Hammar-skjold's request for a status agreement for UNOGIL and to his suggestions as to the role and authority of the UN observers.

THE CONTROVERSY over the possibility of some form of summit meet-ing, which occupied the last week of July, gave Hammarskjold a brief respite in which to think about a more comprehensive approach to the Middle East situation. His main concern was to suggest forms and arrangements for the increasingly dynamic Arab unity movement that would not create acute international problems, and his thoughts on this matter became the basis of the general agreement reached late in August. Four main problems had to be faced: the status of Gaza, Jordan, and Lebanon; the policy of the big powers in the Middle East; some "mutual assistance-noninterference"[80] arrangement among the Arab states themselves; and some method of safeguarding Western oil supplies. The situation in Gaza, with UNEF coexisting with an

Egyptian civil administration and with no Egyptian troops, was for the moment satisfactory. On the other hand, Jordan and the regime of King Hussein were extremely vulnerable, and a heavy-handed UN move within Jordan would threaten Hussein's prestige almost as much as a threat from Israel. Hammarskjold therefore envisaged stepping up the UN observer operation on the West Bank of the Jordan and establishing a larger UNTSO office in Amman to lessen the risk of incidents and to add an element of stability in Amman itself, which would in turn strengthen Hussein in relation to Syria and Iraq. In Lebanon it seemed likely that President Chehab would soon want to reduce the UNOGIL operation or even have it withdrawn altogether. In this case Hammarskjold hoped that UNOGIL might be succeeded by some form of UN presence in Beirut—a UN commissioner perhaps —to guarantee Lebanon's special status as recognized by the UN. The effect of such UN arrangements in Gaza, Jordan, and Lebanon would be to establish a sort of "cordon sanitaire,"[81] which would break the trend toward a military encirclement of Israel.

Hammarskjold hoped that after the alarms and excursions of the summer the big powers might try to develop what he called a "shared self-discipline,"[82] which ideally should include an embargo on arms shipments to the area, although he recognized that this was almost certainly wishful thinking. To encourage inter-Arab cooperation he intended to resume his efforts of the past year to develop institutions for economic cooperation and to promote a wider agreement among the Arab states covering nonaggression, noninterference, and mutual assistance.

Western oil supplies would best be safeguarded by a general détente in the region, reinforced perhaps by an agreement between the oil-producing countries such as Iraq and oil-transmitting countries such as the U.A.R., guaranteeing noninterference with the transit of oil. Hammarskjold hoped that it might also be possible at a summit meeting to get the U.S.S.R. to recognize formally the Western interest in the oil supply. He deliberately excluded from his thinking for the time being the basic questions of the Palestinian refugees and a permanent territorial settlement with Israel because he felt that the first necessity was to deal with the causes of the current crisis.

At the end of July, Khrushchev's efforts to persuade the United States to join in some form of summit meeting finally failed, and on August 5 the Soviet Union requested an emergency meeting of the Security Council to consider the Soviet proposal for an emergency special session of the General Assembly "to discuss the question of the withdrawal of United States forces from Lebanon and of United Kingdom forces from Jordan."[83] On August 7, after a six-hour meeting, the Security Council unanimously adopted an amended U.S. draft resolution calling for an Emergency Special Session of the Assembly.[84]

By this time, Western fears of an impending Moscow-inspired Nasser-executed take-over in the Middle East had largely evaporated. In Lebanon the election of General Chehab had brought the government and the opposition together, while Washington had changed its initial interpretation of the republican coup in Iraq to such an extent that on July 30 the United States recognized Brigadier Kassem's government. A steady thinning out of U.S. troops in Lebanon had already begun.

The relaxation of Western anxieties over the Middle East was not matched by any lessening of tension among the Arab states. In particular, distrust and mutual recrimination still dominated the relations between Jordan and the U.A.R. The main problem before the Assembly, therefore, was to achieve some measure of reconciliation among the Arab states themselves. The Jordanian problem was now potentially much more serious than the Lebanese situation, but no UN solution could be evolved without consultation with both the Jordanian authorities and other Arab governments. In any case, nothing could be done until after the Emergency Special Session of the Assembly, and Hammarskjold's main worry was that the Assembly might fail to make any progress at all.

The Third Emergency Special Session of the General Assembly convened at 5 p.m. on Friday, August 8, 1958. Hammarskjold addressed the session[85] on "some of the basic needs for action"[86] and set out ideas for a Middle East détente that he had worked out the week before. The Assembly then agreed to adjourn until August 13 to enable some twenty Foreign Ministers, including Dulles, Lloyd, Gromyko, Fawzi, and Maurice Couve de Murville of France, to attend.

Eisenhower addressed the Assembly on August 13[87] and put forward a comprehensive program for peace in the Middle East, much of which resembled the program which Hammarskjold had outlined five days before. Eisenhower's six points were: (1) United Nations concern for Lebanon; (2) United Nations measures to preserve peace in Jordan; (3) an end to the fomenting from without of civil strife; (4) a United Nations standby peace force; (5) a regional economic development plan to assist and accelerate improvement in the living standards of the Arab nations; (6) steps to avoid a new arms race in the area. While in general agreement with five of these points, Hammarskjold considered Eisenhower's proposal for a standby peace force ready for immediate action to be dangerous, as well as unacceptable to a large number of member states.

The debate in the Assembly lasted from August 13 to 21 in a general atmosphere of moderation, which prevailed also in the Middle East itself. On August 12 the Observation Group reported[88] that since the election of General Chehab there had been "virtually a nation-wide truce"[89] in Lebanon, and on August 18 the British and U.S. governments stated[90] that they would withdraw their troops from Jordan and Lebanon if the UN took steps to ensure the peace and security of those countries.

Speaking for the U.S.S.R., Andrei A. Gromyko welcomed Eisenhower's plan for economic assistance to the Middle East but insisted that the primary duty of the Assembly was to secure the immediate withdrawal of U.S. and British troops. Selwyn Lloyd emphasized that Britain had gone to the assistance of Jordan at King Hussein's request and that the troops would immediately be withdrawn when the UN had taken action to safeguard Jordan's independence and integrity. Jordan and Lebanon repeated their charges against the U.A.R., which Fawzi vehemently denied.

Behind the scenes, the search for a resolution that would be generally acceptable to all the interested parties was pursued in intensive private consultations among Dulles, Gromyko, Lloyd, Fawzi, and Hammarskjold, the meeting between Lloyd and Fawzi being their first since the Suez crisis. Hammarskjold also worked closely with the Norwegian Ambassador, Hans Engen, who on August 18 sponsored with six other countries a resolution*[91] that took note of the British and U.S. declarations of withdrawal. It reaffirmed "that all member states should refrain from threats or acts, direct or indirect, aimed at impairing the freedom, independence or integrity of any State, or of fomenting civil strife and subverting the will of the people of any State,"[92] and urged all nations to put this principle into effect in relation to the Middle East. The resolution went on to request the Secretary-General to make such practical arrangements, in consultation with the governments concerned, as might help to uphold the principles of the Charter in relation to Lebanon and Jordan, noted that the Secretary-General was already studying the feasibility of establishing a standby UN peace force, and asked him to continue his studies and also to consult with the Arab countries on the assistance they might require in establishing an Arab development institution.

In presenting this compromise resolution, Engen admitted that it was not perfect but maintained that it embodied "very fundamental elements representing some of the positions of all the parties directly

---

* Engen dined with Hammarskjold on Sunday, August 17, and they worked on the text of the resolution. After dinner they went to see a play and lost the first draft of the text in the taxi on the way to the theater. After the performance Hammarskjold sat down at his own typewriter and reconstructed the draft.

concerned."[93] Despite intensive efforts to enlist the support of the twenty-eight–nation Afro-Asian group in the Assembly, no agreement on the resolution could be reached, particularly because it did not demand the withdrawal of foreign forces from Jordan and Lebanon. At the final meeting of the Afro-Asian group on August 20, Fawzi suggested that in view of the prevailing differences in the group, the representatives of all the Arab states should meet separately among themselves to try to evolve a formula satisfactory to all. This Arab meeting produced the next day a resolution[94] that was presented to the Assembly by Mohamed A. Mahgoub, the Foreign Minister of Sudan. It contained much of the Norwegian resolution and an added reference to the obligation stated in the pact of the Arab League that the Arab states should strengthen the close relations and numerous ties linking them. It also referred to measures by the Secretary-General in relation to Lebanon and Jordan that would facilitate the early withdrawal of foreign troops from the two countries and invited the Secretary-General to continue to study and consult with the Arab countries concerning an Arab development institution for economic growth.

The Arab resolution was unanimously adopted by the Assembly on the evening of August 21,[95] bringing the proceedings to an unexpectedly triumphant close. Its adoption was hailed by Dulles as a new opportunity, by Lloyd as a constructive first step, by Gromyko as useful work, by Mahgoub as the beginning of "a glorious future"[96] for the Arab nations, and by Arthur Lall as "the beginning of a new era of cooperation and prosperity, a new era of peace in the Middle East."[97] Charles Malik even went as far as to tell Hammarskjold, who gave a luncheon in his honor on August 23, that the Lebanese opposition leaders were good patriots and personal friends of his, devoted to their country. Abba Eban, understandably, expressed "certain profound and serious reservations,"[98] since the principles enunciated in the resolution were clearly not intended to apply to the relationship of the Arab states to Israel, an omission that was also pointed out by the representative of Australia, Dr. Ronald Walker. On the whole, however, the outcome of the Emergency Special Session was regarded as a triumph for patience, moderation, and common sense.

Only two weeks earlier, Ralph Bunche had written to Blickenstaff that the Emergency Special Session was a meeting "which no one really wants, and out of which no good is likely to come unless Dag can pull a miracle of education and persuasion among the delegations that count. He is all set to make a game try at it."[99] By contrast, on August 26 Dayal wrote: "The unanimously adopted Arab resolution, which has been described as a miracle, has the unmistakable stamp of the 38th floor."[100] Hammarskjold himself was both relieved and delighted at the result. "To my mind," he told the press on August 22,[101] "yesterday was one of those days in the life of this Organisation when it showed its invaluable contribution to present politics in the international field and to present diplomacy. . . . For those who sometimes like to sharpen their wits on the weaknesses of the Organisation, it is for that reason a day they should remember before starting all over again." Then, evidently feeling he might have gone too far, he asked the correspondents to "excuse me for banging the drum a little bit." Asked what he would do next, he replied: "That is very obvious. I shall talk to those who know more about it than I do."[102]

11

MORE PREVENTIVE
DIPLOMACY

THE GENERAL ASSEMBLY RESOLUTION on the Middle East,[1] which Hammarskjold described as "one of the strongest" ever adopted by the
UN and which "re-establishes ... some very basic Charter rules as
immediately applicable rules of behaviour,"[2] gave the Secretary-General
new responsibilities, especially in relation to Jordan. Hammarskjold
arrived in Beirut on the evening of August 26 and left for Amman the
next morning. The twin objectives of this trip were to begin the dis-
mantling of the UN operation in Lebanon and to set up a mission of a
very different kind in Jordan.

After three days of discussion in Amman, King Hussein, Prime
Minister Samir Rifai, and Hammarskjold agreed that "neither a UN
force, nor a border observation group, would adequately serve the
purposes which the General Assembly had in mind."[3] Instead they
developed the idea of a "representative office" in Amman with counterparts in other Arab capitals, the object of which would be to promote
a good-neighbor policy among Arab states as well as to create an
atmosphere favorable to the withdrawal of U.S. and British troops.
Specific objectives would be the resumption of normal communications between Jordan and Syria and the cessation of the radio battle
between Cairo and Damascus on the one side and Amman on the
other.

On August 30, Hammarskjold left Beirut for Geneva, where he opened the huge Second International Scientific Conference on the Peaceful Uses of Atomic Energy[4] and discussed the Middle East situation at length with Bunche and with Piero Spinelli, the head of the Geneva Office. On September 3 he resumed his Middle East tour via Cairo, Jerusalem, and Baghdad, where for the first time he met Brigadier Kassem and the new Iraqi leaders. He was in Amman again on September 8 and 9, and ended his tour with a four-day visit to Beirut.

By early September the Lebanese situation had much improved. The opposition had relaxed its hostile attitude and closed down its clandestine radio stations, while the political organizations on both sides had begun collecting arms from their followers. The situation was still confused, however, and after Hammarskjold's talks in Beirut with Chehab and Chamoun it was decided as a temporary measure to increase the number of observers in UNOGIL substantially.

Hammarskjold, who returned to New York on September 13 to prepare his report on the Middle East to the General Assembly, was by no means sanguine about the future. "I do not," he wrote to Fawzi on September 17, "find a peaceful and constructive development in the Middle East probable, but I continue to consider it quite possible,"[5] and he took occasion again to mention the inflammatory broadcasts of Radio Cairo.

His report to the General Assembly[6] dealt with arrangements in relation to Jordan and Lebanon, with the withdrawal of the U.S. and British forces, and with ideas for promoting economic cooperation in the region. He reported his agreement with the Jordanians on the establishment in Amman of a UN "presence" that could "keep under purview the adherence of all the principles set out in Part I of the resolution in relation to Jordan."[7]

Spinelli, who was to be the Secretary-General's special representative in Jordan, came to New York on September 17 for a full briefing on the situation in Jordan and on the new and somewhat elusive concept of the UN "presence." When a German correspondent asked Hammarskjold to define this concept, he replied: "There is an infinite variety and I may quote to you as a German: '*Name ist Schall und Rauch*' "[8] ("A name is noise and smoke"). A more explicit definition was given in 1960 by Ralph Bunche: "The important aim of the UN 'presence' is the establishment of some sort of UN arrangement on the spot with a purpose of watching local developments, holding a finger on the pulse and keeping UN Headquarters fully informed about developments in that area. For the most part those who constitute and lead the 'presence' operation, whatever its form, are expected to play their role pretty much by ear, to give well considered advice where needed and requested, to intervene as necessary but always delicately and diplomatically, and to keep constantly in consultation with the Secretary-General for advice and guidance."[9]

Spinelli had some difficulty in following the finer and more abstract points of Hammarskjold's exposition, for the latter's Swedish accent became more and more pronounced as his enthusiasm for the idea increased. He was, however, left in no doubt that this was a new experiment in preventive diplomacy with critical practical objectives. The immediate aim was to secure the withdrawal of British troops as soon as possible by giving a new kind of guarantee to Hussein and to the British which would also show Nasser that the UN was following the Jordanian situation closely.

Spinelli arrived in Amman on September 27, more convinced of the importance of his mission than clear as to exactly how he was to carry it out. Some of the signs were promising. The government of Iraq had assured Hammarskjold that it wanted normal relations with Jordan, and the U.A.R. had stated that there would be no objection to the resumption of the oil supply to Jordan from the port of Tripoli in Lebanon just as soon as the British troops had left. The U.A.R. had also agreed to discuss the resumption of Air Jordan flights into Cairo, and Fawzi had expressed his intention to "do our best to simplify all difficulties."[10] Hammarskjold hoped that Spinelli, in transmitting this information privately to Prime Minister Rifai, might be able to influence public reactions in Jordan in favor of the withdrawal of the British troops. Spinelli found the situation in Amman calmer than he had expected, and on October 1 King Hussein announced that the British troops would withdraw. On the same day, Dixon informed Hammarskjold that the British withdrawal would begin on October 20.

This first experiment in establishing a UN presence showed, among other things, that in Spinelli Hammarskjold had found a collaborator after his own heart. Spinelli's sharp political intelligence and strong will were concealed behind a kindly and somewhat rumpled appearance and a notably obscure though charming mode of expression in English. A modest and highly professional man, Spinelli was not interested in personal success or prestige, never appeared to be in a hurry nor showed off his great ability, and was perfectly prepared to sit around and be kept waiting. He thus gained not only the confidence but the real affection of the harassed and apprehensive people with whom he dealt, after which his position was both a strong and a useful one. His political judgment was independent and shrewd, and he was also entirely unintimidated by Hammarskjold, with whom he was quite prepared to disagree if he thought it necessary. From this time on he became one of Hammarskjold's most trusted colleagues for difficult emergency assignments.

In Lebanon, General Chehab's formal accession to the Presidency on September 23 had been followed by clashes in Beirut in which some twenty people were killed and forty wounded. The army soon moved in to restore order, and Chehab appointed the former opposition leader, Rashid Karame, Prime Minister, to the intense resentment of Chamoun's supporters. The situation in Beirut remained uncertain for some days until the President announced, on October 15, the formation of a coalition Cabinet consisting of two government and two opposition leaders. On October 6, Hammarskjold agreed with Plaza and Dayal that the total strength of the UN Observation Group should be fixed at five hundred. On October 8 the State Department announced that the U.S. evacuation would be completed by the end of the month "barring unforeseen developments."

Although UNOGIL's relationship with the new government was excellent, its *raison d'être* was now obviously disappearing and on November 6 Hammarskjold agreed to reduce its strength to three hundred observers. The Lebanese government had asked that a formal decision by the Security Council on UNOGIL's withdrawal be taken before November 22, which was the Lebanese national day, and it particularly wished to avoid a debate in the Council, so that the episode could be closed on a noncontroversial note acceptable both to Lebanon and to the U.A.R. On November 16, the Lebanese government formally requested deletion of the Lebanese item from the Security Council agenda,[11] and on November 25 the Council agreed to this request.[12]

UNOGIL's last function was to assist in the British evacuation from Jordan.[13] The surrounding Arab countries and Israel were reluctant to give overflying rights to British military aircraft. General Bull therefore set up the necessary ground-to-air communications and an international flying control team that arranged for the routings and air clearances of the British aircraft with Jordan, the U.A.R. and Lebanon.*

UNOGIL officially closed down on December 10. In congratulating Blickenstaff, who had carried a very heavy load in advising the Observation Group, in administering a large and improvised operation, and in resisting a variety of strong pressures from the interested parties, Hammarskjold wrote on December 13, "I hope that you will be able to bring back from this mission also personal satisfaction

---

* The manifest for the last British plane included as passengers two horses, a gift from King Hussein to Queen Elizabeth II.

and the experience of what the UN can do in very difficult circumstances and with untried means."[14]

As soon as the British troops were withdrawn, Hammarskjold pressed Nasser to call off the blockade of Jordan, accept the flights of Air Jordan, and restore overland traffic across Jordan's frontiers. Nasser replied that Air Jordan could fly over Syrian territory between Beirut and Amman, and that the overland traffic would be restored on November 1.

The decision of King Hussein to leave for Europe on November 10 gave rise to an incident[15] that threatened for a time to put Jordan's relations with the U.A.R. back to where they had been in July. On the first leg of the flight to Europe, the King's private aircraft was intercepted by Syrian fighter planes which attempted to force it to land in Damascus. Hussein's British pilot took evasive action and contrived, virtually at ground level, to get back to Amman. On landing, the King broadcast an account of the incident, declaring that Jordan would take "all necessary measures to answer this act of hostility."

This incident, which was widely interpreted as an attempt to kidnap Hussein, caused intense anger and a prolonged series of public demonstrations of loyalty to Hussein in Jordan. Cairo and Damascus immediately denied that Syrian aircraft had tried to force down Hussein's plane, explaining that an unidentified plane had entered Syrian airspace without prior clearance and that its pilot had refused to give information about its mission or destination. Hammarskjold asked Spinelli to get from the Jordanians the exact facts about clearance of the plane, and it turned out that no clearance had in fact been requested from Syria, an omission unknown to the King's pilot. In an effort to avoid further repercussions, Hammarskjold suggested to Nasser that even if the U.A.R. was technically in the right about the clearance of the flight, he might express his regrets as a simple matter of courtesy. He instructed Spinelli to inform Rifai of this message, emphasizing that its effectiveness would depend on the discretion shown by the Jordanians, since, as they must well know, Nasser would never agree to anything under public pressure.

Rifai was in a difficult position, partly because he himself was indirectly responsible for the failure to obtain proper clearance for the King's plane and partly because the Jordanian Army was urging retaliatory action on the Syrian border. He therefore favored an appeal to the Security Council, which might turn popular indignation into less dangerous channels. Thus, despite all Spinelli's arguments, Jordan formally requested the Secretary-General to bring the incident before the Council. Hammarskjold instructed Spinelli to tell Rifai that he could not regard the incident as a threat to peace and security under Article 99 of the Charter. He was, however, prepared to offer his good offices in the matter and if necessary to circulate the Jordanian letter as a document.

Late on November 12, King Hussein informed Spinelli that, after reflecting on the whole incident, he felt that since he had been able to forgive those who in the past had attempted to harm his country, it would not be difficult for him to take the same attitude when only his own person was involved. He had therefore instructed Rifai to find a way to settle the problem in a conciliatory manner and to avoid putting Hammarskjold in a difficult position. Rifai accordingly withdrew the request for Security Council action and accepted the Secretary-General's good offices. In spite of this conciliatory attitude, the Western press continued to lambaste Cairo on the basis of the original Jordanian account of the incident, and Nasser evidently considered that Amman was still exploiting it. No apology was therefore made by Cairo.

By the end of 1958 there was considerable disappointment in Amman over the failure of the Spinelli mission and of the UN to stop economic restrictions against Jordan, in particular the holding up of oil trucks at the Syrian border. Hammarskjold pressed Cairo on this matter as well as on the establishment of liaison offices for the Spinelli mission in Damascus and Beirut, to which the Jordanians attached great importance. The delay, he told Fawzi, put the whole stature of his office in jeopardy. "Do not believe," he wrote, "that I have lost the serenity inspired by the mild light of the Fatimite lanterns,* but I am getting worried by the possibility of running into a situation that could be construed as a bad slip backwards."[16] He received Fawzi's assurances on both these matters on December 31 while he was in Jerusalem after spending Christmas with UNEF in Gaza, and when he arrived in Amman on January 3, 1959, he was amused to hear that the Syrian customs chief, when his Jordanian counterpart had told him that he was now satisfied with the way Jordanian trucks were allowed to go through Syria, had replied: "Good. Well, kindly inform your friend Mr. Hammarskjold immediately."[17]

By April 1959 the Jordan situation had sufficiently improved for both Fawzi and Hussein to agree with Spinelli that the UN presence could gradually fade out once diplomatic relations were reestablished between Jordan and the U.A.R. On July 30, the opening of the Jordan-

---

* Two Fatimite lanterns, a present from Fawzi, hung in Hammarskjold's East Seventy-third Street apartment.

Syrian border cleared the way for the resumption of relations, but once again the calm was short-lived. On October 3 and 4, Radio Cairo suddenly attacked Jordan again, and on October 7 an attempt to assassinate General Kassem in Iraq revived the old danger that the Jordanians might react by sending troops to the frontier. Spinelli cautioned the Jordanian government firmly against any such dramatic reaction, and the King promised that no move would be made unless the situation deteriorated to a point where the U.A.R. seemed likely to intervene. Once again calm was restored, and starting in October Spinelli based himself in Geneva, making only periodic visits to Amman.

On August 29, 1960, relations between Jordan and the U.A.R. received another and serious setback when a violent explosion in his office killed the Jordanian Premier, Hazza Majali. Spinelli, who was en route to Togo, was immediately diverted to Jordan, where he arrived on September 1. The announcement by Radio Cairo the night before Majali's death that sooner or later all traitors would meet their doom was taken in Jordan as a clear reference to the intended assassination, and it was only with some difficulty that Spinelli persuaded the King and his Ministers to restrict their reaction to demanding the extradition of the two plotters, who had taken refuge in Syria. The radio war between Amman and Cairo was resumed with full fury, and a week later rumors of a new plot against him decided Hussein to move troops up to the Syrian border. On September 11, in an effort to forestall military moves by the Jordanian authorities that might have unforeseeable consequences, Hammarskjold offered his personal good offices to Hussein. The King was unenthusiastic, although he asserted that he was not contemplating any aggressive action as long as there was a hope of a peaceful solution, which he hoped Hammarskjold would try to achieve.

The presence of Nasser, Fawzi, and Hussein in New York for the General Assembly during October seemed to provide the opportunity for some kind of rapprochement. The Jordanian government suggested that Hussein and Nasser meet under Hammarskjold's auspices in an attempt to reach a real understanding once and for all. Hammarskjold was doubtful whether the time was ripe for such a confrontation and wished in any case to test the mood of Nasser and Fawzi before committing himself. Although Hussein had assured Spinelli that his speech to the Assembly would be moderate in tone and substance, the fevered atmosphere of New York apparently gave him second thoughts and, despite the advice of Hammarskjold and Spinelli, in his speech to the General Assembly[18] he attacked the U.A.R. for its hostility to Jordan, mentioning in particular Majali's assassination.

The U.A.R. mission promptly denounced Hussein's statement, and all possibility of a meeting with Nasser was over. From early 1961, however, the relations between Jordan and the U.A.R., despite temporary setbacks, steadily improved.

HAMMARSKJOLD'S OTHER EFFORTS at peaceful settlement and long-term solutions in the Middle East were on the whole a disappointment. Once UNEF became reasonably well established, he began to search again for a solution to the underlying causes of the Middle East conflict and especially the Palestine refugee question. Initially he pursued an idea that had arisen during his talks with Fawzi in July 1956, with the intention of narrowing as much as possible the gap between the Arab states and Israel on the refugee problem and then defining in clear terms the remaining disagreements. After this process was completed, he hoped to evolve a plan to which the UN could require the parties to acquiesce on the basis of "co-responsibility" for the refugees.

This idea proved totally impracticable, and by the end of 1957 Hammarskjold decided instead to base his efforts on a new kind of Middle East development organization to be established in Beirut with the assistance of the UN and the International Bank.[19] Humphrey Trevelyan, the former British Ambassador in Cairo who had joined his staff in January 1958, was given the task of persuading the Arab governments to accept this idea, the object of which was to coordinate the development programs of the Arab states and to finance them without the political strings usually attached to bilateral arrangements, through an Arab Development Board that would have international status and would be as nonpolitical as possible. Trevelyan's efforts were frustrated first by the rivalry of the governments of Iraq and Egypt and later by Arab suspicions that the scheme was in reality a back-door solution to the Palestine refugee problem. The idea of an inter-Arab development institution was also proposed in the resolution adopted by the Third Emergency Special Session of the General Assembly on August 21, 1958.[20] In his report to the General Assembly in September 1958,[21] Hammarskjold recognized that a revival of inter-Arab economic cooperation might require some further progress in the political field.

In his report to the fourteenth session of the General Assembly in 1959,[22] Hammarskjold set out his ideas on the relationship between the economic development of the Middle East and the reintegration of the Palestine refugees. He maintained that "the reintegration of the refugees in the Near East would have to run parallel to an increase in the national income at least proportional to the number reintegrated,"[23] and went on to outline a plan for capital imports to increase national income and for capital formation sufficient to encompass the reintegration of the refugees into the Arab world. In this perspective, he wrote, "the unemployed population represented by the Palestinian refugees should be regarded not as a liability but, more justly, as an asset for the future; it is a reservoir of manpower which in the desirable general economic development will assist in the creation of higher standards for the whole population of the area."[24]

The political obstacles to such a scheme were formidable, and Hammarskjold conceded that no progress was likely unless the refugees were given freedom of choice between repatriation and compensation in accordance with the 1948 decision of the General Assembly,[25] for this freedom was the "means through which the wrong that they consider themselves to have suffered could be put right and their individual self-respect safeguarded."[26] He suggested, however, that a de facto economic integration would not prejudice any rights established by the 1948 resolution. "The perspective," he concluded, "is not a discouraging one, provided that the world is willing to assist the region in its economic development and provided, further, that, step by step and as economic conditions permit, progress regarding the political and psychological obstacles is sought in a constructive spirit and with a sense of justice and realism."[27] Hammarskjold's logic and the practical common sense of his ideas evoked no response from the Arab governments, although he remained convinced that in the end a solution of the Palestine refugee problem along these lines would prove to be the only way out.

AFTER THE REOPENING of the Suez Canal in April 1957, Hammarskjold urged Fawzi to open negotiations with the old Canal Company and offered his good offices on such matters as compensation. In July he visited the executive director of the Canal Company, Jacques Georges-Picot, who agreed that he should transmit to Fawzi a proposal on compensation and other related matters and an offer of immediate negotiations. These negotiations, which eventually got under way with the help of Hammarskjold and the International Bank, were concluded to the satisfaction of both parties on July 13, 1958.

The surcharge system devised by Hammarskjold to pay for the Canal clearance operation was approved by the General Assembly in December 1957[28] and came into effect on September 15, 1958, at the rate of 3 percent of the regular Canal toll. Having achieved its objective, it was finally discontinued on March 15, 1961. The proceeds of the surcharge were used first to repay the difference between the total of the loans made by governments for the clearing of the Canal and the actual cost of the clearing operation, and thereafter to repay the governments themselves. The $11.2 million originally lent by eleven governments in response to the appeal that Hammarskjold had made on Christmas Day 1956 was finally repaid in full on July 10, 1963.

The reopening of the Canal in barely four months at a cost of $8.2 million, a third of the original estimate, was a remarkable achievement, but the failure to secure freedom of navigation for Israeli ships also made it in part a hollow one. For a time things went well enough, and Egypt did not interfere with Israeli cargoes carried by non-Israeli ships going through the Canal. On February 26, 1959, however, the peaceful passage through the Canal of cargoes to and from Israel came abruptly to a halt when the Egyptian authorities detained and impounded the cargo of the *Capetan Manolis*, flying the Liberian flag, with a cargo going from Haifa to Southeast Asian ports. This action was followed up on March 13 by the impounding of the cargo of the *Leglott*, flying the flag of the German Federal Republic, coming from Cyprus and going to Southeast Asia and the Far East with Israeli cement on board.

Hammarskjold was in New Delhi when on March 17 he received news that Israel had complained formally to the Security Council[29] of the Egyptian action, on which he himself had already protested to Cairo. From Srinagar on March 21 he sent an urgent message to Fawzi expressing his deep concern and pointing out that flag discrimination was a very vulnerable point for Egypt if it wished to make its Suez Canal Declaration fully respected internationally. He begged Fawzi to arrange for a speedy and satisfactory settlement of the problem and suggested that they should meet in Geneva early in May. Fawzi did not answer this message, but on April 20 he told Ralph Bunche, who had gone to Cairo to discuss the situation, that because of a conspiracy to undermine Egypt's maintenance of a state of war with Israel, Egypt's policy was now to hold the cargo of any ships chartered by Israel, although it was possible that the cargo of such ships would be released after inspection if it was already owned by the legitimate purchasers. Hammarskjold commented, "The formula which seems to be emerging is of course legally utter nonsense."[30]

On May 9, Hammarskjold and Bunche met with Fawzi in the Hotel Beau Rivage in Lausanne for an elegant but unproductive exchange, best summed up by Hammarskjold's remark that Fawzi's recent letter assuring him that the seizure of the cargo of the two ships did not mean any change in the Egyptian policy was an unusually dry lemon from which not much juice could be obtained. Fawzi replied that lemons in Egypt were unusually dry at that time of the year and must be squeezed very hard to get even a little juice.

On May 21 a Danish vessel, the *Inge Toft*,[31] with a cargo from Haifa for the Far East, was detained at Port Said. The Egyptian authorities requested the master to unload the cargo, which he refused to do, and the ship remained in Port Said. This affair seemed to Hammarskjold to be entirely irreconcilable with the Egyptian declaration on the Canal. "In all frankness," he wrote to Fawzi, "I would believe that a statement to the effect that freedom of navigation is maintained if a ship flying a non-Israeli flag is permitted to pass after you have taken away the cargo, would be generally regarded as nothing but a lawyer's ploy."[32] He strongly urged Fawzi to take no further steps to confiscate the cargo of the *Inge Toft* and, above all, to detain no more ships until they could have a further discussion. When in June Israel retaliated by seizing an Egyptian vessel, the *Karim*, he told Fawzi that he was not at all surprised.

On July 2, during talks in Cairo with Fawzi and Nasser, Hammarskjold evolved an ingenious formula designed at the same time to save Egypt's face in the Arab world and to ensure that Israeli cargoes carried in ships not flying the Israeli flag could go through the Canal. Under this formula Cairo's *formal* position would be that no Israeli-flag ships would pass, that ships chartered to Israel would be treated on the same basis as ships flying the Israeli flag, and that no Israeli commodities would be permitted to pass through the Canal whatever the flag. *In practice*, however, although no ships flying the Israeli flag would pass, the decisive factor for Cairo in relation to chartered ships would be the formal ownership of the cargo. Thus, cargoes *from* Israel F.O.B.* and commodities shipped *to* Israel C.I.F.** would both be regarded as not being owned by Israel while they were going through the Canal. The success of this plan, which came to be known as "the effective stand," would depend entirely on discretion and lack of publicity, so that Egypt's position in the Arab world was protected. From a legal point of view Hammarskjold could not endorse either the formal position of the Egyptian Government or its effective position, nor would he be prepared to defend either from any point of prin-

---

* F.O.B., Free on Board, means that the ownership of a cargo passes to the buyer at the free on board point, i.e., when the cargo is loaded.
** C.I.F., Cost Insurance Freight, means that the ownership of a cargo passes to the buyer with the documents when they are handed over against the payment of the price or acceptance of the bill of exchange at the port of destination.

ciple. He suggested the plan only because he felt it was his duty, in the interests of all concerned, to try to find some way out of an impossible situation which was already having repercussions far beyond the Canal problem.

On July 5 it was learned that a Norwegian ship, the *Spero*, chartered by an Israeli company and destined for Elath in the Gulf of Aqaba, was to sail without cargo from Haifa for the Canal in two days' time, under the assumption that on the basis of the "effective stand" arrangement it would be allowed through the Canal. Hammarskjold was alarmed at Israel's decision to send an empty ship through the Canal to Elath, apparently as a test both of the freedom of passage of chartered ships through the Canal and of the right of innocent passage through the Gulf of Aqaba. Obviously the Egyptians would find it very difficult to close their eyes to the publicized passage through the Canal, and between two Israeli ports, of an empty ship chartered by Israel. The mystery deepened on July 7 when Norwegian sources revealed that the ship that was to sail through the Canal was not the *Spero* but her sister ship the *Pronto*, which was in Haifa, and that its cargo had been rerouted overland to Elath for loading there. To make matters worse, a story in the New York *Herald Tribune* of July 6 gave the main substance of the "effective stand" arrangement.

Cairo regarded the proposed passage of the *Pronto* as a trap by which Egypt would either suffer a serious setback in its efforts to improve its relations with the West or create a decisive precedent in favor of Israel that would cause Cairo a serious loss of face in the Arab world, and Hammarskjold began to wonder whether the *Inge Toft* had not also been a deliberate test case. Israeli cargoes had previously passed through the Canal without publicity, but in the case of the *Inge Toft* the ship's position had been given by radio practically every hour during its approach to the Canal.

On July 9 the representative of Israel in New York told Bunche that Jerusalem's first reaction to the "effective stand" arrangement was unfavorable and that the sailing of the *Pronto* had been postponed, but on July 13 he reported that the *Pronto* was now in Elath, although nobody seemed to know how she had got there. Hammarskjold believed that the Egyptians had let the ship through the Canal to avoid falling into the trap.

Meanwhile Danish efforts to get the *Inge Toft* released had run into trouble, because, according to Fawzi, unexpected publicity about the "effective stand" had made the Egyptian position impossible. Cairo insisted that the *Inge Toft* could leave Port Said only if her cargo was unloaded. Disappointed as he was at this negative attitude, Hammarskjold still hoped that Fawzi, at Denmark's urging, and Ben-Gurion, with whom he was exchanging views through their mutual acquaintance Jacob Blaustein, would both find it possible to make sufficient concessions to get the *Inge Toft* episode out of the way.

Mounting indignation in Israel gave rise to a press campaign against Hammarskjold and against the UN that was, he told the Israeli representative in New York in early September, "of a scope and intensity I do not remember having seen since the termination of the Suez crisis."[33] As usual, Hammarskjold refused to pursue his objectives through the press. "We observe strictly here in the Secretariat," he told the Israeli representative, "some few rules in our diplomatic and political actions. We do not distort information to anybody or about anybody. We do not try to pry into anyone's secrets. We do not use anyone as a scapegoat. We try to keep our promises, and if we cannot do so for reasons beyond our control, we frankly admit that that is the case. We try to assist irrespective of the reaction of the assisted. And for that reason I will not cease to continue in my efforts on the *Inge Toft* and the Canal. We try to maintain as balanced a picture of political events as possible, and we do that not in order to placate anybody or to balance our guilt—two words very often used in discussions with me in Jerusalem—but because we believe that peace is not possible without justice also in that sense. Finally, we do not betray any of these principles even if this might seem to yield a short-term advantage in the direction of the aims we are serving. . . . Were we to work in any other way on the basis of any other principles, it would indeed be a house built on sand."[34]

Hammarskjold expected little help over the problems of the Canal, for, as he told Mrs. Meir on October 7, "the majority of Members basically is sick and tired of the story,"[35] but he continued his own efforts in the hope that it might be possible eventually at least to return to the 1958 situation, when passage of Israeli cargoes through the Canal was tacitly accepted. He regarded the "effective stand" formula merely as a pragmatic step through which it might be possible to get back to 1958.

In December Mrs. Meir informed Hammarskjold that, in order to test the "effective stand" formula, Israel intended to try putting another cargo ship, the Greek-flag *Astypalea*, through the Canal, carrying cement from Haifa to Djibouti. Hammarskjold notified Fawzi on December 12 that, although Israel had formally rejected the "effective stand" procedure, she was prepared to apply it as a transitional measure in the hope of an eventual return to the 1958 pattern of Canal passage. The *Astypalea* was due to arrive in Port Said early in the following week. There would be no publicity, and he urged Fawzi to ensure that this first real test of the "effective stand" formula went smoothly with strict observation of the rules of the game on both sides.

The reply to this message came not from Fawzi but from the Deputy Foreign Minister, Zulficar Sabry, who thanked Hammarskjold for his selfless efforts but stated that the Egyptians had no confidence in the idea that there would be no publicity about the *Astypalea*. "The matter has already been given all available publicity," Sabry wrote, "shortly after it was broached out by you. Publicity is obviously redundant. How can one find a basis when the prerequisite foundations have already been demolished?"[36] Hammarskjold was incensed both at the tone and the origin of this reply. The allegation that the Israeli assurances were hollow was offensive, he told Fawzi, in the light of his own declaration to Fawzi that he found them to be satisfactory, nor was he aware of any publicity given by Israel to the intended passage of the *Astypalea*.

The *Astypalea* was held up by storms and only on December 17 did it reach Port Said, where it was promptly detained by the Egyptian authorities, despite Hammarskjold's insistence on the telephone to Fawzi that his assurances concerning her cargo should be accepted and the ship allowed to pass. This new incident coincided with the International Bank's consideration of a loan to Egypt for the development of the Canal. In spite of strong Israeli pressure to defer consideration of the loan until the situation about Israeli cargoes was clarified, the Bank's president, Eugene Black, insisted that the proposed development of the Canal was technically and economically sound and necessary to provide the users of the Canal with the required facilities, and that only economic considerations were relevant to the Bank's decision. Hammarskjold had given him to understand, Black told the governors of the Bank, that he was working actively on a solution of the freedom-of-navigation problem and that there seemed to be a chance that before long it would be possible to get back to the 1958 situation. Once again Hammarskjold and Black faced a typical dilemma. In Israeli eyes the granting of the Canal loan would indicate acquiescence in Egypt's policy, while Cairo was apt to feel that a delay in granting the loan until the *Astypalea* was released would be a surrender to Israel. Hammarskjold believed that the Egyptians would let the ship go as soon as the loan was granted, and on December 21, the day on which the board of the Bank unanimously approved the loan, he sent a message to Fawzi urging prompt and positive action on the *Astypalea*. His hopes were soon dashed, for Fawzi continued to maintain that the *Astypalea*'s papers showed that the cargo still belonged to Israel. This was intensely embarrassing both for Black and for Hammarskjold, who cabled Fawzi that "a speedy straightening out is a condition of my possibility to maintain my personal usefulness on related questions."[37]

On December 22, Mrs. Meir told the Knesset that Israel's patience was now at an end and she hoped that everyone, including the World Bank, who thought that Nasser was to be trusted, would no longer be convinced of it. "The Egyptian policy in respect of the Suez Canal," she said, "is the direct outcome of the tolerant attitude of the UN to Nasser's policy of boycott and threats against Israel who is also a Member of the UN, and to his violations of the UN Charter.... The Secretary-General of the UN told us on more than one occasion that he had reason to assume that this arrangement would work. We have no doubt that when he made this statement he had something to rely on. Now he stands helpless at the Egyptian dictator's door."

Hammarskjold, who was on an extended tour of Africa, received a copy of Mrs. Meir's speech in Monrovia, Liberia, and he could only admit that its substance was justified if the information as now known about the *Astypalea* was true. He instructed Bunche to go to Cairo early in the new year to prepare the ground for his own arrival there by some very plain speaking with Fawzi. When Bunche arrived in Cairo, however, he was systematically kept at arm's length, Fawzi saying that he preferred not to see him until Hammarskjold himself arrived on January 20. In Israel the press reaction to these events was bitter. Both Hammarskjold and Mrs. Meir were in Cameroon for the celebration of independence from France, but since they met only on New Year's Eve as members of the jury at a beauty contest, they had little chance to talk. In any case, there was little to discuss until Hammarskjold had held further talks in Cairo.

Hammarskjold finally arrived in Cairo on the evening of January 20 and, with Bunche, spent all of the following day and most of the night in conversation with Fawzi. Fawzi was unforthcoming about the *Astypalea* and claimed that Israel had sent her in an attempt to block the World Bank loan to Egypt and that the cargo was Israeli-owned. For good measure, he also warned Hammarskjold that sooner or later the continued presence of UNEF on Egyptian soil would be raised. Nasser also strongly denied to Hammarskjold that he had gone back on his word. In the first place there was no agreement on the Canal, and Israel, by first publicizing the "effective stand" arrangement and then rejecting it, had seriously embarrassed Egypt. Hammarskjold, although he had questioned the timing of the *Astypalea*'s voyage, insisted that it met the conditions of the "effective stand" and should have been let through.

Hammarskjold was deeply disappointed by his talks with Nasser and Fawzi, which he described as "very extensive, intense, unpleasant and somewhat disturbing,"[38] and on the plane leaving Cairo he was unwilling to discuss the previous two days at all. Nasser was equally bitter and on January 26 announced that both detained ships could leave Port Said if they unloaded their cargoes, which Egypt considered to be "the property of the Palestinian nation." He denied that there was any previous agreement on the passage of Israeli cargoes in any form and asked: "Why should Egypt obey UN resolutions when Israel has ignored all UN resolutions on Palestine since 1948?"[39]

In Jerusalem the "effective stand" formula was denounced as being neither practical nor an arrangement, since its conditions were so complicated as to allow Nasser, whenever he thought fit, to find a pretext to detain all cargoes.[40] The *Jerusalem Post* termed Hammarskjold's Cairo visit "a disgraceful failure"[41] and "the greatest defeat of his career,"[42] and as far afield as Whitehall in London a spokesman told a *Jerusalem Post* correspondent that "Hammarskjold holds his cards so close to his person that he can hardly recognise them."[43] Washington also was strongly criticized.

By early February, Hammarskjold concluded that the period during which quiet diplomacy should take precedence over public debate in the Security Council had come to an end, because attitudes and actions on both sides had deprived his diplomatic efforts of the necessary setting. On February 14 the *Inge Toft*, having unloaded her cargo, which was promptly seized by Egypt, left Port Said. On April 8 the *Astypalea* was unloaded and her cargo confiscated, and she too finally sailed away on April 10.

Hammarskjold's efforts to solve the Canal problem had failed, and other developments soon served to make matters even worse. In April 1960 the National Maritime Union boycotted the Egyptian ship *Cleopatra* in New York, resulting in a counterboycott of U.S. ships in Arab ports, and anti-Egyptian feeling in the U.S. Congress gave rise to amendments to the foreign-aid bill directed against Egypt. Such developments, Hammarskjold told Jacob Blaustein in May 1960, made it "time lost for me to argue the Suez case in the Arab world,"[44] and so it remained for the brief remainder of his life.

HAMMARSKJOLD USED VARIATIONS of the "good offices" technique in contexts other than the Middle East problem. The special value of this method of resolving disputes is its confidential nature, which allows the search for a face-saving formula to go on in private until the governments concerned can change or adjust their policies on contentious problems without public embarrassment.

Hammarskjold normally undertook "good offices" missions only at the request of governments, and he refused to take initiatives if he believed that either his right to do so or his chances of success were seriously in doubt. As early as 1955 he was under considerable pressure from the Afro-Asian group in the UN to use his good offices on North African questions, and especially on Algeria. Asked about this in August 1955, he replied[45] that as a matter of courtesy he had informed the other party concerned, France, of the Afro-Asian approach, but the UN's right to interfere in the internal affairs of states was very limited, and Algeria was legally under the domestic jurisdiction of France. Even when it proved impossible to avoid a debate in the UN on Algeria, he refused to make any further move on the grounds that France itself was attempting to negotiate a solution of the Algerian problem.

Hammarskjold was similarly circumspect in other situations where he felt he had no chance of useful action. When, for instance, Malaya, in an attempt to forestall Indonesian ambitions, suggested in November 1960 that West Irian—then still Netherlands New Guinea—should become a UN Trust Territory and that the Secretary-General should send a personal representative there, he replied that he could not possibly do so without the consent of all the parties concerned, and the idea lapsed.

Hammarskjold played a more active role in the events that followed the French bombing of Sakiet-Sidi-Youssef in Tunisia on February 8, 1958, an action justified by France on the grounds that Tunisia was allowing the Algerian rebels to operate from Tunisian territory. Tunisia, which had become a member of the UN in November 1956, brought the matter to the Security Council, where all the parties concerned accepted the "good offices" of the U.S. and Great Britain.[46] After the bombing of Sakiet-Sidi-Youssef the Tunisian government decided on a policy of *"encerclement populaire"* of all French posts, garrisons, and barracks in Tunisia—a tactic which was repeated in 1961 over the Bizerte naval base—with the result that the French supply lines were seriously threatened. Anxious to avoid any increase in tension, Hammarskjold persuaded the Tunisians to allow supplies to go through to the French military posts in Tunisia on the basis of his personal assurance that the French would not exploit the arrangement to bring in further military supplies.[47] The affair dragged on, and when at the end of March the American and British mediators, Robert Murphy and Harold Beeley, could make no further progress, Britain suggested that Hammarskjold visit Paris and Tunis in an attempt to break the deadlock. Not wishing to take over the "good offices" function from Britain and the United States, he met Beeley and Murphy in London. In late May, Mongi Slim requested him to bring the Tunisian situation to the Security Council as a threat to peace and security under Article 99 of the Charter. Hammarskjold declined to do this, but he immediately informed the French representative, G. Georges-Picot, of the Tunisian request and was informed in return that the French negotiator, Armand Bérard, would be sent back to Tunis with conciliatory instructions. On June 17 the Franco-Tunisian negotiations were successfully concluded.[48]

LATE IN 1958 the government of Cambodia, which had broken off diplomatic relations with Thailand because of border incidents and a dispute over the ancient temple of Preah Vihear, complained to Hammarskjold of Thai troop concentrations on the border, an accusation that Thailand strongly denied.[49] In an effort to find a solution to this problem without resorting to the public procedures of the UN, Hammarskjold told the representatives of the two countries in New York that he would be prepared to send a personal representative to assist their governments, provided both governments wished it. He informed all members of the Security Council of this offer. When Cambodia and Thailand accepted, he appointed Baron Johan Beck-Friis, an experienced Swedish diplomat, as his personal representative, and on February 6, 1959, he was able to congratulate Beck-Friis and the two governments on the reestablishment of diplomatic relations.[50] "You can see," he told a press conference in February 1959, "how much more effective and smooth-working such a technique is than the regular one, which involves all the meetings and debates, and so on. That is a good case in point to demonstrate how, pragmatically, we can find better ways to do the job, without at all departing from the Charter but, so to speak, adjusting the procedures so as to meet a concrete situation as conveniently and efficiently as possible."[51] This effort was something of an innovation which, as Hammarskjold told the government of Thailand, "has enhanced our possibilities to assist in other cases and ... has broken new ground for fruitful UN assistance to member countries."[52]

But the trouble was not over and on September 16, 1960, Thailand again requested the Secretary-General's "good offices." By this time Soviet and French reactions to the UN Congo involvement had made independent initiatives by Hammarskjold liable to criticism in the

Security Council. Instead, therefore, of sending a representative, he coopted Hans Engen, who, as Norwegian Deputy Foreign Minister, was in New York for the General Assembly, and on November 5 they met with the representatives of Thailand and Cambodia to discuss an exchange of letters to settle their differences. A month later, on December 15, an agreement between the two countries was signed.[53]

A FAR MORE COMPLEX "good offices" exercise arose from the dispute between Great Britain and Saudi Arabia over the Bureimi Oasis. Sovereignty over Bureimi and the allegiance of its inhabitants were claimed by the Kingdom of Saudi Arabia on one side, and by the Sheikh of Abu Dhabi and the Sultan of Muscat and Oman, both under British protection, on the other. The Oasis, covering an area of about fifty-four square kilometers with a population of approximately 10,000, belonging to a number of tribes and settled in nine villages, was a communication center of some importance.

This ancient feud had been revived by the rumor—since proved unfounded—that oil might be found in the Oasis. In the summer of 1952 the Saudi Arabian government had reasserted its sovereignty over Bureimi by sending a party of some forty men, who promptly came into conflict with rival forces. After an unsuccessful effort to arbitrate the dispute, the governments of Saudi Arabia and Britain accepted a "standstill agreement" that lasted until October 26, 1955, when British-led troops, the Trucial Oman Scouts, occupied the entire Oasis and expelled the Saudi party. Subsequently, in 1959, when the Oasis was partitioned between Abu Dhabi and Muscat, a number of sheikhs loyal to King Saud left the Oasis with their families and retainers and became refugees in Saudi Arabia.

Diplomatic relations between Britain and Saudi Arabia had been suspended since the Suez crisis of 1956, and other efforts at pacific settlement had been unavailing. Azzam Pasha, the former Secretary-General of the Arab League who had played a major role in trying to solve the Bureimi problem, was still convinced of the basic common interests of Britain and Saudi Arabia in the Persian Gulf area, and he persuaded the Saudi Arabian Government that it was worth using Hammarskjold's exceptional talents as a negotiator and his special flair for Middle East problems in a further effort to solve the Bureimi question.

While in Riyadh in early 1959 after a Christmas visit to Gaza, Hammarskjold learned for the first time of the Saudi Arabian intention to bring the Bureimi problem to the Security Council. After consulting with Sir Pierson Dixon, he advised Prince Faysal, the Saudi Arabian Prime Minister and Foreign Minister, against making this public move while there was still a possibility of negotiating privately with the British. He suggested that a useful first step would be to reestablish diplomatic relations with Britain, after which the two countries should try to reach an agreement on the Bureimi problem, either with or without the asistance of a third person.

In April 1959 Faysal suggested that Hammarskjold himself take part in the search for an agreement, and Britain also welcomed his participation provided that Saudi Arabia was prepared to restore diplomatic relations with Britain. On June 23, in a long and complex letter to Faysal,* Hammarskjold suggested that a special diplomatic representative might initially explore "some general conditions—or some general unbinding terms—which might constitute an area of agreement"[54] between the two countries. He also suggested that the discussions of frontier problems might be "conducted with the participation, in an appropriate form, of the UN as represented by the Secretary-General."[55] Saudi Arabia was unwilling to restore diplomatic relations without having some idea of what solution might be found to the frontier problem. To get around this difficulty, Hammarskjold proposed that the two governments agree to reestablish diplomatic relations provided the frontier questions were taken up in special negotiations under his own auspices.

Late in November, he began a series of separate exploratory meetings with Harold Beeley, the deputy British representative in New York, and Azzam Pasha, representing the interests of King Saud and Prince Faysal. On December 15 he proposed to Faysal and British Foreign Minister Selwyn Lloyd that the representatives of both sides meet at his invitation for informal talks to be based on five main understandings. First, both parties were determined to solve their problems "in the spirit of their traditional friendship and with recognition of the shared interests in peace and stability in the area"[56] and should make this clear in their public statements. Second, neither would complicate matters by additional moves to change the situation. Third, once the talks were started, the village of Khour-el-U'daid, a police post in the Oasis, would be evacuated by the British, and diplomatic relations would be reestablished without delay. Fourth, means other than the talks might be agreed on—mediation, arbitration or plebiscite, for example—to settle particular problems. Last, the Secretary-General

---

* Azzam Pasha appreciated Hammarskjold's subtleties and shared his passion for delicate nuance, but even he found the task of translating into Arabic Hammarskjold's exact meaning formidable and very time-consuming.

would take part in the talks to the extent that the parties wished and would be available through most of the spring.

Although by the end of January 1960 Faysal and Lloyd had agreed in principle that the talks should begin, further hesitation from the Saudi Arabian side, which Hammarskjold believed to be due to the pressure of the Bureimi sheikhs on King Saud, persuaded him, despite British objections, that the refugee question also had to be included in the negotiations. By June 1960 there was still no progress, and in another long and even more complex letter to Faysal, he proposed that a "neutral personage"[57] should first consult the two governments, the Sheikh of Abu Dhabi, and the Sultan of Muscat and Oman on the possibilities for useful action and report to him, and he would then decide what to do next. A second stage might be a full study of the refugee question, after which the "neutral personage" might turn to other problems associated with Bureimi. The point of dividing the representative's work into stages was to ensure "that no one by his acceptance of one step, would be committed to the next one without prior consideration of the experiences reached in the previous stage."[58] Hammarskjold hoped that this method, which he admitted was complicated, would avoid "frustrating discussions concerning conditions and terms of reference" and would build up pragmatically, step by step, "the best possible setting for our discussions"[59] as well as providing for immediate consideration of the refugee situation.

In July, Hammarskjold asked the Swedish government for the loan of a Swedish diplomat, Herbert de Ribbing, to act as the "neutral personage." "If time had permitted," he wrote, "I would have undertaken it myself."[60] He himself was now heavily involved in the Congo crisis, and de Ribbing, whom he briefed in New York in late August, was by no means encouraged by his initial contacts with the British and Saudi Arabian governments and with the local rulers and some of the refugee sheikhs. In October de Ribbing reported from London that the Arab states were going to press for consideration by the General Assembly of the closely connected problem of Oman, while the British disagreed with the course of action outlined in Hammarskjold's last letter to Faysal and were generally skeptical about the usefulness of the de Ribbing mission.

Despite his other preoccupations, Hammarskjold maintained an active interest in the Bureimi problem. In January 1961, just before Harold Beeley was due to leave his post in New York, Hammarskjold had a further discussion with him and Azzam Pasha. The appointed time for this meeting happened to coincide with a meeting of the Security Council on the Congo at which Hammarskjold came under heavy attack from the Soviet Union, and he had to postpone the meeting for one hour so that he could reply to the Soviet attack. As soon as he had delivered his reply, however, he joined Beeley and Azzam in a detailed and enthusiastic discussion of possible solutions to the Bureimi question.

In May, after further talks with Azzam Pasha, Hammarskjold went over the problem at length with Colin Crowe, Beeley's successor. He told Crowe that if the British government was not prepared to discuss the withdrawal of the police post at Khour-el-U'daid and the refugee question, both he and Azzam Pasha would be put in such a difficult position that they would be unable to continue their efforts to find a solution, a failure that might well invite interference in the Trucial States by other Arab countries. After following up this approach with Lloyd and Edward Heath, the Lord Privy Seal, at the end of May when he went to England to receive an honorary degree at Oxford, Hammarskjold felt sufficiently reassured to ask de Ribbing to return to the area[61] to study the refugee question and to complete a registration of refugees from the Bureimi Oasis. Little further progress was made during his lifetime, but sixteen months after his death, Britain and Saudi Arabia reestablished diplomatic relations. No oil was found in Bureimi, but plenty in the Sheikhdom of Abu Dhabi, and the Bureimi question lost much of its interest for all concerned.

12

DISARMAMENT

DISARMAMENT IS ONE OF THE MAIN objectives of the United Nations under the Charter. Since it engages both the vital interests of the great powers and the concern for survival of the lesser ones, it has been the source of more continuous effort and debate than any other single item on the UN agenda. The achievement of a major degree of disarmament is a prerequisite for the effectiveness of the system of world order outlined in the Charter, but this is not the only compelling reason for continuing the efforts to achieve it. World-wide alarm at the rapid development of nuclear weapons and at the increasingly horrific dimensions and possibilities of the nuclear arms race was compounded in the early 1950's by fears of the consequences of atomic fallout from increasingly frequent nuclear-test explosions. The probable consequences of a nuclear war are so appalling as to numb the ordinary imagination, and it is one of the peculiarities of post-World War II life that humanity has more or less accustomed itself to living in the shadow of the most risky, destructive, and indiscriminate military confrontation ever devised. Disarmament discussions at the UN[1] or elsewhere, which tend to be technical and lengthy, are seldom followed with the passionate interest reserved for less important but more topical political subjects.

Hammarskjold had few illusions about the possibility of early or rapid progress on disarmament, but he was also deeply convinced that the effort must continue, both within and outside the UN, and that even a few intermittent gains amply justified the time and energy expended in the search. In 1955, to what he regarded as a defeatist question on disarmament, he answered:

> I react very strongly against pessimism couched in those cynical terms. I think it is even irresponsible. . . . There have been no precedents or experiences which entitle us not to try again. It is quite true that there is an interplay between . . . the political atmosphere, on the one side, and disarmament, on the other. But, when people say, in these simple terms, that if the political situation improves, disarmament will follow and that, for that reason, it does not make sense to discuss disarmament, they overlook one essential factor: that the very study of disarmament may be the vehicle for progress towards greater international political understanding. This is to say, disarmament is never the result only of the political situation; it is also partly instrumental in creating the political situation. . . . We must, I think, show greater patience in this whole field than ever before. When . . . I said that I felt that the disarmament question was a hardy perennial which might give us a pleasant surprise by producing a few new leaves and even flowers but that I doubted the possibilities of fruit, I was merely expressing that kind of patience.[2]

On May 10, 1955, the U.S.S.R. submitted to the United Nations Disarmament Commission what was, up to that time, its most comprehensive and detailed disarmament proposal.[3] The main features of the Soviet plan were acceptance of the specific ceilings for armed forces proposed by France and Great Britain, postponement of the prohibition on nuclear weapons until after 75 percent of the reduction of armed forces had been carried out, and a detailed proposal on controls. After long years of frustration, this was a major development. Hammarskjold, who had discussed the new Soviet proposals with Arkady Sobolev, the able and respected Soviet permanent representative to the UN who had previously been the first Soviet Assistant Secretary-General in the Secretariat, thought that these proposals might well provide the basis for real progress and that the Secretary-General might even play a role "discreetly and in all modesty—as a kind of catalyst or initiator."[4]

In the two following years, Hammarskjold kept in touch with disarmament questions through Dragoslav Protitch, a senior official in the Political Department of the Secretariat, but refrained from taking any initiatives himself. In October 1957, however, he engaged with Selwyn Lloyd, U.S. disarmament representative Harold E. Stassen, and V. V. Kuznetsov in talks concerning the possibility of the suspension of nuclear-test explosions. The idea of nuclear-test suspension had first been publicly suggested by Nehru on April 2, 1954,[5] but the Indian idea was not embodied in a General Assembly resolution until December 16, 1955,[6] when, also at the suggestion of India, the Assembly established a Scientific Committee on the Effects of Atomic Radiation to collect and coordinate data on both the immediate and the long-term consequences of nuclear radiation as well as on the known effects of hydrogen-bomb and nuclear-bomb tests.[7] The question of test suspension was taken up again in October 1966 in an exchange of letters between Premier Bulganin and President Eisenhower, but there was disagreement on the question of international supervision. The Soviet Union maintained that any nuclear explosion would be detectable, while the U.S. insisted on the necessity of a system of inspection and control as part of a comprehensive disarmament program.

In June 1957, in the UN Disarmament Subcommittee, the U.S.S.R. proposed immediate cessation of nuclear tests for a specific period and the establishment of an international commission to supervise the agreement and to set up control posts in the countries concerned.[8] The Western countries, while welcoming this proposal, still wished it to be part of a first-stage comprehensive disarmament agreement. They maintained this position during the 1957 session of the General Assembly, a year in which there was a higher level of nuclear testing than ever before by the U.S., U.S.S.R., and Britain. The resulting concern over the effects of fallout was dramatized on January 13, 1958, by the American scientist, Linus Pauling, when he presented to Hammarskjold a petition from nine thousand scientists in forty-three countries urging an international agreement to stop nuclear testing at once.

The technological race between East and West took on a new dimension on October 4, 1957, when Sputnik, the first space satellite, was launched by the Soviet Union. In the same month, in order to avoid the appearance of complete stagnation until some wider agreement could be reached, Hammarskjold suggested, as an interim measure, that the Secretary-General be requested to make a technical and scientific study of an adequate international control system for the suspension of nuclear tests. The Soviet Union had so far declined to agree to any such study unless the question of suspension itself was agreed upon first. Stassen and Lloyd welcomed Hammarskjold's willingness to attempt to break the stalemate between East and West on what had seemed earlier to be a hopeful development. Hammarskjold's object was to find out, in talks with Kuznetsov, what controls the Soviet Union would accept for the suspension of tests and what its position was on the limitation or cessation of further nuclear production for weapons. The U.S.S.R. was suspicious of the Western insistence that nuclear-test suspension not be separated from other disarmament problems and stiffened its own position accordingly. Hammarskjold believed that an initial technical study should cover the cessation of nuclear tests only and that if it proved to be useful the same technical group could be asked to study control over nuclear production. In November, however, disarmament questions came to a standstill again when the U.S.S.R. walked out of the Disarmament Commission to emphasize its dissatisfaction with the Assembly's decision to enlarge the membership of the Commission.[9]

In March 1958 during a visit to Moscow, Hammarskjold discussed the disarmament question with Khrushchev, emphasizing in particular that the current situation did not correspond to the assumption of the cooperation of the great powers on which the United Nations was based. For his part, Khrushchev expressed his disappointment with the Disarmament Commission. He complained that the United States was trying to impose its views on the U.S.S.R. by its control of the majority in the UN in a matter that could be settled only between the two great powers. Khrushchev was in favor of a summit conference where the question of disarmament could be brought out into the open for all to see.

To Andrei Gromyko, Hammarskjold expressed his regret that the promising discussions that had taken place in the UN in the last year now seemed to be closed. Gromyko was not encouraging about the possibility of further talks and also spoke of the necessity of a summit meeting to discuss disarmament. Hammarskjold tried to convince him of the value of his proposed technical study on the cessation of nuclear tests as a means of clarifying the picture. Gromyko was gloomy about the Disarmament Commission, which he referred to as a "vaudeville performance."[10] Hammarskjold suggested that the Security Council might sponsor the idea of a summit meeting on disarmament.

In February 1958, Hammarskjold was credited in the press with having suggested a meeting of the Security Council at the Foreign Minister level to break the disarmament deadlock. He vigorously denied this story,[11] saying only that he had reminded the powers about the possibilities of a meeting of Foreign Ministers such as had shown some promise of reaching a successful agreement on the Suez Canal in 1956 before the Anglo-French-Israeli invasion. He was, he admitted, determined that a procedure be found by which the disarmament question should remain "on the UN rails,"[12] even if a summit meeting of the great powers did take place.

On April 29, 1958, Hammarskjold took the unprecedented step of making a statement on disarmament in the Security Council.[13] The occasion was the consideration by the Council of a Soviet request for "urgent measures to put an end to flights by U.S. military aircraft, armed with atomic and hydrogen bombs, in the direction of the frontiers of the Soviet Union."[14] In the course of the debate, the United States had suggested the establishment of a zone of inspection in the area north of the Arctic Circle and had proposed that, without waiting for the renewal of disarmament talks, negotiations should begin on an international inspection system designed to remove the fear of surprise attack. Hammarskjold took this proposal as a pretext for appealing for real progress on the disarmament problem, stressing the importance of such separate measures as the suspension of nuclear-weapons tests, which had been proposed formally by the U.S.S.R. the previous June, and inspection zones to prevent surprise attack, as suggested by the United States. He had taken this opportunity to make an appeal of his own, he said, because the impasse was too dangerous to be allowed to continue. He had welcomed[15] the decision of the U.S.S.R. on March 31, 1958, to suspend unilaterally its nuclear tests. He now intervened "in the same spirit and on the same basis ... to welcome the initiative taken by the U.S. in presenting a proposal which might break up the stalemate from the angle of a limited system of inspection,"[16] a proposal that had been made in response to Soviet concern over the possible consequences, in an area of immediate concern, of "the present state of extreme preparedness in the field of armaments."[17]

Hammarskjold went on to analyze the disarmament deadlock and the reasons for "this deeply worrying failure."[18] One reason, he told the Council, was "that in a sense governments have been too ambitious, not being satisfied with just making a dent in this intricate and vital problem from which a rift could develop, opening up the possibilities of a true exchange of views. Another reason has been a tendency for each government to wait for others to take the first step. Still another reason, and, of course, the basic one, is the crisis of trust from which all mankind is suffering at the present juncture and which is reflected in an unwillingness to take any moves in a positive direction at their face value and a tendency to hold back a positive response because of a fear of being misled."[19] The recent Soviet and U.S. initiatives could make a dent in the disarmament problem and have a major impact "if treated in good faith—which is not the same as to let down one's guard"[20]—and might provide the first frail basis for the development of some kind of trust. The government that took an initiative of this kind would be hailed as a benefactor by the peoples of the world, who were "anxiously expecting leadership bringing them out of the present nightmare."[21] These were the peoples "whose voice is reflected in the Charter under which I am acting."[22] Hammarskjold's remarks were, he said, merely an "expression of profound feelings which are current all over the world and which have a right to be heard here also outside the framework of government policies. I hope that each of the governments, represented around this table, will wish to try out the line of trust as a way out of the disintegration and decline under which we now all suffer."[23]

This intervention was taken amiss by both sides—by the West because of the wish to link the Soviet proposal for nuclear-test suspension to the other aspects of disarmament, and by the U.S.S.R. because Hammarskjold appeared to be speaking publicly in favor of the U.S. proposal for an inspection zone in the Arctic. Only two members of the Security Council commented on his statement. G. Georges-Picot, the French representative, said that the Secretary-General's statement was very important and reflected his customary impartiality and objectivity and his constant care to ensure the application of the principles of the Charter.[24] Sobolev, on the other hand, criticized it as being in support of the U.S. position.[25] On May 2, 1958, the U.S. resolution[26] and the Soviet resolution[27] were both rejected, the former by the Soviet veto.

When at Hammarskjold's next press conference[28] some concern was expressed that he might have gone too far in his statement to the Security Council, he confidently replied, "I do not for a second believe that the Secretary-General, with due reserve and due tact, going on record with his general views on one of the key UN problems, will shake such trust."[29] He characterized his Security Council speech, which he admitted was a calculated risk, as

a general appeal to all Governments, first of all, of course, the big powers, to get all the positive value they possibly can out of any honest initiative taken by any Government. . . . There is a point in the development of disarmament where every time an initiative is taken in good faith and its possible consequences, its possible values, are not fully explored, I have the feeling that we have missed the bus. And we should not be too sure that the road will remain open for busses in all the future. That sense of urgency, that sense of responsibility, in the face of every new opening, from wherever it comes and whatever its immediate limited substance, was what prompted me, what made me feel that it was one of those occasions where public statements by the Secretary-General are very much part of his duty and a very adequate supplement to private diplomacy. . . . I did feel that this was a move which changed the constellation on the chessboard in a way that the possibilities . . . had to be fully explored. . . . You see, even a very small dent may lead to a rift, and a rift may lead to an opening and you may break in through the wall. . . . The interesting thing is, is this a dent which may lead to a rift?[30]

The immediate answer was negative, and efforts to reconvene the enlarged Disarmament Commission in the summer of 1958 were unsuccessful. Thus ended the first UN effort, which had begun in 1952, to draft a comprehensive and coordinated treaty for the regulation, limitation, and balanced reduction of all armed forces and armaments.

The idea of an expert technical study and exchange of information on the implications of a cessation of nuclear tests proved more fruitful. On March 26, 1958, Eisenhower had invited the UN to send a group of qualified observers to witness a large nuclear explosion in which radioactive fallout would be drastically reduced. Five days later the Supreme Soviet adopted a decree ending nuclear testing, and on April 4 Khrushchev wrote to Eisenhower calling on the Western nuclear powers to do the same. In his reply Eisenhower, saying that the forthcoming U.S. tests had been arranged for a long time, proposed, as Hammarskjold had done the previous October, that technicians from both sides study specific control measures upon which a test suspension agreement could be based. Despite the fact that the United States and Great Britain shortly afterwards embarked on the most intensive nuclear test program in history, the exchange between Eisenhower and Khrushchev finally resulted in the meeting in Geneva, from July 1 to August 21, of a conference of experts from Canada, France, Britain and the United States on the one side, and the U.S.S.R., Poland, Czechoslovakia, and Romania on the other, with the Secretary-General being represented at his own request by a personal representative, T. G. Narayanan.

The experts agreed[31] in a surprisingly short time that the available methods for detecting nuclear explosions made it possible, within limits, to detect and identify them. Hammarskjold hailed their report as a "signal contribution in making an effective dent in the hitherto rather intractable problem of disarmament. It will hereafter lie with the governments concerned and the UN to follow through the opening you have created."[32] Ever since the First UN Conference on the Peaceful Uses of Atomic Energy, he had been convinced of the value of the exchange of scientific information as a means of improving the political atmosphere and reducing distrust and suspicion. The progress made by the nuclear-test experts supported this view as applied to the whole problem of disarmament.

"It may be worth considering," Hammarskjold wrote in the introduction to his annual report for 1957–8,[33] "whether those elements of the problem lending themselves to objective study by experts in science and technology, in military experience, and in law might not be singled out for separate treatment—despite their inter-relationship —in a manner similar to that recently tried at Geneva. Certainly, such an approach would not in itself bring about disarmament, but it might help to improve the atmosphere and clarify many of the problems involved, thus preparing the ground for a time more politically propitious than the present seems to be for a general disarmament agreement."

In proposing the inclusion of an item on disarmament on the agenda of the 1958 session of the General Assembly, Hammarskjold pursued this thought a little further. "The General Assembly," he wrote, "might wish to consider the value of endorsing the principle of openness of information in the armaments and allied fields as one which could contribute significantly to reduce international tension and promote progress toward disarmament. Furthermore, were Governments to be invited to endeavour to apply this principle progressively and in widening areas, consistent with the requirements of international peace and their own security, it might lead to still further encouraging initiatives similar to those to which the results of the Geneva talks have given rise and which also Members have noted with satisfaction."[34]

The United States and Britain agreed on August 22, subject to reciprocity, to suspend nuclear testing for one year.[35] It was also agreed that the U.S.S.R., the United States, and Britain should begin negotiations on a nuclear-test-ban treaty in Geneva on October 31, 1958. Progress on a nuclear-test ban, however, was slow. The Geneva Conference on the Discontinuance of Nuclear Weapons Tests finally transferred its work to a subcommittee of the eighteen-nation United Nations Disarmament Committee in March 1962. On August 5, 1963, two years after Hammarskjold's death, the Treaty banning Nuclear Weapons Tests in the Atmosphere, in Outer Space and Under Water was signed in Moscow.

HAMMARSKJOLD HAD ALWAYS BEEN convinced that disarmament, as a legitimate concern of all member states, must remain a central preoccupation of the UN, and he opposed whenever possible the tendency to treat it as a purely great-power or East-West concern that could best be considered outside the UN framework. It was for this reason that in 1958 and 1959, when the Disarmament Commission was in abeyance, he insisted on the inclusion of an item on disarmament on the General Assembly agenda.

He had always resisted the kind of great-power elitism that led to the discussion of important subjects, such as disarmament or the future of atomic energy, only by a small number of privileged countries outside the framework of the UN. When, for example, the new

International Atomic Energy Agency was being set up, he had fought against[36] the decentralizing and proliferating tendencies that aimed at separating the Agency as far as possible from the political merry-go-round of the UN. Since the Agency might play a key role not only in the development of the peaceful uses of atomic energy but also in a future system of arms control, nuclear safeguards, and inspection, Hammarskjold had originally tried to get the Agency set up as an organ within the framework of the UN itself. When he failed in this, he insisted that the Agency remain in the closest possible relationship to the UN. To the objections of scientists and anti-internationalists, who maintained that the International Atomic Energy Agency should stay as far away as possible from the UN's political wranglings and frustrations, he retorted that this was an unrealistic view since, whether scientists liked it or not, atomic energy was a primary factor in world politics. His insistence on a special relationship of the Atomic Energy Agency to the General Assembly and the Security Council was formally embodied in the agreement[37] between the UN and the Agency, and his proposal that the United Nations Scientific Advisory Committee also advise the Agency was also accepted.[38] Nonetheless, the International Atomic Energy Agency, once established in Vienna, tended to become increasingly remote from the UN.

In August 1959, Hammarskjold was dismayed to learn that the Foreign Ministers of France, the U.S.S.R., Britain, and the United States, who were then meeting in Geneva to consider the Berlin problem, had decided to create a new Ten Nation Disarmament Committee outside of, but linked to, the UN, consisting of themselves, Bulgaria, Canada, Czechoslovakia, Italy, Poland, and Romania, i.e., an East-West parity arrangement of five on each side. He reacted strongly and immediately to this step in a memorandum to the three Western representatives in New York. This new disarmament body, which contained no representation from Africa, Asia, Latin America, or the neutral countries of Europe, had a "purely bilateral build-up"[39] and could not possibly be claimed to act on behalf of the UN. It was true that the Disarmament Commission, which had been constituted by the General Assembly in 1958[40] to contain the whole membership, was not capable of doing the necessary work properly, but Hammarskjold felt that the big powers could not entirely disregard its existence. At the very least the Disarmament Commission should have been informed of the decision to set up the Ten Nation group, and the Ten Nation group itself should also report to the Commission.

Hammarskjold suggested that either he or the four great powers should immediately convene the Disarmament Commission, which, after electing a neutral chairman, should be informed that the Big

Four had asked six other countries to join them in their disarmament talks. No claim should be made that this group was to replace the Disarmament Commission, which would continue to report to the General Assembly so that all members would have an opportunity to discuss disarmament problems. The General Assembly might even set up a new disarmament commission with a more workable composition and representing equitably the various interests in the UN in order to avoid general resentment among the members. Such a step would prevent disarmament, which under the Charter was an objective of the United Nations, from being lifted out of the Organization and would apply a brake to "the present trend into a kind of bi-lateralism in international polititics, which—apart from being dangerous— negates the fact that the majority of the nations of the world are not lined up in the Eastern or Western camps."[41]

On August 22 a draft communiqué of the four powers, which was eventually issued on September 8,[42] showed that Hammarskjold's reaction had had its effect. The decision of the Big Four to establish a group outside the UN, the communiqué stated, "in no way diminishes or encroaches upon the UN responsibilities in this field," but rather "takes into account the special responsibility resting on themselves to find a basis for agreement."[43] The group's efforts would, it was hoped, "provide a useful basis for the further consideration of disarmament in the UN,"[44] and the Disarmament Commission would be kept fully informed. "As a first step in this direction they have requested the Secretary-General . . . to convene the Disarmament Commission during September 1959 if feasible, in order that the members may be fully informed of the nature and purpose of the deliberations."[45]

In September 1959 there was a new and dramatic development. On September 17, Selwyn Lloyd submitted to the General Assembly a three-stage comprehensive disarmament plan.[46] The next day, Khrushchev presented his item on "general and complete disarmament,"[47] aimed at eliminating, within four years and under international control, all armed forces and armaments. A revised version of this proposal was submitted to the Ten Nation Committee which met in Geneva in March of the following year. The General Assembly transmitted all these ideas to the Disarmament Commission and to the Ten Nation Committee.[48] The latter body soon justified Hammarskjold's apprehensions by considering a Western proposal, strongly opposed by the Soviet and Eastern European delegations, for setting up a separate International Disarmament Organization. The Western proposal purported to provide peace machinery that could not be frustrated or rendered impotent by the actions of a single power or group of powers.

Hammarskjold was shocked at the irresponsibility and lack of realism of this kind of "playfulness,"[49] which he regarded as a self-deluding attempt to create a new UN in order to get around some aspects of the Charter that displeased the authors of the International Disarmament Organization plan. On March 15 he wrote to Christian Herter, the U.S. Secretary of State:

> It is said that previous experience should be taken into account. That experience, in my view, very convincingly indicates that an independent agency set up only for control functions will not have a sound life or become an effective member of the family of international organizations. The International Atomic Agency is a case in point, which also demonstrates that there is no half-way house between a specialized agency, completely independent of the UN, and an organ *within* the UN like, for example, the UNRWA [United Nations Relief and Works Agency for Palestine Refugees]. By opening the discussion about a disarmament organ as you do, I am afraid you have tipped the scales in the direction of a specialized agency, and the result, in my view, would undoubtedly be a very weak agency and a hollowing out of the UN of one of its main fields of activity.
>
> I suppose that it has been thought that disarmament control would be too much for and would surpass the capacity of the UN Secretariat. If so, the answer is a UN organ of the type we already have used for other major operations within the framework of the UN proper. The same argument could well have been put forward in the case of Technical Assistance. Fortunately, it was not done.
>
> There seems to be at present a tendency in the thinking of the West which I find worrying. The peaceful uses of atomic energy, for no good reasons, were pushed outside of the UN. The proposed atomic test organ is another example of the same approach. Both of these cases may be defended as marginal, but no such deference is possible when we reach disarmament.
>
> If the disarmament control were to be lifted out of the UN, and if present efforts to build up an international organ with wide membership for assistance to under-developed countries were to succeed, the result would be a weakening of international cooperation all around as the UN would be robbed of a main part of its substantive content without new and really viable substitutes being created.[50]

Hammarskjold was particularly disturbed by the statement of Gaetano Martino, the Italian representative on the Ten Nation Committee, that the United Nations lacked the means to ensure peace and security and that special machinery had to be created, whether within or outside the UN framework. Gaetano's statement, Hammarskjold wrote to Lodge on March 25,

> . . . if taken at face value, confirms my worst fears. It is recognized that the UN has "as one" of its purposes and goals the maintenance of peace and security, but the speaker adds that it has not the means to ensure this. He draws the conclusion that special machinery would have to be created—obviously with the somewhat unexpected hope that a new body could have "the necessary arms and men to impose respect," although the UN could not get it—and winds up by leaving it as an open question whether the new machinery should be within the framework of the UN.
>
> I find it difficult to formulate my reaction to the present trend, but I guess that the most adequate word would be "irresponsible." Instead of discussing what, if any, changes of the Charter might be desirable and possible, one scraps, by implication, all that has been done and argues as if a new start would be all that is needed in order to get over the difficulties with which we have been battling within the UN.
>
> Similar observations apply to the talk about an international peace organization which has now been elaborated by [Jules] Moch in the Sixth Committee. What he paints before us—this year when it is impossible to get rid even of the Connally amendment*—is a developed International Court with compulsory jurisdiction and disposing of an international force so that it can order an enforcement of its decisions. It would seem that the normal distinctions between the legal and political elements, and the need to keep them apart, as well as the accepted distinctions between judiciary and executive, have been forgotten.
>
> With the frankness to which I feel that I am entitled with you, I confess I am at a loss to understand what is happening. I am deeply frustrated to see what strikes me as a mixture of dilettantism and utopianism tainted by what appears as a predominant desire to get away from the UN while paying lip service to it.[51]

The Soviet representative in the Ten Nation Committee, Valerian Zorin, evidently shared Hammarskjold's view and pointed out forcefully the damage that would be done by the Western proposal to the UN as the organization specially created to maintain international peace and security. "If the United Nations is still in existence," Zorin asked, "why should we think of setting up a new organization? This

---

* The declaration of acceptance by the United States of the optional compulsory jurisdiction clause of the Statute of the International Court of Justice (Article 36, para. 2) deposited on August 26, 1946, originally contained the provision that the declaration should not apply to "disputes with regard to matters which are essentially within the domestic jurisdiction of the United States of America as determined by the United States of America . . ." The words "as determined by the United States of America" were rejected by the Senate Committee on Foreign Relations, but were added on the floor of the Senate in an amendment by Senator Tom Connally.

is not clear to me at all. I am even afraid that perhaps Mr. Hammar-skjold might find himself out of his job once we begin setting up such a new organization—and I doubt very much whether this can be our common purpose."[52]

As Secretary-General, Hammarskjold was much concerned with the predominant desire of some Western European statesmen, what-ever their motives might be, to sidetrack the UN as an effective inter-national instrument. In a letter to U.S. Assistant Secretary of State Francis Wilcox, he asked where, since a disarmament organization must be fully integrated with the "international policy-making of the UN,"[53] the ultimate political responsibility for it should lie. Experience had shown that organizations like the Specialized Agencies, with their own assemblies and councils, were very difficult to coordinate with the UN, not least because "we have no reason to hope that govern-ments will get over their normal 'schizophrenia' and speak with the same tongue in different assemblies."[54] The Western plan for a new independent disarmament agency had a basic fallacy. "I have heard the objection that a new operation must be free from the weaknesses of the UN in three respects: it must be able to include members which are not admitted to the UN, it should preferably have a weighted voting system and there should be no veto. I do not consider those arguments against ultimate political responsibility for the UN as in any way valid, as it seems obvious to me that the moment these three questions could be resolved to your satisfaction in a new organ, they could just as well be resolved within the UN itself."[55]

Hammarskjold's arguments apparently convinced the United States of the impracticability of the Western plan, and he was able to address the Ten Nation Committee itself with considerable confidence when other duties brought him to Geneva on April 28. Disarmament, he pointed out, was inseparable in the policies of member governments from the pacific settlement of disputes and action with respect to threats to the peace, for these were functions of the UN that would become of critical significance if progressive or complete disarmament were to come about. "Organizational arrangements ... do not change realities; what at a given time politically is attainable on one organiza-tional basis, is equally attainable on another one. Essential difficulties encountered within the UN are based on realities and not on the specific constitution of the Organization. In the work for achieving and maintaining disarmament they would not be experienced with less force, were an attempt to be made to start, so to say, all over again."[56]

On May 18, 1960, the shooting down of an American U-2 spy plane over the Soviet Union broke up the Paris summit meeting, and on

June 27 the Ten Nation Committee on Disarmament came to an end when the five Eastern European delegations withdrew from it.

Following the collapse of the Ten Nation Committee, the United Nations Disarmament Commission reconvened to review the situation, and on August 18, 1960, it called for the earliest possible resumption of negotiations on disarmament.[57] "It is certainly not productive," Hammarskjold wrote on the eve of the General Assembly's fifteenth session, "to approach the disarmament problem solely on a pragmatic basis, without integration of the steps taken into a plan ultimately aiming at full disarmament. Likewise, however, it seems unrealistic to approach the total problem oblivious of the fact that all political experience and all previous negotiation show that the road to progress lies in the direction of efforts to contain and reduce the area of disagreement by mobilizing such common interests as may exist and as may override other and special interests tending in the opposite direction."[58]

During 1961, U.S.-Soviet relations on disarmament steadily improved, and on September 20, 1961, three days after Hammarskjold's death, the two governments issued a joint statement of agreed principles as a basis for multilateral negotiations on disarmament.[59] Eleven years later the endless search continues, and an occasional step forward justifies Hammarskjold's contention that as regards disarmament in the second half of the twentieth century, cynicism and defeatism are as indefensible as they are unrealistic.

13

LAOS

"THE SITUATION IN LAOS,"[1] Hammarskjold wrote in October 1959, "is hardly the most auspicious for launching the United Nations in a far-reaching initiative in South-East Asia. It would have been far better to bring about a presence gradually, perhaps based on Phnom Penh [in Cambodia], which would have political and economic responsibilities. Unfortunately developments in and *about* Laos have combined almost to dictate the path which the United Nations must now follow."[2]

The collapse of French power in Indochina and its withdrawal after the Geneva Conference of 1954 revealed, in the stark context of the cold war, the basic regional instability that the French empire had masked for nearly a century. The Geneva settlement had envisaged Laos as a neutral buffer state between Western-oriented Thailand, to its south and west, and Communist North Vietnam. The area now called Laos had in fact played this neutral role for a time before the arrival of the French in the nineteenth century, but the ethnic and political factors that had made this role possible were no longer present. The frontiers of modern Laos were the result of French empire building, and its population was ethnically divided in such a way that in any dispute between North Vietnam and Thailand the lowland half would side naturally with Thailand and the upland half with North Vietnam. Since after 1954 these countries were backed by the United States and China respectively, Laos, far from being a buffer state, became a natural area of confrontation in the cold war.

This outcome was not foreseen in 1954 at Geneva, where the major issue for the West had been the disengagement of France from a hopeless, costly, and irrelevant conflict. The fact was, however, that at the end of the Indochina war Laos had in effect been left physically divided between the two sides. The validity of the country as an independent political entity depended on the reconciliation of the two main factions: the lowland Lao, who were politically dominant and who by tradition, race, and education were oriented toward Thailand and the West, and the relatively undeveloped highland peoples, whose traditional dislike of the Lao had been exploited by a handful of anti-Western, pro-Communist leaders in alliance with the North Vietnamese in order to form the dissident Pathet Lao.

The Laotian Premier, Prince Souvanna Phouma, set about the task of reconciliation as soon as the Geneva settlement went into effect. The leader of the Pathet Lao was his half-brother Prince Souphanouvong, and it looked at first as if integration of the dissidents might be relatively speedy. Before the end of 1954, however, French political, economic, and military commitments in Indochina as a whole were already being replaced by those of the United States. At a time when Washington was trying to build up the new Southeast Asia Treaty Organization, based on Thailand, into a credible anti-Communist bastion and to create a stable anti-Communist regime under Ngo Dinh Diem in South Vietnam, the last thing it wanted was to see significant concessions to Communism in Laos on the very frontier of South Vietnam. U.S. and Thai opposition led to the failure of Souvanna Phouma's first attempt at reconciliation in 1954, and it was three years before he finally achieved a settlement with his half-brother by the so-called Vientiane Agreements of November 1957.

In the interval, the Pathet Lao had made considerable political progress in the country as a whole. When this became clear at the partial elections held in 1958 to implement the Vientiane Agreements, Thai and American fears became predominant. American aid was suspended on a pretext, and Souvanna Phouma was forced from the scene. A right-wing pro-Western government under Phoui Sananikone took over, and the Royal Laotian Army was further built up with covert American military advice. At the beginning of 1959, all possibility of political opposition was stifled by the grant of emergency powers to the government on the dubious pretext that a Communist rebellion was imminent. The National Assembly was suspended, and protests

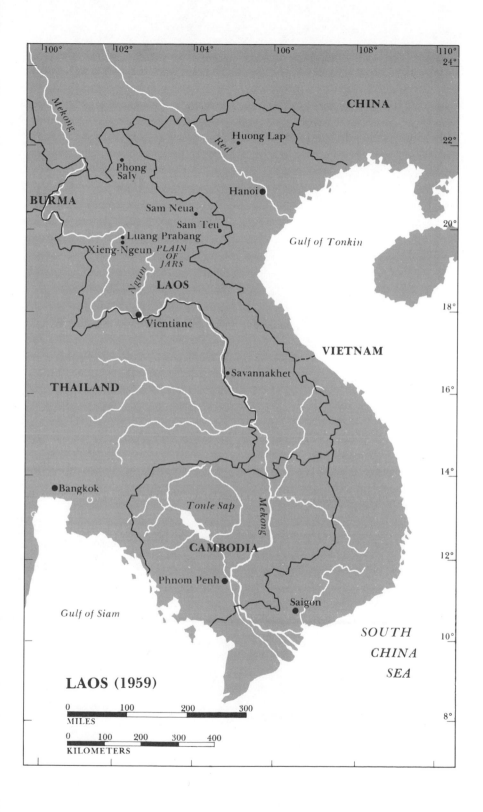

CHINA

Huong Lap

Phong
Saly

Hanoi

BURMA

Sam Neua

Sam Teu

Luang Prabang

Xieng-Ngeun PLAIN
OF
JARS

LAOS

Gulf of Tonkin

Vientiane

VIETNAM

Savannakhet

THAILAND

Bangkok

Tonle Sap

Mekong

CAMBODIA

Phnom Penh

Saigon

Gulf of Siam

SOUTH

CHINA

SEA

LAOS (1959)

| 0 | 100 | 200 | 300 |
MILES

| 0 | 100 | 200 | 300 | 400 |
KILOMETERS

Mekong

Red

Ngum

100°   102°   104°   106°   108°   110°

24°

22°

20°

18°

16°

14°

12°

10°

8°

from Hanoi and Peking were rejected. The strongest military figure in the country, Phoumi Nosavan, became a member of the government, which proceeded to ask the United States officially for military aid. A Soviet protest that this request contravened the Geneva Agreement was rejected by both the United States and Great Britain.

At this point the government of Laos decided to integrate into its expanding army the two Pathet Lao battalions that were to have been integrated under the Vientiane Agreements but which had remained separate owing to lack of agreement on the terms of integration. When the battalions rejected integration, it was decided to use force. From the Pathet Lao point of view, integration was indeed unacceptable. They had surrendered their territory in 1957–8; they had been deprived of their political voice by the suspension of the Assembly; now they were to lose the remains of their independent military position. One of the battalions decamped to the North Vietnamese frontier at the end of May, and the greater part of the other followed its example in August.

By the end of June, before the Pathet Lao forces could have reorganized themselves for rebellion—which they were in any case unlikely to start while Prince Souphanouvong and their other leaders were still in Vientiane, the administrative capital, and while the monsoon that had just started made serious military operations in the area almost impossible—the Laotian government was alleging that a full-scale Communist invasion of northeast Laos was under way. In retrospect it may be said that this allegation was false. The reality was small-scale guerrilla activity in remote areas that achieved limited success partly because of the spreading of rumor. Nevertheless the fanciful reports of the journalists who flocked to Vientiane were accepted by the world press and by the U.S. government, as well as by the Premier of Laos himself, Phoui Sananikone. Toward the end of August the situation seemed to deteriorate dramatically, and on September 4 Laos appealed to the United Nations[3] to dispatch an Emergency Force to Laos to halt North Vietnamese aggression.

HAMMARSKJOLD HAD FOLLOWED the Laotian situation closely ever since the crisis of January 1959, of which he had been officially informed by the Laotian government at the time.[4] A year earlier the frontier incidents that led to the crisis would have come within the purview of the Laotian section of the International Control Commission [ICC], which had been set up in 1954 to supervise the implementation of the Geneva Agreement, but this body had been disbanded upon the request of the previous Laotian government in 1958 under strong Western pressure, ostensibly because its task had been completed. Its members, Poland, Canada, and India, which provided the chairman, had departed with some dissatisfaction on the Communist side, and in the crisis of 1959 Hanoi and Peking demanded that the ICC be recalled to Laos, a demand firmly rejected by the Laotian government.

When, in January 1959, Hammarskjold had been asked by the Laotian Foreign Minister for his informal advice and active interest, he replied that he would think over the problem and revert to it if and when he had any advice to give. The right-wing government in Laos deeply distrusted the ICC and greatly preferred the UN, of which North Vietnam was not a member, as a court of appeal. North Vietnam, however, regarded the ICC as alone competent to undertake conciliation. Hammarskjold's problem, therefore, in considering the Laotian Foreign Minister's request was to find a course of action that would offer a role for the ICC as well as for the UN.

This was precisely the moment at which the Laotian government, with Western connivance, was about to create a new situation by stating that it regarded itself as no longer bound by the limitations on foreign military aid that it had accepted under the Geneva Agreement of 1954 and had confirmed as still valid less than a year earlier. The Geneva Agreement provided that apart from French training and defense establishments already in the country, no reinforcements of troops or military personnel from outside Laotian territory were to be allowed. Having in effect denounced this provision on February 11, 1959, the Laotian government asked for American military assistance. This was promptly furnished in the form of eighty Filipino military technicians and in the establishment of a training section of the so-called Programs Evaluation Office (PEO) of the U.S. Operations Mission in Laos.[5] The PEO was headed by a brigadier general of the U.S. Army who had doffed his uniform and whose name had been removed from the appropriate military lists to conceal his status.

One of the possibilities which Hammarskjold had in mind, and which he put to the Laotian permanent representative on February 9, was to get the member nations of the ICC to suggest to the governments of North Vietnam and Laos that they ask the Secretary-General to appoint a representative, or some third party, to assist them in the settlement of their dispute. Obviously Laotian acceptance was vital to this plan. On February 19 the permanent representative of Laos told Hammarskjold that it was acceptable, and two days later he asked him to approach North Vietnam and Laos through India. On February 24, Hammarskjold asked Nehru to approach both Laos and North Vietnam on the procedure for reconciliation he had devised, suggesting further that India itself, another state, or United Nations "good offices" as provided by the Secretary-General to Cambodia and Thailand* might constitute the necessary third party in the case.

As part of a previously planned Asian tour, Hammarskjold visited Vientiane from March 9 to 11 and gained some insight into the views of the members of the Laos government. In spite of its strong aversion to the ICC, the government agreed that Hammarskjold should try to get some kind of negotiation going with North Vietnam, especially to resolve the problem of the two Pathet Lao battalions that were supposed to be integrated into the Royal Laotian Army. In these discussions he emphasized the necessity of using the ICC as a bridge to Hanoi and Peking. His interlocutors listened politely but without conviction, and their subsequent actions indicated that they and their backers did not share his enthusiasm for reconciliation and negotiation.

In Delhi later on in the tour, Hammarskjold pursued with Prime Minister Nehru, Defense Minister Krishna Menon, and Finance Minister Morarji Desai his idea that India should sound out Hanoi and Vientiane and lay the ground, if possible, for a joint request for mediation. The Indians were exceedingly cautious and undertook only to sound out Poland on Hammarskjold's plan, while Hammarskjold agreed to inquire if the Canadian government would be willing to resume its seat on the ICC so that India could consult the Canadian member as well. Several months of unproductive discussion with the various parties followed.

On his return to New York from Asia, Hammarskjold was extremely noncommittal. The object of his visit to Vientiane, he told a press conference, was "to give them [the Laotians] a chance to talk matters over and lay a basis for continued close contact, so that we can to some extent jointly judge what can best be done. Whither that may lead I cannot tell now."[6]

The Laos situation took a turn for the worse when the Phoui government decided to bring to a head the question of integrating the two Pathet Lao battalions into the Royal Laotian Army, a matter that had long been held up by disagreement on the number of Pathet Lao officers to be accepted and on their ranks. Toward the end of April, Phoui agreed to commission the 105 officers nominated by the Pathet Lao and named May 11 as Integration Day.

In view of the fact that only two Pathet Lao battalions were to be integrated into an army that already numbered twenty-four battalions and a substantial roster of ancillary units, the Pathet Lao demand for

---

* See Chapter 11.

105 officers was high. Government acceptance, however, involved a trick, as Sisouk Na Champassak, the Laotian Information Minister at the time, has made clear: "Once the agreement was reached, the weapons surrendered, and the two battalions scattered through the country, the commissions could be nullified by demanding, for example, that the new officers pass examinations appropriate to their rank."[7] Most of the proposed officers had spent the past ten to fifteen years in the jungle and could be expected to fail such examinations.

Prince Souphanouvong and his colleagues undoubtedly knew that this was nothing but a ruse to deprive him of what military resources he had left. Nevertheless the two battalions apparently had orders to accept integration provided the Prince or his military commander was present. The military commander was not invited, and the Prince only at the last minute. On this and several other pretexts, the two units refused integration.

On May 13 the government arrested the Pathet Lao leaders and surrounded the two battalions in their camps. Four days later one of them accepted integration, but the other escaped from its camp at night and made for the North Vietnamese border. This action caused the government to state that the Pathet Lao had openly rebelled. In fact it had been forced, perhaps intentionally, back to the jungle. In any case the government declaration that only a military solution now seemed possible opened a new phase of activity.

In a note to Britain on May 30, the Soviet Union suggested that the two governments, by virtue of their continuing responsibility as cochairmen of the Geneva Conference of 1954, send a joint message to the Laotian government urging it to observe the Geneva Agreements and to resume its cooperation with the ICC. The British rejected the Soviet proposal, saying that to reinstitute the ICC without the concurrence of the Laotian government would be "inconsistent with the duty resting on all members of the Geneva Conference to respect the sovereignty and territorial integrity of Laos and to refrain from any interference in Laos' internal affairs."[8] The British replied in a similar vein to allegations made by the Chinese government against Laos, and on May 29 the United States roundly accused the Communists of violating both the Geneva Agreement of 1954 and the Vientiane Agreements of 1957, adding that the United States was not involved and had taken no part in the Laotian government's efforts, despite Communist propaganda to the contrary.

In a cable to Hammarskjold on May 28, Nehru expressed grave concern over both Laos and Southeast Asia in general and begged him to pursue his efforts to get Canada to nominate its representative on the ICC, which Nehru regarded as the only organ capable of reducing tension between Laos and North Vietnam. Nehru complained of U.S. military activities in Laos, including the arrival of U.S. military advisers in civilian clothes and of military equipment. He asked Hammarskjold to do his best to promote a constructive approach in Washington "so that peace may be maintained in Indo-China and a grave conflict averted."[9]

In a letter to Secretary of State Herter on the following day, Hammarskjold admitted his lack of real knowledge of the Laos situation: "Insufficiently informed about the true situation as I am, I do not consider it possible to do more for the moment than to inform you about this démarche [Nehru's], to consult Ottawa, to request the Ambassador of Laos to give me as full a picture of the situation and of the present stand of his Government as he can, and, finally, to inform Selwyn Lloyd—as one of the co-chairmen of the Geneva Conference— of this new development."[10] The situation was now deteriorating to the point where Hammarskjold felt he must abandon his ingenious formula for marrying the ICC and the UN in a conciliation effort. "The stakes being what they are," he wrote Herter, "I would be quite willing to play the United Nations card for what it is worth—in this case it might mean assuming a personal role in the field—if I saw any opening in that direction."[11]

If the idea of Hammarskjold's taking the field was likely to be unacceptable to the Soviet Union, it was also the last thing the United States wanted, and Herter's reply of June 9 was a masterpiece of polite discouragement. U.S. military and economic aid, he wrote, had been given to Laos for a number of years, and Laos could not survive without it, nor could it threaten its neighbors with the aid provided by the United States. The Communists "readily create provocations to justify actions which they plan to take in the international field,"[12] but the United States would do nothing to provoke them. "I think we should continue to follow this situation closely," Herter concluded, "and I look forward to the opportunity of talking with you about it."[13]

Hammarskjold gained a more realistic, if less pleasant, impression of the U.S. attitude from a talk on June 12 with Walter S. Robertson,* the Assistant Secretary of State for Far Eastern Affairs. He noted that Robertson "considered himself to have the only true version"[15] of events in Laos, which differed widely from his own. Robertson made little effort to conceal his conviction that Hammarskjold was unduly influenced by Communist propaganda, while his obvious contempt

---

* In *A Thousand Days*, p. 305, Arthur Schlesinger, Jr., writes: "Robertson, like Dulles, judged Chiang Kai-shek moral and neutralism immoral and established policy on those principles." [14]

for normal diplomatic and governmental approaches to the problems of Indochina seemed to indicate a commitment to the covert operations prevalent in Laos in flat contradiction of publicly stated U.S. policy.

Writing to Nehru on June 11, Hammarskjold agreed that the difficulties between Laos and North Vietnam could all too easily lead to a dangerous and unmanageable situation, especially with the increasing undercover U.S. involvement. He had, he added, told the Foreign Secretaries of the major power blocs that the countries of Indochina should be allowed to concentrate on their economic and social development without cold-war alignments or interventions. He again asked for Nehru's help in setting up some kind of mediation between Laos and North Vietnam. On June 10, Nehru had publicly urged that the ICC be reconstituted in order to keep Indochina out of the cold war, into which the activities of various other countries were tending to pull it.

It soon began to seem likely that a military solution was already under way in Laos. Reports of attacks on frontier outposts in the northeastern province of Sam Neua, which borders on North Vietnam, began to be circulated on July 20. On July 23 the Laotian government asked for more American military aid, which was promptly granted, and on July 29 it announced that the attacks had been carried out by Pathet Lao forces stiffened by Viet Minh elements. Prince Souphanouvong and the other Pathet Lao leaders in Vientiane, who had been released from arrest, were once again put in jail. During August the military situation appeared to deteriorate. It is uncertain how far the crisis was real and how far a series of relatively small incidents was exaggerated by the Laotian military in order to keep American money coming in spite of a recently published U.S. government report about the mismanagement and corruption surrounding U.S. aid in Laos.[16] It is enough to say that later information did not justify the degree of panic into which the American press and the Laotian and American governments were thrown. The main result was a double escalation. The American commitment to the Laotian government and particularly to its dominant military member, General Phoumi, was substantially increased, and the Pathet Lao was reactivated by North Vietnam as a serious guerrilla force.

Hammarskjold soon found himself involved in this strange crisis. On August 2 the Laotian Foreign Minister, Kamphan Panya, had declared that "should the situation become graver in the next forty-eight hours, the Laotian Government would call on the United Nations,"[17] adding that the real objective of the Pathet Lao was to force the government to accept the arbitration of the ICC and the revision of military assistance arrangements with the West. On August 4, after a few incidents in Luang Prabang Province, Kamphan Panya cabled Hammarskjold that the situation was very grave and accused North Vietnam of having supplied arms and provisions to the Pathet Lao.[18] On the following day Selwyn Lloyd informed Hammarskjold that Britain, France, and the United States were anxious to find a method of fact-finding and mediation to calm the situation down. Lloyd, as one of the cochairmen of the Geneva Conference, suggested that if Gromyko, as the other cochairman, agreed, Hammarskjold should be asked to appoint a mediator. Hammarskjold immediately assented to this idea and on August 6 alerted Nehru to the possibility that he might set up some form of fact-finding machinery for the Laos situation. Gromyko's negative response to Lloyd's approach put an end to this plan for the time being, although rumors of a UN involvement compelled Hammarskjold in mid-August to deny any plans for UN action. "I have not the slightest intention," he told the press, "to send Ambassador Beck-Friis, or, for that matter, anybody, under present circumstances, to the region. The initiative must come from the region, not from me."[19]

Such an initiative was not slow in materializing. On August 14 the Laotian Premier sent his brother, Ngon Sananikone, to New York to ask for UN observers who would "soon be fully educated as to the effective aid given by the Democratic Republic of North Vietnam."[20] When Sananikone was received by Hammarskjold on August 20, he did not, as had been expected, make a formal complaint against Laos' Communist neighbors, but instead handed Hammarskjold a letter inviting him to suggest "such procedures or such measures as he might consider designed to achieve a peaceful settlement of the difficulties at present experienced by Laos."[21] Forbearing to point out that this was exactly what he had been trying to do since the previous February, Hammarskjold replied that to send a fact-finding representative would require either General Assembly or Security Council action or a request from the governments of Laos and North Vietnam jointly, or alternatively a joint invitation from the two cochairmen of the Geneva Conference. There was some possibility that he might be able to send a representative to exercise good offices simply at the request of the government of Laos, but he seriously doubted whether such a move would be wise unless Hanoi's consent to it could be obtained. In response to press speculation, his spokesman announced on August 22 that the permanent representative of Laos and the Secretary-General had agreed on the next step to be taken, but that "as this step is wholly in diplomatic channels, there is nothing further that can be said at the present time."[22]

The next step was, in fact, yet another letter to Nehru repeating Hammarskjold's idea of working out an acceptable formula for mediation with Hanoi and Vientiane and begging India to take on the job. Should India be successful in evolving such a formula, he envisaged an "absolute neutral"[23] (i.e., not an Asian) as a mediator, to be appointed perhaps by himself at the request of the ICC. In his reply, which Hammarskjold received on August 25 after setting out on a Latin-American tour, Nehru declined to contact Hanoi and Vientiane unless he had the active support of the ICC and of Great Britain and the U.S.S.R. as cochairmen of the Geneva Conference, as well as of Laos and North Vietnam.

Hammarskjold had been reluctant to leave on his long-planned official visit to Argentina, Brazil, Paraguay and Uruguay. He was especially worried, he wrote to Alexis Léger on the day of his departure, about the outcome of "Western policies in S.E. Asia after the Geneva Conference."[24] Not the least of his worries at being away from Headquarters was the mood of the U.S. government. On August 24, Herter had told the Senate Foreign Relations and House Foreign Affairs Committees that the dangerous situation in Laos warranted the sending of a UN observer team, but that Hammarskjold had felt that these observers should not be sent unless both North Vietnam and Laos requested them. As Hammarskjold had foreseen, the U.S. press reacted to this statement by complaining that he had not taken immediate action on the cable from the Foreign Minister of Laos on August 4. The New York *Herald Tribune* commented, "If the communists maintain their present pace, Laos could collapse before you could say Dag Hammarskjold,"[25] and another article in the same paper criticized him for taking off on a Latin-American tour immediately after receiving the Laotian appeal, Latin America being "about as far away as anyone could get from the explosion in South-East Asia."[26]* The fact was that no one could have been less enthusiastic than Hammarskjold himself about the timing of the Latin-American tour, but he knew that to cancel it would only serve to heighten international tension over Laos.

Hammarskjold had taken steps to maintain momentum on the Laos question during his absence. In view of Nehru's hesitation about approaching Laos and North Vietnam, he was increasingly inclined towards Lloyd's idea of an impartial fact-finder to examine the border situation, and on August 27 he issued a statement "on principles regarding political fact-finding or 'good offices' missions."[28] Political fact-finding or good-offices missions had always been based on decisions of the General Assembly or the Security Council, unless the Secretary-General, after agreeing with the government concerned, went on a

---

* Bernard Fall awarded "the crown in alarmist reporting" in this "crisis" to the *Herald Tribune*'s columnist Joseph Alsop.[27]

mission personally. Lately, however, without specific sanction from the Charter or decision by the General Assembly or the Security Council, Hammarskjold had gone a little further. In the conflict between Cambodia and Thailand he had sent a personal representative at the joint request of the two countries, and in Jordan he had acted on the invitation of the Jordanian government alone. It would be outside his constitutional competence to arrange a fact-finding mission on the border situation in Laos without a prior decision by the General Assembly or the Security Council or an invitation from Laos and the other country concerned. An alternative, which might make it constitutionally possible for him to act, might be a joint initiative, after consultation with Laos and North Vietnam, by the two cochairmen of the Geneva Conference, in view of their special responsibilities under the Geneva Agreements.

In Latin America, through the routine occasions of an official tour, Hammarskjold fretted over the Laotian situation. Speaking no Spanish or Portuguese, he felt more inhibited in Latin America than in other parts of the world, and the daily cables from Andrew Cordier kept him in constant uncertainty whether to cut short his tour. Finally, on the afternoon of Friday, September 4, on returning to his hotel in Rio de Janeiro from a luncheon with President Juscelino Kubitschek of Brazil, Cordier called to inform him that the Foreign Minister of Laos had requested the Secretary-General to dispatch immediately a UN Emergency Force to Laos "to halt aggression and to prevent it spreading."[29] The message specifically accused the North Vietnamese of taking part in attacks on Laos but was reticent on the scale of the alleged aggression and totally silent on the question of casualties.

Hammarskjold's first reaction to this message was that his immediate return to New York would be reply enough, but on second thoughts he instructed Cordier to ask the President of the Security Council to convene it for Sunday or Monday. He took this constitutionally risky and unprecedented step for two reasons. He feared that if he did not do so, the Western powers would call for a Council meeting anyway— a step which from the outset would make the issue a cold war problem. If he could forestall this move by an initiative of his own, it might be possible to avoid an acrimonious debate. Secondly, since the request for an Emergency Force had been addressed to him, he believed that he either had to convene the Council or risk the accusation that he had done nothing because he had been away or, even worse, because he was afraid of the Soviet attitude and had left it up to the Western countries to take the initiative. Such a public reaction would certainly be detrimental to his future possibilities for action.

Hammarskjold was fully aware of the constitutional and political difficulties involved in his request for a Security Council meeting but made the decision anyway, trusting to luck that during his flight back to New York he would find some suitable formula. During the flight he concluded that he could not use Article 99 without grossly over-dramatizing and prejudging the situation in Laos. There were various alternative possibilities. He might, after consultations with Ngon Sananikone, the Laotian permanent representative in New York, act on behalf of the Laotian government in asking for a Council meeting. With this in mind he cabled from Trinidad to tell Cordier not to produce a written text of his request or of the Council's agenda until he had seen Sananikone. Another possibility was to try a totally new procedure and to act as Secretary-General without invoking Article 99. His request for a Council meeting would then be simply for the purpose of reporting orally to the Council on a problem facing the UN. By the time his plane reached Puerto Rico, Hammarskjold had decided that this idea was far preferable to the first possibility, and he cabled it to Cordier. When he arrived in New York, Cordier reported that he had already mentioned this procedure to Anatoly Dobrynin, the Soviet Under-Secretary, and to James Barco of the U.S. mission, and that both had reacted favorably.

Hammarskjold found Sananikone, whom he received on Saturday, September 5, noncommittal as to what his government, having made a sensational request, wished him to do. He consulted Egidio Ortona, the permanent representative of Italy, who was the President of the Security Council, and then, at Lodge's request, received Lodge at his apartment. Before this meeting he had learned on the phone from Pierson Dixon that Lodge was going to put an "ingenious"[30] proposal to him.

The United States had only reluctantly come around to the idea of some form of UN intervention in Laos as a means of gaining time and cooling down a situation largely created by alarmist reporting.* Washington was far from happy at the prospect of Hammarskjold's involvement in Laos, no doubt remembering the difficulties of the year before in Lebanon. His insistence on a role for the ICC and his criticism of covert U.S. activities in Laos had only increased Washington's determination to find a UN formula that would not give the Secretary-General a major role. Lodge told him that a Security Council meeting on Monday, September 7, was essential and showed him a draft resolu-

---

* In his memoirs Eisenhower states that when he met with Macmillan on August 29 at Chequers "we decided to ask the United Nations to send Observers to Laos, at least to determine the accuracy of our suspicion that the aggressors—the Pathet Lao units—were communists."[31]

tion setting up a subcommittee of the Security Council to study the Laos situation. Hammarskjold replied that he had nothing against the idea but was worried about the procedural situation. How could he go ahead and request a Council meeting without any support from Ngon Sananikone, whose brother's government's request for a UN force had started the whole process in the first place? Lodge said that to retreat now would put the Secretary-General in a most exposed position and added that Laos had already requested military assistance from SEATO, which would certainly take up the request if there seemed to be any delay at the UN. Hammarskjold rejoined that Lodge's first argument for going ahead was unacceptable and that SEATO intervention in Laos would be a disaster.

Sananikone was still noncommittal when he met Hammarskjold again at 10 p.m. that same Saturday. Seeing that no help was forthcoming from Laos, Hammarskjold explained the situation to Ortona and formally requested an emergency meeting of the Council.[32] Shortly before midnight Ortona announced[33] that the Council would meet at 3 p.m. on Monday.

On Sunday Hammarskjold saw Armand Bérard, the French permanent representative, and Dixon, to both of whom he explained that his request for a meeting was a procedural move designed to give the Council the possibility of making up its mind whether or not to inscribe the substantive issue of Laos on its agenda. The purpose of the subcommittee, which the British and French were to join the United States in proposing, would be solely to collect further information on which the Council could base this decision. The appointment of the subcommittee would also be a purely procedural move and would, if properly handled, avoid an acrimonious substantive debate as well as the problem of inviting the other parties concerned to attend the Council meeting. The resolution establishing the subcommittee could be taken up under the item proposed by Hammarskjold, entitled "Report by the Secretary-General on the letter received from the Minister for Foreign Affairs of the Royal Government of Laos,"[34] a wording specifically designed to avoid the use of Article 99.

This delicate procedural plan was rudely shaken on Monday morning when Lodge requested that the draft resolution[35] establishing the subcommittee be circulated before the meeting of the Council. Hammarskjold protested that the prior circulation of a draft resolution under the agenda item he had proposed would push him into a contradictory position that he could not accept from a constitutional point of view. Lodge insisted, and Hammarskjold reluctantly agreed that the resolution should be circulated, but without any reference to the item he had put on the agenda. He noted at the time that Lodge seemed to have failed totally to understand the suggested procedure and its implications. This judgment was perhaps overcharitable, as he was to find out later in the day when the procedure initiated by the United States in the Council gravely compromised his own position and initiative.

Even without such maneuvering, Hammarskjold's position was extremely precarious, for in trying to forestall a cold-war confrontation in the UN by bringing the question of Laos to the Security Council himself, he was bound to invite criticism from the Soviet Union. Already on September 6 the Premier of North Vietnam, Pham Van Dong, had violently criticized the Laotian appeal to the UN[36] as a fabrication and had demanded the reinstatement of the ICC. The civil war, he said, had been started by the United States and by the Sananikone government as a pretext for liquidating the Pathet Lao forces. The danger of Hammarskjold's approach to the Council was that it might easily be interpreted both as a recognition of the Laotian charge of foreign aggression and as a deliberate move against the ICC. By insisting on the procedural nature of his approach, he hoped to emphasize that his knowledge of the real situation in Laos was insufficient to judge the validity of the Laotian request for UN action. To his acute discomfort, the proceedings in the Security Council tended completely to blur this distinction.

When the Council met on the afternoon of September 7, it had before it a draft resolution proposed by France, Britain, and the United States, "to appoint a sub-committee consisting of Argentina, Italy, Japan and Tunisia . . . to examine the statements made before the Security Council concerning Laos, to receive further statements and documents and to conduct such inquiries as it may determine necessary, and to report to the Council as soon as possible."[37] This cautious and moderate text avoided any accusation of North Vietnam and did not specifically call for a fact-finding mission in Laos itself.

Hammarskjold explained that he had asked for the inclusion of the item on the agenda in order to make a statement on a subject within the range of the responsibility of the Council.[38] "Just as the Secretary-General can ask for, and is granted the floor in the Council," he said, "I feel that he is entitled to request an opportunity to address the Council publicly on a matter which he considers necessary personally to put before the Council. In doing so . . . the Secretary-General does not introduce formally on the agenda of the Council anything beyond his own wish to report to the Council."[39] He emphasized that his action was not based upon his rights under Article 99, a procedure that "would necessarily also have involved a judgement as to facts for which, in the present situation, I have not a sufficient basis."[40]

The Soviet representative, Arkady Sobolev, immediately questioned this procedure, saying that since Laos had not brought the
matter to the Security Council and the Secretary-General was not
doing so under Article 99, the Secretary-General could not address the
Council on the matter, because it was not, under the terms of Rule 22,*
under consideration by the Council. The meeting of the Council, Sobolev said, was in violation of its own rules of procedure, and he could
see no necessity for it. To this Hammarskjold answered[42] that he was
not asking to make a statement to the Council on the substance of the
question until the Security Council itself had decided to take the
question up for consideration, and that his request to make a statement was made under Rule 6, which reads: "The Secretary-General
shall immediately bring to the attention of all representatives on the
Security Council all communications from States, organs of the United
Nations, or the Secretary-General concerning any matter for the consideration of the Security Council. . . ."[43] Sobolev repeated his objections, and the agenda was adopted by 10 votes to 1, the U.S.S.R.
opposing.**

Hammarskjold then described to the Council[44] his efforts during
the past year to find a procedure by which the political difficulties
of Laos could be resolved by diplomatic means. The Laotian request
for a UN force had put an end to this effort by confronting the UN and
the Secretary-General with a new and entirely different problem, for
by requesting a UN force the Laotian government had transferred the
problem into a field where the Security Council had responsibility.
This was why he had felt obliged to report this request personally to
the Council.

The ensuing debate followed predictable lines. Sobolev put the
blame on the Laotian government and on U.S. interference. Pierson
Dixon maintained that the first thing to do was to establish the facts
of the situation through what he termed the "procedural" device of
appointing a subcommittee. Sobolev insisted that a resolution appointing the subcommittee was substantive, not procedural, and was therefore subject to the veto.

Up to this point the debate had gone more or less as Hammarskjold
had foreseen. When, however, as Hammarskjold described it the next

---

* Rule 22 of the Rules of Procedure of the Security Council reads:
   The Secretary-General, or his deputy acting on his behalf, may make either oral
or written statements to the Security Council concerning any question under consideration by it.[41]
** An opposing vote by one of the permanent members of the Security Council on
a *procedural* question does not count as a veto. The veto does apply, however, on a
vote *whether* a question is procedural or substantive.

day, Sobolev raised the issue of substance or procedure, the Council President "bungled the situation by permitting the question to be put to the vote. In doing so he admitted that the question, whether it was procedural or not, was controversial (which was difficult to avoid as at that stage no one had given a reasonable and consistent explanation why it should not be considered substantial) and as he, himself [the President], had obviously not understood or been briefed on a reply which would have kept him on safer ground in relation to the request for a vote."[45] In accepting a vote on the question of procedure or substance, the President was trapped under the San Francisco Declaration of the great powers concerning the procedure of the Security Council, in which it had been agreed that if there was a doubt on whether a question was procedural or substantive, the matter should be decided by a vote in which the veto applied.

In Hammarskjold's view the Western representatives on the Council, as a result of the position they had been obliged to take, were forced to define the task of the subcommittee in terms that would rob it of its practical usefulness. In fact, however, it seems more likely that both he and the Soviet Union were the victims of a highly organized maneuver to use the technique of negating the "double veto" to get the subcommittee appointed over the objection of the Soviet Union, a step that may also have been intended by the United States to keep fact-finding in Laos out of Hammarskjold's own hands. Sobolev complicated the scenario* by insisting on a preliminary vote on whether the establishment of the subcommittee was a procedural matter. When the Council voted 10 to 1 that the appointment of the subcommittee *was* a procedural matter, the resolution itself also went through quickly by 10 votes to 1. Ortona ruled that despite the two opposing votes by the Soviet Union it had been adopted, leaving Hammarskjold surprised and indignant** and Sobolev outmaneuvered. Sobolev immediately denounced the President's ruling and the resolu-

---

* The intended plan was probably as follows: the resolution itself would be voted upon and would be declared adopted by the Council President. The Soviet Union would then challenge the ruling of the President on the ground that the resolution was not carried in view of the negative vote of a permanent member. The ruling of the President would then be upheld by the majority of the Council, a vote to which the veto did not apply.
** Hammarskjold was much annoyed nearly two years later to read in *Storm over Laos*, by Sisouk Na Champassak, the Laotian permanent representative to the UN, fulsome praise for his alleged part in this procedural stratagem for getting around the Soviet veto so that the subcommittee could be sent to Laos.[46] He wrote angrily to Sisouk that it was *"un rôle que je n'ai jamais joué: je n'étais pas en faveur de cette procédure et je m'y suis opposé"*[47] ("a role that I never played: I was not in favor of this procedure and I opposed it").

tion itself as "non-existent, illegal and hence not binding upon anyone."[48]

Hammarskjold was profoundly disturbed by the outcome of the Security Council proceedings. For the sake of a tactical success, the Western powers had compromised both the procedures of the Council and the practical usefulness of the Laos subcommittee itself. So strongly did he feel the need to dissociate himself from this procedure that on September 9 he took the unusual step of circulating a memorandum to its organizers, the representatives of the United States, France, Italy, Great Britain, and Canada. He also gave a copy to Dobrynin and to the members of the subcommittee. He was obliged, he wrote, to accept the decision taken by the Security Council on its own responsibility, but "the Secretary-General is in a sense the guardian of the Charter and in a position to guide and supervise executive United Nations activities. He must, for that reason, form a view on the legal situation with regard to various decisions in the implementation of which he may be involved."[49] In the Council's proceedings, the question whether the subcommittee was of a procedural nature should not have been put to the vote, the relevant question being whether the subcommittee was set up under Article 29 of the Charter, which is part of the section headed "Procedure" and which allows the Security Council to set up subsidiary organs for the performance of its functions. The only criteria for making such a judgment were "the concrete tasks of the sub-committee"[50] and how those tasks fitted into the proceedings of the Security Council. The way the Laos subcommittee had been set up was ambiguous and would inevitably affect its work, not least because there was a suspicion that the ambiguity of its terms of reference was intended to allow the subcommittee to exceed the functions allowed by Article 29 of the Charter. Another procedure in the Council could have achieved the same results while also giving the Security Council proceedings "uncontradictable legality."[51] These sophisticated arguments seem to have made little impact on the procedural organizers, but Kuznetsov and Sobolev sharply disagreed with Hammarskjold's views on the permissibility of another procedure and mildly reproved him also for his "suspicious zeal"[52] and "exaggerated efficiency"[53] in bringing the Laos question before the Council. For his part, he found the Soviet position on the constitutional question reasonable even if it differed from his own.

The names of the members of the Security Council subcommittee were announced on September 9,[54] and the next day Hammarskjold made known that David Blickenstaff, the head of the UN Paris Office who had been principal secretary in Lebanon in 1958, would be the principal secretary, with another experienced Secretariat official, Jacques Engers, as his deputy.[55] The subcommittee, after receiving a detailed briefing from Hammarskjold on his efforts over the last year and on the diplomatic situation in Laos, arrived in Vientiane on September 15.

The already dubious nature of the subcommittee's task was not made any clearer by the situation in Laos, for on September 7, as the Security Council was meeting, the Vientiane government had announced that all the "foreign invaders"[56] had departed and that whatever Communist forces remained were native to Laos. At the same time martial law was declared, and the Defense Minister told the press that Laos would not hesitate to call on SEATO if the UN turned Laos down. Reports on the military situation continued to be wildly contradictory, and doubts about the existence of an external threat to Laos began belatedly to be expressed in the Western press.*

The Laos government obviously intended to use the subcommittee's presence to the limit for propaganda purposes, and impressive arrangements, including crowds of schoolchildren waving Laotian and UN flags, large numbers of motor vehicles with UN license plates, and a tremendous hospitality program, confronted the group on its arrival in Vientiane.** Specially detailed American officers were soon urging the subcommittee to make use of U.S. logistical support, including aircraft and helicopters, for an extensive inspection of the frontier regions. Hammarskjold had briefed Blickenstaff carefully on his duties in Laos and had especially warned him that the subcommittee should at all costs avoid rushing around the country. Blickenstaff's reception in Laos fully justified this warning and he soon found that much of his time and energy had to be spent in resisting various attempts to take over the subcommittee.

The subcommittee's efforts to elicit from the Laos government a report on the real situation proved to be frustrating. The Sam Neua crisis, headlined as an invasion a few days before, had faded with the group's arrival in Laos, and there were no more accusations of aggres-

---

* Typical was the *Wall Street Journal*, which on September 10 ran a front-page story under the headlines "Looking into Laos—UN Will Find Little Red Invasion Evidence, Much Political Turmoil—Fear of Army Coup Underlies Premier's Call for Help, Bars Deals with Rebels—A Direct Plea to the U.S.?" The story itself began: "Vientiane, Laos.—When United Nations observers land in Laos this weekend, their first look behind this nation's appeal for UN troops will uncover more evidence of a political tug-of-war here in the Laotian capital than of foreign military invasion."
** When Blickenstaff reported to Hammarskjold that the government had expressed the desire to pay for everything that the mission used and consumed, including its food and drink, he commented: "I agree entirely with you on desirability of fading out exaggerated hospitality. One thing is to collect evidence presented by a government, another thing, as inquirer, to let the government pay for one's ink," [57] to which Blickenstaff replied that he had "undertaken discreet preliminary steps for buying our own ink." [58]

sion by North Vietnam. Even the tone of pronouncements from Hanoi became more conciliatory, and the Pathet Lao leaders asserted that they were ready to negotiate with the government on the basis of the 1954 and 1957 agreements. While members of the Laos government attributed this improvement to the influence of the subcommittee, others tended to be increasingly skeptical as to the facts of the Laos "crisis." The government and its supporters thus had a problem in living up to some of their earlier communiqués and in producing credible evidence of foreign intervention* and its submissions to the subcommittee were no less puzzling and contradictory than its previous announcements to the press. An elaborate social program did not compensate for this shortcoming, and the subcommittee soon became restive.

It was perhaps partly to remedy this situation that the government suggested a seven-day tour of the northern provinces. An immediate difficulty was that this tour could be made only by helicopter, and the only helicopters available were American. Hammarskjold, when consulted, declined to express an opinion on where the subcommittee should go or what it should do, although he advised against the use of U.S. helicopters as a matter of principle in order to keep clear of any involvement with one of the permanent members of the Security Council. Ultimately the subcommittee contented itself with visits to Sam Neua, Sam Teu, and Luang Prabang, the royal capital, and no helicopters were required. The helicopter affair, however, was to have a sequel in the form of a U.S. attack on Blickenstaff that served to reveal to Hammarskjold the influence of the more covert parts of the U.S. establishment in Laos.

While the subcommittee was finishing its task and preparing to return to New York, Hammarskjold was actively considering the next stage, and in a long letter to Secretary Herter on September 29 he reviewed the current situation and outlined some ideas for the future. He first restated his own uneasiness about the "procedural" vote by which the subcommittee had been set up and his sympathy, on legal grounds, with the Soviet objection to this action. There was a growing tendency in some quarters to say that the subcommittee had had a salutary effect in Laos, that no one wished to have another showdown in the Security Council, and that therefore the right thing to do was to find a pretext to keep the subcommittee in Laos indefinitely. He felt that this course, however tempting, could only have very bad long-

---

* One weapon of Communist-bloc origin was in fact produced for the subcommittee's inspection, although it had no connection with the current scare and had been taken some time before from a Viet Minh deserter.[59]

term results. The subcommittee's report would not, in all likelihood, warrant any drastic steps, although it might show that the UN could still play a useful role in the Laos situation. If the Council, on the tacit assumption that the subcommittee would stay on in Laos, did not meet to consider this report, it would turn the "procedural" decision de facto into a substantive activity, the establishment of a continuous UN presence in Laos. This would be a mockery of the assurances given by the Western powers in the Security Council that the subcommittee had a limited and procedural function.

"There is in my view," Hammarskjold wrote, "no more dangerous way of a majority to undermine the United Nations than to flout the rules and to be less than straight in its actions when that suits its interests. The precedent is good as long as it stands firm on a *bona fide* basis, but it will break down under the pressure of any abuse— and, as such, I feel that one has to consider the injection of a clearly substantive element into a decision repeatedly stated to have been only procedural."[60] The Security Council should discuss the subcommittee's report and go on to consider a proposal to establish a United Nations presence in Laos in consultation with the royal Laotian government. He intended to try, without much hope of success, to persuade the Russians to agree to such a proposal, or at least to abstain on it.

Hammarskjold's idea of a UN presence was not a committee, but a mission headed by one man who would report to the Secretary-General, who would in turn report to the Security Council or the General Assembly. Thus the Secretary-General would be able to use his judgment as to what extent matters would be thrown into public debate, and he could also act as a buffer—a situation in which he would find himself anyway—just as he had done hitherto in the Laos situation. The terms of reference of the UN presence should make proper reference to the Geneva Agreements so as to make it clear that the UN arrangement did not set them aside, and the UN representative should also be empowered to assist other UN member governments in the region and would be concerned with events in the whole of Indochina, just as the UN representative in Jordan had been concerned with developments in the Middle East. He had already discussed his ideas with the Foreign Ministers of Burma, Cambodia, Laos, and Thailand, who had agreed in principle to his proposals. Hammarskjold himself was prepared to go to Vientiane to launch the whole arrangement properly.

This daring and far-sighted plan, designed to develop a UN presence in Southeast Asia as a whole and to transfer to the Secretary-General the main responsibility for the continuing role of the UN in the area, was hardly likely to commend itself either to the United States or to the Soviet Union. In retrospect, nonetheless, it is tempting to speculate on the possible effects of a strong UN presence in Indochina as a whole on the developments of the next ten years. Herter somewhat guardedly agreed that a continuing UN presence in Laos and in Indochina was desirable, but he disagreed with Hammarskjold's ideas about his own future role. "You will also recognize," Herter wrote, "that there are times when it is necessary and desirable for the Security Council and the General Assembly to create inter-governmental bodies or appoint individuals directly."[61] The United States and the Soviet Union had more in common in their feelings about Hammarskjold than they seem to have realized.

To Herter's last point Hammarskjold replied:

> Our solid experience leads me to the conclusion . . . that a field operation on a semi-permanent basis gives rise to continuous politico-administrative problems, which make it both very difficult and quite risky to run them with direct subordination to the General Assembly, the Security Council or any other inter-governmental body. This is true especially in the case of field operations with a cold-war aspect, regarding which the work, if subordinated to a group, is either stymied, if the group has a balanced composition, or given a dangerous slant, if the group is composed of countries only from "one side." You see that the basic distinction for me is one between what I might call shorter "crash operations" and more regular operations of a more lasting and continuous nature. Furthermore, a "crash operation" sometimes is more easily staged via the Secretary-General for the reason that not only the Soviets but likewise the governments directly concerned often seem to find it a lot easier to acquiesce informally in certain actions than to go on record with a formal approval or even a simple abstention in the Security Council or the General Assembly.[62]

Hammarskjold found Kuznetsov very suspicious of Western intentions in Laos and of the possible use that might be made of the subcommittee's report as a cover for some drastic intervention. He asked Kuznetsov if he would hang him if, after the report had been received and he had consulted with the governments of the region, he were to go to Vientiane to install a special representative there in an effort to make it unnecessary for the Security Council to have an extended debate or to take any formal action. Kuznetsov personally was favorable to this idea, and although Hammarskjold realized that Moscow might not take the same view and that Kuznetsov might change his mind, he felt sufficiently encouraged to take the risk of going ahead with his plans for a UN presence in Laos as an alternative to a prolonged cold-war debate in the Security Council.

The first opposition to Hammarskjold's ideas came from the West.

On October 14, United Press International published a story from Tokyo to the effect that the UN subcommittee had evidence that the Chinese Marshal Peng Teh-huai was directing the operations of the Pathet Lao from across the border in Yunnan.[63] This obviously planted story, which was immediately denied[64] categorically by the members of the subcommittee, was quickly followed by an announcement from Vientiane that the Premier, the Minister of Defense, and the Foreign Minister would leave at once for New York for the forthcoming debate on Laos in the Security Council. This highly publicized trip of the entire nucleus of the Laos government made a debate in the Security Council virtually unavoidable, as well as making Hammarskjold's projected trip to Laos unnecessary and ridiculous.

Increasingly suspicious of a U.S. maneuver to sabotage his proposals, Hammarskjold told Herter on October 15 that this new episode "unavoidably . . . puts some questions in my mind which I hope are unwarranted."[65] He noted that these developments, of which there had been no hint in his recent talks with the Laotian Foreign Minister, had coincided with renewed attacks on the French in Laos and with a press statement in New York by the permanent representative of Laos in which he anticipated the possible findings of the subcommittee by new accusations of North Vietnamese aggression. Someone was clearly interested in giving the Laos crisis a new impetus at precisely the moment when the subcommittee was finishing a report that gave no support to the broader Laotian allegations and when he was trying to devise a procedure that would satisfy all the parties and remove the question from a public cold-war debate. Even Sisouk Na Champassak, the Laos permanent representative at the UN, expressed his amazement, and later on characterized the Laotian government's trip to New York as the "worst conceivable diplomatic blunder."[66] In the end only the Laotian Foreign Minister came to New York. The Premier stayed in Washington for a medical checkup, and the death of King Sisavang Vong on October 29 caused the whole party to return immediately to Laos.

Hammarskjold's growing suspicions were in no way abated by his talks with Lodge. The American was at pains to dispel his notion that somebody or some group consistently worked at cross-purposes with the UN and in directions of which he strongly disapproved, but an official attempt by the United States to discredit Blickenstaff caused him, in his own words, to "permit himself to fly into a rage."[67] Blickenstaff, an experienced international official familiar with similar pressures, had proved in Laos to be a far greater stumbling block to outside pressures than the relatively inexperienced members of the subcommittee, and Hammarskjold resented this crude attempt by U.S.

agencies in Laos to get Blickenstaff out of the way. He was tempted, he told the U.S. mission to the UN, to write a rejoinder that would force Blickenstaff's accusers to identify themselves, but instead he gave Lodge a detailed rebuttal of the charges against Blickenstaff, and the matter went no further.

With Kuznetsov and Sobolev, Hammarskjold had equally frank talks of a different kind. The idea of a UN presence in Laos would almost certainly command a majority vote in the General Assembly, and he hoped that the U.S.S.R. might therefore tacitly accept the Secretary-General's arrangements for that presence rather than risk having the matter transferred to the Assembly because of the Soviet veto and then being outvoted. Kuznetsov found his ideas, including his own visit to Laos, unacceptable and insisted instead on the reestablishment of the ICC and the restoration of the Geneva Agreement. Although the Soviet attitude was negative, Hammarskjold still felt that as a practical matter, although for the record it would protest against it, the U.S.S.R. might see advantage in some sort of UN presence in Laos that could head off and discourage extreme right-wing military moves sponsored by the Vientiane government and its supporters. This course would also avoid an acrimonious public debate in the Security Council or the General Assembly. In spite of Washington's disillusionment with the Secretariat and with the Laos subcommittee, the United States would also probably still favor a continuing UN presence in Laos as a restraining influence both on the Laotian government and on Communist elements within and outside Laos. On balance, therefore, he decided that the best and safest course would be to try by quiet diplomacy to establish some kind of UN representation in Laos.

This delicate and carefully calculated gamble was upset by the rumors that began to appear in the press in the last days of October, and on October 30 the Soviet Union issued a blistering denunciation of the idea of a UN presence as undermining the Geneva Agreement.[68] This outburst dispelled once and for all the hope that the Soviet Union would not object to Hammarskjold's plan.

The Laos subcommittee, which had returned to New York on October 20, published on November 5 a relatively inconclusive report[69] that gave no support to stories of the invasion of Laos from North Vietnam, although it conceded that varying degrees and kinds of support might have been given to dissident Laotian elements from abroad and that some of the guerrilla operations must have been centrally coordinated. The report provided no basis for dramatic initiatives in the Security Council from any quarter. The United States made the best of it by hailing the "tranquilizing effect"[70] of the subcommittee on the situation in Laos, and by claiming that the "aggressive actions of the attacking forces were immediately reduced upon the Subcommittee's arrival."[71] The Soviet Union denounced the report of the "so-called sub-committee"[72] but noted that "in spite of all their efforts the sub-committee members could not, naturally, find any proof for these fabricated charges of the alleged 'aggression.' "[73] In asserting once again the sole legality of the ICC and the Geneva Agreement, the U.S.S.R. sternly warned against any further attempts "to utilize the United Nations for the interference in the internal affairs of Laos."[74]

On November 6, Hammarskjold announced through a spokesman[75] that he had not yet decided on a course of action. A visit to Laos was one possibility, but this visit would not have any connection with the report of the Security Council subcommittee. On the next day he received an invitation from the government of Laos and decided to leave for Vientiane at once.[76] "In considering this invitation," he wrote to all the members of the Security Council:

> I have taken into account my obligations under the Charter and all the information at present available regarding the difficulties facing Laos. I have concluded that it is highly desirable that I avail myself of this opportunity to get, at first hand, as complete a picture as possible of conditions and developments in Laos of relevance from the point of view of the general responsibilities of the Secretary-General. I have therefore decided to go to Laos within the next few days for a short visit in order to inform myself about the present problems of the country. Were my experiences to indicate that such an arrangement would be warranted—and this seems probable—I would, with the consent of the Government, temporarily station a personal representative in Vientiane through whom I could maintain contact after my departure. . . . It may be noted that an individual stationed in Vientiane as my personal representative would be under the exclusive authority of the Secretary-General; constitutionally, he would, thus, be in a position different from the one held by the United Nations missions, as, for example, the Special Representative stationed in Amman under a resolution approved by the General Assembly, or the Observation Group in Lebanon the mandate of which had been decided by the Security Council. The legal basis for a decision to leave a personal representative in Laos, apart from the consent of the Government of Laos, would be the general responsibilities of the Secretary-General regarding developments which may threaten peace and security, combined with his administrative authority under the Charter.[77]

This letter elicited from Sobolev an immediate reminder of Soviet disapproval of attempts to use the UN to annul the Geneva Agreement. There was no aggression against Laos, and the Secretary-General's visit and the idea of a personal representative "can only further complicate the situation obtaining."⁷⁸ The Secretary-General's assertions concerning his administrative authority under the Charter were also unjustifiable.

Hammarskjold's decision to go to Laos in spite of the negative Soviet reaction was a calculated risk, for he felt that in the circumstances only some form of UN presence might possibly in the end achieve a return to peaceful and stable conditions. By taking the initiative himself, he sought to avoid the danger of the UN presence emerging as a direct response to the original Laos request and from a Soviet defeat in a public cold-war debate. As he wrote to Nehru:

> You will appreciate that, in fact, I was faced with the necessity of choice. If I had decided not to go I would, so to say by default, have thrown my weight back of an effort, through the Security Council and the General Assembly, to establish a "presence" in Laos which, due to its history and political setting, would practically have blocked the road to the national reconciliation and international diplomatic moves which sooner or later will be necessary. On the other hand, by going—even if that were to lead finally to a "personal" representation—I would avoid aggravating the story here and the above-mentioned outcome while instead establishing such links with Vientiane as to enable me to work towards the goals we had in mind in our previous correspondence and which I still think are fully valid. In a situation like the present one there enters necessarily an element of gambling. In this case I have taken a risk, but in order to have the chance to avoid something which would certainly be detrimental.⁷⁹

Hammarskjold was convinced that Kuznetsov, Sobolev, and Dobrynin understood his line of action and respected his motives and his courage in taking it. Herter also appreciated and understood what he was trying to do, no matter what other U.S. interests were active in Laos itself, and on November 11 he received warm support from Selwyn Lloyd. The Soviet opposition to his trip persisted, although in a restrained way. *Izvestia* on November 11, the day of his departure, in an article entitled "A Not Too Respectable Junket," maintained that the Secretary-General's trip was a violation of the Charter and also constituted interference in the internal affairs of a sovereign state.*

---

* During its opposition to Hammarskjold at the 1960 session of the General Assembly, the U.S.S.R. was far less restrained concerning his visit to Laos, and he replied: "If the Secretary-General is entitled to draw the attention of the Security Council to threats to peace and security, has he to rely on reports in the press or from this or that government? Has he to take the word of Moscow or Washington? No, certainly not. He has to find out for himself and that may mean, as in the case of the criticized journey to Laos last November, that he has to go himself. . . . The mission to Laos of the personal representative of the Secretary-General, charged with the coordination of widespread and important practical activities in the social and economic

In Vientiane, Hammarskjold discussed with Premier Phoui Sananikone and Foreign Minister Kamphan Panya what should be done now
that the Security Council subcommittee phase was over. He showed
them a press release he had drafted on the night of his arrival announcing that Sakari Tuomioja, the Executive Secretary of the UN Economic
Commission for Europe,* would establish the UN presence in Laos.
While Tuomioja's primary role would be to review the economic
situation and suggest the kind of help that the UN could most usefully
give, he would also "follow up the discussions initiated by the
Secretary-General and provide him with such further information as
would be of importance for the judgement regarding the assistance
he might most appropriately render under the Charter, taking into
account also other international agreements which provide a framework for the development of Laos."[81] This draft initially got a cool
reception from the Laotian officials.

After this meeting, King Savang Vatthana gave Hammarskjold the
traditional account of events leading up to the Laotian appeal to the
UN but also expressed his desire for a new start. The particular
problems of Laos were the economic situation and tribal integration.
The King greeted Hammarskjold's proposals for the UN presence with
enthusiasm and remarked, *"du point de vue politique, je trouve ce que
vous proposez d'une très grande finesse"*[82] ("from the political point of
view, I find your proposal has great finesse"). Later in the day Hammarskjold learned that his text had been unanimously approved by the
Cabinet, and from an interview with the U.S. Ambassador he got the
impression that Washington's views also were at last beginning to
converge with his own.

The next day he got down to longer-term problems. The value of
the UN presence would depend entirely on the policies that Laos pursued in other respects. In particular, the impending trial of Prince

---

fields, was arranged at the request of the Chief of State and his legitimate Government. It has been endorsed by succeeding governments, including the present one.
Obviously, the criticism means that the Secretary-General would not be allowed to
respond to a practical request of a government, and all legitimate authorities of a
country, unless such a move had the approval of the Security Council, under the
unanimity rule, or by the General Assembly, which may not be in session when the
need arises. Those countries who wish to have the independent assistance of the
United Nations, in the modest forms possible for the Secretary-General and without
running into the stormy weather of a major international political debate, will
certainly be interested in this attitude of the delegate of the Soviet Union."[80]
* Tuomioja had been in the ECE post since September 1957. Before joining the UN
he had been Finnish Minister of Finance in 1944–5, of Commerce in 1950, of Foreign
Affairs in 1951–2, and Prime Minister in 1953–4. He was also governor of the Bank of
Finland from 1945 to 1955 and later served as Finland's Ambassador to the United
Kingdom.

Souphanouvong, the government's attitude toward the ICC and the forthcoming elections were issues that vitally affected the relationship between Laos and North Vietnam. For the moment he left it at that, hoping the Laotians would revert to these delicate issues later.

The whole of Sunday, November 15, was spent at the stadium for the That Luang festival which surrounds the annual rededication of government officials and generals to the King. There were medal-giving, games, and horse races, and finally a vast dinner, during which competing loudspeakers boomed Laotian music and winning numbers for the national lottery. This convivial day gave Hammarskjold a chance to get to know Phoui Sananikone better.

The next day's main event was a three-hour luncheon with the King, whose high style and intelligence had already charmed Hammarskjold. After a brilliant analysis of the basic ethnic problems of Laos, the King engaged him in one of those allusive, circumlocutory dialogues which Hammarskjold loved but for which he could rarely find a worthy partner. As the King himself said, he and Hammarskjold seemed to share a love for the classical French diplomacy of the eighteenth century, after which "we both happily embarked," Hammarskjold wrote later, "on an intense discussion of the acute problems of Laos without ever mentioning them by name."[83] Evidently enjoying this esoteric form of dialogue, the King lamented that "nowadays one had to deal only with *'des inspecteurs de finances.'* "[84]

On the following day, on an expedition by helicopter to two mountain villages, Foreign Minister Kamphan asked Hammarskjold for his frank personal views on the trial of Souphanouvong. Tuomioja and U Nyun, the Executive Secretary of the Economic Commission for Asia and the Far East, were awaiting them on their return to Vientiane, where they all dined with Kamphan. By November 18, Hammarskjold felt the time had come to press his views on the three most delicate issues: the ICC, the trial, and the elections. Faced with the usual arguments against the ICC, he pressed for a renewed contact between the government and the Commission. As for the trial, he argued that at least no further judicial steps should be taken and at best Souphanouvong should be set free. He also urged that the Assembly be convened to decide on its future, a move that would automatically entail freeing Souphanouvong as a member of the Assembly.

At his farewell audience next day, Hammarskjold found the King still much opposed to the reactivation of the ICC. The King surprised him by saying that he had been, and was still, in regular correspondence with President Ho Chi Minh of North Vietnam. On his way back to New York, Hammarskjold took the opportunity to see Thanat

Khoman, the Foreign Minister of Thailand, who seemed satisfied that his arrangements in Vientiane represented the best the UN could do to moderate the situation.

The Soviet reaction to the announcement[85] of Tuomioja's mission in Laos was negative but relatively mild. "The visit of the UN Secretary-General to Laos and his subsequent actions," the Soviet statement read, ". . . do not, however, contribute to this in any way [i.e., to peace and security in Laos]. Whatever may be the pretext for them, these actions are designed to cover by the name of the United Nations further interference of the Western powers in Laos and can only make the existing situation still more complicated."[86]

Hammarskjold came back from Laos with a much deeper understanding of the problems of the country and with a new concept of the UN approach to the Laos situation as a full-scale attack on basic economic and social problems within the context of a reaffirmation of Laotian neutrality. He now understood far better than before both the appalling economic situation of Laos—its lack of even rudimentary communications, transport, and basic industrial facilities—and the ethnic differences between the Lao people of the plain and the nomadic tribes of the mountains that made national integration so difficult. Until its economic and social conditions could be transformed, Laos, situated on a sensitive frontier in the cold war, would inevitably be dependent on foreign aid. If this major challenge was not taken up urgently by the UN and its Specialized Agencies, Laos would remain a vacuum and a standing invitation to foreign intervention and to politically motivated foreign-aid programs. This primarily economic and social United Nations approach also had the advantage of not cutting across the Geneva Agreements.

He instructed Tuomioja to submit to him as soon as possible a detailed study of the economic situation of Laos with recommendations as to the contribution the UN and its Specialized Agencies could best make to the economic growth and stability of the country. Anticipating the necessity for help in surveying national resources and for planning a rudimentary communications and transport network, a system of settlement and integration of nomadic tribes, and a program of basic education, he also wrote to the Directors-General of UNESCO, the Food and Agricultural Organization, and the World Health Organization. This work, he warned them, could be carried out efficiently only under UN coordination. Although the final outcome was uncertain, he asked their help in meeting a challenge "which, quite realistically, must be described as a question of war and peace."[87]

The principal recommendations of Tuomioja's report[88] included the points that Hammarskjold had foreseen as well as some short-term projects to be undertaken at once, such as the acceleration of the Mekong River development program. It provided for surveys of natural and human resources, agricultural development and marketing, basic education and vocational training, public health, community development, transport and communications, and public administration. The report both outlined a solution for the political and economic problems of Laos and suggested a pattern of activity that might have wider application in the area. Hammarskjold sent another UN official, Robert Huertematte, to Laos to discuss with the authorities various technical and organizational questions with regard to the implementation of Tuomioja's recommendations and to hold the fort in Vientiane over Christmas while Tuomioja was away.

The situation in Laos did not stand still over the holiday season, and a military coup d'état against the Phoui Sananikone government on December 29 started a chain of events that was eventually to frustrate any useful UN activity in the country. The coup followed a series of disagreements within the government. The Premier himself probably agreed that the time had come for a return to moderate policies of reconciliation. The Committee for the Defense of National Interests (CDNI), however, believed that the situation demanded an intensification of pressure against the Pathet Lao, with dictatorial powers for the government and an indefinite postponement of the elections which under the Constitution were due by the end of the year. The result had been a government reshuffle that excluded the CDNI Ministers. A special meeting of the Assembly confirmed the new government, but Phoumi Nosavan, newly promoted to brigadier-general, and the CDNI clique decided to resort to force. On December 30, the day after the military had seized control, the King dismissed Sananikone. Whether or not this change was brought about by American CIA influence as some have alleged,* Phoumi could not have acted without some assurance of American support.

The emergence of a military regime in Laos was neither likely to enhance the possibilities of a successful UN presence on the lines that Hammarskjold had envisaged nor to maintain the "sense of direction"[90] that he had hailed in December when Tuomioja's report came in. He observed these developments anxiously from afar on his African tour and for a time contemplated returning at once to New York. From Brazzaville on January 4 he cabled Cordier, "I need desper-

---

* David Wise and Thomas Ross, in *The Invisible Government*, describe Phoumi Nosavan's cooperation with the CIA in easing out the Sananikone government and in rigging the April/May 1960 elections. They note that the policies pursued by the CIA contact man with Phoumi, Jack Hazey, bore little relation to the public U.S. policy on Laos as represented by the U.S. Ambassador.[89]

ately some basis for decision,"[91] and, in spite of a reassuring telephone conversation with New York from Leopoldville, his anxiety persisted. On January 5 from Leopoldville, he sent a message to the King of Laos urging him to hold strongly to a line of independent neutrality and *"travail démocratique pour le progrès économique et l'intégration de la population"*[92] ("democratic effort for economic progress and social integration") and reminded the King of his undertaking that no changes would be made *"qui pourraient mettre en doute cette base essentielle de la politique du pays et de la confiance qu'elle a créée"*[93]* ("which could put in question the essential basis of the policy of the country and the confidence it has created"). According to Sisouk Na Champassak, this telegram later proved to be "decisive in quieting the ambitions of certain military men,"[94] whose inclusion in the government he feared would nullify the efforts of Hammarskjold and the "friendly big powers"[95] to keep Laos out of the cold war. A somewhat similar approach to the King was made on January 4 by the ambassadors of the United States, France, Great Britain, and Australia.

The military coup in Vientiane was decried both in the Communist world and elsewhere. The King himself, doubtless with such criticisms in mind and strengthened by Hammarskjold's cable, managed to convince Phoumi's revolutionary committee that constitutional government must be restored. On January 7 a government under Kou Abhay was appointed by the King, the army having previously terminated the legislature by decree. From Mogadiscio on Janaury 14, Hammarskjold sent a message to the new Premier assuring him that the UN would continue to give what support it could to Laos. The new government announced the date of April 24, 1960, for general elections.

As the crisis in Laos seemed to abate, Hammarskjold's cable to the King was credited in some quarters with having played a major part in restoring a civilian regime. At a press conference on February 4, 1960, a reporter introduced his question thus: "It is a widely recognized fact that thanks to you the situation in Laos, which looked very bad indeed a few months ago, appears to have been stabilized, at least on the surface. Also you have been credited, while the army was seizing power, with having restored political order and a democratic

---

* Hammarskjold was much annoyed over the leakage of this cable and demanded that an investigation be made in the UN mission in Laos as to how the message had reached the press. The mission was equally annoyed by this demand because it had never even received a copy of the message, which had, in fact, been transmitted by telephone from Leopoldville to the WHO office in Brazzaville, which had sent it on to Vientiane via Geneva by commercial cable. It was later discovered that the King's entourage itself had released the cable, believing it to be a useful and calming document, as indeed it turned out to be.

regime in Laos with a mere telegram to King Savang Vatthana...."[96]
To this Hammarskjold replied, "As to . . . your writing of history, I
have some strong reservations."[97]

Tuomioja, whose ebullient and outgoing personality had endeared
him to the Laotians and to the diplomatic community in Vientiane,
had been only temporarily detached from his job as Executive Secretary of ECC. On February 18, Hammarskjold announced the appointment of Dr. Edouard Zellweger[98] as his special representative to
coordinate UN economic activities in Laos. Zellweger, a Swiss jurist
and diplomat, had been constitutional adviser to the Libyan government since 1955. Hammarskjold explained to Zellweger that although
he was going to Laos to coordinate economic assistance, his seniority
of rank also gave him the latitude discreetly to do what he could in the
political field as a reassuring presence. Zellweger arrived in Vientiane
on March 4.

After measures had been taken by General Phoumi to assure a
successful result,* general elections were held between April 24 and
May 8. All fifty-nine seats in the National Assembly were won by supporters of groups represented in the outgoing caretaker government,
which had been a right-wing coalition composed chiefly of members of
the strongly anti-Communist CDNI group supported by the army.
None of the few candidates presented by Souphanouvong's party, the
Neo Lao Haksat or Pathet Lao, were successful. Souvanna Phouma,
however, from his family constituency of Luang Prabang, was among
the successful candidates and was elected president of the Assembly.

Hammarskjold was happy neither with the method nor with the
result of the elections. Zellweger had warned him early in May that it
was the intention of the CDNI leaders to establish a government based
on their newly organized majority rather than on a coalition. The
political monopoly thus created could easily lead to a military dictatorship, an evolution that would inevitably destroy Laos' neutrality
and be disastrous equally for the integration and development of the
country and for its relations with its Communist neighbors. Zellweger
suggested that a message from Hammarskjold to the King might once
again provide a moderating influence. On May 5, Hammarskjold sent
a message to be delivered by Zellweger. "It seems to me," he wrote,
"that now a unique occasion has offered itself for the consolidation
and integration of the Kingdom and its people reflecting a real agreement between all the Lao. To this end the formation of a national
union government including all those who are animated by love of

---

* Sisouk describes how electoral districts were revised to break up Pathet Lao
zones of influence and the eligibility requirements for candidates were stiffened in
a way that excluded more than half of the less educated Pathet Lao leaders.[99]

the kingdom and interested in its peaceful development would, without doubt, have a decisive value. Such a government, in which all the national parties in the parliament would be represented, would take its inspiration, I am sure, from the points contained in the declaration made by your Prime Minister, Mr. Kou Abhay, in his important speech of 10 January 1960, which seems so well to have represented the main lines of the policy of the kingdom."[100]

The new government, formed on June 2, was headed by Prince Somsanith, with Kamphan Panya as his Foreign Minister. It was in fact a coalition government, although five of its Ministers had been members of the previous caretaker government. Somsanith himself was a moderate, but there was little doubt that the real power still lay with General Phoumi. The conservative triumph had been somewhat marred by the escape, on the night of May 23–24, of Prince Souphanouvong and seven other former Neo Lao Haksat deputies, who had been in prison for ten months. The escapees would, it was said, seek to rejoin the Pathet Lao guerrillas in northern Laos or escape to North Vietnam, and the new Premier warned the National Assembly on June 3 that the internal situation of the country was grave and that an intensification of subversive activities must be expected as a result of Prince Souphanouvong's escape. He also declared, however, that the government would adopt a policy of neutrality, good-neighborliness, and peaceful coexistence in accordance with the Buddhist temperament of the Laotians as well as with the geographical situation and conditions of existence of Laos. The country, he said, was placed between the two worlds and was subject to the effects of the antagonistic forces in them, and neutrality was its only possible foreign policy. For the time being it seemed possible that the situation might settle down again, and the King and the new government appeared to have appreciated rather than resented Hammarskjold's and Zellweger's efforts.

Because of bureaucratic obstacles and the difficulties of traveling, especially in the monsoon season, the UN mission was unable to come to grips with the real problems of Laos or to penetrate far beyond the limits of Vientiane and Luang Prabang. Nor could Zellweger, for all his intelligence and devotion, do much to influence the new trend toward civil war compounded by foreign support of the opposing elements in Laos.

On August 9 another army coup occurred from an entirely unforeseen quarters. A young parachute captain, Captain Kong Lae, motivated apparently by distaste for the long civil war against the Pathet Lao and disgusted by false reports of sham battles against a nonexistent invader, by foreign interventions of all kinds, and by corruption in

Vientiane, took advantage of a moment when practically the whole government had flown to Luang Prabang, the royal capital, to prepare for the cremation ceremonies for Sisavang Vong, the King's father, to take over in Vientiane.

The coup of August 9 occurred when Hammarskjold was totally involved with the Congo problem and was poised between New York and Leopoldville on the eve of his entry with UN troops into Katanga. He did not, therefore, react to the reports which Zellweger, present at the center of the coup in Vientiane, was sending him. In Vientiane it soon became apparent that Captain Kong Lae had no particular political alignment and was mainly concerned with forming a broad-based coalition government under Souvanna Phouma that would achieve a settlement of the national schism. The right wing of the old government under General Phoumi Nosavan and Foreign Minister Kamphan Panya obviously had no intention of taking part in any such coalition, and it was rumored that these two Ministers had gone to Thailand. Souvanna Phouma refused to form a new government except through the proper constitutional procedures, which required the government to resign and the King to appoint a new Premier. Somsanith resigned of his own accord to avoid bloodshed, and on August 14, at the King's request, Souvanna Phouma agreed to form a new government. While Souvanna Phouma was in Vientiane, most of the Ministers remained with the King in Luang Prabang, which was firmly under the control of General Phoumi, who had now returned to his home in Savannakhet. On August 15, Phoumi declared martial law and was able to withhold from the King the documents for the investiture of the new government, and it seemed likely that his next step would be to march on Vientiane. Zellweger suggested that, in order to avert a civil war, he might attempt to play the role of mediator provided that the two parties requested it, and he urgently pressed Hammarskjold for instructions. Lacking instructions, Zellweger remained in contact with Souvanna Phouma and with various ambassadors in an effort to reestablish contact with Phoumi Nosavan before the latter embarked on a military expedition against Vientiane.

On August 17, Hammarskjold authorized Zellweger to assume the role of mediator provided both parties asked him to do so. When Zellweger finally arrived in Luang Prabang on August 19, he had difficulty getting permission from the colonel in charge of the airport to go into the town, and when this was finally obtained he waited in the Hôtel du Gouverneur for some hours. During this wait he received an invitation from Phoumi Nosavan to visit him at Savannakhet. He also saw Kamphan Panya, who told him that Phoumi Nosavan was convinced that Captain Kong Lae was a Communist agent, to which Zellweger replied that most of the diplomats in Vientiane did not agree with this assumption.

Zellweger had brought with him to Luang Prabang, at Souvanna Phouma's request, copies of the royal *ordonnance* appointing the Souvanna Phouma government, which was presumably why the military authorities prevented him from seeing the King. In any case he was warned by the secretary-general of the royal palace that the King must be kept out of the confrontation between two military groups. *"Le Roi n'est pas visible et ne le sera pas"* ("The King cannot be seen, nor will he be"), Zellweger was told.[101] When he asked why the royal *ordonnance* had not been signed, he was told that no such documents had been received at the palace. He then offered his copies to the secretary-general of the palace, who replied that under martial law he was not authorized to receive them, adding that in any case the Assembly had acted under pressure and would have to nominate the government again after the military quarrel was settled. Zellweger returned in frustration to Vientiane.

On August 23, Souvanna Phouma decided to go to Savannakhet to meet Phoumi Nosavan. He was to be accompanied by the new commander of the Royal Laotian Army, General Ouan Rathikon, who at the last minute asked Zellweger to send a UN representative with him, apparently both to assure his personal security and to provide a neutral witness for his negotiations with Phoumi. Zellweger at once assigned a member of his staff, John Gaillard, to go with the party. The two-hour negotiations with Phoumi Nosavan seemed both to satisfy Souvanna Phouma that there would be no march on Vientiane and to convince Phoumi that Captain Kong Lae was not an agent of the Pathet Lao. A new meeting of the Assembly at Luang Prabang was agreed on, and on August 31 it again unanimously approved a new government headed by Souvanna Phouma, this time with General Phoumi as Vice-Premier and Minister of the Interior.

This new government was one of national union committed to a policy of neutrality and national conciliation, and for a moment it seemed possible that a new and more hopeful chapter, with fewer cold war pressures, might be beginning in Laos. This hope soon faded when Phoumi, at the very moment of boarding an aircraft for Vientiane, was informed by the U.S. Embassy of a plot against his life. Phoumi refused to proceed and returned to his base at Savannakhet, where, to the accompaniment of a new Vietminh invasion scare, he set up a "Revolutionary Committee" presided over by Prince Boun Oum.

On August 23, Hammarskjold had written a letter to the King concerning the situation resulting from the military coup. It was a flowery production of two pages but the basic message was his concern that *"influences néfastes"*[102] ("nefarious influences") might infiltrate the Laotian situation, and he strongly urged conciliation, especially between Souvanna Phouma and Phoumi Nosavan. No means was found to deliver this letter, a sure sign of the decline of the UN influence. Retroactively approving Zellweger's efforts, Hammarskjold cabled, *"Espérons le mieux. Du côté Nations Unies nous avons fait tout ce qui nous est permis, par votre action, la présence de Gaillard, et peut-être ma démarche auprès du Roi. La ligne des Nations Unies comme partie intéressée, amicale et non engagée, doit ainsi avoir été maintenue."*[103]* In the kaleidoscopic atmosphere of Laos, the UN presence was fading fast.

On September 10, Prince Boun Oum, at the instigation of Phoumi Nosavan, announced that he was seizing power, abrogating all the constitutional rights of the coalition government and putting the entire country in a state of siege. At the same time Thailand restricted the arrival of goods in Vientiane, a move which operated against Souvanna Phouma and in favor of Phoumi Nosavan. One important result was the diversion of American military supplies to Savannakhet. The situation deteriorated steadily, and on September 18 Vientiane came under mortar fire for three hours. The government of Thailand simultaneously announced that it would prefer to intervene now rather than later and that Souvanna Phouma would pave the way for a Communist take-over in Laos. Souvanna Phouma charged that the mortar and shellfire on the morning of September 18 had come from the Thailand side of the Mekong. Hammarskjold feared that if Laos filed a complaint against Thailand in the Security Council, the only result would be a cold-war debate which would be of no help to the government in Vientiane and would also put in doubt the neutrality of Laos and the efforts being made to establish some form of political equilibrium. The fact that he himself was now a prime cold-war target reduced his possibilities of useful action to a minimum, and he was therefore compelled to leave Zellweger, whom he trusted as a man of wisdom, experience, humor, and political judgment, to do what he could locally in Vientiane.

During the autumn the mutual disillusionment of Souvanna Phouma and the United States steadily increased. On October 7 the United States suspended financial aid to Laos, but Souvanna Phouma still refused to break off his talks with the Pathet Lao. At the same

---

* Translation: "Let us hope for the best. On the UN side we have done all that we are permitted to do, by your action, the presence of Gaillard, and perhaps my démarche to the King. The line of the UN as a concerned, friendly, and disinterested party should thus have been maintained."

time, substantial American military aid was given direct to Phoumi, and it became increasingly obvious that Washington had decided that Souvanna Phouma must go. On November 11, the Luang Prabang garrison declared for Phoumi, and on November 23 Phoumi's drive on Vientiane began. In early December, Souvanna Phouma, failing to get from the United States even the supplies of rice and oil he had requested, turned for assistance to the Soviet Union, which started a supply airlift from Hanoi on December 4. His efforts to come to an agreement with Phoumi had merely led to a further weakening both of his own position and of Captain Kong Lae's small force in Vientiane, and he asked Zellweger if there would be any point in appealing to the UN. Zellweger undertook to consult Hammarskjold, but it was already too late to save Souvanna Phouma, for Phoumi was now in a position to take Vientiane.

On the evening of December 9, Souvanna Phouma, realizing that a fight for Vientiane was inevitable, went to Cambodia with his Ministers, leaving Kong Lae's small force to be dealt with by Phoumi. After three days of desultory fighting, during which the civilian population suffered considerably, resistance ended on December 16. Phoumi entered Vientiane to celebrate his triumph over the opposition, which could now be conveniently classified as "Communist." For the moment, the fight for Laotian neutrality had been lost.

On December 19, Kamphan Panya, who was Minister of Works in the new emergency government, sent a telegram to Hammarskjold recalling their old friendship and speaking also in his capacity as Acting Minister for Foreign Affairs. He assured him that the policy of the new government was for internal peace, neutrality, and social progress, and that the confidence of the government in the role of the UN remained limitless. These words did little to conceal the fact that a hard-line right-wing regime had been established which was unlikely to follow a policy of neutrality and conciliation which would either keep Laos out of international complications or make a serious UN assistance effort possible. On December 20, Hammarskjold replied that the aim of the UN was and had always been to give Laos all possible economic and social assistance and that he was encouraged by Kamphan's assurances of a policy of internal peace, neutrality, and social progress. *"C'est là, j'en suis convaincu, la base essentielle pour le succès ultime des efforts de donner au Laos une vie en paix extérieure et indépendance assurée par la stabilité à l'intérieur."*[104]*

---

* Translation: "That is, I am convinced, the essential basis for the ultimate success of efforts to give Laos an existence in external peace and in independence assured by internal stability."

In the unpromising state of affairs in Laos this message had a hollow ring, but Hammarskjold made one more effort. In the last days of December, through Zellweger, he urged the King to establish a government on as broad a base as possible and with a regularized constitutional position, as the prelude to a public declaration of neutrality. His efforts to get American support for this line were met with the declaration that the United States would never back Souvanna Phouma, who was a Communist sympathizer, and two days later Sisouk Na Champassak, the Laotian representative at the UN, sent Hammarskjold a letter to be circulated to all the member states,[105] denouncing Soviet intervention and aid to the rebels in Laos. In Laos, meanwhile, the King had informed Zellweger that he favored a policy of internal peace and strict neutrality and would be happy if Souvanna Phouma would return and join the government. The King also favored Hammarskjold's idea of a "statute of neutrality" to be recognized by all the interested powers.*

The power to influence events in Laos no longer lay with the King, or with the Secretary-General for that matter. The situation was dominated instead by public charges and countercharges between the United States and the U.S.S.R., wild allegations by General Phoumi of another Vietminh invasion, and by the practical support that continued to flow in to General Phoumi's faction from various U.S. agencies. On the Plain of Jars there was a temporary alliance between the Pathet Lao and the small force of Captain Kong Lae, whose simple virtues, integrity, and ability to speak to his own people in terms they could understand were soon reinforced by a Soviet airlift and intensive military training. This combination produced a military enclave that defeated all of General Phoumi's effort to reduce it, and the Laotian civil war dragged on in the wider context of the East-West struggle.

President Kennedy had his own views on Indochina, and soon after his inauguration in January 1961 U.S. policy began to shift from the effort to turn Laos into a pro-Western bastion toward the policy of neutralization that Hammarskjold had always advocated. Kennedy soon found that the military reverses suffered by Phoumi, the continuing activities of U.S. agencies, and the anxiety of Thailand made the

---

* On September 29, 1960, Norodom Sihanouk of Cambodia had suggested to the General Assembly[106] the establishment of a neutral zone in Southeast Asia consisting of both Cambodia and Laos which would be guaranteed by all the interested powers, thus removing the two countries from the zones of rivalry between the blocs and making them buffer states. On October 13, Khamking Souvanlasy, Souvanna Phouma's Foreign Minister, had endorsed this idea in the General Assembly,[107] and asked the UN to study it, but the General Assembly was too preoccupied with the Congo and other matters, and the proposals were ignored.

realiza ion of his new policy a slow and complex business, and it was only af.er various alarms, involving warnings that the United States would intervene to prevent a Communist take-over, the movement of the Seventh Fleet to the South China Sea, and the alerting of U.S. troops in the Pacific, that on March 23 the President finally accepted the idea of a cease-fire to be followed by a new Geneva Conference on Laos. The cease-fire was eventually proclaimed at the end of April, by which time the Pathet Lao had succeeded in occupying almost without opposition some three-fifths of the territory of Laos, including those areas long coveted by the North Vietnamese in the context of the South Vietnamese insurgency, which now began to move toward full-scale guerrilla warfare.

The change in U.S. policy, the cease-fire, and the decision to convene a conference on the Laotian question in Geneva on May 16 took the Laotian problem out of the United Nations context and also set aside Hammarskjold's ideas of a UN presence. "As regards Laos," he told a press conference on May 29, "our mission was basically a mission which depended for its success on reasonably peaceful conditions. We were setting up teams for work in the villages, for an integration of the villages with bigger markets, and similar things. This operation, which would have done much, I believe, to mould the various areas into one nation, had not really started when the trouble on the political level began. From then on the situation has been one which increasingly has made it difficult to get anything useful out of what we tried to do. For the moment, and pending a solution of the purely political problem, the operation is therefore kept, so to say, in abeyance, in a kind of icebox, with its potentialities maintained but without any real activity."[108]

The Geneva Conference on Laos, which began in May 1961, finally ended on July 23, 1962, with an agreement on Laotian neutrality endorsed by a provisional government of national union headed once again by Souvanna Phouma. The internal conflicts persisted nonetheless, and national conciliation remained an elusive hope. At the same time, the spreading war in Vietnam began to cast its shadow over Laos, and as the use of Laotian territory and the Ho Chi Minh Trail became more important for the Vietminh, the necessary conditions for the neutralization of Laos began once again to vanish. After a further ten years of civil disturbance and war, the news reports from Laos had a familiar ring. On July 10, 1970, a Reuters dispatch from New Delhi read: "The International Control Commission (I.C.C.) in Laos has offered to try to bring together the country's two rival factions, the Government and the Pathet Lao, Indian sources said here today. The offer came in a unanimous resolution, forwarded to the Laotian Government in Vientiane, offering to make the I.C.C.'s good offices available. . . . It was the first unanimous resolution by the three-nation Commission . . . in several years." On July 14, 1970, Agence France-Presse reported from Vientiane, "A spokesman for the left-wing Pathet Lao said here today that the only obstacle to talks between his organization and the government of Prince Souvanna Phouma was the acts of aggression committed by the American imperialists," and on August 3, 1970, "Prince Souvanna Phouma, the Laotian Prime Minister, today received a personal letter from Pathet Lao leader Prince Souphanouvong by the hand of Prince Souphanouvong's special envoy to Vientiane, Prince Soukvongsak." In January 1971 the South Vietnamese Army, with overwhelming U.S. air and logistical support, invaded Laos in order to smash the North Vietnamese supply lines.

Hammarskjold's efforts in Laos did not achieve their long-term objectives, and his ideas were sidetracked by great-power rivalries, by the twists and turns of Laotian politics, and, later, by his own personal embroilment in the turmoil of the cold war. His highly moral and personal view of politics may also have led him to overestimate the possibilities of influencing the situation through personal relationships with the leaders concerned, and his efforts finally became redundant when the 1961 Geneva Conference was set up to achieve, outside the framework of the UN, many of the aims for which he had worked.

Hammarskjold had taken considerable risks in his effort to remove the very real problems of Laos from the arena of great-power rivalries. In his great sympathy and liking for the Laotians he had tried to understand and to help with their problems and to counteract the baneful influence of the cold war on the divisions and rivalries of a small, ancient, and helpless country. In the end he failed to find the way to a peaceful solution of the problems of Laos, and perhaps even of Indochina as a whole, because his good intentions and his ingenuity were not high enough cards to play in a competition for influence between superpowers.

14

THE DEVELOPING COUNTRIES

HAMMARSKJOLD'S PUBLIC CAREER, until he became Secretary-General of the United Nations, had been largely concerned with economic matters. At Uppsala University, after studying social philosophy, political economy, and the history of French literature for two years, he majored in economics and received his degree in 1928 at the age of twenty-three. In 1927 he had studied economics at Cambridge under John Maynard Keynes.* In 1930 he became secretary of the governmental Commission on Unemployment and wrote his doctor's thesis in economics, entitled "Konjunkturspridningen" ("The Spread of the Business Cycle"). On receiving his doctor's degree from the University of Stockholm in 1933, he became assistant professor in political economy in that university. At thirty-one, after having served one year as secretary under Ivar Rooth in the National Bank of Sweden, he was appointed to the post of Permanent Under-Secretary of the Ministry of Finance, serving concurrently after 1941 as chairman of the board of the Swedish National Bank, a post he held until 1948. He seems

---

* Keynes had thought Hammarskjold highly intelligent but not original or creative as an economist. "I don't think we can expect much from *him*,"[1] Keynes told the Swedish economist and political leader Bertil Ohlin.

early in life to have rejected the idea of becoming a theoretical economist in favor of more practical work, and at the Finance Ministry, under
the great intellectual Fabian socialist Ernst Wigforss, Hammarskjold's
skill in putting ideas into action, reinforced by an acute sense of
political realities and possibilities, met its first major challenge.

The Second World War brought severe problems even to neutral
Sweden, and Hammarskjold was concerned with countering supply
difficulties and inflationary pressures by means of price-control laws
and other measures. Early in 1945 he left the Finance Ministry and
was appointed to the Cabinet as adviser on financial and economic
problems. Here he organized and coordinated, among other things,
governmental planning to deal with postwar economic problems. He
played an important part in shaping Sweden's financial policy and led
a series of trade and financial negotiations with other countries, including the United States and Great Britain. In 1947 he was appointed
Under-Secretary in the Foreign Office, where he was responsible for
all economic questions, and in the same year he was Sweden's representative to the Paris Conference at which the Marshall Plan machinery
was established. In 1948 he was Sweden's chief delegate to the Paris
conference of the Organization for European Economic Cooperation
and for some years thereafter served as vice-chairman of the OEEC
Executive Committee. His enthusiasm for an international civil service
as an instrument of multilateral diplomacy, as well as his reputation
in Europe as a brilliant and ingenious negotiator, dated from this
time. In the Swedish Foreign Ministry, as Secretary-General in 1949
and from 1951 as Minister Without Portfolio, he specialized in economic
problems and international economic cooperation.

At the United Nations, in spite of the growing pressure of political
responsibilities, Hammarskjold followed with particular attention the
economic activities of the Organization. His lasting interest remained
in what has traditionally been known as "political economy," and economics was for him one aspect of a wider picture of society, an
instrument for the achievement of political, social, and ethical objectives. In his last message, the introduction to his Report to the 1961
Assembly[2]—he once again referred to a fundamental aspect of his UN
philosophy, the principle of equality and its economic consequences.
His first task in public life as secretary of the Swedish Government
Commission on Unemployment had given him an experience of social
problems and of the necessity of mediating for an equitable solution
between conflicting groups and interests which he never forgot.

Hammarskjold came to the UN at a time when the economic activities of the Organization were at a low ebb. Even when the cold war
began to recede, the major industrial countries, fearful of an emerging

majority of newly independent developing countries, were not prepared to entrust to the UN really important activities in the economic and social field. They preferred the problems of trade to be handled through the General Agreement on Tariffs and Trade (GATT) and matters affecting the transfer of capital through the more conservative channels of the International Bank for Reconstruction and Development (IBRD) and the International Monetary Fund (IMF), where weighted voting procedures gave predominance to the developed countries. In these circumstances the relatively small program of UN technical assistance to developing countries, apart from its specific purposes, was important in staking out the UN role in a field of activity strongly emphasized in the Charter. Hammarskjold had high hopes of the potentialities of this program and was determined that it should grow from being a clearinghouse for fellowships and for the placement of experts into an important vehicle for economic development.

Hammarskjold's deep sense of the inequality of nations, in terms both of opportunity and of actual position, led him to believe that some form of international social consciousness should be fostered through a well-equipped and powerful system of international organizations, and he was determined to preserve and develop the possibilities of the UN system in this role. He was indignant, for example, when the OEEC, in the creation of which he had played a major role, was transformed into the Organization for Economic Cooperation and Development (OECD) and claimed a responsibility for the development problems of the Third World. He regarded this change as the intrusion of a rich man's club into problems that were within the rightful jurisdiction of the more democratic and broadly based United Nations.

Hammarskjold did not live to see the growth of the UN's role in economic development from a marginal one into an important instrument of assistance. This change was brought about under the impact, in the early 1960's, of the admission of some seventy new members to the organization, and the resulting emergence of the Third World as an important force in United Nations decision-making. His hopes, however, aspired to and foreshadowed this development.

Hammarskjold's approach to the UN's economic activities was essentially pragmatic and undoctrinaire. When, on the occasion of Gunnar Myrdal's departure from the Economic Commission for Europe in 1957, he was asked as "one of the few surviving Keynesians"[3] whether there was any change in the basic economic thinking of the Secretariat, he replied,

I think that our duty is collectively to reflect as well as we can not this

or that trend in political thinking in economics, but certainly the development of economic thinking at its best. It is eclectic; it is pragmatic, if
you want. From that point of view the scientist may sometimes feel a
little unhappy because everyone who has this kind of academic background, whether it is Mr. Myrdal or Mr. Hammarskjold, of course likes
to think in his own way. But I think we are all solidly and well coordinated and subordinated to the major responsibility. The reply, therefore,
is just simply that there will be no change of policy.[4]

From the outset he was insistent that the UN should concentrate on
the type of economic activities it was uniquely suited to carry out, and
should not spend its meager resources on the kind of economic
research and analysis which could be done as well or better in uni-
versities and other national institutions. He believed that the world
organization's most important role lay in the economic development
of the new and less developed countries, which was crucial both to
the ultimate success of the decolonization process and to the foundation of a more stable political order in the world. In the statements
he made each year to the Economic and Social Council on general
economic policy, the problems of the developing world occupied an
increasingly important place.

The UN system of autonomous Specialized Agencies, sometimes
referred to as the "United Nations family of organizations," presented
a special challenge to Hammarskjold's orderly mind, and he made a
continuous effort to transform this unwieldy grouping into a coordinated machine for economic and social development. "Wherever we
may find ourselves on the weather map of international policies," he
told a joint meeting of the boards of governors of the International
Bank and International Monetary Fund in September 1953, "we have to
maintain a calm awareness of the urgency of the demands facing us.
Working closely together in such an awareness we have a fair chance
of reaching safely an area of fair weather and steady winds."[5]

The heads of the Specialized Agencies meet periodically under the
chairmanship of the UN Secretary-General in a body called the Administrative Committee on Co-ordination (ACC). Hammarskjold tried to
use his chairmanship of this group to develop, as far as the autonomous constitutions and special objectives of the Agencies would allow,
common and coordinated policies on major problems. His mastery of
detailed and specialized subject matter and his powers of analysis and
leadership soon won the respect and admiration of the heads of the
Agencies, and at first he had some success in mitigating the natural
divisiveness of the system. The honeymoon period with the Specialized
Agencies was relatively short-lived, however, for their Directors-
General soon found that Hammarskjold's leadership entailed practical

consequences that seemed likely to circumscribe their autonomy. In practice his policy of "unity in diversity" turned out to put more weight on the first than on the second part of the proposition, and he himself became increasingly exasperated or amused by turns at the tendency of his Specialized Agency colleagues to go their own way and politely to ignore his leadership.

The resentment of the heads of the Agencies over efforts to establish a firmer central control of their activities was demonstrated in the reactions of some of them to a passage in a speech delivered by Hammarskjold in Chicago in May 1960:*

> Historically we have to register a tendency to create new organs for each new major field of activity [a reference to the creation of the International Atomic Energy Agency and to proposals for a new agency for the control of nuclear tests and disarmament]. . . . If I am permitted to fall back again on a parallel with biological developments, it is as if we were to permit the growth of a tree to be weakened by the development of too many branches, finally sapping its strength so that it breaks down under its own weight. . . . We must seek the optimum balance between a system with a large number of autonomous bodies and a system with strong concentration of tasks within a lesser number of organizations. . . . Probably, new forms will have to be devised, not only, as already indicated, for an integration of activities among autonomous organizations, but also for the delegation of powers within this or that organization without a breaking up of its inner unity.[7]

Two months later, the urgent and complex demands of the Congo operation provided the first occasion when Specialized Agency missions actually came under the direct control and coordination of a United Nations operation in the field. The success of the civilian operations branch of the UN operation in the Congo provided a practical demonstration of the merits of Hammarskjold's attempts to provide for strong central coordination of Specialized Agency activities, but the pattern necessitated by emergency conditions was not soon repeated.

Hammarskjold summarized his ideas of the economic role of international organizations in an address to the Economic and Social Council on the World Economic Situation in Geneva in July 1955:[8]

> A great deal, admittedly, has been achieved, but we cannot be complacent as regards the rate of achievement. Much remains to be done before we shall have mastered the techniques for utilizing the manpower now

---

* Earlier in 1960 he had had another example of this resentment. He had heard that one of the Agencies was going to have an official flag of its own and inquired about this "matter of mutual interest."[6] To his surprise, he received a furious reply that revealed the deep suspicions aroused by his mild expression of interest.

wasted in disguised unemployment, for tapping the natural resources now unused owing to lack of sanitation, irrigation, power and transportation, for creating a spirit of dynamic entrepreneurship, private and public, in areas where it is nonexistent, for introducing modern technology and economic, social and political institutions appropriate to a market economy, for developing effective demand to absorb the newly produced supplies, and above all, for obtaining the financing, both internal and external, necessary to support a program of balanced economic development without crippling inflation and without unmanageable balance of payments problems. We have by now gained considerable insight into the problem of bridging a gap which may emerge between effective demand and the capacity to produce in developed countries. We have yet to acquire adequate experience and wisdom, however, in the matter of closing the large divide between productive capacity and human requirements in underdeveloped countries.

This is the major long-term economic problem facing our generation, the greatest economic challenge to nations, both individually and collectively. As I have said on other occasions, it defines the major task of the UN. It calls for all the collective wisdom, patience, and earnest desire for mutual assistance which the nations of the world are capable of mustering. Above all, it calls for flexibility of mind and realistic examination of problems.[9]

He developed this theme over the years with increasing emphasis on the obligation of the UN to the developing countries. He told the Economic and Social Council in 1956:[10]

Unfortunately, the achievement in stabilizing the national economies of the developed countries finds no parallel in the stabilization of the national economies of the underdeveloped countries. Nor has sufficient progress been made in stabilizing and integrating the world economy as a whole. The world continues to be divided into two economic regions with only marginal trade relations between them. While trade has grown significantly, the flow of international capital has never regained its importance of only a generation ago, either in relation to trade or to income and investment. . . . If the underdeveloped countries are even to maintain, let alone increase, their relative share of the world's total output, they cannot rely exclusively on expanded exports of primary products to industrial countries, but must embark upon a program of broad economic development. . . . A reasonable target for economic development should at least provide for a higher percentage rate of growth in the underdeveloped than in the developed countries; otherwise, it would be impossible ever to increase the share of the underdeveloped countries in the distribution of the *per capita* income of the world. That we have thus far fallen short of the target only dramatizes how great is the need to intensify our efforts, both national and international, to speed the process of economic development.[11]

Hammarskjold was especially disturbed by the problem created by the fluctuations in world commodity prices for developing countries whose economies were largely dependent on a single primary product, and he strongly supported the attempt to regulate commodity price fluctuations by international agreement. As he noted in 1956:

> Disappointingly little progress has been achieved in stabilizing world commodity prices. Much more can be done if we show the same understanding and good will we do in developing programs of technical assistance. Wild fluctuations in the prices of primary products, the main foreign exchange earners, paralyze the efforts of underdeveloped countries for long-term development. Nor do these fluctuations serve any useful purpose in the developed countries. What these fluctuations mean to underdeveloped countries can be readily grasped from the fact that *a change of only 5 per cent in their average export prices is about equal to the entire annual inflow of private and public capital and government grants to underdeveloped countries.*[12]

By 1958 Hammarskjold was referring to himself as "an ex-economist ... because in the last few years I have not been able to follow in detail the literature in the field,"[13] but he continued his efforts to improve the organization and procedure of economic work in the UN. Not all of these efforts were effective. In June 1959, recognizing that the UN system of economic assistance was becoming highly diversified, he set up a Secretariat Economic Policy Board designed to ensure that requests from governments for assistance were referred to the organization or unit within the UN system that could respond to them most effectively. He himself was chairman of this board, which consisted of all the senior officials concerned with economic matters, including Paul G. Hoffman, the director of the UN Special Fund for Economic Development. The board was supposed to meet once a month, but after the first meeting Hammarskjold's other preoccupations made it impossible for him to attend, and after three more meetings the board ceased to meet and was forgotten.

He also tried to put new life into the workings of the Economic and Social Council, whose proceedings had shown a tendency to become stale and bureaucratic. "There is a difficulty," he said, "with UN procedures as they are at present in the sense that they tend to develop into what I might call routine. There are very many questions partly of a household nature which have to be tackled by, for example, the Economic and Social Council or the appropriate committee of the General Assembly, and it is difficult to get concentration on the key issues. ... It is also difficult to organize the work in those permanent bodies in such a way as to make it possible for key people in governments to attend. They cannot spare too much time."[14] He gave much thought to this problem. He rejected the often proposed idea of large economic conferences and tried instead to reorganize the procedures of the Economic and Social Council itself to allow for concentration on a few key problems for a short period during which the most senior and responsible government officials would attend. His idea was to "hold a concentrated top-level debate, half conference and half seminar, which will, on the one hand, give new life to the debate within the UN. . . . and also have a different kind of impact on world opinion from the one we now get from the regular procedures to which people have become a little bit too accustomed."[15]

The sole practical result of this idea was a ministerial-level meeting of the Economic and Social Council in Geneva in July 1960. Despite the threatening situation in the Congo, Hammarskjold flew over to make the opening speech to this meeting on July 11 and had to return to New York the same evening. He hoped, he said, "that out of your deliberations will come an increased awareness of the services that the UN is in a strategic position to render."[16] This hope was not fulfilled, at least in the form that he had proposed. His own enforced absence detracted seriously from any momentum or success the first meeting might have had, and there were some who thought that a group of Ministers reading prepared speeches would make the Council's meetings even more lifeless than before. Hammarskjold's own enthusiasm, knowledge, and leadership conceivably could have been able to instigate a useful discussion, but without him a stimulating exchange of ideas was unlikely to occur.

In his last address to the Economic and Social Council, in July 1961,[17] Hammarskjold spoke of the profound revolution in international thinking which consisted in "accepting as a basic postulate the existence of a world community for which all nations share a common responsibility. . . . We have thus assumed an international responsibility to reduce the disparities in levels of living between nations, a responsibility parallel to that accepted earlier for greater economic and social equality within nations. Axiomatic as this has now become, it would have been considered as rank national heresy only a short while ago."[18] He saw this side of the UN's economic work not only as a moral obligation but also as a field in which multilateral aid programs through the UN were especially suited to the political, psychological, and economic problems of the developing countries, particularly the newly independent ones.

Hammarskjold naturally detested patronizing, paternalistic, or neocolonial attitudes. The term "underdeveloped countries" was, he pointed out to the Swedish Chamber of Commerce in 1954,[19] "a rather curious term . . . if you realize that a few of them have civilizations dating back far beyond anything we know of; they have attained a maturity of the individual which makes you feel rather humble. They are underdeveloped only in the economic sense."[20] These governments were fighting for their place in the world economy, and in order to meet the claims of their peoples for a way of life comparable to that of developed countries they had to achieve in a couple of decades goals that had taken most developed countries at least two hundred years to reach. In the anticolonial climate of the time, aid had to be free of any taint of dependence or submission to political pressures. The United Nations was uniquely suited to meet this requirement. In "bringing the underdeveloped countries into the world market in the proper way,"[21] the UN would also be laying the indispensable foundation for a world in which the basic causes of political conflict might be reduced. "For us in the UN," he said in 1956, "and for all governments with a feeling for the future of this world, it is an imperative challenge to live up to the economic needs of the vast majority of mankind. I say this with a cold mind and thinking only of the political problem."[22]

The resources of the UN are pathetically small in relation to the vast and complex problems of world poverty, and Hammarskjold never ceased to stress this contrast in appealing for funds for technical assistance for economic development. He also brooded over the necessity of training the right kind of staff to carry out a global economic development program. One new form of assistance with which he experimented came to be called the OPEX (Operational and Executive Personnel) program. He first mentioned this idea in a speech at McGill University in May 1956, in which he welcomed Lester Pearson's idea of establishing "an international professional and technical civil service of the UN with experts especially trained for work in the underdeveloped areas."[23] The OPEX scheme would recruit qualified people who, although they would maintain their international status, would work in developing countries as part of the national administration of the country concerned, the idea being to provide experienced executives who were actually part of the government machinery rather than temporary consultants from outside. OPEX personnel would serve until local people were sufficiently trained to take over. They would be paid by the government, but if necessary the UN would make up the difference between their salary and the normal pay they would have received at home.

Hammarskjold was enthusiastic about this new idea, which in 1956 he called "my favorite child at present,"[24] and he proposed it for the consideration of the Economic and Social Council in the summer of that year. In presenting it as a formal proposal to the General

Assembly in 1958,[25] he called OPEX one of the most important issues since the UN's technical assistance program had been started in 1949. "It is, of course," he said, "the complete antithesis of anything in the nature of a colonial arrangement. It will be started only when it is requested by a government; it can be stopped at any time by the government's own decision."[26]

The General Assembly approved the OPEX plan on November 14, 1958,[27] but in practice, despite Hammarskjold's hopes, it did not develop fast or easily. His enthusiasm was by no means unanimously shared even within the "UN family," and it also proved difficult to get the right kind of qualified people to serve as OPEX experts. Their assignments, he said in 1960, "are exacting; they are not rewarding either in terms of money or in visible results, or in terms of formal merits, so we have to build on the idealism of people. Thank God, there are enough people who have this kind of idealism and this kind of pioneer spirit. But we have to find them and that becomes increasingly a somewhat tough job."[28] He had also underestimated the psychological problems at the receiving end and the possibility that governments and officials in newly independent countries, however great their need for expertise, might not welcome a new visitation of foreign experts, however high-minded and selfless.

Despite these difficulties, Hammarskjold was able to announce[29] in 1960 that the experimental period was over and that OPEX would be made a permanent part of the technical assistance program. The idea slowly gained momentum, and ten years later there were sixty-nine OPEX officials from the UN alone serving throughout the world.

In his concern to make UN economic and technical assistance effective, the emerging countries of Africa increasingly occupied Hammarskjold's attention. From 1958 the avalanche of independence in Africa gathered speed and momentum, leaving in its wake a landscape strewn with new and challenging problems—economic, social, and political. The UN membership from the continent rose from ten states at the end of 1958 to twenty-seven by September 1961.

On December 29, 1958, Hammarskjold went to Addis Ababa, Ethiopia, to open, in the presence of the Emperor Haile Selassie, the first session of the UN Economic Commission for Africa. "In the days when international cooperation was not so well founded as it is today," he told the Commission, "His Imperial Majesty, in the adversity then experienced, was a symbol to the whole world of the principles of international order. It is certainly a vindication of his faith that now, in happier times ... the UN is to make its African home in Addis Ababa."[30] The "happier times" were also anxious ones and were soon to become more so. "For the longer run ahead," Hammarskjold asked the Economic and Social Council in the summer of 1959, "are we sure that there is a sufficient awareness of the problems and frustrations which are building up progressively in the underdeveloped countries as their peoples grow more and more conscious of the fact that time is slipping away from them? Can we rest content with the fact that all the efforts of recent years—and I do not wish to underestimate them—have still not sufficed to prevent the gap between rich and poor countries from continuing to increase? There is a widespread feeling in the underdeveloped countries of the need for some new break-through on the road to economic development."[31]

HAMMARSKJOLD'S FIRST PRACTICAL EFFORT to assist a new African country arose from the circumstances following Guinea's achievement of inde-pendence. During de Gaulle's African tour in August 1958, Sékou Touré had greeted him in Conakry with a strongly worded speech[32] in which he declared that he and his party, the Rassemblement Démocratique Africain, would not support the French referendum on the Constitu-tion because the right of Africans to full independence was not clearly written into the text. He added that although Guinea wished to remain in the French African community as an independent state, "we prefer poverty in freedom to riches in slavery."[33] In the referendum on the Constitution of the French Fifth Republic on September 28, the people of Guinea, alone of the French African Community, voted "no" by an overwhelming vote of 636,381 to 18,012. On September 29 the French informed Sékou Touré that Guinea should no longer expect to receive either the normal assistance from the French administration or funds for equipment, and that French officials in Guinea would be transferred to similar posts in other territories within two months. Two months later French officials left Guinea lock, stock, and barrel.

Guinea celebrated its independence on October 2, 1958, and became a member of the UN on December 12, but the government of Sékou Touré, who had been elected President, faced its new independence with the minimum of organization and resources. After an exchange of letters with Touré, on July 8, 1959, Hammarskjold appointed Adrian Pelt, formerly the UN Commissioner in Libya, his special representa-tive in Guinea. This unprecedented arrangement, he explained, was designed "to see to it that the limited resources we have are put to the best possible use"[34] and to provide a link between Guinea and the UN, the Specialized Agencies, and governments that might give bilateral aid.

President de Gaulle evidently did not share Hammarskjold's view that there was "nothing remarkable"[35] about his interest in Guinea, and during Hammarskjold's visit to Paris at the end of July 1959 the President reacted brusquely to his wish to discuss the question. Guinea, he told Hammarskjold, had chosen its own road and had to solve its own problems. He might give Guinea some assistance but *"rien qui me coûte cher"*[36] ("nothing which costs me much"). He was personally convinced of *"la descente inévitable da la Guinée"*[37] ("the inevitable decline of Guinea"). When Hammarskjold pointed out that it was in the interest of France and of the world in general to forestall such a decline and to avoid the creation of a political vacuum, and that France, in cooperation with the UN, should try to do this, de Gaulle repeated that he was *"complètement désintéressé"*[38] ("completely uninterested"). "As you see," Hammarskjold told Pelt, "there is considerable 'pique' in the air, and as the General is an autocrat, we shall hear more of it."[39] Hammarskjold seems to have underestimated the resentment that his interest in Africa, and especially in the French Community, had already aroused in de Gaulle and among his entourage. The UN intervention in the Congo turned this private resentment into public denunciation.

In November 1959, Sékou Touré visited New York to discuss in detail the nature of UN aid to Guinea. The relationship between Hammarskjold and the young radical African leader was frank and cooperative, and they shared a taste for political philosophizing that also gave the talks a broader basis. Through Pelt and his successor in Guinea, Ansgar Rosenborg, Hammarskjold remained in close touch with the problems of Guinea and spent Christmas there in 1959 during his African tour.

In June 1960, Sékou Touré asked for Hammarskjold's comments and suggestions on his plans for monetary, economic, and administrative reforms, including a triennial economic development plan and the principles of Guinea's foreign policy. Hammarskjold was both gratified and embarrassed by this expression of confidence and friendship. He could not, he told Sékou Touré, be absolutely sure of responding to this gesture in the manner that Sékou Touré wished. The options facing a new country sometimes went beyond the *"domaine où les organisations internationales, si impartiales soient-elles et sympathiques aux problèmes du pays intéressé, peuvent offrir une contribution valable"*[40] ("the field where international organizations, however impartial and sympathetic they may be to the problems of the country concerned, can offer a proper contribution"). Such questions as the choice of a monetary system, the definition of the objectives of economic growth, or the setting up of an administrative and institutional system were major decisions which a government and its people themselves had to make and in which helpers from outside should not play a determining role. The role of UN assistance was in a more technical sphere—to deal with the consequences and the problems of application of policies already adopted. For this reason, far removed as he was from the realities of Guinea, he was reluctant to make a detailed commentary on Sékou Touré's plans, which should rather come from experts within or near the government. There was already a UN monetary expert, M. Bellec, in Guinea, and other experts could be sent for consultation on economic planning. On one point in Sékou Touré's letter, however, he was very positive. Sékou Touré had mentioned that an African common market was one of his objectives, and Hammarskjold referred to his own recent suggestions along these lines to the Economic Commission for Africa in Tangier[41] as a means for new African states *"surmonter les obstacles imposés par des frontières politiques qui, souvent, ne sont que la conséquence d'accidents historiques"*[42] ("to surmount the obstacles created by political frontiers that are often only the result of historical accidents"). He urged Sékou Touré to push for action in the Economic Commission for Africa on the study of regional economic arrangements.

In Hammarskjold's apartment on October 10, 1960, at a dinner *à deux* which was to be their last private meeting, Sékou Touré made a remark that stuck in Hammarskjold's mind as a vivid description of the problems of the new Africa: "You Western democracies already had a nation when you got a national government, but many of us are expected to govern a country without a nation."[43] The UN involvement in the Congo and the ensuing political complications had an inhibiting effect on Hammarskjold's efforts in Guinea, and the violent recriminations that followed Patrice Lumumba's death finally put an end to his personal relationship with Sékou Touré.

The main purpose of Hammarskjold's extensive tours to member countries was to meet their leaders and to get a firsthand idea of their problems. His first such tours, in January and February 1956, had taken him to twelve countries in the Near East and Asia, and to Australia and New Zealand; a second tour in March 1959 took him to nine Asian countries. Late in 1959 he decided to make an extended tour of Africa. He told a press conference in announcing this tour:

> I have wanted first of all, to all the extent I can do so, to get at least the personal contacts necessary for the right kind of discussions and exchanges. . . . I may perhaps quote as an example—and I do not think it is indiscreet in any way—that I would not have felt able to do whatever I managed to do in the Laos question this fall, unless I had had the advantage of personal acquaintance from a previous visit with those who now carry the responsibility. . . . I quote it just as an example of

how the personal contact in itself may add essentially to what we can do from the UN angle. I want to have that advantage, and in order to get it I have to put in these several weeks of personal contacts.[44]

His African tour, which lasted from December 21, 1959, to the end of January 1960, was an intensive visit by special aircraft to some twenty-four countries, territories, or regions, with twenty-seven stops of one or two days each. The journey took him to Senegal, Liberia, Guinea, Ghana, French Togoland, Lagos, Yaoundé in the French Cameroons, British Cameroons, Kaduna in Northern Nigeria, the French Congo, Leopoldville and Stanleyville in the Belgian Congo, Ruanda-Urundi (later to become Rwanda and Burundi), Tanganyika, Zanzibar, Mombasa and Nairobi in Kenya, Uganda, Somaliland, Ethiopia, Khartoum in the Sudan, and, after discussions in Cairo, to Tunisia and Morocco. On his way back he also paid official visits to Madrid and Lisbon. To a less energetic and involved man such a tour might have proved to be a totally exhausting and frustrating succession of formal airport welcomes, meals, and conversations, but Hammarskjold lived every minute of it with passionate enthusiasm and curiosity and gained a vivid first impression of the diversity of problems, attitudes, and traditions of the African continent. It provided, he cabled Andrew Cordier from Leopoldville, "increasingly challenging food for thought at UN."[45]

For Hammarskjold this tour provided an opportunity both to explain his own views to the leaders of the new Africa and to hear their point of view and make their personal acquaintance. He took every possible opportunity to emphasize the difference between UN experts and colonial officials. "Within strict limits and for specific tasks," he told a press conference in Dar es Salaam, Tanganyika, "where there is just no possibility to fill a vacancy due to a lack of candidates of national origin, we have gone in and sent a man or found a man for the government. I have established two very strict rules in that respect. It must be on the initiative and at the request of the government concerned. We do not want to poke our fingers into it uninvited. In the second instance, if a man goes in, half of his duty should be to see to it that, as quickly as possible, he schools somebody who can take his place. . . . A major part of his service should be to render himself unnecessary."[46]

Hammarskjold was greatly inpressed by the new generation of African leaders, many of whom he found remarkable and, in their directness and style, unlike anything he had previously encountered. He was equally struck by the immense problems of Africa. He was impressed not only by the obviously imminent difficulties of a country like the Belgian Congo, which was to become independent with virtually no preparation at all for self-government, but he also now saw at first hand the crippling legacy that the crazy colonial quilt, imposed on Africa by the European colonial powers in the late nine-teenth century without regard for economic or tribal facts, would inevitably bequeath to the new nations as they became independent. On his way back to New York he urged, in an address to the Economic Commission for Africa in Tangier,[47] direct economic cooperation through the harmonization of policies, the expansion of regional trade, and concerted action in transport and basic investments. "This may for some countries represent something of a sacrifice," he said,

> or at least an additional effort; for others, it may mean the forming of a new habit; but it is clear that advancement will be much more difficult if each country must proceed on its own and only with whatever direct help it can get from outside this continent. We must recognize the fact, inevitable under historic circumstances, that very often political borders will cut across natural economic regions in a manner which will make useful development schemes impossible without concerted action among contiguous areas. Coming from a cross-continental tour, it is perhaps not unnatural that I should mention the overriding importance of a national network of inland transport and communications and of international rivers without which the economic potentialities of Africa cannot be realized.[48]

This far-sighted view seemed, in the honeymoon atmosphere of the great year of African independence, less naive than it might now appear, but the next eighteen months were to show how soon more immediate political problems were to cloud Hammarskjold's vision of a continent launched on the road to cooperative success by new and able young leaders with the help and advice of the UN. Later it was said that his tour had given him an unrealistic and overly hopeful view—a view which could only invite the disillusionment that came before he died—but it is also true that the stresses of the Congo crisis would certainly have been far more difficult for him to bear without this earlier personal contact with the new African leaders.

His African tour greatly stimulated Hammarskjold's determination that the UN should play a leading role in the proper development of Africa. "The journey makes me both a little bit wiser and a lot more humble," he said on his return. "One most encouraging fact is that over a wide range of countries you find the people of the present generation of African leaders of the highest seriousness, devotion and intelligence. I am sure that in their hands those countries will go on to a happy future."[49] "The image I take back with me," he had told the Economic Commission for Africa in Tangier, "is a refreshing one of youth and vigor, and generally speaking of a remarkable aptitude on the part of the leaders to grasp facts and adhere to facts, notwithstanding the understandable impatience and the strong ideological currents which are necessary ingredients of the rapid changes now taking place."[50]

After his tour, Africa became the dominant theme in his press conferences, speeches, and letters. "There are extremely able people all around the continent," he said in February 1960, " . . . but they are few. The period of growth, of education and of political formation in Africa has been a very short one . . . and in such a short period . . . it is quite natural that there has not emerged the kind of social grouping, the kind of social classes, from which you can recruit a broad administration and a broad political leadership. The countries will have to live with few people, and quality will have to make up for numbers and quantity."[51]

The new countries would temporarily require foreign experts, technicians, and officials, and Hammarskjold noted that while "some striking investments have been made, and some good development schemes are under way . . . it is quite common to note that we lack what I would call the economic infra-structure for a national life as a political unit." A huge educational effort would also be required to "bring people not only to national awareness but to the point where they form as free individuals their judgement on political issues."[52]

Finally, he was acutely aware of what he called the "necessity of moral support . . . because people and money and education do not mean a thing unless they are given and provided in the right spirit . . . neither a feeling of false superiority, nor a feeling of sterile pessimism, nor a feeling of facile optimism. What is needed is realism and understanding. . . ." This was a special challenge to the UN, for it was much easier for the new countries to receive financial and technical assistance from an international body than from a single government. "It is not," he said, "until and unless the receiving country feels that this is an act of solidarity within an organization where they have equal rights with the donors that you really reach the optimum point not only psychologically but politically and economically."[53]

Hammarskjold hoped that the UN, having no past in many African countries, could play a special role in their future, and he announced that as a result of his African tour he would make certain proposals and initiatives, of which the first would probably be submitted to the spring session of the Economic and Social Council.

HAMMARSKJOLD'S NEW ENTHUSIASM for Africa was not likely to be widely appreciated in some Western European circles. Even a veteran international socialist like Paul-Henri Spaak was to write many years later: *"Son influence sur les pays d'Afrique et d'Asie était certaine. Il la consolidait en n'étant pas toujours très juste pour l'Europe et les blancs en général. Il a vécu l'anticolonialisme exacerbé et triomphant. Il y participait par devoir, mais aussi, j'en suis sûr, par conviction."*[54]*

Hammarskjold had shown his awareness of European attitudes to decolonization in a speech at the University of Lund in Sweden on May 4, 1959.[55] "One may reach back," he said, "for the imagined calm of the closed world. One may find one's spiritual home in the very disintegration and its drama. Or, one may reach ahead towards the glimpse of the synthesis, inspired by the dream of a new culture in which there is achieved, on a level encompassing the whole world, what once seemed to have become a regional reality in Europe.... I used the word solidarity. It is a key word in this connection, and to me it is the answer to the irritable questions and reactions which are still sometimes forthcoming from those who have entrenched themselves in the past and view almost as a traitor any European who does not weep over the receding power of Europe."[56]

He reacted strongly against the clubmanesque view held by some at the UN, that the arrival of the new African nations would upset and disrupt the world Organization. "I do believe very much," he said in 1960, "in the ability of those various States to make valuable contributions as soon as they have found their way in the maze of the United Nations.... I believe that ... they will add life to the debates and to the consideration of questions. There is something very shocking in the idea that new States must take so-called irresponsible stands. I myself do not believe it for a moment.... It is quite natural that they, like all of us, will have to find their way through a political system and a framework of procedures which so far have been unknown to them."[57]

Hammarskjold's views about Africa seem from the first to have aroused President de Gaulle's worst suspicions. At their meeting in July 1959, Hammarskjold spoke at length of the form and political orientation of the inevitable independence of the French colonies in Africa. While conceding that French guidance and assistance would be vital in this development, he argued that France would need the wider

---

* Translation: "There was no question of his influence on the countries of Africa and Asia. He consolidated it without always being altogether fair to Europe and to whites in general. He experienced anticolonialism both exacerbated and triumphant. He shared in it from a sense of duty, but also, I am sure, out of conviction."

setting provided by the UN, so that its help could be given not as an act of patronage but as from a senior to a junior brother, both having equal rights, self-respect, and potentially equal status. The bridge from the past to the future that all Western colonial powers would have to find in Africa would, in Hammarskjold's view, best be provided by the UN, which was free of the Africans' suspicions of Western initiatives. De Gaulle received this notion coldly, and things were probably made worse by one of Hammarskjold's less felicitous metaphoric efforts when, comparing French relations with Africa to a good martini, he told André Malraux that "France might be the gin, but the UN was definitely the angosturas"[58]—a flight of fancy unpalatable in more ways than one. De Gaulle certainly resented what seemed to him and his colleagues to be Hammarskjold's self-righteous views about Africa, which arose, they believed, from the fact that he came from a European country without a recent colonial past.

Hammarskjold feared that European attitudes such as de Gaulle's might fatally impede the far-ranging tasks that he believed the UN should undertake. At a Western summit meeting in Paris on December 19, 1959, which was attended by de Gaulle, Eisenhower, Macmillan, and Konrad Adenauer, it was decided to call an informal meeting in Paris to consider how the industrialized Western European countries could take measures for further development of the less developed countries. Obviously these discussions, to be held in the spring of 1960 in Paris, would be particularly relevant to Africa. Hans Engen, who was to represent Norway at these meetings, consulted Hammarskjold on the best approach to the problem of assisting the new countries. "Only the UN," he replied to Engen, "of which they are themselves members, breaks the colonial spell and puts the matter outside the orbit of the cold war."[59] The first and most urgent need was for "pre-investment projects in a proper form."[60] Such assistance, being close to central government activities, would come better from the UN than through bilateral aid programs.

"I find it rather surprising," he wrote to Engen, "that—apart from a personal contact with the Italian delegates—'the eight' in Washington have not taken any contact with us or shown any interest in the coordination of their thinking with our experiences. Alas, it is symptomatic of an effort at all costs to avoid this mixed company and to try and make the world safe for the West." This attitude, he felt, would in fact "reduce their own chances to make the contribution they want, while having only slight possibilities to reap the national or group benefits they are hoping for. My worry is that, in our race against time, all of us, and not least the West, are losing out as the situation develops very quickly. It is in these circumstances only a modest consolation that I am sure that experience and hard facts sooner or later will bend the help to under-developed countries back into UN channels. . . .

"The idea to launch assistance to the under-developed countries as an operation outside the UN at the summit meeting seems to me to be substantially dangerous and tactically poor. However, I see back of it the hand of de Gaulle with his 'directorate of four' approach and his nearly pathological attitude *against* the UN. However, I would hope that the Americans and the British would be strong enough to resist such an 'idée saugrenue.' "[61]

"The African development," Hammarskjold wrote to Alexis Léger in March 1960, "puts the international community to the test, and I worry at the thought of the lack of unity and the lack of vision which characterizes the Western approach to this new continent. In the UN we have to fight against heavy political odds, and with very meagre resources, to do the very minimum necessary and fervently requested by the African leaders. The ex-colonial powers look at this with disapproval, others with jealousy, and the result is the same in both cases. However, we have to live up to our own appraisal and to those duties which critics themselves have forced upon us as signatories of the Charter."[62]

Hammarskjold felt that too much bilateral aid to Africa could develop into an assistance competition that would inevitably project great-power rivalries onto the African scene. "I have a feeling," he said in March 1960, "that Africa is a part of the world which at present is outside the conflict, the competition, the cold war, if you want to put it that way, under which we are all suffering at present, and I would like to see that part of the world remain outside."[63] He was convinced that the African preference was for aid through the UN. Julius Nyerere, soon to become President of Tanganyika, had told him, "If we have to choose between 'X' millions bilaterally and 'X-minus' through the UN, we choose 'X-minus,' "[64] and generally speaking he had found the new African leaders anxious to avoid being committed by receiving aid from a country or group of countries whose assistance had a political accent, whether it was Soviet or pro-NATO, or Western European and ex-colonial.

To set the tone for the ministerial-level July meeting of the Economic and Social Council, which was to concentrate on the difficulties of underdeveloped countries and their relations with the rest of the world, Hammarskjold made proposals to the spring meeting of the Council on how the UN could meet the transitional needs of countries which had just attained independence. Countries attaining independence in 1960 would include the Trust Territories of the Cameroons,

Togoland and Somaliland, as well as Nigeria, Mali, Madagascar, and the Belgian Congo:

> They face a situation, first of all, where naturally very great expectations have arisen, where the people in general are looking for guidance, for initiative, for an opening up of the future of their government. . . . On the one side, they have had a richly developed administration with people from other territories, from the ex-colonial power. Even with the happiest of cooperation between an ex-colonial power and a newly independent state, it is unavoidable that this or that official, this or that administrator, feels that this may be the time when he should go back home, that this may be the occasion for him to switch back to his previous occupations. That is to say, there will be necessarily and unavoidably a certain outflow of administrators, quite irrespective of any political stands, on the basis of natural individual initiatives.
>
> In the same way, the first period after independence necessarily is one when there is a certain atmosphere of uncertainty. People who previously invested more or less automatically in the country may hold back, not out of distrust, but because they want to see a little bit of the trend of the development. And further, resources which were available under the budgetary arrangements of the metropolitan power are no longer available in any sense automatically. They have to be solicited; there have to be special decisions. And even with the best of relations, the best of cooperation, this is bound to introduce a certain amount of red tape, a certain delay.[65]

The new countries would be members of the UN, which was thus not an outside factor. "The UN should be there and, as a kind of stopgap organization, it can come in with the assistance needed during those days when assistance is a necessity, but when, on the other hand, the government needs leisure to look around, to orient itself, to find its lines."[66] The UN could provide assistance without pressure and without committing a new government to decisions from which there was no way back. The assistance might be modest but would provide "a little bit of elbow room which they need during the first period. . . . What we need,"[67] Hammarskjold told the Council, "is not so much money or people as to be able to grant the assistance, within the framework already established by the UN for its assistance to underdeveloped countries, with the necessary speed, at the right moment, when there is a kind of sur-value on all that we can do. . . . What is needed is the possibility to help those countries to catch up with others."[68]

Hammarskjold experimented with the UN "presence" approach in other African countries besides Guinea. In April 1960, he sent Piero Spinelli to Togoland ten days before the independence ceremonies to serve as a UN presence "during the politically sensitive period of transition with well known and publicized possibilities of international conflict."[69] Specifically at this juncture, Kwame Nkrumah of Ghana, which had been merged in 1957, following a UN-supervised plebiscite, with the adjacent trust territory of British Togoland, was waging against Sylvanus Olympio, the President-elect of Togo, a press and radio campaign which indicated that Ghana might have designs on what had been French Togoland. Although theoretically Spinelli was on a technical assistance mission, Hammarskjold had in mind that a UN presence, similar to Spinelli's previous mission in Jordan, might also have a deterrent effect on such designs. Spinelli attended the independence celebrations on April 27 and stayed on to make a long report on the technical assistance requirements of Togo. He returned for brief visits in December 1960 and August 1961 to maintain the UN interest until the possible threat from neighboring countries was past.

In May 1960 Hammarskjold wrote to Abdullah Issa, the Prime Minister of Somalia, saying that he was interested in Somalia's needs for UN assistance after independence and proposing to send a personal representative. He also informed Emperor Haile Selassie of this intention. Constantin Stavropoulos, head of the UN Legal Office, attended the Somalia independence ceremonies from July 1 to 4, and Hammarskjold himself intended to visit Somalia in July on his way to Pretoria but the Congo crisis supervened and he never got there. In June 1960 a technical assistance team of six experts was sent, and on March 3, 1961, he appointed a representative in Somalia with whom he remained in touch until his death.

In June 1960, Ralph Bunche was detailed to act as the UN "presence" during the independence ceremonies in the former Belgian Congo, which Hammarskjold believed might have exceptional transitional difficulties. In this case, however, a UN "presence" was not sufficient and served only as the prelude to the largest and most difficult operation the UN had ever undertaken in the field.

15

THE CONGO,
JULY–AUGUST 1960

THE CRISIS IN THE FORMER BELGIAN CONGO, which erupted within a week
of that country's accession to independence on June 30, 1960, was to
dominate the rest of Hammarskjold's Secretary-Generalship. It was to
bring him into a head-on collision with one of the major powers, the
Soviet Union, and into serious disagreements with the three other
great powers and with many smaller ones as well, and it was to pose
problems concerning the role and nature of the United Nations, and
especially of the Secretary-Generalship, which haunt the Organization
still. It was also to cost him his life.

Hammarskjold was never in any doubt about the risks of the UN
involvement in the Congo, but he was also deeply concerned over the
probable consequences of a failure to act. In January 1960, during his
tour of Africa, he had seen the Congo in the last months of its colonial
state and had realized that its independence, and the lack of preparation for it, would, in view of the country's size and natural wealth,
inevitably produce a series of extraordinary problems. Foreseeing
trouble, he arranged in May 1960 that Ralph Bunche should arrive
in the Congo well before Independence Day and should stay on for
a while to be available to the new government for consultation and
advice. After independence, the breakdown in the Congo was even

more sudden and catastrophic than Hammarskjold had foreseen, and within a few days the country became the center of a new and extraordinary world crisis.

The collapse of the Belgian system of colonialism in the Congo occurred with lightning speed. In one sense, the Congo was the most highly developed of all colonial territories. It was based on a bureaucracy of ten thousand Belgian civil servants, a highly developed system of economic exploitation involving international corporations and enormous investments and profits, and a complex rail, water, and road transport system. A structure of religious missions constituted the third major pillar of Belgian colonialism. But this elaborate creation had been unable to change direction in time to meet the new wave in Africa, and its last-minute attempts to do so were rendered futile by the onrush of events. As a result, when independence came, the great colonial structure lapsed almost overnight into anarchy and confusion.

Until 1957, little if any political activity by Africans had been permitted in the Belgian Congo, and the very idea of independence was hardly discussed, let alone its timing. The first serious anticolonial disturbances, led by Joseph Kasavubu in Leopoldville* in 1959, caused arrangements for independence to be hastily made in early 1960 at a round-table conference in Brussels in which the new Congolese leaders, Moise Tshombe included, participated. The first legislative elections ever held in the Congo took place in May 1960, and Parliament met for the first time in the second half of June. The first central government of the Congo, an uneasy partnership of rivals, President Joseph Kasavubu[1]** and Prime Minister Patrice Lumumba,[2] was established on June 24, only a week before independence. When the Congo became independent there was not a single African officer in its army, not one Congolese doctor or engineer, and no experienced Congolese administrators. Only a handful of political leaders had had even the smallest experience of public life. No one in the Congo, African or European, was prepared either emotionally or practically for the consequences of independence, and in the ensuing tragedy no single group or person led or controlled events. All were more or less at sea in a storm of chaos, fear, and mutual recrimination.

In the absence of long-term preparations for independence, much hope had been invested in the signed but unratified Treaty of Friend-

---

* Leopoldville is now Kinshasa. In these chapters the place names given are those in use at the time.
** Biographical notes on personalities in the Congo are given (by footnote number) in the Notes section at the back of the book. They are based on those given in G. Heinz and H. Donnay, *Lumumba—The Last Fifty Days* (New York, 1969).

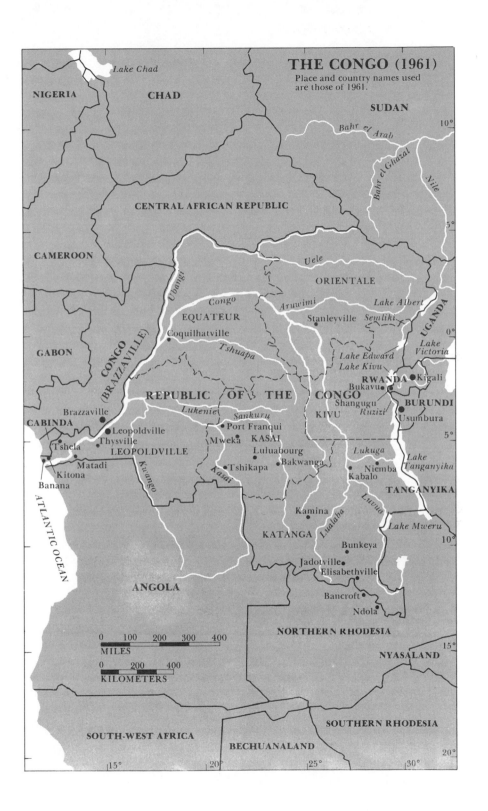

THE CONGO (1961)
Place and country names used
are those of 1961.

NIGERIA   CHAD   *Lake Chad*

SUDAN   10°

CENTRAL AFRICAN REPUBLIC

Bahr el Arab

Bahr el Ghazal

Nile

5°

CAMEROON

Uele

ORIENTALE

Ubangi

Congo   EQUATEUR   *Aruwimi*   Lake Albert

Coquilhatville   Stanleyville   *Semliki*   UGANDA

GABON   *Tshuapa*   Lake Edward   0°

CONGO (BRAZZAVILLE)   Lake Kivu   Lake Victoria

REPUBLIC   OF   THE   CONGO   RWANDA   Kigali

Bukavu

Brazzaville   *Lukenie*   *Sankuru*   KIVU   Shangugu   *Ruzizi*   BURUNDI

CABINDA   Leopoldville   *Port Franqui*   Usumbura   5°

Tshela   Thysville   Mweka   KASAI

LEOPOLDVILLE   Luluabourg   *Lukuga*

Matadi   *Kwango*   *Tshikapa*   Bakwanga   Niemba   Lake Tanganyika

Kitona   *Kasai*   Kabalo

Banana   TANGANYIKA

Luvua

Kamina   *Lualaba*   Lake Mweru   10°

KATANGA   Bunkeya

ANGOLA   Jadotville

Elisabethville

Bancroft

Ndola

ATLANTIC OCEAN

0 100 200 300 400
MILES

0   200   400
KILOMETERS

NORTHERN RHODESIA

NYASALAND   15°

SOUTH-WEST AFRICA   BECHUANALAND

SOUTHERN RHODESIA

20°

15°   20°   25°   30°

ship and Cooperation between Belgium and the Congo, under which much of the Belgian administration and all of its technical personnel were to have stayed on in the Congo after independence. The mainstay of law and order was to be the Force Publique, the Congolese Army of more than 25,000 men, in which the officers were exclusively Belgian. The equation which the commander of the Force Publique, General Emile Janssens, had caused to be inscribed on blackboards in the officers' messes of the Force Publique, *"Avant l'indépendance = Après l'indépendance"*[3] ("Before independence = After independence"), perfectly symbolized the notion that independence would be largely a formality. The emotional, political, racial, and personal frictions and crosscurrents that were soon to destroy forever the dream of a slow and peaceful transition to independence were largely unanticipated.

A note of warning was sounded at the independence ceremonies by the new Prime Minister, Patrice Lumumba, who, in response to a speech in the old paternalistic style from the King of the Belgians, denounced Belgian colonialism in uncompromising terms. "We have known," Lumumba said, "ironies, insults, and blows which we had to undergo morning, noon, and night because we were blacks. Who will forget that blacks were addressed as 'tu,' certainly not as friends, but because the honorable 'vous' was reserved for the whites alone?"[4] Although on the very same day Lumumba went out of his way to be conciliatory at a ceremonial luncheon, the Belgian population of the Congo were given a first inkling of the fiery and volatile nature of the new Prime Minister. More serious developments soon followed.

Ralph Bunche kept Hammarskjold informed of the twists and turns of events in newly independent Leopoldville. The Congo's application for membership[5]* in the UN was accepted by the Security Council on July 7[6] in an atmosphere of harmony that the alarming reports from the country itself were not yet insistent enough to disturb.

From the very beginning, relations between Kasavubu and Lumumba were strained, and Bunche foresaw that the compromise, which had at the last minute made the formation of a Congolese government possible, could at best last only a few months. There was, however, a slim hope that with judicious advice and assistance, the challenge of independence would overcome the temptation of the new leaders to indulge in individual power struggles. The Congo was a vast country with little or no national cohesion or consciousness and

---

* The competition for the name "Republic of the Congo" between the leaders of the ex-French and the ex-Belgian Congos was not resolved until 1971, when the former Belgian Congo became the Republic of Zaïre.

in which loyalties were overwhelmingly tribal, and there were already
alarming undertones of strife and violence. A further warning of things
to come occurred a few days after independence during a talk in
Leopoldville between Bunche and Moise Tshombe,[7] the president of
Katanga Province. Tshombe had shown an unhealthy interest in the
early federal system of the United States. "He seemed only to be
encouraged," Bunche wrote later, "when I protested strongly that the
U.S. Articles of Confederation had failed woefully to work."[8] Tshombe
told Bunche that he favored a loose—and weak—federation in the
Congo rather than the unitary system imposed by the provisional
constitution of the Congo, the Loi Fondamentale.

Hammarskjold had sent Sture Linnér to the Congo in early July as
Resident Technical Assistance Representative, and after the independence ceremonies Linnér held discussions with Lumumba on the
Congo's requirements for UN assistance, but events were soon to dictate a new and unusual aid priority: the maintenance of law and
order. The idea of independence had encouraged many Congolese to
expect immediate and sweeping improvements of their way of life.
This expectation was especially strong in the barracks of Leopoldville
and Thysville among the soldiers of the Force Publique, who were
dissatisfied over the failure of the new government immediately to
Africanize their officer corps and to improve their conditions of service. On July 5 the Leopoldville garrison mutinied and rejected its
Belgian officers. A visit by Lumumba to the main military complex,
Camp Leopold II, during which he promised a one-step promotion for
all and called for discipline, failed to stem the tide of discontent, and
the mutiny soon spread to other towns in the Congo. Belgians were
manhandled by the mutinous soldiers, and there were cases of rape
and other atrocities.

On July 7 the Belgian commander of the Force Publique suggested
that Belgian forces stationed in the great military bases of Kamina
and Kitona should be called in to maintain law and order, but the
Belgian Ambassador refused to sanction such an action. That evening
Congolese soldiers, fully armed, suddenly surged out of their barracks
into the city of Leopoldville. Some went to the airfield in response
to an unfounded rumor that a Soviet aircraft had landed there, while
others searched the hitherto sacrosanct European quarter for weapons. Next morning the soldiers forcibly stopped a panic evacuation of
Europeans across the Congo River to Brazzaville. During the night of
July 7–8 the Belgian Ambassador suggested to Lumumba that Belgium
provide him with military assistance to restore order under the Treaty
of Friendship. Lumumba responded angrily with accusations of various
Belgian plots, including one on his own life. On the morning of the

eighth, Bunche and his staff were ordered out of their rooms in the Stanley Hotel at gunpoint by the mutinous soldiers and spent an uneasy period under military detention in the hotel lobby.

In New York, Hammarskjold temporarily postponed his departure for Geneva to address the Economic and Social Council in order to await Bunche's suggestions on what useful action the UN might take. On July 9, Bunche described the government's total lack of control, the growing African hostility to Belgians and to all Europeans, the disorderliness of the mutinous soldiers, and the imminent paralysis of organized life. Seeing as yet no prospect of useful UN action, Hammarskjold left reluctantly for Geneva. His greatest fear was that European military intervention might become a psychological necessity, causing not only a complete breakdown in African-European relations in the Congo but also serious repercussions in the outside world as well. Events were not slow in justifying his fears.

On July 9, mutinies broke out in Luluabourg and in Elisabethville, where for the first time some Europeans were actually killed by the mutineers, and the next day Belgian airborne troops from the Kamina base intervened in both places to protect the white population. This military intervention was undertaken over the strongly worded objection of Bunche, who clearly foresaw its consequences. Nor was the consent of the Central Government, as required under the Treaty of Friendship, obtained.

The first intimation that the Congolese leaders might seek some kind of military assistance from the United Nations came on July 10 through the US Ambassador, Clare Timberlake, who had been talking with Kasavubu and Lumumba. That same afternoon Bunche attended a meeting of the Congolese Cabinet at which it became clear that the Congolese government urgently wanted help from the UN but had no clear idea either of what was required or what might reasonably be expected. After Bunche had explained in detail the possibilities and limitations of UN military assistance, the government decided to ask the UN for technical assistance of a military nature, including military advisers, experts, and technicians to assist it in developing and strengthening the national army for the twin purposes of national defense and the maintenance of law and order.

In Geneva, Hammarskjold anxiously waited to hear from Bunche whether the Congolese government would formally appeal to the UN for military assistance. On the evening of Sunday, July 10, he called Andrew Cordier in New York and told him to call a meeting of the African group in his office for the afternoon of Tuesday, July 12, with the further possibility of an informal meeting of the Security Council on the following day. At this point in their conversation,

Cordier, who had been trying all day to call Bunche in Leopoldville, announced with some surprise that the call had come through. Through the expertise of Loretta Cowan, the Secretary-General's switchboard operator, Hammarskjold, Bunche, and Cordier in three different continents had a joint discussion. Bunche reported the outcome of the meeting of the Congolese Cabinet, which had decided to ask the UN for "technical assistance in the military field."[9]

Hammarskjold at once decided to return to New York on the evening of the following day, July 11. Later in the evening he called Cordier again to suggest that the terminology be changed so that his discussions with the African group and the Security Council would be on "technical assistance in the field of security administration."[10] This change was also communicated to Bunche so that he could get it included in the official request of the Congo government. On the morning of July 11, Thomas Kanza, the Congolese representative-designate to the UN, told Bunche that the official request would be sent to New York immediately, but for practical reasons it did not reach Hammarskjold until very much later.

After delivering his speech to the Economic and Social Council,[11] Hammarskjold spent July 11 in Geneva impatiently awaiting further word from Bunche. Before leaving for the airport he sat for some time in Piero Spinelli's office, deep in thought. Then, walking to the windows overlooking the park of the Palais des Nations, he began to talk to Spinelli about the future. The Congo operation, he said, would be the most difficult and complex one ever undertaken by the UN, not least because the Security Council would be involved in it from the very beginning. There would be no question of his conceiving and executing the operation himself with his chosen representatives on the spot, as he had been able to do in some of the crises of the Middle East—in Jordan, for instance, with Spinelli. Nor could there be any doubt that the Congo government would soon ask the UN to send troops. A UN force in the violent and unpredictable context of the Congo would inevitably give rise to endless difficulties and controversies. It would be a very difficult, even a dangerous, affair. "I am not optimistic,"[12] he told Spinelli, but it was necessary to put aside such troubled and negative thoughts and to devote all possible energy to organizing whatever UN action might be required in the Congo.

Hammarskjold arrived back in New York late in the evening of Monday, July 11. On the following morning he consulted with the African representatives to the UN[13] on the probable needs of the Congo for assistance of all kinds. He then called José Correa, the permanent representative of Ecuador who was the current President of the Security Council, and asked him to find out if the Council members were willing to meet to hear an oral report from him on the situation in the Congo. The meeting could be either without agenda or with a single item, "Report from the Secretary-General."[14] Correa feared that after the experience with Laos the previous year this might cause a procedural discussion with the Russians, and it was finally agreed that "in the name of the President, at the request of the Secretary-General,"[15] the members be invited to meet in the Secretary-General's office. The Russians were doubtful even about this innovation, and the meeting finally became a luncheon in Hammarskjold's office on July 13.

Meanwhile the crisis in the Congo had taken on a new dimension. On July 11, Moise Tshombe, who had requested Belgian troops to intervene in Elisabethville, announced the secession of Katanga, which he declared to be an independent state. Belgian troops also occupied other major towns in the Congo, and occasional armed clashes between them and the Congolese Army led to a renewal of panic. This panic in turn led to the exodus of much of the Belgian population, including almost all of the administrators and technicians who were to have been put at the disposal of the Congolese government under the Treaty of Friendship. The collapse of law and order was thus compounded by an almost complete breakdown of essential services and economic activity.

Tuesday, July 12, was a day of considerable confusion. Just before noon Hammarskjold learned from Assistant Secretary of State Francis Wilcox in Washington that the Congo government had asked the United States to send troops. He called Secretary of State Christian Herter just before 1 p.m. to inform him of the request to the UN for "technical assistance in the field of security administration"[16] that Bunche had mentioned two days before. Herter said that the United States would under no circumstances respond to the Congolese request for American troops unless the UN endorsed such an action. At about 2 p.m. Hammarskjold received, by commercial cable, a request from Kasavubu and Lumumba for UN military assistance. This request originated in Luluabourg, where Kasavubu and Lumumba, who had wished to go to Katanga, had been taken by their Belgian air crew after being refused permission to land at either Elisabethville or Kamina. It came as a complete surprise to Hammarskjold, since it appeared to supersede both the request for U.S. troops and the request to the UN for technical assistance that Bunche had relayed by telephone. In this new appeal the emphasis was no longer on internal order but on fighting Belgian aggression.

This change had come about because of developments all over the Congo. On the afternoon of July 11, heavy fighting had broken out in the port of Matadi between the Congolese Army and Belgian troops and naval units. This action caused another mutiny in the garrison town of Thysville, where a number of Belgian officers were beaten up and their wives raped. A similar pattern repeated itself in other parts of the country, giving rise to an increasing demand from the remaining European inhabitants for the use of Belgian troops to restore order.

The decision of the Belgian authorities to send troops to Elisabeth-ville, the capital of Katanga, had been interpreted by the central gov-ernment as direct Belgian support for the secession of Katanga. This was the main reason Kasavubu and Lumumba had changed their original appeal for UN assistance to restore the internal situation into a request for the protection of the territory of the Congo from Belgian aggression. If UN assistance was not speedily forthcoming, they cabled Hammarskjold, they would be obliged to appeal to the Bandung Treaty powers.

On the morning of July 13, Belgian paratroops expelled Congolese troops by force from the main airport of Leopoldville and occupied the European areas of the town, in which the Government and Parlia-ment buildings were situated. News of this action created new tensions throughout the Congo, and Lumumba informed Bunche that Ghana had been asked for military assistance pending the arrival of a UN force. These developments forced Hammarskjold to conclude that an immediate and conspicuous military intervention by the UN was the only hope of getting the Belgian troops out and of avoiding both a complete breakdown of public order and administration and the risk of various forms of outside intervention. A further cable from Kasa-vubu and Lumumba clarifying their request for military assistance only served to fortify this conclusion, and on that morning, July 13, Hammarskjold decided to ask immediately for a Security Council meeting under Article 99, which had never formally been invoked for this purpose before. He therefore informed Correa in writing that he had "to bring to the attention of the Security Council a matter which, in my opinion, may threaten the maintenance of international peace and security"[17] and requested him to call a meeting of the Council for 8:30 that night. He also informed Lodge and asked G. P. Arkadiev, the Soviet Under-Secretary, to explain to Sobolev the new developments that had caused him to take this action.

When the members of the Security Council arrived for lunch on July 13, Hammarskjold urged them to accept his suggestion for a meeting that very night. After luncheon their advisers were called in, and he gave a long presentation of the Congo situation. He made three main proposals for UN action: technical assistance in the field of security administration, the introduction of UN troops, and the shipment of emergency food supplies. The Council members, having no instructions, merely asked a few questions. No one opposed Hammarskjold's ideas, and even when he raised the problem of financing none of the members seemed to think that it would present any insuperable difficulty.

During the afternoon Hammarskjold worked over his formal statement to the Security Council. He also called Henry Labouisse, who was working for the World Bank in Washington, and asked him to come up and help. "How soon should I arrive?" Labouisse asked. "This afternoon at the latest,"[18] Hammarskjold replied. At 7 p.m. Kwame Nkrumah called from Accra to say that, in response to the request of the Congo government, two Ghanaian battalions were available for service in the Congo, and he asked Hammarskjold to get air transport for them as soon as possible.

The Security Council, which met at 8:30 on the hot, humid evening of July 13, attracted world-wide attention and even competed successfully for television coverage with the U.S. Democratic Convention, which was then under way in Los Angeles. The violence in the Congo, with its strident racial overtones, the recent appeals for help from Kasavubu and Lumumba, the strange and new character of the Congolese problem, and the secession of Katanga with its fabulous mineral wealth, had all contributed to the drama of the occasion, as had Hammarskjold's formal use, for the first time in the history of the United Nations, of Article 99 of the Charter to convene the Security Council.

In his opening statement,[19] Hammarskjold outlined his proposals for meeting the Congolese Government's request for assistance. Quite apart from the maintenance of order and the protection of life, the Congo's difficulties were of a nature that could not be disregarded by other countries. His reaction to Kasavubu's and Lumumba's requests[20] for help was emphatically positive because the only lasting solution to the Congo problem would be to create conditions in which the government could become capable of taking care of the situation itself. His idea, therefore, was to provide assistance during the intermediate period when the government might find it difficult to operate efficiently, or even at all, in the field of public security.

The activities of the Belgian troops in the Congo, whatever the reasons for them, unquestionably constituted a source of internal, and potentially also of international, tension. Their presence could in no sense be regarded as a suitable stopgap arrangement for reestablishing order, an objective that could best be achieved by the UN providing military assistance to the government. If this could be done, it was to be assumed that the Belgian government would see its way to withdrawing the Belgian troops.

Hammarskjold proposed that the composition and method of operation of the UN force should be based on the principles and conclusions drawn from previous experience. Its main elements would be contingents from African states, and in no circumstances would its operational units be provided by any of the permanent members of the Security Council. If the Council approved his plan, he undertook to move in token groups of soldiers at the earliest possible minute, although there would inevitably be a few days' delay in assembling any sizable military force. He concluded his statement by urging the Council to act with the utmost speed that very night, so that initial practical steps could be taken to meet the crisis.

The Council meeting went on through the night, and when delays seemed inevitable it was Hammarskjold who argued for immediate action. At one point, speaking against a proposal to delay the meeting until a representative from the Congo could be present, he said, "It cannot be a question of a delay of a few hours; it is a question of a delay of a few days and I would say, in all seriousness, that we have not got them."[21]

The Council debate centered on a Soviet draft resolution[22] condemning Belgian armed aggression in the Congo and a milder resolution proposed by Mongi Slim of Tunisia,[23] which merely called upon Belgium to withdraw its troops and authorized the Secretary-General to provide the Congo government "with such military assistance as may be necessary until through the efforts of the Congolese Government with the technical assistance of the United Nations, the national security forces may be able, in the opinion of the Government, to meet fully their tasks."[24] If the Tunisian resolution should run into opposition, Hammarskjold was prepared to propose a short resolution simply putting UN troops into the Congo; if this also failed, he was ready to take steps to ensure that the question was transferred to an emergency session of the General Assembly, where there would be no doubt of a majority vote in favor of action. As it turned out, the Tunisian resolution proved tough enough not to be vetoed by the U.S.S.R. and mild enough not to be vetoed by Belgium's allies France, Great Britain, and the United States. It was the first of many occasions during the Congo crisis when Mongi Slim's wisdom and powers of persuasion effectively bridged a dangerous gap. The resolution was adopted with no votes in opposition and with only China, France, and Great Britain abstaining, the last on the grounds that, with the Suez precedent in mind, it could not vote for a plan which would allow for an interval between the departure of Belgian troops and the arrival of the UN force. The Council adjourned at 3:25 a.m. on July 14.

Hammarskjold went immediately to his office on the thirty-eighth floor to put in train the series of arrangements that would give reality to the Council's decision. He consulted Slim on how best to approach the African governments for the provision of troops and addressed a message to them all, sending an immediate appeal for troops only to Ghana and to the French-speaking countries. He had in mind Guinea, Mali, Morocco, and Tunisia, all French-speaking countries, as the first governments to provide troops, and told Bunche to clear the acceptability of all these units with the Congo government. In the next three hours the necessary messages were sent, while Great Britain, the United States, and the U.S.S.R. were requested to provide transport aircraft for an immediate airlift of the troops. In another room, which Hammarskjold visited from time to time, administrative arrangements were being made to dispatch staff, to establish a staging area at Kano in Nigeria, and to set up the headquarters in Leopoldville. He also chose a name for the operation, ONUC, the initials of Organisation des Nations Unies au Congo—later changed to Opération des Nations Unies au Congo.* He also decided to appoint the Swedish general Carl von Horn, then chief of staff of UNTSO, who had already been warned to hold himself in readiness, as commander of the new operation. By 6:30 on July 14, when Hammarskjold and his staff went out into the moist morning air for breakfast and a shave, the UN operation in the Congo was under way. Harold Beeley, who was called in at 11 a.m. to get British clearance for the use of Kano airfield in Nigeria as a UN staging area, was astonished that Hammarskjold, who appeared as fresh as ever, had mounted the entire operation since 3:30 that morning and had also found time before receiving Beeley to discuss the UN presence in Southeast Asia with Thanat Khoman, the Foreign Minister of Thailand.

The decision of the Security Council had imposed a sudden and crushing additional burden upon the UN Secretariat and upon the Secretary-General. The Secretariat bears only a superficial resemblance to the civil service of a government, and its lack of great civilian or military establishments and of the normal resources of a government was highlighted more harshly than ever by the size and complexity of

---

* The acronyms of UN operations are a favorite source of tired jokes, as if they were some form of willful caprice of the Organization. The fact is that efficiency of communication demands a one-word title that not only describes an operation but is also easily pronounceable. Hence Hammarskjold's interest in this apparently minor detail.

the Congo problem.* In the first stages of the operation, however, the UN's dependence for practical support on the good will and cooperation of governments was offset by the general enthusiasm, and it was revealed sharply only later, when a wide divergence of views developed among the supporting governments. The nature and the demands of the Congo situation were still largely unknown when the decision was taken to launch the operation, but it was already obvious that its every aspect would have delicate political implications. The operation therefore had to be kept under close and detailed control by the one person to whom the Security Council had given authority, the Secretary-General himself.

To launch, without preparation or planning, an emergency multinational military expedition with a large civilian component into a vast and little-known tropical country six thousand miles away was a tremendous challenge to the ingenuity of Hammarskjold and the Secretariat, and their problems were complicated by other factors peculiar to the Congo. Although there was no well-established governmental authority to deal with, it was essential at every step to maintain the cooperation of the inexperienced Congolese leaders with the UN action and to conduct the operation in such a way that they would not feel that it was some kind of new colonial tutelage.** It was also vital to maintain the support of the members of the UN, and especially of the Security Council. The decision of the Council to authorize the Secretary-General to go ahead—taken overnight in the face of a desperate situation—had to some extent blurred the reservations and

---

* An example of the UN's practical limitations involved getting General von Horn to Leopoldville. The SAS plane that had been immediately chartered for this purpose turned out to be both unsuitable and unserviceable, and when a U.S. C-130 was finally made available, it was delayed by engine trouble at Wheelus Base in Libya. Thus von Horn did not arrive in Leopoldville until July 17. This delay of almost three days, apart from its effect on the General's temper, created another complication. On July 15, Hammarskjold read an Associated Press dispatch from Leopoldville reporting that General H. T. Alexander, the courageous British chief of staff of the Ghana Army, was exercising the functions of UN Commander in Leopoldville and had said that the Congo Army had "laid down its arms in the Leopoldville area" and that he would act as UN commander until von Horn arrived. The unsuitability of Alexander's nationality and his obviously mistaken view of the UN role in the Congo caused Hammarskjold to send a top-priority cable through several channels appointing Bunche immediately as commander of the force until von Horn arrived. Alexander's idiosyncratic view of the Congo operation seems to have persisted. In his book he writes: "I can remember the late Dag Hammarskjold telling me that it was a political, not a military problem in the Congo. How wrong he was."[25]
** The UN was a total novelty to the Congolese. Already on July 10, Bunche had to explain to Lumumba that the UN would not be in the Congo to fight anyone; and a district administrator in Thysville had asked him, *"L'ONU, c'est quelle tribu?"*[26] ("The UN, what tribe is that?")

anxieties of many governments about a quite unprecedented UN action.

Apart from these difficulties, there were the practical problems involved in raising a military force of as yet unknown size from a number of yet unspecified countries, transporting it, equipping it, organizing it, and then deploying it, commanding it, and supporting it in a task the very nature of which was still obscure.

Bunche's small staff in Leopoldville was rapidly reinforced from Headquarters. Sture Linnér, who had been formally appointed Resident Representative for UN technical assistance on July 12, became chief of ONUC Civilian Operations. The force commander, Carl von Horn, arrived from Jerusalem on July 17. Bunche, as Special Representative of the Secretary-General, was the overall chief of the entire operation. Others were brought in as needed. Maurice Pate, the executive director of UNICEF, arrived to set up an emergency food program. Lieutenant General R. A. Wheeler, who had directed the clearance of the Suez Canal in 1956–7, was enlisted to clear the port of Matadi and to advise on other practical engineering problems. Galo Plaza, the ex-President of Ecuador who had served on the UN Observation Group in Lebanon, came out to study the problem of what to do with the vast military bases at Kamina and Kitona.

Hammarskjold's appeal for troops to the heads of all independent African states was in line with the view he had already expressed in the Security Council that the operation should be mainly a manifestation of the willingness and ability of African nations to help a sister state within the framework of the UN. Troops from other regions and specialized personnel for logistics, air transport and communications would be asked for as necessary. The first contingents from Ethiopia, Ghana, Morocco, and Tunisia began arriving in the Congo in a miraculously short time. Slim had called Bourguiba from Hammarskjold's office at 4 a.m. on July 14 and was told that the troops would be waiting on the Tunis airfield from five that very morning. The first Tunisian troops arrived by U.S. military air-transport aircraft in Leopoldville during the evening of July 15. They were quickly followed by the Ghanaians in British and Soviet transport aircraft. More troops from Tunisia, Morocco, and Ethiopia were picked up by U.S. transport aircraft on July 16 and began to arrive in Leopoldville on the evening of the seventeenth. The lack of reception facilities and other arrangements made it necessary to stagger the arrival of later contingents until the requisite logistical support could be improvised.

The first objective was to establish a UN presence in as many of the disturbed areas in the Congo as possible, if necessary even before the commander's headquarters staff was set up or logistic arrangements had been made. By July 18, when Hammarskjold made his first report[27] to the Security Council, about 3,500 troops from four countries had arrived in Leopoldville and had been deployed around the Congo. It was already obvious that the situation would require a much larger force, four battalions being required in Leopoldville alone. It was also apparent that if the remaining Europeans, who were vital to the day-to-day economic and administrative life of the Congo, were to be persuaded to stay, it would be necessary to include at least one non-African continent in the UN force. After explaining this to Arkady Sobolev, who had strongly urged that only African troops be used, Hammarskjold decided temporarily to move the UNEF Swedish battalion in Gaza to the Congo. On July 20 the government of Ireland agreed to send a battalion, which soon arrived in Leopoldville, bagpipes and all, good-humoredly sweating in its nontropical clothing, and was immediately flown into the eastern province of Kivu.

Since the Congo situation was quite unlike anything that had occurred before, there was no precise immediate directive as to the method of operation of the UN force. ONUC's initial function in the Congo was threefold: to remove the threat to international peace and security by effecting the withdrawal of Belgian troops from the entire territory of the Congo; to assist the government in restoring and maintaining law and order, a task that included the training and reorganizing of the mutinous Force Publique, now rechristened the Armée Nationale Congolaise (ANC); and to assure the continuation of essential services, to restore and organize the administrative machinery of government, and to train the Congolese to run that machinery. To put it briefly, the UN operation was to fill a vacuum that would probably otherwise be filled by the conflicting forces and influences of East and West, and by a variety of racial, economic, ideological, political, and tribal conflicts as well.

The leaders and people of the Congo could be expected to be intensely sensitive to anything that smelled of paternalism or foreign interference. Thus the UN had to provide the maximum assistance while giving the minimum impression of domination or take-over. The UN force itself would be composed of contingents from a number of countries whose governments might at any time develop views or involvements that would not coincide with UN policy or would conflict with Hammarskjold's daily decisions on particular problems. The force, operating on an entirely improvised basis, was made up of contingents of national armies that had never worked together before. They would be commanded and controlled by a commander they had never seen and by a staff that did not yet exist, in a situation about which there was virtually no reliable information at all.

The Congo crisis had aroused strong emotions in the world at large as well as in the country itself. By July 18 some twenty-five thousand Belgians had fled, and their accounts of their experiences had created, especially in Europe, grave resentments and fears that would inevitably influence interpretations of future events. Stories of rape and violence, considerably exaggerated in the world press, had had a particularly emotive effect. Strong racial overtones were already inherent in the situation, and no amount of idealism, sincerity, or disinterestedness would keep the UN operation immune from them.

Hammarskjold had devoted much thought to the principles upon which the Congo operation should be carried out, and throughout the hectic weeks that followed he did not cease to elaborate, largely for his own guidance, a firm basis in principle for all of the variety of actions that had to be taken. He also went back again and again to the Security Council for endorsement of the basis for his actions. His brief acquaintance with the new African leaders and his desire to help them were no preparation for the kind of difficulties, especially with the Congolese leaders, that he was to experience repeatedly in the succeeding months. To give the maximum possible assistance to the government of the Congo and at the same time to stay within the political realities of the UN, to remain afloat amidst all the crosscurrents and conflicting interests that were soon to emerge in the Congo, was a task of enormous complexity. All too soon every move would be questioned, every action criticized, and every failure to act regarded as a gross dereliction of duty by one or other of the UN member governments or of the factions in the Congo. The simplest actions would be misinterpreted, and a choice would have to be made daily between acting in almost impossible conditions or not acting at all. A firm grasp of basic principles, and a determination to stick to them, would be the best—perhaps the only—hope of ultimate success.

The terms of the original Security Council resolution on the Congo were clear in one respect only, namely that the Secretary-General had the responsibility for doing something about the Congo crisis. Precisely what, the resolution did not and could not say. It gave, for example, no time limit for the Belgian withdrawal and no description of what "military assistance"[28] was supposed to mean. It made no mention of Katanga and no reference to the maintenance of the territorial integrity of the Congo, an omission remedied on July 22.[29] In this expedient vagueness, which had for the time being papered over the real differences among the members of the Council, lay the seeds of many future problems. Moreover, in directing the Secretary-General to eliminate any justification for foreign intervention by restoring law and order, as far as possible with the help of the Congo government but without using force or interfering in internal affairs, the Council from the start injected an inherent contradiction into the Congo operation.

The principles on which the operation would be based had been outlined by Hammarskjold in his first statement to the Council,[30] and he expanded upon them in his first report to the Council on July 18.[31] The force might never use its weapons except in self-defense and might take no action that would make it a party to internal conflicts. It was in the Congo to assist the Congolese government, at its request, and to restore and maintain order and law, the absence of which, combined with the Belgian intervention, was a threat to international peace. It would make it possible for the Belgian government to "see its way to a withdrawal."[32] It would at all times be under the exclusive command of the UN and not under the orders of the Congolese government. It should enjoy freedom of movement throughout the entire territory of the Congo.

All these principles were to be tried severely in the months to come, and their application, or allegations of their nonapplication, would be the subject of increasingly violent criticism from widely different quarters. A basic agreement with the Congo government[33] embodying these principles was initialed on July 27, but no amount of legal drafting could protect the Secretary-General and his representatives in the Congo from relentless and conflicting pressures to take action or to refrain from action, according to the views and preferences of whatever party happened to be giving the advice.

The first prerequisite to reestablishing some degree of public confidence throughout the country was to secure the withdrawal of the Belgian forces, whose paratroops had intervened by July 18 in twenty-three different places in the Congo. The Belgian government originally claimed that its troops should remain in the Congo until the UN force was in a position to maintain order effectively. This aim, while understandable enough from the point of view of the European inhabitants of the Congo, whose frantic appeals for Belgian military intervention continued to arrive from all over the country almost hourly at European embassies in Leopoldville, soon became a primary source of suspicion and resentment among the Congolese and in turn led to a deep suspicion and fear of whites in general on the part of the Congolese population.

On July 14, there were some ten thousand Belgian soldiers in the Congo. By July 16, UN soldiers had replaced Belgian detachments in the European sector of Leopoldville and were progressively taking over in other main centers. The Belgian troops' activities and the humiliations that Kasavubu, Lumumba, and other Ministers had suffered at their hands, soon became an obsession with the new government, and on July 18 Lumumba presented Bunche with the first of a series of ultimatums, in which he declared that if all Belgian forces were not withdrawn within forty-eight hours the government would appeal for aid elsewhere, specifically to the Soviet Union. Two days later in Stanleyville, Lumumba told General Alexander that the UN's delay in expelling the Belgian forces was an "imperialist trick"[34] and repeated his ultimatum. Bunche took the only realistic course, namely to go ahead with the speediest possible deployment of UN troops and to put constant pressure on the Belgians to withdraw at the earliest possible moment.

In New York, Hammarskjold also was subject to conflicting pressures. The Belgian permanent representative urged delaying the Belgian withdrawal, while V. V. Kuznetsov and Anatoly Dobrynin, when they visited Hammarskjold on the afternoon of July 18, insisted that a fixed date for the Belgian withdrawal should be set, for example "within three days."[35] Hammarskjold replied that he could not take responsibility for such a decision, since the decisive point was whether or not human lives could be properly protected. He would not, he said, support a withdrawal of Belgian troops from any point unless ONUC headquarters in Leopoldville was prepared to assume responsibility for security. The next day Sobolev protested the presence at the Leopoldville airfield of twenty U.S. Air Force personnel, who were, in fact, the indispensable administrative end of the troop and food airlift. When Hammarskjold explained this the meeting ended with a general laugh, but the cold-war thunder, though still distant, was already distinctly audible.*

Hammarskjold quickly sensed the impending change in the political climate. When the Belgians, with Bunche's support, asked for U.S. planes to take the Belgian troops out of Leopoldville to one of the Belgian bases in the Congo, he flatly opposed the request for this U.S. involvement in view "of the heavy cold war aspect which the whole operation was on the verge of taking on."[37] He suggested instead that the Belgian troops should be flown in Sabena (Belgian) planes chartered for refugees and that the U.S. planes should carry the refugees. The Belgian government agreed to this, and Hammarskjold enlisted Lodge's support in putting the complicated plan into effect. He was also adamant against various delays in the withdrawal plan proposed by the Belgian government.

---

* The first distant rumble had been heard as early as July 13, in the first Security Council meeting on the Congo, when Sobolev had charged that the U.S. Ambassador in the Congo was using Bunche to develop plans for the intervention of the Western powers in the Congo.[36]

On July 20, prior to another meeting of the Security Council, Hammarskjold persuaded the Congo representative to the Security Council, Thomas Kanza,[38] to take a realistic view on the Belgian withdrawal. The Belgian Foreign Minister, Pierre Wigny, although praising the UN action in general, was unhappy about Hammarskjold's insistence on immediate Belgian withdrawal and especially about his demand for the withdrawal of Belgian troops from Katanga. One hour before the Council meeting was due to start Lumumba requested a postponement of the session so that he could attend it in person. Lumumba evidently felt that it was time to make his debut on the international scene before the Organization which he had summoned to his assistance, and he also may have felt a strong desire to escape for a few days from the frustrations and confusions of Leopoldville.

The Security Council met, despite Lumumba's request for a delay, on July 20–22, in three sessions marked by violent interchanges between Wigny and Kanza. The Council again called urgently upon Belgium to withdraw its troops, authorizing the Secretary-General to take all necessary action to that effect.[39] No member of the Council challenged any part of Hammarskjold's detailed interpretation of the status and functions of the UN force, and the American and Soviet attitudes were still not far apart. "Each," a historian later wrote, "was prepared to back the Organization if the other did not seem to be gaining too obviously from its decision."[40]

Hammarskjold himself was in no doubt of the potential dangers of the situation. "There should not be any hesitation," he told the Council,[41] "because we are at a turn of the road where our attitude will be of decisive significance, I believe, not only for the future of this Organization but also for the future of Africa. And Africa may well in present circumstances mean the world. I know these are very strong words, but I hope that this Council and the Members of this Organization know that I do not use strong words unless they are supported by strong convictions."[42]

He asked the representatives of the African states contributing troops to attempt to explain to Lumumba that his violent criticisms, ultimatums, and threats could only complicate the position of all African states as well as endangering the UN operation, which had started so well. The Congo must make the choice between African solidarity and the cold war, or to put it more generally, it must choose between assistance from the UN and dependence upon one or other of the superpowers.

On the morning of July 20, Lumumba repeated over the radio his ultimatum on the withdrawal of Belgian troops and his threat to seek help elsewhere. On the same day he asked for UN troops to replace

Congolese soldiers at the Parliament Building on the grounds that the latter were involved in sinister plots, including one to assassinate Lumumba himself. On July 22 he decided to come to New York. Hammarskjold had intended to leave New York on July 23 and to stop off in Leopoldville for a few days on his way to South Africa, where he was due to discuss the problem of apartheid, but he decided to postpone his departure until July 26 so that he would have at least three days to talk to Lumumba. The Security Council resolution of July 22[43] had temporarily allayed the impatience of the Congolese authorities, and it seemed possible that Lumumba's absence from the Congo would give the UN operation a short respite from ultimatums and threats, during which it could concentrate on expediting both the Belgian withdrawal and its own deployment.

Lumumba, accompanied by a large party, arrived in New York on July 24. He was in a conciliatory mood, and the African ambassadors in New York, led by Slim of Tunisia and Alex Quaison-Sackey of Ghana, were anxious that he should get along well with Hammarskjold. The latter had, nonetheless, to be patient and firm on a number of points, including unrealistic expectations as to the timetable of UN deployment, Belgian withdrawal, and Lumumba's threats to use the Congolese Army for military enterprises. On July 25, Hammarskjold gave a lunch for Lumumba and the members of the Security Council, at which the Prime Minister was at his most moderate and persuasive. Hammarskjold left for Leopoldville on July 26.

When, after visiting Washington and Ottawa, where he was informed that all aid to the Congo should be channeled through the UN, Lumumba returned to New York, his mood had changed and he complained of the slowness of the Belgian withdrawal, of the failure to dispatch UN troops to Katanga, and of the alleged disarming of Congolese troops by the UN force. In a meeting with .Cordier on August 1, he was at first curt and irritable, and made a thinly veiled attack on Hammarskjold's impartiality, alleging that he had fallen in with the wishes of the Belgians that the UN should not intervene in Katanga and had sided with Belgium against the Congo. Cordier told him that in Brussels the Secretary-General was believed to be strongly biased in favor of the Congolese position. Such reactions were only natural; to be blamed by both sides in a conflict was the traditional fate of the Secretary-General of the UN. He also explained that the UN was obliged to get into Katanga by negotiation, not by force. Lumumba left New York on August 2 and visited London, Tunisia, Morocco, Guinea, Ghana, Liberia, and Togo before returning to Leopoldville.

Hammarskjold was determined, if possible, to carry the Belgians with him in implementing the decisions of the Security Council, and with this end in view he stopped in Brussels on his way to Leopold-ville. The Congo situation presented a serious dilemma for the Belgian government, for while Belgian public opinion demanded that it maintain and use its military power in the Congo, every use of that power and every delay in its withdrawal only served to increase the hostility and resentment of the Congolese. Hammarskjold's insistence that the Security Council resolution[44] required the withdrawal of Belgian troops from the whole territory of the Congo, including the military bases and Katanga, had been a severe shock to the Belgian authorities. One of the Belgian generals in Leopoldville had told Bunche that if the UN forced the Belgian troops to leave the bases there would be a revolution in Belgium, while another said it would take three years to evacuate them. Brussels claimed that the Belgian forces were present in Katanga "at the request of the government."[45] Hammarskjold's most pressing task was to convince the Belgian government that both the future of the Congo and the preservation of Security Council support for the UN operation demanded the total and immediate withdrawal of all Belgian troops.

As the Belgian forces withdrew from other parts of the Congo, the Katanga problem took on an increasing importance. Apart from Katanga's extraordinary wealth and its importance to the Congolese economy, there had been a traditional rivalry between Leopoldville and the Katangese capital, Elisabethville. It was thus doubly intolerable for the central government to see Katanga setting itself up as a separate state with the connivance of the Belgians and with the apparent sympathy of much of the Western world, which had large financial interests in its phenomenal resources. Whatever the intentions of the Belgian government, Belgian troops had in fact made Tshombe's secession possible, for it was they who had disarmed the Congolese Army units in Katanga that were loyal to Leopoldville, and Belgian officers and civilian advisers soon became the mainstay of Tshombe's régime.

FROM THE OUTSET, Hammarskjold had declined to give any recognition to Katanga's secession or independence. On July 14, Tshombe had urged him to come to Elisabethville to see for himself that peace, order, and legality reigned in Katanga, and had sought to justify the presence of Belgian troops and the secession of the province. Hammarskjold had replied firmly that the structure of Congolese independence was established by the Loi Fondamentale, to which all

Congolese leaders, including Tshombe, had agreed. The Congo government had also concluded a Treaty of Friendship and Assistance with Belgium.* The UN had admitted the Congo to membership as a single territorial entity on July 7, and on July 14 the Security Council had decided to give assistance to the Congo Government. These four juridical actions, which envisaged the Congo as a single territory, were binding on the Secretary-General and formed the basis of his actions over the Congo. The right of self-determination described in the Charter and in the Universal Declaration of Human Rights did not outweigh national constitutions, and a secession could only take place according to forms prescribed in the Constitution. Lumumba was delighted when Bunche showed him this exchange.

On July 26 Hammarskjold asked Bunche and von Horn how soon they would be in a position to put troops into Katanga without weakening UN deployment elsewhere. As soon as he had their answer he proposed to inform the Belgian government, and perhaps Tshombe as well, of the date on which the UN planned to enter Katanga. The earliest possible date given by Bunche and von Horn was the weekend of July 30–31, provided sufficient aircraft were available.

During Hammarskjold's talks in Brussels on July 27, the Belgians questioned whether the Security Council resolution was clear in demanding their withdrawal from Katanga and insisted that the UN's arrival in Katanga would cause a full-scale exodus of the European population. This would not necessarily be because of distrust of the UN but because the UN's arrival would indicate a take-over by Lumumba. The Belgian authorities also insisted that any moves must be preceded by contact with Tshombe and perhaps with the representatives of the European population as well. Since the UN had neither the right nor the military potential to enter Katanga by force, Hammarskjold, for purely practical reasons, was also privately convinced that every possible effort had to be made to ensure a peaceful entry and to avoid a breakdown of economic life in Katanga. In Brussels, however, he insisted on the legal case for UN action and stressed the international implications and the political risks for Belgium as well as for the UN if a speedy Belgian withdrawal from Katanga did not take place.

Hammarskjold arrived in the Congo via Brazzaville** on July 28. His arrival was not without that note of *opéra bouffe* that so often char-

---

* The treaty was never ratified.
** He had not wished to arrive by Sabena, the Belgian airline which was the only airline then flying into Leopoldville, and had therefore taken a KLM flight to Brazzaville.

acterized Congolese events at the time. Bunche had arranged for a ferryboat to bring him from the pier in Brazzaville across the Congo River to the landing beach in Leopoldville, but he had not reckoned with the guile and superior footwork of the President of Congo-Brazzaville, the Abbé Fulbert Youlou. The Abbé, resplendent in a white silk soutane, greeted the Secretary-General at the Brazzaville airport and then sidetracked him onto his own much faster launch, which easily outdistanced the slow-moving UN ferryboat. Hammar-skjold thus arrived at the Leopoldville beach some twenty minutes ahead of schedule and of the welcoming party of Congolese Ministers and UN officials, who had come to meet him on the ferry. The guard of honor of Swedish and Ghana troops was quickly called on parade, and Hammarskjold, looking somewhat irritable after his experiences with Youlou, inspected them before driving to the ONUC head-quarters.

The physical, psychological, and emotional reality of the Congo situation was in bewildering contrast to the staid proceedings of the Security Council or the civilities of ordinary diplomatic life. This was Hammarskjold's first direct experience not only of the confused and emotional state of mind of the Congolese leaders but also of the improvised conditions of the UN operation itself and the shortcomings of a great enterprise undertaken at a moment's notice and under severe political limitations. During his stay in Leopoldville, Hammar-skjold lived and worked, as most of the ONUC staff did, in the apartment building that housed the UN Congo headquarters. The build-ing, which had been chosen for want of anything better, was quite unsuited to its new function. The small size and mechanical caprices of its elevators alone were enough to account for any amount of con-fusion and delay, and the telephone system was equally inadequate. Most of the staff worked in one or two large rooms where the only available telephones were located, the disadvantages of this arrange-ment being to some extent balanced by the fact that all information and most decisions were instantly shared. Communications to other points in the Congo were still spasmodic at best. The only two sources of food were military field rations and a Greek restaurant that had survived on the ground floor of the building. The whole staff normally ate together and worked as it ate. Hammarskjold vastly enjoyed these informal arrangements.

Hammarskjold intended to use his time in the Congo to explain the possibilities and the limitations of the UN and to enlist, if possible, the full support of the government for his efforts. Above all, he was anxious to instill a sense of reality and a modicum of patience. The proceedings of the Cabinet of the Congo and its Council of Ministers at this stage were also refreshingly unusual.* His first formal meeting with the government was presided over, in the absence of Lumumba, by Vice-Prime Minister Antoine Gizenga,[46] who soon proved to have many of the more distracting qualities of the Prime Minister with few of his redeeming virtues. The meeting started an hour late for no particular reason and took place in the presence of the press corps, who, to Hammarskjold's surprise, were suddenly revealed by the drawing of a curtain.

The objectives of the UN in the Congo, he told the government, had to be realized in a manner and according to a timetable that would cause the least disturbance of public order and economic life in the country. The Belgian withdrawal might be the present problem, but the real problem for the future would be the internal political settlement of the country, and in that process the UN could not interfere. While leaving the Cabinet in no doubt on his own position on Katanga, Hammarskjold explained the problem presented for the UN, which could not use force and had to stay out of the internal politics of the country. Moreover, the preservation of the economic life of Katanga was vital to the country as a whole, and this meant that the attitude of the Europeans of Katanga had to be considered.

The obvious obsession of the Central Government with the Katanga question made such an impression on Hammarskjold that he immediately sent an urgent new appeal to the Belgian Foreign Minister. "I did not believe," he began, "that we were in any way around the corner, but I must confess that I had not fully realized the continuing deep seriousness of the situation. It may still easily trigger a major conflict."[47] Hope for peaceful settlement now depended on the Belgian government's declaring that it would withdraw its troops from Katanga as soon as the UN troops arrived. As soon as this declaration was made, Hammarskjold would make arrangements for a peaceful entry of the UN force into Katanga and for the security of the Europeans there.

Behind a façade of pleasant official occasions, the pressure from the Congolese side on the Katanga issue steadily mounted. On the evening of July 31, Gizenga gave a reception in the Secretary-General's honor in the low hills outside Leopoldville at a restaurant called La Devinière. To music by the band of the Congolese National Army in full ceremonial uniform, members of the government, the diplomatic corps, the UN mission, and the press talked and drank in an atmos-

---

* Lumumba's first government consisted of twenty-seven Ministers, including representatives of virtually all political groups; ten Secretaries of State with ambassador's rank were also appointed to various ministries.

phere of seeming cordiality, until Gizenga suddenly asked for silence. He then delivered a long speech, of which mimeographed copies were eagerly distributed among the bewildered guests. This surprise maneuver left the guest of honor standing awkwardly, glass in hand, beside his host, who proceeded to berate him and the UN in the most exaggerated terms. He could not understand, Gizenga said, why the Congolese people, who had appealed to the UN, had been systematically and methodically disarmed, while the Belgian aggressors, acting as if they were in a conquered country, still kept their arms. The UN force was allowing the secessionist regime to consolidate itself because of the incomprehensible delay of its departure for Katanga. The Congo government demanded the unrestricted implementation of the Security Council resolutions, and was confident that the Secretary-General would meet this demand.

Gizenga's accusations, especially in regard to the Belgian forces and the disarmament of the Congolese Army by the UN, were gross distortions, but in this public gathering Hammarskjold decided to answer them indirectly and in a more than usually oblique manner.[48] In this charming place, he said, he felt that he was very far from the Security Council, but all the same he permitted himself for a moment to talk about the ends and principles of the UN. The phrase "peace with justice,"[49] so often used in the UN, might this evening be reversed to read "justice with peace,"[50] and he hoped the significance of this change of order would not be lost on his audience. History must not be allowed to enslave people, for the future was what was important. The happiest people were those who had the courage to get rid, not of their great national memories, but of their resentments and their bad memories. The essential thing was to try to be as creative as possible and to build something new based on human values that existed everywhere. He had come to Leopoldville to discuss the assistance the UN might give the Congo in this creative process. The UN was an organization for peace and for justice with peace. "Do not expect from us action," he concluded, "which might jeopardize the future happiness of those we wish to help. . . . We shall not . . . act in a manner which goes against our convictions, which were based on thorough study of the problems of the country and its people, and which were guided by the views expressed by their representatives. We will not abandon a line of action which, in our eyes, tries to meet our responsibilities toward the community of nations and toward the peoples whom we serve."[51] Gizenga's guests, somewhat bemused, dispersed quietly.

Hammarskjold's plan for urgent action in Katanga envisaged an approach that would enable the UN at the same time to continue to neutralize the Congo crisis, to achieve the peaceful entry of UN troops into Katanga, and to provide some reasonable hope of preserving law, order, and economic life in Katanga itself. Negotiations in Elisabethville and a firm declaration of Belgian intentions were essential to this plan. He therefore planned to send Bunche to Elisabethville, while he himself would accompany one or two of the Congolese Ministers on short visits to the presidents of other provinces to avoid the appearance of giving preferential treatment to Tshombe. As soon as arrangements were made in Katanga, he would himself go to Elisabethville. Hammarskjold fully realized the extreme delicacy and difficulty of this plan, but nothing else seemed likely to succeed. He was already hampered by the unanimous view of the Congolese Cabinet that he could not negotiate with Tshombe except in the presence of members of the central government, whose very arrival in Elisabethville would certainly provoke violent opposition and a total breakdown of law and order. The diplomatic and political complications and the risks experienced in previous UN operations, he told Cordier, had been nothing compared to this.

Hammarskjold's apprehensions were well founded. Until the end of July the UN operation in the Congo, and his leadership of it, had been generally regarded with admiration and approval. In the face of fantastic complications and difficulties, ONUC had seemed to be moving steadily and miraculously toward a successful fulfillment of the Council's resolutions. The world press was full of praise. Walter Lippmann wrote of the invaluable role of the UN "as it is now administered with the genius of Mr. Dag Hammarskjold" and continued, "This UN enterprise is the most advanced and the most sophisticated experiment in international cooperation ever attempted. Among all that is so sad and so mean and so sour in world politics, it is heartening to think that something so good and so pure in its purpose is possible. No one can say that the experiment will succeed. But there is no doubt that it deserves to succeed."[52]

Hammarskjold knew very well that the whole effort might easily and rapidly go very sour indeed. He had observed the warning signs— the possibility that the U.S.S.R. might eventually by-pass the UN in supplying equipment and aircraft directly to Lumumba, the increasing mutual antagonism of the Congolese leaders, the volatility and lack of consistency of Lumumba and Gizenga, the endless and often farcical intrigues in Leopoldville, the procrastination of the Belgians, and the growing crisis of Katanga. He was in no mood for premature rejoicing.

On July 31, Hammarskjold received from King Baudouin a personal message written on July 28. In it, after referring to the civilizing mission started in the Congo by Leopold II, the King affirmed once more that Belgian forces had intervened in the Congo only to protect human life and to guarantee the security of Europeans, and expressed grave concern at the possibility of a complete economic collapse and the outbreak of intertribal warfare. The King noted that, amid the anarchy prevailing in the rest of the Congo, order and calm characterized life in Katanga—a line to be heard frequently from Katangese sources over the next two years—and that a withdrawal of Belgian troops from Katanga could only create insecurity among the Belgian population and risk extending to Katanga itself the chaos prevailing elsewhere in the Congo.

Hammarskjold regarded this letter, which put all the responsibility squarely on the Secretary-General if anything went wrong, as an expression of maximum practical resistance, short of a definite refusal to comply with the Security Council resolution, to the UN entry into Katanga. He replied that, after weighing all of the factors, both national and international, he was convinced that the Security Council resolution on Katanga had to be implemented just as soon as the UN was capable militarily of doing so, and preferably after a direct contact with the Katangese provincial authorities to ensure that UN troops would enter peacefully. In this process the help of Belgium was vital. Although economic collapse and violence had to be avoided at all cost, the real work of pulling the Congo together could start only when the current political crisis over Katanga, which was creating a strong trend toward extremism in Leopoldville, had been overcome. The solution of the Katanga problem was thus the key to the future of the Congo.

He followed up this reply by sending Heinz Wieschhoff, his chief adviser on African affairs, to Brussels with a personal message for the Foreign Minister, Pierre Wigny, in which he again asked for a declaration of intention from Belgium. Without some progress in Katanga, the moderate men in Leopoldville upon whom the Congo's political future depended would vanish from the scene. Worse still, a series of violent actions might well be undertaken by the Central Government with appalling consequences, and there was a further possibility that the Congo government might take the Katanga issue to the Security Council and make a direct attack on Belgium, the UN, and the Secretary-General. In this case the African members in the Council would have to take sides in a way that could only result in a complete breakdown of the UN approach to the crisis. The Congo government would then almost certainly try to get bilateral military assistance for the purpose of dealing with Katanga, in the first instance from African states. One or two states that already had troops in the UN force in the Congo might then combine their units with the Congolese Army and try to restore the government's authority in the Congo, creating a situation far bloodier than anything that had happened hitherto. If in this situation Belgium felt obliged to take countermeasures, it seemed unlikely that a wider war, or at the least something along the lines of the Korean conflict, could be avoided. If the mood of the Belgian public prevented the Belgian government from issuing the kind of declaration that Hammarskjold was asking for, he asked the Foreign Minister to accept, admittedly as a very weak alternative, a public statement by himself that he was convinced that Belgium was determined to comply with the Security Council resolution on Katanga and would not oppose the execution of the resolution by the Secretary-General.

While Wieschhoff was delivering this message in Brussels, Hammarskjold took steps to obtain further troops. He asked for a second battalion from Ireland, a third battalion from Morocco, and a fourth battalion from Ethiopia, and at the same time asked Sweden to raise another battalion for Gaza so that the existing Swedish battalion might remain in the Congo. He received favorable answers to all of these requests.

Wieschhoff reported on August 2 that the climate of Belgian public opinion was such as to make a firm statement of intention to withdraw from Katanga very difficult for the government. In its formal reply the Belgian government stated that it was not opposed to the implementation of the Council's resolution of July 22 as interpreted by the Secretary-General, that is to say as covering Katanga, but, because of difficulties with Tshombe as well as with Belgian public opinion, it would make no public statement.

The situation, in Hammarskjold's view, allowed of no further delay. The only hope of forestalling any or all of the risks he had outlined to Brussels was an initiative, either by the Belgians or by himself, that would eliminate any ambiguity about Katanga. The military possibilities of the UN were strictly limited, and urgent reinforcements would have to arrive before the entry into Katanga could be undertaken. August 6 or 7 seemed to be the earliest possible date for such a move. It was also essential to make sure that the Belgian forces in Katanga would not resist the UN troops, since the UN force was neither entitled nor equipped to fight. If this could be done, the entry of the UN troops and the Tshombe problem would be one of political maneuvering that should not involve the UN Force in any armed conflict. The preliminary discussions with Tshombe and the Belgians in Katanga would have to be followed up within twenty-four hours by the entry of UN troops, and if the plan failed he would have to report to the Security Council immediately.

On August 2, Hammarskjold learned that Lumumba had ordered Gizenga to dismiss Foreign Minister Justin Bomboko[53] and UN representative Thomas Kanza, two moderate members of the Cabinet who had been most cooperative with the UN. He had also learned of Lumumba's remark to Cordier that he might, if necessary, resort to an attack on the UN force. August 2 was a Tuesday, and Lumumba was likely to be back in Leopoldville on Thursday morning. If nothing was done about Katanga there was a risk that Lumumba, elated by his tour of various capitals, would use his considerable demagogic powers to carry the issue into the streets of Leopoldville. In the absence of a positive declaration of Belgian intentions, Hammarskjold could at least publish the assurance that Belgian troops would not oppose the entry of UN troops. With all these factors in mind, he decided that he could no longer delay the attempt to secure the entry of the UN force into Katanga.

On the afternoon of August 2, in a statement to the commission of the Council of Ministers that had been appointed to work with the Secretary-General, Hammarskjold announced[54] that he would send Ralph Bunche to Elisabethville for talks on the withdrawal of Belgian troops as the first step toward complete execution of the Security Council resolution on Katanga. Bunche would be followed on Saturday, August 6, by the first UN military contingents, and the Belgian withdrawal would begin immediately.

Various reactions to this announcement[55] showed how very difficult and dangerous a course Hammarskjold was now set on. The Belgian Foreign Minister issued a public statement[56] which did not explicitly confirm his acceptance of the Secretary-General's interpretation of the Belgian position but emphasized again that law and order prevailed in Katanga and that, on declaring secession, the Katanga government had proposed the reconstitution of the Congo as a federation. From Katanga the reaction was stronger. Tshombe had replied to Hammarskjold's message of July 18 with a long cable justifying his secession with copious references to the Balkan States, the Ottoman Empire, and other historical cases. Hammarskjold had told Tshombe on July 25 that he had warned the Security Council of the impending Katanga operation and had received its unanimous endorsement.[57] Now Tshombe addressed him in terms that were to become familiar in succeeding months. "The Katanga Government," he wrote, "is unanimous in its determination to resist by every means the Lumumba Government, its illegal representative . . . and the dispatch of UN forces to Katanga."[58]

To this threat Hammarskjold replied that resistance by a member state to a decision of the Security Council had legal consequences laid down in the Charter that would also apply to subordinate territorial organs of a State. The Council had unanimously agreed that its resolutions applied to the entire territory of the Congo. He hoped that Tshombe's expressed intentions would be reconsidered with full knowledge of their extremely serious character. As much for Lumumba's benefit as for Tshombe's, he went on to restate the principles upon which the UN operation was based.[59] The troops were under sole command of the UN. They were not permitted to interfere in the internal affairs of the country. They could not be used to impose any particular political solution of pending problems or to influence the balance of political forces. They could use force only in self-defense, and this categorically prohibited them from taking the initiative in resorting to armed force, although it did permit them to reply by force to an armed attack, especially when such an attack might be made with the object of forcing them to evacuate positions they had occupied on the order of their commander. He concluded by saying that if Tshombe's negative attitude was maintained he would be compelled to request an immediate meeting of the Security Council, which undoubtedly would not fail to take whatever urgent measures might be necessary.

The Vice-Premier, Gizenga, also reacted to Hammarskjold's plan.[60] On the afternoon of August 3, Hammarskjold was informed by Gizenga that he had "decided" that Bunche should be accompanied on his mission to Katanga by three representatives of the Central Government, escorted by twenty Ghanaian soldiers. Hammarskjold replied that he had already rejected a similar proposal in a meeting with the full Cabinet, which had not insisted upon it. "In this respect," he wrote, "I have to tell you again that the mission of Mr. Bunche is purely a UN mission, the character of which should not be compromised by the arrangements made."[61] The next day Gizenga and Foreign Minister Bomboko informed him that the "Council of Ministers had decided to postpone sending members of the Government to Katanga for the time being."

In case Bunche should find it necessary to advise against the immediate entry of UN troops into Elisabethville, Hammarskjold instructed Cordier to have a report ready for immediate transmission to the Security Council, to which, if necessary, he would add his own conclusions and recommendations. In his detailed instructions to Bunche for his trip to Elisabethville,[62] which had been put forward to August 4, he briefly restated the plan by which military units would enter Katanga on August 6 and again expounded the legal basis for the operation. Bunche's task was to discuss with the Belgian authorities the withdrawal of the Belgian troops and their replacement by UN troops, who would be charged with the maintenance of security in Katanga. Bunche was entitled to meet such authorities, including Tshombe and other representatives of the population, as might be necessary to make these arrangements. No opposition would be offered by the Belgian authorities or forces, but "disorder may all the same develop, either at the instigation of local leaders or spontaneously."[63] If Bunche concluded that resistance by force was a serious risk and therefore advised against the entry of UN troops, Hammarskjold would immediately request the Security Council for further instructions.

Bunche left Leopoldville early in the morning of August 4. On the way to the airport it occurred to him that, having no UN base in Katanga, he would have to use Belgian channels to communicate with Hammarskjold in Leopoldville. He therefore devised a simple code that he sent to Hammarskjold in a penciled note. If the entry of the troops was to proceed, Bunche would signal "Will report soonest."[64] If it was not to go ahead, he would signal "Reporting fully,"[65] with other phrases to indicate various periods of delay.

Arriving in Elisabethville on the afternoon of August 4, Bunche found a surprisingly friendly reception, including a guard of honor and a band, although he noted that fully equipped soldiers with arms at the ready were also on hand, as was an impressive supply of oil drums to block the runway. He was met by the chief Belgian officials, Ambassador Robert de Rothschild and Count Harold d'Aspremont-Lynden, who immediately warned him that the arrival of UN troops without a proper preparation of the population would result in violence and chaos. The stock bogeys of Katanga propaganda were all paraded for Bunche's edification, including the immediate departure of all Europeans, the outbreak of tribal warfare, the descent upon Elisabethville of warriors from the bush, and the use of poisoned arrows, scorched-earth tactics, and the like. Guerrilla warfare would be used against the UN troops wherever they went, and it would be far wiser to send them elsewhere in the Congo where there was real trouble. While enthusiastic for consultations between the Belgian and UN military representatives, the Belgian representatives were insistent that all UN officers should be in civilian clothes.

Bunche's efforts to explain the objectives of the UN in the Congo to Tshombe and his Interior Minister, Godefroid Munongo,[66] were met politely but with a truly provincial lack of understanding,* and on the evening of August 4 Tshombe announced to the press that the decision to send UN troops to Katanga had been canceled. This characteristic trick, which did not fail to find takers in Leopoldville, compelled Bunche to issue a counterstatement that he was reporting fully to the

---

* Munongo was much surprised to learn that Bunche was not a Swede.

Secretary-General and had taken no decisions, since he was not authorized to do so. The inadvertent use of the words "reporting fully" caused some confusion in Leopoldville, where Hammarskjold was puzzled as to whether Bunche was trying to send him the pre-arranged signal or not.

The position taken by Tshombe and his Belgian advisers about the consequences of the arrival of UN troops obviously contained a con-siderable element of bluff, but even taking this into account Bunche was uneasy about the kind of violence that might be stirred up by the skillful propaganda of the provincial government. Tshombe was too deeply committed to change his attitude immediately, and as long as his attitude was unchanged there was a serious risk of disorder and even of violent resistance. One emotion was unquestionably and sin-cerely shared by almost everyone in Elisabethville. It was an unaffected terror of Lumumba.

On the morning of August 5, while Bunche was conferring with Tshombe and had not yet made up his mind whether the. UN troops should come in on the following day, Rothschild and D'Aspremont-Lynden arrived at Tshombe's residence in a state of great agitation and demanded to see Bunche urgently. Feverish preparations were being made at the airport to oppose by force the landing of the UN plane carrying the military advisers in civilian clothes, which was due to land in an hour. Bunche refused the frantic demands of the two Belgians that he should have the plane diverted to Kamina and at once went to the airport, where he found an alarming situation. In spite of assurances that no UN troops were on the plane, the airport commandant had been instructed by Munongo to block the runway. Munongo himself soon appeared, wild with excitement and rage. He had, he said, just ordered the Belgian officer in charge of the troops at the airport to fire if the UN plane landed. Bunche managed at last to calm Munongo down, and the plane was allowed to land, but the episode, combined with Tshombe's continued opposition, convinced Bunche that it was too risky for the time being to bring in planeloads of UN troops in uniform. He therefore postponed the military opera-tion by sending to Hammarskjold through Belgian channels the pre-arranged message "reporting fully," and took off immediately for Leopoldville.*

---

* Looking back, and in light of the brilliant series of deceptions carried out later by the Katanga authorities, it is possible to construe Bunche's reception in Elisa-bethville as a gigantic bluff. But to call this bluff would have involved a tremendous risk, which the UN contingents, in unarmed, unescorted transport planes, were neither prepared nor authorized to take.

How seriously Hammarskjold regarded this setback can be judged by a handwritten note which he sent to Bunche by the plane bringing the military advisers to Elisabethville on August 5 and which Bunche received only after he had taken his decision. Hammarskjold had already, through the inadvertent use of "reporting fully" in Bunche's statement of the previous evening, anticipated Bunche's apprehensions. "You know, of course," he wrote, "that if we call off Simba* without recognizable and visible reason and without immediate alternative action here, I am in very deep waters."[67] Later reports, however, left him in no doubt of the wisdom of Bunche's decision.

On receiving Bunche's message, Hammarskjold cabled instructions to Cordier to call for an urgent meeting of the Security Council and left Leopoldville for New York on the night of August 5. In the face of the threat of resistance by force, further efforts to enter Katanga could be made only after the Security Council had given the Secretary-General new authority.

The rapidly growing number of critics of the UN Congo operation were not slow to react to this setback. In a memorandum to the President of the Security Council,[68] the Soviet government for the first time severely criticized the UN command in the Congo—although not yet the Secretary-General himself—for failing to enter Katanga, for the alleged disarming of the Congolese National Army, and for including European contingents in the force. The memorandum ended with a demand that if such shortcomings continued the present command of the UN force should be replaced by a new command and that troops be sent to the Congo who would be prepared to take the right kind of action to deal with the Katanga situation.

Although Lumumba, from Morocco, sent a message praising Hammarskjold's decision to send troops to Katanga and complimenting him on his farsightedness and wisdom,[69] Gizenga in Leopoldville took a different line. On the morning of August 6 he broadcast an attack upon Bunche and Hammarskjold, recalling that they had refused to allow representatives of the government to accompany Bunche to Elisabethville and accusing Bunche of collaboration with Tshombe in calling off the UN entry into Katanga. He also complained that the Secretary-General had left for New York without consulting him or informing him of the details of Bunche's mission to Elisabethville. He insisted that UN troops go immediately to Elisabethville. Gizenga sent this same message to the members of the Afro-Asian group at the

---

* "Simba" ("Lion") was the code name for the entry of UN troops into Katanga. It was also the name of one of the two brands of beer available in Leopoldville.

UN in New York. Reacting to Gizenga's message,* Hammarskjold pointed out that the Council of Ministers had not taken the decisions mentioned by Gizenga and that he himself was not authorized to commit UN troops to situations not envisaged by the Security Council.

In New York, Hammarskjold set about preparing the ground for the Security Council meeting. Owing to the late arrival of the Congo representatives the meeting was postponed until August 8, which gave him time for talks with the four big-power representatives and the African group. On August 6, he had submitted a written report to the Council[71] on the events of the last few days. The problem was a vicious circle. The Belgian troops would not leave Katanga before the UN troops arrived, and the UN troops could not arrive if their arrival was likely to be resisted by force. Since events had shown that the Council's aims could not be achieved by the use of the UN force under its present mandate, the Council must either change the character of the force, which appeared to Hammarskjold to be impossible both for constitutional reasons and in view of the commitments that had been made to the governments contributing troops, or resort to other methods that would enable him to implement the Council's decisions without going beyond his present instructions. On the withdrawal of Belgian forces from Katanga there could be no argument, but the hostility between the Central Government and the provincial régime was an internal political problem to which the UN could not be a party and on which it could not take sides. The Council would have to take this problem into account in writing new rules for the UN operation.

The situation was rapidly deteriorating. On August 7, Lumumba requested the Council to send to the Congo a group of observers from the Afro-Asian countries to ensure on the spot and without delay the withdrawal of Belgian troops, especially from Katanga.[72] On the same day, Bunche suggested that the best and perhaps the only way to avert a complete shambles in Leopoldville, where tension was mounting alarmingly, was the immediate and total Belgian withdrawal from Katanga and the Kamina base at so speedy a rate that the ground would be cut from under the feet of those who were maneuvering to disrupt the UN operation and carry on with non-UN military support and action. On August 6, Ghana had offered to lend armed assistance to the Congo government if no UN solution was forthcoming,[73] and

---

* The Gizenga campaign included the rumor that Hammarskjold was working for Belgium because King Baudouin's mother was a Swedish princess. Hammarskjold characterized this slander as an "illustration of political life in a world of stupidity abused by evil."[70]

similar moves from some other African countries were to be expected. Bunche doubted if the UN operation could survive these disruptive tendencies unless the Belgians withdrew at once from Katanga.

Hammarskjold, although he shared Bunche's concern, believed that the Security Council might still reach a decision that would break both Belgian and Katangese resistance. Meanwhile he alerted the UN command to be ready to move into Katanga at twelve hours' notice at any time after the end of the Council meeting, which he undertook to keep going, if necessary through the night, until a decision was reached.

In his opening speech on August 8,[74] Hammarskjold regretted the necessity for coming to the Council again with the Congo problem, but Tshombe's attitude required him to take a military initiative that he was not entitled to take without formal authorization. The central government's impatience had degenerated into distrust that had, in turn, created an atmosphere most harmful for the UN effort. This dangerous tendency had not been without support from quarters outside the Congo. Nor had the UN effort been aided by those governments which had threatened to break away and pursue a unilateral policy. On the other hand, he was more than ever convinced that the UN effort must, and could, be carried to a successful conclusion in the best interest of the people of the Congo, who must remain free to choose their political orientation independent of any foreign influence or control.

"I do not hesitate," he told the Council, "to say that the speediest possible—I would even say immediate—achievement of such a solution of the Congo problem is a question of peace or war, and when saying peace or war I do not limit my perspective to the Congo. . . . Efforts to safeguard national or group interests now, in a way that would hamper the UN effort, would risk values immeasurably greater than any of those which such action may be intended to protect."[75] He urged the Council to state explicitly that its resolutions on the Congo applied fully and specifically to Katanga, and to request the immediate and active support of all member governments. The Council should also formulate principles for the UN operation that would safeguard democratic rights and protect the representatives of all different political views in the Congo. The vicious circle by which the entry of the UN troops into Katanga was obstructed and the Belgian withdrawal thus rendered impossible had to be broken, and those who opposed the entry and encouraged obstruction would shoulder full responsibility for subsequent events. The Europeans of Katanga should understand that the UN entry into Katanga was their best and most realistic hope for the future, for it would make it possible for them to work in harmony with the people among whom they had lived and wished to continue to live.

The Congolese Foreign Minister, Bomboko, delivered a slashing attack upon Belgian interference and demanded again the immediate withdrawal of Belgian troops.[76] The Belgian Foreign Minister stated[77] once again that Belgium had intervened in Katanga solely to protect Belgian nationals and had no part in the secessionist plot. Kuznetsov, the Soviet representative, attacked the actions and motives of Belgium and strongly criticized the conduct of the UN operation,[78] whose presence, he said, had become a cover for the continued occupation by Belgian forces both of Katanga and certain regions of the Congo. While paying tribute to the energy shown by the Secretary-General and his colleagues, he interpreted the refusal to send UN troops into Katanga as a concession to the aggressor and to its puppet Tshombe. Kuznetsov maintained that the UN force had full powers to proceed into Katanga to eliminate armed resistance, and he repeated that should the UN command fail to take this action, it should be replaced along with contingents that were not prepared to fight.

In answer to another of Kuznetsov's charges, Hammarskjold pointed out[79] that far from his high-handedly disarming the Congolese National Army, the decision to call upon Congolese soldiers to lay down their arms wherever UN forces were present was a decision originally made by the government of the Congo. He himself had given the order to postpone the entry of UN troops into Katanga. "The Representative of the Soviet Union," he told the Council, "expressed a sincere wish to help the Congolese people. That wish is certainly shared by everybody, and for me it is a guiding inspiration. I do not believe, personally, that we help the Congolese people by actions in which Africans kill Africans, or Congolese kill Congolese, and that will remain my guiding principle for the future."[80]

The Council met for the third time on the evening of August 8, and, after a debate that lasted until 4:25 the next morning, adopted, with the concurring vote of the U.S.S.R., a resolution[81] put forward by Tunisia and Ceylon that closely followed Hammarskjold's requirements. Kuznetsov withdrew a Soviet proposal with good grace, but in the course of the debate he made a statement which was to be remembered later on, in which he affirmed the right of governments to respond to appeals for bilateral help from the government of the Congo. The Council called upon the Belgian government to withdraw immediately from the province of Katanga under "speedy modalities determined by the Secretary-General."[82] It declared that the entry of the UN force into Katanga was a necessity, and reaffirmed that the force would not be a party to, or in any way intervene in or be used to influence, the outcome of any internal conflict, constitutional or other. As was to become increasingly clear in succeeding months, this was more easily said than done.

The Council's latest resolution, by calling on Belgium to assist the UN actively and by singling out Katanga as a special problem, put the Secretary-General in a much stronger position to adopt a forceful line of action.[83] He immediately asked Foreign Minister Wigny whether Belgium would actively cooperate in the implementation of the Council's decision and requested him to clarify a number of points of detail concerning the Belgians in Katanga.[84] He requested Lumumba[85] to give urgent assurances that he would apply the rules of cooperation that derived from the resolution and from Article 49 of the Charter.* He asked Tshombe[86] whether he accepted the same duty of cooperation as was imposed upon the Congo government and on the Belgian government and undertook to hold the necessary conversations with him should his reply be favorable.

Lumumba's reply,[87] which Hammarskjold did not receive before once more leaving New York for the Congo, was forthcoming but not reassuring. He promised the Secretary-General his complete cooperation and expressed deep gratitude to the Council for its action. He would soon enter Katanga with all the members of his government and he was awaiting Hammarskjold's arrival to determine with him what measures should be taken. Lumumba added that he had declared a state of national emergency.

Tshombe was obviously becoming uneasy. Before receiving Hammarskjold's message he had sent one of his own, protesting that his government had no wish to be the cause of an armed conflict and that he was most anxious to study immediately with a UN representative the modalities of the UN entry into Katanga. To this, Hammarskjold replied[88] that he proposed personally to discuss with him the method of deployment of UN troops in Katanga. There could be no question of conditions, but for practical reasons it was urgently necessary to have a frank exchange of views. He told Tshombe that he expected to fly to Elisabethville on Friday, August 12, with military and civilian advisers and two companies of Swedish troops.

Hammarskjold's decision to become his own agent for breaking the vicious circle in Katanga was a bold and extremely risky step. If it was to succeed, it would have to be put through with maximum speed before any of the parties could raise the kind of objections that could be expected if they were given time for second thoughts. He informed Gizenga and Bomboko, who had been in New York for the Council meeting, that he intended to go almost directly to Elisabethville for

---

* Article 49 of the Charter reads:
    The Members of the United Nations shall join in affording mutual assistance in carrying out the measures decided upon by the Security Council.

his discussions with Tshombe, which meant that there would be no question of Lumumba or any other member of the government accompanying him. The Congolese representatives in New York raised no objection, although Lumumba's reply, which Hammarskjold had not yet received, showed that the Prime Minister expected to take an active role in the expedition, regardless of the fact that his participation would almost inevitably ensure total failure, if not disaster.

Hammarskjold and his party left New York on the evening of August 10, stopping briefly at Accra for a meeting at the airport with Nkrumah, whose close relationship with Lumumba was a factor to be reckoned with, and arriving in Leopoldville at 9:30 p.m. on August 11. By this time a telegram had been received from Tshombe accepting Hammarskjold's suggestion for a frank exchange of views and agreeing to his arrival the next day with military and civilian advisers and two companies of Swedish troops under his personal and exclusive authority. This message was rapidly followed by some second thoughts from Tshombe, who mentioned the serious disadvantages and disorders that might result from the arrival of troops before he and the Secretary-General had discussed the deployment of the UN force, to which Hammarskjold replied immediately that a reconsideration of his plans was entirely out of the question.

On the plane from New York, Hammarskjold had written the outlines of a memorandum on the implementation of paragraph 4 of the Council resolution of August 9,[89] which had affirmed that the UN force would not be a party to or in any way intervene in, or be used to influence, the outcome of any internal conflict, constitutional or other, in the Congo. He felt obliged to give both Tshombe and Lumumba a detailed explanation on this point, for if he did not make the position clear in advance he would obviously be criticized for granting concessions to Tshombe as a condition for the entry of the UN troops. He recalled that in Lebanon the UN had carried out its observation activities throughout the country without supporting either the constitutional government or the opposition party, and that in Hungary the Organization had directed its decision solely against the intervention of foreign troops without taking any stand on the relationship between the government and the insurgents. It followed that in Katanga the UN was directly concerned with the attitude of the provincial government to the extent that it was based on or influenced by the presence of Belgian troops. Once these troops were withdrawn, the political and constitutional question would be a matter for negotiation between the provincial government and the central government, and the UN would have nothing to do with it. The UN force could not be used to compel the provincial government to take a specific line of action, nor could UN facilities be used to transport civilian or military representatives of the Central Government to Katanga if such a decision was against the will of the provincial government. On the other hand, the UN had no right to forbid the Central Government to take any action by its own means with relation to Katanga. This declaration was not subject to negotiation and was his own.

When Bunche presented this memorandum to Lumumba on the afternoon of August 12, the Prime Minister reacted very strongly against it. He was already indignant that Hammarskjold had not seen him during his overnight stop in Leopoldville and told Bunche that he would be compelled to deal with the Congo situation with the aid of those countries which had already offered to assist him. He demanded a UN plane to fly Victor Lundula,[90] the senior general of the Congolese Army, and some of his ministers to Elisabethville to join Hammarskjold.

Hammarskjold took off for Elisabethville at 8 a.m. on August 12 in the UN force commander's white Convair, followed at brief intervals by four DC-4's carrying two companies of Swedish troops. As his aircraft was approaching Elisabethville, the control tower informed the pilot that the Secretary-General's plane alone would be permitted to land and that the following aircraft with the Swedish troops would be turned back. While his plane circled the airfield, Hammarskjold told Tshombe over the aircraft's radio that if permission for all the aircraft to land was not received within five minutes, all five aircraft would return to Leopoldville. Tshombe answered that the previous order was a misunderstanding. The landing was nonetheless an uneasy one, for from the air massive military preparations could be clearly seen on the airfield, and little if anything was known of the true state of mind of the Katangese.

In greeting Hammarskjold, Tshombe was all smiles and, with characteristic aplomb, stationed his visitor under the new Katangese flag while the band struck up the new Katangese national anthem.* Irritated at being maneuvered into even a fleeting recognition of the independent status of Katanga, Hammarskjold stared grimly ahead. He insisted on staying at the airfield until the first planeload of Swedes had begun to disembark. The Swedes put on a fine ceremonial show, and as soon as he was satisfied that there would be no trouble at the airport, Hammarskjold left for the Union Minière** guesthouse, which had been assigned as his residence for his stay in Elisabethville.

---

* Each stanza of this anthem concluded with the rousing refrain *"Avec vos bras et votre sang! Avec vos dents!"* ("With your arms and your blood! With your teeth!")
** Largely Belgian-owned and -operated, the Union Minière du Haut Katanga was the largest mining company in the Congo.

Since Hammarskjold had stipulated in advance that there were to be no conditions to the discussions, he simply handed Tshombe his memorandum on the implementation of the Council's resolution, and during the subsequent talks he stayed well within the lines he had laid down in that document. On the morning of August 13 a joint communiqué was issued[91] stating that there had been a broad exchange of views on the resolutions of the Council and that special attention had been given to the means of introducing UN troops into Katanga. The military advisers on both sides had been holding parallel discussions on the relief of the Belgian troops by the UN force, and as a first step it was announced that the two Swedish companies would immediately take charge of the protection of the Elisabethville airport. UN troops, of which more would be arriving on August 15, were also to move to the main towns of the province within three or four days. When a sizable delegation of young Baluba opponents of the Tshombe régime appeared at Hammarskjold's residence to deliver a petition and were dispersed by tear gas and bayonets, Ham.narskjold also demanded a written agreement from Tshombe and Munongo guaranteeing free access to UN premises. Otherwise the atmosphere was peaceful and friendly, and on the next day, August 14, Hammarskjold departed for the Kamina base for a brief inspection before returning to Leopoldville.

Hammarskjold's personal intervention in Katanga was daring and unprecedented. By persistence and forceful diplomacy, he had obtained without fighting—which the UN troops were in no position to engage in anyway—the presence of the UN force all over Katanga, a move that only a week before was supposed to be resisted by armed force, not to mention popular resistance, poisoned arrows, and guerrilla warfare. His plan had required not only brilliant timing and the mobilization at exactly the right moment of the support of the Security Council, but also considerable physical courage, for during the twenty-five minutes he was circling over Elisabethville and speaking to Tshombe in the control tower, it seemed entirely possible, at least to Hammarskjold's companions, that he might be descending into a violent and potentially fatal situation.

The operation proved extraordinarily successful. The total withdrawal of Belgian troops from the Congo had been brought miraculously nearer to realization, although to Hammarskjold's indignation the last Belgian combat troops did not in fact leave Katanga until September 9. For the time being, both the Belgians and Tshombe were cooperating with the UN, and it seemed likely that they would continue to do so unless their fear of Lumumba got the better of them.

Unfortunately, Hammarskjold's visit made Tshombe feel that he too had improved his position. His administrative and financial arrangements were not interfered with, no Central Government officials had appeared, and he was still free to surround himself with whatever foreign advisers he chose. Although Hammarskjold had succeeded in bringing UN troops into Katanga, many people in Elisabethville regarded his visit as a success for Tshombe, for the arrival of the UN troops had not put an end to secession. It was true that Hammarskjold had forced the withdrawal of the Belgian troops, but by mid-August, after having crushed the ANC mutiny and disbanded the army units loyal to the Central Government, the Belgian army was no longer vitally necessary to Tshombe. Provided that he did not lose the services of individual Belgian officers such as Major Guy Wéber, the chief of the new Katangese gendarmerie, or of the key civilian advisers, the withdrawal of Belgian troops might even strengthen his position by making him appear to be less dependent on Belgian support. Hammarskjold was not yet sufficiently well informed about Katanga to realize that the individual military and civilian advisers, supported by the money and influence of the Union Minière, had replaced the Belgian army as the real backbone of the Katanga secession. His success, therefore, contained the seeds of future difficulties.

On his way back to Leopoldville, Hammarskjold landed at Kamina to inspect the enormous strategic base, with its two airfields, elaborate living quarters, and giant workshops. Once the Katanga problem was solved, the Belgian bases at Kamina and Kitona would inevitably be the next hurdle. Even when the Belgian evacuation had been achieved, the UN would still have a formidable problem at Kamina in administering this strategic white elephant and in looking after its fifteen thousand Congolese workers.

As Hammarskjold flew back to Leopoldville he may well have felt that he had surmounted a major obstacle and that the way ahead might be somewhat easier. In fact he was flying into another storm which was only the beginning of much more far-reaching opposition to his policy and his efforts. Any lingering hope that his success in Katanga would cause an improvement in ONUC's relations with the government in Leopoldville was soon rudely dispelled. The practical and legal reasons, unanswerable as they were, for not including Lumumba, his Ministers, or his soldiers in the Katanga operation were not likely to commend themselves to the Prime Minister, for in personally achieving a breakthrough in Katanga, Hammarskjold had dealt a blow to Lumumba's pride, and Lumumba had decided to seek military help directly from the Soviet Union.

THE CONGO, AUGUST–SEPTEMBER 1960: THE CONSTITUTIONAL CRISIS

ALREADY ON AUGUST 13, Lumumba had expressed violent dissatisfaction with the UN and demanded that the Leopoldville airport be controlled jointly by the Congolese Army and a nonwhite UN contingent. He criticized Hammarskjold for passing through Leopoldville on his way to Katanga without notifying him or consulting him, for exchanging messages with Tshombe, and for sending only white troops—and a small number at that—to Katanga—an act, he said, which proved the maneuvers of the Belgian government and the Secretary-General.[1] He also demanded that all white UN troops leave the Congo. *"Les Suédois,"* he said, *"ne sont que des Belges en déguise"* ("The Swedes are only Belgians in disguise").

On his return to Leopoldville on the afternoon of August 14, Hammarskjold informed Foreign Minister Justin Bomboko[2] that he had now returned from Elisabethville and Kamina and wished to report to the Congolese government on the action taken thus far by the UN in carrying out the Security Council resolution on Katanga. The following morning Gizenga asked him to receive Lumumba and himself. Hammarskjold immediately invited them to UN heaquarters, and Gizenga accepted for 3:30 p.m. At noon, however, he received from Lumumba a letter containing a sweeping attack on his actions, and neither the Prime Minister nor Gizenga appeared for the afternoon appointment. The Congo government, Lumumba wrote, totally disagreed with the Secretary-General's interpretation of the Security Council's resolution because Hammarskjold had ignored the provision of an earlier resolution that the Secretary-General was to provide military assistance "in consultation with" the government. This in Lumumba's view meant that the UN was to place all its resources at the disposal of the government for the purpose of subduing by force the rebel government of Katanga. He accused Hammarskjold of acting in connivance with Tshombe and at the instigation of the government of Belgium, by whose wish only Swedish and Irish troops had been sent to Katanga.* He demanded again that the Congolese Army replace UN troops at all airfields, that African troops be sent immediately to Katanga, and that all non-African troops be withdrawn. UN aircraft should transport Congolese Ministers to Katanga.

Hammarskjold replied immediately that there was no reason at this time for him to enter into a discussion either of what he considered to be Lumumba's unsound and unjustified allegations or of his interpretation of the Security Council's resolution. Lumumba's letter would be immediately circulated to the Security Council, to which Hammarskjold would give his comments on it, and he hoped very much that Lumumba would also see fit to present his case to the Council in person. Lumumba answered on the same day, denying that he had made allegations against Hammarskjold but going on to distinguish between the Secretary-General's position and that of the Security Council, in which, he wrote, the government of the Congo continued to have confidence. Hammarskjold at once replied that he assumed that Lumumba's letters had been approved by the Council of Ministers and that the Ministers had also seen his own replies to these letters, to which he had nothing further to add. He proposed, unless the Council of Ministers asked him to do otherwise or had further proposals to make, to return to New York that very night to consult with the Security Council.

Lumumba replied with another tirade, this time to the effect that the government and people of the Congo had lost confidence in Hammarskjold and would ask the Council to send immediately a group of observers from Afro-Asian countries to supervise the proper application of the Council's resolution. He concluded with the request that Hammarskjold delay his departure for New York by twenty-four hours so that the Congolese delegation to the Council could travel in his

---

* This accusation was without any foundation, since the Swedish troops had been quickly followed into Katanga by Ethiopians and Moroccans.

,ersonal aircraft. Hammarskjold replied that it was for the Council to judge the validity of Lumumba's allegations against him and to assess the confidence of the member states in the Secretary-General. He declined to delay his departure for New York but gave assurances that the Council would await the arrival of the Congolese delegation. He would have been happy, he added, to delay his departure had the President, the Prime Minister or the government wished to consult him, but in the absence of any such request he felt obliged to put himself as quickly as possible at the disposal of the representatives of the member states in New York.

The last communication in this "somewhat lively correspondence"[3]* —as Hammarskjold later described it to the Security Council—was a letter from the Secretary-General to President Kasavubu, saying that he would willingly have seen the President if the latter had indicated any desire to see him and that he regretted deeply the misunderstandings which now seemed to have arisen within the Congolese government and the lack of confidence they indicated, in spite of all the UN had managed to do in the short time it had been in the Congo.

Two dangerously disruptive extraneous elements had now been superimposed on Hammarskjold's original concept of the UN operation in the Congo—racial feeling and the cold war. Irish and Swedish contingents had been included in the force as a reassurance to the European population of the Congo, and in demanding the departure of all white contingents Lumumba had raised an issue on which Hammarskjold, for all his sympathy with the new leaders of Africa, could not possibly compromise. This kind of inverted racialism was in conflict with the principles on which the UN was based and would be a manifest affront to many members, which the Organization could never accept. Moreover, from a purely practical point of view, the economic life of the Congo depended for the time being upon non-African technicians, including both those who had stayed on and those who had been provided by the UN, and their position would become difficult or even impossible if the UN were to bow to a racist policy. If the removal of the white contingents was insisted upon, he felt that he would have no choice but to recommend to the Security Council that the whole force be withdrawn, in which case it would be impossible to maintain the UN civilian operation which was the backbone of the day-to-day life of the Congo. Even if bilateral assistance should be forthcoming, the Congo government would soon find that, unlike assistance from the UN, it would not be given without strings. For all

---

* Lumumba's last letter began with the sentence "I have just this moment received your letter of today's date in reply to the one I sent to you an hour ago."[4]

these reasons, Hammarskjold was determined to resist all pressures to remove the European contingents of the force.

After the Katanga breakthrough, Soviet opposition to Hammarskjold came out in the open. The "strange role"[5] that *Pravda* had imputed to Hammarskjold on August 3 had by August 13 become his "disgraceful role"[6] in dealing with Tshombe, to whom he, as a "traitor to the cause of African freedom,"[7] was alleged to have surrendered the control of the UN troops in Katanga. In the Security Council meetings on August 8 and 9, the Soviet representative had been critical of the conduct of the operation but had centered his criticism largely upon the UN command in the Congo. After the breakthrough in Katanga, Hammarskjold was called a puppet of the West and the organizer of a new form of colonial enslavement in the Congo. On August 20 the Soviet government rejected his plan for the UN civilian operation in the Congo.[8] For the first time, the role that Hammarskjold had envisaged for the UN as a buffer between rival great powers in Africa was seriously threatened.

The change in Lumumba's attitude toward the UN also had immediate repercussions in the Congo itself, and organized harassment of UN personnel began. On August 17 two UN security officers, delivering a letter to Lumumba late at night, were arrested by the Prime Minister's guards and threatened with death before they were released through the intervention of UN Ghanaian soldiers and of General Indar Jit Rikhye, the Secretary-General's military adviser. On the eighteenth, Congolese soldiers at the airport boarded a UN plane and arrested and manhandled fourteen Canadian soldiers. It even seemed likely that in the not too distant future it might be necessary to use force to hold the airport, which was the lifeline of the UN operation. Hammarskjold's strong protests about these incidents and his demand that the government take all necessary measures to prevent any recurrence received a twofold response—a derisive rejection by Lumumba and a letter of apology[9] from Colonel Joseph Mobutu,[10] Lumumba's chief of staff and the deputy commander of the ANC. Although the Prime Minister still alternated his tirades against the Secretary-General and the UN with requests for assistance of various kinds, the split between Lumumba and ONUC was steadily widening.

Most African states had been reluctant to take sides in Hammarskjold's dispute with Lumumba over Katanga, and the harassments of UN personnel in Leopoldville and Lumumba's increasingly erratic performance made them even more unwilling to do so. The Soviet Union, however, in a letter to the Secretary-General on August 20,[11] sought to justify the attack on the Canadians at the airport by accusing Hammarskjold of having continued to bring in troops from

Canada, one of Belgium's NATO allies, against his own pledge and of thus arousing the fully justified indignation of the Congolese people.* The Soviet note went on to attack him for his conduct of the Katanga operation and his failure to consult with Lumumba in Leopoldville, and hinted at his involvement in a NATO plot under U.S. leadership.

In the Council meetings that began on Sunday, August 21, Hammarskjold faced his accusers and critics head-on. He dealt first with Lumumba and his series of "unprecedented allegations. . . . In order to carry out my mandate," he said, "I have been forced to act with great firmness in relation to many parties. One of them has been the Central Government itself. I do not believe that I have ever failed in courtesy. On the other hand, I do not excuse myself for having stated clearly the principles of the Charter and for having acted independently on their basis, mindful of the dignity of the Organization—and to have done so whether it suited all those we are trying to help or not. Nor have I forgotten that the ultimate purpose of the UN services to the Republic of the Congo is to protect international peace and security, and that, to the extent that the difficulties facing the Republic are not of a nature to endanger international peace, they are not of our concern."[12] He went on to describe the Katanga operation and gave the reasons for his conduct of it, pointing out that it had worked and that the Security Council resolution was now fully implemented in Katanga. As for Congolese criticism of his action in Katanga, "Let me ask what were then their aims: the speediest possible withdrawal of Belgian troops while order and security were maintained by the UN troops? If so, my approach proved to be adequate. Or was it something different?"[13]

Before the Council met, the Soviet Union had submitted a proposal[14] that a group representing all countries providing forces in the Congo should meet daily with the Secretary-General and with the Congo government. Hammarskjold suggested the same idea in a more formal and regular way, asking for the setting up of an Advisory Committee of the troop-contributing countries, as had been done for the United Nations Emergency Force in the Middle East. He concluded by urging the Council to rise above the tensions of the moment and to look toward the real problems of the future.

The subsequent proceedings soon showed that this appeal had fallen on deaf ears. Vice-Prime Minister Antoine Gizenga, representing the

---

* Canada was not providing infantry or combat troops, but was the sole available source of trained signalers and communications units which could work in both English and French. It was for this compelling reason that Canadian units had been included in the force.

Congo, went so far as to accuse Hammarskjold of having taken Swedish troops to Katanga so that Belgian soldiers and civilians could disguise themselves as UN troops. To this Hammarskjold replied: "I can assure the representative that the discipline of the Swedish Army is such that no people in disguise are able to figure as members of the Swedish troops. . . . If I used two Swedish companies as my personal support at the Katanga breakthrough while, as he knows, the troops following the vanguard had an overwhelming majority of Africans, it was simply because I wanted to reduce the risks of a failure of the breakthrough to an absolute minimum by establishing an identity between myself and the troops."[15]

The assault launched by the Soviet representative,[16] Kuznetsov, was far more serious. He attacked the UN command, which, he maintained, was largely composed of officers drawn from NATO countries,* and demanded the total withdrawal of the Canadians, whom he again accused of provoking the incident at Leopoldville airport. He maintained that Hammarskjold's interpretation of the resolution of August 9 was wrong because it put Tshombe on the same footing as the government of the Congo. He again rejected Hammarskjold's civilian operations plan as a step toward putting the Congo under American-directed tutelage. The tone of these accusations was still mild enough, and Hammarskjold answered them mildly,[17] even going so far as to agree that the distribution by nationality of the staff in the Congo was, after five hectic initial weeks, not yet satisfactory. Mongi Slim of Tunisia strongly supported Hammarskjold and provided, in a reasoned and eloquent speech, a rallying point for the African countries.

Hammarskjold was not unduly concerned at the political situation. The meetings of the Council, which ended at 1:45 a.m. on Monday, August 22, had indicated that despite verbal support for Lumumba, neither the African states nor the Russians had any real taste for actively taking Lumumba's side in his quarrel with Hammarskjold. The African states had considered adding to the Soviet draft resolution a vote of confidence in the Secretary-General. The Russians, however, had no instructions, and Hammarskjold pointed out that once such a vote of confidence had been submitted and discussed he could not possibly accept a resolution from which it had been dropped. The Russians agreed not to insist upon their proposal to set up a group of observers, provided the Africans did not insist on a vote of confidence in Hammarskjold. The U.S.S.R. alone had sought to challenge his interpretation of the resolution of August 9 upon which the break-

---

* Actually the commander was from Sweden, not a member of NATO, the deputy commander a Moroccan, and the chief-of-staff an Ethiopian.

through in Katanga had been based. "I have the right to expect guidance," Hammarskjold told the Council on August 21, ". . . but it should be obvious that if the Security Council says nothing I have no other choice than to follow my conviction."[18] In effect the Council rejected Lumumba's position, and Hammarskjold's essential authority for directing the operation was not seriously impaired.

Events in the Congo did not echo this subdued note, and Hammarskjold realized that his representatives in Leopoldville faced an even rougher time ahead. A further crisis erupted in Leopoldville on August 24, when Bunche was informed that the Prime Minister had ordered the Congolese National Army to take over control of the Leopoldville airfield. ONUC was thus faced with the possibility of having to defend its lifeline by force, and Hammarskjold had no doubt that it must do so if necessary. Matters were complicated by Lumumba's refusal to receive Bunche, who had asked urgently to see him when the ANC was about to attack the airfield, and Bunche warned Hammarskjold that in the circumstances his usefulness in the Congo was at an end. In the event, Lumumba's generals were more cautious than he, and the issue was not pressed to a test of military strength, although minor harassments of ONUC continued.

A far more tragic development began on August 23 when, at Lumumba's orders, Congolese soldiers began to be airlifted into Kasai Province. This move was intended to be the build-up for an attack on Katanga by the ANC for which Lumumba had requested Soviet aid, but in fact the troops, who had no logistic support and therefore had to live off the land, immediately became entangled with the Baluba secessionist movement led by the Mulopwe (King), Albert Kalonji,[19] based on the town of Bakwanga,* and with the traditional tribal rivalry of the Lulua and Baluba in Kasai. The resulting massacre of the Baluba by the ANC was an important link in the chain of events which were shortly to lead to the constitutional crisis. It also changed Hammarskjold's opinion of Lumumba. Before the Bakwanga affair he had regarded Lumumba as a talented if inexperienced young leader, who, however exasperating and volatile he might sometimes be, both deserved and desperately needed help. The almost casual ordering of the military movement that led to the Kasai massacres deeply shocked him and led him to think that Lumumba had become totally irresponsible.

A visit by Lumumba to Stanleyville on August 27 was the occasion of another and more serious incident involving UN troops. A rumor

---

* Kalonji had proclaimed separate statehood, to which the diamond production of Bakwanga gave revenue and importance, and had set up a personal army and issued his own postage stamps.

spread among the crowd that had gathered at the airport to greet Lumumba that an American Globemaster aircraft bringing in UN Canadian signals personnel was a Belgian plane landing paratroops, whose intention, some said, was to assassinate Lumumba. After the plane landed, the crowd and the police beat up and abducted the Canadians and the American air crew, most of whom were seriously injured before being rescued by the UN Ethiopian troops. This outrage created a strong reaction not only among UN personnel in the Congo but also among the member states supporting the UN operation.

Although Brussels confirmed that the withdrawal of troops from Katanga would start forthwith, the Belgian commanders in Katanga indulged in various stratagems of delay. They maintained, for example, that the UN had not fully taken over from the Belgians, and that fifteen Belgian paratroops were being held by the Government in Leopold-ville. It was even suggested that the Belgian commander, General Gheysen, might stay on in Katanga as a "technician"—a proposal, Hammarskjold observed, that showed "a sense of humor but an utter lack of judgment."[20] He gave instructions that no delay in the Belgian withdrawal either from Elisabethville or from the Kamina base could be allowed and that he would, if necessary, report on further delays to the Security Council.

On August 25, Hammarskjold learned that ten Russian IL-14 transport aircraft were refueling in Athens en route to the Congo. On the night of August 27 he had a long talk with the Soviet Representative, Kuznetsov, who upbraided him for the continuing use of Canadian troops, for setting up the Advisory Committee on the Congo,[21] and for sending another American, Andrew Cordier, to Leopoldville to take over temporarily from Bunche, who had, now that he could no longer communicate with Lumumba, asked to be relieved.* After the meeting, Hammarskjold assessed the Soviet attitude to himself as "that I had good intentions, bad judgment and impressive energy,"[22] but he foresaw that it might not be long before Moscow took a sterner line.

In effect the Soviet Union had declared its full support for the Prime Minister, Lumumba, as distinct from the President, Kasavubu. This meant that the initial threat to international peace and security, the presence of Belgian troops in the Congo, had been superseded by an even graver potential danger, the possible intervention in the internal affairs of the Congo by greater powers than Belgium. If

---

* Cordier, in fact, was going to Leopoldville for a few days only, for a review of the whole administrative organization of ONUC and to hold the fort until the arrival of Rajeshwar Dayal, whom Hammarskjold had asked Nehru in early August to make available as Bunche's successor.

in these circumstances Lumumba were to go through with his often repeated threat to ask the UN to leave the Congo, the decision could no longer be made on a unilateral and arbitrary basis by the Congo government, since it would involve a potential threat to international peace and security that would have to be considered by the Security Council.

Hammarskjold met with the Congo Advisory Committee for the first time on the evening of August 24, and for the next year these confidential meetings were to provide his best means of consulting, getting advice, and rallying support for the UN operation in the Congo. The meetings were strictly private, and only agreed communiqués were released to the press. There was no voting, but at the end of the debate the Secretary-General as chairman gave a summary of his conclusions, and anyone who disagreed could record a dissenting view. In the two former committees of this kind, the UNEF Advisory Committee and the Atomic Energy Advisory Committee, no member had ever gone on record as disagreeing with the Secretary-General, because it had always been possible to thrash out differences and to reach a consensus. The Congo Advisory Committee was never asked to take formal decisions, a right that in any case belonged constitutionally to the Security Council. The principal object of the meetings was to keep the members informed of the immediate problems in the Congo and to keep the Secretariat in close touch with the views of the countries most closely interested in the Congo problem.

The representatives of some African states obtained a firsthand view of the realities of the Congo situation when Lumumba summoned an African conference to meet in Leopoldville on August 25. Several of the representatives, including Mongi Slim of Tunisia and Alex Quaison-Sackey of Ghana, were detained in Brazzaville for some time, and others arriving by ferry at Leopoldville were initially refused permission by the ANC to land. At the first meeting of the conference the Congolese police, after spotting some anti-Lumumba banners, opened fire over the heads of the crowd which had gathered to welcome the African delegates, and Lumumba informed the assembled representatives that any one of them, including himself, might be assassinated in the streets when they left the conference hall. Such experiences gave the African representatives a new understanding of the problems of the UN operation, and all except the representative of Guinea expressed, both in a resolution at the end of the conference and in private talks, strong support for the UN operation and for the Secretary-General personally and made a determined if ineffective effort to persuade Lumumba to adopt a policy of moderation and cooperation.

Early in August the U.S.S.R. had sent a hundred trucks to the Congo. They were originally to have been donated to the Congo government through the UN, but on their arrival they were made available to Lumumba and were delivered directly to the ANC in Kasai. By August 31 there were eleven Soviet transport aircraft in Stanleyville. These aircraft, with their fuselages painted with the Congolese colors and the words "République du Congo," were used to fly ANC reinforcements into Kasai. Hammarskjold felt compelled to react to this new development, because the UN could not stand aside in what he called "a case of incipient genocide."[23] "Where ultimate responsibility must be ours," he wrote, "we cannot with open eyes, in order to placate the Government, do things we know to be harmful to the best interests of the Congo."[24] The Bakwanga situation, where the Congolese Army was almost fortuitously engaged in a tribal massacre, was a delicate one for the UN to interfere in, because the government could easily reply to the Secretary-General's protests that it was dealing with another secessionist movement and that the ends justified the means. "Prohibition against intervention in internal conflicts," he cabled Cordier, "cannot be considered to apply to senseless slaughter of civilians or fighting arising from tribal hostilities."[25] After a full discussion with the Congo Advisory Committee, he instructed Cordier, on September 2, to recommend strongly to Foreign Minister Bomboko that immediate steps be taken to control and discipline the army in Kasai. He also authorized the interposing of UN troops, using force if necessary, to stop the massacre.

DESPITE ALL THESE DEVELOPMENTS Hammarskjold remained relatively optimistic, and at the end of August he was still hoping that the military phase of the UN operation in the Congo might soon be ended and that a large-scale program of civilian assistance might take its place. His optimism was to be short-lived. On September 5 the latent rift between Kasavubu and Lumumba flared into an open conflict which left the Congo for nearly a whole year without a constitutional government, and in the ensuing confusion the UN operation, far from being transformed into a program of civilian assistance, found itself in the impossible position of trying to maintain a modicum of law and order and the bare necessities of public administration in the face of constitutional chaos and intermittent factional violence.

The atmosphere in Leopoldville immediately prior to and during the Kasavubu-Lumumba rift was an important factor in subsequent events. President Kasavubu, as was his habit, seldom left his residence, and little, if anything, was known of his feelings or of his intentions. The activities and statements of Lumumba, on the other hand, although in their own way equally incomprehensible and far more inconsistent, exercised a strong influence on the state of mind of almost everyone else. His outbursts against the UN were still interspersed with requests for assistance and discussions of future plans. He was surrounded by a multinational coterie of hangers-on and advisers, many of whom had apparently settled in on him of their own volition.* He was known to see much of the Ghanaian Ambassador, Andrew Y. K. Djin, and of the Guinean diplomats in Leopoldville, and was believed by many to be increasingly under the influence of the Soviet Embassy. His alternating moods of excitability and listlessness gave rise to all sorts of rumors about his health and his alleged use of various stimulants.

The garrison of Leopoldville, some four thousand strong, was sulking in its camps, unpaid, only spasmodically rationed, fully armed, and torn by tribal differences. Its commander, General Victor Lundula, who had shown himself to be a decent and responsible man, exercised only a tenuous control of his troops either in Leopoldville or elsewhere in the Congo and seemed to be almost as apprehensive of them as everyone else. Congolese Ministers and politicians were for the most part frightened, confused, and deeply preoccupied with their own safety.

The foreign embassies in Leopoldville also contributed in their own way to the general confusion. The Western embassies, fearful of Lumumba and of growing signs of Soviet influence, were inexhaustible sources of rumor and suggestions for impossible courses of action by ONUC. The African envoys were more realistic though equally apprehensive, and for the most part did their best to exercise a moderating influence. Little was known of what the Soviet Embassy was doing or not doing, but the existence of fifteen Soviet transport aircraft based in Stanleyville under Lumumba's direct control haunted the imagination of those who already feared Lumumba and hung like a sword of Damocles over the capital city. Reports of the atrocities and brutalities committed by the ANC in Kasai added a note of horror to the already near-hysterical atmosphere. In this strange situation, ONUC headquarters was a last resort and a focus of exaggerated hopes, requests for protection, protests, rumors, and conflicting demands for action from all sides. Caught between the passivity of the President and the frenetic activity of the Prime Minister, the ONUC staff did its best to

---

* *Uhuru Lumumba,* by Serge Michel, a French journalist whom the Algerian FLN office in Tunis had lent to Lumumba as a press adviser, gives some impression of the atmosphere of Lumumba's entourage.[26]

separate truth from rumor, to act where action was really needed, to protect people who were in real danger, to keep public utilities and services running, and not to get involved in the internal political imbroglio. All possible opportunities were taken, both by direct contact with Ministers and politicians and through intermediaries such as the African envoys, to counsel moderation and conciliation and to urge the Congolese factions to compose their differences and face up to the real and daunting problems of their country.

The ONUC deputy commander, General Ben Hammou Kettani, who had also become Lumumba's military adviser at the Prime Minister's request, had embarked, with a large team of Moroccan officers, on the vital task of instilling order, discipline, and training into the Congolese Army. As Lumumba's military adviser, Kettani unceasingly urged that the army be kept out of the political struggle.

In the first days of September, Cordier warned Hammarskjold that serious clashes between different tribal elements of the ANC in Leopoldville might well occur. The tension and complete lack of communication between Kasavubu and Lumumba had become even more acute since Lumumba had ordered the army into action in Kasai, and direct Soviet support for the Prime Minister had certainly increased the President's hostility toward him. The foreign embassies were alive with rumors of plots and counterplots.

Cordier got his first direct indication of what was in the wind early on September 3, when, at Kasavubu's request, he visited him at his residence. The President told Cordier that for the good of the Congo he was going to exercise his constitutional right to dismiss Lumumba. When Cordier immediately dissociated the UN from any part in this plan, Kasavubu gave him a letter which began by saying that he had already dismissed Lumumba. When Cordier pointed out that this was untrue, Kasavubu said he had wanted to give Cordier the letter first. Cordier refused to accept it on the grounds that it attempted to make the UN a party to the dismissal of the Prime Minister. Kasavubu then urged that ONUC close the Parliament. Cordier again declined. The President then asked that ONUC arrest some twenty-five persons. Cordier refused, and did so again when Kasavubu finally reduced the list to one man, whom Cordier assumed to be Lumumba. Cordier asked Kasavubu if he had discussed his ideas with his colleagues in the government, to which Kasavubu replied that he had not and that no one ever told him anything either. Before leaving, Cordier warned the President of the probable disorders that would result from his proposed action.

This strange interview caused Cordier to consult Hammarskjold by Telex on the position that ONUC should take in the event of a political showdown. Hammarskjold felt that "even hypothetical discussion of later possibilities and our action in situation which may arise would place us in a most exposed position."[27] He realized, however, that the pressing realities of the situation in Leopoldville might make a cautious and agreed course of action impossible. "If you have to go ahead," he told Cordier, "time may be more important than our comments. . . . At any time you may face the situation of complete disintegration of authority that would put you in a situation of emergency which in my view would entitle you to greater freedom of action in protection of law and order. The degree of disintegration thus widening your rights is a question of judgment."[28] Later on the same day he sent more precise instructions to Cordier, evidently wishing to avoid any possibility of misunderstanding. "Prior to any change in political situation your line to Kasavubu is only possible one: We maintain law and order under UN rules, not being a tool for anyone. Another UN stand taken prior to drastic action—even hypothetical discussion now of possible moves after such action—would make us parties to possible internal conflict."[29]

Nothing further of interest happened until the afternoon of Sunday, September 4, when Cordier was visited by Joseph Ileo,[30] the president of the Congolese Senate, accompanied by several tribal leaders of the Kasai Baluba, who asked for UN help in stopping the massacre by the ANC. Cordier assured Ileo that the UN force now had instructions to intervene in tribal killings such as had occurred in Bakwanga. The Baluba leaders expressed the fear that the persecution of the Baluba might soon spread to Leopoldville.

In New York, Hammarskjold called a Sunday meeting of his closest advisers to review the latest developments. The Soviet intervention with transport planes, trucks, and some directing personnel had, he believed, revived the possibility of a Korean type of situation with a distinct threat of wider war. The threat of a Soviet intervention at Lumumba's request, with all its possible consequences, now seemed too real to ignore.

His idea for meeting this new danger was for the UN to concentrate on the future financial and technical assistance needs of the Congo and to elaborate a convincing plan for assistance requiring $150 million to $200 million for one year, for which he proposed to appeal to member governments.[31] If this imaginative plan was to have any hope of success, law and order in the Congo had to be reestablished and the risk of civil war eliminated. This would require that the Security Council appeal again to all governments to abstain from any action that might complicate or delay a solution to the Congo problem. This appeal would apply equally to Belgium, the U.S.S.R., and any other government giving unilateral aid to any one of the factions in the Congo.

When, at Kasavubu's request, Cordier again visited him on the afternoon of September 5, there was a desultory discussion of various trivial matters. Only when Cordier was actually leaving did Kasavubu inform him, almost casually, that he was going to dismiss Lumumba at 8:30 that very evening. Cordier pointed out that Kasavubu would be solely and entirely responsible for any such action, and suggested only that ONUC be informed of his final decision. At 7:30 p.m. Kasavubu's Belgian adviser, A. J. van Bilsen, appeared at ONUC headquarters to inform Cordier that Kasavubu was indeed going ahead with his plan. He also communicated a request from the President that ONUC provide guards for the Presidential residence, for the Parliament—which Lumumba had some weeks before asked ONUC to guard—and for the radio station.

At 8:15 p.m., Kasavubu appeared at the Leopoldville radio station and made a short anouncement dismissing the Prime Minister and six Ministers. He accused Lumumba of betraying the task entrusted to him, of governing arbitrarily, and of plunging the country into civil war. In accordance with his constitutional powers under the Loi Fondamentale, he appointed the president of the Senate, Joseph Ileo, as Prime Minister and asked him to form a new government immediately. He pledged himself to end the civil war and to resolve the difficulties of the country, and concluded by appealing for calm. Immediately after his broadcast, Kasavubu requested Cordier by letter to make arrangements forthwith for ONUC to take over responsibility for the maintenance of law and order throughout the whole territory of the Congo. In a second letter he requested the immediate closing of all airfields in the Republic of the Congo to all except ONUC aircraft.

Thirty minutes after Kasavubu's broadcast Lumumba delivered a highly emotional speech, which was repeated three times over the radio during the evening, once in Lingala and twice in French, declaring that Kasavubu was no longer Chief of State. He called upon the people to rise and upon the army to die with him.

Kasavubu's requests put Hammarskjold and his representatives in the Congo in a new and uniquely difficult position, which Rajeshwar Dayal, who was to take over from Cordier on September 8, described a few days later as follows: "It has been made clear, times without number, that the UN is here to help but not to intervene, to advise but not to order, to conciliate but not to take sides. . . . We have refused to take any position if it could only remotely be considered as an act of intervention. But how can the duty of maintaining law and order be discharged without taking specific action when necessary? That is the problem which faces us daily and which is yet to be solved."[32]

For Hammarskjold, the split between Kasavubu and Lumumba presented an even deeper dilemma. His representatives in the Congo had to be given a free enough hand to allow them to react effectively to the immediate situation, but he himself must also be able to justify their actions to the Security Council in New York, far from the turmoil of the Congo. The predominant reality in the Security Council was that East and West had now taken sides, the East backing Lumumba and the West Kasavubu. All UN actions in the Congo would henceforth be judged from the standpoint not of their real objective in terms of law and order or the protection of human life, nor of how they gave effect to the original mandate given to ONUC by the Security Council, but rather of which Congolese faction they might seem to benefit.

The Bakwanga massacre, the mood of the Leopoldville garrison, the threat of a clash between the rival youth movements of Kasavubu and Lumumba, and the lively expectation of further trouble had already caused Cordier to instruct ONUC unit commanders that they might have to use force in legitimate self-defense to hold positions necessary to the performance of their duties, and that they should intervene for the maintenance of law and order subject to the judgment of the local commander in a given situation. As soon as the constitutional crisis began, Hammarskjold sent general instructions designed to strengthen Cordier against pressures both from the various Congolese factions and from the foreign embassies in Leopoldville. Action by the UN for the maintenance of law and order, provided it was in line with the general principles of the Organization and for the general purposes indicated by the Security Council, could be undertaken in consultation with the constitutional government of the Congo or at its request and would be within the mandate provided by the resolutions of the Council.

But now there was a new and highly controversial question—who was the "constitutional government"? Hammarskjold's understanding of the position after studying the provisional Constitution of the Congo, the Loi Fondamentale, was that the Chief of State clearly had the authority under Article 22 to dismiss the Prime Minister and appoint a new one, provided his action was countersigned by at least one Minister—and in this case it had been by Foreign Minister Bomboko and the Resident Minister in Belgium, Albert Delvaux[33]— although if a new government had not yet been established, the Constitution made no express provision for the resulting situation. It was theoretically possible either to consider that the Head of State was the only person legally competent to speak for the government in an emergency, or alternatively that the government might be regarded as continuing in a caretaker capacity. On the other hand, there could be no doubt that the Prime Minister's attempt to dismiss the President

was unconstitutional and had put Lumumba in a very doubtful position. For all practical purposes, it seemed that in the present circumstances the UN must inevitably regard the Chief of State as the only
unquestioned constitutional authority.*

The provisions of the Loi Fondamentale notwithstanding, the three
requests that Kasavubu had made to Cordier posed an awkward problem. Under the Organization's function of maintaining law and order,
both the President's requests for personal protection and his general
request that ONUC be responsible for the maintenance of law and
order could be granted, although in both respects it was for the UN
command to decide how and to what extent it could carry them out
without affecting the balance in the internal political struggle. In any
case, ONUC was already guarding Lumumba's residence. The request
to close the airports and the radio station, on the other hand, could
only be met if the UN command believed such action to be essential for
the avoidance of serious disorders. While ONUC should obviously take
due account of the views of the legitimate constitutional authority,
which in the existing circumstances could only be the President, the
principle of nonintervention in internal conflicts also had to be preserved without jeopardizing ONUC's capacity to deal with a highly
explosive situation.

In Hammarskjold's view, the apparently imminent threat of large-
scale violence automatically gave the people on the spot a right to act
as they thought best in the circumstances. He therefore added what
he called an "irresponsible observation" to his instructions to Cordier.
"In such a situation," he cabled, "responsible people on the spot might
commit themselves to what the Secretary-General could not justify
doing himself—taking the risk of being disowned when it no longer
mattered."[34]

On the night of September 5, Leopoldville was full of alarms and
rumors. Colonel Mobutu, the Chief of Staff and deputy commander
of the ANC, brought his whole family for safety to the house of General
Kettani. Kettani, as Lumumba's military adviser, had urged Lumumba
and Mobutu to ensure that the four thousand ANC soldiers in Leopoldville remain outside the conflict and put their arms and ammunition
under UN supervision. The Russian transport planes in Stanleyville
were another source of fear and speculation, and when it was reported
that there was a plan for them to take off from Stanleyville at 9:30 p.m.
on September 6 with a full load of Congolese troops, it was widely
assumed that they would be coming to Leopoldville.** During the night

---

* An excellent discussion of this constitutional question is given by Catherine
Hoskyns, op. cit., pp. 208–10.
** It was later learned that their destination was Luluabourg.

of September 5, ONUC received many calls from political leaders of all factions asking for protection.

Cordier spent the night of September 5–6 thinking over the interlocking dilemmas of the situation and consulting with his military and civilian advisers. It was generally agreed that the mobility of the ANC must be reduced by closing the airfields, and that incitements of the population, especially of rival youth groups, must be stopped by closing down the radio station. Cordier therefore decided to close all major airports in the Congo, and on September 6 he also gave orders to close down the Leopoldville radio station.[35] Having in mind Hammarskjold's "irresponsible observation" and feeling that he must take the responsibility himself, he did not attempt to consult the Secretary-General on this decision. The transmitters of Radio Leopoldville were switched off soon after midday, and at the same time steps were taken to close the airfields throughout the Congo to all except ONUC aircraft.

Hammarskjold was taken aback when he first heard of Cordier's action through a news-agency report, for he immediately foresaw, with a clarity which was not possible for those directly involved in Leopoldville, how the action would inevitably be interpreted outside the Congo. Cordier and his advisers did not know that Kasavubu, through his Bakongo contacts and his friendship with the Abbé Youlou across the river in Brazzaville, would be given access to the even more powerful transmitters of Radio Brazzaville. Thus what was intended to be a general ban on political broadcasts put Lumumba at a considerable disadvantage, especially since Lumumba was a far more effective demagogue than Kasavubu, whose normal reaction to any crisis was to lock himself in his house and go to bed. This fortuitous consequence of Cordier's decision was later cited as evidence that both his and Hammarskjold's primary intention had been to hamper Lumumba. The closing of the airports also had a greater effect on Lumumba than on Kasavubu, who had no Soviet or any other aircraft at his disposal, and was in any case not engaged, as Lumumba was, in shuttling troops about the country for military purposes. The immediate reason for closing the airports was to reduce the very real risk of civil disorder, fratricidal war, and pointless violence, but later on Lumumba's partisans argued that it was a patently anti-Lumumba measure.

Apart from immobilizing the fifteen Soviet transport planes which General Lundula, under Lumumba's orders, was using to ferry ANC troops into the murderous confusion in Bakwanga, the most important immediate effect of closing all Congolese airports was the prevention of further shipments of arms to Tshombe through the Elisabethville Airport and the halting of the deployment of the Katangese gendarmerie into the disaffected areas of North Katanga, where they too were persecuting the Baluba.

Rajeshwar Dayal, who had arrived in Leopoldville on September 5, the first day of the crisis, was also taken aback by Cordier's decisions, for he saw that he would both be associated with them and would have to do his best to rescind them as soon as possible. The situation in Leopoldville was so different from the rational UN policy which he and Hammarskjold had just discussed in New York that for a moment he considered resigning, but he soon realized the monstrous complexity of the circumstances and the necessity of preserving the UN operation as the sole potential element of stability.

In reporting on the closing of the radio and airfields, Cordier cabled Hammarskjold that "we have not chosen sides, but the constitutional party has chosen to follow UN line,"[36] while the other party had long insisted that the UN should give support to political and military aims leading to civil conflict and against the UN mandate to maintain peace and order. This interpretation, though perfectly valid from the perspective in Leopoldville, was naive in the wider political context of the Congo operation. Hammarskjold, dismayed though he was by Cordier's decisions, gave full public support to a subordinate who was in difficulties. He informed Cordier of the arguments he would use to defend the closing of the radio station, "which, according to agencies, is now a—basically regrettable—fact."[37] The words "basically regrettable," written into the typed draft of the cable in his own handwriting, give an indication of his true feelings. The ultimate responsibility was his, and he would defend the actions of his representatives in the field.* He doubtless also remembered his "irresponsible observation," giving Cordier a free hand in case of emergency.

Cordier was under heavy pressure from all sides. On September 6 he refused to see either Kasavubu or Lumumba pending efforts by Jean David, a Haitian UN official who had been lent as an assistant to Kasavubu, to effect a reconciliation between the two Congolese leaders. It was not only Lumumba's supporters who were unhappy. The U.S. Ambassador, Clare Timberlake, who on the previous day had infuriated Cordier by calling several times to insist that the UN "fight it out,"[39] was outraged that Kasavubu was excluded from the radio

---

* A year later, when the question of taking over Radio Katanga arose, Hammarskjold commented that taking over Radio Katanga under paragraph A-1 of the February 21, 1961, resolution, which had been adopted in the interim, "has justification and validity which did not exist in case of similar action September 5, 1960 in Leo[poldville]; this action was justified in Secco [the Security Council] solely on 'emergency rights' basis."[38]

and that the UN was not supporting the President against Lumumba. On the evening of September 6, Colonel Mobutu followed up Lumumba's protests by visiting Cordier to protest again about the closing of the radio and airfields and about the long-standing UN guard on the Leopoldville post office. Mobutu stated that Lumumba, as Minister of Defense, had ordered the ANC to take over the radio and post office. A compromise arrangement was finally agreed upon whereby the UN and the ANC were stationed together at both places.

During Cordier's all-night consultations with his staff on September 5–6, the danger of leaving the four thousand ANC soldiers in Leopoldville unpaid and unfed had been discussed, and General Kettani, who as Lumumba's military adviser shared Colonel Mobutu's fears on this score, suggested that the UN try to provide food and pay in order to forestall another irruption of the army into the political conflict. This gave rise to an episode which was subsequently extensively misrepresented. On September 6, Cordier asked Hammarskjold to raise immediately the million dollars required to pay the ANC. The next day Hammarskjold told Cordier that the amount would be transferred on September 9 to the Banque du Congo and should be used by Cordier through Kettani to meet the pay and food costs of the ANC as a measure in aid of law and order. On September 9, Lundula, Mobutu, and the ANC commanders from Leopoldville, Stanleyville, and Luluabourg met to discuss pay and logistical problems. At this meeting the soldiers argued against Lumumba's order to seize the Leopoldville Airport, especially because they were relying on the UN for the army's pay and food. Later in the day, Kettani informed Lumumba of the arrangements to pay the ANC, and Lumumba, in approving them, proudly told Kettani that it was he who had refused to let the ANC attack the UN guard on the Leopoldville airfield. The actual payment of the ANC began on September 10 under the supervision of Generals Lundula and Kettani and of Colonel Mobutu. On September 11, Lumumba expressed to Dayal his warm appreciation for this and other financial assistance given by the UN.*

Dayal took over from Cordier on September 8. Between Lumumba's extremes of cooperation and furious denunciation and the total inactivity of Kasavubu, there lay an increasing risk of disorder and violence

---

* Another unfounded charge subsequently made against ONUC in order to prove bias against Lumumba was that it had permitted Ileo, Kasavubu's Prime Minister designate, to fly all over the Congo drumming up support, despite the closing of the airfields. Already on September 8, Dayal had categorically denied this rumor, saying that Ileo was incommunicado in Leopoldville in Kasavubu's house. Ileo was certainly in touch with other parts of the Congo, as were the other leaders, but his contacts were by cable or telephone.

if ONUC, now on bad terms with both sides, failed in its efforts at conciliation. The airports and radio could not remain closed for long, both for practical reasons and because of the wider political storm which the action had stirred up. While Dayal searched for a way out of the impasse, Hammarskjold decided to take the matter to the Security Council. On September 7 he had asked the President of the Security Council to convene a meeting[40] to consider his Fourth Report on the Congo.[41] Two days later he asked for an urgent meeting of the Council on the night of September 9.[42] At this meeting, within the context of the longer-term problems of the Congo, he asked for the Council's guidance in the immediate crisis.

He began his opening statement to the Council[43] by "an appraisal of the true character of the vast problem in which the United Nations has had to engage itself in order to forestall the worst."[44] Despite its great natural resources the Congo was financially bankrupt. Because of the complete disruption of normal life it had no revenue or foreign exchange or taxes, and the government was making no effort to provide them. A vivid example of the consequences of this situation was the behavior in Kasai of the ANC units, which Lumumba had sent into the field unpaid and without rations. The government, if it wished to avoid complete collapse, must choose to be financially dependent either on another state or group of states and thus tie its fate to that group, or else depend on the UN and remain politically free. Unless law and order and economic activity were restored, money put into the Congo would be money lost. When the Security Council decided to assist the Congo, it had expected the cooperation of the Congolese government in using to the full the assistance given, but now it was being said that the UN was working against the Congolese government. In the present crisis, "where there was on the one side a Chief of State whom the United Nations must recognize and whom the statements of the Prime Minister had not deprived of his rights, but where there was, on the other side, a Cabinet which continued in being, but the chief of which had put himself in sharp opposition to the Chief of State,"[45] the UN representatives in the Congo had to "avoid any action by which directly or indirectly, openly or by implication, they would pass judgment on the stand taken by either one of the parties in the conflict."[46] In the event, they had had to act on their own responsibility in the emergency because "there was nobody, really nobody with whom they could consult without prejudicing the constitutional issue."[47]

The Secretary-General then described the circumstances in which the radio station and the airfields had been closed, an action "not preceded by any reference of the matter to me, because of the extreme urgency of the problem our people were facing on the spot. This latter fact," he added, "throws, in my view, considerable light on the character of a situation which it is easy to sit in New York and discuss in terms of protocol, but which it requires wisdom and courage to handle when you are at the front. . . . I was not consulted, but I fully endorse the action taken and I have not seen any reason to revise the decisions of my representatives. Naturally, I assume full personal responsibility for what has been done on my behalf, and I do it convinced of the wisdom of the actions and of their complete accordance with the spirit and the letter of the Security Council decisions, adjusted to a situation of unique complication and, of course, utterly unforeseeable when the resolutions of the Council were adopted."[48] He had hoped that conciliation and compromise might have produced an improvement that would make it possible to reopen the radio and the airports quickly, but failing this he now submitted the problem to the Council for its consideration and instructions.

Hammarskjold went on to denounce the barbarities of the ANC's Kasai expedition and the build-up of arms and foreign mercenaries in Katanga, and appealed to all the Congolese leaders to reconcile themselves and cooperate with the UN. The UN operation must continue, he said, because of the hazard the Congo presented for international peace. It was not only the Belgians who had given unilateral assistance to a faction in the Congo. "There are others who follow a similar line, justifying their policy by a reference to the fact that assistance is given to the constitutional government of the country. . . . I believe that the Security Council has now come to a point where it must take a clear line as regards all assistance to the Congo. I believe it will achieve its aims only if it requests now that such assistance should be channelled through the United Nations, and only through the United Nations. It would, thereby, solve the problem of military assistance to Katanga, and it would also solve the problem of abuse of technical assistance in other parts of the Congo, thus at the same time serving the vital interest in a localization of the conflict and the interest in a peaceful solution of the domestic problems of the Congo, without any interference from outside influencing the outcome. Thus, and only thus, could it justify its appeal to member nations for the funds now so desperately needed by the Congo, whether the need is seen by the leaders of the country or not."[49]

On September 9, the Soviet Union issued a statement[50] taking Lumumba's side entirely. "The outrageous colonialist behaviour of the representatives sent by Hammarskjold to the Congo really knows no limits," the Soviet statement read, and it went on to accuse the

Secretary-General of an "unseemly role" and of having failed "to display the minimum of impartiality required of him in the situation that has arisen."[51]

After two meetings, the Security Council showed no desire or intention to respond to Hammarskjold's request for instructions on the closing of the radio station and airports. On September 10 he again urged the Council to give guidance, pointing out that it had communications from both parties before it and should "shoulder its responsibility"[52]—but to no avail. "I doubt whether we shall get anything out of the Secco [Security Council] in their present mood,"[53] he cabled Dayal. They must therefore try to find an agreed basis with Kasavubu and Lumumba upon which the emergency measures could be liquidated as soon as possible. On the other hand, since Kasavubu and Lumumba had now formed rival governments, the UN could not be responsible for a decision that would give a decisive advantage to either of them.

Hammarskjold instructed Dayal to negotiate with Lumumba and Kasavubu on the reopening of the Leopoldville radio station on the firm condition that it would be used for peaceful purposes only, and on an equal basis for all political parties. If this approach succeeded, the airfields could be reopened on similar conditions.

Dayal saw Kasavubu and Lumumba on September 10. Lumumba started by threatening to use force at once. When Dayal advised patience and moderation, Lumumba changed his tone and said that he would not order the use of force but feared that the army and the people might take matters into their own hands. He thanked Dayal for UN financial assistance and offered him his full cooperation.

The next day, among other wild accusations, Lumumba charged that UN troops had invaded his house. On investigation this charge proved to refer to the UN Ghana guard which Lumumba himself had requested. Lumumba also made a halfhearted attempt to take the radio station by force, but was easily dissuaded by the UN Ghana troops. Lumumba and Kasavubu then agreed to Dayal's conditions, and the radio was reopened at 11 a.m. on Monday, September 12. The airports were reopened, for nonmilitary flights only, on the following day.

The reopening of the radio and the airports did not altogether bear out the argument that their closing had been predominantly to Lumumba's disadvantage, and the sang-froid of Lumumba's principal military supporters seemed to be considerably shaken at the thought of what might happen next. On September 12, Colonel Mobutu, Lumumba's chief of staff, appeared at ONUC headquarters in civilian clothes and stated he was going to resign because of political interference with the army. Dayal urged him to stay at his post for the good of the country. The next day General Lundula put himself under UN protection. Everyone seemed extremely nervous and confused. The Prime Minister designate, Ileo, begged Dayal to resume control of the radio station. Dayal refused and was surprised the next day to receive, through the Ghana Ambassador, a request from Lumumba that the UN guards both at the radio and at the airport be increased.

This series of unexpected and inconsistent events reached its climax on the evening of September 14, when Colonel Mobutu announced over the radio that he was neutralizing the Chief of State, the two rival governments, and the Parliament until the end of the year and would meanwhile call in "technicians" to run the country. Dayal and his staff were astonished at this development, not least because Mobutu was actually in the ONUC heaquarters when his recorded message was broadcast. Dayal quickly dispelled any idea that ONUC would have anything to do with the coup, and Mobutu was requested to leave the ONUC headquarters at once. Later in the evening, during a press conference at the Hotel Regina, Mobutu stated, in an apparently off-the-cuff response to a question, that he was giving the Soviet-bloc embassies in Leopoldville forty-eight hours to leave.

Next day Lumumba, who had gone to the army camp to find Mobutu, was attacked by Baluba soldiers and was rescued and escorted out only with extreme difficulty by Dayal and soldiers of the UN Ghana contingent. On September 17, despite Dayal's urgent insistence to Kasavubu that the insulting expulsion of the Soviet-bloc embassies be rescinded and that instead the President should firmly state that all aid must be channeled through the UN, the personnel of the Soviet-bloc embassies, under a UN escort requested by them, were taken to the airport and flown out of the country.

Soviet opposition to Hammarskjold's policies in the Congo, which found an echo in the lofty statements of de Gaulle,* was rapidly developing into a full-scale attack on himself and on the office of the Secretary-General. To Hammarskjold's inquiry about the status of the Soviet aircraft flying troops into Kasai,[55] the Soviet representative

---

* De Gaulle said at a press conference on September 5: "If the United States, Great Britain, and France had concerted their positions in this matter from the beginning of the crisis; if these three powers had first encouraged the Belgians and the Congolese to establish their mutual relations on a practical and reasonable basis; and if these three powers had also taken steps to help the young state of the Congo get started and finally to make it understood that once the emancipation of the Congo had been assured and guaranteed by the West, no intervention from elsewhere would be permitted, I feel that the result would have been preferable to the bloody anarchy that now exists in this new state. I believe, furthermore, that the prestige and cohesion of the West would have been better assured in this way than by playing second fiddle to the so-called 'United' Nations, whose action is inadequate and very costly." [54]

replied on September 10 that the Security Council[56] had made no restriction on the right of the Congo government to ask another government for assistance nor had it given UN officials the right to control such assistance.

At the Council's meeting on September 12, Valerian A. Zorin took Kuznetsov's place as the representative of the Soviet Union, and the tone as well as the substance of Soviet interventions on the Congo changed sharply. Zorin assailed Hammarskjold's conduct of the Congo operation with a new violence.[57] Repeating all the previous Soviet accusations, he added that Belgium, the United States, and France had been preparing a conspiracy to overthrow the Lumumba government. He attacked the cease-fire that ONUC had declared on the borders of Katanga, which constituted, he maintained, a ban on the entry of Central Government troops into Katanga—a military feat of which the ANC was entirely incapable anyway, even if this had been the real intention of the cease-fire. Zorin maintained that all these actions showed that Hammarskjold and his representatives had taken a definite position in the political conflict in the Congo and, in the words of Khrushchev, delivered from the *Baltika* in mid-Atlantic to the London *Daily Express*, "that Mr. Hammarskjold's actions in fact dovetail with the policy of countries which have always espoused positions of colonialism."[58]

To Zorin's long tirade Hammarskjold replied at some length[59] and in a tone unusual for the Secretary-General replying to the representative of a member state:

> The representative of the Soviet Union said himself, and quoted both from the Soviet Government and from Mr. Khrushchev's statements to the effect that I was the conscious tool of imperialist plans and consciously served the interests of colonialists. I understand that the spokesman of the Soviet Union in this respect feels that he voiced the opinion of the peoples of Africa and Asia, for which the Soviet Union regards itself as an interpreter.
>
> I am sure that these peoples will have followed and will study with greatest interest the statements of the representative of the Soviet Union. They are able to form their own opinion. I have no doubt that they will express it, and I would deem their reactions to be those of the peoples directly interested and with direct and complete knowledge of of my activities both in the Congo and through the years in Asia and Africa.
>
> My record is on the table of the Security Council and of the United Nations with such completeness that there is no need for me to add anything or to explain anything. I stand by it, and that is all I have to say.
>
> . . . It was mentioned that for the first two months my personal representative in the Congo [Bunche] was an American, but it was

omitted that this was the natural function of the person in question in view of the position he holds in the United Nations Secretariat, and also because of his unmatched personal record of fighting for the interest of the African peoples and for minorities.

It was also mentioned that for some ten days or a fortnight my Executive Assistant, an American, was in Leopoldville; but it was not mentioned that the present Personal Representative, who will be staying there until further notice, is an Indian. . . .

I may again draw to the attention of the Council, and especially to the attention of the representative of the Soviet Union, that this United Nations Command, which is now said to represent a colonizing element, apart from the Supreme Commander, who is from a country which never had any colonies, consists of one Moroccan and one Ethiopian general, at present assisted by an Indian general. But, of course, in official statements I have recently seen it hinted that even some African countries have now turned colonizers. I begin, quite frankly, to feel uncertain about what this word means in modern political terminology. . . .

Let me only, in concluding, say that among a total of 127 civilian experts 87 are from countries which, by no stretch of the imagination, can be linked with NATO. And after that, of all the Force—now, I think, some 18,000 men—some 500 are from NATO countries, and half of that number we have had to take because Poland did not find it possible to help us.[60]

Mongi Slim of Tunisia once again came to Hammarskjold's aid, blaming the Belgians and the situation in Katanga for the tension between ONUC and the Congolese authorities, and supporting the UN action in closing the radio and airports. Since Slim himself had just returned from the Congo, his opinion carried considerable weight; as Hammarskjold said, he had "seen the nightmare for himself."[61] Slim suggested that the Security Council now try to bring the Congolese leaders together and finished by expressing his wholehearted support for the UN operation.

There were now signs that the radio and airport crisis might cause the withdrawal of some of the contingents of the UN force. On September 13, Hammarskjold addressed a long message to Kwame Nkrumah giving an account of the crisis and pointing out the role that Lumumba's inconsistencies had played in it. "If grave unrest threatens because of actions for which part of the responsibility rests with those who have asked the Organization to assist them in the maintenance of law and order," he wrote, "the Organization is not therefore forced to forget its own responsibility for law and order."[62] On September 14, he appealed to the Heads of State of Yugoslavia, Indonesia, the United Arab Republic, Ceylon, Guinea, and Morocco not to withdraw their troops, a movement that would inevitably lead to "a disintegration within the country provoking open and active involvement of major powers."[63]

Hammarskjold was now inclined to present to the Council, in the barest and starkest form, the realities of the situation in Leopoldville as described in Dayal's cables, and he drafted such a speech on September 15. In it he referred to the total incoherence of all the Congo's political institutions and leaders, the empty treasury, growing unemployment, and the total lack of administration, of a judiciary, of tax collection and even of functioning schools. "With complete and utter recklessness," he wrote, "the political struggle—if it can be so called—is going on without logic or sense. Meanwhile the country is hustling headlong on the road to disintegration and chaos. The leaders resent any action taken which is aimed at saving them from the consequences of their own actions."[64] The partisanship of the army not only increased the danger of violence but added a third party to the constitutional authorities that had to be dealt with. Dayal advised strongly against such outspokenness on the ground that it would hamper his mission's efforts at conciliation, whereupon Hammarskjold asked Dayal to submit a comprehensive report of his own.

The Security Council had before it an American and a Soviet draft resolution. The U.S. resolution[65] asked for financial contributions, for the settlement of internal conflicts by peaceful means, and for all states to refrain from sending the Congo military aid except through the UN. The Soviet resolution[66] instructed the Secretary-General to remove the present command of the UN force because its actions constituted a "flagrant violation of the Security Council decisions."[67] On September 16, Alex Quaison-Sackey of Ghana, also just back from the Congo, addressed the Council in very moderate terms and supported the idea that all aid should be channeled through the UN. Although "Ghana had not been very happy over certain matters,"[68] he concluded with a warm personal tribute to the Secretary-General.

When the Council reached a total deadlock with all resolutions being voted down or vetoed, including the compromise resolution of Ceylon and Tunisia,[69] the question was transferred,[70] at the instance of the United States and over the protests of Zorin, to an Emergency Special Session of the General Assembly.[71]

The Emergency Special Session[72] opened on the evening of September 17 and heard much the same speeches as had been given in the Security Council. Zorin attacked the Secretary-General more personally and harshly than before and goaded Hammarskjold to a reply in which he even hinted at resigning: "The representative of the Soviet Union used strong language which, quite frankly, I do not know how to interpret. The General Assembly knows me well enough to realize that

I would not wish to serve one day beyond the point at which such continued service would be, and would be considered to be, in the best interests of this Organization."[73] The obvious complexities and dangers of the situation were such, however, that even those governments which were critical of Hammarskjold's Congo policy saw that more was to be gained by supporting him than by destroying his authority and wrecking the UN operation.

On September 16, Lumumba had issued a violent statement demanding the total withdrawal of all UN personnel, whose blood would flow if they failed to leave. He threatened that in eight days' time Soviet troops would come to the Congo *"chasser brutalement l'ONU de notre République. . . . S'il est nécessaire de faire l'appel au diable pour sauver le pays,"* he rather tactlessly added, *"je le ferai sans hésitation, persuadé qu'avec l'appui total des Soviets, je sortirai malgré tout victorieux."*[74]* Lumumba followed up this statement four days later by a letter to Hammarskjold enclosing a reconciliation agreement with Kasavubu which *"met pratiquement fin à la crise Congolaise"*[75] ("virtually puts an end to the Congo crisis"), asking for full UN assistance, and assuring Hammarskjold of his total cooperation.

In the Assembly, the African states agreed upon a resolution that supported the UN operation and Hammarskjold's interpretation of the principles on which it should be based, and demanded that all military aid be channeled to the Congo through the UN. The African resolution also appealed to the Congolese to solve their differences by peaceful means. It was adopted[76] in the early morning of September 20, by seventy votes with eleven abstentions—the Soviet bloc, France, and the Union of South Africa. This overwhelming vote of confidence gave the Secretary-General moral support both for a further effort to reconcile the Congolese leaders and for preventing the shipping of arms and military personnel to any faction in the Congo. He was also authorized to set up a Congo Fund for technical assistance. "I have been happy indeed," Hammarskjold told the General Assembly, "to note the correspondence between the attitude reflected in the resolution and that of the Secretariat as presented most recently in the fourth report. I believe that I am right in finding in this fact evidence of a fundamental agreement with and within the African world regarding the aims and the very philosophy of this major United Nations operation."[77]

Although the vote was widely regarded in the West as a triumph

---

* Translation: "To expel by force the UN from our Republic. . . . If it is necessary to appeal to the devil to save the country, I shall do it without hesitation, persuaded as I am that, in spite of everything, with the full support of the Soviet Union, I shall emerge victorious."

for Hammarskjold, the congratulations that came pouring in gave him no illusions that the path ahead would be easier. A violent reaction could be expected from Khrushchev, who had just arrived in New York. The Assembly vote also concealed the fundamental disagreement between Western countries and African governments on the future direction to be taken in the Congo. The fact was that a new and active United Nations policy of reconciliation and reconstruction in the Congo, as suggested by Hammarskjold, would now be hampered by those Western countries which supported Mobutu, which were covertly sympathetic to Tshombe, and which wished above all to have Lumumba out of the way.

17

THE GENERAL ASSEMBLY, SEPTEMBER–DECEMBER 1960

THE FIFTEENTH SESSION OF THE GENERAL ASSEMBLY, which convened on the afternoon of September 20, 1960, was by any standard an extraordinary gathering, attended as it was by twenty-three Heads of Government and fifty-seven Foreign Ministers. "Somewhere a voice is calling," a journalist wrote at the time, "and the world rumbustiously responds."[1] This Assembly session was to be a demonstration both of the new significance of the United Nations in a period of rapid decolonization, and of the enormous difficulties with which the Organization was faced. Any gathering that included Khrushchev, Castro, Nkrumah, Nehru, Sukarno, King Hussein, Nasser, Sékou Touré, Macmillan, Eisenhower, and Tito was not likely to be dull.

The Assembly meeting was marked from the beginning by dramatic interludes, the first of which took place just before the session opened. On the evening of September 19, before the final meeting of the Special Emergency Session on the Congo, Hammarskjold and his staff were settling down to a quick supper in the office dining room when the guards at the Secretariat entrance to the building called to say that a group of bearded men in olive-drab uniforms were approaching the main gates. Hammarskjold just had time to prepare his office as for the visit of a Head of State, with the double doors of the reception room open and himself stationed at the open door of his office, when Premier Fidel Castro of Cuba and his companions came surging down the corridor of the thirty-eighth floor. Hammarskjold's dignified preparations had a steadying effect on the impromptu occasion, and as if by long-standing appointment Castro, whom Hammarskjold had met in 1959,[2] was ushered into the Secretary-General's office. During the pause until a Spanish interpreter arrived, Hammarskjold and Castro made friendly but more or less unsuccessful efforts to converse. When the interpreter arrived Castro explained that he and his party had been thrown out of the Hotel Shelburne on Lexington Avenue because the proprietor was anti-Cuban.* Hammarskjold offered to find alternative accommodation and meanwhile arranged for sandwiches and drinks to be served to Castro's entourage in the lounge adjacent to the Security Council chamber. After a suitable interlude for refreshment, the Cuban party left for the Hotel Theresa in Harlem where they stayed for the rest of their time in New York.

In the introduction to his annual report,[3] Hammarskjold had tried, as usual, to provide an analysis of the current political situation in the UN as a guide for the Assembly's deliberations. The introduction centered on the Congo experience, which was "putting the United Nations to a test both as regards the functions of its parliamentary institutions and as regards the efficiency and strength of its executive capacity."[4] His underlying theme, "the possibilities of substantive action by the UN in a split world,"[5] was a call, addressed especially to the new and the nonaligned states, to use the UN to keep "newly arising conflicts outside the sphere of bloc differences."[6] In the Middle East, Laos, and the Congo the UN's role had been to fill a power vacuum between the main blocs "so that neither of the blocs will attempt to fill it. . . . Temporarily," he wrote, "and pending the filling of the vacuum by normal means, the United Nations enters the picture on the basis of its non-commitment to any power bloc. . . . As a universal organization neutral in the big Power struggles over ideology and influence in the world, subordinated to the common will of the Member Governments and free from any aspirations of its own to power and influence over any group or nation, the UN can render

---

* The hotel management later maintained that the Cubans had merely been asked not to cook in their rooms, and since it afterwards transpired that the Cubans had made reservations in the Hotel Theresa in Harlem several weeks before, it seems possible that Castro had wanted to make a show of leaving the Shelburne for Harlem anyway. An additional reason may have been to protest against the restrictions imposed by the United States authorities, for security and other reasons, on Khrushchev and some of the other Heads of State.

service which can be received without suspicion and which can be absorbed without influencing the free choice of the peoples."[7]

Hammarskjold's subsidiary theme, that the UN "has increasingly become the main platform—and the main protector of the interests— of those many nations who feel themselves strong as members of the international family but who are weak in isolation," was unlikely to commend itself strongly to any of the great powers. The small nations, he wrote, "look to the Organization as a spokesman and as an agent for principles which give them strength in an international concert in which other voices can mobilize all the weight of armed force, wealth, and historical role and that influence which is the other side of a special responsibility for peace and security."[8] This constituency of smaller states was well represented among the Heads of Government who attended the session.

The Assembly session opened happily enough with the admission of thirteen new African states* and Cyprus to membership. It received a message from Emperor Haile Selassie regretting the failure of the summit conference in Paris in May because of the U-2 spy-plane incident and hoping that the Assembly, with the presence of so many Heads of State, would do better. President Eisenhower spoke in support of Hammarskjold's actions in the Congo and demanded again that individual governments should not intervene but should channel all assistance to the Congo through the United Nations. Tito, in the context of colonial interference in the new countries, took a stand only moderately critical of the Congo operation. Nkrumah, although he strongly defended Lumumba and criticized the UN for what he called a failure to distinguish between legal and illegal authorities, specifically refused to blame either the Security Council or the Secretary-General for these shortcomings and merely urged an African solution in the Congo and the withdrawal of all non-African troops.

Khrushchev, on September 23, departed drastically from the prevailing tone of moderation. Starting off by denouncing Eisenhower and the United States over the U-2 incident and over its policy toward Cuba, he proceeded to a violent attack upon colonialists in general and upon their alleged activities in the Congo in particular. "It is deplorable," he said, "that they have been doing their dirty work in the Congo through the Secretary-General of the United Nations and his staff. . . . The Assembly should call Mr. Hammarskjold to order and

---

* Cameroon, Central African Republic, Chad, Congo (Brazzaville), Congo (Leopoldville), Dahomey, Gabon, Ivory Coast, Madagascar, Niger, Somalia, Togo, and Upper Volta.

ensure that he does not misuse the position of the Secretary-General but carries out his functions in strict accordance with the provisions of the United Nations Charter and the decisions of the Security Council."[9] Later in his speech, after a wide-ranging survey of the political problems before the Assembly, Khrushchev returned to the attack on Hammarskjold. "Conditions have clearly matured," he said, "to the point where the post of Secretary-General, who alone directs the staff and alone interprets and executes the decisions of the Security Council and the sessions of the General Assembly, should be abolished."[10] Instead the executive organ of the UN should consist of three persons, representing respectively the military bloc of the Western powers, the socialist states, and the neutralist countries. This formula soon came to be known as the "troika."

Khrushchev's speech was not wholly a surprise to Hammarskjold. The events in the Congo, culminating in Mobutu's expulsion of the Soviet-bloc embassies, the overwhelming vote of confidence in the Secretary-General by the Special Emergency Session of the General Assembly, in which all Asian and African States had participated instead of following the Soviet lead, and the very moderation of the preceding speakers, had certainly influenced Khrushchev's mood, quite apart from more fundamental factors.

Hammarskjold deplored the general tendency to personalize his differences with Khrushchev and refused to consider the troika proposal as a question of confidence in himself. He had received an overwhelming vote of confidence from the Assembly only a week before and was strongly opposed to Secretary of State Herter's well-intentioned idea of asking the General Assembly for another vote of confidence in the Secretary-General. Such moves could only make it more difficult to put clearly before the Assembly both the real implications of the troika proposal and the problems of the UN Congo operation. On the latter question Hammarskjold was, in any case, less immediately worried by Khrushchev's denunciations than by Nkrumah's bid for leadership of an all-African Congo operation, which would, he believed, have disastrous results both for the Congo and for peace in Africa.

Khrushchev's troika, which amounted to an attempt to extend the veto power to the working of the Secretariat, involved the future effectiveness of the UN itself, and Hammarskjold felt he must oppose it by all possible means. On September 26 he addressed the Assembly[11] with what amounted to a declaration of principle, designed to bring home the significance and potential seriousness of the situation for the middle and smaller countries, and especially for those which had recently become independent, for whom membership in the UN was the best protection against great-power pressures. "The General Assembly," he began, "is facing a question not of any specific actions but of the principles guiding United Nations activities. In those respects it is a question not of a man but of an institution. . . .

"It is common experience that nothing, in the heat of emotion, is regarded as more partial by one who takes himself the position of a party than strict impartiality." This strict impartiality might "at any stage become an obstacle for those who work for certain political aims which would be better served or more easily achieved if the Secretary-General compromised with this attitude. But if he did, how gravely he would then betray the trust of all those for whom the strict maintenance of such an attitude is their best protection in the world-wide fight for power and influence. . . . I would rather see that office [the Secretary-Generalship] break on strict adherence to the principle of independence, impartiality and objectivity than drift on the basis of compromise. That is the choice daily facing the Secretary-General. It is also the choice now openly facing the General Assembly, both in substance and in form. I believe that all those whose interests are safeguarded by the United Nations will realize that the choice is not one of the convenience of the moment but one which is decisive for the future, their future."[12] Khrushchev greeted this exposition, according to one observer, "by thumping the table enigmatically with his brawny fists while gazing around with a mischievous, almost pixie-like smile."[13]

Fidel Castro, who addressed the Assembly for four hours and a half, and later Nasser and Sukarno, all studiously avoided public attacks on the Secretary-General or harsh criticisms of the Congo operation, and they expressed no support for the troika. Nehru, Sukarno, and Nkrumah, however, represented a general anxiety to reduce tension and to make it possible for Khrushchev to retreat from the extreme position he had taken. Wishing to channel this general anxiety in the right direction, Hammarskjold engaged in an effort to clarify the implications both of the troika proposal and of the situation in the Congo. When Nkrumah lunched with him on September 26 they discussed the Congo situation and the difficulties created for the Ghana contingent by the partisan activities of Nkrumah's ambassador in Leopoldville. The U.A.R. contingent in the UN force in the Congo had also shown signs of partisanship that had aroused the suspicions of Mobutu's régime, but Hammarskjold found Nasser, who dined with him on September 29, unexpectedly realistic and desirous above all for a stable Congolese government, independent of either Eastern or Western influence.

Efforts to meet the troika halfway disturbed Hammarskjold

deeply, for he was not prepared to accept any compromise on the authority of the Secretary-General and was also convinced that no compromise would satisfy Khrushchev. Nkrumah's suggestion, in a speech to the United Nations Correspondents Association,[14] for establishing three deputy Secretaries-General disturbed him only slightly less than Nehru's idea of a consultative council to advise the Secretary-General. Much to Hammarskjold's annoyance, Nehru, who was guest of honor at an informal dinner in his apartment on September 30, was reluctant to discuss the subject at all, letting Krishna Menon do most of the talking. Frederick Boland, the Irish President of the Assembly, and Walter Nash, the Prime Minister of New Zealand, who was an old friend of Nehru's, worked hard to dissuade Nehru from publicly putting forward his compromise proposal, and unexpected support came from Nasser, who, perhaps remembering Hammarskjold's firm dealings with France, Israel, and Great Britain over Suez, strongly opposed both Khrushchev's ideas and Nehru's compromise.

On Saturday, October 1, Khrushchev addressed the General Assembly on the question of Chinese representation and took the opportunity, provided by an inept U.S. suggestion that Chinese criticism of Hammarskjold was a factor against Peking's admission, to attack Hammarskjold again. This time his language was so insulting to some other Heads of State that Boland called him to order, and the African and Asian reaction was so strong that the group even considered proposing that the General Assembly adjourn until January. Sékou Touré called Hammarskjold at home the same evening to express his sympathy and concern.

When Khrushchev spoke again two days later,[15] he went to new lengths. The responsibility for executing all decisions of the Security Council and the General Assembly fell upon one man. "Let those who believe in saints," he said, "hold to their opinion; we do not credit such tales."[16]* Hammarskjold, Khrushchev told the Assembly, was the agent of imperialist countries, and "If he himself cannot muster the courage to resign in, let us say, a chivalrous way, we shall draw the inevitable conclusions from the situation. There is no room for a man who has violated the elementary principles of justice in such an important post as that of Secretary-General."[18] Seated beside Boland on the podium, Hammarskjold, although outwardly calm, was so enraged that he asked Boland to give him the floor immediately to reply. Boland, sensing his violent indignation, advised him to wait

---

* This remark foreshadowed Khrushchev's comment to Walter Lippmann that "there are no neutral men," which Hammarskjold took as the text for his Oxford speech in May 1961.[17]

until the afternoon to give a considered reply, and Hammarskjold gratefully accepted his advice.

After Khrushchev had finished addressing the Assembly, King Hussein of Jordan roundly denounced "an obvious attempt to wreck the United Nations"[19] by weakening the Secretary-General's powers, and he gave full support to Hammarskjold's policies in the Congo. Nehru, speaking next, stuck to his prepared text, cautiously rejecting the troika and saying nothing about Hammarskjold or the Secretary-General's authority, but he did not propose his compromise formula on the troika.

Hammarskjold dictated his reply to Khrushchev before meeting Bunche, Cordier, and Spinelli in his office for lunch. When the typed draft was brought to the table he passed it round, asking for comments only on the style. The speech remained as he had first dictated it, and in the afternoon he delivered it in tense and incisive tones to an unusually attentive meeting of the Assembly. He spoke as follows:[20]

The Head of the Soviet Delegation to the General Assembly, this morning, in exercising his right of reply, said, among many other things, that the present Secretary-General has always been biased against the socialist countries, that he has used the United Nations in support of the colonial powers fighting the Congolese Government and Parliament in order to impose "a new yoke on the Congo," and finally, that if I, myself, and I quote, "do not muster up enough courage to resign, so to say in a chivalrous manner, then the Soviet Union will draw the necessary conclusions from the obtained situation." In support of this challenge the representative of the Soviet Union said that it is not proper for a man who has "flouted elementary justice to hold such an important post as that of the Secretary-General." And later on he found reason to say to the delegates of this session that they should not "submit to the clamorous phrases pronounced here" by me "in attempts to justify the bloody crimes perpetrated against the Congolese people."

The General Assembly can rightly expect an immediate reply from my side to a statement so directly addressed to me and regarding a matter of such potential significance.

The Assembly has witnessed over the last weeks how historical truth is established; once an allegation has been repeated a few times, it is no longer an allegation, it is an established fact, even if no evidence has been brought out in order to support it. However, facts are facts, and the true facts are there for whoever cares for truth. Those who invoke history will certainly be heard by history. And they will have to accept its verdict as it will be pronounced on the basis of the facts by men free of mind and firm in their conviction that only on a scrutiny of truth can a future of peace be built.

I have no reason to defend myself or my colleagues against the accusations and judgments to which you have listened. Let me say only this, that *you*, all of you, are the judges. No single party can claim that authority. I am sure you will be guided by truth and justice. In particular, let those who know what the United Nations has done and is doing in the Congo, and those who are not pursuing aims proper only to themselves, pass judgment on our actions there. Let the countries who have liberated themselves in the last fifteen years speak for themselves.

I regret that the intervention to which I have found it necessary to reply has again tended to personalize an issue which, as I have said, in my view is not a question of a man but of an institution. The man does not count, the institution does. A weak or nonexistent executive would mean that the United Nations would no longer be able to serve as an effective instrument for active protection of the interests of those many Members who need such protection. The man holding the responsibility as chief executive should leave if he weakens the executive; he should stay if this is necessary for its maintenance. This, and only this, seems to me to be the substantive criterion that has to be applied.

I said the other day that I would not wish to continue to serve as Secretary-General one day longer than such continued service was, and was considered to be, in the best interest of the Organization. The statement this morning seems to indicate that the Soviet Union finds it impossible to work with the present Secretary-General. This may seem to provide a strong reason why I should resign. However, the Soviet Union has also made it clear that, if the present Secretary-General were to resign now, they would not wish to elect a new incumbent but insist on an arrangement which—and this is my firm conviction based on broad experience—would make it impossible to maintain an effective executive. By resigning, I would, therefore, at the present difficult and dangerous juncture throw the Organization to the winds. I have no right to do so because I have a responsibility to all those states members for which the Organization is of decisive importance, a responsibility which overrides all other considerations.

It is not the Soviet Union or, indeed, any other big powers who need the United Nations for their protection; it is all the others. In this sense the Organization is first of all *their* Organization, and I deeply believe in the wisdom with which they will be able to use it and guide it. I shall remain in my post during the term of my office as a servant of the Organization in the interests of all those other nations, as long as *they* wish me to do so.

In this context the representative of the Soviet Union spoke of courage. It is very easy to resign; it is not so easy to stay on. It is very easy to bow to the wish of a big power. It is another matter to resist. As is well known to all Members of this Assembly, I have done so before on many occasions and in many directions. If it is the wish of those nations who see in the Organization their best protection in the present world, I shall now do so again.[21]

The Assembly listened in silence until the words "a responsibility which overrides all other considerations," when an ovation broke out which lasted a full minute. Again, when Hammarskjold began the sentence "I shall remain in my post..." another ovation began which he tried to stop by holding up his hands. He had to begin the sentence over again, and when he had finished, the Assembly rose to its feet with a roar of approval and applause that lasted for several minutes. Throughout the uproar, Khrushchev and Gromyko, who remained seated, pounded their table with a circular motion of their fists, with broad grins on their faces.

For once in his life Hammarskjold had transgressed his own rule against the use of oratory, and as the ovation continued, he soon began to look acutely uncomfortable. He wrote a brief penciled note to Ralph Bunche saying, "Did I read it all right?"[22] to which Bunche wrote back, "Perfectly. The voice was the most resonant I have ever heard from you; the pace was measured and the enunciation crystal clear—all of which did full justice to the superb text. Thus the greatest and most spontaneous demonstration in UN annals. Congratulations."[23] The General Assembly slowly settled down again to its debate.

Did I read it all right?

Perfectly. The voice was the most resonant I have ever heard from you; the pace was measured and the enunciation crystal clear — all of which did full justice to the superb text. Thus the greatest—& most spontaneous demonstration in UN annals. Congratulations.

The future relations between Hammarskjold and Khrushchev were naturally in some doubt after this extraordinary scene. About an hour later, Hammarskjold, who was still on the podium, received a folder containing an invitation to a Soviet reception on the following day, October 4. Since the envelope containing the invitation was postmarked October 1, he asked his staff to check informally with the Soviet mission whether the invitation still stood. The mission replied in the affirmative and stated that it was up to the Secretary-General whether he wanted to attend or not. Making a distinction in his own mind between personal and political questions, Hammarskjold decided to attend. At the Soviet reception, Khrushchev received him warmly and kept him in conversation for some time in full view of the assembled diplomats and journalists, as if to show that he too distinguished between personal and political considerations.

In the week until his departure from New York on October 13, Khrushchev scaled down his public attack, and in his farewell speech on the afternoon of October 13 he made what could only be interpreted as a conciliatory reference to Hammarskjold. On that morning Sékou Touré, who had prolonged his stay in New York to speak again to the Assembly, had made a remarkable attempt to bring the Assembly back from its increasingly acrimonious and disorderly debate on colonialism to a more dignified level. The serious and responsible tone of his speech, coming as it did from one of the younger and more radical African leaders, may have made an impression on Khrushchev, who spoke as follows: "I should like to ask the Assembly to bear with me a little longer so that I may revert once again to the question of the Secretary-General of the United Nations. I am not making war on Mr. Hammarskjold personally. I have met him and we have had very pleasant conversations. I consider that Mr. Hammarskjold is in my debt, because he exploited me when he was our guest on the Black Sea. I took him around in a rowboat and he has not paid off that debt; he has not done the same for me."[24] He went on to say that it was not a question of personalities but that he was a Communist, while Hammarskjold was a representative of big capital who acted in the interests of a certain group of states, as was demonstrated by his actions in the Congo. He then restated his troika proposal.

To this Hammarskjold replied briefly: "... I was very happy to hear that Mr. Khrushchev has good memories of the time when I had the honour to be rowed by him on the Black Sea. I have not, as he said, been able to reply in kind. But my promise to do so stands, and I hope that the day will come when he can avail himself of this offer. For if he did I am sure that he would discover that I know how to row—following only my own compass."[25] After this cryptic exchange the President suspended the meeting for a few minutes to give Khrushchev the opportunity to leave the building. Hammarskjold came down from the podium and made his way through the hall to the U.S.S.R. desk to bid Khrushchev good-bye and wish him a pleasant journey.

THERE HAVE BEEN MANY speculations as to the origins of this dramatic confrontation, and there is probably a grain of truth in most of them. The immediate pretext for Khrushchev's attack was certainly Hammarskjold's conduct of the Congo operation in opposition to Soviet policy, his refusal to take sides by backing Lumumba against Kasavubu, his insistence that all aid to the Congo government be channeled through the UN, and his failure to prevent the expulsion of the Soviet-bloc embassies from Leopoldville.* Khrushchev did not mention that at the same time Hammarskjold had also frustrated the efforts of other outside interests in the Congo, as he had been required by the Security Council to do.

There were undoubtedly other and more basic reasons for the change in the Soviet attitude since July 1958, when Khrushchev had suggested that the summit meeting of the great powers should include the Secretary-General of the United Nations. When Hammarskjold visited Khrushchev in March 1959 at Sochi, on the Black Sea, he had made a determined effort to establish with the Soviet leader a personal relationship, based on frankness and mutual respect, such as might transcend even serious political differences. This effort was perhaps misguided in relation to a leader in Khrushchev's position, and it may even have given rise to suspicion on Khrushchev's part. When, at the conclusion of their formal talks, which had been largely concerned with the German question, Hammarskjold had said that if he took positions which were not agreeable to the U.S.S.R. he felt he could trust Khrushchev not to misconstrue his motives, Khrushchev had replied with a smile, "Please do not do anything which will force us to criticize you."[27]

At dinner that evening, Hammarskjold had brought the conversation round to Boris Pasternak's novel *Doctor Zhivago* and to his own part, as a member of the Swedish Academy, in awarding to Pasternak

---

* In February 1961 in a letter to Östen Undén, the Swedish Foreign Minister, Hammarskjold wrote: "The first attempts at solid penetration in the Congo flopped. They were followed by two further defeats—which in my view should never have come about—the dismissal of Mr. Lumumba and the ousting of the Soviet embassy." [26]

the Nobel Prize for literature.* Khrushchev asked angrily how the prize could have been given to an author who was rejected by the Russian people, and Hammarskjold explained at length how the nomination had come about, saying that literary merit had outweighed the fact that some three or four pages of the book might be objectionable to the Soviet government. When Presidium Vice-President A. I. Mikoyan criticized Hammarskjold's judgment, the latter replied that it was essential to keep aesthetic judgment apart from political considerations. The Secretary-General had no views on literature, but Mr. Hammarskjold as an individual had the right to such views, provided he also accepted the consequences. When Mikoyan asked if Hammarskjold approved of the antisocial actions of the hero of the book, Hammarskjold retorted that the general view that *Crime and Punishment* was a very great novel did not mean that he and Mikoyan thought it was a good idea to murder old widows.

In an effort to change the mood of the conversation, Hammarskjold proposed a toast to "honest sinners now on record."[28] Both Khrushchev and Mikoyan were disconcerted and asked if he meant "repentant sinners,"[29] and, when Hammarskjold replied in the negative, they refused to drink the toast. After a discussion of the relative merits of Soviet authors and bourgeois émigrés, Hammarskjold proposed a new toast to "living Soviet art."[30] When Khrushchev asked what he meant by that, Hammarskjold said each should define it for himself, and Khrushchev and Mikoyan finally joined in the toast.

Hammarskjold's own conclusion was that these interchanges, while demonstrating how different were the worlds in which he and Khrushchev lived, did not leave any bad feelings and might even have done some good, but Anatoly Dobrynin, who had accompanied him, was probably nearer the mark when he told him that the evening had only shown that Khrushchev and he were equally stubborn.

The next day Khrushchev took his guest for a row in a very small boat on the Black Sea, thus effectively blocking further literary conversation. As Hammarskjold remarked in his letter of thanks to Khrushchev, "Although the boat trip was a bit on the silent side, not because of a lack of will but because there was no place for an interpreter, I shall always remember it with great pleasure. I have carefully noted that next time you will leave it to me to row you. A third time we may perhaps arrive at rowing with four oars."[31]

Hammarskjold's African tour in late 1959 and early 1960, and his

---

* The Swedish Academy had awarded the prize to Pasternak in 1958. Although Pasternak had recently become internationally famous for *Doctor Zhivago*, the prize was for his literary work as a whole.

often stated view that the UN should fill the power vacuum left by the departing colonial powers, may also have aroused in Khrushchev misgivings that were brought to a head by the UN Congo operation. Khrushchev was not the only Head of State to be irritated by Hammarskjold's African ideas. De Gaulle, for slightly different reasons, also regarded them with the utmost distaste, and other governments had strong reservations about them.

Disagreements over Africa and the right way of filling the post-colonial vacuum were probably not the whole story either. The Soviet government had not reacted adversely, or indeed at all, to Hammarskjold's 1957 reelection statement that the Secretary-General would, where necessary, attempt to fill the gaps left by the frustration of the Security Council or the General Assembly. The Soviet government's attitude toward his initiatives in Lebanon and in Laos had been restrained and understanding, although it viewed his Laos initiative with considerable misgivings. By September 1960, however, Khrushchev evidently felt that Hammarskjold was dangerously exceeding his powers, although it seems likely that the Congo developments were more the occasion than the basic cause of this change of attitude.

The change in superpower relationships provided another important element in Hammarskjold's confrontation with the U.S.S.R. From 1956 to 1960 the notion of "peaceful coexistence" between the United States and the U.S.S.R. had allowed him to take initiatives in the Middle East and elsewhere based on general U.S.-Soviet agreement—or at least lack of active disagreement—in the Security Council. Thus, in situations where neither superpower wished to be too closely involved or to confront the other, the Secretary-General could act in a way that was not prejudicial to the interests of either. When, with the collapse of the Paris summit meeting in May 1960 over the U-2 incident, the "peaceful coexistence" period temporarily came to an end, the U.S.S.R., with its minority voting position in the UN, naturally became more sensitive about the activities of the Secretary-General in delicate areas—activities over which it had little control. Soviet suspicions were also undoubtedly aggravated by the fact that in the early months of the Congo operation, Hammarskjold had a high proportion of senior American assistants, who, although no one who knew them doubted their objectivity and impartiality, naturally appeared to the U.S.S.R. to be a proof of pro-Western bias in the Secretariat. Hammarskjold himself was slow to appreciate the seriousness of this problem, and he tended to dismiss the warnings of his senior American officials themselves, saying that he must have colleagues whom he trusted and knew to be objective, regardless of their nationality.

Khrushchev himself suggested another reason for the troika proposal. In the General Assembly in 1959 he had launched his proposal for general disarmament,[32] and in 1960 he explained that since the U.S.S.R. now accepted the Western idea that disarmament would necessitate the creation of armed forces under the UN, the UN executive must be reshaped as a troika to avoid the risk of this force being "used for reactionary purposes."[33]

Hammarskjold came to accept this basic explanation for Khrushchev's change of attitude. In March 1961, in a letter to Östen Undén, the Foreign Minister of Sweden, he gave a long analysis of the reasons for the Soviet attack on him which was largely an elaboration of Khrushchev's own justification of the troika. Khrushchev's commitment in 1959 to general and complete disarmament, he argued, would, if it ever came about, require an international police force, which in turn would require that the Secretary-General as UN executive be superseded by the troika arrangement, constituting a built-in veto. The Congo operation and its dramatic ramifications had provided Khrushchev with a pretext for proposing this change, although there was considerable evidence that the Soviet Foreign Office had been unhappy about Khrushchev's attack on Hammarskjold.

In these circumstances Hammarskjold felt that his own stand was required by the general international interest, even though by March 1961 he had begun to feel that he could no longer bear the sole responsibility and that governments must share it with him through the General Assembly. Thus, he told Undén, if the U.S.S.R. were to put a proposal for the troika on the General Assembly agenda for the resumed Fifteenth Session, he would feel obliged to intervene at the beginning of the debate to make the implications of such a move, both in principle and in practice, perfectly clear to the members. He had, in fact, drafted such a statement pointing out what the destruction of the concept of an international civil service would mean for the future of the UN. The occasion to give this statement in the General Assembly never arose because the Russians did not formally present the troika proposal to the resumed General Assembly, but much of the thinking in it later appeared in Hammarskjold's Oxford speech in May 1961.

Undén gave a simpler explanation for Khrushchev's reaction. "He has become aware," he wrote to Hammarskjold, "of your being a power-factor in international politics which he is not able to manage. It must be unbearable for Khrushchev to know that the right of veto cannot be used when the Secretary-General is applying the directives of the Security Council. This shows that the mechanism of the UN can function under the leadership of an effective Secretary-General, also in important questions, without unanimity in the Security Council or when the Assembly cannot muster the sufficient majority."[34]

Developments in the Communist world may also have influenced Khrushchev's attitude at the UN and pushed him into playing an anti-Western role that could best be dramatized by a violent personal attack on an individual who, as Hammarskjold said, could serve as a "symbolic target for their attack on 'colonialists' and imperialists."[35] The Soviet disagreement with China was coming to a head in early 1960. In early June a session in Peking of the General Council of the Federation of Trade Unions had resounded with the clashes between the Soviet and Chinese delegates. On June 18, at a Communist summit meeting in Bucharest, Khrushchev had delivered a sharp counterattack on Chinese Communism. In July various Chinese publications in the U.S.S.R. were stopped, and all the 1,390 Soviet experts working in China were recalled. One of Peking's main accusations against Khrushchev was of an East-West, and specifically a U.S.-U.S.S.R., détente. In November 1960 there was to be a conference of world Communist leaders in Moscow. In the circumstances it was only natural that Khrushchev should wish to stress the basically anti-Western nature of Soviet policy; and the development of the UN operation in the Congo, which the U.S.S.R. had voted for in the initial crisis, provided a pretext for a dramatically anti-Western move.

Whatever the basic reasons for it may have been, the Soviet attack on Hammarskjold and on the authority of the Secretary-General dominated his last year and, like a recurrent thunderstorm, threatened the serenity and the effectiveness of all his activities. It also tended to obscure his differences with France, the United States, Great Britain, and a number of African and Asian countries over the conduct of the Congo operation. The very violence of Khrushchev's attack swung a large majority of the Assembly in Hammarskjold's favor and highlighted his defense of his position in such a way as to turn him, quite unexpectedly, into a public hero in large areas of the world. In standing up to Khrushchev, Hammarskjold symbolized both the struggle and the potential of the UN itself. As an American commentator put it:

> Krushchev's charge is that Hammarskjold is a stooge of the West and not genuinely neutral. The fact is the exact opposite: Hammarskjold's sin was exactly his neutrality, which was unyielding to the Soviet designs in the Congo when Khrushchev wanted him to be pliant. Krushchev does not want a neutral UN Secretariat that will act justly, but one that is paralyzed and will not act at all.
>
> That is why the David-like struggle of Hammarskjold against the Russian Goliath may prove a turning-point in the history of the UN. If Khrushchev wins out, the UN will become as ineffectual as the League of Nations was, and the only law we shall have will be the law of the nuclear jungle. If Hammarskjold musters enough support from the

small nations of Africa, Asia, Latin America and the Middle East and rides out his term, the principle will be established that a UN official need not panic before any of the great-power Goliaths, and perhaps some day we shall have a body of men capable of building precedents for a body of world law and capable of enforcing it.[36]

Heroics and public admiration, as Hammarskjold knew better than anyone, are not the stuff of effective day-to-day work, and Soviet opposition was a severe and continual handicap as well as a heavy psychological strain. Although not prepared to compromise on matters of principle, he certainly wished for the earliest possible improvement in his relations with the U.S.S.R., and he maintained, where possible, a scrupulous correctness in his relations with the Soviet representatives. It is perhaps a measure of how much he hoped for a rapprochement with the U.S.S.R. that he was carrying in his wallet at the time of his death a note from Heinz Wieschhoff, his adviser on African Affairs, informing him of the remark of a member of the Soviet mission in March 1961 that the Soviet attacks on him were Khrushchev's own idea and a mistake—"just one of those things in politics."[37] Khrushchev expressed his own feelings when he presented his condolences to the Swedish Ambassador in Moscow three days after Hammarskjold's death. "Our relations," he said, "were somewhat special, but I am now having regard to the humanitarian aspect. This is not the way to solve problems.* Hammarskjold was a great man."[38]

For his part, Hammarskjold was surprisingly slow to comprehend the difference between his own Western style of thinking and the point of view of Khrushchev and the Soviet leadership. After his talks with Khrushchev in 1958 and 1959 he may have believed, and certainly wished to believe, that with Khrushchev—as, for example, with Ben-Gurion—he could temper public disagreement with private friendship and mutual understanding. By the time he began to realize fully the complete unreality of any such idea, he was already confronting Khrushchev on a vital matter of principle on which he could accept no compromise.

ALTHOUGH MUCH OF THE DRAMA went out of the General Assembly's proceedings with the departure of Khrushchev and the other Heads

---

* Khrushchev was here referring to the manner of Hammarskjold's death and to the view, also expressed by Sobolev and Kuznetsov when they had presented their condolences to the Swedish Ambassador, that Tshombe, supported by the British and by Sir Roy Welensky, Prime Minister of Rhodesia and Nyasaland, was to blame for Lumumba's and probably also for Hammarskjold's deaths.

of State, the problems of the Congo showed no signs of abating. Every day after the Assembly proceedings were over, Hammarskjold retired to his office on the thirty-eighth floor to go over other business and eventually to settle down with his advisers on the Congo to discuss the day's events and the plans for the morrow. These discussions usually went on through dinner, and often far into the night, in a group that came to be known informally as the "Congo Club."* Out of these meetings came a steady stream of comments and instructions to Rajeshwar Dayal, most of which Hammarskjold himself dictated. He enjoyed the daily exchanges with Dayal, whose intelligence and sense of duty were illuminated by a vivid descriptive style and humor, and whose analyses of the Congo situation were invaluable to him in the preparation of his own public statements. Hammarskjold's efforts in these cables to try to explain his own concept of the UN position to his representatives in the field were not always easy to understand. "As regards political situation," ran a typical cable to Dayal, "one major difficulty is that we can never get inside the skin of our Congolese friends or disentangle outsider maneuvers. For that reason we are constantly under handicap which we cannot overcome. For that reason also I find it dangerous to base our actions on anything but rather general concepts as to interplay of forces to extent we find our analysis supported by confirmed facts. Believe that on the whole we will get safer results with this skeptical approach. Believe also that this may save us from danger of getting tied up in Congo type intrigues which grow like mushrooms and die like mushrooms and mostly, like mushrooms, are rather poisonous."[40]

Despite Dayal's efforts to reconcile Lumumba and Kasavubu, the situation in the Congo was, if anything, more confused than ever. There was no legitimate constitutional government, and the refusal of the UN to recognize Mobutu's regime made Dayal's relations with it increasingly sour. Dayal's policy was to keep scrupulously aloof from the political merry-go-round while doing his best to promote reconciliation, to keep the country going, and to protect all parties from actual physical harm. Lumumba had a UN guard of the same strength as Kasavubu's. Mobutu had also initially sought and received UN protection, and Dayal had prevailed on him, for the time being at any

---

* This innocent appellation which originated casually as a convenient term to describe the group of officials dealing with the Congo at any given time, was later given a quite unwarranted importance in some quarters, and as late as 1967 the representative of the U.S.S.R. in the Security Council referred indignantly to the "Congo Club." Such writers as Conor Cruise O'Brien and Ian Colvin both imply erroneously, to support their very different points of view, that the "Congo Club" was a clique dominated by the views of the U.S. State Department.[39]

rate, to give up his attempts to arrest Lumumba and to release Gizenga,* Mpolo,[41] and Okito,[42] who had been detained. Since their rivalries left the Congolese political leaders little time to engage in the work of government or administration, UN civilian experts were largely responsible for keeping public administration and public services going as best they could. The bloodshed in Kasai was brought to a halt by the UN force by late September, and a relief operation for the 250,000 Baluba who had become refugees was undertaken by ONUC.

Another of Dayal's problems was the partisan activity of some of the ambassadors in Leopoldville and their efforts to pressure him into adopting impossible positions. Thus, on September 25, he was surprised to be asked by a group of African ambassadors, who only three weeks previously had been the loudest in protesting against the similar and much less sweeping measures taken by Cordier, to take over the radio station, airfield, government offices, and Parliament. Dayal still hoped that, with patience and good advice, the political balance might be restored. Hammarskjold too was not despondent. "In spite of all the real difficulties," he wrote on September 30 to Paul-Henri Spaak, "and all the misunderstandings, created with all the diligence of certain powers mounting an offensive for their own ends, I still have the firm hope that, thanks to all the good and reasonable forces, we shall manage to get over this crisis."[43]

Hammarskjold was still inclined not to take too gloomy a view of the strong criticisms of his actions voiced in many quarters. To Eisenhower, in a courtesy letter after the President's visit to UN Headquarters, he wrote on October 5: "I believe that our record stands up well, although few representatives of any one of the states in the major world conflict may be satisfied with all of it. It has been as common to meet, from some, the criticism that we did not intervene to settle matters in favor of one faction, as it has been to meet objections from the other side because our neutrality was considered to favor that very faction. However, this is the destiny of the United Nations in every major operation and we do not evaluate what we do in the terms of praise or criticism from any one side."[44] Walter Lippman described the situation in different words after Hammarskjold's death: "The cause of the opposition from East and West is a determination not to have the UN succeed in what it is attempting to do. For if the UN succeeds, there will not be a communist government in the Congo. That is what Khrushchev hated about Hammar-

---

* Gizenga, on his release, promptly went to Stanleyville.

skjold and the Secretary-General's office. And if the UN succeeds, there will not be a restoration of white supremacy in the Congo, and that is why money, propaganda, and clandestine intervention are being employed to frustrate the UN."[45]*

The pressure and partisanship that were soon to destroy Hammarskjold's and Dayal's hopes for a political reconciliation in the Congo were now coming largely from the West, and from the United States in particular. As Hammarskjold remarked, if his difficulties with the Russians seemed greater than with the Americans, it was only because the former had been publicized, as had been his one-month quarrel with Lumumba, to the almost total exclusion of his three-month struggle with the Belgians. Lumumba, who had little support in Leopoldville, was in the process of establishing his own political base in Stanleyville. He was still the only Congolese leader who attached more importance to national unity than to local tribal interests and thus had a real national following. From the UN point of view it was vital to reconcile Lumumba and Kasavubu and to restore constitutionality as soon as possible. If that could be achieved, it would be possible to work for the reopening of the Parliament and a return to constitutional government and to deal with the Katanga problem by taking firm measures to end foreign civil and military assistance to Tshombe.

At the beginning of October, Hammarskjold sent a message to the permanent representative of Belgium[46] asking for the withdrawal of all Belgian military, paramilitary, and civilian personnel, so that in the future, in accordance with the September 20 Assembly resolution, all aid to the Congo would be channeled through the UN. Three weeks later he protested to Belgium[47] that the Belgian technicians who were returning at the request of the Mobutu régime had in general taken an attitude hostile to the UN. With Western support for Mobutu and Tshombe increasing, Belgian reaction to these notes was uncooperative, and the Belgian Foreign Office complained[48] that Belgium had not been treated with adequate respect or dignity.

Dayal's persistent refusal, with Hammarskjold's full support, to recognize the legitimacy of the Mobutu regime or to permit the army to arrest Lumumba had repercussions far beyond the borders of the Congo, and a campaign against him began to take shape, led by Mobutu and the Western embassies in Leopoldville. Dayal responded, with Hammarskjold's full backing, by issuing, on November 2, a devastatingly frank report[49] on the situation, in which he especially

---

* A reference to Western opposition to the UN effort to solve the Katanga problem.

singled out for criticism the activities of Belgian advisers in Leopold-ville and Katanga and the indiscipline and brutality of the Congolese Army. He concluded by suggesting that if minimum conditions of noninterference and security could be established, the Congolese lead-ers might still be able to find a a peaceful solution through the office of the Chief of State and the Parliament. Dayal's report caused an uproar in the Congo and in the West, where it was widely interpreted as an attempt by the UN to bring Lumumba back to power. Wigny, the Belgian Foreign Minister, went so far as to state in New York on November 14[50] that Belgium might have to consider withdrawing from the UN, while the U.S. State Department publicly declared that it could not accept Dayal's criticisms of Mobutu's Belgian advisers. Lumumba, for his part, in a letter of November 11 to the President of the General Assembly and to the Secretary-General,[51] warmly endorsed Dayal's report, which, he said, told the truth about the situation in the Congo.

During October, Hammarskjold's relations with the United States over the Congo situation became increasingly strained. On October 21 he received a memorandum from Ambassador Wadsworth criticizing his views on the constitutional situation, Dayal's recent activities, and his demand to Belgium to withdraw Belgian civil and military advisers. Professing faith in Tshombe's willingness to cooperate in a unified Congo, the U.S. note asked if Hammarskjold would be able to replace im-mediately all Belgian advisers in Katanga. The memorandum went on to criticize the UN for favoring and protecting Lumumba and his support-ers against the Mobutu régime and concluded with a thinly veiled threat of withdrawal of U.S. support for the Congo operation if Hammarskjold persisted in his current policies. Hammarskjold reacted strongly to this approach, deploring the harmful talk of a new U.S. policy in the Congo as reflected in the State Department's comments on Dayal's latest report and in a *New York Times* article of November 10 hinting that U.S. support would be withdrawn if the Secretary-General facili-tated Lumumba's return to power. He pointed out that he would not act in support of Lumumba or of any other Congolese politician out-side the framework of law and order, and he hoped that the United States would not use its key financial position "in a way which would force us out of our impartiality—or indeed integrity—by actions intended to block the road for anybody by a political interference in the Congo."[52] He warned strongly against "an American influence game,"[53] which would certainly antagonize all African States.

In the Assembly meanwhile, there began a development that was to have serious, and ultimately tragic, consequences. The Advisory

Committee on the Congo had decided in early November, under the terms of the General Assembly resolution of September 20, to send to the Congo a Conciliation Commission consisting of representatives of African and Asian countries with troops in the Congo, to help in the process of national reconciliation. Before this group could leave for the Congo, a controversy began in the General Assembly that was to result in destroying the basis for Hammarskjold's effort to reconcile Kasavubu and Lumumba.

Since the two rival factions both claimed it, the Congo seat in the Assembly had remained vacant since the beginning of the session. On October 10, Sékou Touré proposed that Lumumba be represented in the General Assembly.[54] This move proved to be a tactical error, for it alarmed Kasavubu's and Mobutu's Western supporters, who were determined to ensure that the Congo should be represented in New York by Kasavubu's delegation only. As a result, the U.S. mission to the UN mounted a massive vote-gathering operation on behalf of Kasavubu. Secret meetings of sympathetic delegations were held outside the UN Building, U.S. embassies throughout the world put pressure on other governments, and potentially favorable votes were pursued relentlessly in the corridors. Kasavubu himself came to New York to take part in this campaign. Greatly to the displeasure of the U.S. mission, Hammarskjold made no secret of his strong disapproval of the campaign to seat Kasavubu's representatives and maintained the view that neither Congolese delegation should be seated in the prevailing constitutionally dubious circumstances. He was equally firm with Sékou Touré, who at a private dinner on October 10 told him that he would not press publicly his objections to some aspects of the Congo operation if Hammarskjold would support the seating of Lumumba's representatives. Hammarskjold replied that he would not hesitate for a second to open the UN dossier on the Congo for public view if the members wished it.

On November 8, Kasavubu, in his capacity as Chief of State of the Congo, addressed the Assembly[55] and later announced that he would stay in New York until the Congo seat was occupied by his own representatives. Kasavubu's apparent moderation made a good impression on the majority in the Assembly, and his stronger constitutional position, as well as the U.S. campaign for votes, soon began to tell in his favor. Guinea and other supporters of Lumumba thereupon changed their tack and urged, somewhat disingenuously, that the question of Congolese representation in New York be adjourned indefinitely in order to avoid prejudicing the work of the Conciliation Commission. Their change of tactics came too late, for the Western countries were now confident of victory and, after an acrimonious debate, they pressed the matter to a vote in which Kasavubu's representatives were seated by 53 votes to 24, with 19 abstentions.[56]

Hammarskjold knew well that the decision of the Assembly, and the circumstances in which it had come about, could only result in new and even greater difficulties for him and for the UN operation in the Congo. He could not know that it would also lead to a historical tragedy with world-wide repercussions. This partisan decision, which as a result of Western pressure formally put the Assembly on the side of one of the factions in the political conflict in the Congo, exacerbated a dilemma that had plagued Hammarskjold throughout the Congo operation, namely that he depended on the African countries for troops and political support and on the West for financial and logistic support, both of which were indispensable to the UN operation. Far from promoting reconciliation and reducing partisanship, the Assembly's decision had intensified both the political crisis in the Congo and the division between the members within the UN itself over the Congo question.

Hammarskjold had tried, in a speech to the General Assembly in mid-October,[57] to give a new perspective to the Congo operation. He had taken as his text Sékou Touré's appeal[58] that the Assembly give more attention to the plight and to the future of the people of the Congo, and less to the struggles of its individual politicians. He paid an eloquent tribute to the unsung Congolese officials who were trying to keep the country going and to the UN personnel who were helping them and who had been so recklessly accused by some of the speakers in the Assembly. "You try to save a drowning man," he concluded, "without prior authorization and even if he resists you; you do not let him go even when he tries to strangle you. I do not believe that anyone would wish the Organization to follow other rules than those you apply to yourself when faced with such a situation."[59]

The task of saving "a drowning man" had been simultaneously complicated by the Assembly's decision to seat Kasavubu's representatives and by developments in the Congo. On the night of November 21 the Tunisian UN troops guarding the Ghana embassy in Leopoldville clashed with Mobutu's troops, who had come to expel the Ghana chargé d'affaires, Nathaniel Welbeck. In the ensuing fight the Tunisians suffered one fatal casualty and nine wounded, while five Congolese, including the commander, Colonel Kokolo, were killed and several wounded. Two days later Dayal expressed his anxiety about the situation around Lumumba's house because Mobutu's régime, misinterpreting the Assembly's decision, apparently intended to renew its attempts to arrest Lumumba.* At Dayal's suggestion, Hammarskjold made urgent representations to Kasavubu and Bomboko to restrain the Mobutu régime from making political arrests or provoking clashes with UN forces, and especially with the UN guard at Lumumba's house, which, he warned, would have to use force if an attempt was made to break in and arrest Lumumba. With Lumumba also there was trouble.[61] He had asked ONUC to fly him and the coffin of his infant daughter, who had died in Switzerland on November 18, to Stanleyville. Dayal had felt obliged to refuse this request, despite the pathetic circumstances, for to have flown Lumumba to his political base at such a time could only have constituted a flagrant interference in the internal political conflict. Instead Dayal offered to have the coffin flown to Stanleyville for burial.

Lumumba himself was apparently taken by surprise by Kasavubu's victory in New York and seems to have decided that his best course would be to regroup his supporters in Stanleyville and set up a rival regime. He, like Dayal, may also have been worried about the possibility of a new threat to his freedom and safety. On the night of November 27 there was a big official banquet in Leopoldville to celebrate the return of Kasavubu from New York. At 10 o'clock the same evening, during a tropical rainstorm, a large black car left Lumumba's house. It was seen by the inner ring of troops, UN Moroccan soldiers whose function was to prevent outside forces from getting in and arresting Lumumba but not to restrict his movements in any way. It passed through the outer ring of Mobutu's soldiers without difficulty. The same night Dayal reported his suspicion that Lumumba had left his house for an unknown destination. Lumumba's departure was confirmed the next day when the Moroccans found that his house was empty.

Lumumba's escape caused a flurry of rumor and speculation. In New York the UN was widely suspected of collaboration in his escape, while in Leopoldville Dayal's refusal, in accordance with Hammarskjold's instructions, to supply air and ground transport for the ANC to pursue Lumumba strained even further Dayal's relations with Kasavubu and Mobutu. Acting on the same principle, Dayal, even supposing he had known where Lumumba was, could not provide protection for Lumumba while he was touring the country at large in pursuit of political aims, an activity from which, no matter what

---

* Already on October 10, Justin Bomboko had stated that "the ANC is ready to do battle with the UN in order to arrest Lumumba,"[60] but, perhaps because of the restraining hand of Mobutu, this threat had not been followed up.

faction was involved, Hammarskjold had always maintained that ONUC should completely dissociate itself.*

Although he was believed to be headed for Kasai en route to Stanleyville, and ANC officers were sent by Mobutu to arrest him, Lumumba's whereabouts remained a mystery for more than three days. His chief ANC pursuer, a Major Pongo,[62] arrived in Tshikapa, 120 miles west of Luluabourg, on November 30 and demanded the assistance of the UN Ghana Brigade, which was stationed in Kasai. The Ghana Brigade headquarters thereupon asked ONUC headquarters to confirm its assumption that Major Pongo should not be given assistance, and that if Lumumba appeared in a locality where there were Ghanaian troops and seemed either to be causing disturbances or to be in danger of arrest, he should be taken into protective custody. The reply from ONUC headquarters, which had already sent a message saying that UN troops should not get involved in any way, explained that ONUC was responsible for Lumumba's personal safety only in his official residence in Leopoldville and that he had been told repeatedly that, if he ventured out of it, it would be at his own risk and responsibility. Before this message reached the Ghana Brigade headquarters on December 1, Lumumba arrived at Port Francqui in northern Kasai, where he appeared to be on good terms with the ANC and attended a lunch given in his honor by the provincial administrator. He asked for a UN escort to go to Mweka. This was refused in accordance with the directive from Leopoldville, and he and his party left by car, having refused the offer of a five-man ANC escort. In Mweka he spent some hours in consultation with his local supporters at the government rest house, made a speech to a friendly crowd outside the administration building, and then went to the Grand Hotel. In Leopoldville, meanwhile, Dayal received a furious protest from Mobutu that the Ghana troops in Port Francqui had forcibly released Lumumba from arrest. This was passed on to the Ghana Brigade, which replied that Lumumba had neither been arrested nor released.

---

* In the light of the subsequent series of political killings in the Congo, some later polemicists have interpreted this line of action as a callous refusal of responsibility, or even as a deliberate pretext for letting Lumumba be arrested in the certainty that he would be killed. Quite apart from the UN's previous record of actively protecting Lumumba in his residence, a policy that had aroused the wrath of Mobutu and Kasavubu as well as of their Western supporters, the possibility of political assassination was not uppermost in anyone's mind in the Congo at the time of Lumumba's escape. In fact, one of the minor wonders of the Congo situation up to that time had been that in nearly five turbulent months no political leader had been hurt, let alone killed.

On the evening of December 1, forty ANC soldiers arrived in Mweka and accused the Ghana platoon stationed there of protecting Lumumba. Early next morning the Ghana platoon commander saw three cars drive past his post and stop a short way down the road. Lumumba was taken out of one car and hit, slapped, and kicked. The Ghana officer intervened to stop this maltreatment, and the cars then drove off apparently in the direction of Luluabourg. This was the first indication that Lumumba's pursuers had caught up with him. He was later taken to Port Francqui, where there was a large ANC garrison, and flown to Leopoldville with a strong ANC guard. On landing, the aircraft, under the direction of Major Pongo, was ordered to a hangar outside the UN-controlled area, whence Lumumba and his companions were taken at once to an unknown destination.*

On December 2, before he knew of Lumumba's arrest, Dayal issued a press statement designed to clear up misunderstandings concerning the UN role in regard to Lumumba's movements. "While protection was afforded to Mr. Lumumba at his request while he was in residence in Leopoldville," Dayal stated, "the UN is in no way responsible for his movements thereafter. Firm orders have been issued to UN troops to refrain from any interference whatsoever in regard to Mr. Lumumba's movements or those of his official pursuers, and these orders have been strictly complied with."[63]

Had Hammarskjold or Dayal known what was going to happen to Lumumba, would they, or should they, have given different orders? If they had tried to hinder Lumumba's pursuers or had taken him into protective custody after having refused to cooperate in his pursuit, it would have certainly been regarded by Kasavubu, by Colonel Mobutu, and by the majority of states in the Assembly that had recognized Kasavubu, as a flagrant interference in the internal political struggle in the Congo. By any objective standard it would have been an act of partisanship, and it would probably also have been violently resented by Lumumba's supporters both within and outside the Congo. It would also have put the UN troops, dispersed in small detachments all over the country and with specific orders not to use force, in a new and general military confrontation with the overwhelmingly more numerous ANC, a confrontation in which they would almost certainly have been defeated. An attempt to rescue Lumumba after his arrest, quite apart from far exceeding the ONUC

---

* The best detailed account of Lumumba's escape and arrest is to be found in G. Heinz and H. Donnay, *Patrice Lumumba: les cinquante derniers jours de sa vie* (Editions du CRISP, Brussels), published in English as *Lumumba: The Last Fifty Days* (New York, 1969).

mandate, would not only have put his own life in danger but would also have provoked a battle between the small ONUC detachments and the ANC in which ONUC would have been at a hopeless disadvantage.

On December 2 the U.S.S.R. accused ONUC of having been an accomplice in Lumumba's arrest,[64] while on the next day Kasavubu formally protested again to Dayal that UN troops in Port Francqui had intervened and released Lumumba. Strict impartiality, as Hammarskjold had said two months before, was regarded as partial by all sides in the conflict.

The panicky reaction in Leopoldville to the news of Lumumba's escape soon gave way, when the news of his arrest arrived, to other preoccupations. The reaction of Lumumba's supporters in Stanleyville was violent. Alphonse Songolo,[65] the president of Orientale Province, and other parliamentarians were arrested in reprisal for Lumumba's arrest, and the gravest fears were entertained for the safety of Europeans residing in that city. No lesser fears were felt about the fate of Lumumba himself. On his arrival at Leopoldville Airport on the evening of December 2 he had been wearing torn and dirty clothes, with his hands tied behind his back, and he was reported to have been taken to the military camp at Thysville. On December 2, Hammarskjold addressed a strong personal message to Kasavubu, pointing out forcefully the disastrous effect upon the international prestige of the Congo, as well as the shock to the UN and its members, that would result if Lumumba was treated contrary to recognized rules of order and decency and outside the framework of due process of law. He urged Kasavubu to be sure that due process was observed, and to take account of Lumumba's position as a member of the Congolese Parliament as well as his special status with large sectors of international opinion.

Hammarskjold himself was in no doubt of the effect upon the UN, and especially upon the operation in the Congo, if things ran wild or summary justice was executed upon Lumumba, and he urged Dayal to try to bring home to Mobutu and Bomboko the necessity for treating Lumumba in a civilized manner and to search for all possible means, compatible with the principle of noninterference, to follow up his message to Kasavubu on Lumumba's behalf.

The safety of Lumumba was not by any means the only source of anxiety. The Leopoldville authorities, with the support of the Western powers and a considerable measure of material support from Belgium, were becoming increasingly hostile toward ONUC; Belgium continued to provide essential military and administrative advisers to Tshombe in Katanga; and in Stanleyville another secessionist government was likely soon to be set up by Gizenga, who might expect diplomatic recognition and material assistance from a number of African states as well as the Soviet bloc. It was also clear that several countries which had provided troops for the UN operation might soon withdraw them, thus weakening the UN force at the very moment when its relations with all the competing authorities in the Congo were under the maximum strain. Worst of all, the renewed flare-up of old antagonisms and fears, both in the Congo and in New York, destroyed Hammarskjold's and Dayal's hopes of an early reconciliation and the possibility of effective action by the UN Conciliation Commission, which was still awaiting Kasavubu's agreement for it to go to Leopoldville. The danger of civil war in the Congo began to loom large on the horizon.

In a further letter to Kasavubu on December 5, Hammarskjold pointed out that Lumumba and the others who had recently been arrested were members of one or other of the chambers of Parliament and therefore enjoyed parliamentary immunity, a point to which world public opinion would certainly attach great importance. He also referred to reports of the violent and degrading physical treatment accorded to Lumumba, and urged Kasavubu immediately to permit a representative of the International Red Cross to examine the detained persons and the places and conditions of their detention, and to obtain all the necessary assurances for their safety. This letter was taken by special emissary to Tshela in the Bas-Congo, where Kasavubu was staying. Mobutu reacted to Hammarskjold's efforts in a press conference on December 6. Lumumba, he said, was comfortably housed, and he and his companions were costing the government a thousand francs a day. "Does Mr. Hammarskjold think Lumumba would have done as much for me if I had been a prisoner?"[66] Kasavubu replied the next day that "Mr. Lumumba is our legal prisoner, duly imprisoned by a warrant of arrest dated the month of September 1960, and the normally rapid execution of which was only prevented by the United Nations."[67] At the same time Hammarskjold asked Gizenga in Stanleyville for fair treatment for Songolo and other anti-Lumumbist parliamentarians who had been detained in Stanleyville in reprisal for Lumumba's arrest. He also protested against the maltreatment both of the UN staff and of the European inhabitants of Stanleyville, where the authorities had threatened to arrest, and if necessary kill, the two thousand Belgians living in Orientale Province.

In appealing for Lumumba, Hammarskjold was in a weak position, for the strongest ground upon which he could protest and appeal was on the basis of due process of law, general humanitarian principles, and Lumumba's parliamentary status, and his possibilities for effective action were extremely limited. Dayal was disgusted that his appeals for Lumumba found no echo among those Western ambassadors in Leopoldville who might have exercised a moderating influence on the régime but instead seemed more interested in running down ONUC. Hammarskjold protested against this attitude strongly to the British and U.S. missions in New York. The drift in Leopoldville toward a military dictatorship violently hostile to the UN continued, and it seemed likely that not only the effort to retrain the ANC but also the UN civilian operations on which the civil life of the Congo largely depended would soon become virtually impossible.

In the midst of these difficulties, Hammarskjold had to face a serious crisis in the command of the UN force itself. The initial doubts of many of his staff as to the wisdom of appointing General Carl von Horn as commander in the Congo had been increasingly justified by the general's performance. Von Horn was suited neither by temperament nor by experience to the task of commanding a multinational force in a critical and complex situation,* and during the battle for the Ghana embassy on November 21 he had been unavailable, having been given a strong sedative, and remained in his house, leaving General Rikhye, who was acting for Dayal while the latter was in New York, and General Alexander, who had come from Ghana to fetch the Ghanaian chargé d'affaires, to manage as best they could. On November 28, von Horn informed Hammarskjold that on medical advice he must take four weeks' leave at once. Dayal was deeply worried at the weakness of the UN military command, which required, he told Hammarskjold, outstanding qualities of military leadership and political consciousness notably lacking in the existing setup. There was no proper coordination of political and security decisions by the military staff, and there were also unexplained delays, lack of foresight in planning, and lack of discipline in complying with orders. "I must reluctantly point out," Dayal wrote, "that a more vigorous, alert and politically conscious high command is essential for the proper execution of your policies."[69] Dayal suggested that General Sean McKeown of Ireland succeed von Horn as soon as possible.

Dayal's forthright approach, which represented the unanimous opinion of UN officials who had dealt with von Horn, put Hammarskjold in a difficult position. He had made a bad appointment, and a bad appointment of a fellow Swede at that. Faced with the consequences, he acted hesitantly and with an unusual lack of frankness.

---

* An impression of von Horn's personality is to be found in his own book *Soldiering for Peace* (London, 1966), a subjective and revealing account of his time with the United Nations.[68]

On December 5 he cabled von Horn that he was worried about the situation in Jerusalem, to which he wished von Horn, as Chief of Staff of UNTSO, to return as soon as he had recovered his health. He could leave the Congo, he wrote, with a good conscience and with the feeling of a job well done. Von Horn went on leave, and the Irish government agreed to release McKeown. Hammarskjold gave no hint to von Horn that his performance in the Congo had been anything but satisfactory, with the result that it never seems to have occurred to the General that he himself was to blame for many of the difficulties of which he later complained so loudly and publicly. Three months later he even reproached Hammarskjold himself, in a letter full of criticisms of his former colleagues, for having removed him from the Congo.

"As time passes and madness flourishes," Hammarskjold wrote to U.A.R. Foreign Minister Mahmoud Fawzi on December 3, "quickly and continuously changing the assumptions on which we first undertook our responsibilities in the Congo, our work is becoming increasingly complicated. On our assembly line of quarrels we have now passed the initial clash with Lumumba and consecutive quarrels with the Russians, the Belgians and Mobutu, seeming for the present to come back to a quarrel with the Russians (which, of course, in no way means that things have been straightened out with the Belgians). There is very little understanding and response from the delegations to the problem in general, and my difficulties in particular, and I often regret not to have the possibility to get your wise counsel. But, at least, we do not give up and maybe we will last longer than this perpetuum mobile of crises and quarrels."[70] Hammarskjold was especially bitter about the attitude of the West in general and of the Belgians in particular. "I shall not complain," he wrote to Joseph Luns, Foreign Minister of The Netherlands, "about the way in which they have treated the UN and myself. I am used to worse; but I would be less than frank if I did not note my own sadness at seeing this kind of reaction coming from people to whom I regard myself as being quite close. . . . The future of the world, and of the West, will depend on the quality shown at the present juncture by the West."[71]

Only a few representatives seem to have understood Hammarskjold's policy at this point. Chief among them was Mongi Slim of Tunisia, whose wisdom and level-headedness were reflected in a long, constructively critical, and sympathetic letter from President Habib Bourguiba on November 28, and there were a few others such as Adnan Pachachi, the representative of Iraq, who had personally come to the conclusion that Hammarskjold was doing the best he could in an impossible situation and supported him strongly and courageously both as chairman of the Fourth Committee of the General Assembly

(dealing with Trusteeship and Colonial matters) and in the meetings
of the Afro-Asian group. But from the extremities of East and West,
and for the most part in the area between, there was a general attitude of carping criticism and defeatism with occasional flashes of ill-
concealed glee at the trials and tribulations of ONUC.

Hammarskjold did his best to promote a deeper understanding of
the Congo situation among the Asian and African representatives in
meetings with the Congo Advisory Committee in the first week of
December. He had just received two cables from Sékou Touré[72] protesting the attitude of the UN representatives in the Congo to the
arrest of Lumumba, threatening to "seek other means within purely
African framework to support Congolese people in struggle against
all forms of colonialism,"[73] and charging the "unpardonable indifference"[74] of the representative of ONUC to the expulsion by Mobutu of
the U.A.R. and Ghana embassies.* He started out by reading these
messages to the Advisory Committee, and went on to discuss Kasavubu's lack of enthusiasm for receiving the Conciliation Commission
in Leopoldville, and the best means of getting it, or at least some
members of it, to the Congo right away. These meetings revealed the
deep differences of opinion that now also divided the African governments on the situation in the Congo, and the extreme difficulty of
charting an impartial yet constructive course between all the conflicting views and emotions the Congo crisis had aroused.

On December 6 the Soviet representative called for a meeting of
the Security Council,[75] violently denounced Hammarskjold as "a
lackey of the colonialists,"[76] accused ONUC of complicity in a plot to
eliminate the true leaders of the Congolese state and people, and
demanded the immediate liberation of Lumumba and the disarmament
of "Mobutu's bands of terrorists"[77] by the UN force. The previous day,
Hammarskjold had circulated a factual report from Dayal on the
circumstances of Lumumba's arrest as far as they were then known,[78]
and he also published the texts of his letters to Kasavubu and a report
on the situation in Stanleyville.[79] For good measure, the Council had
before it a violent denunciation by the Belgian government of Dayal's
report of November 2, which it characterized as "tendentious judgments based upon a series of purely subjective allegations and
interpretations, ambiguous innuendoes, unfounded insinuations and
arbitrary interpretations of the decisions and resolutions of the UN."[80]
The Council also received a telegram from Kasavubu, who accused
ONUC of protecting Lumumba and used the curious and ominous

---

* In late November 1960 the Mobutu régime had broken off relations with Ghana,
Morocco, and the U.A.R. because of their support of Lumumba.

argument that "in view of its unwillingness to alter its position regarding the protection of Mr. Lumumba, the UN cannot now evade the responsibility for the consequences of his escape."[81]

The Council met on December 7 in an atmosphere of acute East-West tension. Valerian Zorin, who was President of the Council for December, called upon the Secretary-General to give a general report "on his execution of the Security Council resolutions on the present situation in the Congo."[82] In an attempt to bring a sense of reality into the overheated atmosphere, Hammarskjold responded with a long and detailed statement[83] dealing with the whole spectrum of criticism from East to West. "It should be a reason for reflection," he said, "that the very day the Soviet Union repeats its well known criticism against the Secretary-General and his representatives we are under equally heavy criticism from people whom the Soviet Union in the same document characterizes as those to whom we show servile subservience."[84] All of the accusations were "no excessive price to be paid for avoiding the thing for which no one in my position should be forgiven: to compromise, in any political interest, with the aims and principles of this Organization. It has not been done and it will not be done with my knowledge or acquiescence."[85] The Security Council had never modified the principle that the UN force should not "be used to influence the outcome of any internal conflict, constitutional or otherwise,"[86] and this had meant, for example, that, although the UN might protect political leaders, it could not oppose the ANC acting under the orders of the Chief of State. The Secretary-General and his Representatives in the Congo were thus limited to making representations for elementary human rights, as in the case of Lumumba, and to trying to promote conciliation and peaceful settlement by persuasion. "What is now laid at the doorstep of the United Nations as a failure," he concluded, "is the failure of the political leaders of the Congo and of its people to take advantage of the unparalleled international assistance for the creation of normal political life within the country. These are harsh words and I hesitate to pronounce them but I do believe that this Organization is too often and too easily used as a whipping horse by those who wish to unburden themselves of their own responsibilities—this Organization which, however, represents values and hopes which go beyond that of any single man, any single political group and—why not—any single country."[87]

A week later he attempted even more bluntly to bring home to the Council what was at stake in the Congo.[88] If the UN operation ceased or was forced out of the country, the almost certain consequences would be civil war, tribal conflict, political disintegration, and economic collapse, accompanied in all probability by military aid from outside to the various warring factions. "If and when that were to happen," Hammarskjold said, "the world would be facing a confused Spanish war situation, with fighting going on all over the prostrate body of the Congo. . . . In these circumstances it seems obvious that the United Nations operation must continue. It is, however, necessary to consider under what circumstances it can continue. It cannot continue if it is being pushed around by various leaders and factions in the Congo, able to activate, against the United Nations, this or that member country, or group of member countries, willing, for whatever reason, to keep the operation under a fire of criticism and suspicion. It cannot continue if it is enfeebled from within by divisions, or by withdrawals, or by a lack of financial and material support, depriving it of its weight as a serious and authoritative factor in the local situation."[89]

Hammarskjold challenged the Council to clarify its intentions and to provide him with the means by which he could fulfill a broader mandate. He also asked the Council to consider how member governments could assume formally their part of the responsibility for day-to-day policy in the Congo, "which I and my collaborators now have had to take alone for five months."[90] If this could be done and those countries which had announced the withdrawal of their troops from ONUC would reconsider their position, it might still be possible to view the future with increased confidence. "Were that not to happen," he concluded, "we would continue to do our best on the Secretariat side, knowing, however, that we would still be weakened by ambiguities and that our efficiency might continue to be reduced by a political war waged around our activities."[91]

The Council adjourned in total frustration at 3:45 a.m. on December 14. Its failure to adopt either a Soviet resolution[92] demanding the release of Lumumba and the disarmament of Mobutu's "terrorist bands," or a Western resolution[93] calling for the humane treatment of political prisoners and the intervention of the Red Cross, left the Secretary-General and his colleagues once again without a precise mandate.

The Congo debate was immediately resumed in the General Assembly in the context of a controversy among the African states over whether to withdraw from the UN operation and try to operate in the Congo on their own or to stay with the UN and try to change its Congo policy. The latter view was embodied in a draft resolution sponsored by Ceylon, Ghana, India, Indonesia, Iraq, Morocco, the U.A.R., and Yugoslavia.[94] This draft urged, among other things, the immediate release of all political prisoners, the immediate convening of Parliament, the withdrawal of Belgian advisers, the channeling of

all aid through the UN, and the appointment of a "standing delegation" to act with Dayal in Leopoldville. Hammarskjold publicly
opposed this resolution,[95] not because he did not favor national
reconciliation and legality but because he was convinced that the UN
could work only through the normal political and diplomatic means
of persuasion and advice. To a demand by Krishna Menon that the
UN force stand up to Colonel Mobutu and his army, he replied, "I
would like to ask the honourable Assembly if it or the Security Council
has ever permitted me, or the Force, to take the initiative in military
action."[96] He went on to deal once again with the Soviet accusation
that he had dealt differently with the threat to the European population of Stanleyville and the threat to Lumumba. In Stanleyville, he
pointed out, the population was assembled in certain houses for protection, and the action required no military initiative by the UN.
Lumumba had deliberately left UN protection in his house for an
undisclosed destination, and thus, when he was later arrested, any
effort to release him would have meant ordering the UN force to attack
units of the ANC. The Security Council had given no authorization for
such an action. The Soviet delegate had said of the situation in
Stanleyville that Hammarskjold was prepared to take "immediate and
effective measures to defend the Belgians."[97] "I think," Hammarskjold
commented, "that the Members of the General Assembly should be on
guard against what I would call inverted racialism."[98]

In the face of increasingly violent attacks from the Soviet bloc,
Hammarskjold intervened four more times before the Assembly
adjourned. "The methods used in interventions," he said, "have
brought us to a point where many may have been tempted to ask
whether facts, or truth, or law no longer count, and whether it is
possible to debate without respect for some basic rules of debate as
developed in Parliamentary life, either as regards form or as regards
substance."[99] He pointed out that the welter of accusations from all
sides laid everything at the door of the Secretariat and excluded "even
the possibility of any responsibility of the Security Council, and its
members, or of the General Assembly and its Members, or of anybody
in the Congo ... Even the imperialists and colonialists seem to fade out
of the picture. Why?"[100]

On December 19, before the vote on the various draft resolutions,
Hammarskjold intervened to give a solemn warning of the dangers of
UN withdrawal and of civil war in the Congo. "Everything should be
done," he said, "by the Organization and its representatives to forestall such a crisis, but if our efforts are of no avail it is better for the
future of this Organization to look the situation in the eye and to
draw the conclusions."[101]

The Assembly failed to agree on any resolution on the Congo before it adjourned on December 21, and only at the very last minute did it vote the financial appropriations necessary to support the Congo operation. "Naturally," Hammarskjold told the Assembly before it adjourned, "the operation will be continued under the previous decisions with all energy, within the limits of the law, with an adjustment —to the best of our understanding—of the implementation of our mandate to the needs, and with aims which, in spite of all, I believe remain common, at least, to the vast majority of Member States. However, the outcome here, as it now stands, has not given us the moral or political support of which the operation is in need."[102]

Hammarskjold's position was now even more isolated than before. The more radical African states would obviously soon withdraw their troops from the operation and throw their support to Gizenga's Stanleyville régime. A group of the French-speaking African states would try to bring Kasavubu and Tshombe together, while the Western countries would step up their support of Mobutu's régime. Hammarskjold's independent position had alienated him to a large extent from all three groups, and yet the fact remained that his dogged maintenance of this independent position had allowed ONUC to prevent a lethal civil war between the factions in the Congo, supported by various outside powers. The 19,500 UN troops in the Congo, frequently resented and publicly derided by all the factions, were still the only guarantee of a minimum of personal safety, law, and order, just as the UN civilian operation alone preserved the basis for public administration, services, and finance upon which the possibility of future development would depend. That the majority of the member states tacitly recognized this state of affairs was indicated by the fact that in voting for the financing of ONUC they voted for its continuation.

The recess of the Assembly session gave Hammarskjold time to concentrate again on essentials. There were, he told Dayal, "strong elements of bluff and even blackmail in the picture, and we shall have to try to call the bluff and resist the blackmail."[103] In particular, he was as yet not sure how seriously the various threats to withdraw troops from ONUC must be taken. So far only Yugoslavia, which had a very small contingent, had actually insisted on withdrawing its personnel.

He followed up his warning to the General Assembly on the possibility that the whole UN operation might have to be withdrawn, by a letter to Kasavubu[104] which he asked the United States and Great Britain—Kasavubu's principal sponsors—to follow up. The letter emphasized the features of the various draft resolutions, which, despite the lack of any final resolution, had had wide support in the General Assembly. These included deep and general concern for the safety of Lumumba and other political prisoners, the necessity of cooperation between Kasavubu and the UN Conciliation Commission, whose advance party had at last arrived in Leopoldville on December 19, the danger of the bilateral provision of arms and military advisers to the various factions from outside, and the wish to see an end to the interference of the ANC in politics. He stressed again the probability that UN withdrawal would lead to civil war.

Hammarskjold had hoped to spend Christmas in Leopoldville with ONUC, as he had done with UNEF in Gaza in past years, but he found there was too much to be cleared up in New York to permit him to leave before the New Year for Leopoldville and South Africa. He spent Christmas Eve with Bill Ranallo and his wife. When Wieschhoff asked him to Christmas dinner at his home in Bronxville, Hammarskjold had refused, evidently not wishing to intrude on a family occasion, but on Christmas morning he called Wieschhoff to ask if he could come out to Bronxville for a walk. Wieschhoff, realizing how lonely Hammarskjold must feel to have made this call, drove into New York to fetch him. Back in Bronxville they walked through the snow for an hour, and Hammarskjold stayed on for the family dinner. The next day he spent quietly in his apartment.

The last days of the year were complicated by several unexpected developments. On December 30 the permanent representative of Laos informed him of an invasion of Laos by the North Vietnamese and the next day complained of the "intrusion of the Soviet Union into the internal affairs of Laos."[105] On New Year's Eve the Cuban Foreign Minister, Raul Roa, flew to New York to demand an immediate meeting of the Security Council because a U.S. attack on Cuba was imminent "within a few hours."[106] Hammarskjold had considerable difficulty in contacting the members of the Council at this festive time, and Roa finally agreed to a meeting of the Council four days later. In view of the Bay of Pigs expedition four months later, the Cuban Foreign Minister's anxieties, which included the training in Guatemala of an invading force of Cuban exiles, proved less fanciful than Hammarskjold believed them to be at the time.

The Congo did not fail to continue to provide its quota of complications. On December 13 the ANC, apparently without orders, had seized the Kitona base from the UN by force, and long negotiations were necessary before it was returned to UN control. On December 15 the entire UN Austrian Field Hospital, which had just arrived in Bukavu, was arrested by the ANC, again acting without orders and under the misapprehension that the Austrians were Belgians. When negotiations failed, Lieutenant Colonel J. T. U. Aguiyi-Ironsi,* the UN Nigerian commander on the spot, ran into strong opposition in attempting to release the Austrians. In the ensuing fight the Nigerians suffered one fatality and five wounded, the ANC losses being considerably higher. Colonel Mobutu apologized for this incident.

Hammarskjold also learned in mid-December that the Organization for Economic Cooperation and Development (OECD) was planning to extend a $60-million grant to the Mobutu regime. He expressed to the United States and Great Britain his concern over a Western gesture that could only be considered as an interference in the Congo by the six European ex-colonial powers, including Belgium, which constituted the Commission. Such gestures might, he warned, "easily give rise to a situation in which the United Nations civilian operation in the fields of finance and trade should be discontinued,"[107] and he quoted the declarations of the American and British representatives in the Assembly in favor of channeling all aid to the Congo through the United Nations.

The year 1960 ended with another Congolese complication that was particularly serious because Belgium was directly involved. During December the eastern province of Kivu had fallen under Gizenga's control, and Mobutu decided to send an ANC detachment to reconquer it. On December 30 this detachment, under the command of the same Major Pongo who had arrested Lumumba, arrived by air in Usumbura in the Belgian-administered Trust Territory of Ruanda-Urundi.** Belgian military trucks drove the Congolese troops to the Congolese border at Shangugu, where they entered Kivu and promptly surrendered to the local troops loyal to Gizenga's Stanleyville régime. Although the Belgian government claimed that it had been as surprised as anyone else at the arrival of the troops and had merely wished to repatriate them as quickly as possible, Hammarskjold protested strongly on what he knew would be generally interpreted as an act of collusion by Belgium with the Mobutu régime.[108]

Hammarskjold's mood at the year's end was one both of exasperation and of determination. The Assembly session had been a disillusioning experience, reflecting certain ugly underlying tendencies and trends in world politics that he was determined to resist from whatever quarter they came. "The job," he wrote to Hans Engen, who was

---

* Ironsi became commander of the UN force (January to June 1964) and later President of Nigeria when President Balewa was assassinated in January 1966. Ironsi himself was murdered in July 1966.
** Which in 1962 became the independent countries Rwanda and Burundi.

now State Secretary for Foreign Affairs of Norway, "has become a bit like fighting an avalanche; you know the rules—get rid of the skis, don't try to resist but swim on the surface and hope for a rescuer. (Next morning historians will dig up the whole rotten mess and see how many were buried.) A consolation is that avalanches, after all, automatically always come to a stop and that thereafter you can start behaving like an intelligent being again—provided you have managed to keep afloat."[109]*

---

* The letter ends: "As a little New Year's gift, I send you two results of pre-Congo extra-curricular activities." These were Hammarskjold's translations of Saint-John Perse's *Chronique* and a copy of the January 1961 issue of *National Geographic* with his article "New Look at Everest," illustrated by his photographs.

18

1961: THE FIRST MONTHS

ON JANUARY 3, 1961, Hammarskjold left New York for Leopoldville. There, apart from a brief meeting with Kasavubu, he spent three days in intensive consultations with Dayal and his colleagues concerning the political and constitutional situation, the widespread outbreaks of violence, often directed against the UN troops, the unresolved question of Katanga, the problem of the Baluba refugees in Kasai, and the difficulties created by the withdrawal of several contingents from the UN force.

For a week thereafter, Hammarskjold was in South Africa where, in contrast to his preoccupations in the Congo, he engaged in a staid and almost academic discussion of a basically far more difficult problem. From the UN's earliest years, the racial policies of the South African government had been the subject of a continuous and frustrating debate. The massacre at Sharpeville on March 21, 1960, had caused twenty-nine members of the Afro-Asian group to make a formal complaint to the Security Council, which on April 1 had passed a resolution[1] requesting the Secretary-General, in consultation with the government of the Union of South Africa, "to make such arrangements as would adequately help in upholding the purposes and principles of the Charter and to report to the Security Council whenever necessary and appropriate."[2]

Hammarskjold had no illusions about the possibility of any quick or considerable success in this vaguely worded assignment. "How do you go about building bridges?" he asked a press conference on April 8, 1960. "The building of a firm bridge, of course, over which you can pass without any difficulties may be a long story, but you can at least put the first stones down into the water or get a first piece of wood across the water, a little bit out into it. And I would say that is what I think the Security Council was hoping for when they put me into the picture. . . . Of course, this all rests very much with the Government of South Africa itself. However, I am in duty bound to seek such contact."[3]

Since the South African government held that the UN had no competence in what it regarded as a purely internal affair, Hammarskjold decided to use once again the "Peking formula" which had been the basis for his talks with Chou En-lai on the release of the American airmen. This formula was not merely a face-saving device for reluctant governments; it also provided a means by which the UN, through the physical presence and activities of the Secretary-General, could move into situations where other UN organs would not be acceptable. The essence of this formula was as follows: The Secretary-General functions on the basis of his authority under the Charter. Any challenge to his authority must therefore be either because he is acting *ultra vires* or because the party concerned refuses to acknowledge the Charter itself, which had been recognized even in 1955 by the Peking government as a universally valid instrument. Thus a member state of the UN cannot reject an initiative of the Secretary-General except on the basis that he is exceeding his authority under the Charter. Article 2, paragraph 7, of the Charter, which safeguards the domestic jurisdiction of states against international interference, is not a limitation if the Security Council has found, as it had done in the case of the Sharpeville massacre, that a domestic situation is also a threat to international peace and security. "Neither Chou nor South Africa," Hammarskjold said later, "considered that discussion with the Secretary-General activated Article 2 (7). Any government can do this [i.e., talk with the Secretary-General] as an act of sovereignty. The next step is what you can do with it. That I don't know. My first care was to establish a working relationship with South Africa."[4]

Hammarskjold told the permanent representative of South Africa in New York that his action would be "limited to consultation rendered necessary by the instructions addressed to me for certain action to be undertaken on the basis of the authority of the Secretary-General under the Charter"[5] and that his actions would not require the prior recognition by South Africa of the UN's authority in the question of apartheid. Eric Louw, the South African Foreign Minister, replied that this formulation removed South Africa's difficulty of appearing, by consenting to talks with the Secretary-General, to recognize the UN's right to intervene in South Africa's internal affairs.[6] On May 13 and 14, after the Commonwealth Prime Ministers Conference, Hammarskjold had preliminary talks with Louw in London.

He had given a great deal of thought to the approach that he should adopt in these preliminary conversations upon an apparently hopeless problem. The South African government's dogmatic views on questions of race had become so inured to international criticism that only a completely new approach was likely to have any effect whatsoever. He had no fixed ideas except to encourage the government to make arrangements that might at the same time provide some reassurance to the outside world in regard to the protection of human rights in the Union and eliminate the risk of further tragedies such as Sharpeville. As an example of the kind of arrangement that might prove useful, he suggested the appointment by the South African government of some kind of ombudsman who would receive, review, and act upon complaints concerning human rights, could deal with Ministers or initiate court actions, and could report to the South African Parliament or even to the Secretary-General. He emphasized that when he visited South Africa he would wish to have free access to all persons he might wish to see.

At the close of the London talks it was announced that the Secretary-General and Louw had agreed on the "character and course"[7] of the further discussions to be held between them in Pretoria in July. Hammarskjold told Selywyn Lloyd, the British Foreign Secretary, that "the discussions with Louw turned out surprisingly well, and the road is paved to Pretoria, not only through good intentions but, I hope, by some solid realization of the need for substantive progress, be it ever so modest."[8]

In June 1960, Hammarskjold had decided that he would visit South Africa between July 27 and August 7, but the sudden crisis in the Congo compelled him to curtail his program drastically, and in July he proposed to the South African government that he should arrive on August 2 and see Prime Minister Henrik Verwoerd on the next day. When the necessity of securing the entry of UN troops into Katanga caused him once again to postpone his arrival, Louw suggested that his visit be postponed until after the session of the General Assembly. Hammarskjold was anxious to avoid further delay and insisted that he would go to Pretoria, if only for a day or two, in August. August 11 and 12 were agreed on but soon canceled because at that moment he was leading the UN troops into Elisabethville. After two further dates had had to be canceled, he was obliged to tell Louw that he hoped to have further discussions with him during the session of the General Assembly. He finally reached Pretoria on January 6, 1961, accompanied by Heinz Wieschhoff, Wilhelm Wachtmeister, and Bill Ranallo. His aircraft was diverted at the last minute from Jan Smuts Airport to the Waterkloof military airfield in order to avoid the crowds which had gathered to greet him.

The immediate purpose of Hammarskjold's visit to Pretoria was less concerned with racial policy than with finding arrangements for safeguarding human rights in accordance with UN principles. Integration was in any case not only totally unacceptable to Verwoerd but also politically unrealistic in view of the parliamentary situation. Hammarskjold therefore resolved to find out whether and how the policy of the Union government could be developed into "a competitive alternative"[9] to integration, and how the arrangements required by the Security Council might become a possible part of such a "competitive alternative."

In his meetings with Verwoerd,[10] Hammarskjold began by criticizing both the theory and the practical application of the Union government's Bantu "homelands" policy. How, he asked, could the Union on the one hand relegate the Bantu to the "homelands" as territory to which they had historic rights and then claim authority within and over those same "homelands" for the central government, which in this case did not represent the will of the governed? Furthermore, the "homelands" were in no sense on a basis of economic equality with the areas the Bantu would have to leave, and to make them sufficiently prosperous to remedy this problem would require huge investments as well as territorial readjustments.

As to the segregation policy, he expressed himself as frankly shocked both at the South African legislation itself and at its application. The Union had never managed to explain its approach to the Bantu problem in terms that had convinced world public opinion, and world public opinion had never accepted either the "homelands" concept or the racial policies which were practiced outside the "homelands." Both the unpracticability and the unacceptability of the current policy created a risk that the whole structure might crumble in the most tragic circumstances. Eventually the South African government would have to choose between the present slow progress toward the probably unrealistic targets it had set itself and a much bolder approach that not only would benefit the Bantu but would in the end also be the best protection for the white population. If the South African government wished to continue to insist on separation of the races, a "competitive alternative" to integration was urgently required which might provide a solution to the apparently irreconcilable problem of a country whose economic base, patterned on integration, supported a political structure patterned on segregation.

If there was to be territorial separation of the races—which Hammarskjold doubted was possible in the long run for both economic and demographic reasons—a sufficient and coherent territory must be set aside to serve as the basis for the national life of the Bantu state. This in turn would require a radical plan for economic development to provide, within the Bantu territory, for industry and economic growth of sufficient scope to encourage the voluntary return of those who were earning their living in other parts of the Union. The political institutions necessary for full independence and self-government of the Bantu territory on a democratic basis would also have to be urgently established. In the meantime, Bantu working outside the "homelands" or the future independent Bantu state must enjoy the normal human rights generally recognized elsewhere, and prolonged residence should also entitle them eventually to acquire citizenship and full civic rights in the Union, which was, after all, dependent on their labor. These admittedly utopian requirements were the logical consequence of the "homelands" concept, which the Prime Minister had described as the basis of the Union's approach to the racial problem. Otherwise the "homelands" concept itself and the sincerity with which it had been formulated were bound to be put in question.

Time was of the essence, and since important problems would obviously arise in the transition to any such new concept, Hammarskjold suggested that the government might set up an impartial and objective institution to receive and consider complaints and to draw the attention of the government and Parliament to deviations from the approach to the established objectives. This institution might also maintain contact with the UN through the Secretary-General, thus providing the "arrangement" requested by the Security Council.

Hammarskjold talked with Verwoerd in Pretoria on January 6 and 7, then flew over the Rand and Orange Free State goldfields to Cape Town. On the ninth he flew to Umtata, in the Transkei native reserve, and then went on, at his own request, to Pondoland, the scene of recent disturbances. He returned to Pretoria on January 10 for further talks with Verwoerd, then went on to Johannesburg, where he was shown an African township. He concluded his talks with the Prime Minister on the afternoon and evening of the eleventh and spent January 12 in the Northern Bantu Territories.

This officially sponsored and highly organized tour gave Hammarskjold little opportunity to have private talks with African representatives, and the distorted press reports of an impromptu speech he had made during discussions after a dinner given by the Commissioner General for the Transkei Territory in Umtata on January 9 created some dismay, which a correction published in the press the next day did not wholly dispel. He was wrongly reported as having said, "I hope you will achieve your destiny as you see it," and this was taken by African leaders and white liberals alike to be an endorsement of apartheid policies. Among those who protested were Chief Albert Luthuli—who in 1961, shortly after Hammarskjold's death, was to share the Nobel Peace Prize with him—and the novelist Alan Paton, who wrote, "The hopes of millions of South Africans whose representatives you have not yet met lie in your visit."[11]

The communiqué published on January 12 described the talks between the Secretary-General and Verwoerd as "frank, constructive, and helpful,"[12] and on January 23 Hammarskjold reported to the Security Council that although "so far no mutually acceptable arrangement has been found,"[13] he did not regard this lack of agreement as conclusive.

In spite of Hammarskjold's plain speaking the atmosphere of the talks had been surprisingly good, but he had no illusions that Verwoerd would welcome or even comprehend his proposals, however persuasive their logic or ingenious their substance. He had felt that he had been speaking to Verwoerd across a gulf of three hundred years, although he had the impression that Verwoerd was in earnest and took the talks seriously. The most that could be hoped for was that the exchange would at least prove useful in opening up contacts that might be pursued later on, since the Union government had officially stated that it wished to continue the consultations. Other preoccupations, and then Hammarskjold's death, prevented any further explorations.

Hammarskjold had intended to return from Pretoria to New York via Cairo, Gaza, and Delhi. Although he had at first refused to curtail his visit to South Africa when the U.S.S.R. called, on January 7, for another urgent meeting of the Security Council on the Congo,[14] he finally left two days ahead of schedule direct for New York, where he arrived on January 13. His visits to Cairo and Delhi were postponed until July, when they again had to be canceled because of the Bizerte crisis.

BEFORE LEAVING FOR SOUTH AFRICA, Hammarskjold had put before the Council a report on the transit of Mobutu's troops through Ruanda-Urundi and the text of his own immediate and sharp protest to the Belgians and to the Leopoldville government,[15] but the Soviet Union strongly criticized his handling of the incident anyway and accused him of connivance with the Belgians and of protecting the lives and property of Europeans. "I think that the substance of the line now taken by the U.S.S.R. makes it clear," he told the Council, "why these accusations have been made. By trying to give the impression that the Secretariat and its representatives, in particular the Secretary-General, are inspired by racial prejudice, they want to drive a wedge into the collaboration, based on confidence, which has been established between the African States and the Secretariat in this operation."[16]

The campaign in Leopoldville against Dayal came into the open in mid-January when Kasavubu publicly accused him of failing to help the government to deal forcibly with the Stanleyville régime of Gizenga and demanded his recall.[17] This demand was curtly refused by Hammarskjold, who pointed out that Kasavubu had made no mention of it earlier in the month, when he had seen him in Leopoldville. "It is regrettable," he said, "that such an opportunity to exchange views personally about such a delicate and important matter was not utilized."[18] He took the opportunity further to point out to Kasavubu that his accusation of UN complicity in the murder of the Minister of Education of Kivu Province was somewhat ludicrous, since the said Minister was at present comfortably lodged in the Hôtel des Chutes at Stanleyville and was recovering from an attack of malignant malaria for which he had just been hospitalized. He also explained again the inability of the UN force, short of new instructions from the Security Council, to enter into Kasavubu's struggle against Gizenga and his military commander, Victor Lundula, or to disarm the ANC groups they controlled. Dayal believed Kasavubu's move to be largely the result of pressures from some of the Western embassies in Leopoldville. "I keep my cases packed," he cabled, "to avoid becoming a political liability to the UN, whose cause I shall always endeavour, to the utmost limit of my ability and strength, loyally and devotedly to serve."[19]

Although Lumumba was in prison in Thysville, Kasavubu and Mobutu felt threatened by his dynamic presence in a large army camp so near to the capital. The New Year's Day fiasco in Kivu had been followed on January 9 by the capture of Manono in northern Katanga by Gizenga's forces and by rumors of a Gizengist offensive to take Coquilhatville, the capital of Equateur Province. The feeling of near panic in Leopoldville had been increased by the pro-Lumumba demonstrations that had greeted Hammarskjold on his arrival in Leopoldville in early January. On January 13 there was a mutiny over inequalities of pay and lodgings at the Thysville military camp, which caused Kasavubu, Mobutu, Bomboko, and Victor Nendaka[20] to rush to the scene. Lumumba's cell door had been opened by the mutineers, but, fearing a trap, he had refused to come out. Nonetheless the Leopoldville regime was determined that Lumumba be transferred to a safer place, and approaches had apparently already been made to Tshombe with a view to sending him to Katanga. Tshombe had been noncommittal, but Kalonji, and later on his mercenary army commander, Colonel J. Gillet, had urged that Lumumba be sent to Bakwanga, where the Baluba could be counted on to avenge themselves on his person for the events of August. Since the Bakwanga airfield was occupied by UN troops, the Leopoldville government eventually decided to send Lumumba, Senator Joseph Okito, and General Maurice Mpolo to Elisabethville, with or without Tshombe's consent. None of these doings were known to Dayal and his staff, and the details of the events that followed became known only much later. The transfer of Lumumba was made in an Air Congo DC-4 on January 17. The all-Baluba escort was under the command of the Commissioner of Defense, Ferdinand Kazadi,[21] whom Lumumba had imprisoned in Luluabourg in August. In the plane during the five-hour flight the Baluba guards beat up the prisoners so brutally that the Belgian crew became nauseated and, after attempting unsuccessfully to intervene, finally locked themselves in the flight deck.

Particular pains were taken to keep Lumumba's transfer secret from ONUC, which had no inkling of it until the plane arrived in Elisabethville. There it was directed to the Katangese military aviation hangar, which was not included in the area patrolled by UN troops. The UN troops at the airfield, a Swedish detail of a warrant officer and five soldiers, had their first sign of any extraordinary activity when police vehicles drove up to the plane and it was surrounded by a cordon of 130 Katangese gendarmes. The Swedes had only an interrupted view of the scene from a distance of about a hundred yards. They did not know who the prisoners were, and Lumumba and his companions had been driven away before the Swedes began to realize what was happening, but even their fragmentary account was shocking enough. They reported that the prisoners had been beaten savagely on leaving the plane, that all were blindfolded and with their hands tied behind their backs, and that one of them had a small beard. They were driven swiftly away under heavy escort and disappeared through a gap cut specially in the airport fence. This proved to be the outside world's last glimpse of the Congo's first Prime Minister, Patrice Lumumba.

For nearly a month, Hammarskjold and the officials of ONUC reacted to these events in ignorance of the fact that the tragedy they were trying to avert had already occurred. Hammarskjold was deeply concerned about the transfer of Lumumba and his companions to Elisabethville, about the reports of their brutal treatment, and about what might be in store for them in Katanga. He urged Dayal to find out all he could and to do everything possible to ensure humane treatment, but he realized all too well that in this situation the UN was almost completely impotent. He asked Dayal to suggest at once any possible action that might be taken for the safety of Lumumba and his two companions. On January 18 the ONUC representative in Elisabethville, Ian Berendsen, talked to Tshombe,[22] who confirmed that it was indeed Lumumba who had arrived and that he and his companions were in a sad state from the maltreatment they had sustained in the aircraft. The transfer to Elisabethville was Kasavubu's idea, Tshombe said, and he had always been against it. He refused to give any further information and refrained from saying what he almost certainly must have already known, that Lumumba and his companions were dead. Berendsen urged Tshombe to return the prisoners as quickly as possible and meanwhile to allow them to be visited by the International Red Cross. The next day the Katanga Information Ministry stated that at the request of Kasavubu and with Katanga's consent "the traitor Patrice Lumumba has been transferred to Katanga, as the prison of Thysville no longer offers sufficient guarantees."[23]

On January 19, Hammarskjold appealed again to Kasavubu for the application of humane methods and due process of law.[24] He demanded that Kasavubu immediately take steps to have Lumumba brought back from Katanga and that he be allowed to answer the accusations made against him in an equitable legal process in public and with all the necessary guarantees for his safety and for his own defense. On the same day he also addressed a strong message to Tshombe through his representative in Elisabethville. On January 20, after meeting with the Congo Advisory Committee, he addressed Kasavubu again, protesting against the brutality with which Lumumba had reportedly been treated. By February 1, Tshombe had recovered his sang-froid sufficiently to express astonishment at the UN's concern for Lumumba and its comparative indifference over developments in Stanleyville and Bukavu. Kasavubu responded in the same tone.

The Soviet Union promptly accused Hammarskjold of connivance in Lumumba's transfer and brutal treatment, which had, as Zorin put it in a note on January 20,[25] been "carried out before the eyes of the 'United Nations Command' in the Congo. Thus, neither the 'United Nations Command' nor the Secretary-General can divest themselves of responsibility for these acts organized for the benefit of the colonialists."[26] Much more serious from a practical point of view was the reaction of the governments of Indonesia, Morocco, and the U.A.R., which immediately withdrew their contingents from the UN force. This move, which Hammarskjold had been trying to stave off since December, drastically weakened the force at precisely the time when growing disorders all over the Congo made its presence more necessary than ever.

Nehru too was highly critical of the UN's "more or less passive attitude in the face of what is happening,"[27] which would, he said, make it difficult for India to provide troops to fill the place of the contingents that had been withdrawn. He urged Hammarskjold to try to get an agreement between East and West on some minimum policy in the Congo, with the aim of keeping the Congo out of the cold war and restoring a legitimate and representative government. Otherwise, Nehru feared, the UN operation would fizzle out for political and financial reasons, and a civil war with large-scale outside intervention would result. Hammarskjold responded to Nehru's letter by asking for an Indian battalion for the force. Although for the most part he agreed with Nehru's views, he made a strong defense of the UN operation, which was working under conditions of near anarchy for objectives that few people seemed to understand.

Hammarskjold took up the idea of a "minimum common policy" on the Congo with Adlai E. Stevenson, the new U.S. representative at the UN, on January 26. He suggested that the West show its neutrality by avoiding backing Kasavubu and Mobutu to the exclusion of any possibility of compromise. He also asked for support for his effort to get more troops and concluded by suggesting that the Kennedy administration approach Moscow with a view to reducing their differences over the Congo and to removing the Congo from the arena of the East-West struggle. For a short time he seems to have felt that this suggestion to Stevenson might bear fruit and that the tide might turn. The ANC's reverses in Kivu and the formation in Leopoldville on February 9 of a provisional government under Joseph Ileo had curbed Mobutu's power, and it seemed possible that the new U.S. administration, which wished to improve its relations with the U.S.S.R. and with the African states, would even support the idea of including Lumumba in a government of national conciliation. Such a development might in turn make it possible for the Security Council to agree on an extension and a clearer definition of the UN's mandate in the Congo. It was toward this end that Hammarskjold worked in the first days of February during the meetings of the Security Council, which had been summoned at the request of the U.S.S.R.[28]

These efforts to bring the members of the Council together and to increase the effectiveness of ONUC were overshadowed by mounting fears and increasingly alarming rumors over the fate of Lumumba.

The Secretary-General's urgings, Dayal's efforts, and the promptings of various governments had all failed to elicit Lumumba's whereabouts. On February 10, Godefroid Munongo, Tshombe's Interior Minister, released an elaborate story of Lumumba's escape,[29] following it up with a second installment on the next day, in which a reward was offered for information leading to Lumumba's capture. The highly detailed nature of Munongo's story, and the constant evasiveness of Tshombe and Munongo in the face of frantic efforts by Dayal's representatives to contact them indicated strongly that Lumumba was already dead. Munongo provided the last episode of this cynical charade on February 13 by announcing that Lumumba and his companions had been massacred by the inhabitants of a village he refused to name, and that he and three other Katangese Ministers had flown to the spot and identified the bodies. The village, he added, had received a reward of forty thousand Congolese francs. "We shall be accused of having murdered them," Munongo said. "My reply is: prove it";[30] and he concluded with a long and incoherent attack on the United Nations.

Although many details are still in dispute and are likely to remain so, the known circumstances of Lumumba's death can be reconstructed from later evidence as follows.* When the aircraft carrying Lumumba was approaching Elisabethville, Tshombe was watching a Moral Re-Armament film, *Liberté*, and could not be reached by the control tower, which finally got through to Munongo instead. Munongo organized a large police escort and rushed to the airport. On January 15, Tshombe had told Justin Bomboko that he would accept the transfer of "Lumumba the Communist" to Katanga provided his rival, Jason Sendwe,[31] the Baluba leader of northern Katanga, was sent too. Apparently he had no idea of the exact date or time of arrival of the prisoners, for on January 18 the Belgian consul in Elisabethville reported that "the authorities were surprised by this sudden but expected arrival."[32] The prisoners were taken from the airfield under heavy escort to a small unoccupied house called "Le Pondoir" (the Chicken Coop), while Tshombe summoned his Cabinet to decide what should be done next. The Cabinet apparently decided to send the prisoners to the home of Munongo's brother, the *Grand Chef* of the Bayeke, at Bunkeya, and Munongo was told to make the necessary arrangements.

What happened next is obscure. On January 18, Tshombe had told the UN representative in Elisabethville that he had seen the prisoners

---

* G. Heinz and R. Donnay, *Lumumba: The Last Fifty Days* (New York, 1969), contains the most convincing and detailed account of the fate of Lumumba yet written, and is the basis for this account.

the evening before and that they were in a sad state. In January 1964, however, he denied that he had seen them at all. Later, while in exile in Madrid, he told a journalist that he had seen them at 9 p.m. on January 17 and that Lumumba was at his last gasp. Certainly some of the Katangese Ministers went out to gloat over the prisoners, and one, Lucas Samalenge,[33] boasted that night in a bar that he had kicked Lumumba's dead body. For this he was rebuked by Tshombe, and later, in 1961, he died in suspicious circumstances in a "hunting accident."

Whether Lumumba and his two companions were executed or died of their injuries is not known for certain. The many different versions of the story of their end have in common only one characteristic, that they exonerate their tellers, and the truth has been further obscured by initial bragging and later efforts at self-exculpation, and by rivalries and feuds between mercenaries, Belgian officers, and other Europeans in Katanga. There are four main versions of Lumumba's end: (1) the fabrication of Lumumba's escape and capture put out by Munongo in February 1961, (2) the story that Munongo and/or the Katangese authorities executed the prisoners, (3) Tshombe's story that the prisoners were already dying when they reached Elisabethville, and (4) the allegations of Nkrumah and other African sources that Europeans were the executioners. The UN Commission of Inquiry concluded[34] tentatively that Lumumba and his companions were killed on the night of their arrival in Elisabethville, very probably in the presence of Tshombe, Munongo, and Finance Minister Jean-Baptiste Kibwe,[35] and probably by a Belgian officer, Colonel Huyghe, assisted by a Captain Gat, also Belgian. A similar profusion of stories surrounds the disposal of the corpses, but no trace of them has ever been uncovered. All that seems certain is that Lumumba, Okito, and Mpolo were killed, or died, during the night of January 17–18 in Katangese custody.

Hammarskjold circulated Munongo's statement on Lumumba's death to the Security Council on the same day it was issued. The fears and doubts were now over, and uproar began. Munongo's sickening and obviously mendacious account of a violent tragedy was a blow felt almost universally, even by those who had good reason to dislike Lumumba. For Hammarskjold, apart from his revulsion at the event itself, it was a disaster that might well put an end both to the hope of making a new start in the Congo and to his own possibility of playing a useful role in the future. Lumumba's murder appalled him as an act of criminal brutality and stupidity, but he was too honest to indulge in false sentimentality or conventional and insincere expressions of personal grief. He had begun by liking Lumumba and wishing to help him, but experience had persuaded him that under the temptations and pressures of public office the Congolese Prime Minister had become an unstable and irresponsible man with dangerous dictatorial tendencies, who was also being exploited by various external forces for their own ends. "I incline to the conclusion," he wrote to the American writer John Steinbeck at the end of February, "that *no* one, in the long pull, will really profit from Lumumba's death; least of all those outside the Congo who now strain to do so but should one day confront a reckoning with truth and decency. There may be immediately some propaganda exploitation of this blunder; indeed, we have been seeing it in staged bursts in many parts of the world, but to what avail, really, and even those efforts have required unbridled distortion. It is, I imagine, at its earliest that the big lie shines brightest; does one ever endure? Events in the Congo move quickly and, it seems, so far always badly or in bad directions; memories, even of ghosts and legends and certainly of synthetic martyrs, are short, and everything soon gets swallowed up in the confusions, frustrations and sheer imbecilities of that arena."[36]

In the Security Council on February 13, Hammarskjold confined himself to confirming the news of Lumumba's death and to suggesting that a full and impartial investigation should be undertaken at once.[37] In many parts of the world the reaction to the murder was violent. In Cairo the Belgian embassy was sacked and burned, and demonstrations took place in many other capitals. Zorin flatly charged Hammarskjold with direct responsibility, claiming that as "a participant in and organizer of the violence committed against the leading statesmen of the Republic of the Congo," [he] deserved "the contempt of all honest people,"[38] and he proposed that the Council impose sanctions on Belgium, authorize the arrest of Mobutu and Tshombe, terminate the UN operation, and dismiss Hammarskjold himself.* The letter went on to say that the Soviet government would have no further relations with Hammarskjold and would support the "lawful Government of the Congo."[40]**

On the morning of February 15 the Security Council itself was interrupted by a well-organized riot in the public gallery. In the ensuing melee, twenty of the unarmed UN guards were injured by brass knuckles, spiked-heel shoes, and other weapons. The main targets of the demonstrators, who had gained admittance on protocol passes

---

* Coincidentally on February 16, Tshombe charged the UN with bathing the Congo in fire and blood and accused it of "passivity and dereliction"[39] with regard to the pro-Lumumba rebels.
** On February 23 a note from Hammarskjold to the Soviet mission was returned with the comment that the Soviet Government no longer recognized Mr. Dag Hammarskjold as an official of the UN. The Soviet mission continued to deal with the Secretariat.

normally issued to UN delegations for their guests, were apparently Hammarskjold and Adlai Stevenson,* and it took some time to round the rioters up and get them out of the building.

After Lumumba's assassination Hammarskjold became, for the first time in his life, an object of hatred among a small minority. He was shocked to learn that one of the UN elevator operators had heard a girl from the Ghana Mission say, after the riot in the Security Council, that she hoped the demonstrators would get to Hammarskjold and kill him. Extra security guards were assigned to him wherever he went, but he disliked being guarded, and the security measures were soon somewhat relaxed.

On the afternoon of February 15, he addressed the Council[41] about the "revolting crime against principles for which this Organization stands and must stand. It is vain to argue with those for whom truth is a function of party convenience and justice a function of party interest, but for others it may be essential that some facts are recalled and clearly and simply put on record."[42] He next gave a lengthy account of the events, as far as they were then known, that had led up to Lumumba's murder, a tragedy which the UN had had neither the authority nor the means to prevent. He spoke of the new element in the Soviet attack, the "preposterous allegation"[43] that the murder of Lumumba could be laid at the doorstep of the Secretary-General. Although under normal circumstances such an accusation might have caused him to resign, the fact that the Soviet position made it clear that no new Secretary-General could be appointed made it impossible for him to do so unless the majority of the members so wished.

He then turned to the history of the UN Congo operation:

> For seven or eight months, through efforts far beyond the imagination of those who founded this Organization, it has tried to counter tendencies to introduce the big-power conflict into Africa and put the young African countries under the shadow of the cold war. It has done so with great risks and against heavy odds. It has done so at the cost of very great personal sacrifices for a great number of people. In the beginning the effort was successful, and I do not now hesitate to say that on more than one occasion the drift into a war with foreign power intervention of the Korean or Spanish type was avoided only thanks to the work done by the Organization, basing itself on African solidarity. We countered effectively efforts from all sides to make the Congo a happy hunting ground for national interests. To be a road-block to such efforts is to make yourself the target of attacks from all those

---

* Hammarskjold watched this riot from his seat at the Council table until his aide, Don Thomas, hearing the rioters shouting "Get Hammarskjold, get Hammarskjold," prevailed upon him to leave the Chamber.

who find their plans thwarted. In the case of some the opposition against the United Nations line was for a while under the surface, but it was not long before it broke out in the open. In other cases the disappointment in meeting this unexpected obstacle broke out at once in violent and vocal attacks on the Organization. From both sides the main accusation was a lack of objectivity. The historian will undoubtedly find in this balance of accusations the very evidence of that objectivity we were accused of lacking, but also of the fact that very many Member Nations have not yet accepted the limits put on their national ambitions by the very existence of the United Nations and by the membership of that Organization.

Now, under basically identical although superficially more dramatic circumstances, we have again reached a point where a local armed conflict is threatening in forms which are only too likely to lead to a widening of the conflict into the international arena.[44]

Hammarskjold concluded by suggesting five points as a basis for future action: an investigation of Lumumba's assassination, authorization for the UN force to protect the civilian population against attacks from armed units, efforts by the UN to forestall clashes between armed units, reactivation of efforts to reorganize the ANC and to remove it from the political conflict, and finally the elimination of foreign, and especially Belgian, political and military personnel. To do all this, he pointed out, he would need both more men and more money.

In the atmosphere of horror, disillusionment, and violence that followed Lumumba's death, the only practical hope for the future in the Congo seemed to lie in a Security Council resolution giving ONUC a stronger mandate such as Hammarskjold had suggested. As long ago as October 8, 1960, he had addressed himself to the government of Belgium and to Tshombe, pointing out the necessity of eliminating the Belgian political and military element in the Congo. "I do not remember," he told the Council, "that I got any active support from any Member country or from any organ of the UN for that stand at that time. I was attacked violently by Belgium and by various leaders in the Congo. I still hold the same view, for which I have been trying to get respect all through these months, alas without effect. It is still, in my opinion, as essential a need as it was in the early autumn. May I now hope that it may gain the moral support of the Council?"[45]

On February 17, Ceylon, Liberia, and the U.A.R. submitted a draft resolution[46] that urged the UN to take all measures to prevent the occurrence of civil war by the use of force, if necessary; it also urged that measures be taken for the immediate withdrawal and evacuation from the Congo of all Belgian and other foreign military and paramilitary personnel and political advisers not under the UN command, along with mercenaries; it called upon all states to take immediate measures to prevent the departure of such personnel for the Congo; finally, it demanded an immediate and impartial investigation into the death of Lumumba and his companions. This resolution, while proposing a considerable extension of the use of force by the UN, made no mention, such as had been customary up to that time, either of the past actions of the Secretary-General or of his future role in the implementation of the resolution, apparently because its sponsors felt that only by this omission could the Soviet Union be persuaded to abstain in the vote. In its second part, the resolution urged the convening of the Congolese Parliament under the necessary protective measures and further urged that the Congolese Army be reorganized and brought under discipline and control. In this part of the resolution also there was no reference to the Secretary-General.

On the morning of February 20, Hammarskjold, "with revolt and shock," informed the Council of the murder of six political supporters of Lumumba in Bakwanga.[47] This new atrocity seems to have been instrumental in causing Stevenson to announce unconditional U.S. support for the Afro-Asian resolution,[48] stating only a reservation concerning the omission to any reference to the Secretary-General and his assumption that the resolution would in any event have to be carried out by the Secretary-General. The resolution was adopted by the Council[49] in the small hours of February 21 by nine votes to none, with France and the U.S.S.R. abstaining.

Hammarskjold greeted this decision with some reserve.[50] It gave, he said, "a stronger and more clear framework for UN action although, as so often before, not providing a wider legal basis or means for implementation,"[51] and he appealed for the provision of additional troops to help carry out the resolution. He knew all too well that once again the Council had passed the buck to him, this time without even the courtesy of mentioning the Secretary-General's role at all. It was perhaps the lowest point of his entire career. To Dayal he curtly described the Security Council resolution as "noble aims and no new means or legal rights,"[52] and after a few meetings with the Congo Advisory Committee he was even more disgusted. None of the members were prepared to commit themselves on controversial points, although, as in the past, they obviously reserved their full right to criticize. In a letter to Fawzi,[53] which he called "a few lines about recent developments which have shed a cruel light on the standards of integrity and courage in present international life,"[54] his bitterness overflowed: "It is not only," he wrote,

> a question of distorting facts as soon as you believe that they may be forgotten, but also a question of picking up old correct facts to which

previously there has been no reaction, and fitting them into a totally new picture so as to make them take a totally new and utterly unjustified significance. That of course is combined with intimidation based on the experience that few countries and few persons are guided by so strong inner criteria that they will not give in to pressure, continued for a sufficient time and concentrated on their feeling of safety and self-respect. . . .

I am of course rather hardened, especially by beatings which I took from France and Israel and, to a lesser extent, from the British over one year or more when I threw all our resources in back of the resistance against attempts to turn the clock backward, around and after Suez. Also, it is not the beatings which matter now. I feel much more strongly the absence of support from quarters who, of course, know the full story.

. . . Naturally I understand why it was considered wise not to mention the Secretary-General in the U.A.R. sponsored resolution—although I think that it was a great tactical mistake—and, naturally, I understand that Loutfi (and the other sponsors) found it difficult to say anything when Zorin in the debate interpreted this omission as an expression of no confidence. But, it must be sad to have to bow in this way, with fresh memory of your own experiences. For me, your doing so is still something I have to get over.

The world goes on, and the man about whom I had the privilege to talk with President Nasser at the luncheon out on Long Island is dead. I remember well the President's frank evaluation which was so realistic. Sorry I did not get a chance to compare notes with him again, and hear what, if anything, has changed his evaluation.

Yes, the world goes on, and we have to try to mend fences and to stop gaps and to forget in order to permit things to move forward. I am certain that you are aware that only an ultimate and hard tested sense of duty not to desert the ship in a storm keeps me prisoner here. But even a prisoner in that position should have access to sporadic radio communication, and that is really the reason for this message.[55] *

Certainly Hammarskjold was more disillusioned than ever before with the failure of the majority of the member states to stand up to great-power pressures. To Karl Ragnar Gierow, his co-translator of *Antiphon*, he cabled, "Lack of resistance to Khrushchev by too many may give me new chances to help you."[57] To Östen Undén, the Foreign Minister of Sweden, he expressed his regret that he seemed to have become a liability to his native country.[58]** After a review of the legal basis for his conduct of the Congo operation, he wrote:

---

* Hammarskjold seems to have felt that he had been unfair to Fawzi in this bitter letter, for a week later he wrote him a short note saying that the previous letter was only "permissible on the basis of solid personal friendship."[56]
** Undén at once replied that if Swedish-Russian relations were strained, "this is the result of the position which we ourselves have chosen to take."[59]

It may be said that in the Congo case I have always had to choose between the risk that the Organization would break down and die out of inertia and inability, and the risk that it might break up and die because I overstretched its possibilities in relation to what the cold war situation permitted. . . . Naturally, I am guided solely—and I really mean solely—by what is in the best interest of the UN, and the world community through the UN. But the judgment on where this criterion leads must primarily be mine. Of course, the Soviet line can claim only a weak minority in the General Assembly, but how many abstentions may they squeeze out and how should these abstentions be evaluated? In the case of a quasi "vote of confidence," I personally regard abstentions as negative votes. And with the special weight I have to give to the votes of the Afro-Asians, I can see the possibility of an outcome in the General Assembly which, under the very terms I explained in the Security Council, should in principle lead me to resign. . . . Even in this situation, I would be open to severe criticism for desertion with ensuing consequences, a criticism which it would not surprise me to see coming from the very countries abstaining, as well as, of course, from those casting a positive vote. In the reverse, with such a show of the weakening of the steadfastness of the Afro-Asian support, I could, should I stay on, be accused—however unjustly—of acting in a provocative way to protect ultimately Western interests. This, obviously, would cut down my usefulness to zero and certainly would not help the Organization. . . . Here I have on the one side the howling from the East and on the other side the Western attitude regarding my staying on as the absolutely obvious thing, while the Afro-Asians express their strong hopes that I stay, when they talk in private, prepared, no doubt, in many cases later not to give expression to that attitude in a vote.[60]

By the end of the month, Hammarskjold's natural resilience and humor had begun to reassert themselves. "As I said yesterday to one of the Soviet people," he told Dayal, " 'Kasavubu has again broken with Dayal and your Government has broken with me; are there any relations left but those between Dayal and me?' . . . We all have to work within imperfect means and human frailties, but the outcome is in the long run determined more by steadfast adherence to principles and endurance than by the current shifts in the situation."[61]

The new authority that the February 21 resolution provided for the use of force in the Congo was not accompanied by any substantial clarification of the circumstances in which force might be used, while withdrawals and threats of withdrawal from the Congo force had greatly weakened its military strength. To make matters worse, despite a long letter of explanation from Hammarskjold,[62] the Kasavubu régime, encouraged by its European advisers, reacted violently to the new Security Council resolution, which it regarded as an infringement of its sovereignty. "Our country is threatened with being placed under

United Nations trusteeship," Kasavubu said in a radio broadcast on February 27; ". . . the United Nations is betraying us."[63] In Leopoldville a rumor was put about that ONUC would use force to disarm the ANC and reconvene Parliament. Dayal, with whom the régime had severed all contact, was powerless to counteract such misunderstandings. Tshombe chimed in by announcing that the UN had declared war on Katanga and on the rest of the Congo, and throughout the country UN personnel were increasingly harassed and insulted.[64] Fighting that broke out on March 3 between UN Sudanese troops and the ANC in Banana and Kitona soon spread to the vital port of Matadi, where the Sudanese, heavily outnumbered, had to evacuate the port and were disarmed by the ANC. ONUC thus not only lost control of a vital point in its supply line, but sustained a severe blow to the morale of the UN force.

Hammarskjold had no doubt that much of the misunderstanding in Leopoldville had been fostered by certain Western embassies, which had stepped up their campaign against Dayal when it was announced that Indian troops for ONUC would be arriving in March. Typical of the wild rumors being circulated was a Reuters report[65] that Dayal was smuggling Gizenga out of the Congo, and a story, traced to a British embassy employee, that India was planning to send two million of its surplus population to the Congo. Hammarskjold requested Adlai Stevenson to have the U.S. embassy in Leopoldville instructed to do everything possible to counteract misunderstandings, rumors, and anti-Indian propaganda.

The key to the withdrawal of foreign military and civilian advisers from the Congo, and especially from Katanga, still rested with the government in Brussels, whose attitude toward the UN Congo operation remained hostile, although there was hope that elections scheduled for March 26 might produce a change. Meanwhile the Belgian government still maintained that it did not control Belgian political and military advisers in Katanga or elsewhere. Another prerequisite for future action was to replace the contingents that had been withdrawn from the UN force, and the situation began to improve in early March when an additional unit of six hundred Tunisians and a brigade of five thousand Indian troops were made available for service in the Congo. Nehru's decision, taken in the face of considerable opposition in Delhi, made it possible to envisage once again a reasonably effective deployment of the UN force. For the time being, however, Hammarskjold's main weapon was still the pen, and he poured out an endless series of letters to governments, urging, cajoling, and demanding that they, each in its own way, contribute to making a reality of the new directive of the Security Council.

In the Congo itself the limits of the Secretary-General's possibilities for useful action were even narrower. Among other tasks, the Council had charged ONUC with preventing civil war, which now threatened in several parts of the Congo, and protecting the lives of political prisoners all over the country. With their very limited authority and practical means, Hammarskjold's and Dayal's attempts to carry out these tasks were still for the most part confined to firm and persistent representations to Kasavubu, Tshombe, Gizenga, and Kalonji, all of whom were being encouraged by their various external supporters to defy ONUC. The news that Alphonse Songolo and fourteen other political opponents of Lumumba had been executed in Stanleyville on or about February 21 was a gruesome reaffirmation of ONUC's relative impotence in protecting political prisoners.

In a new twist of the Congo kaleidoscope, Kasavubu, Tshombe, and Kalonji, representing Leopoldville, Katanga, and South Kasai respectively, announced on February 28 that they had joined together in a military pact and would meet in early March in Tananarive, Madagascar, to discuss the setting up of a loose confederation of separate states in place of a centralized government. Hammarskjold's attempt to make this conference representative of all the Congolese factions fell through when Gizenga, having failed to get the conference moved to a more neutral African state, refused to attend and became hostile to the whole idea. The conference was a considerable triumph for Tshombe and for Belgian policy, and served to accentuate the split between Leopoldville and Stanleyville as well as the disagreement on Congo policy between various groups of countries in the UN itself.

In New York, once the debates were over, a dispute arose as to the precise meaning of the Security Council's February 21 resolution and what degree of real action it authorized the UN force in the Congo to take. ONUC's authority to take action had been considerably increased by giving it the right to use force for the prevention of civil war, a condition now latent throughout almost the entire territory of the Congo. On the other hand, the UN still had no authority to impose a political solution by force or, specifically, to bring Katanga back into the Congo by any means other than persuasion and negotiation. Although the resolution had provided increased authority to deal with foreign personnel, both civilian and military, it still did not give ONUC the right to remove these personnel by force unless it could be shown that their removal was essential to the prevention of civil war. Thus the basic split in the UN over what the Organization could and could not do in the Congo remained as wide as ever and, as before, produced a new round of accusations, recriminations, and disagreements. These differences were especially evident in the Congo Advisory Committee, on whose counsel and support Hammarskjold had hoped to rely, and after many meetings its members seemed more inclined than ever to leave all difficult decisions to the Secretary-General. The only matter upon which there was fairly general agreement was the objective of reuniting the country under a parliamentary system, and Hammarskjold decided to concentrate his immediate efforts on this relatively noncontroversial aim.

Obviously any improvement in the Congo would depend on some measure of cooperation from the Kasavubu régime, and on March 15 Hammarskjold put before the Congo Advisory Committee the draft of a letter to the President[66] in which he suggested a new approach to two of the demands of the Security Council, the withdrawal from the Congo of Belgian and other foreign political advisers (paragraph A-2 of the Security Council resolution) and the reorganization of the ANC. He proposed[67] that three African members of the UN Secretariat— Robert Gardiner of Ghana, Francis Nwokedi of Nigeria, and Mahmoud Khiary of Tunisia—discuss with the Congolese government the best means of giving effect to the Security Council's decisions, and he sent Taieb Sahbani of Tunisia to Brussels to pursue the same questions with the Belgian Government.[68] This new approach soon began to produce results.

THE FIFTEENTH SESSION of the General Assembly, which had resumed on March 7, lasted until April 21. Although the General Assembly's six weeks of discussion did little either to clarify or to extend the mandate of the Congo operation, by the time it adjourned the degree of support shown for Hammarskjold's efforts, as well as a more promising atmosphere in the Congo itself, gave reason to hope that smoother waters might be ahead.

The Soviet attack continued unabated. On March 21, Gromyko denounced Hammarskjold again to the Assembly,[69] and three days later it was announced that the Soviet government would not pay any financial contribution toward the Congo operation.[70] A similar statement from France soon followed.[71] Hammarskjold addressed the Assembly briefly on March 29,[72] and on April 5[73] he delivered an extensive survey of the military and political situation in the Congo, in which he also replied at some length to the charge that he was responsible for the murder of Lumumba and his comrades. "One can admire," he told the Assembly, "the ingenious way in which, with a skillful combination of unrelated facts, a careful choice of data, and appropriate changes of emphasis and lighting, for example the delegate of Romania has built up history which to the uninformed may have a semblance of veracity. But such admiration cannot hide the fact that the skill shown has no application to the way in which United Nations organs must deal with a serious international problem however effective they may have proven for political purposes in this or that national setting."[74] As to the demand for his resignation: "I do not consider that I am entitled to present the General Assembly with a *fait accompli* by resigning because I have been requested to do so by a big Power and its likeminded supporters. On the other hand, I regard the will of the General Assembly in this respect as my law, and the General Assembly may thus consider itself as seized with a standing offer of resignation, were the Assembly to find it to be in the best interest of the Organization that I leave."[75]

The opportunity for a vote of confidence in the Secretary-General arose fortuitously early in April, when the Afro-Asian group submitted two draft resolutions,[76] one giving Belgium twenty-one days to withdraw its civilian and military personnel from the Congo and the other calling for the release of political prisoners, the reconvening of Parliament, and a new conciliation commission. The first of these resolutions made no mention of the Secretary-General, and in the debate on the second the representative of Guinea proposed[77] that the words "by the Secretary-General" be replaced by the words "by all interested authorities."[78] This effort publicly to record dissatisfaction with Hammarskjold's conduct of the Congo operation got surprisingly little support; eighty-three members voted to retain "by the Secretary-General," with only the Soviet bloc, Guinea, and Cuba voting against them.[79] The Assembly also voted down the proposal to put a time limit on the withdrawal of foreign personnel and to impose sanctions against Belgium.[80]

The problem of getting financial support for the Congo operation was becoming increasingly serious. The refusal of the U.S.S.R. and France to contribute had already cast doubt on what otherwise might have been an ordinary budgetary question. Although Hammarskjold pointed out that the total annual cost of the Congo operation was less than half the world's daily bill for armaments,[81] the General Assembly failed at first to authorize the necessary appropriations.[82] Mongi Slim forced the matter to be put to the vote again[83] in the early hours of April 22, when the Assembly, as its last act of business, authorized the Congo appropriation—$100 million for the period from January 1 to October 31, 1961.[84]

THE DEBATES in the General Assembly had shown that in practice most governments still wished to work with Hammarskjold. His effort to work through Kasavubu toward some kind of reconciliation of the various factions in the Congo bore fruit when, on April 17, after nearly a month of intensive negotiations, Nwokedi, Gardiner, and Khiary initialed an agreement with Kasavubu on the general principles for cooperation between him and the UN in the Congo.[85] Under this agreement Kasavubu accepted the Security Council's resolution of February 21 and endorsed its aim of the elimination of all deleterious foreign influence in the Congo.

The efforts of Sahbani, Hammarskjold's representative in Brussels, also began to show results, and the formation in late April of a new Belgian coalition government, headed by Théo Lefèvre, with Paul-Henri Spaak as Minister for Foreign Affairs, Deputy Prime Minister, and Minister for African Affairs, gave hope that Belgium might be willing to cooperate in securing the withdrawal of Belgian political advisers and military personnel from Katanga. Gardiner's and Nwokedi's contacts with Tshombe, however, gave less cause for optimism, and it was obvious that very firm action would be required in the months ahead if the Katanga problem was not to be allowed once again to poison the possibilities of reconciliation and political reconstruction in the Congo.

Despite the general improvement in the atmosphere, Rajeshwar Dayal's position as the Secretary-General's Special Representative in the Congo had become increasingly untenable. Hammarskjold had repeatedly refused to consider demands for his removal[86] on the grounds that the policies pursued by Dayal, in whom he had full confidence, had faithfully and scrupulously reflected the mandate established by the major organs of the UN for the operation in the Congo and that, in these circumstances, criticisms of Dayal must be considered as directed against himself. Hostility to Dayal had steadily mounted, and it was reported that elements of the ANC had even contemplated an armed assault on his residence on the banks of the Congo River. The British and American ambassadors, Ian Scott and Clare Timberlake, had never concealed their misgivings about Dayal, and their attitude was reflected in the reports of Western journalists as well as in the behavior of the Leopoldville régime. They had been joined in this campaign, much to the embarrassment of his colleagues, by Jaja Wachuku, the Nigerian chairman of the UN Conciliation Commission.

Hammarskjold was thus compelled to weigh his personal loyalty to a respected senior member of his staff against the demands of the Congo operation itself. He was never more unswervingly loyal to his representatives in the field than when they were faced with difficulties or unjustified criticism, and as a matter of principle he would not bow to the preferences or prejudices of any government concerning

Secretariat appointments. Dayal was an old and trusted friend who had been released only with the greatest reluctance by the Indian government from his vital position as Indian High Commissioner in Pakistan, and in him Hammarskjold had found the kind of colleague he was always looking for, thoughtful, courageous, loyal to the UN, and fearless in attempting to carry out the most difficult policies even in the most impossible conditions. In the almost continuous nightmare of the past five months in the Congo, Dayal had never complained and had continued to act and to report, even in the most alarming circumstances, with judgment, perception, and humor.

The accusations against Dayal were grossly exaggerated and fanciful. It was said that he was arrogant and high-handed and did not sympathize sufficiently with the Congolese. He was alleged to be pro-Lumumbist, anti-Western, a Communist supporter even, and, by his obstinacy and aloofness, to have alienated Kasavubu and Mobutu. A series of fantastic stories had been added to these basic criticisms, with the connivance, as Hammarskjold well knew, of a number of people who ought to have known better. Hammarskjold shared the unanimous view of Dayal's Secretariat colleagues that he was an immensely able, high-minded, and dedicated man of rare integrity and courage. Dayal's plight was largely the result of his having served loyally and unswervingly the Secretary-General's directives and policies, and Hammarskjold was determined to support him to the ultimate possible limit. Another consideration was that Dayal's removal under pressure might well create serious difficulties for Nehru, whose decision to provide Indian troops for ONUC had finally been carried through only by his own personal insistence with the Parliament.

Hammarskjold decided to play for time. He recalled Dayal to New York for consultations in early March, replacing him temporarily by Mekki Abbas, the Sudanese Executive Secretary of the UN Economic Commission for Africa. He explained frankly to Adlai Stevenson the dilemma, which was attributable in considerable part to American attitudes and to the U.S. press. He pointed out that any action in relation to Dayal that might be construed as bowing to American pressure would be as bad for him and for the UN as it would be for the United States itself. He again urged Stevenson to take measures to curb the pressures and accusations against Dayal, which he believed to be entirely unjustified and unfair.

Hammarskjold was determined that Dayal should go back to the Congo at least for a short time, but his repeated approaches to Kasavubu on this score were met by blank refusals and by threats of violence and disorder if Dayal returned. In mid-May, he sent Mekki Abbas to Coquilhatville, where Kasavubu and his colleagues were attending yet another abortive constitutional conference, to press again for the return of Dayal, but the Congolese reaction was even more violent than before, and Kasavubu refused to take responsibility for Dayal's safety if he should return. This latest threat finally convinced Hammarskjold that Dayal's return would not only put him personally in danger but would also jeopardize the more cooperative attitude Kasavubu had recently begun to display toward ONUC. On May 20 he gave Nehru a detailed account of the sorry affair and expressed his feelings of revulsion at the decision he had had to take. It was another of those occasions in which "I have had to take the lesser of two risks, when even the one taken, I fully realize, is most serious."[87]

A lesser man than Dayal would have made this painful affair even worse, but by the dignity, generosity, and restraint of his attitude and behavior he turned his rejection into a sort of moral triumph. Nehru, too, quickly showed his understanding. "We will be happy," he wrote, "to have him back with us."[88] In announcing Dayal's[89] withdrawal, Hammarskjold went into no details except to pay tribute to his ability, loyalty, and unfailing integrity. He also took the occasion to announce that the Congo operation would no longer be headed by a Special Representative, and that administrative arrangements for its future conduct would be announced later.

THE CONGO OPERATION brought to a head Hammarskjold's perennial problem of finding enough first-rate senior officials to handle sensitive missions. Anatoly Dobrynin, the invaluable Soviet Under-Secretary whom he had liked and trusted, had left in the spring of 1960, and Hammarskjold failed to establish a comparable relationship with his successor, Georgy P. Arkadiev. His experiments in taking on senior officials from outside the Secretariat were on the whole disappointing. It was not only that the UN pay scale was unlikely to attract the caliber of public servant which he was looking for. A far graver problem was to find people who could quickly grasp and live up to the standard of international conduct that Hammarskjold required. A brilliant man who had risen to high position in his own country's service often found—and still finds—that it is difficult, if not impossible, to accept and to live with the restrictions, frustrations, and anonymity of a civil service working for an embryonic international organization, more especially when the most important tasks require a degree of objectivity and aloofness that is seldom popular with any of the parties to a conflict. Even if suitably qualified men from nonaligned countries could be found, there was no certainty that Hammarskjold could get them posted to the Secretariat. In November 1960 he approached Adnan Pachachi, the permanent representative of Iraq to the UN, with the suggestion that he become the Under-Secretary for Special Political Affairs in charge of the New York end of the Congo operation. Pachachi had impressed him both by his ability and by his fair-mindedness. Although Pachachi was willing and his Foreign Minister, Hashim Jawad, would have liked to help, the Iraqi government finally turned down Hammarskjold's request because the Congo situation was so controversial.

For difficult political assignments Hammarskjold had been compelled more and more to fall back upon the few well-tried career officials whom he knew and trusted—Bunche, Cordier, Labouisse, Pelt, and later Spinelli, Wieschhoff, and a few others—and as the political responsibilities of the Secretariat increased, these officials became more and more overburdened.

By the fall of 1960 another and more serious difficulty became apparent. Hammarskjold was incapable of giving his confidence, or of delegating authority or responsibility, to people he did not trust. His experience in the Swedish civil service had imbued him with an ideal of politically impartial and dedicated public service that made considerations of nationality or political representation seem trivial and unworthy as compared with ability and integrity. He had complete confidence, for instance, in Bunche, Cordier, Labouisse, and Wieschhoff —all Americans—of whom the first three had worked with him closely throughout his time as Secretary-General, and he was convinced that their loyalty to the UN would never allow them to succumb to influence or pressure from their own or any other government. In fact, the U.S. State Department had on occasion complained that they tended to show more resistance toward suggestions coming from the United States than from any other source. Hammarskjold was reluctant to believe that his own confidence in them was not shared by others, although his American colleagues themselves warned him of the danger. In September 1960, he was surprised when Labouisse refused to stay on as a fourth American member of his directorate on Congo affairs on the grounds that he had too many senior American assistants already. The events of the winter of 1960–1 at last convinced him that he must diversify the geographical pattern of his immediate senior staff. The staff in the Congo was now broadly representative. The commander was an Irishman, General McKeown; the Chief of Staff an Ethiopian, General Iyassou; while Gardiner (Ghana), Nwokedi (Nigeria), and Khiary (Tunisia) operated as a kind of African triumvirate. The officer in charge was Sture Linnér, the Swede who had formerly been in charge of civilian operations in the Congo.

The problem was in New York, and Hammarskjold decided that Cordier, his Executive Assistant of nearly eight years who had reached retiring age, would have to be moved. This decision was announced on June 26[90] in an exchange of letters in which Hammarskjold referred to Cordier's "wish to resign as Executive Assistant to the Secretary-General in order to assist in the adjustment of posts at the Under-Secretary level."[91] Cordier would, for the time being at any rate, remain the official responsible for General Assembly affairs in the Secretary-General's office as a transitional step toward leaving the Organization altogether, a step that Hammarskjold hoped would not take place before he himself left the UN. To Cordier, who knew better than anyone else the circumstances in which this decision had had to be taken, this was nonetheless a bitter blow. His place as Chef de Cabinet, the new title for the Executive Assistant, was taken by C. V. Narasimhan, an Indian who had served as Executive Secretary of the UN Economic Commission for Asia and the Far East (ECAFE) until a year before, when he had become Under-Secretary Without Portfolio in succession to Sir Humphrey Trevelyan.* Bunche also submitted his resignation in order to make it easier to change the senior staff, but Hammarskjold was not prepared to give up another experienced and dedicated colleague** and refused to accept it.

The decision to replace Cordier was a particularly painful one. The painter Bo Beskow, who was in New York to discuss the large mural he was to paint for the new UN Library, observed Hammarskjold's efforts, during the weekend after it had been taken, to get his mind onto other things. He was reading Julien Gracq's *Un Balcon en Forêt* and trying to translate a work by Martin Buber,*** and Beskow remembers him sitting with his books on the raft**** in the middle of the little lake at Brewster, while Bill Ranallo and another guard water-skied around him. Hammarskjold was profoundly disturbed by the political pressures that were imposing themselves more and more both on his loyalties and on his concept of an independent international civil service.

---

* Cordier remained in his old office next to the Secretary-General's until some months after Hammarskjold died. He then left the UN to become Dean of the School of International Affairs at Columbia. He was President of the university from 1968 to 1970.

** Hammarskjold's regard for Bunche was reciprocated. Years later Bunche wrote: "Dag Hammarskjold was the most remarkable man I have even seen or worked with. . . . I learned more from him than from any other man."[92]

*** The first part of *Die Legende des Baalshem*.

**** The maintenance personnel at UN Headquarters had made this raft as a present for Hammarskjold, who had responded by giving a party for them and their wives at Brewster one summer Saturday afternoon.

1960–1961:
THE INTERNATIONAL
CIVIL SERVICE

HAMMARSKJOLD HAD NEVER HAD any illusions about the difficulty of making the concept of an objective and independent international civil service work in a world of independent sovereign states, but the pressures of the Congo crisis had raised problems concerning the authority of the Secretary-General and the operation of the Secretariat that even he had not anticipated. The necessity of coping with the emergencies of the Congo situation in the absence of clear directives from the intergovernmental organs of the United Nations had raised a central and highly controversial issue of principle over the independence and authority of the Secretary-General. He was convinced that the outcome of the controversy would have a vital bearing on the future effectiveness of the United Nations as an instrument for maintaining international peace and security, and he was determined not to make any compromises that would prejudice the possibilities of future Secretaries-General playing a useful role.

Although the Secretary-General as chief administrative officer of the United Nations had long since taken second place to the Secretary-General as executive peace-keeper and go-between, the loyalty and respect of the Secretariat for Hammarskjold had become steadily stronger as the years went on. Inevitably there were many staff members who felt neglected or insufficiently appreciated, and under the pressures of political crises his regular contacts with the various departments became increasingly spasmodic, but the staff as a whole was immensely proud of him and appreciated the effect of his activities in putting the UN, and the Secretariat itself, on the map. "The staff takes pride," the chairman of the Staff Committee said in the staff meeting held to mark the beginning of Hammarskjold's second term of office in 1958,[1] "in the many achievements you have accomplished which have added greatly to the stature of your office and of the Organization as a whole. Through your single-minded devotion to the cause of the UN and through your matchless skill derived from an inner strength, you have put the principles and purposes of the Charter into the forefront of the world scene. You have created a new style in contemporary diplomacy which you carry out with imagination and with verve. You have provided a quiet centre and a calm course in the turbulent and troubled times in which we live."[2] Hammarskjold responded with a heartfelt statement of his own. "We are no Vatican, we are no republic, we are not outside the world—we are very much in the world. But, even within the world, there can be this kind of sense of belonging, this deeper sense of unity. I hope that we are on our road to that sense. I feel that we have moved in that direction and, to the extent that it depends upon me, I can give you one assurance: whatever I can do for that purpose, I will do."[3]

In his earlier years as Secretary-General, Hammarskjold had had moments of considerable optimism about the development of the international civil service. "I have an impression," he told a press conference in December 1954, "that the Secretariat, in relation to the other main organs, is coming more into what I consider it to be its rightful position. On the one side, it is necessarily the servicing machinery, a servant, as I have always said. . . . A servant should at the right moment tell his master a little bit about what he thinks about the right development."[4]

The Suez crisis had accelerated the development of the Secretariat as an operational and executive instrument. The Congo crisis and the ensuing confrontation with the U.S.S.R., however, brought the principle of an independent international secretariat into the center of the controversy over the nature of the UN itself; and by October 1960, Hammarskjold found himself once again engaged, this time publicly and with the other superpower, in the struggle for the independence of the Secretariat that had been his first challenge when he arrived in New York in 1953. "The Charter talks about 'efficiency, competence, and integrity' as the decisive elements,"[5] he told the Fifth Committee of the General Assembly in one of many responses to Soviet criticism. ". . . To me, integrity means that the officials should have only *one* loyalty in the performance of their duties, and that is the one to the UN. . . . To accuse people who serve this Organization in the true spirit of the Charter, with an integrity beyond praise and a loyalty which does not suffer any reservation, to accuse such people of being the spokesmen of one power bloc or another because of their passports, is a slight to men and women who deserve much better."[6]

During the General Assembly in the fall of 1958, the Advisory Committee on Administrative and Budgetary Questions had expressed some misgivings about the working of the Secretariat. The feeling persisted that Hammarskjold had gone too far in diminishing the authority of the Administrative and Financial Services and the Bureau of Personnel and had taken on his own shoulders a burden that was too heavy and too time-consuming. He disagreed. "Almost five years have passed since the adoption of the new arrangements," he told the Fifth Committee in October 1958. "They have therefore by now been tried and tested to the full and under conditions which for long periods have been unusually exacting. My personal experience does not lead me to share the misgivings of the Advisory Committee. Indeed, I should like to register the view that the present arrangements have proved entirely sound, and in practice have worked well. I do not myself see the slightest justification for proposing any changes."[7]

In December 1959 the Assembly called for another overall review of the organization of the Secretariat by a committee of six outside experts to be appointed by the Secretary-General.[8] On the basis of the experts' report, Hammarskjold was to make provisional recommendations to the 1960 General Assembly and to put forward final recommendations to the 1961 Assembly. He found it impossible to appoint a six-member committee with fair geographical representation and therefore appointed eight members:[9] G. Georges-Picot of France was chairman, and there were experts from Colombia, Ghana, India, the U.A.R., the U.S., Great Britain, and the Soviet Union. In its first report[10] the Committee of Eight made no specific recommendations, and the General Assembly, with some of its members expressing disappointment over the lack of progress, served notice that except in emergencies no additions to the UN budget or to the Secretariat should be made until the experts' final report was received.

On June 24, 1960, only a week before the Congo crisis began, Hammarskjold gave the Committee of Eight an account of his problems that anticipated accurately some of the difficulties soon to beset him and the Secretariat. The unexpectedly rapid change in the nature and membership of the UN had greatly enlarged the political, economic, and social challenges to which the Organization had to respond. The member governments had not yet fully appreciated the magnitude of this change, which had placed new and heavy burdens on the Secretariat, and seemed to expect the Secretariat, in Hammarskjold's words, to go on a lion hunt without being willing even to provide it with a bird gun. "In looking at it as a political proposition," he told the experts, "the work of the Secretariat, of the Organization as an administrative body, one can and one must realistically face the possibility that we will fail in Africa, fail here and fail there because we are not, so to say, good enough."[11] It would be frustrating and unworthy if the cause of such a failure were to be the lack of a few million dollars, or because administrative savings had been deemed more important than political needs.

Hammarskjold had followed a conservative budget policy, first severely cutting the budget and staff and then forcing the Secretariat to absorb new tasks without increasing its size, but on both the political and the economic sides he had reached the limit in this process. Nor was it wise to cut essential activities for reasons of economy. "If," he told the Committee of Eight, "we, because of our wish to maintain the UNEF, were to cut down what has to be done in, for example, Africa, I think we have a good chance to get one or two other additional UNEF's started in that area before very long, and the economy seems to me, in such circumstances, to be doubtful. The outstanding tendency in recent policy-making through the UN and in the UN has been, as much as possible, to switch to what may be called preventive action from corrective action. Corrective action, as you know, is infinitely more costly than preventive action."[12]

By October 1960, the Congo crisis had led Hammarskjold much further in his thinking about the nature and importance of the independence of the Secretariat. In reply to a speech by the Soviet representative in the Fifth Committee of the Assembly, he said:

> If I am to draw my general conclusions from the observations made in the statement of yesterday, it would be, as I have already said, that technical assistance should be reduced to marginal expert work and that the Secretary-General should forget the responsibilities and needs which flow from Article 99, and serve only as chief administrator of a Secretariat technically assisting a vast conference machinery. This would mean that the United Nations organization should be reduced to the role of a framework for public multilateral negotiations and robbed of its possibilities of action in the preservation of peace in prevention of such conflict as might come before the various organs of the United Nations.
>
> The United Nations is the instrument of its member governments, and those governments decide the destiny of the Organization. They can choose the line which slowly has been emerging in response to current

needs over the last few years, or they can choose to fall back on the pattern of the League of Nations or of the most conservative interpreters of the Charter of the present Organization. The Secretariat as a body will certainly loyally accept the role for the Organization chosen by its members, but it should be understood that every member of the Secretariat serves in accordance with his own conscience and that the best may withdraw if they were to feel that they can have no faith in the line along which the Organization is permitted to survive.[13]

The new pressures led Hammarskjold to look to a more authoritative source for additional assistance in reinforcing the Secretariat. In early October he invited three ex-presidents of the General Assembly, Mrs. V. Lakshmi Pandit of India, Lester Pearson of Canada, and Víctor A. Belaúnde of Peru, to consult with him urgently on a problem stated in the introduction to his 1960 annual report, namely that the Secretariat "does not dispose of a sufficient number of highly qualified senior officials for all the tasks that now have to be met in spite of the feeling sometimes voiced that the Organization is 'top-heavy.' "[14] It also lacked completely the kind of highly qualified military expertise required for such situations as the Congo. How delicate and controversial the Secretariat situation had become was indicated by Hammarskjold's difficulty even in constituting this group of three. Mrs. Pandit's brother, Prime Minister Nehru, was far from positive in his initial response, and referred to Khrushchev's criticisms of Hammarskjold and the Secretariat. Many Asian and African countries, he wrote, felt the inadequacy of the Secretariat and their lack of representation in it.* Hammarskjold replied that it was precisely with the dual problem of lack of highly qualified senior officials and the narrowness of regional representation at the top level that he needed help. Mrs. Pandit and her brother remained unconvinced, and Hammarskjold asked Prince Wan Waithayakon of Thailand to join the group of three instead.

This distinguished trio, which inevitably came to be known as "the three wise men," after surveying the history of the top-level Secretariat problem, came out firmly against the troika arrangement proposed by Khrushchev and supported Hammarskjold's idea of a single echelon of senior officials. It recommended[15] increasing the Under-Secretaries for Special Political Affairs** from two to five in order to constitute a group that the Secretary-General could consult on political and diplomatic questions. This larger group could also be available for special

---

* At this time one of Hammarskjold's Under-Secretaries for Special Political Affairs, his Special Representative in the Congo, and his Military Adviser were all Indian.
** The new name for the former Under-Secretaries-General Without Portfolio.

assignments and would help to redress the geographical imbalance of the existing top level of officials.

These suggestions were passed on to the Committee of Eight, and in April 1961, in commenting on the Committee's provisional findings, Hammarskjold addressed himself to the problem of how the Executive of the UN should be organized. The Secretary-General, as the only elected official, inevitably carried the ultimate personal responsibility for running the Secretariat. "This creation of a one-man office with very wide ultimate responsibilities and a position detached from all national links, dependent solely on an international staff that the man himself has recruited, has necessarily led to difficult and untried political and administrative problems."[16] He disagreed with the Committee's effort to solve the problem by the introduction of a Cabinet system, because it was based on an analogy with national government for which the basis was lacking at the UN. This was not only true during the current cold-war situation but also "so long as national interests are bound to clash and so long as an only limited number of international civil servants can be counted upon as wholly uninfluenced by national considerations."[17] He also disagreed with the Committee's idea of reducing the responsibilities of the Secretary-General and strengthening the corporate nature of the Secretariat on the grounds that the ultimate personal responsibility of the Secretary-General was based on the Charter. He denied again that too much authority was concentrated in the hands of the Secretary-General. "If publicity gives a false impression and tends to highlight the person of the Secretary-General, this I can tell you from rather bitter personal experience is very much against the efforts of the Secretary-General, and is the result of the present tendency, all over the world, to dramatize issues by personalizing them."[18]

The creation of a new level of six to eight more senior officials as deputies would be expensive and inefficient, quite apart from making life more difficult for the Secretary-General. If the proposed deputies acted as a Cabinet and disagreed on controversial issues, they would embarrass the Secretary-General, who would then have to take one side or another; and if they were merely to act as an advisory committee they would not have enough to do. Hammarskjold conceded that the Committee had "very clearly seen the extremely difficult problem created by the form in which the executive aspect of the Secretariat has been handled in the Charter,"[19] but so far they did not seem to have found a workable solution to the problem.

The Committee of Eight finally agreed to disagree on the organization of the top level of the Secretariat, three of its members favoring the establishment of three Deputy Secretaries-General, while four others favored the designation of not more than eight major areas of responsibility to be run by the eight most senior Secretariat officials.[20] The Soviet member published a separate opinion, strongly criticizing the Secretariat because the senior staff "is composed, in the overwhelming majority, of nationals of countries belonging to Western military alliances,"[21] and went on to repeat the Soviet objections to Hammarskjold and to propose a troika in place of the Secretary-Generalship.

In his formal comments in June 1961,[22] Hammarskjold put forward his own suggestions about the top-level organization of the Secretariat, since he disagreed with most of the views expressed by the members of the Committee either collectively or separately. There should, he said, be one top level, but its members would be grouped into two categories: Assistant Secretaries-General who would be "political" and Under-Secretaries who would be "administrative," although both would have the same rank. The former would serve for one term of three to five years, the latter might serve for up to two terms. Equitable geographical distribution would apply to both categories. Hammarskjold was dead by the time these ideas came before the General Assembly, and it did nothing about them.

Hammarskjold certainly felt that the Committee of Eight had not understood the basic problems involved in the leadership and direction of the independent international civil service for which he was fighting a desperate battle. The Committee members for their part seem to have shared in varying degrees the opinion expressed by their chairman, Georges-Picot, in a letter written on September 14 which Hammarskjold never received, that the Secretary-General was going "too fast and too far"[23] for the member governments of the UN. "The possibility," Hammarskjold had said in 1953, "for a Secretary-General to resist pressure is not in any way dependent on this or that kind of administrative arrangement. . . . It finally boils down to the man."[24] Eight years later this appeared to be truer than ever.

It was in the Sheldonian Theatre at Oxford, where he received an honorary degree on May 30, 1961, that Hammarskjold developed his final ideas on the concept of an independent international civil service as the keystone of an effective future international order. His speech,[25] composed with unusual care in collaboration with Oscar Schachter of the UN Legal Department, took as its text Khrushchev's remark to Walter Lippmann that "while there are neutral countries, there are no neutral men."[26] He took issue with Khrushchev's view that there could be no such thing as an impartial civil servant, a notion which if accepted would throw the world back to 1919 and necessitate a searching reappraisal of all current ideas of international cooperation. Describing the hard reality of the Secretary-General's role in controversial political situations, Hammarskjold pointed out that while the Secretary-General must carry out the decisions of the main organs of the UN, he must also live by his own sense of responsibility, especially when for various reasons no precise directive from one of the main organs was available. "Should he, for example," he asked, "have abandoned the operation in the Congo because almost any decision he made as to the composition of the Force or their role would have been contrary to the attitudes of some Members as reflected in debates, and maybe even in votes, although not in decisions? . . . the responsibilities of the Secretary-General under the Charter cannot be laid aside merely because the execution of decisions by him is likely to be politically controversial. The Secretary-General remains under the obligation to carry out the policies as adopted by the organs; the essential requirement is that he does this on the basis of his exclusively international responsibility and not in the interests of any particular State or group of States."[27]

In practice the international Secretariat would from time to time inevitably be exposed to heated political controversy and to accusations of a lack of neutrality, but it could not be accused of a lack of neutrality simply for taking a stand on a controversial issue when this was its duty and could not be avoided. "But there remains a serious intellectual and moral problem as we move within an area inside which personal judgment must come into play. Finally, we have to deal here with a question of integrity or with, if you please, a question of conscience.

"The international civil servant must keep himself under the strictest observation. He is not requested to be a neuter in the sense that he has to have no sympathies or antipathies, that there are to be no interests which are close to him in his personal capacity or that he is to have no ideas or ideals that matter for him. However, he is requested to be fully aware of those human reactions and meticulously check himself so that they are not permitted to influence his actions."[28] In the last resort it was a question of integrity, even when that integrity drove an international civil servant into positions in conflict with this or that interest. The demise of the concept of a truly international civil service, Hammarskjold concluded, might well prove "to be the Munich of international cooperation,"[29] and if this were to happen, the price to be paid might all too well be peace itself.

Although Hammarskjold's speech, delivered in his flattest tones at five o'clock on a hot summer afternoon, had a generally soporific effect on his Oxford audience, it stimulated the Soviet authorities to denounce it as "an attempt . . . to create a sort of a theoretical basis for that vicious practice which, in spite of protests by many states, was being carried out by Hammarskjold in the UN Secretariat during the last years."[30] His usurpation of power, the statement went on, had constituted a flagrant violation of the basic provisions of the Charter, and it rejected the idea that "he allegedly has pursued and is pursuing now an 'independent' political course obeying only the voice of 'conscience and honour.' . . . The so-called 'independent' course of Hammarskjold expresses the interests of the imperialist powers, whose will he obediently executes."[31]

On September 8, 1961, five days before he left for the Congo and ten days before he was killed, Hammarskjold addressed the staff for the last time. He spoke once again of the necessity of an independent Secretariat. "If the Secretariat," he said, "is regarded as truly international, and its individual members as owing no allegiance to any national government, then the Secretariat may develop as an instrument for the preservation of peace and security of increasing significance and responsibilities. If a contrary view were to be taken, the Secretariat itself would not be available to member governments as an instrument, additional to the normal diplomatic methods, for active and growing service in the common interest."[32]

SUMMER 1961:
BIZERTE

THE VISIT OF PRESIDENT HABIB BOURGUIBA of Tunisia to United Nations Headquarters on May 12 was of special significance for Hammarskjold. Bourguiba had given him unfailing support and understanding through all the trials and tribulations of the Congo situation, and his representative to the UN, Mongi Slim, had always had the courage to talk reason at critical moments and to suggest conciliatory solutions. Bourguiba's son, Habib Jr., had also been a loyal friend and colleague, first as a member of the subcommittee on Laos and, later on, at several junctures in the Congo operation. To Slim, who was returning home to become Tunisia's Foreign Minister, Hammarskjold expressed *"ma profonde gratitude pour l'appui et la collaboration inébranlables que j'ai toujours trouvés auprès de vous et de votre gouvernement"*[1] ("my deep gratitude for the unshakable support and collaboration which I have always had from you and your government"). With Slim's departure he was losing an incomparably loyal and understanding friend whom he would next see at the height of the crisis over Bizerte.

Hammarskjold was still feeling to some extent the isolation of the winter. To Per Lind he wrote that "the continued weakening of the top level staff here"[2] would prevent him from coming to Sweden in the summer, and he offered the Lind family his house in southern

Sweden if they wanted to use it. To Karl Ragnar Gierow, recalling their work together on the translation of *Antiphon* at Brewster the year before, he wrote, "the birds are back but otherwise the atmosphere is very changed."[3] This dark mood was expressed in another letter to Gierow two weeks later, in which he said that politics and diplomacy were after all just another "corvée"[4] (chore). "The big shoe-thumping fellow continues as a dark thunderhead to threaten all unrepentant non-communists with hail and thunder. . . . Some believe in umbrellas and some in propitiating sacrifices and others go for a holiday. . . . I am in this situation constantly reminded of the good old story about Jehovah's willingness to save the 'cities of the plain' if he could find ten righteous men."[5]

At the end of May, Hammarskjold went to Oxford to deliver what was to be his last major public address[6] and to receive an honorary degree. Humphrey Waldock, who had accompanied him to Peking in 1955, was in charge of the arrangements. Hammarskjold had originally suggested for his speech the awkward title "International Civil Service as a Problem of Law and Fact," which Waldock had amended with his agreement into "The International Civil Servant in Law and in Fact." Hammarskjold greatly enjoyed this interlude and the ceremonial of the Encoenia at Oxford at which his own address was the central event. The splendor and calm of the academic atmosphere in the Sheldonian Theatre and later at dinner in the great eighteenth-century Codrington Library at All Souls were a soothing change from the abrasive routine of New York. The Vice-Chancellor, in conferring the degree of Doctor of Civil Law, addressed him as *"Vir fortis et integer, pacis defensor, qui spem gentium omnium, velut alter Atlas, onus gravissimum sustines"* ("A man of strength and integrity, defender of peace, who sustains, like another Atlas, the heaviest of burdens, the hope of all peoples").

June was a relatively peaceful month and gave Hammarskjold time for a number of uncontroversial activities, including the problems of the construction and decoration of the new UN Library which after his death was to become his memorial. News from the Congo seemed to be improving. "I think that the grievous stage is past," he told a press conference on June 12 "—that is to say, with the reservation that the unexpected is always possible."[7] This qualified optimism seemed justified when on June 19 the Leopoldville and Stanleyville régimes announced their agreement that the Parliament should be reconvened, with the UN making the necessary security and travel arrangements.

In July, Hammarskjold went to Geneva for the meeting of the Economic and Social Council. He had intended to go on from Geneva to Cairo and Delhi to pay the visits he had had to cancel in January, but ominous news from Tunisia caused him instead to return to New York. "Indeed we are the pawns and not the masters of world developments,"[8] he told Mahmoud Fawzi in apologizing for once again canceling his visit to Cairo.

After the French bombing of the village of Sakiet Sidi Youssef in 1958, when Hammarskjold as well as the British and U.S. governments had acted as intermediaries, all French troops in Tunisia had been withdrawn except for those in the naval base near Bizerte and in a frontier zone in the south of the country. When, after two years, President Bourguiba again raised the question of the evacuation of the French troops, the French government indicated that the French garrison at the base in Bizerte was necessary for France's security and gave the impression that the troops might stay there indefinitely. In February 1961 a meeting between de Gaulle and Bourguiba at Rambouillet resulted in conflicting accounts as to what, if anything, had been agreed, and during the spring further approaches to de Gaulle by Bourguiba remained unanswered.

On July 6, Bourguiba, facing an increasingly tense situation at home, requested new talks concerning the total evacuation, within a reasonable time, of French troops from the Bizerte base and from the frontier zone in southern Tunisia.[9] De Gaulle replied a week later[10] that it was impossible to respond to Bourguiba's request since it came in the form of a threat, and that talks on Bizerte, much as he desired them, could not be started under pressure or blackmail. On July 18, Tunisian troops and civilians surrounded the French naval base in Bizerte and set up a full-scale blockade, while Tunisian volunteers moved south to Garet el Hamel in the disputed part of the Sahara. Shooting broke out in Bizerte during July 19, and France accused the Tunisians of opening fire. Tunisia claimed that its troops had only fired warning shots and blamed the French garrison for firing directly on the Tunisians. On the following night the French forces launched a full-scale attack and, after reinforcements had been flown in, occupied the city of Bizerte on July 21.

On July 20, Tunisia asked for an urgent meeting of the Security Council,[11] and, when the Council convened on the following day, charged France with aggression, to which the French replied that they had acted in legitimate self-defense. Worried that the Security Council might fail to reach any decision, Hammarskjold told Slim that he was considering intervening at the end of the debate to try to get the minimum action required to forestall the disaster that might easily come about if nothing was decided. Slim visited him before the Council met on the following morning to tell him that the news from Bizerte was very bad. The killings were going on with no end in sight, and some effort must be made to stop a further deterioration.* In these circumstances, Hammarskjold decided to appeal to the Council for an immediate cease-fire as a means of halting the killing pending the working out of a solution. Shortage of time did not allow him to consult the French representative, and after dictating his statement he went straight into the Council, which had delayed its proceedings until he arrived. He urgently appealed to the Council,[13] "in view of the obligations of the Secretary-General under Article 99 of the Charter,"[14] to consider without delay taking an intermediary decision requesting a cease-fire and an immediate return to the *status quo ante* by the withdrawal of forces until an agreed settlement could be reached. With the abstention of France, the Council adopted a resolution to this effect on the morning of Saturday, July 22.[15]

After the meeting, Slim asked Hammarskjold if he could send a military unit or observers to consolidate and supervise the cease-fire. Hammarskjold replied that even observers could be sent only at the joint request of Tunisia and France, and that the step would be of dubious constitutionality even in the highly unlikely event that France agreed to it. With the object of finding some way of stabilizing the cease-fire, he suggested that he himself might go to Tunisia if President Bourguiba invited him. On Saturday afternoon, after talking on the telephone with Slim, Bourguiba decided to invite the Secretary-General to come to Tunis if the Council reached no decision on the major issue of the French presence in Bizerte. The invitation would be sent, if necessary, on the following day.

The Council adjourned on Saturday afternoon without reaching any decision on the major issues involved, and Hammarskjold drove out to Brewster. He was anxious to inform the French about his plans as soon as possible but could not do so until the formal invitation from Bourguiba had been received. He had understood, however, that Bourguiba did not expect him to leave New York before Monday night, so there would be plenty of time to talk to the French permanent representative. In any case, his visit to Tunis would be welcome to the French if their wish for a cease-fire was sincere, and he intended

---

* Robert Daley, in the *New York Times* on July 23, 1961, vividly described the bloody fighting in Bizerte with the French troops "cleaning up" the Tunisians. On August 21, Slim gave the official casualty figures as 800 dead and 1,115 wounded.[12] Napalm was used and there were widespread reports of atrocities against the cilivian population. The material damage was immense, and the French forces were accused of deliberately bombing economic targets such as a large cement plant. On August 24 the Tunisian government gave a revised figure of 1,300 dead and 639 prisoners. The French losses were 21 killed and 101 wounded.

to stop in Paris on his way back if the French government wished to talk to him.

On Sunday afternoon, when Hammarskjold saw Slim again and received Bourguiba's formal invitation,[16] the news from Bizerte was worse than ever, and Slim strongly urged him to leave for Tunis that very night. Hammarskjold said this was impossible because he had to consult the French, and it was finally agreed that he would aim to leave on Monday morning. He then tried to get in touch with the French mission, but both the Ambassador, Armand Bérard, and his deputy, Pierre Millet, were away for the week-end. A meeting with Millet was finally arranged for 7 p.m., and Hammarskjold occupied the intervening time by dictating a reply to Bourguiba. He also discovered that the Monday morning plane he had planned to take was stopping over in Paris, which might in the circumstances be awkward. Since there was no other suitable flight until Monday evening and Bourguiba's invitation was couched in the most urgent terms, he decided to leave New York that very night, and when Millet arrived he informed him of this change of plan.

Hammarskjold gave Millet copies of Bourguiba's message and his own reply[17] and explained that the object of his visit was to apply the brakes (*"un coup de frein"*) to the developments on the spot. He would, of course, stop in Paris on his way back from Tunis if the French government wished him to do so. Millet, who had no instructions, raised no objection to these plans, but on leaving Hammarskjold he telephoned Foreign Minister Couve de Murville. It was 1 a.m. in Paris, and Couve merely said, *"Il n'y a pas de communication à faire à M. Hammarskjold"*[18] ("There is no message for Mr. Hammarskjold"). Millet saw no point in passing on this non-answer, since he had undertaken to contact Hammarskjold only if Couve had any message for him. Hammarskjold therefore left New York under the mistaken impression that the French government had no objection to his visit to Tunis. In this he had once again seriously misjudged the state of mind of President de Gaulle.

His admiration for de Gaulle seems to have made Hammarskjold reluctant to recognize de Gaulle's view of him as an international interloper attempting under false pretenses to gain admission to the hallowed fraternity of leaders of powerful sovereign states. Describing his first meeting with de Gaulle, he wrote of a "kind of warm simplicity which was in no way immediately visible, but could be elicited by a refusal from my side to treat either him or myself as an official personality. In everything he struck me as a very lonely man, far more used to listen to himself than to others. This left me with a great uncertainty regarding the extent to which I managed to get across to him what I wanted to say. This also in a way explains the discrepancy between the liberal and nearly Goethian philosophy of French politics which he developed and the realities of the policy of France as apparent to the world. When I pointed it out to him he did not understand me, but said that there could be no such discrepancy since—and this without any irony and quite unselfconsciously—*'La France c'est moi!'* "[19] With de Gaulle, Hammarskjold had felt a "thin link of mutual human sympathy which may come to be needed with the strains on France-UN relations which undoubtedly are in front of us."[20]

Hammarskjold's hopes of a "thin link of mutual human sympathy" as a lifeline in a crisis proved illusory with leaders like de Gaulle or Khrushchev, and de Gaulle's own feelings were made crystal clear when he visited the U.S. in April 1960, and the Secretary-General, as is customary when a Head of State comes to New York, invited him to lunch at the UN. De Gaulle replied:

> *Paris, le 26 Mars 1960.*
>
> *Monsieur le Secrétaire Général,*
>
> *J'ai bien reçu votre lettre et puis vous indiquer qu'au cours de mon prochain voyage aux Etats-Unis, mon intention n'est pas de faire visite aux Nations-Unies. D'ailleurs, cette organisation ne tiendra pas, à ma connaissance, de session lors de mon passage à New-York. Comment pourrais-je la rencontrer?*
>
> *Il me sera, par contre, Monsieur le Secrétaire Général, très agréable de vous recevoir....*

After this, it is the more surprising that Hammarskjold did not foresee the repercussions that his activity over Bizerte would inevitably have in Paris.

PIERO SPINELLI JOINED HIS FLIGHT at Zürich, and Hammarskjold briefed him during the trip to Rome, whence a Tunisian DC-4 brought them

---

*Translation:
Mr. Secretary-General,
   I have received your letter and can tell you that in the course of my coming visit to New York it is not my intention to visit the United Nations. Furthermore, this organization will not, as far as I know, be in session at the time of my visit to New York. How would I be able to meet it?
   It will, on the other hand, Mr. Secretary-General, be entirely agreeable to me to receive you. . . .

to Tunis on the afternoon of July 24. His original intention had been merely to listen, assess the situation, and return to New York, but his talk with Bourguiba not only gave him explicit and horrifying details of what had happened in Bizerte but also indicated the extent and danger of the deadlock between the Tunisians and the French. Bourguiba had flatly rejected the overtures of the French, the object of which seemed to him to be some kind of permanent French-Tunisian coexistence in Bizerte, and efforts to reach a settlement were at a standstill. Hammarskjold was obliged to reject Bourguiba's suggestion that he should ask representatives of both sides to meet with him in Tunis as being far outside his own authority or possibilities.

The talk with Bourguiba convinced Hammarskjold that he must do more in Tunis than he had originally intended and that he might even have to make a report to the Security Council right away. Spinelli doggedly counseled patience, pointing out that if he made an immediate report, the French would inevitably say—as in fact they later did—that he had made his report under the influence of the Tunisians, and by 3:30 a.m. on July 25 he had persuaded Hammarskjold to put off a decision until breakfast time. Hammarskjold, however, continued to think over the problem, and at 6:30 a.m. he awoke Spinelli to tell him that while he understood his arguments, he had decided that it was his duty under the Security Council cease-fire resolution to cable Couve de Murville at once asking him to provide information on the French attitude as to the conditions under which the Secretary-General could help to establish direct contact between the two sides. Apart from establishing this contact, he would play no role in the affair. This time Spinelli failed to dissuade him, although over breakfast he prevailed on him to tone down the original draft of his cable to Couve. Hammarskjold told the French consul, through whom the message[21] was dispatched, that he could leave Tunis in sufficient time for a reasonable stopover in Paris if the French government so wished. He also told the consul that he was considering paying a visit to Bizerte on the following day but would take into consideration the answer from Paris before making up his mind. He suggested that if the French government agreed, the French commander in Bizerte, Admiral Amman, might talk to him.

Hammarskjold's message was received in Paris at 3:30 p.m. on Tuesday, July 25, and he anxiously awaited a reply until 11 a.m. the following day. He then decided to go to Bizerte with Spinelli, Bill Ranallo, and the Tunisian Governor of Bizerte and told Spinelli to ask the French consul to inform Admiral Amman that they were on their way. Spinelli, from the evident dismay with which the French consul had received this news, foresaw trouble, but Hammarskjold was determined to go anyway. At 3:40 p.m. the party arrived at the canal outside Bizerte, where they were stopped by French paratroops. The Secretary-General's car was followed by several press vehicles, while other newsmen had cameras already mounted when he arrived, so that the paratroops could have been in no doubt as to his identity. They demanded, nonetheless, to search the car for weapons. Hammarskjold protested strongly, but the paratroopers insisted that they had their orders and could not know for sure whether he was really Hammarskjold or not. During this episode other cars were let through without a search. As was evidently intended, the incident created a good press story and ended only when a French officer arrived and said casually to the paratroops, *"C'est bien Monsieur H"*[22] ("It is indeed Mr. H.").

Hammarskjold and his party went on to the Governor's residence in Bizerte, where Spinelli telephoned to Admiral Amman. The Admiral expressed his regrets at the incident, claiming that there had been no time to warn the French paratroops of the Secretary-General's arrival, and then, evidently under instructions, excused himself from meeting Hammarskjold. Apart from these discourtesies, Hammarskjold's main impression was of the general exercise of sovereign rights on Tunisian territory by the French troops and of the overwhelming presence of French tanks and paratroops around public buildings in Bizerte.

On his return to Tunis he cabled to Cordier, "We are very far indeed from even the most modest demonstration of willingness to bow to the Security Council decision."[23] There was still no reply from Paris, and in stopping him from seeing the French base commander in Bizerte, the French authorities had frustrated a contact that "would have presented a less formal and more amiable approach"[24] to executing the Council's decision. Meanwhile the provocative deployment of French forces in Bizerte could all too easily lead to renewed violence. Hammarskjold instructed Cordier to give the French Ambassador the facts of the incident with the paratroops and to protest, "not for any inconvenience or embarrassment which was caused to the Secretary-General personally but for the disregard of the Organization."[25]

Couve de Murville's reply,[26] which finally arrived late in the evening of Wednesday, July 26, both increased Hammarskjold's indignation and revealed fully the extent of de Gaulle's anger at his part in the Bizerte affair.* It completely ignored his request for information as

---

* The attitude of de Gaulle is best described by the General himself. In his memoirs nine years later, de Gaulle wrote:
> Nor did the agitation at the UN or the attempt at intervention by its Secretary-General Dag Hammarskjold induce us to modify our actions. Hammarskjold, who was already in open disagreement with us at the time because he was inter-

well as his offer to go to Paris, and dismissed in icy terms the Security Council cease-fire resolution by stating that the cease-fire had come about solely because the French forces had secured all their objectives. Hammarskjold particularly resented Couve de Murville's remark that his message *"me paraît exposer les vues du Gouvernement tunisien"*[28] ("appears to me to set out the views of the Tunisian government"). He no longer doubted that the events of the afternoon had been a deliberate and petty insult to the United Nations and to himself. It took all Spinelli's tact and several hours of conversation to turn his mind to more agreeable matters, an effort for which Hammarskjold later warmly thanked him.* Before finally retiring at 3 a.m., he wrote a reply to Couve that he cabled to New York for Cordier's and Wieschhoff's comments. He left for New York via Rome on July 27.

Hammarskjold's reply to Couve noted *"non sans étonnement"*[29] ("with some surprise") Couve's insinuation that he was acting as spokesman for the Tunisians, and said that his sole intention had been to establish the contacts necessary to secure the cease-fire and the withdrawal of the armed forces of both sides in accordance with the Council's decision. He regretted deeply that he had failed to achieve such a result.

To the Council, on the afternoon of Friday, July 28, Hammarskjold again explained the limited purpose of his visit to Tunis.[30] He could fulfill his duties under Article 99 only if he was in a position to form a personal opinion about the relevant facts of a situation that might represent a threat to the peace, and for this reason he had accepted Bourguiba's invitation to go to Tunis. He had been able to get from Bourguiba and his collaborators a full picture of their own views and their problems, but all efforts had so far failed to establish a contact between the two parties so that a withdrawal of forces could be arranged. The French forces still occupied Bizerte, and "by personal experience I can also confirm that these troops, at the time of the visit, exercised functions for the maintenance of law and order in the

---

fering directly in the affairs of the Congo, sided personally with Bourguiba. He went to see him in Tunis, held friendly discussions with him, and on July 26, when the fighting was over, proceeded to Bizerte as though it was for him to settle the dispute on the spot. This move rebounded to his discomfiture. For, following instructions, our troops paid no attention to the comings and goings of the self-appointed mediator and Admiral Amman refused to see him. There was nothing left for President Bourguiba to do but write the whole thing off as a dead loss. In any case he would get over it eventually, just as the damaged friendship between France and Tunisia would one day be repaired.[27]

* It was to be the last evening Hammarskjold and Spinelli were to spend together, and Spinelli saw him alive for the last time when he got off the plane next day in Rome. The next time he saw Hammarskjold was in the morgue in Ndola.

city which normally belong to organs of the sovereign Government."[31] The Security Council failed, in the face of U.S. and British opposition,* to adopt any of the three draft resolutions[32] before it, and a special session of the General Assembly was accordingly summoned to meet on August 21.

During the period before the Special Session of the Assembly the situation in Tunisia remained tense. Despite all efforts by Secretary of State Dean Rusk and others, de Gaulle continued to insist on the presence of the French troops in Bizerte, and there was a widespread fear that the smallest incident might provoke a march on Tunis by the French forces. On August 9, Adlai Stevenson asked Hammarskjold if he was in a position to send observers, or even a UN force, to Tunisia. Hammarskjold replied that such an action was inconceivable without an invitation from Tunisia and a decision by the Security Council, but undertook to advise Bourguiba to do everything possible to avoid any incident that might provide the excuse for further French military adventures. He urged the United States to continue to put all its weight behind the request for the withdrawal of the French troops.

Hammarskjold was profoundly disturbed by the Bizerte episode. The Tunisian government, which had been unfailingly helpful and understanding through all the ups and downs of the Congo affair, had a very special claim on his support in its own crisis, but there were wider considerations. A small and relatively new state that had already proved itself especially loyal to the United Nations had the right to expect from the Secretary-General a public gesture in its struggle with a great power which was also a member of NATO. Such a gesture, apart from Hammarskjold's sympathy with the plight of Tunisia, might also serve to maintain the confidence of small states in the straightness of the UN Secretariat even when it might mean a conflict with the big powers. He was under no illusions, however, about his mission to Bizerte. "The moral problem was such," he wrote to Fawzi, "that I felt I might make a real contribution by taking the risk. . . . The French are pleased to say that I side with the Tunisians. . . . I side with the principles of the UN. . . . I fear that I have played my cards now."[33] To Bourguiba, on whom he urged patience and restraint, he wrote, "*Hélas, j'ai fait tout ce que j'ai pu, et ça s'est montré bien insuffisant*"[34] ("Alas, I have done all that I could, and it has proved to be far from enough").

The Bizerte affair brought Hammarskjold's already strained relations with de Gaulle to a breaking point. The episode had started with a misunderstanding and had ended in a deliberate slight followed by

---

* France boycotted the meeting.

a public rebuff. The depth of Hammarskjold's feelings were expressed in an eight-page letter to his friend Alexis Saint-Léger Léger (Saint-John Perse), whom he regarded as the embodiment of the France and of the European tradition he so deeply admired. It was a story, he wrote, *"tellement typique pour les hommes et les peuples engagés—et peut-être pour nous tous. Dans le sens légal, tous ont tort. Dans le sens moral, La France. Dans le sens de la sagesse politique, Bourguiba—et, aussi, de Gaulle"*[35] ("so typical for involved men and peoples—and perhaps for us all. In the legal sense everyone was wrong. In the moral sense, France. In the sense of political wisdom, Bourguiba—and also de Gaulle"). What had resulted was a tragedy not only for Tunisia but also for France and the West, and for the moral principles the West claimed to defend. Hammarskjold believed that de Gaulle had reckoned on British and American support in preventing any decision in the Security Council, and when instead the Council had adopted the Secretary-General's proposal—designed solely to stop the killing—for a cease-fire and withdrawal of troops, de Gaulle had blamed him for disrupting his plans. The French official and press reaction to his message to Couve and the text of the French reply had shown *"la main du maître"*[36] ("the hand of the master") and had treated him as insolent and partisan. The French Ambassador had called Hammarskjold's approach to Couve stupid, *"et bien sûr, cela a été une démarche stupide si le but des Nations Unies n'est que d'éviter la pire en ce qui concerne le jugement du Général sur 'ce machin'***"*[37] ("and certainly that was a stupid approach if the aim of the United Nations is only to avoid the worst as far as the General's judgment is concerned about 'this thing' ").

The disillusionment of the Tunisians themselves had not been confined to France but had extended to the United States, which, in its desire to maintain good relations with Paris, had turned its back on its weaker friend, Tunisia. Hammarskjold had even failed to persuade the United States to provide transport aircraft to bring home the three Tunisian battalions in the Congo that Bourguiba had asked for urgently.** He feared that among the small nations, and especially the African states, the result would be a threefold crisis of confidence—in France, in the West, and in the UN as the protector of small nations.

Many people, including Östen Undén, the Swedish Foreign Minister, to whom Hammarskjold had sent a copy of his letter to Léger, felt

---

* A reference to de Gaulle's contemptuous epithet for the UN.
** Rusk had queried the wisdom of Hammarskjold's request for these aircraft on July 23 and, when Hammarskjold had insisted, had said that "technical problems" would cause a delay of several days in making the aircraft available.

that he had allowed himself to become too emotional over the Bizerte crisis. Nor was his pessimistic evaluation of his own efforts universally shared. Six years later Bourguiba told Spinelli that Hammarskjold's visit had bolstered the morale of the Tunisian population at a critical time and had never been forgotten by them, and that it had also helped him in his later negotiations with de Gaulle. Certainly his courage in standing up to a great power and in at once going to the scene of conflict did not pass unnoticed among the majority of small nations in the UN.

France boycotted the meetings of the Special Session of the General Assembly on Bizerte, as it had boycotted the last series of meetings of the Security Council, and the session was dominated by the brilliance, moderation, and elegance of the speeches of Mongi Slim. A resolution was adopted on August 25[38] which supported Tunisia's sovereign right to call for the evacuation of forces present on its territory without its consent and urged the two governments to get together for negotiations. Among the thirty abstentions on this resolution were the United States and Britain. On October 1 the French troops began to withdraw from the town of Bizerte to the base, and the last French forces withdrew from the base on October 15, 1963. Diplomatic relations between France and Tunisia, broken off over the Bizerte crisis, were reestablished in July 1962.

APART FROM THE SPECIAL SESSION of the General Assembly on Bizerte, and the usual preoccupations with the Congo, August was a relatively quiet month in New York, and Hammarskjold was able once again to go to Brewster for weekends that started at the earliest at noon on Saturday and ended during Sunday afternoon, when he always made an appearance in his office. He even toyed with the idea of going to Sweden for a few days to see his farm, "Backåkra," near Löderup in the south of Sweden, which at last was ready to receive his books and furniture, but because of developments in Katanga he decided to remain in New York.

On August 21, Hammarskjold published the introduction to his Annual Report on the work of the Organization.[39] Most of it had been dictated without notes and virtually without a pause on a Sunday afternoon in August, and only very minor changes were made to the original draft. It was Hammarskjold's personal, and last, analysis of the state of development of the UN, and he himself regarded it as the most comprehensive and far-reaching statement of his views. In it he again compared the two conflicting basic views of the UN. The first of these envisaged the Organization as a static conference machinery for resolving conflicts of interests and ideologies, served by a Secretariat which was to be regarded not as fully internationalized, but as representing within its ranks those same interests and ideologies. The second view was of the UN as a dynamic instrument of governments through which they could seek reconciliation but through which they should also try to develop forms of executive action, undertaken on behalf of all members and aimed at forestalling or resolving conflicts in a spirit of objectivity and in implementation of the principles and purposes of the Charter. This dynamic concept of the UN could be served only by a Secretariat whose actions were guided solely by the principles of the Charter, by the decisions of the main organs of the UN, and by the interests of the Organization itself.

The static concept of the UN was related to the traditions and national policies of the past. The dynamic concept was related to the needs of the present and of the future in a world of ever closer international interdependence, where nations had at their disposal armaments of a hitherto unknown destructive strength. The first concept was firmly anchored in the time-honored philosophy of sovereign national states in armed competition; the second envisaged possibilities of intergovernmental action overriding such a philosophy and opened the road toward more developed and increasingly effective forms of constructive international cooperation. Hammarskjold argued that the United Nations Charter itself went far beyond the static concept of the UN, and that those who now wished to reduce the development of the UN to the limits of the static concept might also have to shoulder the responsibility for a return to a state of affairs which governments had already found too dangerous after the First World War.

The Charter says little about how United Nations decisions are to be actually carried out, and the fact that circumstances had required Hammarskjold on occasion to shoulder responsibility for certain limited political functions had lately given rise to controversy. This was natural, indeed unavoidable, in the light of the different concepts of the role of the Organization held by various countries. If the dynamic concept was to be adopted, however—and Hammarskjold left no doubt that he viewed any other course as inconceivable—the principle of the international and independent character of the Secretariat was of decisive significance, and there could be no compromise upon a Secretariat composed along party lines, representing the interests of groups of member states. An independent and objective Secretariat was perfectly possible, provided it contained people of integrity.

On September 8, Hammarskjold returned to this theme in addressing the staff at the annual Staff Day. After paying his colleagues the warmest tribute he had ever paid them, he concluded: "It is false pride to register and to boast to the world about the importance of one's work, but it is false humility, and finally just as destructive, not to recognize—and recognize with gratitude—that one's work has a sense. Let us avoid the second fallacy as carefully as the first, and let us work in the conviction that our work *has* a meaning beyond the narrow individual one and *has* meant something for man."[40]

The entries in *Markings* for the summer of 1961 show a mixture of moods—determination, resignation, fatigue, loneliness, and a growing faith. Perhaps the most important is the entry for Whitsunday, 1961, which combines all these elements:

I don't know who—or what—put the question. I don't know when it was put. I don't remember answering. But at one moment I answered *yes* to someone—or something.

From that moment stems the certainty that existence is meaningful and that therefore my life, in submission, has a goal.

From that moment I have known what it means "not to look back," to "take no thought for the morrow."

Led through the labyrinth of life by Ariadne's thread of the answer, I reached a time and a place where I knew that the way leads to a triumph which is a fall and to a fall which is a triumph, that the price of one's effort in life is defamation and the depths of debasement the only exaltation open to man. After that, the word courage had lost its meaning since nothing could be taken from me.

As I continued along the way I learned, step by step, word by word, that behind every saying in the Gospels stands *one* man's experience. Also behind the prayer that the cup might pass from him and his promise to drink it. Also behind each of the words from the Cross.[41]

The last entry, on August 24, is a poem of a dream landscape that ends:

The seasons have changed
And the light
And the weather
And the hour.
But it is the same land.
And I begin to know the map
And to get my bearings.

The last introduction, the last entry in *Markings*, and Hammarskjold's final talk to the staff sounded a note of tranquillity and hope that had been lacking from many of his statements during the preceding year. It is the voice of one who has passed through great storms, has had his beliefs tested and tempered by adversity, and who is looking with few illusions and with the realism of experience to a calmer future. One of his last personal letters, to the poet Erik Lindegrén, expressed this mood in another way:

> Sten Selander*—who, as you know, never outgrew the adventurous explorer spirit of action of a boy—wrote me once with an accent of envy about those who create poetry by action. It is a beautiful concept and there may be some little element of truth in it, but basically it is an illusion. We all remain free to form our personal life in accordance with standards which otherwise may find their expression in poetry. But obligation to action, especially in the political field, is more of a danger than of a privilege. At the present phase, events on all levels and the basic stone-age psychology of men make it rather difficult to translate contemplation into action and to make action the source material for contemplation. However, we do not ourselves choose the shelf on which we are placed.[42]

---

*Sten Selander (1891–1957), Swedish poet and essayist; president of the Swedish Association for the Protection of Nature; member of the Swedish Academy. He visited Lapland extensively and wrote about it.

VINDICATION
AND TRAGEDY

Different interests and Powers outside Africa have seen in the Congo situation a possibility of developments with strong impact on their international position. They have therefore, naturally, held strong views on the direction in which they would like to see developments in the Congo turn and—with the lack of political traditions in the country and without the stability which political institutions can get only by being tested through experience—the doors have been opened for efforts to influence developments by supporting this or that faction or this or that personality. True to its principles, the United Nations has had to be guided in its operation solely by the interest of the Congolese people and by their right to decide freely for themselves, without any outside influence and with full knowledge of facts. Therefore, the Organization, throughout the first year of its work in the Congo, up to the point when Parliament reassembled and invested a new national Government, has refused—what may have been wished—to permit the weight of its resources to be used in support of any faction so as thereby to prejudice in any way the outcome of a choice which belonged solely to the Congolese people. It has also had to pursue a line which, by safeguarding the free choice of the people, implied resistance against all efforts from out-

side to influence the outcome. In doing so, the Organization has been put in a position in which those within the country who felt disappointed in not getting the support of the Organization were led to suspect that others were in a more favored position and, therefore, accused the Organization of partiality, and in which, further, such outside elements as tried to get or protect a foothold within the country, when meeting an obstacle in the United Nations, made similar accusations. If, as it is sincerely to be hoped, the recent national reconciliation, achieved by Parliament and its elected representatives of the people, provides a stable basis for a peaceful future in a fully independent and unified Congo, this would definitely confirm the correctness of the line pursued by the United Nations in the Congo. In fact, what was achieved by Parliament early in August may be said to have done so with sufficient clarity. It is a thankless and easily misunderstood role for the Organization to remain neutral in relation to a situation of domestic conflict and to provide active assistance only by protecting the rights and possibilities of the people to find their own way, but it remains the only manner in which the Organization can serve its proclaimed purpose of furthering the full independence of the people in the true and unqualified sense of the word. *

HAMMARSKJOLD THUS SUMMED UP, in August 1961, the policy which he had steadfastly followed in the Congo over the previous year. His decision to visit Leopoldville in September reflected not only the new possibilities for progress provided by the reestablishment of a constitutional government,[1] but, above all, his anxiety to tackle the residual problem of Katanga before the General Assembly met. "Dag Hammarskjold did not go to the Congo," Ralphe Bunche wrote later, "in gracious response to a polite and not at all pressing invitation[2] received from Prime Minister Adoula, but for more compelling reasons. He had it definitely in mind to try to induce Mr. Tshombe to enter into talks with Mr. Adoula, preferably in Leopoldville. He knew that if this could be achieved it might well relieve the Assembly of the necessity of extensive and poisonous debate on the subject of the Congo, which would do neither the Congo nor the UN any good."[3]

Throughout the spring and summer, Hammarskjold's two main objectives had been to remove the foreign advisers and mercenaries in Katanga, in pursuance of the Security Council's decision of February

---

* A/4800/Add. 1; SG/1052, August 21, 1961.

21, and to encourage national reconciliation and a return to legality through the reconvening of the Parliament in Leopoldville.

On April 24, two hundred Congolese political leaders met at Coquilhatville, the capital of Equateur Province. At this meeting, which lasted until May 28, the fundamental conflict of interest between Kasavubu and Tshombe reemerged, and Tshombe was arrested by the Central Government. Hammarskjold noted that the arrest of Tshombe at Coquilhatville posed an interesting problem both for those who had opposed the protection of Lumumba and now demanded that the UN rescue Tshombe, and for others who had demanded that the UN rescue Lumumba and now kept resolutely quiet. Tshombe was finally released on June 24 on the understanding that he would send Katangese representatives to the Parliament in Leopoldville, but on his return to Elisabethville he reneged on this undertaking, claiming that the Katanga Assembly was against it. He also denied that he had declared his intention to end the secession of Katanga. Disillusioned by yet another failure to come to terms with Tshombe, the Kasavubu régime began to display a more conciliatory attitude toward the Gizenga regime in Stanleyville.

Another development, in late April, was to have an unexpected and adverse effect upon the Katanga problem. On April 22, elements of the French Army attempted a military coup in Algeria with the aim of preventing talks between France and the insurgent FLN. When the coup failed, some of the French officers involved joined the small French group of military advisers and mercenaries already in Katanga, where their fanaticism and capacity for intrigue added a formidable new component to the problem.

In late May, in a directive to Sture Linnér about the reconvening of the Congolese Parliament, Hammarskjold wrote: "It is for the Congolese to decide what they want. We cannot be anything but, so to say, midwives in this operation, and the greater discretion we show, the less we formalize our part in the story, the better I believe it is."[4] To get the Congolese Parliament together again in any constructive way required agreement between Leopoldville and Stanleyville, and he noted with some satisfaction that "the fervour, which was shown in some quarters in the beginning, to make this and that kind of bilateral approach has somewhat abated."[5] The unique complexities of the Congo seemed at last to have begun to discourage foreign partisanship.

After Rajeshwar Dayal's departure, Hammarskjold had decided to spread the responsibility for the direction of the UN Congo operation, a decision that was to have unfortunate results in September. Linnér became the "Officer in Charge," though not the Special Representative of the Secretary-General, while Mahmoud Khiary took over the civilian operations and also did a considerable amount of political contact work. Khiary, Francis Nwokedi, and Robert Gardiner were especially concerned with the effort to reconvene the Parliament.

In mid-May, Hammarskjold made another appointment which was to influence future events. Ian Berendsen, a New Zealand Secretariat official whom he had brought out with him to the Congo in August 1960, had been his representative in Elisabethville for nearly a year. Berendsen's relief from this most frustrating, nerve-racking, and isolated of all the UN posts in the Congo was long overdue. Georges Dumontet, a French member of the Secretariat, had ably filled the gap for the time being, but his nationality made him unsuitable as the permanent occupant of this post.

The February 21 Security Council resolution required a new and firm hand in Katanga, and Hammarskjold was anxious to make this clear by putting as strong a representative as possible in Elisabethville. For this purpose he chose Bibiano Osorio-Tafall, a Spaniard who had taken Mexican nationality after the Spanish civil war and who was currently serving as the UN Technical Assistance representative in Indonesia. Osorio-Tafall was known as a tough, experienced, and resourceful member of the Secretariat, and he was recalled to New York and briefed extensively on his new functions in Katanga. When, as a result of his briefing, he realized the political delicacy and exposure of his new position, he felt obliged to warn the Secretary-General of a part of his own background of which Hammarskjold was evidently unaware. Osorio-Tafall knew that the wild and groundless accusations originally made by Senator Joseph McCarthy against another member of the Secretariat with a Spanish civil war background similar to his own, Gustavo Durán, had recently been resurrected in the right-wing press in the United States while Durán was serving as the UN representative in Stanleyville. Osorio-Tafall was even more liable to this kind of attack, for he had been the Commissar-General for Defense and Minister of the Interior in the Spanish Republican Government during the civil war. The day he was to leave for Katanga, therefore, during a final briefing by Hammarskjold, Osorio-Tafall made known his anxieties on this score. Hammarskjold, who had been unaware of Osorio-Tafall's Spanish background, told him that much as he appreciated his willingness to go to Elisabethville, it would be idiotic and quite unfair thus to expose him in such a place at such a time. Osorio-Tafall's assignment to Katanga was therefore canceled at the last moment.

A substitute of suitable nationality had to be found urgently. Conor Cruise O'Brien, a member of the Irish Foreign Service, had served in the Irish delegation to the General Assembly for several

years past and was known to be a talented, high-spirited, and courageous man. O'Brien had been sounded out earlier about his willingness to serve in the UN Secretariat, and Cordier now telephoned him
in Ireland to ask him if he would accept the Katanga assignment.
O'Brien agreed to come to New York at once to be briefed, but stipulated that officially he should be asked merely to join the Secretariat
without specific mention of the Congo or Katanga, because he thought
that the Irish government would be reluctant to see an Irish official
"assume the unpredictable responsibilities of the UN representative
in Katanga."[6] Thus it was only after O'Brien had already agreed to
come to New York that Hammarskjold asked Frank Aiken, the Irish
Foreign Minister, to release O'Brien. This request took Aiken by surprise. Although the Irish authorities respected and admired O'Brien's talents, they were by no means convinced that he was best suited either by
temperament or background for the Elisabethville post, and had they
been consulted in time they would almost certainly have suggested
another candidate. Since O'Brien had already been approached, however, the Irish Foreign Office gave its consent, and O'Brien came to
New York for briefing before going to Katanga on June 8. Hammarskjold did not know O'Brien but had read and liked his *Maria Cross*,
a series of essays on a group of French and English Catholic writers.
The two men met only briefly in New York, and neither seems to have
got any real idea of the other's character or way of thinking. This
failure was an important factor in the events of the following September.

After many delays and difficulties, the Congolese Parliament finally
met on July 15 at Lovanium University outside Leopoldville. The members were under the protection of the UN, which also provided all the
administrative services and transport at, to, and from the meeting.
This promising development was complemented by the change of
government in Brussels. The new Belgian government was much less
favorable to the Katanga secession than its predecessor, and Paul-
Henri Spaak, the Foreign Minister, was prepared to help as far as
possible in the implementation of the Security Council's resolutions,
although he had his own difficulties, for Belgian public opinion was
on the whole sympathetic to Katanga and was still very hostile to the
UN. Spaak had therefore to move cautiously over the withdrawal from
Katanga of the Belgian advisers upon whom the maintenance of the
secession still largely depended, and he was concerned that UN
policies should not cause damage or suffering to the European population and that the operations of the Union Minière du Haut Katanga*

---

* Crawford Young in his *Politics in the Congo* describes the position of large cor-

should not be disrupted. In spite of Spaak's preoccupations and difficulties, by the end of June the attitude of the Belgian government was, for the first time since the Congo operation began, fully cooperative.

Tshombe, on the other hand, was in no mood to end the secession of Katanga. Apart from the practical support of the Union Minière, his régime enjoyed the moral support of large sections of the press and of the financial establishment in Great Britain, the United States, Belgium, and France, as well as the active sympathy of Sir Roy Welensky across the border in the Federation of Rhodesia and Nyasaland and of the government of the Union of South Africa. Despite their votes in the UN Security Council, there was little sign that Britain or even the United States was enthusiastic about cooperating in any active UN measures to remove foreign influences in Elisabethville and thus clear the way for bringing Katanga back into the Congo.

Tshombe's régime relied on various categories of foreign advisers. The Belgian political advisers were largely responsible for the attitude of the provincial government toward the UN. The original leadership of Tshombe's army, the Gendarmerie, had consisted of former Belgian Force Publique (Congo Colonial Army) officers and Belgian regular officers on loan. Katanga also had a small and heterogeneous group of aircraft flown by mercenary pilots, to which three Fouga Magister jet trainers from France had been added in February. These overrated aircraft, of which only one ever became operational, were to play an important psychological role in the events leading up to Hammarskjold's death. The main strength of Katanga's air force lay in the

---

porations in the Congo as follows:

> The role of the large corporations, especially Union Minière and the Société Générale, is much more complex than is generally believed. . . . One must carefully distinguish between the activity of the companies as such and that of their employees, and also between the Brussels and Elisabethville offices. . . . There can be no doubt . . . that UMHK fully supported the secession in July 1960.

The companies supported different factions at different times,

> and there was too much at stake for the companies to risk betting on a losing horse. . . . The most reasonable interpretation of the behavior of colonial corporations is that they were simply bewildered by the pace of events, had had little experience in other countries to provide perspective in survival techniques for periods of political effervescence, and pursued simultaneously several contradictory policies in order to hedge as many bets as possible.[7]

Hammarskjold's private efforts to persuade the UMHK, both for UN reasons and for its own ultimate good, to change its ambiguous and uncooperative attitude toward the Central Government fell on deaf ears.

On December 31, 1966, it was officially announced in Leopoldville that the previously announced intention to nationalize the UMHK had come into effect without compensation. In October 1968 both parties, Belgium and the Congo, asked Robert McNamara, president of the International Bank, to help them negotiate an agreement. A year later both parties informed him that they had worked out their difficulties and had come to an agreement on the terms of the nationalization.

fact that at this time neither the UN nor the Congolese Central government had any military aircraft at all.

As soon as the new Belgian government showed signs of cooperating with the UN in the withdrawal of Belgian military personnel from Katanga, the mercenary element in Tshombe's army assumed a new importance, and the Katanga government engaged in an urgent recruiting campaign in Western Europe, Rhodesia, and South Africa. The mercenaries thus recruited had an effect upon both the political and the military situation far in excess either of their numbers or of their military skill. They were for the most part the riffraff of declining colonial empires, variously motivated by greed, by addled notions of white racial superiority, and by a love of violence and trouble in someone else's country at someone else's expense. In their ranks were to be found a bizarre collection of professional killers, hard-core failures, and one or two idealists. Misfits and braggarts for the most part, the mercenaries tended to quarrel among themselves and to bewilder the luckless African soldiers they had been hired to command. Among this rabble the newly arrived French officers stood out as professional, fanatical, and experienced and they soon gained an ascendancy over Tshombe, Munongo, and the Katangese military organization. After their embittering experiences in Indochina and Algeria, they tended to regard Katanga not only as a ready source of high wages but as a bastion of white civilization in Africa to be defended against the sinister forces represented by the UN.* At Kabalo in northern Katanga on April 7, in the process of resisting Tshombe's efforts to subdue the hostile Baluba, UN Ethiopian troops arrested thirty mercenaries of English stock whose interrogation revealed for the first time the widespread recruiting network that Tshombe had organized abroad.

During the period of Tshombe's detention by the Central Government in May and June, the Katanga Minister of the Interior and supposedly the most die-hard secessionist of all, Godefroid Munongo, professed his willingness to cooperate with the UN in getting rid of the foreign military and civilian personnel, whom he professed to hate even more than the UN did, but it soon became obvious that Munongo

---

* When Colonel Egge, a UN Norwegian officer in Katanga, attended the July 14 party at the French consulate in Elisabethville in 1961, one of the French mercenaries stuck a hard object in his back, saying dramatically: "You are betraying the last bastion of the white man in Central Africa. You will get a knife in your back one of these days" (O'Brien, *To Katanga and Back*, pp. 101–2). Tshombe's chief military adviser, the French mercenary Lieutenant Colonel Faulques, grumbled: *"On est décidément en pleine négritude"* ("We are decidedly in the heart of blackness") (*Notre Guerre au Katanga* [Paris, 1963], p. 148. This weird production by Colonel Trinquier, Jacques Duchemin, and Jacques Le Bailly, with its fantasies, bragging, and ludicrous distortions, gives a vivid idea of the state of mind of the mercenaries).

was only playing for time. O'Brien's arrival in Elisabethville on June 14 more or less coincided with Hammarskjold's conclusion that a tougher line must be taken against the mercenaries and foreign advisers in Katanga. In the next few weeks O'Brien succeeded, by persuasion and negotiation, in getting a number of the political advisers withdrawn, but as the summer wore on it became evident that more drastic measures would be required to deal with the mercenary problem. In early July, ONUC Headquarters asked the Secretary-General whether, since peaceful and civilized methods seemed to be getting nowhere, it was not time to consider a swift take-over of Katanga by force as being the only means of avoiding another disastrous deterioration throughout the Congo. Hammarskjold immediately replied that such an extreme departure from approved policy was inconceivable. Instead, he told Linnér, ONUC must build up a position of strength to back up its demands for the expulsion of the foreign officers and advisers, although this position of strength should not be used in action.

In July, O'Brien, with Hammarskjold's full support, began to use more stringent methods. George Thyssens, who was considered to be one of the more pernicious of Tshombe's political advisers, was arrested and expelled on July 7, and O'Brien announced that such forceful actions would be repeated unless real progress was made in reducing foreign influences. O'Brien and Khiary urged Tshombe to speed up the expulsion of the foreign political and military advisers, and O'Brien made persistent efforts to persuade Tshombe to send Katangese parliamentary representatives to take part in the reconvened Parliament in Leopoldville. At the same time, during talks with Hammarskjold in Geneva, Spaak undertook to inform Tshombe that he could not count on either political or military support from Belgium, agreed to withdraw all Belgian officers, and also asked for a complete list of the political advisers to be withdrawn.

Tshombe intermittently hinted that he was about to expel certain key foreign personnel, including some of the Belgian political advisers and the more extreme French officers. Munongo, on the other hand, after an incident between UN troops and the Katanga Gendarmerie near Niemba on July 17, began again to make inflammatory statements against the UN and even announced that he would request assistance from the Soviet Union.

Tshombe employed his usual technique, promising O'Brien cooperation one day and prevaricating or withdrawing it the next. He grumbled about the arrival of Gurkha troops in Elisabethville and about UN activities in northern Katanga but agreed that Munongo was going too far. He was friendly but stopped well short of real cooperation.

O'Brien commented that in the existing circumstances almost every Belgian in Katanga was capable of becoming a political adviser, and he also observed that some members of the foreign consular corps in Elisabethville were anything but wholehearted in their cooperation with the UN and were particularly averse to speeding up the withdrawal of the foreign advisers.

On August 1 the Congolese Parliament unanimously elected Cyrille Adoula[8] as "formateur" of a coalition government. This success for the UN's policy of national conciliation made it possible for Hammarskjold for the first time to think of scaling down the UN operation in the Congo. "If," he wrote to Fawzi on August 4, "the solution chosen by the unanimous Parliament, as I sincerely hope, proves reasonably stable, it would from my point of view be a signal for the beginning of the liquidation of the UN operation: what can be achieved more with the limited task that has been ours, and to give the Congolese a possibility to settle their own affairs in their own way, but in democratic and peaceful forms? . . . I fail to see how the separatist movement [in Katanga] can survive very much longer, once Leopoldville and Stanleyville unite."[9] On August 31, Adoula's government was recognized by the U.S.S.R. Three days later, after persistent efforts by Khiary, Gizenga was persuaded to leave Stanleyville and take up his post in Leopoldville as Vice Prime Minister.

Hammarskjold instructed Linnér to take up with Adoula the retraining of the ANC, the progressive take-over from the UN by the ANC of responsibilities for law and order in the safer areas of the Congo, the question of the future of the bases of Kamina, Kitona, and Banana, the future of the Central Bank, and the Africanization of key posts in the civil service. When Linnér came to New York for consultations in mid-August, Hammarskjold indicated that he would be prepared to go to Leopoldville for a few days to discuss the place of the UN in the present and future Congo picture, but that such a visit would have to be at the invitation of either Adoula or of Kasavubu and with the concurrence of the Congolese Cabinet.

Hammarskjold was encouraged by the UN's constructive and friendly relationship with the new government, but he knew it would not be long before Adoula brought up the Katanga problem. On August 16, Justin Bomboko indicated that the government, if it was to survive, urgently needed UN assistance on the problems both of Stanleyville and Katanga, and a few days later Adoula told Hammarskjold through Khiary that he was already having difficulties with his Cabinet on the Katanga problem and would soon be in danger from its more extreme members if nothing could be done about it. He asked urgently what assistance he could expect from the UN. Tshombe, meanwhile, continued to resist all attempts to bring him and Adoula together.

The Adoula government was not alone in pressing for UN action over Katanga. The African and Asian representatives in New York had for some time been advocating stronger measures to secure the objectives of the February 21 Security Council resolution, and they were now openly critical of the Secretary-General on this score. In these circumstances Hammarskjold found doubly irritating the sympathy and moral support expressed for Tshombe in large sectors of the Western press and public opinion, and the lack of any real effort by Western governments to support the UN's objectives in Katanga.*

When, at the beginning of August, all progress in removing Tshombe's foreign officers and advisers had come to a halt, Hammarskjold asked urgently for the cooperation of the Belgian government with a view to completing the whole operation within three months, and the Belgian government agreed in principle to the withdrawal of 208 Belgian officers. This would leave 304 foreign officers of various nationalities in Katanga, including the hard core of the problem, the mercenaries over whom their countries of origin claimed to have no control. Their removal was particularly desirable because of their influence in preventing Tshombe, who paid them lavishly, from meeting with Adoula, a meeting that alone could forestall the inevitable effort by the new Central Government to involve the UN in the conquest of Katanga by force.

As August wore on, it became increasingly obvious that the future stability of Adoula's government depended upon an early solution of the Katanga problem. The Stanleyville group in the government, oblivious of the fact that the ANC was in no condition to engage in a military expedition of any kind anywhere, were beginning to insist that the government take military action. The atrocities of Tshombe's mercenary-led mobile groups against the Baluba of northern Katanga lent force to these activist arguments and caused Hammarskjold to give instructions that all possible efforts short of the use of military force must be made to remove European officers from the mobile units in North Katanga. He also suggested that Adoula, as a basis for further UN action, issue an ordinance declaring undesirable all non-Congolese officers and mercenaries in the Katanga forces and demanding their immediate departure from the Congo, and that he should request the UN to help the central government in executing this order in conformity with the obligations of the Organization under the February 21 resolution of the Security Council. He undertook simul-

---

* Katanga's propaganda, conducted by various public-relations firms in Europe and the United States, was spectacularly succesful throughout the period of secession.

taneously to request the Belgian government to withdraw all of the Belgian nationals mentioned in the UN list of foreign personnel.

On August 24 the Congo government issued the ordinance[10] suggested by Hammarskjold—Ordonnance 70/1961—and on the next day he communicated with the Belgian government. O'Brien, who had been away on leave for three weeks, was instructed to go at once to Elisabethville to inform Tshombe that under a formal directive from the Secretary-General he was going to proceed to the expulsion of all non-Congolese officers and mercenaries who had not accepted a contractual engagement with the Central Government. He would ask Tshombe to give the necessary instructions to evacuate all those concerned and warn him that if they failed to go the UN would be compelled to remove them, if necessary by force. It was hoped that Tshombe would cooperate in this move, not least because the African soldiers of the Gendarmerie were reported to be dissatisfied because nearly all their officers were European. Hammarskjold also gave orders for the strengthening of the UN military establishment in Katanga with a view to facing possible trouble ahead.

On August 26, O'Brien failed once again to persuade Tshombe to go to Leopoldville in the UN force commander's plane under UN protection, and Radio Katanga resumed its violent anti-UN broadcasts. The old refrain of the threat to law and order as usual had a powerful effect on the European population, who were further upset by the rumor, started by Munongo, that the UN was about to fly in fifteen hundred men of the dreaded Leopoldville ANC to disarm the Katanga Gendarmerie.

Hammarskjold's anxieties over pressure on the UN to take Katanga by force were not confined to the attitude of the government in Leopoldville. On August 26 he had been concerned about United Press International (UPI) and Reuters dispatches from Elisabethville which quoted O'Brien as saying that if Tshombe did not go to Leopoldville the UN would put its forces at the disposal of the central government. He cabled Linnér:

> This must be misleading quotations and statements which should be corrected. There is no change in our basic principles that we cannot serve as a military arm under the Central Government and for its specific purposes, beyond what is our clear mandate under the resolutions. Thus we cannot "wage war" on the Katanga forces, while we can, if necessary by force, execute paragraph A-2 of the resolution.* That is to the best of

---

* Paragraph A-2 of Resolution 161 (S/4741) of February 21, 1961, urged "that measures be taken for the immediate withdrawal and evacuation from the Congo of all Belgian and other foreign military and paramilitary personnel and political advisers not under the United Nations Command, and mercenaries."

our understanding the instruction to O'Brien and ONUC and that is also all that the Central Government has asked for. It is most unfortunate that the press now overflows with statements about our intention to "disarm the gendarmerie" or, as in these despatches, even worse, to fight down the Katanga regime. The line must be kept clear and erroneous statements corrected. I guess that the stories from Eville [Elisabethville] are explained as ruthless and irresponsible propaganda from Munongo and consorts.[11]

THE UN OPERATION for rounding up European officers and mercenaries* started, with Hammarskjold's approval, at 5 a.m. on August 28,[12] when UN troops in Elisabethville, as a security precaution, occupied the Gendarmerie headquarters, the post office, the radio station and transmitter, and the telephone exchange. There was no opposition and no fighting, and Tshombe cooperated with the UN to such an extent that O'Brien was soon able to cancel the extraordinary security measures that had been taken. On the afternoon of August 28, O'Brien agreed to the request of the foreign consuls concerned that they should arrange, with the help of a number of senior Belgian ex-officers, for the repatriation of their own nationals. Hammarskjold and Linnér were far from happy about this concession, although they congratulated O'Brien warmly on the success of the operation, which by the afternoon of August 28 had netted eighty-one foreign officers. To Spaak's protest against the arrest of Belgian officers, Hammarskjold replied that those concerned had had ample time to leave and had been frequently urged to do so by the Belgian government itself as well as by the UN. There could, he added, be no dishonor involved in detention and expulsion by the UN under a decree of a sovereign government and in accordance with a resolution of the Security Council that was already six months old. He also rejected Spaak's criticism of O'Brien, which was, he said, based to a large extent on misleading press reports of the latter's statements.

By August 31 it was evident that O'Brien's concession to the consuls had justified Hammarskjold's worst fears. The Belgian consul was reported to have given asylum to ninety Belgian officers in the consulate. When Tshombe informed O'Brien that he feared a coup by Munongo if he agreed to go to Leopoldville, O'Brien asked for instructions on how he should deal with Munongo. Hammarskjold replied that while Munongo or anyone else could be arrested if caught

---

* This operation was locally known as "Rumpunch."

in flagrante delicto directing operations against the UN or against the Central Government, his present activities, as reported by O'Brien, would not justify such action unless both Tshombe and the central government were prepared to call for his arrest on the grounds of criminal activity or of preparing for civil war. He told O'Brien to press on as far as possible with the evacuation of the foreign officers and to continue to put pressure on Tshombe to go to Leopoldville.

After the Elisabethville consuls had succeeded in sidetracking the UN roundup operation, the toughest mercenary elements went into hiding and began to plot. On August 31 a defector from their ranks, a Belgian named Crémer, gave O'Brien a detailed and highly sensa-sational account of their plans and told him of plots by Munongo to harass the UN, to murder O'Brien's assistant, Michel Tombelaine, and to continue the persecution of the Baluba. Crémer's information, whether reliable or not, had a considerable impact and caused O'Brien to demand that Tshombe suspend Munongo, while on his own responsi-bility he decided to reduce his own relations with Tshombe to a bare minimum.

At this point Hammarskjold appears to have become aware of the possibility that his people in the field, under the pressure of bizarre and often violent circumstances, might take unauthorized decisions and actions that had wider implications of which they could not be fully aware. On August 31 he cabled to Linnér that he would be more at ease if prior clearance were sought for some of the actions taken in Katanga, as, for example, the provision of a UN honor guard for the departing Belgian officers, a gesture that had struck Hammarskjold as foolish and inappropriate. It would be wise also if UN representa-tives in the field said less to the press, since their words were liable to distortion and misunderstanding and were widely reported through-out the world. Referring to O'Brien's fears of a *"coup de main"* by mercenaries, he wrote: "Extent of reactions of our representatives to such fears raises legal and political problems of which we should be apprised."[13] In relaying this message to O'Brien, Linnér also requested him to consult beforehand on any action affecting general principles, for example his decision to minimize his dealings with Tshombe. O'Brien explained that talking to the press was the only available means of countering the intrigues and machinations of the highly effective Katanga propaganda machine and repeated that the key to the situation was to find a method of dealing with Munongo.

As so often before, events and reactions in the outside world now began to play an important part in internal developments in the Congo. The Katangese leaders found new encouragement from a num-ber of sources. Sir Roy Welensky rose in the Salisbury Parliament on

August 30 to express total sympathy with Katanga and to accuse the UN of subjugating the Katanga government and deliberately threatening law and order. The Federation, he said, would "take necessary measures and legally acceptable steps to help its neighbours." In New York the British representative was instructed to ask the Secretary-General about the scope and purpose of the UN roundup action, to inquire whether force had been used before other means had been exhausted, and to say, in a dim echo of Radio Katanga, that in the view of Her Majesty's Government the UN had no mandate to remove essential foreigners and thereby cause a breakdown in the Katanga administration. To this scarcely disguised support of Tshombe, Hammarskjold replied sharply that the action was fully covered by the resolution of February 21, for which Britain had voted.

In Elisabethville the active and obvious sympathy of much of the consular corps with the secessionist authorities was reflected in the picture painted by some Western correspondents of lawful, prosperous, pro-Western, anti-Communist Katanga being destroyed by the pro-Communist, anticolonial UN juggernaut. O'Brien in particular was singled out for vicious personal attacks, especially in the British and Belgian press. He was even accused of deliberately creating, for political purposes, the Baluba refugee camp in Elisabethville, in which by early September some thirty-five thousand refugees from Munongo's police were being fed and protected by the UN. This concerted propaganda campaign finally destroyed any lingering intention on the part of Tshombe to cooperate with the UN.

Laboring under pressure, vilification, and harassment, O'Brien and the UN commander in Katanga, the Indian Brigadier K. A. S. Raja, not unnaturally favored stronger and more drastic measures, even at the cost of legal niceties. In particular O'Brien suggested that Munongo be neutralized and that legitimate provincial authorities loyal to the Central Government be firmly established in both North and South Katanga. He believed that a clean and total ending of secession would be a relief to all, even to Tshombe himself. This message was not relayed to Hammarskjold in New York, but Linnér arranged for Khiary to meet with O'Brien at Kamina on September 4 to discuss the situation and possible future moves.

Hammarskjold was increasingly apprehensive of the state of mind of his people in the field. On September 5 he told Linnér and the ONUC commander, McKeown, that while he fully understood the pressures and the impossible circumstances under which his representatives in Katanga were working, he must without fail be fully informed in advance of important proposed moves and plans so that he could communicate his views and directives as necessary. He believed that for the moment the best policy in Katanga was "to remain strong but to sit tight, and let the medicine do its work without, if possible, new injections."[14]

After the meeting with O'Brien on September 4, Linnér and Khiary informed Hammarskjold that the situation was now so delicate that an urgent reconsideration of plans was required. About three hundred of the five hundred foreign officers and mercenaries in Katanga had surrendered, but the remainder had gone into hiding and were believed to be organizing guerrilla action. The steadily increasing horde of Baluba refugees in Elisabethville also presented an enormous task of maintenance and protection for the UN, and with Tshombe increasingly under the thumb of Munongo and the French mercenaries it was impossible for O'Brien to make any further progress by purely political means. Radio Katanga's inflammatory broadcasts were becoming a serious danger, and Munongo, in a speech outside the Elisabethville post office, was reported to have demanded O'Brien's death. The tensions between the members of the government in Leopoldville also allowed of no further delay, and it had been learned that the ANC was planning to launch an attack on Katanga from Stanleyville on September 15.

Linnér and Khiary suggested a plan of action. A campaign should be launched to persuade the various governments concerned to stop their consuls in Elisabethville from encouraging Tshombe in his opposition to the UN. One of the Secretary-General's representatives should make a brief visit to Brussels to explain to Spaak the realities of the situation both in Elisabethville and in Leopoldville and to disabuse him, if necessary, of some of the illusions created by Katangese propaganda. At the same time O'Brien would urge Tshombe to put an end to inflammatory broadcasts and to the arrests, terrorism and persecution organized by the Katanga Sûreté (secret police). He would give a twenty-four-hour time limit for the expulsion of all foreign officers, after which the UN would, if necessary, immediately resume its rounding-up operations. If none of these measures worked —and this was paragraph 9(c) of Linnér's and Khiary's plan—the UN would again take over the radio, arrest troublemakers and those who were inciting violence, and at the same time take steps to prevent the Gendarmerie, the police, and the Sûreté from interfering in UN actions. If necessary, O'Brien and Khiary would then visit Tshombe, accompanied by a Commissaire d'Etat* to be appointed by the Central

---

* Under the Loi Fondamentale, the Central Government was to be represented in each province by a Commissaire d'Etat or State Commissioner, who was to be named by the Chief of State and confirmed by the Senate after consultation with the respective provincial president. This provision had never been used.

Government, to get Tshombe's approval for Munongo's arrest and the detention of others guilty of crimes against common law. If Tshombe agreed, the UN would execute the warrants of arrest; if he did not agree, the Commissaire d'Etat would order the Katanga provincial government to conform to the laws and would in effect, temporarily take over control of the provincial administrative apparatus. It was Linnér's and Khiary's belief that Tshombe would cooperate in the first and less drastic course of action and that he could be prevailed upon to announce his return to legality and to summon the Provincial Assembly, to be attended, for once, by all of its members.* Linnér and Khiary explained that only the inevitable alternative, which was an invasion of Katanga by the ANC and civil war, had led them to make such drastic proposals.

Hammarskjold decided to consult the representatives in New York of a number of governments concerned with the Katanga problem before commenting in detail on this suggested plan of action. After talks with the representatives of the United States, Britain, Belgium, Canada, Sweden, the U.A.R., Tunisia, and Nigeria on September 6, he concluded that most of the governments concerned would now be prepared to assist in putting all possible pressure on Tshombe to negotiate and that they now also realized that more drastic measures could be expected if these efforts did not quickly produce the desired effect. Even the British representative, who had protested a week before against the roundup operation in Katanga, had raised no objection at all to the proposed new course of action on Katanga that Hammarskjold had outlined.

The next day, Hammarskjold summarized his view of the UN position for Linnér's guidance. There were four possibilities. The first was to preserve Tshombe's legal status as provincial president and to persuade him to negotiate with Leopoldville on a new constitutional arrangement. The second was for the UN to take drastic measures that would lead to its exercising control in Katanga in a way contrary to the principles on which the whole Congo operation had been conducted. This course could be justified only as a last resort by the fear of the two other possibilities—namely that the central government would be forced by internal pressures to launch the ANC into North Katanga or that it might disintegrate and collapse over the Katanga problem, thereby returning the Congo to the political chaos

---

* The Katanga Provincial Assembly consisted of 30 representatives from Tshombe's Conakat party, 27 from the Cartel Katangais (led by the Balubakat Party, which opposed Tshombe) and 12 from various other groups. The Cartel, which had appealed against the results of the provincial elections without avail, had boycotted the Provincial Assembly almost from the outset in July 1960.

of September 1960. Another firm effort must therefore be made to persuade Tshombe to negotiate. If that failed, more drastic measures would have to be considered if they really seemed to be the sole alternative to civil war or to the collapse of the Adoula government.

Tshombe was still confident that he could maintain the secession of Katanga and seemed less willing than ever to go to Leopoldville. O'Brien therefore asked, on September 6, for authority to react immediately and strongly to all incitements to disorder. This request and O'Brien's statement that "our main need now is to be able to react immediately and decisively if people get killed or badly hurt"[15] worried Hammarskjold, and he asked Linnér urgently to explain what measures O'Brien had in mind. Linnér replied that the action envisaged by O'Brien was to take over the radio station once again and to arrest troublemakers, but that O'Brien had been instructed to take no such action until he was authorized to do so. Linnér hoped, however, that Hammarskjold would be prepared to authorize such measures if there was still no progress after he himself had returned from the one-day trip to Brussels that Hammarskjold had instructed him to make in order to explain the situation to the Belgian government. Meanwhile the Central Government had prepared the necessary ordinances, decrees and warrants to legalize any action necessary.

To clear his mind, and for the guidance of Linnér and O'Brien, Hammarskjold felt it necessary at this point to formulate the legal position of ONUC as he saw it. Since this formulation is important to an understanding of his conception of the role and limitations of the UN in facing the Katanga problem, a summary follows:

1. The mandate of the UN for the protection of law and order authorized it to deploy troops to protect civilians when they were threatened by tribal war or violence.

2. Paragraph A-1* of the Security Council's resolution of February 21 also authorized preventive action by the UN to deal with incitement to or preparation of civil war.

3. The right of UN troops to use force in self-defense covered attempts to overrun or displace UN positions. It also covered attempts to injure or abduct UN personnel.

4. The act of self-defense against attack could include the disarming and, if necessary, the detention of those preparing to attack UN troops.

---

* Paragraph A-1 of the Security Council resolution of February 21, 1961, urged "that the United Nations take immediately all appropriate measures to prevent the occurrence of civil war in the Congo, including arrangements for cease-fires, the halting of all military operations, the prevention of clashes, and the use of force, if necessary, in the last resort."

5. Incitement to or preparation for violence, including troop movements and confirmed reports of an impending attack, would warrant protective action by UN troops, but criticism of the UN, however pungently expressed, or peaceful demonstrations against the UN, could not be held to justify protective action.

6. The maintenance of law and order or the prevention of civil war might justify, in certain circumstances, the closing of radio stations and airports if it was clear they were being used to foment civil war or for other unlawful purposes. The legal basis for taking such measures would be strengthened when the competent authorities of the Central or the provincial government had requested or approved such measures.

7. Arrest or detention of civil leaders was only justifiable if they were engaged in overt military action or were caught *in flagrante delicto* inciting violence. Without such justifying circumstances, the detention of political leaders would run a serious risk of violating the ban on intervention in domestic political conflicts.

8. Political leaders could be arrested by the UN if the UN was requested to do so by *both* the Central Government *and* the provincial authorities. However, it was doubtful if a warrant of arrest issued against a provincial leader by the Central Government alone was sufficient basis for the UN to carry out such an arrest, even if the arrest was requested by the Commissaire d'Etat appointed by the Central Government.

9. The appointment of a Commissaire d'Etat could not change the legal situation of the UN in conflicts between the Central Government and a provincial government, nor did it remove the obligation of the UN to abstain from interference in constitutional conflicts.

If they achieved little else, these observations served to demonstrate the extraordinary complexities and weaknesses of the UN position and to highlight the contrast between its great responsibilities and its minimal right to take action. They can have provided little comfort for O'Brien and his staff in the overcharged atmosphere of Elisabethville.

On September 8, with extremism flourishing in Elisabethville and the two Chambers in Leopoldville meeting in special session on Katanga, Linnér assured Hammarskjold that there would be no abuse of the plans for action by ONUC to deal with the Katanga problem and that all precautions would be taken to avoid mistakes. Nevertheless, urgent and decisive action was necessary. To Khiary, who was in charge in Leopoldville during Linnér's brief trip to Brussels, Hammarskjold cabled on September 9 that he had still not seen the detailed instructions for O'Brien that Khiary was formulating. Linnér had asked for authority to apply 9(c), the plan for more drastic action, immediately after his return from Brussels and had later, in another message, suggested postponing this move to a later date. Hammarskjold told Khiary that "with quick changes of constellations and pending your elaboration of instructions,"[16] further authority for specific action could not be given, except that ONUC might take control of the Elisabethville radio station, as it had done on August 28, if this was considered absolutely necessary. This could be done under paragraph A-1 of the Security Council resolution because of the inflammatory nature of Radio Katanga's broadcasts. Although force could be used in self-defense, "very much ground may be lost psychologically at the first shot from our side, if we can be accused of acting prematurely or in provocative way."[17] Hammarskjold disliked the idea of the UN executing warrants of arrest on behalf of the central government, which would come dangerously close to interference by force in the internal political conflict. On the other hand, the importance of the standing authorization to arrest troublemakers caught *in flagrante* should not be underestimated. "Were one of these gentlemen for example to take active part in or lead a mob demonstration, they certainly can be apprehended."[18]

Tension in Elisabethville increased sharply on September 9 as the result of the simultaneous arrival of the UN Gurkha Battalion and of the news that the Central Government had issued warrants of arrest for the Katangese Ministers, had appointed a Commissaire d'Etat Extraordinaire, and expected the UN to assist it in its efforts in Katanga.

On the same day Khiary, after meeting with the Congolese Cabinet, urged that firm action be taken in Katanga within a few days. As soon as Linnér came back from Brussels and Hammarskjold approved the plan of action, Khiary would go to Elisabethville to brief O'Brien. Khiary also told O'Brien that he was awaiting the Secretary-General's approval for quick action and warned him in general terms to make the necessary preparations. The next day Khiary confirmed to Hammarskjold that the instructions he would give O'Brien would coincide with the Secretary-General's modifications to the plan put forward some days before by himself and Linnér, namely to take over Radio Katanga if necessary and at the same time to ensure that the Gendarmerie, Sûreté, police, and mercenary-led groups could not oppose the UN's action or disrupt public order. This was, in fact, a considerable distortion of Hammarskjold's comments on Linnér's and Khiary's proposals. What he had said was that much would depend on how the plan was implemented and that the UN should avoid antagonizing the Gendarmerie and should, if possible, win them over to its side. Khiary assured Hammarskjold that the instructions to

O'Brien were to be acted on *"avec toutefois réserve d'application après entente avec vous à Leo* [Leopoldville]"[19]—only after an understanding with the Secretary-General himself at Leopoldville. This referred to Hammarskjold's acceptance of an invitation to visit Leopoldville that he had just received from Adoula.[20]

By September 10 the pace of developments in Elisabethville and Leopoldville had convinced Hammarskjold that, short of an unexpected change for the better, more drastic measures would be required, and he authorized Linnér to go ahead with preparations for the plan which they had discussed and for which he had given limited authority to Khiary the day before, although he enjoined him to bear in mind his views on the questions of principle involved. He himself was now planning to arrive in Leopoldville direct from New York on Wednesday, September 13, and to return to New York on September 18.

On September 10, O'Brien's assistant, Tombelaine, was arrested. O'Brien, after securing his release, demanded the immediate expulsion of all the Belgian agents of the Katangese Sûreté, which he described as a small-time Gestapo. Hammarskjold strongly endorsed this demand, apparently believing that if the first steps of the plan were taken firmly, it would be unnecessary to proceed with the later and more drastic ones. He was encouraged in this belief by Linnér's report of Belgian understanding and willingness to help and by O'Brien's impression that the Secretary-General's representations to delegations in New York were beginning to have a salutary effect on the consular corps in Elisabethville.

Hammarskjold certainly had no idea that any major and drastic action might be taken before he himself arrived in Leopoldville. His authorization to Linnér on September 10 to go ahead with the plan they had discussed omitted any precise guidance on timing, but it specifically referred to Khiary's message saying that no action would be taken before consulting with the Secretary-General in Leopoldville. In a second cable to Linnér on the same day, he expressed misgivings about Khiary's absence from Leopoldville to brief O'Brien and hoped he would be "back by Thursday to assist me with his ideas and evaluation regarding latest situation in Katanga,"[21] and in a third cable he suggested that his visit to Leopoldville might be used as a face-saving device which might enable Tshombe to come there to meet Adoula.*

---

* When Khiary and O'Brien suggested this to Tshombe on September 12, he flatly rejected the idea of going to Leopoldville but invited Hammarskjold to come to Elisabethville. Just before he left New York, Hammarskjold saw a news-agency report on the press conference in which Tshombe had repeated this invitation. When asked if he would consider going to see Tshombe, he replied, "Why not, if it helps to get him and Adoula together?"[22]

All these messages indicate Hammarskjold's assumption that no major action would be taken in Katanga before he arrived in the Congo, and later on he was angered by the allegation that *he* had ordered the action in Elisabethville on September 13. "It belongs to history," he cabled Bunche from Leopoldville, ". . . that the first I knew about this development, I learned by tendentious Reuters report in Accra on my way to Leo."[23]

As HE PREPARED to leave for the Congo, Hammarskjold was in a more cheerful frame of mind than he had been for some time. He had hopes that his visit might produce substantial progress on the Katanga problem and that the first steps could also be taken toward phasing out the military side of the UN Congo operation. His target, he told Mekki Abbas, the Executive Secretary of the UN Economic Commission for Africa, in late August, was to reduce the UN force to 8,000 by the end of the year,* but any progress in this direction was dependent on solving the Katanga problem. He told Mongi Slim that this would be his last personal effort to solve the Katanga problem and that if he failed he would be unable to remain as Secretary-General and had decided to resign.** He repeated this thought to Adnan Pachachi of Iraq in a more optimistic way, implying that he would probably resign anyway as soon as the UN force could be withdrawn from the Congo. In his meetings with Ambassadors Frederick Boland of Ireland, Charles Ritchie of Canada, Sievert Nielsen of Norway, and Carl Schürmann of the Netherlands the day before he left New York, he appeared optimistic and explained that his main objective in going to the Congo was to get Adoula and Tshombe together. None of the ambassadors, either at the time or later when they checked their notes on their meetings with Hammarskjold, detected the slightest hint that he was expecting fighting in Katanga, and from what he told them it would have been the last thing he would have wanted. To his Swedish aide, Wilhelm Wachtmeister, he said in parting, "If *this* succeeds, we may have a decent Assembly."[24]

On the evening of September 11, Hammarskjold gave a small dinner party at Seventy-third Street for the American painter Ben Shahn and

---

* In September 1961 the strength of the UN Congo Force was 16,814 officers and men from twenty countries.
** Hammarskjold thought that, of the candidates with a chance of being elected as his successor, either Mongi Slim or U Thant would be best. He mentioned this only to his closest associates, knowing that any support from him might damage their prospects.

Carl Nordenfalk, director of the National Museum in Stockholm, with their wives. The ostensible purpose of the evening was to discuss the portrait of Hammarskjold which the National Museum had commissioned Shahn to paint.* As usual the conversation ranged over a wide variety of subjects, and Hammarskjold spoke in optimistic terms of his forthcoming visit to the Congo, where the worst now seemed to be over.

Hammarskjold, accompanied by Wieschhoff and Bill Ranallo, left New York for the last time on Pan Am Flight 150 at 5:30 p.m. on September 12. At the airport, Bunche, realizing that Wieschhoff had a high fever and was unfit to travel, was about to suggest that he should take Wieschhoff's place, when Wieschhoff, guessing what was in Bunche's mind, begged him to say nothing and assured him he would soon recover. Cordier's parting words were, "Well, Dag, I believe this trip is going to be your most pleasant trip to Leopoldville."[26]

While Hammarskjold was flying over the Atlantic, an action began in Elisabethville which transformed his visit to the Congo from an effort to reconcile Tshombe and the Central Government into a desperate and increasingly bitter attempt to put an end to the unanticipated fighting in Katanga.

The origins of the fighting which started in Elisabethville in the early morning of September 13 are still a matter of controversy and of some mystery. There seems little doubt that, acting partly under the pressure of local events and partly also perhaps in the misguided hope of being able to present the Secretary-General on his arrival in the Congo with a decisive step forward on the Katanga problem, Hammarskjold's representatives went far beyond his admittedly complex instructions. The different temperaments and attitudes of the principal UN officials in the Congo were certainly one ingredient in the confusion that ensued. All three officials principally involved were recent recruits to the UN Secretariat. Sture Linnér, the Officer-in-Charge in Leopoldville, was devoted to the UN and to Hammarskjold personally but lacked the dominating personality and authority necessary to keep subordinates coordinated and under control in a complex and tense situation. Linnér's immediate subordinate, Mahmoud Khiary, the Tunisian Chief of Civilian Operations, had been given a number of important political assignments during the summer and had played a key role in bringing together the Congolese Parliament. Khiary was

---

* When told that Shahn had also painted Freud and Hemingway, Hammarskjold commented, ". . . with Freud and Hemingway—what a 'troika'!"[25] The portrait, painted after his death, is a curious work that now hangs in the collection of pictures of famous Swedes at Gripsholm Castle.

a determined and impressively able official* with strong views on what should be done in the Congo and how. He was convinced that it was impossible to understand the Congo from New York and had told Hammarskjold as much. Much as he admired the Secretary-General, Khiary was not unduly impressed by what he regarded as Hammarskjold's overcautious concept of UN policy in the Congo or by his insistence on the observance of basic principles, and he felt that in the Congo the UN lacked the forcefulness necessary to be effective. He was determined to do what he could to rectify this shortcoming, even if, on occasion, it meant stretching his instructions.

The UN representative in Elisabethville, O'Brien, had since June been carrying out with considerable style and courage the lonely, thankless, and increasingly unpopular task of implementing the Security Council's decisions in Katanga. Whenever he had seemed to be making progress, he had been frustrated by the intrigues of Tshombe, Munongo, the European consuls, and the mercenaries, while the European population held him up to receptive Western press correspondents as an object of execration and the author of all misfortune. As his exasperation increased, O'Brien had naturally favored stronger measures as against Hammarskjold's cautious step-by-step approach. The tense, hate-filled, rumor-laden atmosphere of Elisabethville was a far cry from the order and tranquillity of UN Headquarters in New York. O'Brien was thus in a receptive mood for the orders for action that Khiary apparently gave him on September 11.

A fourth element in the UN setup played a disastrous if secondary role. Linnér, Khiary, and O'Brien were all working with a military organization which, both in Leopoldville and Elisabethville, was poorly organized and lacking in the leadership, political judgment, staff work, discipline, and forceful restraint that are particularly vital in UN operations. In Elisabethville especially, the military preparations to carry out, even at their minimum interpretation, the instructions which Khiary gave O'Brien were totally inadequate and were based upon an entirely unrealistic estimate of the opposition likely to be encountered. In fact, they were largely a repetition of the security measures taken on August 28 and were therefore easily anticipated by the opposition. To make matters worse, the higher ranks of the UN force in Katanga were bedeviled by national and personal rivalries and antipathies. The September 13 operation, apart from lacking the Secretary-General's authorization, was poorly planned and abys-

* O'Brien describes Khiary's "closed, watchful face in conference, looking like some impenetrable and resourceful envoy of Genghis Khan."[27]

mally executed, and the total confidence in a rapid success which the commander, Brigadier K. A. S. Raja, had expressed to Khiary on September 11, quickly gave way, when fighting broke out, to extreme nervousness and caution, and to a constant demand for reinforcements. When the shooting started, the mercenaries, with their much closer contacts with the press and the local population, soon established a psychological superiority over the UN, to which the unopposed activities of the single Katangese Fouga jet made an important contribution.

O'Brien's own description of his briefing by Khiary on September 11 gives an impression of instructions very different, especially in tone, from the plan envisaged in the cable exchanges between Hammarskjold in New York and Linnér and Khiary in Leopoldville.* O'Brien first recalls the glee with which Vladimir Fabry, Linnér's legal adviser, handed him the warrants for the arrest of Tshombe, Munongo, Kibwe, Kimba,[28] and Mutaka.[29] Khiary explained to O'Brien that only the latter four were to be arrested, and that further instructions would be forthcoming on what to do with them. Tshombe was to be arrested only in the last resort, but his residence was to be sealed off and O'Brien was then to parley with him, making it clear that his only hope was to cooperate with the UN and to come to terms with the Central Government. UN forces were to secure the post office and the radio studios and transmitters, and to take over the offices of the Sûreté and the Ministry of Information and remove the files, apprehending the senior officials in these places if possible. The Congo flag would be run up as soon as possible on public buildings and UN buildings. The Central Government would send down a Commissaire d'Etat Extraordinaire to take over the Administration, in cooperation with Tshombe if possible and in cooperation with the UN in any case. Great care should be taken to avoid a clash with the Gendarmerie during these operations.

O'Brien pointed out to Khiary that it would be difficult to carry out these instructions without bloodshed, although he believed that

---

* *To Katanga and Back*, Chapter XV. An earlier and shorter account is given in "My Case," O'Brien's articles in the London *Observer*, December 10 and 17, 1961. These articles are highly subjective, as their title implies, but they give a valuable picture of O'Brien's feelings and views a short time after the events of September. The two accounts differ, as O'Brien himself points out, on a number of important points. The earlier account tends to place the responsibility for confusion on Khiary, while the later one shifts it to Hammarskjold. In the earlier account O'Brien seems to subscribe to the view that the September 13 operation was for the main purpose of rounding up foreign personnel (paragraph A-2 of the Security Council resolution), while in the later account he maintains that he was acting for the broader objective of preventing civil war (paragraph A-1 of the resolution) and with the intention of ending the secession of Katanga.

Tshombe would cooperate if he saw that the UN meant business. According to O'Brien, Khiary told him that the operation should be carried out either before 3 p.m. on the afternoon of Wednesday, September 13, when the Secretary-General was due to arrive in Leopoldville, or after Hammarskjold's departure from the Congo. He said that the Secretary-General had given authority for these operations, but it would be embarrassing for him if fighting was actually going on in Katanga while he was in Leopoldville. Since the Katanga authorities were aware, through informers, both of the UN's plans and of the various actions taken by the Central Government, O'Brien thought that the sooner the UN acted the better. Brigadier Raja also supported the idea of immediate action and stated confidently that any armed resistance could be overcome in two hours at the most. In the light of this conversation, Khiary agreed that the operation should be started early on the morning of September 13. After a final and unsuccessful effort to persuade Tshombe to go to Leopoldville during Hammarskjold's visit, Khiary left for Leopoldville on September 12. According to O'Brien, his last words were *"Surtout pas de demi-mesures!"* ("Above all, no half measures!")

O'Brien had assumed that Tshombe could be persuaded to make a radio statement as he had done on August 28, ordering the Gendarmerie to cooperate with the UN, and that the mercenaries would therefore be forced to fight, if at all, without any semblance of legality and without any African screen. In the event, however, Tshombe was never prevailed upon to make this broadcast, and the loss of contact with him after the early hours of September 13 doomed Khiary's and O'Brien's basic conception of the operation from the start.

Khiary's and Fabry's activities on their return to Leopoldville on the evening of September 12 also went well beyond the cautious step-by-step measures that had been discussed by cable with Hammarskjold in New York. A group of UN technical experts—mostly telecommunications personnel to man the radio and communications centers in Elisabethville—were to be sent down to Elisabethville early in the morning of September 13, accompanied by the Central Government's Commissaire d'Etat Extraordinaire, Egide Bocheley-Davidson.[30] When Khiary briefed this group of experts at 7 a.m. on September 13, he gave the impression that the military part of the operation in Elisabethville was already over, as under Raja's forecast it should have been. At 8 a.m., Khiary briefed the Commissaire d'Etat, Bocheley-Davidson, who appeared nervous, bewildered, and anxious for any support the UN could give him. To Walter Fulcheri, the ONUC official who was to conduct the experts and Bocheley-Davidson to Elisabethville, Khiary gave the same farewell he had given O'Brien the day before: *"Surtout pas de demi-mesures!"* Owing to a series of muddles, Fulcheri's party did not reach Elisabethville until after dark on September 13, and in the then prevailing confusion neither the Commissaire d'Etat nor the experts got further than the Elisabethville Airport.

After 4 a.m. on September 13 everything went wrong in Elisabethville. The UN troops going to the post office, the radio station, and other objectives that they had taken without opposition on August 28 came under fire from the mercenary-led Gendarmerie. This time Tshombe's troops were prepared for the UN moves, and sporadic fighting was soon going on in the center of the city. At 4:45 a.m., Tshombe called O'Brien and seemed anxious to arrange a cease-fire, but the orders to surround his house had not been carried out by the UN troops, and he soon vanished. O'Brien told press correspondents who met him at 8 a.m. and subsequently during the day that the secession of Katanga was at an end, and, with the sound of firing in their ears, it was hardly surprising that they concluded, and reported, that the UN was ending the secession by force.

Hammarskjold's first inkling of these developments had come from the "tendentious" press dispatch he received when his plane landed in Accra. He was not unduly worried at this report since he did not believe that his representative in Elisabethville could possibly have decided, or declared, that the Katanga secession was to be ended by a UN military operation conducted at the request of the central government. This was a course of action he had always rejected, and he believed that this had been made very clear in his recent exchanges with his representatives in the Congo.

Hammarskjold landed at Ndjili, the Leopoldville airport, at 3 p.m. on September 13. To the welcoming crowd of Congolese Ministers, UN officials, diplomats, and press correspondents he was the familiar, slight, hatless figure—radiating confidence, informal and yet dominating. He was greeted warmly by the Prime Minister, Adoula, the Vice-Prime Minister, Gizenga, Colonel Mobutu, and Justin Bomboko, the Foreign Minister. Gizenga, so hostile the year before, seemed particularly affable. The presence of the members of the new government, united and legitimate, was a physical reminder of the success of the policy of national reconciliation for which Hammarskjold had worked tirelessly for a year, and it also gave promise of a future in which the UN's assistance to the Congo might at last be used to full effect. With Adoula, Hammarskjold inspected the guard of honor of Congolese, Nigerian, and Swedish troops, looking, as he often did on ceremonial occasions, preoccupied and a little impatient. From the airport he drove with Adoula to the Prime Minister's house for a brief discussion of the work program for the next two days. It was Adoula's fortieth birthday, and the Prime Minister felt that it was a fitting day to welcome Hammarskjold, whom he trusted and admired and on whose help he knew he must depend if he was to succeed in uniting his troubled country and in setting it on a sound and independent course.

It was only when he arrived at Linnér's villa, where he was to stay during his visit, and had a chance to talk to Linnér alone that Hammarskjold began to realize the full implications and the seriousness of the situation in Elisabethville. From a series of Telex exchanges with O'Brien and Raja during the morning, Linnér already knew that what was supposed to have been a brief, limited, and nonviolent operation, repeating the tactics of August 28, had developed into a sporadic battle in and around Elisabethville between the UN forces and the mercenary-led Katangese Gendarmerie, and that the hope of a quick end to the fighting had vanished with the disappearance of Tshombe and the unexpectedly heavy Katangese opposition to the UN troops. To his insistent questions as to why the operation had gone ahead before he had been consulted, Linnér replied that the deteriorating situation in Elisabethville had evidently made immediate action necessary.

This was obviously no time to engage in recriminations, and Hammarskjold and Linnér soon adjourned from the pleasant, sprawling villa in its large tropical garden to the more businesslike atmosphere of the ONUC headquarters, where he and Wieschhoff set grimly about the task of trying to discover from Linnér, Khiary, and the ONUC commander, General McKeown, what had gone wrong and what was to be done about it. Hammarskjold, as usual, took full responsibility for what had happened. He was above all anxious to stop the fighting, which could in any case no longer contribute to what he understood to be the objective of the operation, namely the roundup of the mercenaries and foreign officers, but he was constantly assured by the military that the fighting would soon be over anyway. Late in the afternoon Linnér cabled O'Brien that it was imperative that he spare no effort to find Tshombe and impress on him the necessity to compose his differences with the Central Government and come to Leopoldville as soon as possible. It was also essential, Linnér told O'Brien, to bring the military action to an end in the shortest possible time.

In the evening Linnér gave an informal dinner for the Secretary-General at his villa. The guests were Adoula; Gizenga; Jason Sendwe, the Baluba Vice-Prime Minister from North Katanga; Christophe Gbenye,[31] the Minister of the Interior; and McKeown and Khiary. What should have been a cheerful occasion was overshadowed by

Hammarskjold's growing anxiety over the continuing fighting in Katanga, its effect on his own mission in the Congo, and its repercussions in the outside world. The first manifestation of these repercussions appeared, soon after the dinner guests had left, in the person of the newly arrived British Ambassador, Derek Riches. Riches told Hammarskjold of the shock and concern of the British government over what was happening in Katanga and asked for an explanation of the day's events and of the various statements which O'Brien was reported to have made. Hammarskjold gave an account of the events that had led up to the outbreak of fighting and stated the main objective of the UN operation, which was to deal with the mercenaries. He recalled that he had already warned the British representative in New York a week before that firmer measures might be required.

Riches left about midnight, and Hammarskjold and Linnér went back to ONUC headquarters to examine the latest reports from Katanga. One urgent task was to transmit to New York a report[32] for the Security Council which Linnér's staff had been compiling from the cables and Telex messages received during the day from Elisabethville. Its first paragraph quoted paragraph A-2 of the Security Council resolution of February 21, urging "that measures be taken for the immediate withdrawal and evacuation from the Congo of all Belgian and other foreign military and para-military personnel and political advisers not under the United Nations Command, and mercenaries." In spite of ONUC's earlier efforts, at least 104 foreign officers, among them the most active and dangerous mercenaries, had remained at large and overtly planning hostile action against the UN. The report described the UN's military moves in the early hours of September 13 as "security precautions similar to those applied on 28 August, and deemed necessary to prevent inflammatory broadcasts or other threats to the maintenance of law and order, while the United Nations resumed carrying out its task of apprehending and evacuating foreign military and para-military personnel. At this point an alert was set since arson was discovered at an ONUC garage. As the United Nations troops were proceeding towards the garage premises, fire was opened on them from the building* where a number of foreign officers are known to be staying. United Nations troops were subsequently also resisted and fired at as they were deploying towards key points or while they were guarding installations in the city. United Nations troops returned fire."[34] The report ended by saying that during the afternoon of Sep-

---

* The original draft had read "the building where the Belgian Consulate is located."[33] Hammarskjold had queried this and discovered that the Belgian Consulate occupied only one floor. He felt that the implications of the original draft were too sweeping and changed it.

tember 13 the Central Government had dispatched to Elisabethville a delegation headed by the Commissaire d'Etat for Katanga, E. D. Bocheley-Davidson, to assist the provincial authorities in the restoration of law and order, and that the UN had sent a team of technical experts to help in the restoration of essential utilities and public services.

Hammarskjold certainly read and approved this report, which was cabled to New York about 2 a.m. on September 14. It described the operation in Elisabethville in the context of the policy which he had consistently pursued in the Congo and which he still assumed to be the policy of his representatives in the field. Linnér had already informed New York early on September 13, before the Secretary-General reached Leopoldville, that the objective of the operation was to "apprehend for evacuation the remaining foreign military personnel and foreign officials of the Sûreté, after taking security precautions necessary to perform this task."[35] That Hammarskjold had not authorized the timing of the action did not alter the objectives that had been agreed upon, nor did the military preparations and moves reported by O'Brien and Raja suggest that the objective of the action had been radically changed or that its purpose was to end by force the secession of a regime supported by an army of some 15,000 men and a small but active and totally unopposed air force. In the continuous exchanges of messages between Leopoldville and Elisabethville on September 13 and on succeeding days, no suggestion was made from either end that the ending by force of Katangese secession was the objective of the action, rather than the objective described in the report to the Security Council.*

---

* Nearly a year later O'Brien, in *To Katanga and Back*, attacked this report as a deliberate misrepresentation by Hammarskjold of the origins of the fighting and of the objective of the UN action, which O'Brien then maintained was the ending of the Katanga secession by force. "The UN action had been designed solely towards that end," he wrote in mid-1962, "and from that end it was now beginning, murkily and irresolutely, to recede."[36] If this was O'Brien's idea of the objective of the operation at the time and he thought that it was also Hammarskjold's objective, he did not see fit to mention the fact either at the time to his colleagues in Leopoldville or later in New York, or in his *Observer* articles[37] written in December 1961. In these, although he did say that he "felt there was some serious misunderstanding, the nature of which we could not grasp, between ourselves and Mr. Hammarskjold,"[38] he stated firmly that the necessity for the instructions given him by Khiary "arose from Tshombe's resistance, encouraged from the outside, to the implementation of the Security Council resolutions," and that "the UN was committed" by the resolution of February 21 "to withdrawal and evacuation of foreign officers."[39] Hammarskjold himself had consistently and publicly refused from the earliest days of ONUC to consider any attempt by the UN to end the Katanga secession by force.

In his book O'Brien adduced, as further evidence of the misleading nature of this report, the fact that the arson in the ONUC garage was not reported by him and never took place—in fact, his chapter on the report to the Security Council is entitled

Thursday, September 14, brought little encouragement. Hammarskjold called on President Kasavubu in the morning and in the afternoon talked with Adoula about the future role of the UN in the Congo, but his mind was on the increasingly serious situation in Elisabethville. O'Brien reported that UN buildings were being fired on and there seemed little hope of contacting Tshombe. It was agreed that the Katangese "Vice-President" Kibwe, the sole Katangese Minister detained by the UN on September 13, should be released in an effort to get hold of Tshombe and to arrange a cease-fire. O'Brien suggested that the British and Belgian consulates, which he believed to have encouraged Tshombe to continue his resistance, should be closed down and that if necessary UN troops should surround Tshombe's residence. He also reported a rumor that Tshombe was in the British consulate and asked urgently for authorization to capture him there if necessary. Hammarskjold firmly turned down this request, saying he would deal with the matter through the British embassy in Leopoldville.

An Irish infantry company, which had been sent, at the insistence of the European consuls and against O'Brien's better judgment, to protect the Europeans in Jadotville was now surrounded and under attack, and the UN rescue party was being held up at a bridge twenty kilometers away. The UN garrison at Kamina had also been attacked. In Elisabethville sporadic firing persisted, and the UN forces continued to suffer casualties, although Raja maintained that the military situation was under control. The single Fouga jet aircraft dominated the skies. The UN was on the defensive, and a long and bitter struggle seemed likely. O'Brien was in favor of stronger measures to avert this possibility and asked for reinforcements and for fighter-bombers.

"The Fire in the Garage." I have been unable to trace the origin of Linnér's mention of this particular incident. However, the first report from Linnér to New York on the Elisabethville operation in the early morning of September 13, which was based on messages from Elisabethville, gives the "burning of UN vehicles" as one of the reasons for the decision to round up the remaining foreign military personnel with the accompanying "security measures," and two months later I was shown the garage in Elisabethville where UN vehicles were said to have been set on fire. In any case, this alleged inaccuracy hardly sustains the broad accusation of misrepresentation that O'Brien, after a year's thought, made against Hammarskjold in his book. O'Brien gave as an additional proof of misrepresentation in the report to the Security Council the fact that "Morthor," the military code name given to the September 13 operation, is the Hindi word for "smash" and would have been quite inappropriate for the limited operation which was described in the report. In fact, "Morthor" was a purely local code-name and was unknown at the time to anyone in New York. The first time New York became aware of the existence of an operation called "Morthor" was in a military situation report from McKeown, received at Headquarters at 11:47 Greenwich Mean Time on September 13, some seven hours after the operation had started.

The repercussions of the fighting in Katanga and of O'Brien's statements to the press, heralded by the British Ambassador's visit the night before, began to build up in earnest. Bunche reported that President Kennedy and Dean Rusk were "extremely upset" that there had been no consultation with the U.S. government, which provided the largest share of the financial and logistical support for the UN operation in the Congo. Rusk had urged that Hammarskjold bring Adoula and Tshombe together and warned that U.S. support would evaporate if the Gizenga line was to become dominant. Hammarskjold was infuriated by this "extraordinary démarche," which seemed to him to be virtually a defense of the mercenaries. The United States had not objected to the expulsion of the Belgian officers on August 28, but what, he asked, had they done since then to bring Tshombe to his senses? The British, too, through their consul in Elisabethville, had done nothing to persuade Tshombe to accept a cease-fire and had simply allowed him to vanish. "It is better," he told Bunche to tell Rusk, "for the UN to lose the support of the U.S. because it is faithful to law and principles than to survive as an agent whose activities are geared to political purposes never avowed or laid down by the major organs of the UN. . . . It is nice to hear these parties urge 'most strongly' that we do everything in our power to bring Adoula and Tshombe together after having gone, on our side, to the extreme point in that direction without any noticeable support at the crucial stages from those who now complain."[40]

While the African and Asian countries applauded the firmness of the UN action, Salisbury, Brussels, and London joined in a swelling chorus of disapproval. Sir Roy Welensky sent troops, armored cars, and planes to the frontier because of a "serious threat"[41] to Rhodesian security and stated in Parliament that "nothing so disgraceful in the whole history of international organisations"[42] had ever happened before. In Belgium, ONUC was accused of a "premeditated crime,"[43] and O'Brien was compared to the Nazis. In Lisbon, Hammarskjold was accused of having a "personal interest"[44] in Katanga because his eldest brother was alleged to be chairman of a Swedish-American firm* with investments in the region, a libel taken up eagerly in some other Western countries. In Britain, Lord Lansdowne, the British Parliamentary Under-Secretary of State for the Foreign Office, was summoned from a grouse moor and told to fly at once to Leopoldville.**

---

* Hammarskjold's eldest brother, Bo Hammarskjold, was a board member of the Swedish-American-Liberian Mining Company, LAMCO.
** Lansdowne had in fact been due to come to the Congo about September 19 anyway to inquire about the August 28 roundup operation, and his visit was simply advanced by a few days.

Spaak also expressed his concern over the events in Elisabethville and at some of the statements attributed to O'Brien.

The world press, radio, and television were having a field day with the Katanga situation and were making it difficult to keep delegates at the UN properly informed and calm. Most unfortunate of all was the statement repeatedly attributed to O'Brien to the effect that the UN action in Elisabethville was taken at the request of the central government and marked the end of the secession in Katanga. It would be helpful, Bunche cabled Hammarskjold, to find out what O'Brien had really said so that the necessary corrections could be made. If by this time Hammarskjold had concluded that something was wrong with O'Brien's conception of UN policy and that the Accra Reuters report had not been "tendentious" after all, his understanding of O'Brien's current difficulties prevented him from adding to them. "We do not know," he replied to Bunche, "what O'Brien may have said and we hesitate to press him on such matters just now but my best guess would be that he said, as a statement of fact, that with the alleged flight of Tshombe and Munongo [from Elisabethville] obviously secession had ceased. If he did, this was diplomatically imprudent but decently intelligent readers should be able to distinguish between a statement of fact concerning result of a specific operation and a statement concerning immediate aim of this same operation. Psychologically such a reaction as his should be understandable in view of the fact that, to my knowledge, all members of the UN are for the cessation of Katanga separatism as established UN aim, although an aim not to be achieved by the initiative of offensive action against Katangese forces."[45]*

Hammarskjold was not unduly alarmed at the reactions of the Western press, which he attributed in large degree to Tshombe's propaganda machine and which, he told Bunche, "may be a nuisance but have as usual very little lasting significance."[47] It was not unusual for the general public to "spontaneously take the side of the bum against the policeman."[48] On the evening of September 14, after a dinner given by Adoula in his honor at the restaurant in the Leopoldville Zoo, Hammarskjold and Linnér again returned to ONUC headquarters to work until 3 a.m. on cables and on the report of the day's events to the Security Council.

---

* After Hammarskjold's death, O'Brien was again asked about his statement to the press on September 13, which was an important part of the historical record, and he finally denied having made it in the form reported. In *To Katanga and Back*, however, he admitted that he had, in fact, made it but had later told UN Headquarters in New York that he had not, "because I was rather childishly anxious to reinstate myself in their good graces."[46]

On the fifteenth, Hammarskjold decided that he would not return to New York as early as he had intended, and that instead he must try to consolidate the UN position and at the same time find a way to end the fighting. The activities of the Katangese Fouga aircraft had prompted both O'Brien and Bunche to suggest independently that the UN must quickly acquire a small number of fighter aircraft, and he instructed Bunche to make urgent requests to Ethiopia, Sweden, and India and to get clearance from Great Britain for the transit and overflight of the aircraft through Kenya and Uganda to the Congo. Ethiopia responded at once, but the request for overflight clearance from the British encountered determined procrastination. Hammarskjold had also asked the United States for transport planes to fly reinforcements to Elisabethville from Stanleyville, but on September 16 he learned that the U.S. planes had been recalled "by higher authority" from Kano [Nigeria] while actually en route to the Congo— "a sad reminder," he commented to Bunche, "of our experience after Bizerte."[49]*

To get a better idea of what was going on, Hammarskjold sent the ONUC commander, General McKeown, to Elisabethville. He also replied to O'Brien's query about how to deal with the Katangese Ministers. Every effort was to be made to complete the removal of non-Congolese military personnel and political advisers. Ministers who had taken part in recent disturbances and had interfered with the UN or incited civil war should be placed in custody by the UN, but not in execution of the Central Government's warrants that Khiary had given O'Brien. Tshombe himself should be protected and brought in touch with the central government's Commissaire d'Etat, or, if that proved too bitter a pill for him to swallow, he should be urged to request the UN to take him to Leopoldville at once. O'Brien reported that Tshombe would meet him at the British consulate in the late afternoon of September 15 and that he would propose to Tshombe an immediate unconditional forty-eight-hour cease-fire with an exchange of prisoners. Tshombe failed to appear for this meeting, and as the evening wore on the news got worse. The Fouga strafed UN troops in Elisabethville, O'Brien's headquarters, the Irish company at Jadotville, and the airfield at Kamina. That evening in Leopoldville there was a UN reception at La Devinière, where the year before Hammarskjold had been harangued by Gizenga. The Secretary-General

---

* Hammarskjold referred to the putting off of his request for U.S. aircraft to repatriate the Tunisian troops from the Congo during the Bizerte crisis the previous July. Both Great Britain and the United States quickly granted his requests on September 18 after his death. It turned out that the Ethiopian fighters would not have made any immediate difference, since they were not ready for active service.

was serious and preoccupied, and even the newly found solidarity of Gizenga and Adoula provided little solace. During a dinner given that evening in his honor by President Kasavubu, Hammarskjold was informed that Radio Katanga had announced that, of the Irish company in Jadotville, fifty-seven were dead and ninety were prisoners. This report soon proved to be as untrue as most of Radio Katanga's broadcasts, but it provided a suitably gloomy ending to a dismal day.

Going over reports at ONUC Headquarters after Kasavubu's dinner, Hammarskjold realized more clearly than ever that a cease-fire was the essential preliminary to any useful action. But a cease-fire depended on talking to Tshombe, and who could do that now? As to Lansdowne, whom he was to meet in the morning, he told Bunche, "I shall receive him simply for information and courtesy."[50] Before he went to bed he drafted a letter to Tshombe, setting out the UN position and holding out the hope of an immediate cease-fire followed by a meeting to bring about national conciliation, to be arranged if necessary at a place outside the Congo.[51]

Saturday, September 16, was a decisive day, and for Hammarskjold a day of mounting frustration. The Fouga triumphantly operated all over South Katanga, strafing the troops trying to relieve the Irish at Jadotville, shooting up a UN DC-3 transport in the air, and dropping bombs on the airfield at Kamina. UN positions all over Katanga were attacked by the mercenary-led Gendarmerie. Sir Roy Welensky met with two of Tshombe's Ministers and later released a message from Tshombe in which he made the cease-fire conditional on all UN troops quitting Katanga and threatened "total war" as the alternative. The Congo Parliament formally decided to invade Katanga. The Secretary-General's civilian and military representatives smarted under the beating they were taking, both in Katanga and in the Western press, and asked for the authorization and the means to hit back. Tshombe and Munongo were reported by British sources to be conveniently poised half a mile from the Rhodesian border.

During the day, Hammarskjold received an almost uninterrupted stream of criticism, advice, and thinly veiled threats, mostly from people who might have been expected to know better. His main impression, he told Bunche, was of total misunderstanding and a complete ignorance of the realities of the Congo. The process began in the morning with Lord Lansdowne. Although Lansdowne himself was restrained and courteous, from Hammarskjold's point of view his mission to Leopoldville was a considerable embarrassment. Lansdowne's arrival was bitterly resented not only by Hammarskjold's own staff, who regarded it as a blatant example of attempted great-power pressure, but also by the Congolese government, whose members felt that the visit was an interference in their relationship with the UN and a direct encouragement to Tshombe. The Congolese Parliament had even considered a resolution expelling Lansdowne from the Congo. Partly as a result of these feelings, a quite unwarranted importance was later attributed to Lansdowne's visit, and in some accounts of Hammarskjold's death Lansdowne has even been cast as the major villain. As far as Hammarskjold was concerned, the talks with Lansdowne were in reality little more than a matter of "courtesy and information," and an additional source of irritation. He already knew the British position from the British Ambassador, and he had long been conscious of the sympathy for Tshombe which underlay Britain's lip service to the UN's objectives in Katanga. He had already decided, in the small hours of September 16, that he himself must meet Tshombe somewhere outside the Congo, and at the beginning of his first conversation with Lansdowne he asked if the British government would agree to make the arrangements for a meeting with Tshombe at Ndola in Northern Rhodesia. Lansdowne, somewhat taken aback, undertook to cable London at once for instructions on this request.

Hammarskjold himself clearly foresaw the interpretation that was likely to be put on Lansdowne's visit. "I am certain," he cabled Bunche at 1 a.m. on September 17, ". . . that every paper will take for granted, if and when the approach to Tshombe is made known, that this is result of 'constructive proposals' made by Lansdowne for Western powers. Both groups of governments would rather like this interpretation. (For the record it may be said that the approach was decided upon and message written before I received Lansdowne.)"[52] Lansdowne's own account[53] confirms that the Secretary-General told him at once that a cease-fire was essential, showed him the draft message to Tshombe, and suggested Ndola as the best meeting place. Hammarskjold explained and strongly defended the September 13 action. "Although he did not disagree with my views," Lansdowne reported, "that his officers had made a quite erroneous appreciation of the resistance that they would encounter, he fully accepted responsibility for the action that they had taken."[54] Lansdowne mentioned the discrepancies between Hammarskjold's account and O'Brien's reported statements and undertook to give him a list of these statements as reported by the British consul in Elisabethville. Hammarskjold told Lansdowne that he would like to examine this question himself before making any comment. "At the end of this meeting," Lansdowne told the House of Lords a month later, "I had formed the impression that many of the apparently more outrageous aspects of the United Nations action as we had seen them from London were inaccurate or exaggerated. I thought that there had been a gross miscalculation of the effect of the United Nations action, and that this was due to ineptitude and bad judgement."[55]

Lansdowne was later alleged to have presented Hammarskjold with an ultimatum to stop the fighting in Katanga or to forego British support. Certainly the major objective of Lansdowne's visit was to make clear the dismay of British public opinion at the action in Katanga and the effect this might well have on the government's attitude toward the UN Congo operation. But Hammarskjold's principal preoccupation since his arrival in Leopoldville had been to arrange a cease-fire, and he had already worked out the first stages of a plan for so doing. In these circumstances a British ultimatum, even supposing the British government had thought of delivering one, could only have weakened his position.

Later in the day Edmund Gullion, the U.S. Ambassador, delivered a démarche on behalf of President Kennedy, Dean Rusk, and Lord Home, the British Foreign Secretary, asking Hammarskjold to remain in the Congo as long as the hostilities continued, in order to show the "seriousness with which the responsibilities of the Secretary-General under UN resolutions are being carried out."[56] Once again the Western powers were pushing on an open door and compromising the Secretary-General's position by appearing to suggest a course of action that he himself had already decided on. "I assume," Hammarskjold cabled Bunche, "that the same seriousness thus supposedly demonstrated is considered by the distinguished Foreign Ministers and the President to apply also to the terms of the resolutions themselves."[57] Dean Rusk had expressed dismay that the UN should have taken such a serious step at an unfortunate time, thus "jeopardizing what it sought to accomplish in Katanga and in the Congo."[58] "The impact of the Katanga problem," Hammarskjold commented, "on reconciliation of the rest of the Congo and on the balance between leading personalities in the Cabinet was such that what we did was indeed the minimum necessary in order not to 'jeopardize what it (the UN) sought to accomplish.' " He had been struck by Lansdowne's ignorance of the Congo situation. "The main reason for complete misunderstanding of UN action," he told Bunche, "is a complete lack of knowledge of the Congo situation and of what would have been unavoidable in case of failure to respond as we did."[59] He noted, however, that the U.S. and British ambassadors were "quite realistic and certainly helpful."[60]

The UN force commander, General McKeown, had left for Elisabethville on the morning of September 16 in his DC-6B, the *Albertina*. The plane was to return at once to Leopoldville in case the Secretary-General should need it. Hammarskjold was convinced that, apart from the dangerous tensions created within the Central Government by the Katanga situation, there were other factors that made a meeting with Tshombe essential and urgent. He believed that Tshombe himself, if he could be removed from the influence of Munongo and his white advisers, genuinely wanted to meet with Adoula and that Katanga's resistance to the Central Government was to a large extent a propaganda creation that would evaporate if a settlement between Tshombe and Adoula could be reached. The situation in Katanga, he told Bunche, had to be brought "closer to the local realities."[61]

On the morning of September 16, O'Brien had offered, through the British consul in Elisabethville, to meet Tshombe anywhere in Katanga without escort. Hammarskjold told O'Brien that if such a meeting should come about, he should use as his main brief the text of the note to Tshombe that Hammarskjold had drafted in the small hours of September 16.[62] This note, after patiently explaining the UN position, suggested an immediate and unconditional cease-fire with the understanding that Tshombe shared the basic attitudes that were binding on the UN, and it emphasized that the solution of the Congo problem must be found through reconciliation within the framework of the Constitution of the Republic. Once the cease-fire was established, he cabled O'Brien, the UN would wish to continue its discussions with Tshombe and try to bring him together with Adoula, "provided as a minimum that, reaffirming his stand of 28 August, he endorses the objective for our last move which is simply that the 104 [foreign officers] be treated the same way as were the 400 last week. Civil war clause [of the February 21 Security Council resolution] has in this context significance that he should strictly observe military standstill which follows already from cease-fire but also that he should understand that a serious civil war risk will remain acute within the Congo, as well as a risk of the breaking-up of the Republic with catastrophic consequences also for Katanga, as long as people have not got together in search of a constructive approach to conciliation between Katanga and the rest of the Congo."[63]*

---

* O'Brien later chose to interpret Hammarskjold's approach to Tshombe as a virtual surrender. This verdict ignores both the fact that Hammarskjold regarded the Katanga fighting as an incidental interruption of his primary objective, which was to bring Adoula and Tshombe together, and that all over Katanga, as well as in the press of much of the world, the UN was on the defensive. Seen in this broader perspective, his instructions to O'Brien appear rather as a firm and realistic attempt to get the UN, and especially O'Brien and the UN Katanga command, out of an impossible situation into which they had fallen through military and other forms of incompetence. Hammarskjold's approach to Tshombe was designed to end the fighting, to restore the effort of August 28 to expel the mercenaries with Tshombe's cooperation, and to pursue urgently his original objective of bringing Tshombe together with the central government to settle the problem of secession peacefully.

Should the British consul fail to bring O'Brien and Tshombe together, Hammarskjold instructed O'Brien that his letter to Tshombe was to be transmitted urgently to him by whatever means could be arranged. An additional paragraph was then to be added proposing that Tshombe meet Hammarskjold personally and without delay *"pour que nous recherchions ensemble les moyens pacifiques pour résoudre le conflit actuel, ouvrant ainsi la voie à une solution du problème katangais dans le cadre du Congo"*[64] ("so that together we can try to find peaceful methods of resolving the present conflict, thus opening the way to a solution of the Katanga problem within the framework of the Congo"). The text of this letter would be published as soon as it was known that Tshombe had received it. Later in the evening, he cabled the text of his message to Tshombe to Bunche in New York with the comment that, although it had been neither approved by, nor written in consultation with, the Congolese Cabinet, it was sent with their full knowledge and without any objection.

Near midnight on September 16, Tshombe offered, through the British consul in Elisabethville, to meet O'Brien at Bancroft, Northern Rhodesia, at 11:30 a.m. the next day.[65] In passing on this message to Leopoldville, O'Brien advised against accepting a rendezvous in Rhodesia as being "tantamount to accepting something resembling the arbitration of Sir Roy Welensky."[66] Hammarskjold, however, told O'Brien that he would stick to his plan to see Tshombe himself, as already suggested in his message to Tshombe, and that he would meet him at Ndola.

O'Brien was horrified at Hammarskjold's decision to meet with Tshombe in Rhodesia. He felt that the Secretary-General did not understand the situation in Elisabethville and that it was essential at least for him to brief Hammarskjold before the meeting. What O'Brien could not realize was that the situation in Elisabethville, the press reports of statements describing the objective of the UN action as an attempt to end secession by force, and the continued and indecisive fighting had put the UN in a weak position from which Hammarskjold was determined to extricate it by his own initiative and on a level above the imbroglio in Katanga.

If O'Brien thought that Hammarskjold did not understand the situation in Katanga, Hammarskjold himself had just received further confirmation that O'Brien and his staff did not understand the position on which he had based his policy in the Congo. On September 16 the *New York Times* correspondent in Elisabethville quoted one of O'Brien's assistants as saying over the UN-controlled Elisabethville radio that the UN was "determined to stand by its decision to implement the Security Council resolution of February 21, and to end the secession of Katanga," adding that all civilians caught as snipers would be shot. This time there was no doubt as to what had been said, since ONUC headquarters in Leopoldville had monitored the broadcast, and Hammarskjold delivered a stinging rebuke. "It is obviously intolerable," he cabled O'Brien in the early hours of September 17, "to read that UN was resolutely decided to carry out the operation it has launched in order to put an end to the Katanga secession, to quote only one of the many erroneous and damaging judgments and statements. Will you please instruct ———— that as long as UN has anything to do with running station, news reporting has to be conducted in as impartial and accurate repeat accurate manner as possible."[67]

To O'Brien's suggestion that Hammarskjold pick him up at Kamina on the way to Ndola, Hammarskjold replied: "You will understand my reasons to desire the present phase to be outside ONUC framework and in my own hands. For those reasons I do not repeat not approve of your going to Ndola but please get through Dunnett [the British consul] across to Tshombe urgently that even without having received his reply to my last message, with observations on his reaction to my original message to him, I shall go as early as possible today to Ndola so as to see to it that no time is lost in reaching the aim which we share. Naturally he should understand that my position as defined in my two messages is the basis on which I go to Ndola and that further developments must depend on his reaction to my reply."[68]

Hammarskjold's final decision to go to Ndola had been influenced by an assessment of Tshombe's state of mind very different from O'Brien's. His relative optimism had been increased by a report from O'Brien's headquarters in Elisabethville, which, like much information from that rumor-befogged town, turned out to be misleading. To Bunche at 5 a.m. on September 17, in a tone very different from the frustration of his previous messages, Hammarskjold cabled as follows:

> We have received two very important pieces of news . . . gendarmerie troops in Jadotville have kicked out white officers and fraternize with Irish. Finally, they seem to have got our point.* Further, Tshombe has, through British Consul, asked O'Brien to meet him tomorrow morning**

---

* The Jadotville development was reported to the Security Council on September 17, but later in the same document a "sudden change" at noon on September 17 at Jadotville was reported. The Irish company was being held as hostages by the gendarmerie, and all communication with them had been cut off.[69]
** This cable was drafted very late on September 16 and was actually transmitted on September 17. "Tomorrow," therefore, was September 17.

11:30 in Bancroft, Northern Rhodesia. In reply to this last mentioned suggestion we ask O'Brien to transmit my message to Tshombe of which you have already got text. [Then follows the paragraph suggesting a meeting at Ndola.]* You will see from this that we shall go tomorrow to Northern Rhodesia provided we get through to Eville [Elisabethville] (always hazardous) and satisfactory reply is received in time. After Jadotville development and in view of other changes of situation, I would expect favorable reaction. Were Tshombe to decide to go back with us to Leopoldville, this would be quite possible.[71]

The tone of this message is hardly that of the desperate appeaser whom O'Brien compared, a year later, to Chamberlain on the way to Munich.[72] After four days of frustration Hammarskjold had decided on a positive course of action.** He hoped that by holding talks with Tshombe away from the hatred, violence, and sinister influences of Elisabethville, an atmosphere of which O'Brien, through no fault of his own, was an important part, he might, by persuasion and forceful argument, still achieve the original objective of his visit to the Congo —to bring Adoula and Tshombe together.

Sunday, September 17, was a relatively quiet day for Hammarskjold. His decision was taken, and he awaited Tshombe's reply. He met with Lansdowne again in the morning and again pressed for British clearance for the Ethiopian jets to fly over Kenya and refuel in Uganda. Lansdowne's response was sufficiently negative to cause him, after the meeting, to tell Bunche to investigate urgently the possibility of the Ethiopian fighters coming to the Congo via Juba in the Sudan. The main point of business with Lansdowne was the

---

*The additional paragraph read: "I have been informed of the message received by Mr. O'Brien from Mr. Dunnett, the British Consul, inviting him to meet you tomorrow at 11:30 a.m. at Bancroft in Northern Rhodesia. I suggest that I should meet you personally, so that together we can try to find peaceful methods of resolving the present conflict, thus opening the way to a solution of the Katanga problems within the framework of the Congo. The proposed meeting obviously requires that orders should be given beforehand for an immediate and effective cease-fire. I therefore propose to you that such a cease-fire should be firmly imposed by both sides, so as to make a meeting possible and to come nearer to a solution of the present conflict within the framework established by the Security Council and already accepted by you. As I shall have to go to the meeting place by air, I suggest that the meeting should be at Ndola. I am dependent on our transport facilities and for this reason the hour which you propose is impossible for me. I shall inform you as early as possible tomorrow morning of my time of arrival, allowing for the fact that before I leave I must have your reply to this message, including your decision regarding the cease-fire. The cease-fire will occur automatically on the UN side, in view of the fact that according to the instructions given and the rules followed by the Organization, it only opens fire in self-defense."[70]

** Bill Ranallo wrote in his last letter to his wife, on the morning of September 17: "The boss has been in such a depressed mood—worse than any time I have known him. . . . He was much better last night because he's set up a parley with Tshombe in Ndoula [sic] for some time today."[73]

Ndola meeting. Hammarskjold turned down Lansdowne's offer to accompany him to Ndola, which would, he said, inevitably be misinterpreted. However, since it was necessary to make proper preparations at Ndola for his arrival, he put at Lansdowne's disposal a UN DC-4 that had previously been slated for his own use. Lansdowne was to precede him and check the arrangements at Ndola, it being understood that he would not talk to Tshombe and that he would leave Ndola before the Secretary-General arrived. Lansdowne also gave him the note he had promised on the previous day, in which O'Brien's statements on September 13, 14, and 15, as reported by Dunnett, were set out in detail together with Dunnett's account of his own part in the events of September 13 and 14.

Hammarskjold's optimism was not universally shared, and his plan to meet Tshombe was viewed with gloom in several quarters. Khiary, who believed, wrongly, that Lansdowne had persuaded him to go to Ndola, felt that for political reasons it was a mistake, and that he himself should go in Hammarskjold's place. Hammarskjold explained to him that *"intérêts supérieurs"* demanded that he should go. Khiary, with Lansdowne in mind, seems to have interpreted these interests as being the fear of the loss of British support, but from Hammarskjold's own communications it is obvious that he was referring to the hope of bringing Tshombe and Adoula together. In any case, he told Khiary, he would be asking him to discuss the details of the Katanga cease-fire plan with Tshombe after he himself had returned to New York. Prime Minister Adoula, although his Cabinet had not objected to Hammarskjold's message to Tshombe, had grave misgivings about the Ndola rendezvous. When Linnér visited him after Hammarskjold had taken off, Adoula upbraided him for agreeing to the plan and said that he would have stopped the plane taking off if he had known the details. Adoula's premonitions turned to grief and horror when he learned that the plane had crashed. But Hammarskjold was a man who made his own decisions, and once he had decided, his particular kind of personal authority effectively discouraged argument.

Tshombe's reply[74] was given to O'Brien by the British consul at 10 a.m. on September 17 and was immediately transmitted to Leopoldville. Tshombe agreed in principle to an immediate cease-fire but stipulated that UN troops should be confined to their camps and that the UN should cease all troop movements and all reinforcement by ground and air. He agreed to go to Ndola, asked for a suitable light aircraft, and stated that he would be accompanied by Kibwe, his "Minister of Finance," Kimba, his "Foreign Secretary," and Mwenda-Odilon, his "Secretary for the Common Market." This arrogant answer was unacceptable to Hammarskjold, who replied at once as follows:

> Kindly inform Mr. Tshombe that the Secretary-General finds it impossible to accept the conditions for a cease-fire and a meeting which have been conveyed to him.
>
> According to the terms of the letter from the Secretary-General, in the existing circumstances, there can be no question of anything but an unconditional cease-fire, and an agreement of both parties to meet together, all other modalities obviously to be discussed in the course of the meeting. The Secretary-General cannot agree to meet Mr. Tshombe unless this preliminary agreement, which is fully in accord with normal practice, is accepted.
>
> The Secretary-General regrets that by introducing conditions, Mr. Tshombe has delayed the taking of measures to protect human life. He sincerely hopes that a favourable reply to his observations by Mr. Tshombe will make possible a meeting without further delay.
>
> As regards military movements and maintaining the positions of the various military groups, the cease-fire order should naturally be interpreted as having no effect on the status quo, which is to be maintained in all respects throughout the period during which an agreement is being sought.[75]

The British consul, who received this reply at 2 p.m. for transmittal to Tshombe, informed O'Brien that Tshombe had chartered a plane and was taking off for Ndola in less than an hour. In the absence of further word from Tshombe, Hammarskjold decided that he would go to Ndola anyway.[76]

The DC-4 originally reserved for the Secretary-General had been assigned to Lansdowne, because the faster DC-6B, the *Albertina*, had returned early that morning from Elisabethville. Lansdowne was having lunch with John Powell-Jones of the British embassy when he was informed that he should take off at once. He called Hammarskjold before leaving for the airport, and, after stopping at the embassy to pick up his luggage, was driven to the airport by Linnér's assistant, Jacques Poujoulat. Lansdowne took off at 4:04 p.m. (3:04 p.m. GMT)* and, flying by a direct route, landed at Ndola at 10:35 p.m. local time, to find that Lord Alport, the British High Commissioner in Salisbury, was already there to make the necessary arrangements. After a brief courtesy meeting with Tshombe, Lansdowne boarded his plane to take off for Salisbury, as he had agreed to do, before Hammarskjold arrived.

When the *Albertina* landed at Ndjili at 8 a.m. local time (7:00 a.m.

---

* Local time in the Congo is one hour ahead of Greenwich Mean Time; local time in Rhodesia is two hours ahead.

GMT) on September 17, the crew reported that it had been fired at on taking off from Elisabethville. A thorough inspection revealed that the No. 2 engine had been hit by a bullet which had penetrated the cowling and struck an exhaust pipe. The exhaust pipe was replaced, and the plane, fully refueled, was ready to take off again by noon. It stood on the airfield with doors locked and all ladders removed but not under special security supervision until about four in the afternoon, when the crew arrived. The crew was the one that had flown McKeown to Elisabethville the day before except for the chief pilot, Captain Per Hallonquist, and they had arranged to take it in turns to sleep on the flight in order to have the requisite hours of rest. Because of the Katanga Air Force's Fouga, it was decided to observe radio silence on the flight to Ndola, but a radio operator, Karl Erik Rosén, was added to the crew to receive and send emergency messages, while a special radio monitoring post was established at Ndjili to maintain a listening watch for the aircraft. The radio operators were to communicate in Morse code in Swedish as an additional security precaution.

Shortly after his arrival at the airport, Captain Hallonquist filed a flight plan for Luluabourg in order to get permission for take-off without revealing the *Albertina's* true destination, although he told Major Ljungkvist of ONUC air operations that he was actually going to Ndola. The last beacon to be used was Luluabourg, and Hallonquist was to plot the remainder of the route in flight, "dependent upon the special conditions." Hallonquist was a navigation specialist and would do the navigation himself.

Expecting to be away for just one night, Hammarskjold took only a briefcase with him, leaving everything else at Linnér's villa, including his wallet, checkbook, key ring, a typed copy of an article he had written during the summer for the Yearbook of the Swedish Tourist Association on his youth at Uppsala Castle entitled "Slottsbacken" ("Castle Hill"), a copy of the first twelve typed pages of his translation into Swedish of Martin Buber's *Ich und Du*, and a book he had been reading, Thomas à Kempis's *Imitation of Christ.** Apart from his personal effects, his briefcase contained a small extra copy of the Charter and a small English edition of the New Testament and Psalms, both of which were always in the briefcase he travelled with; Rainer Maria Rilke's *Duineser Elegien* and *Die Sonette an Orpheus*; Buber's *Ich und Du* and an English edition of it translated by Ronald Gregor Smith; a writing pad to be used for his own translation; a book he

---

* The bookmark left in this book was a slip of paper with the Secretary-General's oath of office typed on it.

had recently bought, Jean Giono's *Noé*, of which the pages were never cut; the letter and notes received that morning from Lansdowne; and a map of New York State with areas around Brewster circled in pencil as suitable for walks.

Shortly after 4:30 p.m. local time (3:30 p.m. GMT) the Secretary-General and his party* arrived at Ndjili. Hammarskjold and Linnér paused at the steps to the aircraft to talk, while Bill Ranallo and Harold Julien, the ONUC acting chief of security who was to fly with the party, searched the cabin as a final check. A last-minute cable was delivered straight from the Telex, still in tape form. The tape fluttered in the warm wind as Hammarskjold read it and then passed it to Wieschhoff and Linnér. The party then embarked, and Linnér, who had gone on board for a last farewell, came out again. The door was closed and the plane quickly taxied to the runway. At 4:51 p.m. local time (3:51 p.m. GMT) it took off into the sultry overcast.

Since there was no flight plan, the exact route of the *Albertina* is not known, but it is thought to have flown two sides of a triangle, first due east from Leopoldville to Lake Tanganyika and then south, skirting the Congolese border, toward Ndola. Hammarskjold's briefcase, which survived the crash intact, gives the only known detail of what went on in the aircraft during the flight. Hammarskjold continued his translation of *Ich und Du*, his flowing script filling the pages of the yellow legal-size pad. The writing was firm and neat, and there were very few corrections.

The *Albertina* was next heard from at 8:02 p.m. GMT, more than four hours after take-off, when it called the Salisbury flight information center and asked for the ETA (expected time of arrival) at Ndola of Lansdowne's aircraft. It gave its own ETA at Ndola as 10:35 p.m. GMT (12:35 a.m. local time). Half an hour later it reported its position at a point over the southern end of Lake Tanganyika. Salisbury informed the *Albertina* that Lansdowne had landed at 10:35 p.m. (8:35 p.m. GMT). When asked, first by the Salisbury flight information center and then by the Ndola control tower, what its plans were, the *Albertina* replied that it would be taking off again almost immediately but was unable to say for what destination. The aircraft informed the Ndola tower that it would give its future intentions after it had landed. Hammarskjold apparently intended to keep the plane at

---

* Hammarskjold's party consisted of Heinrich A. Wieschhoff, Vladimir Fabry, William Ranallo, Miss Alice Lalande, Sergeant Harold M. Julien, Sergeant Serge L. Barrau, Sergeant Francis Eivers, Warrant Officer S. O. Hjelte, and Private P. E. Persson. The crew members were Captain Per Hallonquist, Captain Nils-Eric Aahréus, second pilot Lars Litton, flight engineer Nils Göran Wilhelmsson, assistant purser Harald Noork, and radio operator Karl Erik Rosén.

Ndola for the night and to send it to Elisabethville early the next day to bring McKeown to Ndola. At 11:35 p.m. local time (9:35 p.m. GMT) the *Albertina* told Ndola it would arrive at twenty minutes after midnight (10:20 p.m. GMT), and at ten minutes after midnight (10:10 p.m. GMT) the *Albertina* informed the Ndola tower that the airfield lights were in sight and that it was descending. The tower replied that it should report when it reached 6,000 feet (above sea level), and the *Albertina* acknowledged the signal. This was the last that was heard from Hammarskjold's aircraft.

On the Ndola airfield, Lansdowne's plane was waiting by the runway to take off when the *Albertina* flew over at about 2,000 feet above the airfield (an altitude of 6,000 feet above sea level), with its navigation lights and flashing anticollision beacon on the high tailfin switched on. The Ndola tower told Lansdowne's plane to wait until the *Albertina* landed, but when twenty-five minutes had passed without further word from the *Albertina*, Lansdowne's aircraft was allowed to take off. Lansdowne, puzzled and already anxious, instructed his pilot to try to contact Hammarskjold's aircraft, but in vain. The *Albertina*, while turning into its landing approach to Ndola, with wheels and flaps lowered, had brushed the treetops nine and a half miles west of the airport, cutting a long curving swathe in the forest. After 250 yards its left wing touched the ground, and the aircraft cartwheeled and disintegrated in a mass of flame. The time of the crash, established by the stopped watches of the passengers, was between 10:11 and 10:13 p.m. GMT on September 17.

Only Harold Julien was alive when the search party finally reached the wreckage on the following afternoon, and he died of burns five days later. Hammarskjold was thrown clear of the wreckage and, alone among the victims, was not burned at all. Although the postmortem showed that he had probably lived for a short time after the crash, his injuries—a severely fractured spine, several broken ribs, a broken breastbone, a broken thigh, and severe internal hemorrhaging—were certainly fatal. He was lying on his back near a small shrub which had escaped the fire, his face extraordinarily peaceful, a hand clutching a tuft of grass.

EPILOGUE

AT NDOLA, AFTER WAITING for some time, Lord Alport concluded that Hammarskjold had decided, perhaps because of information received in flight, to land elsewhere. Apparently agreeing with Alport, the airport authorities also ceased to expect him. A police report of a brilliant flash in the sky in the direction of Mufulira was disregarded, and despite the sudden and total loss of communication with the aircraft, no immediate effort was made to find out what had happened.

The *New York Times* for Monday, September 18, published this Associated Press dispatch from Ndola:

> Secretary-General Dag Hammarskjold and President Moise Tshombe of Katanga Province met for more than an hour here tonight to discuss a cease-fire. The two then drove to Kitwe, 30 miles northwest of Ndola, for what informants said would be the crucial phase of the truce talks.[1]

The correspondents at Ndola had evidently mistaken Lansdowne's arrival for Hammarskjold's.

In New York, Bunche and his colleagues worried through Sunday night without any news. It had long been obvious that something was seriously wrong when, at ten o'clock on Monday morning, a message arrived at last from Colonel Ben Matlick of the U.S. Air Force, who had taken charge of the search, that the wreckage had been sighted from the air and that there was no sign of survivors.

There was an immediate and widespread assumption that foul play had caused the disaster, with the British, the Rhodesians, Tshombe, the Belgians, and the mercenaries being credited singly or collectively with the deed.

Joshua Nkomo, president of the National Democratic Party of Southern Rhodesia, called the crash "a serious indictment of the British Government."[2] The *Indian Express* wrote: "Never even during Suez have Britain's hands been so bloodstained as they are now," and similar accusations were made in the *Ghanaian Times*, which declared, "Hammarskjold was the victim of a deliberate attack inspired by Britain and executed by Roy Welensky and that African traitor Moise Tshombe."[3] The general agreement that only a detailed international investigation could establish the facts did little to restrain these wild recriminations.

In Ndola, Tshombe, evidently shaken, placed a wreath on Hammarskjold's coffin and later met with Khiary, with whom, on September 20, he concluded the cease-fire agreement[4] that had been the first item on Hammarskjold's agenda.

Frederick Boland of Ireland opened the annual session of the General Assembly on September 19 "in the shadow of an immense tragedy."[5] At the United Nations, shock, grief, and a pervading sense of acute personal loss were mingled with general dismay. Much though Hammarskjold had been criticized from all sides in the past year, his empty chair on the podium of the General Assembly Hall symbolized the void left in the life of the Organization by the sudden and permanent absence of his active leadership.

The process of identifying the remains of the other victims of the crash took a whole week, and only on Tuesday, September 26, was the chartered plane which was to bring the coffins home finally able to leave Rhodesia. Stopping for brief ceremonies in Leopoldville, Geneva, and Malmö, the aircraft, escorted by Swedish jet fighters, reached Stockholm exactly at noon on September 28. As it came in to land, all traffic around the airport came to a halt until the solemn ceremony at the airfield was over. Sweden was in full mourning, and in the evening a vast torchlight procession filled the center of Stockholm. At the state funeral in the Cathedral of Uppsala on the following day, King Gustaf Adolf and Queen Louise of Sweden led a throng of representatives from all over the world. After the service the mourners followed Hammarskjold's coffin through the streets of the old town to its last resting place in the Hammarskjold family plot.

On October 23, the Norwegian Storting (Parliament) announced that the Nobel Peace Prize had been awarded to Hammarskjold.

At the United Nations the threads of normal life were gradually picked up again. The UN's position in the Congo and in Katanga remained difficult and dangerous and was weakened still further by the lack of a Secretary-General. This vacuum was filled on November 3 by the election—as Acting Secretary-General to serve out Hammarskjold's term of office—of U Thant, the permanent representative of Burma, one of the two men whom Hammarskjold had thought of as a possible successor. Two days later, fighting between the UN and the mercenary-led Katangese forces broke out again in Elisabethville.

On October 26 the General Assembly set up a Commission of Investigation[6] into the conditions and circumstances of the crash. The Federal Government of Rhodesia and Nyasaland also set up a board of investigation and a commission of inquiry, and the Swedish government made its own investigation. All available evidence was exhaustively examined and the wreckage of the plane submitted to the most detailed tests. While these investigations went on, rumors flourished and mythology took a firm hold.

The UN Investigation Commission submitted its report on April 24,[7] 1962, and, like the other inquiries, it reached no firm conclusion as to the cause of the crash. It reported that it had found "no evidence to support any of the particular theories that have been advanced nor has it been able to exclude the possible causes which it has considered."[8] The possible causes listed were sabotage, attack from ground or air, material failure, and human failure. The commission examined, but found no evidence for, the various rumors of foul play that had come to its attention. It did, however, criticize the Rhodesian authorities for taking fifteen hours to locate the wreckage, only nine and a half miles from the Ndola airfield. The only practical result of an earlier and more diligent search might have been the survival of one passenger, Harold Julien. The incontrovertible fact remained that the aircraft, on its normal approach to the airport, had been a few feet too low to clear the trees on the rising ground beneath it.

Certainly the obsession in Leopoldville with Tshombe's single Fouga Magister jet trainer had much to do with the unusual flight plan of Hammarskjold's aircraft, which imposed a severe strain on the crew. In fact, as the pilot of the Fouga himself later pointed out, the range and equipment of the Fouga made an attack at night on the plane a "logistic and physical impossibility."[9]

Although there is a large—and still growing—literature on Hammarskjold's death, it is significant that none of those who cling to the idea that he was murdered in one way or another have seen fit to demand a new inquiry or to present serious evidence. The main conspiracy theories put forward are mutually exclusive—if one is true, all the others must be false—and so far none of them is backed by anything more than rumor, speculation, and fantasy.

In October 1963, the publication of *Markings*, first in Swedish and a year later in English, gave rise to a new round of mythmaking and speculation. The book was taken in some quarters as evidence that Hammarskjold was a religious fanatic, despite all attempts by scholars and friends to point out that a serious reading would show this to be nonsense. Some passages were even quoted as evidence that he had suicidal tendencies that might account for the nature of his death. The book also provoked, and continues to provoke, a variety of serious studies of which the most illuminating to date is the remarkable work of the nonagenarian Swedish Bishop Gustaf Aulén.[10] *Markings* became a best-seller in many countries, and its sales continue.

In the Congo, after two more skirmishes with the UN, the secession of Katanga came to an end in January 1963. The UN force was withdrawn in June 1964,[11] leaving only the large UN civilian operation to assist the government. Tshombe succeeded Cyrille Adoula as Prime Minister of the central government in July 1964 and faced, in his turn, secession and rebellion. When his government was overthrown in October 1965 he went into exile in Madrid, where he dabbled in conspiracies against his successor, General Joseph Mobutu. Tshombe was kidnapped in midair over the Mediterranean in June 1967 and taken to Algeria, where he died two years later.

At the UN the constitutional controversy over peace-keeping, and especially over the Secretary-General's role in it, to which UNEF and the Congo operation had largely given rise, has continued until the present day, although it has not prevented the setting up of other peace-keeping operations such as the UN force in Cyprus. The chronic indebtedness of the Organization caused by the peace-keeping controversy also remains unresolved, although by late 1971 there were some hopeful signs of an eventual solution.

For some time after Hammarskjold's death the Congo operation, which had caused so much controversy and dissension, was generally regarded with varying degrees of disapproval as an example of the type of involvement that the UN should avoid in the future. Later, however, the turmoil in some other newly independent African countries, and the relative stability and prosperity of the Congo itself, caused a widespread reassessment of this judgment, and the Congo operation began to be regarded increasingly as an ultimately success-

ful effort by the world organization in the face of almost insuperable
difficulties.

President Mobutu remained in power in Leopoldville—now Kinshasa—and established an increasingly firm grip on the Congo, which
in 1971 became the Republic of Zaïre. In October 1970, ten years after
independence, in spite of his uneasy earlier relationship with the UN,
Mobutu declared: "The Democratic Republic of the Congo is a living
testimony to what the United Nations Organization is capable of
when it is given the appropriate means. In the Congo, the United
Nations defended the sovereignty of a country which certain covetous
interests were ready to compromise. The United Nations fulfilled one
of the essential functions which the Charter prescribed to our Organization, that of assuring and guaranteeing the respect of the territorial integrity and the independence of each State Member."[12]

As time and the dramatic nature of his death created around
Hammarskjold's career as Secretary-General a romantic glow that he
would have been the first to deplore, there developed a tendency at
the United Nations to judge current efforts by a hypothetical speculation on what Hammarskjold would have done in the circumstances.
Such comparative speculations have little relevance or usefulness, and
in any case Hammarskjold's highly personal style and approach were
impossible to re-create or to duplicate. His successor, U Thant, succeeded at least in one way in which both his predecessors had failed.
He managed to remain on relatively good terms with all the member
governments of the UN, and especially with the great powers, without
giving up his right to disagree with them on specific issues when he
felt it necessary.

EVEN AFTER ELEVEN YEARS it is difficult to assess Hammarskjold's
achievement. Did his work have important lasting effects, or was he a
brilliant phenomenon, a comet flashing through the sky and leaving
little trace after it has gone? Was he ahead of his time, so that his
ideas will eventually gain a new validity and usefulness? Or was he
more *above* his time in the sense that his personality and exceptional
skill made an impression on his contemporaries out of all proportion
to their lasting political or institutional value?

Hammarskjold was certainly a virtuoso of multilateral diplomacy
and negotiation. The circumstances of his Secretary-Generalship also
had much to do with his success, which owed, in the words of one of
the most perceptive historians of the UN,

a great deal to the singular disposition of world forces at that moment of time. A Russia emancipated from Stalinist paranoia but not yet heady with Khrushchevian ebullience, a United States whose Dulles' Manichaeism was moderated by Eisenhower's old soldier's preference for a quiet life, an Africa more conscious of its dependence on the United Nations than deluded into a conviction of the reverse, and a posse of sophisticated neutrals, the "fire brigade," whose predominantly white skins were not yet thought to disqualify them as fire fighters. Add to this the happy accident that the fires themselves broke out in areas to which the United Nations had ready access—the Middle East or Africa—because for various reasons it was in the interest of the super-powers not to aim at total domination there and not to allow conflicts to develop into unquenchable conflagrations. Even the one great exception to this generalization—Hungary—in effect upheld the rule, since here was an intra-bloc flare-up so patently beyond the reach of the machinery of the United Nations that no one who understood the facts of life would blame the organization for not trying to cope with it.[13]

Hammarskjold was very skillful in taking full advantage of this political environment and in using it to foster and increase the UN's effectiveness.

It was when the times began to change, when the cold war reemerged after the summit fiasco of May 1960, emphasizing once again the East-West struggle for influence in the world, and when the real difficulties of the newly independent African states, and the cold-war competition for their allegiance, destroyed the first fine careless rapture of independence, that Hammarskjold's activism ran into serious trouble.

Hammarskjold was essentially a middle-power man. He saw the UN as the protector and helper of small and new states, and as an institution through which the established medium powers could bring their wisdom and expertise to bear on the world scene. As Secretary-General he was a natural leader and coordinator in this process, even when it meant disaffecting the greatest powers.

Hammarskjold believed that a reliable and just world order could only be built pragmatically by making precedents and by case law. By this process he hoped that the UN would be gradually transformed from an institutional mechanism into a constitutional instrument recognized and respected by all nations. During this process the only guarantee that such an evolution would not be subverted by baser motives was a fearless adherence to the principles of the Charter, the nearest thing to a constitution which the nations of the world have yet formally recognized.

How far Hammarskjold succeeded in these infinitely ambitious aims is still hard to judge. Certainly he gave the Secretary-Generalship and the Secretariat—and to some extent the United Nations itself— a new status. He provided the most dynamic and striking leadership an international organization had ever had, and he personified the ideals of the Charter in action in a way that made a profound impression on hundreds of millions of people all over the world. In the end he carried this implicit challenge to national sovereignty further than some of the more powerful states were prepared to tolerate. In doing this he displayed a certain overconfidence born of the successes of previous years —an overconfidence that disturbed many governments in addition to those which actively opposed him.

Hammarskjold perfected a style of active but quiet diplomacy which proved extraordinarily successful in a series of seemingly hopeless situations. He improvised a variety of original instruments of multilateral preventive diplomacy, UN peace-keeping forces, observer groups, UN "presences," and various experiments in "good offices." He gave the Secretariat a new pride in itself and the concept of international service a new involvement and meaning.

Perhaps most important of all, he showed that one man, if sufficiently spirited and courageous, could stand up for principle against even the greatest powers and that in doing so he might sometimes have an influence on important events. He did this in the full knowledge that it might eventually put an end to his own usefulness. In speaking up for the common interest in peace and decency he also showed the potential of the office of the Secretary-General, as a political organ of the United Nations, to act when intergovernmental organs, and especially the Security Council, were frustrated by the conflicting interests of the great powers.

The journey which Hammarskjold undertook from that day in 1953 when, "with a strong feeling of personal insufficiency,"[14] he arrived in New York, to the night when his aircraft plunged to destruction, was long and arduous. History will form a measured judgment of his stewardship. Until then his ideas, his achievements, and his failures must speak for themselves.

Dag Hammarskjold was that most unusual of creatures, a truly good man. His integrity was absolute. His intellect was acute and subtle. His political judgment was by no means infallible, but he erred comparatively rarely. He was alert, responsible, and sensitive. His character was elusive, partly because he deeply disliked the idea of being a public "personality" and went to great lengths to preserve the privacy of his personal life. He was a man involved in momentous issues which he came to symbolize, even in death. He inspired loyalties and affections of remarkable intensity and duration. By his skill, stamina, and resourcefulness he made a new art of multilateral diplomacy. He gave a fresh dimension to the task of international service by the qualities of his mind and of his compassionate nature. He was an outstanding proponent of the conviction that our fate is what we make it.

From among the countless tributes paid to him after his death, perhaps the deepest chord in Hammarskjold himself would have been struck by the words spoken over his coffin by the Archbishop of Sweden, Erling Eidem:

> Death, which so unexpectedly and for us all so poignantly fell upon him, our friend and companion: death forces us to face the old and always so disturbing question of the meaning and fulfillment of our life on earth. The answer may be expressed in one word, serve—so measurelessly simple, yet so overwhelmingly filled with significance.

Some Acronyms and Abbreviations

ACABQ	Advisory Committee on Administrative and Budgetary Questions (UN)
ACC	Administrative Committee on Co-ordination (UN)
ADL	Armistice Demarcation Line(s)
ANC	Armée nationale congolaise
AP	Associated Press
CDNI	Committee for the Defense of National Interests (Laos)
CIA	Central Intelligence Agency (U.S.)
ECA	Economic Commission for Africa (UN)
ECAFE	Economic Commission for Asia and the Far East (UN)
ECE	Economic Commission for Europe (UN)
ECOSOC	Economic and Social Council (UN)
FAO	Food and Agriculture Organization
FBI	Federal Bureau of Investigation (U.S.)
FLN	Front de libération nationale (Algeria)
GA	General Assembly (UN)
GATT	General Agreement on Tariffs and Trade
IAEA	International Atomic Energy Agency
IBRD	International Bank for Reconstruction and Development
ICAO	International Civil Aviation Organization

IDA	International Development Association
IDO	International Disarmament Organization (proposed but never set up)
IFC	International Finance Corporation
ILO	International Labor Organization
IMCO	Inter-Governmental Maritime Consultative Organization
IMF	International Monetary Fund
ITU	International Telecommunications Union
NATO	North Atlantic Treaty Organization
OAS	Organization of American States
OEEC	Organization for European Economic Co-operation
ONUC	Opération des Nations Unies au Congo (UN)
OPEX	Program for the Provision of Operational, Executive & Administrative Personnel (UN)
SCUA	Suez Canal Users Association
SEATO	Southeast Asia Treaty Organization
SECCO	Security Council (UN)
TAB	Technical Assistance Board (UN)
UNCA	United Nations Correspondents Association
UNEF	United Nations Emergency Force
UNESCO	United Nations Educational, Scientific, and Cultural Organization
UNICEF	United Nations Children's Fund
UNOGIL	United Nations Observation Group in Lebanon
UNRWA	United Nations Relief & Works Agency for Palestine Refugees in the Near East
UNTSO	United Nations Truce Supervision Organization in Palestine
UPI	United Press International
UPU	United Postal Union
WHO	World Health Organization
WMO	World Meteorological Organization

NOTES

An Explanation to the Notes

References are to books, published articles, published United Nations material, and unpublished material. The term "unpublished" refers largely to material in Hammarskjold's papers to which the author was granted sole access. The published UN material consists of Official Records (OR), Press Releases (PR), and records of Press Conferences (PC).

Official Records include the following further abbreviations:

DC	Disarmament
ES-I, ES-II,	First, Second, Third, and Fourth Emergency
ES-III, ES-IV	Special Sessions of the General Assembly
GA	General Assembly
Res.	Resolution
SC	Security Council
S-III	Third Special Session of the General Assembly

Among the OR, the following document symbols occur:

DC/...	(Disarmament)
A/..., A/C...,	(General Assembly)
A/C...,/PV...,	
A/L...	
E/...	(Economic and Social Council)
S/..., S/PV...	(Security Council)

Among the PR or PC, the following symbols occur:

CO/...	(Congo)
EC/...	(General economic items)
ECOSOC/...	(Economic and Social Council)
HQ/...	(Headquarters)
Note...	(Most of the press conferences have this symbol; the Background press conferences—Background PC—were issued without a symbol.)
PM/...	(Permanent Missions)
SC/...	(Security Council)
SG/...	(Secretary-General. Almost all of the Secretary-General's statements, announcements, and speeches carry this symbol. Whenever the Secretary-General made an intervention in one of the official organs of the UN, reference is made, wherever possible, to both the OR's and PR's. In most cases, the quotation was taken from the [unedited] PR's. Whenever a speech, statement, or announcement was issued without a symbol, it is referred to as "unnumbered.")
TA/...	(Technical Assistance)

Notes

Chapter 1 / Election

1. OR, GA, 392nd meeting, November 10, 1952, paras. 2–11.
2. Ibid., para. 10.
3. Unpublished.
4. Unpublished.
5. Unpublished.
6. Unpublished.
7. OR, SC, 617th meeting, Annex.
8. Unpublished.
9. Unpublished.
10. Joseph P. Lash, *Dag Hammarskjold: Custodian of the Brush-Fire Peace* (New York, 1961), p. 13.
11. Gunnar Jarring, "Dag Hammarskjold, In Memoriam," *Swedish Pioneer Historical Quarterly*, January 1962.
12. Lash, op. cit., p. 13.
13. *Markings*, April 7, 1953. Translated from the original Swedish.
14. Lash, op. cit., p. 7.
15. Carl Schürmann, Introduction to the Dutch translation of *Vägmärken* (*Markings*), *Merkstenen*, translated by R. F. M. Boshouwers (Bruges, 1966). The translation of the Introduction from Dutch into English was made by Schürmann himself.
16. P. Meuty, *Le Monde*, April 3, 1953.
17. Unpublished.
18. S/2975)
    A/2380) April 1, 1953.
19. OR, GA, 423rd meeting, April 7, 1953.
20. Ibid., para. 107.
21. UN Film Archives. Hammarskjold mentioned this remark in a speech to the staff, SG/299, May 1, 1953.
22. SG/287, April 9, 1953—remarks on arrival.
23. OR, GA, 426th meeting, April 10, 1953.
24. Ibid., para. 3.
25. Ibid., paras. 8–13; SG/289/Rev. 1, April 10, 1953.
26. Ibid., para. 58.

Chapter 2 / Dag Hammarskjold

1. PR, HQ/212, June 11, 1964. The unveiling of "Single Form," UN Headquarters.
2. *Markings*, first page, letter to Leif Belfrage.
3. Speech to Swedish Academy, taking his seat, December 20, 1954. Original Swedish.
4. Ibid.
5. Ibid.
6. Ibid.
7. Ibid.
8. Unpublished.
9. Speech to Swedish Academy, December 20, 1954. Original Swedish.
10. Ibid.
11. Ibid.
12. Ibid.
13. *Markings*, "From Uppsala," 8.9.59, p. 180.
14. Speech to Swedish Academy, taking his seat, December 20, 1954. Original Swedish.
15. Sture Petrén, *Svenskt Biografiskt Lexicon*, Vol. XVIII. Original Swedish translated by Sven Ahman.
16. Background press conference, November 13, 1953.
17. *Markings*, p. 82.
18. André Malraux, *Antimémoires*, U.S. ed. (New York, 1968), p. 103.
19. *Markings*, Whitsunday 1961. Translated from the original Swedish.
20. Ibid., 6.23.57, p. 154.
21. Unpublished.
22. PC, Note No. 1571, April 4, 1957.
23. *This I Believe*, compiled by Edward R. Murrow, edited by Raymond Gram Swing (New York, 1954).
24. SG/643, December 20, 1957, speech to Swedish Academy on Linnaeus. Original Swedish translated by Sven Ahman.
25. Bertrand Russell, *Autobiography*, Vol. II (London, 1968), p. 38.
26. *Markings*, 8.4.59. Translated from the original Swedish.
27. Unpublished.
28. *Markings*, 7.29.58. Translated from the original Swedish.
29. Bo Beskow, *Dag Hammarskjold:*

Strictly Personal—A Portrait (New York, 1969), p. 37.
30. *Markings*, 10.25.59. Translated from the original Swedish.
31. Interview with George Ivan Smith, printed in the *Guardian*, January 30, 1969.
32. *Markings*, 4.7.57. Translated from the original Swedish.
33. Ibid., p. 124.
34. Unpublished.
35. Lester Pearson in the Montreal *Star*, September 19, 1961.
36. Unpublished.
37. Unpublished.
38. PC, Note No. 996, December 22, 1954.
39. Speech to Swedish Academy, December 20, 1954. Original Swedish.
40. SG/643, December 20, 1957, speech to Swedish Academy on Linnaeus. Original Swedish translated by Sven Ahman.
41. Note No. 2116, February 27, 1960. Original Swedish translated by Sven Ahman.
42. "Slottsbacken," published in the yearbook of the Swedish Touring Association, January 1, 1962, was translated into English by Alan Blair under the title "Castle Hill," issued by the Dag Hammarskjold Foundation (Uppsala, 1971).
43. SG/643, December 20, 1957, speech to Swedish Academy on Linnaeus. Original Swedish translated by Sven Ahman.
44. Unpublished.
45. Dictated version of extemporary remarks in reply to a speech by the Foreign Minister of Mexico at an official luncheon, Mexico City, April 8, 1959.
46. A/4800/Add. 1, SG/1052 and Corr., August 21, 1961.
47. *Markings*, 11.19–20.55. Translated from the original Swedish.
48. Unpublished.
49. Walter Lippmann in *International Organization*, Vol. XV, No. 4, 1961, p. 547.
50. PC, Note No. 1601, May 16, 1957.
51. Unpublished.

52. Unpublished.
53. Unpublished.
54. Unpublished.
55. Unpublished.
56. PC, Note No. 1226, December 22, 1955.
57. PC, Note No. 2339, May 29, 1961.
58. Unpublished.
59. *Göteborgs Handels och Sjöfartstidning*, November 14, 1970. Original Swedish translated by Sven Ahman.
60. S/643, December 20, 1957, speech to Swedish Academy on Linnaeus. Original Swedish translated by Sven Ahman.
61. Unpublished.
62. Interview with Alistair Cooke, summer 1955—UN Film Archives.
63. Unpublished.
64. BLM, Vol. 28, No. 1, January 1959; published also in *Honneur à St.-John Perse* (Paris, 1965).
65. Unpublished.
66. Unpublished.
67. Unpublished.
68. PC, Note No. 1706, January 2, 1958.
69. Unpublished.
70. Unpublished.
71. Unpublished.
72. Martin Buber, *Nachlese* (Heidelberg, 1965).
73. Unpublished.
74. Unpublished.
75. Unpublished.
76. Unpublished.
77. SG/400, October 19, 1954.
78. Unpublished.
79. Unpublished.
80. Unpublished.
81. SG/973, October 24, 1960.
82. Henri Hoppenot in *Le Monde Diplomatique* (October 1961).
83. Translated from the French by Hugh Chisholm.

Chapter 3 / The First Stage

1. SG/420, March 28, 1955.
2. Ibid.
3. SG/367, February 13, 1954.
4. SG/336, September 14, 1953, at a dinner in his honor given by the American Association for the United Nations, New York University, and other private organizations.
5. SG/318, July 10, 1953.
6. SG/378, April 14, 1954.
7. Ibid.
8. SG/382, May 13, 1954.
9. A/4132/Add.1, p. 2, August 20, 1959—Introduction to Annual Report.
10. Unpublished.
11. Unpublished.
12. Unpublished.
13. Unpublished.
14. SG/307, May 26, 1953.
15. Unpublished.
16. Res. 705 (VII), April 18, 1953—GA, 427th meeting.
17. Unnumbered.
18. SG/299, May 1, 1953.
19. Ibid.
20. SG/300, May 1, 1953.
21. SG/308, May 26, 1953.
22. PC, Note No. 657, May 12, 1953.
23. PC, Stockholm, May 19, 1953.
24. Note No. 1616, June 19, 1957.
25. *United Nations Review*, November 1961.
26. SG/331, September 8, 1953.
27. UN Preparatory Committee, Committee 6, 22nd and 23rd meetings, December 19 and 20, 1945, Summary Records, pp. 50–51. (Quoted in A/2364, Introduction, para. 5, January 30, 1953.)
28. PC, Stockholm, May 19, 1953.
29. A/2364, January 30, 1953; the appointment was made on October 22, 1952.
30. A/2364, Annex III.
31. Keesing's Contemporary Archives.
32. Ibid.
33. A/2364, January 30, 1953.
34. OR, GA, 413th meeting, March 10, 1953.
35. Ibid., para. 12.
36. OR, GA, 421st meeting, para. 125, April 1, 1953.
37. Res. 708 (VII), April 1, 1953.
38. Unpublished.
39. Unpublished.
40. Staff Regulation 1.1.
41. Staff Regulation 1.4.
42. A/2533, November 21, 1953.

43. Ibid.
44. *New York Times*, November 18, 1953.
45. Unpublished.
46. SG/298, May 1, 1953.
47. Unpublished.
48. E/2501, August 1, 1953; SG/322, July 31, 1953.
49. A/2533, November 21, 1953.
50. Summary, June 16, 1953.
51. SG/329, September 2, 1953.
52. Unpublished.
53. Unpublished.
54. A/2533, November 21, 1953.
55. SG/358, December 4, 1953.
56. SG/331, September 8, 1953.
57. A/2533, November 21, 1953.
58. Ibid., para. 25.
59. Ibid., para. 41.
60. Ibid., para. 43.
61. SG/353, November 18, 1953.
62. Res. 782 (VIII), A, December 9, 1953.
63. SG/338, September 30, 1953.
64. Res. 785 (VIII), December 9, 1963.
65. July 13, 1954.
66. Res. 888 (IX), December 17, 1954.
67. A/2554, November 12, 1953.
68. Summary, June 16, 1953.
69. A/2554, November 12, 1953.
70. Res. 784 (VIII), December 9, 1953.
71. SG/385, May 28, 1954.
72. PC, Note No. 868, June 9, 1954.
73. *The World Today*, signed EB (London, 1954).
74. OR, GA, 470th meeting, December 8, 1953.
75. SG/359, December 17, 1953.
76. Ibid.

Chapter 4 / Settling Down

1. Unpublished.
2. Speech at Church House, London, for Nongovernmental Organizations. Unnumbered.
3. ECOSOC/687, July 5, 1954.
4. A/C.5/591, October 23, 1954.
5. Unpublished.
6. Unpublished.

7. Unpublished.
8. PC, Note No. 902, August 19, 1954.
9. Unpublished.
10. PC, Note No. 902, August 19, 1954.
11. A/2731, September 21, 1954.
12. A/C.5/580, October 11, 1954; SG/397.
13. A/C.5/581, October 11, 1954.
14. Unpublished.
15. August 8–20, 1955.
16. SG/344, October 21, 1953.
17. Unpublished.
18. SG/420, March 28, 1955.

Chapter 5 / The Political Challenge

1. SG/311, June 9, 1953.
2. SG/314, June 18, 1953.
3. SG/318, July 10, 1953.
4. Ibid.
5. Ibid.
6. Unpublished.
7. SG/369, February 18, 1954.
8. Statement of June 18, 1954.
9. S/3232, June 19, 1954.
10. S/3235/Rev. 1, June 20, 1954.
11. S/3236/Rev. 1, June 20, 1954.
12. S/3237, June 20, 1954; see OR, SC, 675th meeting, para. 200.
13. S/3241, June 22, 1954.
14. S/3247, June 24, 1954.
15. S/3241, June 22, 1954.
16. S/3232, June 19, 1954.
17. S/PV. 676, paras. 179, 181, June 25, 1954.
18. Unpublished.
19. Unpublished.
20. Unpublished.
21. Unpublished.
22. "The Charter of the UN—Hearings before the Committee on Foreign Relations," U.S. Senate, 79th Congress, U.S. Government Printing Office, Washington, 1945, pp. 98–9.
23. S/3236/Rev. 1, June 20, 1954.
24. Unpublished.
25. Unpublished.
26. PC, London, June 4, 1953. Unnumbered.
27. PC, Note No. 818, March 24, 1954.
28. Note No. 894, July 29, 1954.

29. Unpublished.
30. Unpublished.
31. Unpublished.
32. Unpublished.
33. Unpublished.
34. Note No. 946, October 15, 1954.
35. OR, GA, 505th meeting, December 8, 1954, para. 196.
36. U.S. Mission Press Release of August 18, 1954.
37. Press Conference, December 3, 1954.
38. Statement at Chicago, November 29, 1954.
39. OR, 9th GA session, items 70 & 71.
40. Ibid.
41. A/2830, December 4, 1954; Note No. 980, December 4, 1954.
42. Unpublished.
43. Unpublished.
44. A/L 182, December 7, 1954.
45. Ibid.
46. Background PC, December 7, 1954.
47. Ibid.
48. Unpublished.
49. Unpublished.
50. Res. 906 (IX), December 10, 1954.
51. OR, GA, 507th meeting, para. 142, December 9, 1954.
52. OR, GA, 509th meeting, paras. 84, 85, December 10, 1954.
53. Ibid.
54. One unpublished.
55. A/2888, December 17, 1954; PM/2964, December 17, 1954.
56. Unpublished.
57. U.S. Mission Press Release No. 2178, June 21, 1955.
58. A/2888, December 17, 1954; PM/2964, December 17, 1954.
59. A/2889, December 17, 1954; PM/2965, December 17, 1954.
60. Ibid.
61. A/2888, December 17, 1954; PM/2964, December 17, 1954.
62. Press Conference, Stockholm, December 18, 1954. Unnumbered.
63. PC, Note No. 996, December 22, 1954.
64. Ibid.
65. Note No. 998, December 24, 1954.
66. PC, Note No. 1024, January 14, 1955.
67. Ibid.
68. Unpublished.
69. Note No. 1013, January 10, 1955.
70. Note No. 1019, January 11, 1955.
71. Unpublished.
72. SG/415, January 13, 1955.
73. PC, Note No. 1023, January 14, 1955.
74. Ibid.
75. Ibid.
76. SG/415, January 13, 1955.
77. *I. F. Stone's Weekly*, Vol. III, Nos. 2 and 3, February 7, 1955.
78. Ibid.
79. *I. F. Stone's Weekly*, Vol. III, January and February 1955; see also Richard I. Miller, *Dag Hammarskjold and Crisis Diplomacy* (New York, 1961).
80. Ibid.
81. Unpublished.
82. Unpublished.
83. Note No. 1027, January 21, 1955.
84. Unpublished.
85. U.S. Mission, Note to Correspondents, January 21, 1955.
86. Note No. 1028, January 21, 1955.
87. Unpublished.
88. Press Release, U.S. Department of State, No. 50, January 27, 1955.
89. Unpublished.
90. Unpublished.
91. Unpublished.
92. S/3354, January 28, 1955.
93. S/3358, February 4, 1955.
94. Unpublished.
95. S/3358, February 4, 1955.
96. Unpublished.
97. Unpublished.
98. Unpublished.
99. Unpublished.
100. Unpublished.
101. Unpublished.
102. Dwight D. Eisenhower, *The White House Years: Mandate for Change, 1953–1956* (New York, 1963), p. 568.
103. PC, Note No. 1078, April 19, 1955.
104. *New York Times*, November 22, 1967.
105. Unpublished.
106. PC, Note No. 1090, May 5, 1955.
107. Note No. 1105, May 30, 1955.
108. SG/422, May 30, 1955.
109. Unpublished.
110. PC, Note No. 1106, June 2, 1955.
111. Unpublished.
112. Unpublished.

113. Unpublished.
114. PC, Note No. 1153, August 12, 1955.
115. SG/434, August 1, 1955.
116. Unpublished.
117. Unpublished.
118. Unpublished.
119. Keesing.
120. Ibid.
121. Unpublished.
122. Unpublished.
123. PC, Note No. 1153, August 12, 1955.
124. Ibid.
125. Unpublished.
126. Note No. 1178, September 16, 1955.
127. Unpublished.
128. A/2954, September 9, 1955.
129. Ibid.
130. Unpublished.
131. Unpublished.
132. Unpublished.
133. Unpublished.
134. "Meet the Press," September 18, 1955.
135. Unpublished.

Chapter 6 / The Middle East, April–May 1956

1. Introduction to Annual Report, 1954–5, A/2911, July 8, 1955.
2. At the Palais des Nations in Geneva from July 18 to 23, 1955.
3. PC, Note No. 1226, December 22, 1955.
4. Interview for "UN Review" television program, Note No. 1605, May 31, 1957.
5. On March 29, 1954, the U.S.S.R. vetoed draft resolution S/3188/Corr. 1 of March 19, 1954, during the 664th Security Council meeting.
6. Res. 95 (S/2322) of September 1, 1951.
7. Anthony Nutting, *No End of a Lesson* (New York, 1967).
8. S/3290, September 14, 1954, para. 11.
9. S/3343, January 11, 1955.
10. S/3373, March 17, 1955.
11. General E. L. M. Burns, *Between Arab and Israeli* (London and Toronto, 1962), p. 18.
12. S/3430, September 5, 1955.
13. Major-General Moshe Dayan, *Diary of the Sinai Campaign* (New York, 1966), p. 12.
14. January 15–February 24, 1956.
15. PC, Note No. 1243, February 27, 1956.
16. Nutting, op. cit., p. 18.
17. Hugh Thomas, *Suez* (New York, 1966), p. 20; Kenneth Love, *Suez, the Twice-Fought War* (New York, 1969), p. 145.
18. PC, Note No. 1248, March 7, 1956.
19. PC, Note No. 1249, March 8, 1956— UNCA luncheon.
20. Unpublished.
21. Unpublished.
22. Unpublished.
23. Res. 113 (S/3575), April 4, 1956.
24. S/3596, VIII, Conclusions, para. 101, May 9, 1956.
25. New York *Herald Tribune*, April 2, 1956.
26. S/3579/Rev. 1, April 9, 1956.
27. Burns, op. cit., p. 143.
28. The exchange of messages during the Secretary-General's negotiations with the governments of Egypt and Israel is published in documents S/3584 of April 12, 1956, S/3586 of April 13, 1956, and S/3587 of April 16, 1956.
29. S/1264/Rev. 1, February 24, 1949.
30. Unpublished.
31. Unpublished.
32. Unpublished.
33. Unpublished.
34. S/3585, April 12, 1956.
35. Unpublished.
36. Unpublished.
37. Unpublished.
38. Note No. 1282, April 19, 1956.
39. Official statement, published in *Pravda*, April 17, 1956.
40. Unpublished.
41. SG/476, April 20, 1956.
42. Unpublished.
43. Statement to press correspondents, summarized in SC/1754 of April 20, 1956; not published in its entirety.
44. Unpublished.
45. *The Jerusalem Post*, April 25, 1956.
46. Unpublished.

47. Unpublished.
48. Unpublished.
49. Unpublished.
50. S/3594, May 2, 1956.
51. Ibid.
52. Note No. 1299, May 6, 1956.
53. Pierre Huss, May 3, 1956.
54. SG/478, May 6, 1956.
55. U.S. Mission Press Release No. 2410, May 4, 1956.
56. S/3596, May 9, 1956.
57. Ibid., VIII, Conclusions, paras. 106–7.
58. Unpublished.
59. Unpublished.
60. Thomas, op. cit., p. 102.
61. S/3596, May 9, 1956, para. 61.
62. Unpublished.
63. PC, Note No. 1303, May 11, 1956.
64. S/3605, June 4, 1956.
65. Burns, op. cit. pp. 143–4.
66. Love, op. cit., p. 124.
67. Ibid., p. 117.
68. Unpublished.
69. Thomas, op. cit., p. 23.
70. Love, op. cit., p. 312.
71. Anthony Eden, *The Memoirs of Anthony Eden: Full Circle* (Boston, 1960), p. 470.
72. Love, op. cit., p. 296.
73. PC, Geneva, July 24, 1956.
74. PC, Note No. 1354, August 2, 1956.
75. S/3632, August 3, 1956.
76. Unpublished.
77. Unpublished.
78. SG/503, SG/504, September 14, 1956.
79. Unpublished.
80. S/3658, September 26, 1956.
81. Report, dated September 12, 1956, published in document S/3659 of September 27, 1956.
82. Unpublished.
83. Unpublished.
84. Unpublished.

Chapter 7 / The Suez Crisis

1. Many works describe this process, including the following: Major-General Moshe Dayan, *Diary of the Sinai Campaign* (New York, 1966); Kennett Love, *Suez, the Twice-Fought War* (New York, 1969); Anthony Nutting, *No End of a Lesson* (New York, 1967); Terence Robertson, *Crisis: The Inside Story of the Suez Conspiracy* (London, 1964); and Hugh Thomas, *Suez* (New York, 1966).
2. Thomas, op. cit., p. 88.
3. Dwight D. Eisenhower, *The White House Years: Waging Peace, 1956–1961* (New York, 1965), pp. 38 et seq.
4. Unpublished.
5. Unpublished.
6. Unpublished.
7. Unpublished.
8. S/3645, September 12, 1956.
9. Nutting, op. cit., p. 58.
10. Unpublished.
11. S/3650, September 17, 1956.
12. Love, op. cit., p. 171.
13. Ibid.
14. Keesing.
15. S/3654, September 24, 1956.
16. Quoted from London *Times*, November 2, 1970.
17. S/3656, September 24, 1956.
18. Thomas, op. cit., p. 96.
19. Love, op. cit., p. 438; Nutting, op. cit., pp. 70–71.
20. Ibid.
21. Thomas, op. cit., p. 100.
22. Eisenhower, op. cit., p. 52.
23. Ibid.
24. S/3666, October 5, 1956.
25. John Robinson Beal, *John Foster Dulles, 1888–1959* (New York), p. 271; first published in 1957 under the title *John Foster Dulles: A Biography*.
26. Unpublished.
27. Unpublished.
28. Quoted from London *Times*, November 2, 1970.
29. Eisenhower, op. cit., p. 53.
30. S/3671, October 13, 1956.
31. OR, SC, 743rd meeting.
32. SG/510, October 13, 1956.
33. S/3728, November 3, 1956.
34. Ibid.
35. S/3685, October 18, 1956.

36. Dayan, op. cit., p. 59.
37. S/3678, October 15, 1956.
38. Statement of October 16, 1956.
39. Unpublished.
40. Keesing.
41. Eisenhower, op. cit., pp. 56–70.
42. Ibid.
43. Ibid.
44. OR, SC, 746th meeting.
45. OR, SC, 747th meeting, October 29, 1956, para. 3.
46. Eisenhower, op. cit., p. 73.
47. S/3706, October 30, 1956.
48. Unpublished.
49. For the debate in the Security Council on the Suez crisis during the last days of October, see OR, SC, 748–751st meetings, October 30–31, 1956.
50. OR, SC, 748th meeting, paras. 13–20; SG/513, October 30, 1956.
51. S/3710, October 30, 1956.
52. S/3713/Rev. 1, October 30, 1956.
53. OR, SC, 751st meeting, paras. 1–6; SG/514, October 31, 1956.
54. S/3721, October 31, 1956.
55. Keesing.
56. Piers Dixon, *Double Diploma: The Life of Sir Pierson Dixon* (London, 1968), p. 278.
57. For the debate in the First Emergency Special Session of the General Assembly on the Suez crisis, see OR, GA, 561st, 562nd, 563rd, 565th, 566th, 567th, and 572nd meetings on November 1, 2, 4, 5, 7, and 10, 1956.
58. Res. 977 (ES-I), November 2, 1956.
59. OR, GA, ES-I, 562nd meeting, para. 299, November 2, 1956.
60. Ibid., para. 307.
61. OR, GA, ES-I, 561st meeting, para. 111, November 1, 1956.
62. Anthony Eden, *The Memoirs of Anthony Eden: Full Circle* (Boston, 1960), p. 598.
63. General E. L. M. Burns, *Between Arab and Israeli* (London and Toronto, 1962), p. 98.
64. A/3268 and A/3269, November 3, 1956.
65. A/3266, November 2, 1956.
66. A/3279, November 3, 1956.
67. Res. 999 (ES-I), November 4, 1956.
68. Unpublished.
69. Res. 998 (ES-I), November 4, 1956.
70. Res. 1000 (ES-I), November 5, 1956.
71. A/3297, November 5, 1956.
72. A/3301, November 5, 1956.
73. A/3295, November 5, 1956.
74. A/3310, November 7, 1956.
75. Ibid.
76. S/3736, November 5, 1956, 755th meeting.
77. Ibid.
78. OR, SC, 755th meeting, paras. 8–10; SG/517, November 5, 1956.
79. Ibid.
80. OR, SC, 755th meeting, para. 28, November 5, 1956.
81. A/3302, November 6, 1956, and addenda.
82. A/3306 and A/3307, November 6, 1956.
83. PC, Note No. 1433/Rev. 1, November 6, 1956.
84. A/3302, November 6, 1956, and addenda.
85. OR, GA, ES-I, 566th meeting, paras. 2–5; SG/518, November 7, 1956.
86. Ibid.
87. Res. 1001 (ES-I) and Res. 1002 (ES-I), November 7, 1956.
88. A/3320, November 8, 1956.
89. Unpublished.
90. Unpublished.
91. Unpublished.
92. Unpublished.
93. Unpublished.
94. Unpublished.
95. Unpublished.
96. SG/525, November 9, 1956.
97. Unpublished.
98. Unpublished.
99. Unpublished.
100. PC, Note No. 1447—SG/528, November 12, 1956.
101. Ibid.
102. Ibid.
103. Unpublished.
104. Unpublished.
105. Unpublished.
106. Unpublished.
107. From the records of the Advisory Committee on UNEF. Unpublished.
108. Ibid.
109. Ibid.
110. Ibid.

111. A/3375, November 20, 1956.
112. Ibid.
113. Ibid.
114. A/3376, November 20, 1956; SG/535, November 18, 1956.
115. From the records of the Advisory Committee on UNEF. Unpublished.
116. Ibid.
117. A/3563, Annex I, February 26, 1957.
118. A/3594, June 25, 1957, p. 23.
119. This private *aide-mémoire* was never published, although the text found its way into print in the *New York Times* of June 19, 1967, during the crisis after the withdrawal of UNEF in May 1967.
120. For a detailed account of the withdrawal of UNEF and the reasons for it, see A/6730, Addendum 3, of June 26, 1967, "Report of the Secretary-General on the Withdrawal of the United Nations Emergency Force."
121. Ibid.
122. Ibid.
123. Ibid.
124. Unpublished.

Chapter 8 / The Aftermath of Suez

1. A/3375, November 20, 1956.
2. A/3376, November 20, 1956.
3. Res. 1121 (XI), November 24, 1956.
4. SG/540, November 28, 1956.
5. SG/546, December 3, 1956.
6. Unpublished.
7. London *Times*, December 15, 1956.
8. Anthony Nutting, *No End of a Lesson* (New York, 1967), p. 147.
9. Eden, op. cit., p. 633.
10. A/3376, November 20, 1956.
11. London *Times*, December 15, 1956.
12. Unpublished.
13. Unpublished.
14. December 17, 1956.
15. Hammarskjold's speech in the 632nd meeting of the General Assembly, paras. 5–21, December 21, 1956; SG/556, December 21, 1956.
16. Unpublished.
17. A/3500, January 15, 1957.
18. A/3501/Rev. 1, January 17, 1957.
19. Res. 1123 (XI), January 19, 1957.
20. A/3511, January 24, 1957.
21. A/3512, January 24, 1957.
22. A/3517 and A/3518, February 1, 1957.
23. Unpublished.
24. Unpublished.
25. OR, GA, 651st meeting, paras. 152–5, February 2, 1957.
26. OR, GA, 652nd meeting, paras. 151–84, February 2, 1957.
27. Res. 1124 (XI) and Res. 1125 (XI), February 2, 1957.
28. *Washington Post*, February 2, 1957.
29. A/3492, Annex III, January 11, 1957.
30. A/3526, February 8, 1957.
31. A/3527, February 11, 1957.
32. Kennett Love, *Suez, the Twice-Fought War* (New York, 1969), pp. 664–6.
33. A/3557, February 22, 1957.
34. OR, GA, 659th meeting, paras. 24–30; SG/563, February 22, 1957.
35. Unpublished.
36. A/3563, February 26, 1957.
37. Unpublished.
38. OR, GA, 666th meeting, paras. 1–24, March 1, 1957.
39. Ibid.
40. Ibid., paras. 25–45.
41. Ibid.
42. Ibid., para. 88.
43. OR, GA, 667th meeting, para. 1, March 4, 1957.
44. Ibid., para. 237. Fawzi had made this reservation before in the 666th meeting, para. 87, March 1, 1957.
45. Unpublished.
46. Unpublished.
47. Unpublished.
48. Unpublished.
49. SG/568, March 12, 1957.
50. Unpublished.
51. In the Advisory Committee on UNEF.
52. Unpublished.
53. Unpublished.
54. Unpublished.
55. Unpublished.
56. Unpublished.
57. Unpublished.
58. Unpublished.

59. Unpublished.
60. Unpublished.
61. Unpublished.
62. Associated Press dispatch of March 29, 1957.
63. SG/583, April 1, 1957.
64. Joseph Alsop in the New York *Herald Tribune* of April 12, 1957.
65. Note No. 1580, April 12, 1957.
66. Unpublished.
67. Unpublished.
68. Unpublished.
69. Unpublished.
70. SG/584, April 8, 1957.
71. S/3817/Rev. 1, April 24, 1957.
72. S/3818, A/3576, April 24, 1957.
73. Advisory Committee records. Unpublished.
74. Ibid.
75. Unpublished.
76. Unpublished.
77. Unpublished.
78. To Advisory Committee. Unpublished.
79. A/3694, October 9, 1957.
80. Unpublished.
81. Res. 1151 (XII), November 22, 1957.
82. Note No. 1693, December 7, 1957.
83. Unpublished.
84. Note No. 1761, March 24, 1958.
85. Unpublished.
86. To Advisory Committee. Unpublished.
87. A/3943, October 9, 1958.
88. To Advisory Committee. Unpublished.
89. Ibid.
90. To the Special Political Committee of the General Assembly, SG/742, November 5, 1958.
91. Ibid.
92. PC, Note 1983, April 30, 1959.
93. PC, Note 1995, May 21, 1959.
94. Ibid.

Chapter 9 / Hungary

1. S/3690, October 27, 1956.
2. Dwight D. Eisenhower, *The White House Years: Waging Peace, 1956–1961* (New York, 1965), p. 82.
3. OR, GA ES-II, A/3251, November 1, 1956.
4. S/3726, November 2, 1956.
5. S/3730/Rev. 1, November 4, 1956.
6. S/3733, November 4, 1956.
7. OR, SC, 754th meeting, para. 76, November 4, 1956.
8. Eisenhower, op. cit., pp. 88–9.
9. A/3311, November 7, 1956.
10. Res. 1004 (ES-II), November 4, 1956.
11. OR, GA, 567th meeting, para. 313; SG/522, November 7, 1956.
12. A/3315, November 8, 1956.
13. Ibid.
14. Ibid.
15. Res. 1005–6–7–8 (ES-II), November 9 and 10, 1956.
16. OR, GA ES-II, 570th meeting, para. 68, November 9, 1956.
17. Ibid., 571st meeting, para. 192, November 9, 1956.
18. Ibid., 573rd meeting, para. 38, November 10, 1956.
19. Ibid., 573rd meeting, para. 78, November 10, 1956.
20. A/3335, November 11, 1956.
21. A/3336, November 11, 1956.
22. A/3340, November 11, 1956.
23. A/3341, November 12, 1956.
24. A/3347, November 14, 1956.
25. A/3346, November 13, 1956.
26. PC, Note No. 1447, November 12, 1956.
27. A/3359–SG/533, November 16, 1956.
28. PC, Note No. 1995, May 21, 1959.
29. A/3358, November 15, 1956.
30. A/3362, November 16, 1956.
31. Unpublished.
32. Unpublished.
33. Unpublished.
34. A/3371 and Add. 1, November 19 and 21, 1956.
35. OR, GA, 586th meeting, paras. 62–67, November 21, 1956; SG/536, November 21, 1956.
36. Ibid.
37. Unpublished.
38. A/3403, November 30, 1956.
39. OR, GA, 608th meeting, paras. 2–4; SG/547, December 4, 1956.
40. A/3435, Add. 6, December 12, 1956.
41. A/3485, January 5, 1957.
42. Ibid.
43. Ibid.

44. A/3487/Rev. 1, January 10, 1957.
45. Res. 1132 (XI), January 10, 1957.
46. A/3493, January 11, 1957.
47. A/3546, February 20, 1957.
48. OR, GA (XI) Supplement 18, A/3592.
49. Speech to the Canadian Women's Club, Toronto, December 7, 1956.
50. A/3594/Add. 1, August 22, 1957.
51. PC, Note No. 1727, February 6, 1958.
52. PC, Copenhagen, May 4, 1959; original Swedish.
53. PC, Note No. 1995, May 21, 1959.
54. Res. 1133 (XII), September 14, 1957.
55. A/3774, December 9, 1957.
56. Unpublished.
57. All quotations regarding this episode, unless stated otherwise, are from "A Chronological Record of Facts Concerning Mr. Povl Bang-Jensen's Period of Duty in the Secretariat Assigned to Serve the Special Committee on the Problem of Hungary and Subsequent Developments Ending in his Dismissal," dated December 22, 1959, and from "A List of Facts about the United Nations and the Case of Mr. Bang-Jensen," dated January 1, 1960. Both documents are unnumbered UN press releases.
58. Unpublished.
59. PC, Note No. 1701, December 16, 1957.
60. Statement by a spokesman for the Foreign Ministry in Budapest.
61. Unpublished.
62. DeWitt Copp and Marshall Peck, *Betrayal at the UN: The Story of Paul Bang-Jensen* (New York, 1961).

Prologue to Part Two

1. Unpublished.
2. Unpublished.
3. Unpublished.
4. Unpublished.
5. OR, GA, 690th meeting, paras. 63–75; SG/616, September 26, 1957.
6. *Markings*, 7.28.57, pp. 155–6.
7. Unpublished.
8. OR, GA, 690th meeting, paras. 63–75; SG/616, September 26, 1957.
9. A/3594/Add. 1, August 22, 1957.
10. OR, GA, 690th meeting, paras. 63–75; SG/616, September 26, 1957.
11. *Markings*, 9.26.57, p. 156.
12. Background PC, April 20, 1954.
13. At meeting of Nongovernmental Organizations, Church House, London, March 19, 1954.
14. SG/585, April 10, 1957, at the 50th anniversary dinner of the American Jewish Committee, New York.
15. Gunnar Jarring: lecture to the Indian Council of World Affairs, New Delhi, February 3, 1956.
16. Extempore speech, Mexico City, April 8, 1959, dictated later.
17. PC, Note No. 1571, April 4, 1957.
18. PC, Note No. 1962, April 2, 1959.
19. A/4390/Add. 1, August 31, 1960.
20. PC, Note No. 1970 and *New York Times*, April 16, 1959.
21. A/4390/Add. 1, August 31, 1960.
22. PC, Note No. 2358, June 26, 1961.
23. Unpublished.
24. Unpublished.
25. PC, Note No. 1934, February 5, 1959.
26. A/4132/Add. 1, August 20, 1959.
27. Extempore speech, Mexico City, April 8, 1959.
28. A/4132/Add. 1, August 20, 1959.
29. OR, GA, 823rd meeting, paras. 146 et seq., October 6, 1959.
30. SG/812, May 2, 1959.
31. PC, Geneva, May 8, 1959.
32. SG/812, May 2, 1959.
33. PC, Geneva, May 8, 1959.
34. *Economist*, January 2, 1960, "Mr. Hammarskjold, We Presume."
35. SG/910, May 1, 1960.
36. Ibid.
37. Press Conference, April 11, 1961, as quoted in Lash, op. cit., p. 165.
38. SG/971, October 18, 1960, to the Fifth Committee of the General Assembly.
39. PC, Note No. 2347, June 12, 1961.
40. SG/1035, May 30, 1961.

Chapter 10 / Lebanon, 1958: Preventive Diplomacy

1. Dwight D. Eisenhower, *The White House Years: Waging Peace, 1956–1961* (New York, 1965), p. 274.

2. Ibid., p. 262.
3. Ibid., p. 265.
4. Ibid., p. 266.
5. Ibid., p. 266.
6. S/4007, May 22, 1958.
7. Ibid.
8. OR, SC, 823rd meeting, para. 11, June 6, 1958.
9. Ibid., para. 74 et seq.
10. Ibid., 825th meeting, para. 86, June 11, 1958.
11. S/4022, OR, SC, 824th meeting, para. 11, June 10, 1958.
12. Res. 128 (S/4023), June 11, 1958.
13. OR, SC, 825th meeting, para. 90; SG/686, June 11, 1958.
14. Unpublished.
15. Unpublished.
16. Eisenhower, op. cit., p. 268.
17. SG/687, June 14, 1958.
18. Unpublished.
19. Eisenhower, op. cit., p. 268.
20. Ibid., p. 269.
21. Unpublished.
22. Unpublished.
23. Unpublished.
24. Unpublished.
25. Unpublished.
26. Unpublished.
27. Unpublished.
28. Unpublished.
29. Unpublished.
30. Note No. 1830, June 26, 1958.
31. Statement on June 27, 1958—Lebanese Mission to the UN.
32. SG/698, June 27, 1958.
33. Unpublished.
34. Unpublished.
35. Unpublished.
36. Unpublished.
37. PC, Note No. 1838, July 3, 1958.
38. Eisenhower, op. cit., p. 269.
39. S/4040 and Add. 1, July 3 and 5, 1958.
40. Keesing.
41. S/4043, July 8, 1958.
42. Ibid.
43. Unpublished.
44. Published in the London *Times*, July 23, 1958.
45. Eisenhower, op. cit., p. 269.
46. Unpublished.
47. Quoted from *New York Post*, January 22, 1972.
48. Eisenhower, op. cit., p. 274.
49. Ibid., p. 273.
50. OR, SC, 827th meeting, paras. 58–70; SG/703, July 15, 1958.
51. Ibid., para. 33.
52. Unpublished.
53. OR, SC, 827th meeting, para. 39, July 15, 1958.
54. Ibid.
55. Unpublished.
56. OR, SC, 827th meeting, para. 123 (S/4047), July 15, 1958.
57. Unpublished.
58. Unpublished.
59. S/4050, July 15, 1958.
60. S/4051, July 16, 1958.
61. OR, SC, 829th meeting, paras. 1–4; SG/704, July 16, 1958.
62. Unpublished.
63. S/4054, July 17, 1958.
64. Unpublished.
65. S/4052, July 17, 1958.
66. S/4053, July 17, 1958.
67. S/4059, July 20, 1958.
68. S/4055 and Rev. 1, July 21, 1958.
69. OR, SC, 835th meeting, para. 7, July 21, 1958.
70. Ibid., para. 12.
71. Ibid., para. 70.
72. OR, SC, 837th meeting, paras. 10–18; SG/708, July 22, 1958.
73. Ibid.
74. Ibid.
75. Ibid.
76. SG/709, July 24, 1957.
77. Ibid.
78. Unpublished.
79. UPI dispatch, July 25, 1958.
80. Unpublished.
81. Unpublished.
82. Unpublished.
83. S/4078, August 5, 1958.
84. S/4083, August 7, 1958.
85. OR, GA (ES-III), 732nd meeting, paras. 34–45; SG/714, August 8, 1958.
86. Ibid.
87. Ibid., 733rd meeting, paras. 2–59, August 13, 1958.
88. S/4085, August 14, 1958.
89. Ibid.
90. A/3876 and A/3877, August 18, 1958.
91. A/3878, August 18, 1958.

92. Ibid.
93. OR, GA (ES-III), 741st meeting, para. 29, August 19, 1958.
94. A/3893/Rev. 1, August 21, 1958.
95. Res. 1237 (ES-III), August 21, 1958.
96. OR, GA (ES-III), 746th meeting, August 21, 1958.
97. Ibid.
98. Ibid.
99. Unpublished.
100. Unpublished.
101. PC, Note No. 1862, August 22, 1958.
102. Ibid.

Chapter 11 / More Preventive Diplomacy

1. Res. 1237 (ES-III), August 21, 1958.
2. PC, Note No. 1862, August 22, 1958.
3. Note No. 1868, August 29, 1958.
4. SG/718, September 1, 1958.
5. Unpublished.
6. A/3934/Rev. 1, September 29, 1958.
7. Ibid.
8. PC, Note No. 1862, August 22, 1958. The quotation is from Goethe's *Faust*.
9. Ralph J. Bunche in a speech to the 9th General Assembly of the International Press Institute, Tokyo, March 25, 1960.
10. Unpublished.
11. S/4113, November 17, 1958.
12. OR, SC, 840th meeting, November 25, 1958.
13. SG/731 and 733, October 18 and 24, 1958.
14. Unpublished.
15. SG/744, November 12, 1958.
16. Unpublished.
17. Unpublished.
18. OR, GA, 882nd meeting, para. 68 et seq., October 3, 1960.
19. PC, Note No. 1701, December 16, 1957.
20. Res. 1237 (ES-III), August 21, 1958.
21. A/3934/Rev. 1, September 29, 1958.
22. A/4121, June 15, 1959.
23. Ibid.
24. Ibid.
25. Res. 194 (III), December 11, 1948.
26. Ibid.
27. A/4121, June 15, 1959.
28. Res. 1212 (XII), December 14, 1957.
29. S/4173, March 18, 1959.
30. Unpublished.
31. See S/4211 of August 31, 1959.
32. Unpublished.
33. Unpublished.
34. Unpublished.
35. Unpublished.
36. Unpublished.
37. Unpublished.
38. Unpublished.
39. Public statement of January 26, 1960.
40. *Haaretz*, January 7, 1960.
41. *Jerusalem Post* of January 26 and 27, 1960.
42. Ibid.
43. Ibid.
44. Unpublished.
45. PC, Note No. 1158, August 25, 1955.
46. OR, SC, 811th meeting, February 18, 1958.
47. SG/658, February 17, 1958.
48. OR, SC, 826th meeting, June 18, 1958.
49. S/4121 of December 2, 1958 and S/4126 of December 8, 1958.
50. SG/782–783–784, February 6, 1959.
51. PC, Note No. 1934, February 5, 1959.
52. SG/797, Bangkok, March 16, 1959.
53. SG/989, December 16, 1960.
54. Unpublished.
55. Unpublished.
56. Unpublished.
57. Unpublished.
58. Unpublished.
59. Unpublished.
60. Unpublished.
61. SG/1049, August 2, 1961.

Chapter 12 / Disarmament

1. For an account of the disarmament discussions at the UN during the period described, see *The United Nations and Disarmament, 1945–1965,* published by the Office of Pub-

lic Information, United Nations, New York.
2. PC, Note No. 1100, May 19, 1955.
3. OR, DC, Annex 15, DC/71.
4. Unpublished.
5. OR, DC Supplement, April 1954, DC/44 & Corr. 1.
6. Res. 914 (X), December 16, 1955.
7. Res. 913 (X), December 3, 1955.
8. OR, DC, 1957, Annex 12, DC/112.
9. Res. 1150 (XII), November 19, 1957.
10. Unpublished.
11. PC, Note No. 1727, February 6, 1958.
12. PC, Note No. 1760, March 20, 1958.
13. OR, SC, 815th meeting, paras. 82–90; SG/675, April 29, 1958.
14. S/3990, April 18, 1958.
15. PC, Note No. 1779 of April 8, 1958.
16. OR, SC, 815th meeting, paras. 82–90; S/675, April 29, 1958.
17. Ibid.
18. Ibid.
19. Ibid.
20. Ibid.
21. Ibid.
22. Ibid.
23. Ibid.
24. OR, SC, 815th meeting, para. 92.
25. Ibid., 816th meeting, para. 22.
26. S/3995 and amendment S/3998.
27. S/3997.
28. PC, Note No. 1794, May 1, 1958.
29. Ibid.
30. Ibid.
31. A/3897, August 21, 1958.
32. SG/715, August 20, 1958.
33. A/3844/Add. 1.
34. A/3936, September 30, 1958.
35. U.S.: A/3895; Great Britain: A/3896/Rev. 1.
36. A/C.1/PV. 770, October 26, 1955.
37. The Agreement came into force on November 14, 1957.
38. SG/505 of September 20, 1956, and SG/507 of October 2, 1956.
39. Unpublished.
40. Res. 1252 D(XIII), November 4, 1958.
41. Unpublished.
42. DC/144, September 8, 1959.
43. Ibid.
44. Ibid.
45. Ibid.
46. OR, GA, 798th meeting, September 17, 1959.
47. OR, GA, 799th meeting, September 18, 1959.
48. Res. 1378 (XIV), November 20, 1959.
49. Unpublished.
50. Unpublished.
51. Unpublished.
52. Records of the Ten Nations Disarmament Committee, March 1960.
53. Unpublished.
54. Unpublished.
55. Unpublished.
56. SG/912, April 28, 1960.
57. DC/182, August 18, 1960.
58. Introduction to Annual Report, A/4390/Add. 1, August 31, 1960.
59. A/4879, September 20, 1961.

Chapter 13 / Laos

1. Among many recent books and articles on Laos, the following have been particularly useful as background: Bernard B. Fall, *Anatomy of a Crisis: The Laotian Crisis of 1960–61* (New York, 1969); Dwight D. Eisenhower, *The White House Years: Waging Peace, 1956–1961* (New York, 1965); Roger Hilsman, *To Move a Nation* (New York, 1967); Hugh Toye, *Laos—Buffer State or Battleground* (London, 1968); David Wise and Thomas Ross, *The Invisible Government* (New York, 1964).
2. Unpublished.
3. S/4212, September 5, 1959—Note No. 2027/Rev. 1, September 4, 1959.
4. Letter of January 16, 1959, circular letter to all member states; Note No. 1919, January 19, 1959.
5. Hilsman, op. cit., p. 112.
6. PC, Note No. 1962, April 8, 1959.
7. Sisouk Na Champassak, *Tempête sur le Laos* (Paris, 1961); *Storm over Laos* (New York, 1961), p. 78.
8. Keesing.
9. Unpublished.
10. Unpublished.
11. Unpublished.

12. Unpublished.
13. Unpublished.
14. Arthur Schlesinger, Jr., *A Thousand Days* (Boston, 1965), p. 305.
15. Unpublished.
16. For this issue, see William J. Lederer, *A Nation of Sheep* (New York, 1961); Toye, op. cit., pp. 126–8.
17. Fall, op. cit., p. 123.
18. Note No. 2017, August 5, 1959.
19. PC, Note No. 2020, August 13, 1959.
20. Fall, op. cit., p. 126.
21. SG/842, August 20, 1959.
22. Note No. 2023, August 22, 1959.
23. Unpublished.
24. Unpublished.
25. New York *Herald Tribune,* August 25, 1959.
26. Ibid.
27. Fall, op. cit., p. 135 et seq.
28. SG/849, August 27, 1959.
29. S/4212, September 5, 1959; Note No. 2027/Rev. 1, September 4, 1959.
30. Unpublished.
31. Eisenhower, op. cit., p. 421.
32. S/4213, September 6, 1959.
33. Note No. 2029, September 7, 1959.
34. S/4213, September 6, 1959.
35. S/4214, September 7, 1959 (same as S/4216, September 8, 1959).
36. Note No. 2030, September 7, 1959.
37. S/4216; Res. 132, September 7, 1959.
38. OR, SC, 847th meeting, September 7, 1959, paras. 11–14; SG/854, September 7, 1959.
39. Ibid.
40. Ibid.
41. Rules of Procedure of the Security Council.
42. OR, SC, 847th meeting, paras. 24–7; SG/856, September 7, 1959.
43. Rules of Procedure of the Security Council.
44. OR, SC, 847th meeting, paras. 43–56; SG/855, September 7, 1959.
45. Unpublished.
46. Champassak, op. cit., p. 124.
47. Unpublished.
48. OR, SC, 848th meeting, para. 139.
49. Unpublished.
50. Unpublished.
51. Unpublished.
52. Unpublished.
53. Unpublished.
54. Note No. 2034, September 9, 1959.
55. Note No. 2035, September 9, 1959.
56. Fall, op. cit., p. 141.
57. Unpublished.
58. Unpublished.
59. Toye, op. cit., p. 131.
60. Unpublished.
61. Unpublished.
62. Unpublished.
63. *New York Times,* October 15, 1959.
64. Ibid., October 16, 1959.
65. Unpublished.
66. Champassak, op. cit., p. 125.
67. Unpublished.
68. Press Release of the U.S.S.R. Mission to the UN, October 30, 1959.
69. S/4236, November 5, 1959.
70. Press Release No. 3283 of the U.S. Mission to the UN, November 6, 1959.
71. Ibid.
72. Press Release of the U.S.S.R. Mission to the UN, November 6, 1959.
73. Ibid.
74. Ibid.
75. Note No. 2072, November 6, 1959.
76. SG/868, November 8, 1959.
77. Unpublished.
78. Unpublished.
79. Unpublished.
80. SG/971, October 18, 1960, to the Fifth Committee of the General Assembly.
81. SG/871, November 15, 1959.
82. Unpublished.
83. Unpublished.
84. Unpublished.
85. SG/871, November 15, 1959.
86. Press Release of the U.S.S.R. Mission to the UN, November 16, 1959.
87. Unpublished.
88. PR, EC/1970; TA/820, December 17, 1959.
89. Wise and Ross, op. cit., pp. 147–54.
90. PC, Note No. 2082, December 11, 1959.
91. Unpublished.
92. Unpublished.
93. Unpublished.
94. Champassak, op. cit., p. 136.
95. Ibid.
96. PC, Note No. 2108, February 4, 1960.
97. Ibid.

98. PC, Note No. 2113, February 18, 1960.
99. Champassak, op. cit., pp. 139 et seq.
100. Unpublished.
101. Unpublished.
102. Unpublished.
103. Unpublished.
104. Unpublished.
105. PM/3952, January 1, 1961.
106. OR, GA, 877th meeting, September 29, 1960.
107. OR, GA, 904th meeting, October 13, 1960.
108. PC, Note No. 2339, May 29, 1961.

Chapter 14 / The Developing Countries

1. Unpublished.
2. A/4800/Add. 1, SG/1052 and Corr. 1, August 21, 1961.
3. PC, Note No. 1601, May 16, 1957.
4. Ibid.
5. SG/335/Rev. 1, September 12, 1953.
6. Unpublished.
7. SG/910, Chicago, May 1, 1960.
8. SG/430, July 12, 1955.
9. Ibid.
10. SG/493, July 16, 1956.
11. Ibid.
12. SG/500, September 26, 1956; published in *IBM World Trade News*, October 1956.
13. PC, Note No. 1760, March 20, 1958.
14. PC, Note No. 2015, July 23, 1959.
15. Ibid.
16. SG/930, July 11, 1960.
17. SG/1045, July 13, 1961.
18. Ibid.
19. Unnumbered, March 30, 1954.
20. Ibid.
21. Ibid.
22. PC, Note No. 1234, February 27, 1956.
23. SG/482, May 30, 1956, Montreal.
24. PC, Note No. 1318, June 7, 1956.
25. SG/739, to the Second Committee of the General Assembly, October 30, 1958.
26. Ibid.
27. Res. 1256 (XIII), November 14, 1958.
28. PC, Note No. 2189, June 30, 1960.
29. Ibid.

30. SG/758, December 29, 1958.
31. SG/831, July 6, 1959.
32. August 25, 1958.
33. Ibid.
34. PC, Note No. 2020, August 13, 1959.
35. Ibid.
36. Unpublished.
37. Unpublished.
38. Unpublished.
39. Unpublished.
40. Unpublished.
41. SG/890, January 26, 1960.
42. Unpublished.
43. Unpublished.
44. PC, Note No. 2082, December 11, 1959.
45. Unpublished.
46. Unnumbered, January 10, 1960.
47. SG/890, January 26, 1960.
48. Ibid.
49. SG/895, January 31, 1960.
50. SG/890, January 26, 1960.
51. PC, Note No. 2108, February 4, 1960.
52. Ibid.
53. Ibid.
54. Paul-Henri Spaak, *Combats Inachevés—de l'Indépendance à l'Alliance* (Fayard, 1969), pp. 244–5.
55. SG/813, May 4, 1959. Translated from Swedish by Sven Ahman.
56. Ibid.
57. PC, Note No. 2176, June 2, 1960.
58. Unpublished.
59. Unpublished.
60. Unpublished.
61. Unpublished.
62. Unpublished.
63. SG/900, March 8, 1960.
64. Unpublished.
65. SG/908, April 14, 1960.
66. Ibid.
67. Ibid.
68. Ibid.
69. Unpublished.

Chapter 15 / The Congo, July–August 1960

1. KASAVUBU, Joseph—President of the Alliance des Bakongo (Abako); national deputy, then President of the republic from June 1960

to November 1965; senator in 1966. Died March 24, 1969.

2. LUMUMBA, Patrice—Born on July 2, 1925, in Onalua, territory of Katako-Kombe (Sankuru-Kasai), of the Otetela tribe. Went through secondary school. In 1954, postal clerk in Stanleyville. In 1957 he was employed by an important brewery in Leopoldville and soon became its commercial director. He left this company in October 1959 to devote himself entirely to the direction of MNC (Mouvement National Congolais).

In 1955 he was a militant in the ranks of the Cercle Libéral. In 1956, as provincial president of the Association du Personnel Indigène de la Colonie (Association of Indigenous Workers of the Colony) for Orientale Province, he traveled to Belgium to study. From October 1958 onward, he was one of the most active promoters of the MNC. In December 1958 he participated in the Pan-African Conference at Accra, the source of his idea of active neutralism. In the Luluabourg Congress of April 1959, he outlined the objectives of a national and supratribal party. On November 1, 1959, he was arrested after the Stanleyville congress. Liberated through intervention of the Minister of the Congo and all the Congolese leaders, he attended the Round Table Conference of the Belgians and Congolese in January–February 1960. Elected national deputy with a majority of 84,602 votes in the Stanleyville district. On June 23, the chambers invested the group he headed with ministerial powers. Lumumba was both Prime Minister and Minister of Defense in this government.

3. Catherine Hoskyns, *The Congo since Independence—January 1960 to December 1961*, Royal Institute of International Affairs (Oxford, 1965),

p. 88.

4. For the full text of the speeches made by the King of the Belgians and Prime Minister Lumumba, see the official documents of the Belgian government, *Chronique de politique étrangère, juillet à novembre 1960*, pp. 630–6.

5. S/4361, July 1, 1960.

6. S/4377, July 7, 1960.

7. TSHOMBE, Moise—President of the Confédération d'Associations Tribales du Katanga (Conakat); elected provincial deputy to Elisabethville in May 1960; president of the province, then of the state (in secession) of Katanga from 1960 to January 1963.

8. *The Quest for Peace: The Dag Hammarskjold Memorial Lectures*, edited by A. W. Cordier and Wilder Foote (New York, 1965), p. 129.

9. Unpublished.

10. Unpublished.

11. SG/930, July 11, 1960.

12. Unpublished.

13. SG/931, July 12, 1960.

14. Unpublished.

15. SG/931, July 12, 1960.

16. Unpublished.

17. S/4381, July 13, 1960.

18. Unpublished.

19. OR, SC, 873rd meeting, para. 18 et seq.; SG/933, July 13, 1960.

20. S/4382, July 13, 1960.

21. OR, SC, 873rd meeting, para. 45, July 13, 1960.

22. S/4386, July 13, 1960.

23. S/4383, July 13, 1960 (same as S/4387, July 14, 1960).

24. S/4387, July 14, 1960.

25. General H. T. Alexander, *African Tightrope: My Two Years as Nkrumah's Chief of Staff* (New York, 1965), p. 80.

26. Unpublished.

27. S/4389, July 18, 1960.

28. S/4387, July 14, 1960.

29. S/4405, July 22, 1960.

30. OR, SC, 873rd meeting, para. 18 et seq.; SG/933, July 13, 1960.

31. S/4389, July 18, 1960.

32. Ibid.

33. S/4389/Add. 5, July 29, 1960.
34. Unpublished.
35. Unpublished.
36. OR, SC, 873rd meeting, para. 103, July 13, 1960.
37. Unpublished.
38. KANZA, Thomas—First Congolese to receive a diploma from a university; Minister-Delegate to the UN in the government of June 1960; Ambassador of the Congo to London under the second Adoula government.
39. S/4405, July 22, 1960.
40. Hoskyns, op. cit., p. 129.
41. OR, SC, 877th meeting, para. 3 et seq.; SG/935, July 20, 1960.
42. Ibid.
43. S/4405, July 22, 1960.
44. Ibid.
45. Unpublished.
46. GIZENGA, Antoine—President of the Parti Solidaire Africain (PSA) and elected to the Chamber by his party in May 1960; Vice-Prime Minister in the Lumumba government in June 1960. He assumed control of the Lumumbist government in Stanleyville from November 1960 to August 1961, at which time he was promoted to Vice-Prime Minister in Adoula's government of reconciliation.
47. Unpublished.
48. SG/937, August 2, 1960. Translated from French.
49. Ibid.
50. Ibid.
51. Ibid.
52. New York *Herald Tribune*, "Today and Tomorrow—The Congo and the UN," August 1960.
53. BOMBOKO, Justin—Elected to the Chamber from the Union Mongo; Minister of Foreign Affairs in the first Congolese government; president of the Board of Commissioners-General in September 1960; Minister in the Ileo and Adoula governments from 1961 to 1964.
54. SG/938/Rev. 1; CO/35, August 2, 1960.
55. For the exchange of messages and statements, and events regarding the Secretary-General's effort to have the UN Force enter Katanga, and its entry, see S/4417 and Addenda, August 6, 1960.
56. Ibid.
57. Ibid.
58. Ibid.
59. Ibid.
60. Ibid.
61. Ibid.
62. Ibid.
63. Ibid.
64. Unpublished.
65. Unpublished.
66. MUNONGO, Godefroid—First president of the Conakat in 1958; Provincial Deputy, then Minister of the Interior, in Katanga from June 1960 to the end of the secession.
67. Unpublished.
68. S/4418, August 6, 1960.
69. S/4421, August 7, 1960.
70. Unpublished.
71. S/4417 and Addenda, August 6, 1960.
72. S/4421, August 7, 1960.
73. S/4420, August 6, 1960.
74. OR, SC, 884th meeting, para. 10 et seq.; SG/940, August 8, 1960.
75. Ibid.
76. OR. SC 885th meeting, August 8, 1960.
77. Ibid.
78. Ibid.
79. OR, SC, 885th meeting, para. 122 et seq.; SG/941, August 8, 1960.
80. Ibid.
81. S/4426, August 9, 1960.
82. Ibid.
83. S/4417 and Addenda.
84. Ibid.
85. Ibid.
86. Ibid.
87. Ibid.
88. Ibid.
89. Ibid.
90. LUNDULA, Victor—Named general commander-in-chief of the national Congolese Army (ANC) in

July 1960; dismissed from his functions by President Kasavubu in September 1960; commander of the Stanleyville group favorable to Gizenga from late in 1960 to 1961.
91. CO/47, August 13, 1960.

Chapter 16 / The Congo, August–September 1960: The Constitutional Crisis

1. Press Conference, August 13, 1960.
2. S/4417/Add. 7, August 15, 1960. This document contains the exchange of letters between the Secretary-General and the Prime Minister, Foreign Minister, and President of the Congo, just before Hammarskjold's return to New York.
3. OR, SC, 887th meeting, para. 25; SG/950, August 21, 1960.
4. S/4417/Add. 7, August 15, 1960.
5. Radio Moscow, August 1; *Pravda,* August 3 and 13.
6. Ibid.
7. Ibid.
8. S/4446, August 20, 1960.
9. S/4449, August 20, 1960.
10. MOBUTU, Joseph-Désiré (now Mobutu Scsc Seko) Ex-journalist; delegate from the MNC Lumumba wing to Brussels in 1960; Secretary of State for the president of the Council in June 1960; named colonel and chief of staff of the ANC in July 1960. Since 1961 commander-in-chief of the reunified ANC; lieutenant general in 1965; President of the Republic since November 1965.
11. S/4450, August 21, 1960.
12. OR, SC, 887th meeting, para. 11; SG/950, August 21, 1960.
13. Ibid., para. 22.
14. S/4453, August 21, 1960.
15. OR, SC, 888th meeting, para. 9; SG/951, August 21, 1960.
16. OR, SC, 888th meeting, August 21, 1960.
17. Ibid.
18. Ibid., para. 100; SG/952, August 21, 1960.
19. KALONJI, Albert—President of the so-called Kalonji wing of the MNC in November 1959; National Deputy in June 1960; President-Mulopwe of South Kasai in 1960–61.
20. Unpublished.
21. SG/953, August 23, 1960.
22. Unpublished.
23. Unpublished.
24. Unpublished.
25. Unpublished.
26. Published by Julliard, Paris, 1962.
27. Unpublished.
28. Unpublished.
29. Unpublished.
30. ILEO, Joseph—Joint founder of the MNC; president of the central provisional government of February 1961, and Minister in Adoula's government of national reconciliation.
31. For this Congo Fund plan see S/4482, Add. 1–4, September 7, 1960, and the Secretary-General's statement to the Security Council on September 9, 1960, 896th meeting; SG/956, September 9, 1960.
32. OR, SC, 904th meeting, para. 74, September 16, 1960; SG/960.
33. DELVAUX, Albert—Resident Minister in Belgium from the first Congolese government, then in the provisional government of Ileo; Minister of Public Works from July 1962–July 1964.
34. Unpublished.
35. S/4531, para. 20, September 21, 1960.
36. Unpublished.
37. Unpublished.
38. Unpublished.
39. Unpublished.
40. S/4488, September 9, 1960.
41. S/4482 and Addenda, September 7, 1960.
42. S/4488, September 9, 1960.
43. OR, SC, 896th meeting, paras. 83 et

seq.; SG/956 and Add. 1, September 9, 1960.

44. Ibid.
45. Ibid.
46. Ibid.
47. Ibid.
48. Ibid.
49. Ibid.
50. S/4497, September 10, 1960.
51. Ibid.
52. OR, SC, 897th meeting, para. 64; SG/957, September 10, 1960.
53. Unpublished.
54. Ernest W. Lefever, *Uncertain Mandate: Politics of the UN Congo Operation* (Baltimore, 1967), p. 115.
55. S/4503, September 11, 1960.
56. Ibid.
57. OR, SC, 901st meeting, September 14, 1960.
58. Ibid., para. 39.
59. OR, SC, 901st meeting, paras. 71–86; SG/959, September 14, 1960.
60. Ibid.
61. Unpublished.
62. Unpublished.
63. Unpublished.
64. Unpublished.
65. S/4516, September 15, 1960; see OR, SC, 902nd meeting, para. 45.
66. S/4519, September 15, 1960; see OR, SC, 903rd meeting, para. 93.
67. Ibid.
68. OR, SC, 905th meeting, para. 73, September 16, 1960.
69. S/4523, September 16, 1960.
70. S/4526, September 17, 1960.
71. Ibid.
72. The Fourth Emergency Special Session of the General Assembly (ES-IV), September 17–19, 1960; OR, GA (ES-IV), 858–863rd meetings.
73. OR, GA (ES-IV), 858th meeting, para. 203; SG/961, September 18, 1960.
74. Public statement of September 16, 1960.
75. Unpublished.
76. Res. 1474 (ES-IV), September 20, 1960.
77. OR, GA (ES-IV), 863rd meeting, para. 276; SG/963, September 19–20, 1960.

Chapter 17 / The General Assembly, September–December 1960

1. James Morris in the *Manchester Guardian*, September 21, 1960.
2. April 22, 1959, at UN Headquarters.
3. A/4390/Add. 1, August 31, 1960.
4. Ibid.
5. Ibid.
6. Ibid.
7. Ibid.
8. Ibid.
9. OR, GA, 869th meeting, paras. 142–53, September 23, 1960.
10. Ibid., para. 282.
11. OR, GA, 871st meeting, paras. 2–11; SG/964, September 26, 1960.
12. Ibid.
13. James Morris in the *Manchester Guardian*, September 27, 1960. ˙
14. September 30, 1960.
15. OR, GA, 882nd meeting, October 3, 1960.
16. Ibid.
17. SG/1035, May 30, 1961.
18. OR, GA, 882nd meeting, October 3, 1960.
19. OR, GA, 882nd meeting, para. 74, October 3, 1960.
20. OR, GA, 883rd meeting, paras. 4–12; SG/966, October 3, 1960.
21. Ibid.
22. Unpublished.
23. Unpublished.
24. OR, GA, 904th meeting, para. 74, October 13, 1960.
25. Ibid., paras. 83–4; SG/968, October 13, 1960.
26. Unpublished.
27. Unpublished.
28. Unpublished.
29. Unpublished.
30. Unpublished.
31. Unpublished.
32. OR, GA, 799th meeting, September 18, 1959.
33. OR, GA, 869th meeting, para. 281, September 23, 1960.
34. Unpublished.
35. Unpublished.
36. Max Lerner in the *New York Post*, October 4, 1960.
37. Unpublished.

38. Unpublished.
39. Conor Cruise O'Brien, *To Katanga and Back* (London, 1962); Ian Colvin, *The Rise and Fall of Moise Tshombe: A Biography* (London, 1968).
40. Unpublished.
41. MPOLO, Maurice—Born at Inongo on March 4, 1928. President of the Lumumba faction at the MNC in Leopoldville; participated in the Round Table Conference in Brussels in January 1960. Elected provincial and national deputy in the district of Lac Leopold II. Minister of Youth and Sports in the Lumumba government; named colonel in the Congolese Army; dismissed on September 12, 1960, by Kasavubu, but named chief of the general staff by Lumumba.
42. OKITO, Joseph—Born in Lusambo (Kasai) on February 5, 1910. President and founder of the Union Rurale du Congo (URUCCO) at the beginning of 1959. In 1960 he became president of the MNC in Sankuru; named senator of Kasai, and elected vice-president of the Senate in June 1960, then president in September 1960; arrested on November 20, 1960, at Kikwit.
43. Unpublished.
44. Unpublished.
45. Walter Lippman, "Dag Hammarskjold, United Nations Pioneer," *International Organisation*, Vol. XV, No. 4, Autumn 1961.
46. A/4557 and Add. 1; S/4557, November 2, 1960.
47. Ibid.
48. Ibid.
49. Ibid.
50. Press Conference of November 14, 1960.
51. A/4571, November 12, 1960.
52. Unpublished.
53. Unpublished.
54. OR, GA, 896th meeting, para. 62, October 10, 1960.
55. OR, GA, 912th meeting, November

8, 1960.
56. OR, GA, 924th meeting, November 22, 1960.
57. OR, GA, 906th meeting, paras. 2–17; SG/970, October 17, 1960.
58. OR, GA, 896th meeting, para. 52, October 10, 1960.
59. OR, GA, 906th meeting, paras. 2–17; SG/970, October 17, 1690.
60. Unpublished.
61. For the UN protection of Lumumba, his escape and arrest, and the Secretary-General's démarches to President Kasavubu regarding the treatment of Lumumba, see S/4571 and Add. 1 (A/4614 and Add. 1) of December 5, 1960.
62. PONGO, Gilbert—Inspector of the Sûreté in September 1960.
63. CO/111 of November 30, 1960.
64. A/4612, December 2, 1960.
65. SONGOLO, Alphonse — Elected National Deputy from the MNC-Lumumba and Minister of Communications in the first Congolese government in June 1960; broke with Lumumba and was arrested by the Gizengist authorities, having been accused of secessionist attempts; executed in February 1961 in Stanleyville.
66. G. Heinz and H. Donnay, *Lumumba: The Last Fifty Days* (New York, 1969), p. 54.
67. Unpublished. For a more formal reply from President Kasavubu, dated December 7, see Note 61 above.
68. Carl von Horn, *Soldiering for Peace* (London, 1966).
69. Unpublished.
70. Unpublished.
71. Unpublished.
72. A/4617, December 5, 1960 (cables of December 3 and 5, 1960).
73. Ibid.
74. Ibid.
75. S/4573—A/4618, December 6, 1960.
76. Ibid.
77. Ibid.
78. S/4571 and Add. 1 (A/4614 and Add. 1) of December 5, 1960.
79. S/4590, December 9, 1960.

80. S/4585—A/4629, December 7, 1960.
81. S/4580, December 7, 1960.
82. OR, SC, 913th meeting, para. 10, December 7, 1960.
83. Ibid., paras. 12–62; SG/979, December 7, 1960.
84. Ibid.
85. Ibid.
86. Ibid.
87. Ibid.
88. OR, SC, 920th meeting, paras. 56–99; S/987 and Add. 1, December 13, 1960.
89. Ibid.
90. Ibid.
91. Ibid.
92. S/4579; see OR, SC, 914th meeting, para. 62, December 7, 1960.
93. S/4578/Rev. 1, December 13, 1960.
94. A/L. 331/Rev. 1, December 19, 1960.
95. OR, GA, 950th meeting, paras. 101–11; SG/988, December 16, 1960.
96. Ibid.
97. Ibid.
98. Ibid.
99. OR, GA, 953rd meeting, paras. 159–98; SG/990, December 17, 1960.
100. Ibid.
101. OR, GA, 957th meeting, paras. 12–23; SG/991, December 19, 1960.
102. OR, GA, 958th meeting, paras. 132–6; SG/993, December 20, 1960.
103. Unpublished.
104. S/4606, January 1, 1961.
105. PM/3952, January 1, 1961.
106. S/4605, December 31, 1960.
107. Unpublished.
108. S/4606 and Add. 1, January 1 and 6, 1961.
109. Unpublished.

Chapter 18 / 1961: The First Months

1. Res. 134 (S/4300), April 1, 1960.
2. Ibid.
3. PC, Note No. 2148, April 8, 1960.
4. Joseph P. Lash, "Hammarskjold's Conception of His Office," *International Organisation*, Vol. XVI, No. 3, 1962; discussion with Hammarskjold on April 20, 1960.
5. Unpublished.
6. See interim report, S/4305, April 19, 1960.
7. S/918, May 15, 1960.
8. Unpublished.
9. Unpublished.
10. All quotes from the Secretary-General's talks with the South African authorities in South Africa are from Hammarskjold's own record, unpublished.
11. Unpublished.
12. SG/999, January 12, 1961.
13. S/4635, January 23, 1961.
14. S/4616, January 8, 1961.
15. S/4606 and Add. 1, January 1, 1961.
16. OR, SC, 927th meeting, para. 86; SG/1000, January 14, 1961.
17. S/4629 and Add. 1, January 16, 1961.
18. Ibid.
19. Unpublished.
20. NENDAKA, Victor—Vice-President of the MNC Lumumba wing in 1959 and until April 1960; head of the Sûreté of the interior from September–October 1960 to 1965.
21. KAZADI, Ferdinand—Ex-student at Lovanium; Commissioner General for Defense in September 1960; in charge of the transfer of Lumumba to Elisabethville on January 17, 1961; Provincial Minister of South Kasai in June 1961.
22. S/4688 and Adds. 1 and 2, February 12, 1961.
23. Ibid.
24. S/4637 and Add. 1, January 23, 1961.
25. S/4634, January 20, 1961.
26. Ibid.
27. Unpublished.
28. S/4644, January 20, 1961.
29. S/4688 and Adds. 1 and 2, February 12, 1961.
30. Ibid.
31. SENDWE, Jason—President and national deputy in 1960 of the Balubakat-Fedeka-Atcar cartel in Katanga; Vice-Prime Minister of the Adoula government of reconciliation in August 1961; assassinated in Albertville in June 1964.

32. G. Heinz and H. Donnay, *Lumumba: The Last Fifty Days* (New York, 1964), p. 107.
33. SAMALENGE, Lucas—National Deputy of the Conakat in 1960; Under-Secretary of State for Information in Katanga during secession; died in November 1961, in a hunting accident (according to the official version).
34. S/4976—A/4964, November 11, 1961.
35. KIBWE, Jean-Baptiste — Provincial deputy of Conakat in 1960; Minister of Finance of Katanga until the end of the secession.
36. Unpublished.
37. OR, SC, 933rd meeting; SG/1006, February 13, 1961.
38. S/4704, February 14, 1961.
39. S/4691/Add. 1 (Annex II).
40. S/4704, February 14, 1961.
41. OR, SC, 935th meeting, paras. 3–37; SG/1008, February 15, 1961.
42. Ibid.
43. Ibid.
44. Ibid.
45. Ibid.
46. S/4722, February 17, 1961.
47. OR, SC, 940th meeting, paras. 2–7; SG/1012, February 20, 1961 (S/4727/Add. 2, Annex 4).
48. OR, SC, 941st meeting, para. 77, February 20, 1961.
49. S/4741, February 21, 1961.
50. OR, SC, 942nd meeting, paras. 216–36; SG/1013, February 20–21, 1961.
51. Ibid.
52. Unpublished.
53. Unpublished.
54. Unpublished.
55. Unpublished.
56. Unpublished.
57. Unpublished.
58. Unpublished.
59. Unpublished.
60. Unpublished.
61. Unpublished.
62. S/4752, Annex IV, February 27, 1961.
63. S/4761, March 8, 1961.
64. S/4750 and Adds., February 27, 1961.
65. March 10, 1961.
66. S/4775, Annex 5, March 30, 1961.
67. Ibid.
68. Ibid.
69. OR, GA, 965th meeting, March 21, 1961.
70. 825th meeting of the Fifth Committee of the GA, March 24, 1961.
71. 831st meeting of the Fifth Committee of the GA, April 4, 1961.
72. OR, GA, 970th meeting, paras. 2–10; SG/1019, March 29, 1961.
73. OR, GA, 977th meeting, paras. 2–44; SG/1020, April 5, 1961.
74. Ibid.
75. Ibid.
76. A/L. 339 and Add., and A/L. 340 and Add., of April 5 and 6, 1961.
77. OR, GA, 982nd meeting, para. 48, April 14, 1961.
78. Ibid.
79. Res. 1600 (XV), April 15, 1961.
80. Res. 1599 (XV), April 15, 1961.
81. SG/1024, statement to the Fifth Committee of the General Assembly, April 17, 1961.
82. OR, GA, 995th meeting, April 21, 1961.
83. Ibid., para. 172.
84. Res. 1619 (XV), April 21, 1961.
85. S/4807 and Add. 1, Annex I, May 17, 1961.
86. SG/1006, February 6, 1961.
87. Unpublished.
88. Unpublished.
89. S/1034, May 25, 1961.
90. S/1040, Note No. 2358, June 26, 1961.
91. Ibid.
92. *Psychology Today*, Vol. 2, No. 11 (April 1969).

Chapter 19 / 1960–1961:
The International Civil Service

1. Note No. 1782, April 10, 1958.
2. Ibid.
3. Ibid.
4. Background PC, December 7, 1954.
5. SG/971, to the Fifth Committee of the General Assembly, October 18, 1960.
6. Ibid.
7. SG/728, to the Fifth Committee of

the General Assembly, October 9, 1958.
8. Res. 1446 (XIV), December 5, 1959.
9. See A/4536, October 14, 1960.
10. Ibid., Annex.
11. Unpublished.
12. Unpublished.
13. SG/971, to the Fifth Committee of the General Assembly, October 18, 1960.
14. A/4390/Add. 1, Section II, p. 3, August 31, 1960.
15. A/4776, Annex I, June 14, 1961 (recommendation dated December 21, 1960).
16. Unpublished.
17. Unpublished.
18. Unpublished.
19. Unpublished.
20. A/4776 and Annexes, June 14, 1961.
21. Ibid., Appendix I.
22. A/4794, June 30, 1961.
23. Unpublished.
24. Background PC, November 13, 1953.
25. SG/1035, May 30, 1961.
26. Ibid.
27. Ibid.
28. Ibid.
29. Ibid.
30. Press Release No. 30/61 issued by the U.S.S.R. Mission to the UN, June 2, 1961.
31. Ibid.
32. Unnumbered.

Chapter 20 / Summer 1961: Bizerte

1. Unpublished.
2. Unpublished.
3. Unpublished.
4. Unpublished.
5. Unpublished.
6. SG/1035, May 30, 1961.
7. PC, Note No. 2347, June 12, 1961.
8. Unpublished.
9. S/4871, July 21, 1961.
10. S/4864, July 21, 1961.
11. S/4862, July 20, 1961.

12. OR, GA, 996th meeting, para. 61, August 21, 1961.
13. OR, SC, 962nd meeting, paras. 2–4; SG/1047, July 22, 1961.
14. Ibid.
15. S/4882, July 22, 1961.
16. S/4885, July 23, 1961.
17. Ibid.
18. Unpublished.
19. Unpublished.
20. Unpublished.
21. S/4894 and Add. 1, July 27, 1961.
22. Unpublished.
23. Unpublished.
24. Unpublished.
25. Unpublished.
26. S/4894 and Add. 1, July 27, 1961.
27. Charles de Gaulle, *Mémoires d'Espoir — Le Renouveau 1958–1962* (Paris, 1970), p. 118, published in English under the title *Memoirs of Hope—Renewal and Endeavor* (New York, 1971).
28. S/4894 and Add. 1, July 27, 1961.
29. Ibid.
30. OR, SC, 964th meeting, paras. 85–95; SG/1048, July 28, 1961.
31. Ibid.
32. S/4903–4–5, July 28, 1961.
33. Unpublished.
34. Unpublished.
35. Unpublished.
36. Unpublished.
37. Unpublished.
38. Res. 1622 (S-III), August 25, 1961.
39. A/4800/Add. 1; SG/1052, August 21, 1961.
40. Unnumbered.
41. Translated from the original Swedish.
42. Unpublished.

Chapter 21 / Vindication and Tragedy

1. S/4913, August 2, 1961.
2. S/4937, September 11, 1961.
3. *The Quest for Peace: Dag Hammarskjold Lectures* (New York, 1965),

"The Operation in the Congo," p. 134.

4. Unpublished.
5. PC, Note No. 2339, May 29, 1961.
6. Conor Cruise O'Brien, "My Case," London *Observer*, December 17, 1961.
7. Crawford Young, *Politics in the Congo: Decolonization and Independence* (Princeton, 1965), p. 503, footnote.
8. ADOULA, Cyrille—Co-founder of the MNC and secretary of the FGTK (Fédération Générale des Travailleurs Congolais) in Leopoldville 1959–60; member of the provisional government of Joseph Ileo in February 1961; Prime Minister from August 1961 to July 1964.
9. Unpublished.
10. S/4940, September 14, 1961, and Addenda. These documents contain the reports of events up to and just after Hammarskjold's death.
11. Unpublished.
12. S/4940, September 14, 1961, and Addenda.
13. Unpublished.
14. Unpublished.
15. Unpublished.
16. Unpublished.
17. Unpublished.
18. Unpublished.
19. Unpublished.
20. S/4937, September 11, 1961.
21. Unpublished.
22. Unpublished.
23. Unpublished.
24. Unpublished.
25. Unpublished.
26. Unpublished.
27. Conor Cruise O'Brien, *To Katanga and Back* (London, 1962), p. 189.
28. KIMBA, Evariste—Senator from Katanga in 1960; Minister of Foreign Affairs in the Tshombe government during the secession; Prime Minister of the central government from October 13 to November 14, 1965; condemned to death and hanged at Kinshasa under indictment for par-

ticipation in the so-called Pentecost plot in 1966.
29. MUTAKA WA-DILOMBA, Charles — Speaker of the Katanga National Assembly.
30. BOCHELEY-DAVIDSON, Egide—Elected to the Chamber in the MNC- Lumumba party; spokesman for the Lumumbist opposition to Cyrille Adoula in 1962–3.
31. GBENYE, Christophe—Minister of the Interior in the first Congolese government in June 1960, and in the Lumumbist government in Stanleyville in November 1960; occupied the same functions in the Adoula government of reconciliation in August 1961.
32. S/4940, September 14, 1961, and Addenda.
33. Unpublished.
34. S/4940, September 14, 1961, and Addenda.
35. Unpublished.
36. O'Brien, *To Katanga and Back*, p. 266.
37. The London *Observer*, December 10 and 17, 1961.
38. Ibid.
39. Ibid.
40. Unpublished.
41. Arthur L. Gavshon, *The Mysterious Death of Dag Hammarskjold* (New York, 1962).
42. Ibid.
43. Ibid.
44. Ibid.
45. Unpublished.
46. O'Brien, *To Katanga and Back*, p. 299.
47. Unpublished.
48. Unpublished.
49. Unpublished.
50. Unpublished.
51. S/4940, September 14, 1961, and Addenda.
52. Unpublished.
53. Hansard Official Report of House of Lords Debate, Wednesday, October 18, 1961, columns 447–9.
54. Ibid.
55. Ibid.
56. Unpublished.

57. Unpublished.
58. Unpublished.
59. Unpublished.
60. Unpublished.
61. Unpublished.
62. S/4940, September 14, 1961, and Addenda.
63. Unpublished.
64. S/4940, September 14, 1961, and Addenda.
65. Ibid.
66. O'Brien, *To Katanga and Back*, p. 284.
67. Unpublished.
68. Unpublished.
69. S/4940, September 14, 1961, and Addenda.
70. Ibid.
71. Unpublished.
72. O'Brien, *To Katanga and Back*, p. 286.
73. Unpublished.
74. S/4940, September 14, 1961, and Addenda.
75. Ibid.
76. For the details of Hammarskjold's flight to Ndola and what followed, see the report of the UN Investigation Commission, A/5069 and Add. 1, April 24, 1962.

Epilogue

1. *New York Times*, September 18, 1961.
2. *East Africa and Rhodesia*, Vol. 38, No. 1929, September 28, 1961.
3. Ibid.
4. S/4940/Add. 7, September 20, 1961.
5. OR, GA, 1007th meeting, para. 3, September 19, 1961.
6. Res. 1628 (XVI), October 26, 1961.
7. A/5069 and Add. 1, April 24, 1962.
8. A/5069, para. 206, April 24, 1962.
9. Interview given by the pilot to the Washington *Evening Star*, August 16, 1962.
10. Gustaf Aulén, *Dag Hammarskjold's White Book: The Meaning of Markings* (Philadelphia, 1969).
11. SG/SM/92, June 30, 1964.
12. CO/364, October 22, 1970.
13. H. G. Nicolas, "The United Nations as a Political Institution: A Personal Retrospect," *International Journal, Canadian Institute of Foreign Affairs*, Vol. XXV. No. 2, Spring 1970.
14. Cf. Chapter 1, Note 10.

INDEX

The abbreviation H in subentries stands for Hammarskjold.

A NOTE ABOUT THE AUTHOR

*Brian Urquhart, an Assistant Secretary-General of the
United Nations, has been a member of the Secretariat
since the earliest days of the Organization. Born in
Dorset, England, in 1919, and educated at Westminster
School and Christ Church, Oxford, he served in the
British Army in North Africa, Sicily, and Europe from
1939 to 1945, and then became Personal Assistant to
Gladwyn Jebb, Executive Secretary of the Preparatory
Commission of the United Nations. After three years
as Personal Assistant to Trygve Lie, first Secretary-
General of the UN, he went on to serve for many years
in the office of Ralph Bunche. He has taken an active
part in the organization and direction of all UN peace-
keeping operations; he served in the Congo at the beginning of the crisis in 1960 and was later, for a time,
the United Nations Representative in Katanga. Mr.
Urquhart is married, and lives in New York City with
his family.*

A NOTE ON THE TYPE

The text of this book was set on the Linotype in Aster, a typeface designed by Francesco Simoncini (born 1912 in Bologna, Italy) for Ludwig and Mayer, the German type foundry. Starting out with the basic old-face letterforms that can be traced back to Francesco Griffo in 1495, Simoncini emphasized the diagonal stress by the simple device of extending diagonals to the full height of the letterforms and squaring off. By modifying the weights of the individual letters to combat this stress, he has produced a type of rare balance and vigor. Introduced in 1958, Aster has steadily grown in popularity wherever type is used.

Composed by Cherry Hill Composition, Pennsauken, New Jersey. Printed and bound by The Haddon Craftsmen, Inc., Scranton, Pennsylvania. Typography and binding design by Anthea Lingeman. Maps drawn for this book by David Lindroth.